THE PICTURE HISTORY OF
PHOTOGRAPHY

Revised and Enlarged Edition

THE PICTURE HISTORY O

ETER POLLACK

PHOTOGRAPHY

rom the Earliest Beginnings to the Present Day

ARRY N. ABRAMS, INC., PUBLISHERS, NEW YORK

Revised and enlarged edition 1969

Milton S. Fox, Editor-in-Chief

Library of Congress Catalog Card Number: 76-76556

Printed and bound in Japan.

*This book is
dedicated to EDWARD STEICHEN
who said: "Photography is a medium of formidable
contradictions. It is ridiculously easy and
almost impossibly difficult."*

Acknowledgments

I WISH TO ACKNOWLEDGE with gratitude the encouragement, advice, and photographs I have received from the distinguished historians Beaumont Newhall, Director of George Eastman House, and Mr. and Mrs. Helmut Gernsheim. My thanks are also due Daniel Catton Rich, former director of the Art Institute of Chicago, and now director of The Worcester Art Museum; Stephen Jarecki, Curator of Photography at the Worcester Art Museum; Hugh Edwards, Curator of Photography at the Art Institute of Chicago; Jacqueline Balish, former editor of Modern Photography; Inge Bondi, Cornell Capa, and Elliot Erwitt of Magnum Photos; The Crerar Library, Chicago; the late Bruce Downes of Popular Photography Magazine and its present editors H. M. Kinzer and John Durniak; the late Oscar Solbert, former director of Eastman House; Minor White, of the Massachusetts Institute of Technology; Howard R. Driggs of American Pioneer Trails Association; W. R. Felton of Sioux City, Iowa, for Laton Alton Huffman material; Raymond Grosset of the Paris office and Charles Rado of the New York office of Rapho-Guillumette; Stanley Rayfield of Time Inc.; Mathilde Kelly of the Chicago Public Library; Carl Maas of Standard Oil Company of New Jersey; Grace M. Mayer, former curator of prints, Museum of the City of New York, and now curator of photography, Museum of Modern Art, New York; John Szarkowski, director, and Peter Bunnell, associate curator of the Museum of Modern Art; A. Hyatt Mayor, curator emeritus of prints, Metropolitan Museum of Art; Janine Niepce of Paris; Georgia O'Keeffe, for Stieglitz material; Mary Frances Rhymer of the Chicago Historical Society; Harold White of Bromley, Kent, England, for Talbot material; Cornelia Otis Skinner for theatrical material; and Nina Adam for help in translations.

I am particularly grateful to Sam Cauman, who not only read my manuscript but edited it and made invaluable suggestions. I am also grateful to Philip Grushkin and Ernst Reichl, who designed this volume.

My deepest thanks are extended to the photographers who have permitted me to reproduce their photographs. Specific acknowledgment is made in each case.

P. P.

CONTENTS

THE PICTURE HISTORY OF
PHOTOGRAPHY

Author's Preface

IT IS WITH PHOTOGRAPHY AS AN ART and with photographers as artists—with the vision of the man behind the camera—that this book is largely concerned. It is a book of many hundreds of pages, despite the fact that lack of space has forced the exclusion of many photographers with a clear title to presentation of their work. In the last thirty-five years, the body of distinguished photographic art has grown to vast proportions. Nevertheless, the art of photography is only a small part of the enormous photographic enterprise, which is one of the momentous developments in the history of human expression and communication.

Photography was invented by nineteenth-century artists for their own purposes. These men were seeking a lasting, literal record of their visual surroundings, and they found it. The new combination of illumination, lens, shutter, and flat surface coated with chemicals sensitive to light produced, within a short interval of time, images more lasting, more convincing in their reality, and more richly detailed than painters could produce manually in weeks and months of effort. This alone was enough to throw consternation into the ranks of fellow artists; and, after their first reaction of pleasure in a new kind of image, art critics rallied with the haughty charge that photography was not and could not be an art. The actual world in which we live had too strong a grip on photography, they said, and pictures so dependent upon mechanical means could not be called acts of man's creative imagination.

Despite the critics, photographers knew that they had found a new art form, a new mode of expression. As artists, they had extraordinary visual sensitivity, and they thought and expressed themselves naturally through visual images. As artists, they used the new tools as other artists before and after them have used brush and pencil —to interpret the world, to present a vision of nature and its structure as well as the things and the people in it.

The most important use of photography was in communication. Here the value of photography was seen in its quality of immediacy, of literal description and convincing presentation of reality. This quality was retained to a large extent even after pictures had been translated into forms that made them available as printing plates for the illustration of books. Almost anything that could be photographed could be printed; and books on travel, medicine, science, and art were published with a wealth and authenticity of visual information never before possible. By now, photography has become as important as the word—perhaps more important as all linguistic barriers fell before this "picture talk."

We use photographs as memories, memories of ourselves when we were younger, of places where we have lived or visited, of friends and relatives who are no longer with us. With the advent of the roll-film Kodak, manageable even by a young child, photography became a folk art—the most democratic art in history. The millions practice it, as well as the few who make of it a medium of high art and a tool of science and industry.

This book cannot go into motion-picture photography, which is a field in itself. Its beginnings are dealt with here, for they belong to still photography. When it was found that the camera could clearly resolve action that was only a blur to the human eye, pioneering still photographers took action sequences and superimposed action pictures. Thereafter, this great new form of art, enter-

tainment, and mass communication took shape swiftly and since then has swept the world.

The production of cameras, photochemicals, and photographic equipment has become a huge, world-wide industry of strategic importance to the life and economy of every great nation.

Our newspapers and periodicals flood us with pictured reports of events as they happen, and employ armies of photographers for this purpose. Merchants expose their goods for sale through photographs, and—especially when they present their products in color—we are so convinced of the reality of what is shown that we accept pictures as samples, as reasonable substitutes for the goods themselves. Photography is used extensively in advertising and publishing, in basic science and engineering, in medicine, commerce, city planning, record keeping, recreation, and defense. It touches almost every aspect of our individual and social existence.

Today we live in a technical and industrial world. We are attuned to an aesthetic in which scientific technique, mass production, and teamwork for creativity have shaped the articles that we drive and wear and put into our homes. In such a society old distinctions between "fine" and "applied" art have come to have less and less meaning. The most creative among us today have accepted the forms and the drives of the technical-industrial world, and have been challenged to express its strength and its beauty.

In accepting this assignment, the creative leaders of our society have accepted also the task of reshaping the technical-industrial world and bringing it into greater harmony and order through their art. Men with cameras, imagination, and sensitive vision show us the actual and potential beauty of our time, so that we are able to remember it, enjoy it, correct it, protect it, and learn about it. In the forward ranks of today's creative workers in the service of industry, advertising, publishing, government, humanity, and—not least—their own creative needs, are today's photographers.

PART ONE

The Beginnings
of Photography

CHAPTER 1

The Long Road to Photography

IT IS A POPULAR BELIEF that photography was invented by one man. When the process was made public in 1839, his name was attached to it. But the "one man," Daguerre, did not actually take the first photograph. Another man did, Joseph Nicéphore Niepce, seventeen years before Daguerre made his momentous announcement in 1839. Four years before Daguerre's announcement, Fox Talbot took a photograph on a one-inch-square paper negative placed in a camera. In the very year of the announcement, Hippolyte Bayard exhibited direct-positive prints in Paris and Sir John Herschel read to the Royal Society his paper on a method he had discovered of fixing photographs with hyposulphite of soda, the same hypo still used in every darkroom.

With photography as with so many other inventions—the electric light, automobile, and airplane, to mention only a few—a number of men working independently of one another conceived a practical solution at about the same time. All the pieces of the puzzle were then at hand, waiting to be put together. The camera box had been ready for two centuries and more, the photochemistry for almost a century.

The first person to prove that light and not heat blackened silver salts was Johann Heinrich Schulze (1687–1744), a physician and professor at the University of

Halle in Germany. In 1725, while attempting to make a phosphorescent substance, he happened to mix chalk with some nitric acid that contained some dissolved silver. He observed that wherever direct sunlight fell upon it the white mixture turned black, whereas no changes took place in the material protected from the sun's rays. He then experimented with words and shapes cut from paper and placed around a bottle of the prepared solution—thus obtaining photographic impressions on the silvered chalk. Professor Schulze published his findings in 1727, but it never entered his mind to try to make permanent the image he secured in this way. He shook the solution in the bottle and the image was lost forever. This experiment, however, started a series of observations, discoveries, and inventions in chemistry that, when combined with a "camera obscura" a little more than a century later, culminated in the invention of photography.

The pieces of the puzzle were first put together in 1760, not physically but in the imagination. In that year Tiphaigne de la Roche, the Jules Verne of his day, prophesied the "sun picture." He was also the prophet of the telephone, the radio, and dehydrated foods. De la Roche's novel *Giphantie* (an anagram of his first name) describes a paradise set in a "tempestuous ocean of sands" and located in an inaccessible desert in Africa. "It was given to the elementary spirits, the day before the Garden of Eden was allotted to the parents of mankind."

Guided by the "Prefect," a disembodied spirit, the narrator walked in an immense gallery, entranced with "images equivalent to the things themselves" and other images depicting historical personages ranging from Nimrod and Nebuchadnezzar to Alexander and Caesar. The guide explained that "rays of light, reflected from different bodies, make a picture and paint the bodies upon all polished surfaces, as on the retina of the eye, on water, and on glass. The elementary spirits have studied to fix these transient images: they have composed a most subtle matter, very viscous and proper to harden and dry, by the help of which a picture is made in the twinkle of an eye. They do over (coat) with this matter a piece of canvas and hold it before the objects they have a mind to paint. The first effect of the canvas is that of a mirror; there are seen upon it all the bodies far and near,

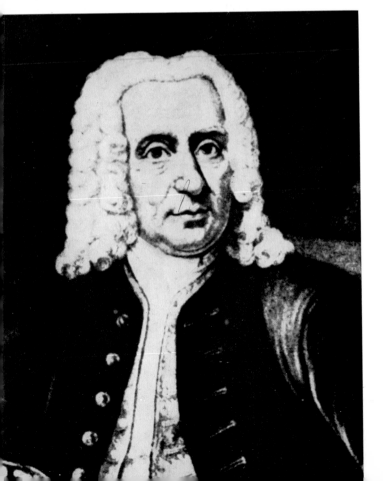

*Johann Heinrich Schulze (1687-1744), German.
He obtained the first images by the action of light
on a mixture of white chalk and silver, in 1727.
Courtesy George Eastman House.*

whose image the light can transmit. But, what the glass cannot do, the canvas, by means of the viscous matter, retains the image. The mirror shows the object exactly but keeps none; our canvases show them with the same exactness and retain them all. This impression of the images is made the first instant they are received on the canvas, which is immediately carried away into some dark place an hour after the subtle matter dries, and you have a picture, so much more valuable as it cannot be imitated by art nor damaged by time.

"We take in their purest source from the luminous bodies, the colors which painters extract from different materials . . . the justness of the design, the truth of the expression, the gradation of the shades . . . the rules of perspective. All these we leave to Nature, who, with a sure and never erring hand, draws upon our canvases images which deceive the eye and make reason to doubt whether what are called real objects are not phantoms."

What an extraordinary prediction from a writer of scientific romances. His imagination was undoubtedly fired by watching eighteenth-century sketch artists work with the camera obscura!

The chemical prehistory of photography goes back to the mists of antiquity. Men have always known that exposure to the sun's rays tans human skin, draws the sparkle from opals and amethysts, and ruins the flavor of beer. Photography's optical prehistory goes back about a thousand years. The original camera obscura may be called "a room with a sunlit view." The tenth-century Arab mathematician and scientist, Alhazen of Basra, who wrote on fundamental principles of optics and demonstrated the behavior of light, recorded the natural phenomenon of the inverted image. He had observed this on the white walls of darkened rooms or tents set in the sunny landscapes of the Persian Gulf area, the image passing through a small round hole in wall, tent flap, or drapery. The camera obscura was first used by Alhazen to observe eclipses of the sun, which he knew were harmful to the naked eye.

The inverted image of the camera obscura is easily explained, for light passes in straight lines through the small hole cut in the center. The lines of light reflected from the bottom of a sunlit landscape will enter the hole and continue upward in a straight line to the top of the wall of the darkened room. In the same way, the lines of light reflected from the top of the landscape will travel downward to the bottom of the wall, and all lines in between the top and bottom will similarly pass through the center, producing an upside-down image.

Alhazen's treatise was known in Europe in the thirteenth century, which was a period of considerable optical activity (for example, the invention of the lens). But the camera obscura was not to become a practical device for a very long time. Meanwhile, a development of great importance was taking place. This development was psychological, not technical. For the first time in a thousand years men began to turn their thoughts away from the hereafter and toward the sensed world of their natural surroundings. Artists became fascinated by the problems of describing animals, plants, and people accurately and

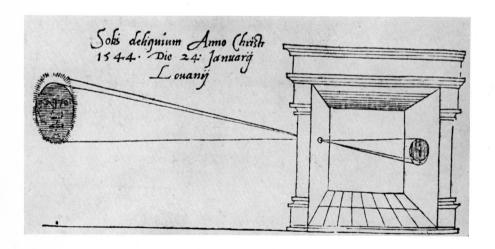

First published illustration of a camera obscura, which is registering the solar eclipse of January 24, 1544. By Rainer Gemma-Frisius, sixteenth-century Dutch scientist. Courtesy Gernsheim Collection, London.

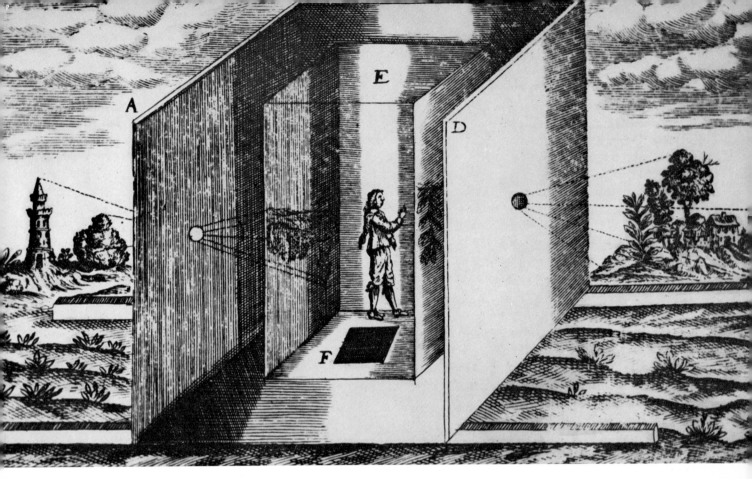

Engraving of a large camera obscura shown with top and front cut away.
A small portable room, it could be easily carried to the scene. The artist then climbed
inside through a trap door, and we see him tracing, from behind, an image cast on
transparent paper which hangs opposite one of the lenses. This was constructed in
Rome by Kircher in 1646. Courtesy George Eastman House, Rochester.

showing them convincingly in space. They studied the world with the utmost determination; and their efforts were as fateful for science as for art, for the artists taught the scientists how to observe.

By the opening years of the fifteenth century, artists were turning to the description of light. On page 22 we see reproduced the first painting in which light was handled as a visual element apart from form and color: a tiny night scene of the Nativity executed by the Italian artist Gentile da Fabriano in 1423. The way things look, Gentile tells us here, depends on the way light hits them. He could not realize it, of course, but he took a big step toward today's photographic vision. The Flemish artist Jan van Eyck, in a little more than a decade, went far beyond Gentile in the study of light, as we may see in his painting *Giovanni Arnolfini and His Bride*. Here is not only a marvelously delicate play of light on forms, but a marvelously precise study of how light and color

are modulated by distance. We call this phenomenon "atmospheric perspective." Linear, or geometric perspective, was a step of even greater importance. It was invented around 1420 by Filippo Brunelleschi, architect, sculptor, painter, mathematician, and the greatest genius of the early Renaissance. In inventing perspective, Brunelleschi envisaged himself as a kind of camera. He assumed that objects are perceived by means of a pyramid or cone of visual rays extending from the eye out into the world. His idea was to intercept this pyramid or cone by a plane a short distance in front of the eye, in this way projecting the visual image on the surface of the plane just as a projector throws a picture on a screen. His first demonstration of the system was a small panel painting of the Baptistery of Florence made from inside the portal of the cathedral a short distance away. A sight hole was bored through the middle of the painting. Brunelleschi would put a friend at the standpoint from which

19

the building had been drawn and have him sight the Baptistery through the hole in back of the painting. That done, he held up a mirror in front of the painting, blocking the actual view of the Baptistery but showing his friend a reflection of the painted view. The two views matched so closely that the beholder never failed to be amazed. The artists Van Eyck and Brunelleschi were making it possible for scientists not only to observe but to observe scientifically.

Leon Battista Alberti's treatise *On Painting* (1435) contains a brief discussion of the perspective system invented by Brunelleschi and an analysis of visual properties of light, both direct and reflected. It also refers (as do other sources) to "miracles of painting that many friends saw me make a while ago in Rome." Alberti's miracles have been interpreted, among other things, as images made with the camera obscura and as boxed peep shows using color transparencies illuminated by sunlight. But the context in which they are mentioned suggests that they were actually perspective constructions fitted with a mirror along the lines of Brunelleschi's painting of the Florence Baptistery. The camera obscura, used as an aid to accurate drawing, did not appear until the second half of the sixteenth century, although Leonardo da Vinci produced a drawing of the instrument in his notebooks (unnoticed until the first publication of his notebooks in 1797). Instead, artists developed rather elaborate and clumsy mechanical devices for making true perspective automatic—*machines pour dessiner*, as they became known in France. On page 21 is reproduced one of four such devices made by the German artist Albrecht Dürer.

The camera obscura was first fully described and illustrated by the Dutch mathematician Gemma-Frisius in 1544. Girolamo Cardano of Milan reported in 1550 that a convex lens could be placed in the window shutter of a darkened room to produce a bright, sharp image. The Venetian Daniello Barbaro, in his book on perspective, described the way in which a double-convex spectacle lens placed in a hole let into the wall of a room would project an image of all the life, color, and movement of the world outside. Giovanni Battista della Porta not only described the double-convex-lens-fitted camera obscura at length in his *Magiae Naturalis* (1558) but recommended its use to artists, suggesting that lines and shapes be copied first and that colors then be added. In the second edition he recommended the addition, inside the room, of a concave mirror placed in such a way that an enlarged right-side-up image would be reflected back onto the wall. Early historians of photography errone-ously ascribed the invention of the camera obscura to Della Porta. In so doing they had been given an assist by Della Porta himself, who was not a modest man.

The lively sixteenth-century interest in optics broke the ground for a new scientific era in the century that followed. In 1604 Johannes Kepler determined the physical and mathematical laws governing reflection by mirrors. In 1609 Galileo invented the compound telescope. In 1611 Kepler worked out the theory of lenses, which now became reliable scientific instruments. Interest in optical phenomena rose to a fever pitch and swept all over Europe. Artists as well as scientists were strongly affected by this development.

If the artists had taught the scientists how to observe, the scientists were now returning the favor. Sixteenth-century painting, especially in Venice and North Italy, had reflected the general interest in optical phenomena. In the seventeenth century this interest became almost obsessive. Architects, stage designers, and sculptors were its captives, falling in love with illusion. Painters drove their vision as far as it would go. Certain Dutchmen—Carel Fabritius, Jan Vermeer, Samuel van Hoogstraten—and the Spaniard Velázquez even went beyond the perceptual limits of the unaided eye to paint phenomena that could be seen only in conjunction with the mirror or lens. Almost certainly, they used the camera obscura. Vermeer's *Girl with Red Hat*, for example, gives us cameralike vision in showing the "circles of confusion" that occur around points of intense illumination when not every ray in a beam of light is brought into the sharpest focus. We can observe a similar phenomenon in the clothing of the little Princess Margarita in Velázquez' *Maids of Honor*. "Photographic" vision, with Van Hoogstraten, reached a point of development that would not be seen again until 1890 or so. Some of his paintings are, for all the world, "tight snapshots."

Although science-minded artists of the seventeenth century could exceed the perceptual limits of the unaided eye through using lenses and mirrors, they could not very well exceed the capacities of the human hand. Artists of the early nineteenth century were to develop an ideal of detailed realism that even the most schooled and disciplined hand of the seventeenth century could not accomplish. The photographic camera would then become an inevitability—and art and science would once again reverse roles in their centuries-old ding-dong game of push and be pushed. The straining of the capacity of the hand as well as of the eye can already be seen in the work of the *veduta* painters of the eighteenth century—painters who concerned themselves to create landscapes and cityscapes with the same relation to actual physical scenes that an accurate portrait bears to a person. The most famous of the *veduta* painters was Canaletto, an enthusiast of the camera obscura whose scenes of Venice are a landmark in the history of art.

The practical usefulness of the camera obscura to artists of the seventeenth, eighteenth, and early nineteenth centuries greatly increased as the size of the instrument diminished. Camera obscura became available for field use when sedan chairs and tents were modified for the purpose in the seventeenth century. In 1620 Kepler, the great astronomer and optical physicist, set up a black tent in a field, inserted a lens in a hole cut in one flap, and traced the image that fell on paper attached to the flap opposite the lens. Gradually, the camera obscura became smaller and more easily portable. It was soon to measure about two feet in length and less than a foot in height, with a lens fitted on one end and a ground glass on the other.

A reflex type of camera obscura was designed by Johann Zahn in 1685. His box had the advantage of a mirror placed inside at a 45-degree angle to the lens, so that the image was reflected upward to the top of the box. Here he placed a sheet of frosted glass, which could be covered with tracing paper so that the image was easily traced. Zahn also invented an even smaller reflex-box

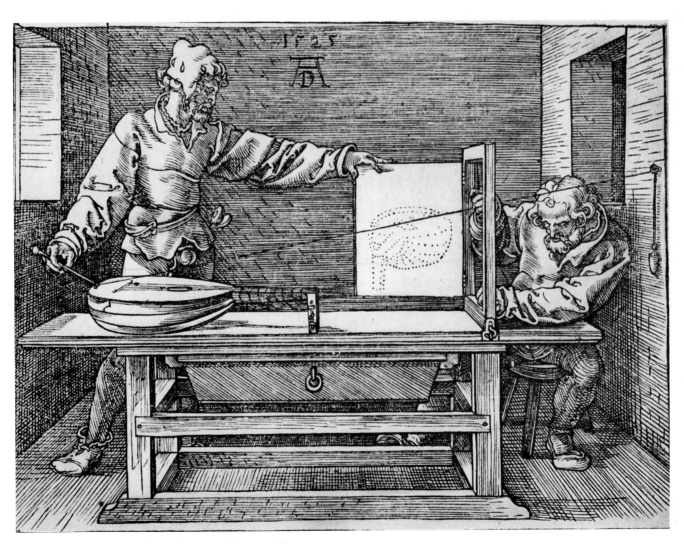

Engraving of 1525 by Albrecht Dürer (1471-1528), German, showing the artist's sighting device for drawing and teaching perspective. Courtesy The Art Institute of Chicago.

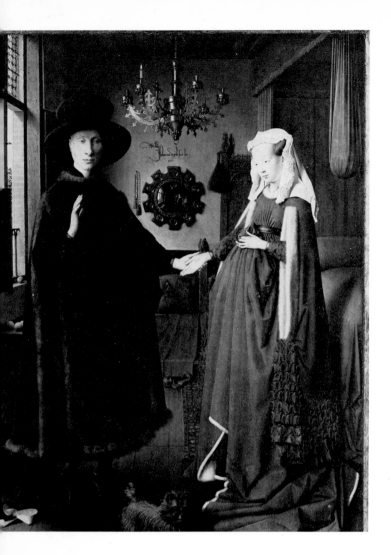

JAN VAN EYCK, Giovanni Arnolfini and His Bride.
*Oil Painting, 1434. Courtesy of the Trustees
of the National Gallery, London.*

Detail

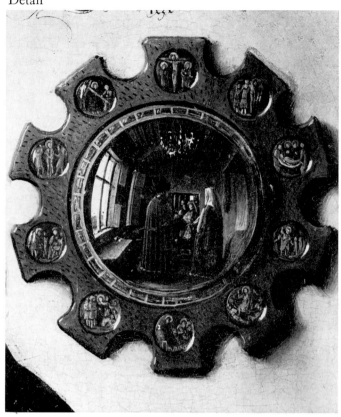

GENTILE DA FABRIANO, The Nativity. 1423.
*Panel from an altarpiece in the
Uffizi Gallery, Florence.*

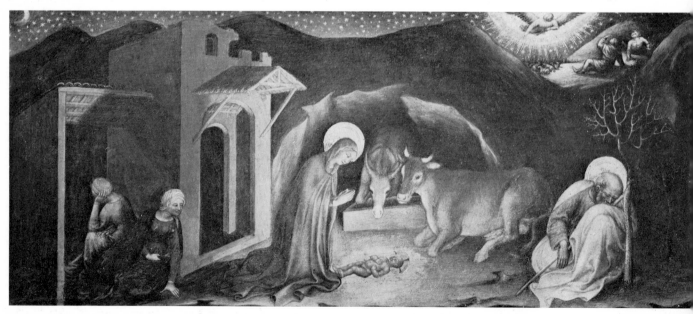

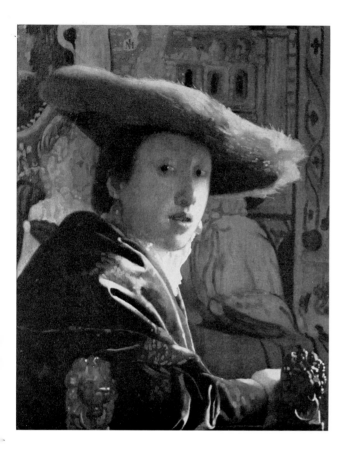

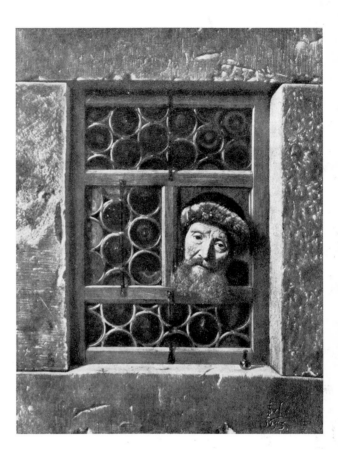

camera obscura fitted with a lens. It resembled the cameras used by Niepce a hundred and fifty years later.

The important growth of the middle class in the eighteenth century created a demand for portraits at reasonable prices. Previously, portraits had been a luxury of the wealthy. The first response to this demand was the development of the "silhouette," which required only that a person trace outlines or shadows cast on a paper and then mount the cut-out likeness.

The "physionotrace," invented by Gilles-Louis Chrétien in 1786, worked on the same principle as the silhouette but had the added advantage that a small engraving on copper resulted from the tracing. This plate could be used to pull an edition of prints.

A third device intended to permit an unskilled operator and a machine to do the work of the artist was the "camera lucida," invented by William Hyde Wollaston in 1806. This enabled the untalented, with the aid of a prism suspended at eye level, to trace images of persons or landscapes reflected on a flat piece of drawing paper. The camera lucida was not a camera at all—its most important asset was its light weight and transportability. Travelers often used it. In 1827–1828 Basil Hall wrote a book, *Forty Etchings Made with the Camera Lucida in North America,* praising the instrument because it freed the traveler and would-be-artist "from the triple misery of perspective, proportion, and form."

The eighteenth-century need for the camera came close to being realized in 1800 by Tom Wedgwood (fourth son of the famous potter Josiah Wedgwood), who secured an image but was unable to make it permanent. In 1796 he experimented with sensitized silver salts to produce images of botanical specimens. He copied the woody fiber of leaves or the wings of insects, which he placed on paper or leather moistened with silver nitrate and exposed to the sun. Had he used ammonia as a fixing agent, a discovery of Carl W. Scheele in Sweden twenty years earlier, or had he washed the image in a heavy solu-

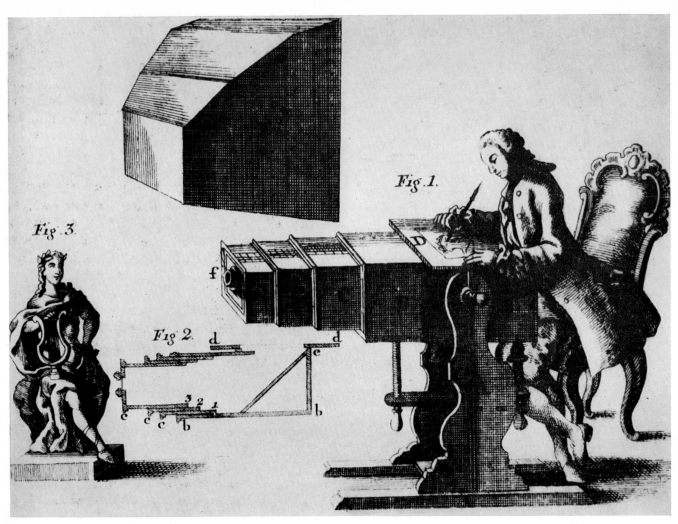

*Table camera obscura, 1769, France.
Courtesy Gernsheim Collection.*

*Reflex box camera obscura, 1685
Germany, invented by Johann Zahn
Courtesy Gernsheim Collection*

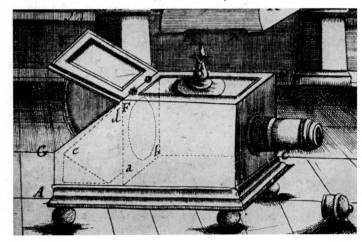

*Sedan-chair
camera obscura,
1711. Courtesy
Gernsheim
Collection.*

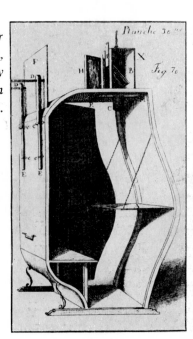

tion of common salt, he could have stopped any further action of light on the sensitive silver salts. Instead, he washed the negative with soap, or he varnished the picture when dry. Though he examined the image by only the weakest of candlelight, it was of no avail, for the image gradually grew black.

How close Tom Wedgwood was to becoming the father of photography! In addition to contact printing he attempted to secure images on prepared paper placed in a camera obscura. As he met with no success, he abandoned further experiments and recorded those he made up to 1802. In that year his friend Sir Humphry Davy wrote a paper explaining Tom's experiments and sent it to the Royal Society. The paper was entitled "On an Account of a Method of Copying Paintings on Glass and of Making Profiles by the Agency of Light upon Nitrate of Silver—Invented by T. Wedgwood Esq." It reads, in part, "the images formed by means of a camera obscura have been found too faint to produce, in any moderate time, an effect upon the nitrate of silver."

The man who first successfully obtained an image from the sun was Nicéphore Niepce of France, who, in 1827, attempted to present a paper to the Royal Society in London while he was in England visiting his brother Claude, like himself a dedicated inventor. Since he kept his process a secret, refusing to describe it in his paper, his proposal was rejected by the Royal Society. Accompanying his paper, however, were several photographs either on glass or metal. In 1853 Robert Hunt, one of photography's first historians, reported several of these plates to be in the collection of the Royal (British) Museum. Mr. Hunt writes, "They prove M. Niepce to have been acquainted with a method of forming pictures, by which the lights, semi-tints, and shadows, were represented as in nature; and he had also succeeded in rendering his heliographs, when once formed, impervious to the further effects of the solar rays. Some of these specimens appear in a state of advanced etchings."

It should not surprise us that these prints resembled etchings, since Niepce actually invented photogravure; and the examples Mr. Hunt saw might well have been "heliogravures" and not photographs taken in the camera obscura.

left: Guyot's table camera obscura, 1770, France.
Courtesy Gernsheim Collection.
below: An early nineteenth-century portable camera obscura.
Courtesy George Eastman House.

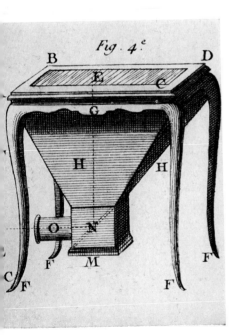

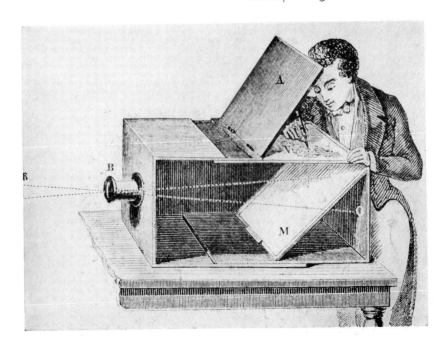

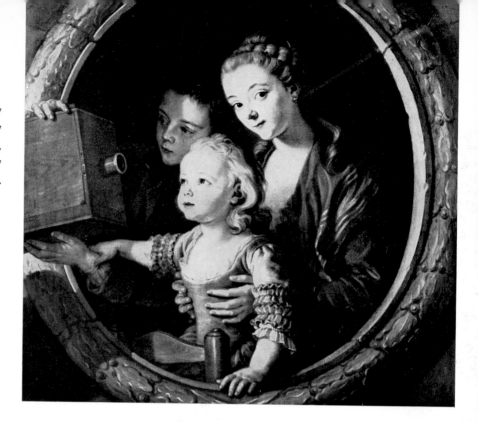

Painting showing the artist's family with a camera obscura, 1764. By Charles A. Philippe Vanloo, (1705-65), French. Courtesy National Gallery of Art, Washington.

Engraving of the German artist Joachim Franze Beich, by Johann Jakob Haid, mid-eighteenth century, showing a small camera obscura as part of the artist's paraphernalia. Courtesy George Eastman House.

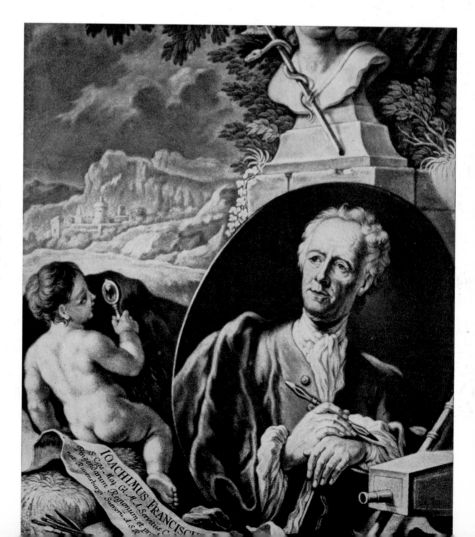

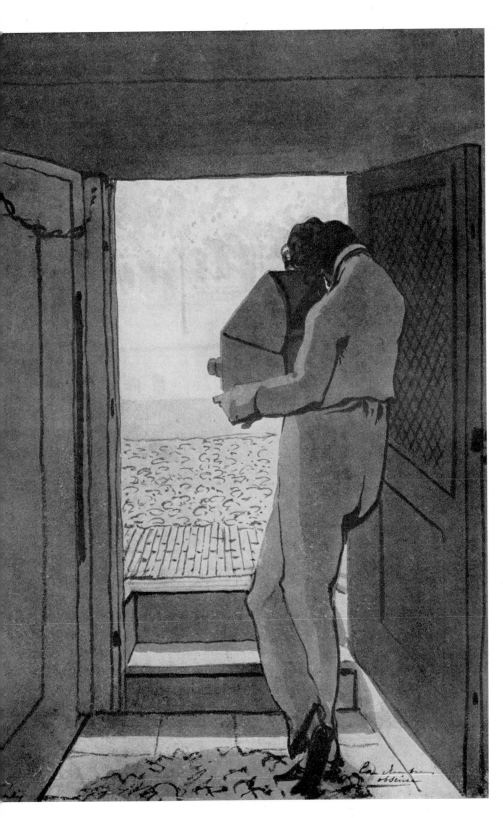

JURRIAEN ANDRIESSEN, The Camera Obscura.
Pen-and-brush drawing, about 1800.
Courtesy Rijksprentenkabinet,
Amsterdam.

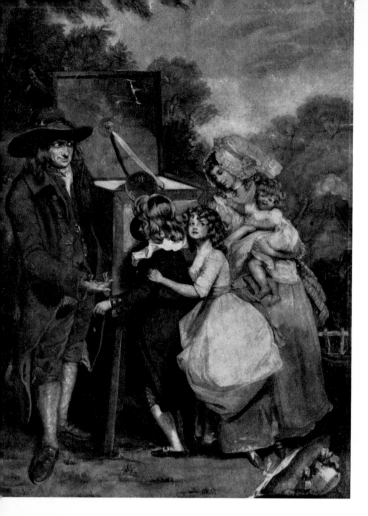

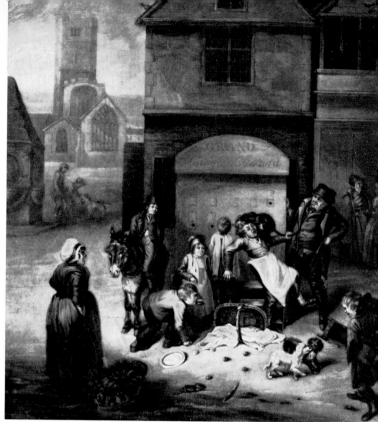

Peep Show. *French mezzotint, around 1790. The sign reads* "camera obscura." *Collection Peter Pollack.*

Street Hawker with Portable Peep Show. *English mezzotint, around 1770. Collection Peter Pollack.*

CANALETTO, Scene in Venice. *Around 1750. Courtesy of the Trustees of the National Gallery, London.*

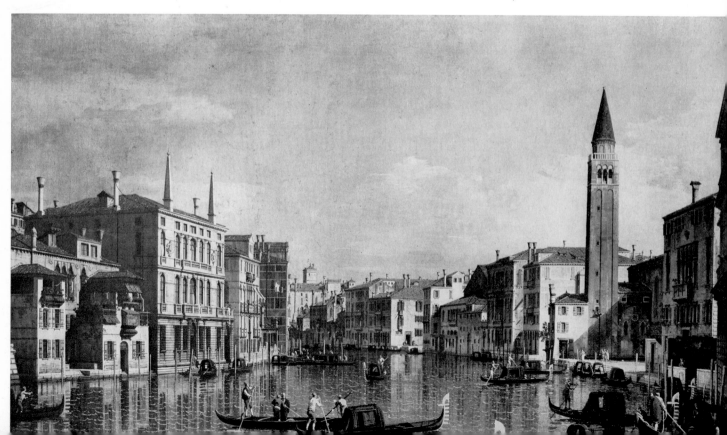

Silhouette. 1786, Germany. The eighteenth-century desire for portraits was satisfied by the simple method of cutting profiles from black paper. These were called "silhouettes," after Etienne de Silhouette, comptroller of finances in the court of Louis XV. Courtesy George Eastman House.

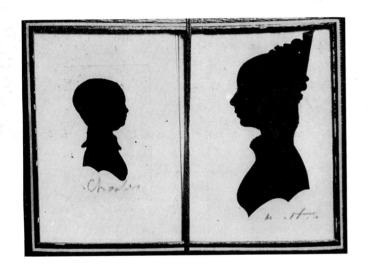

Silhouette. "Hand cut" of Charles Wage, age 2, and his mother. 1824, America. In the early nineteenth century, Rembrandt Peale, the American painter, made silhouettes which he called "profileographs." Courtesy The Art Institute of Chicago.

Portrait of Gilles-Louis Chrétien, 1792, French, who invented the "physionotrace" six years earlier; resembling the silhouette, the physionotrace had the added advantage of tracing small engravings. Courtesy George Eastman House

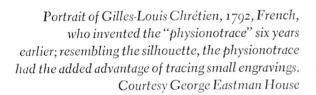

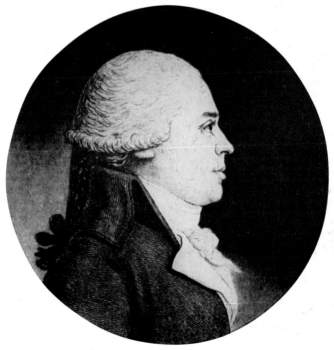

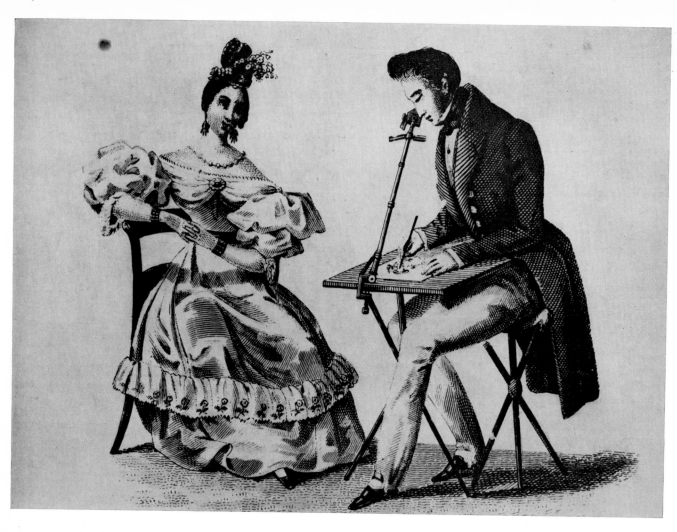

Camera lucida, designed by William Hyde Wollaston in 1806.
This model was made four years later in London. It consists
of three telescoping brass tubes, table clamp, 45° prism,
adjustable peep sight, and spectacle lens to accomodate
individual vision. Courtesy George Eastman House.

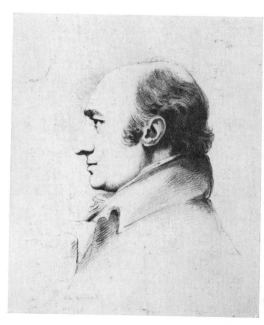

A lithograph of Wollaston from a sketch
made with the camera lucida, which he
invented. Courtesy George Eastman House.

A sketch of the Erie Canal made 1827-28 with the camera lucida by
Captain Basil Hall, R.N. It was copied, printed as an etching,
and published in London in 1830 as one of Forty Etchings from
Sketches Made with the Camera Lucida in North America, 1827-28,
by Captain Basil Hall. *Courtesy Chicago Historical Society.*

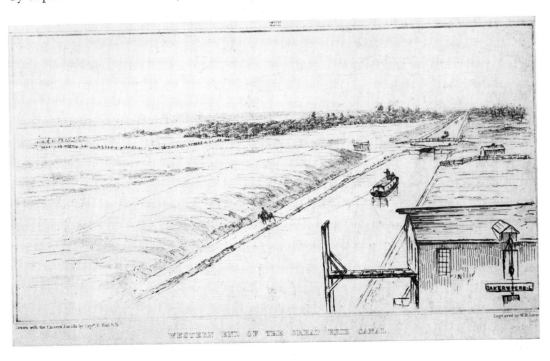

Tom Wedgwood, *the first to conceive the idea of practical
photography, in the year 1800. He was unable, however,
to fix the image. Courtesy George Eastman House.*

Sir Humphry Davy in 1802 *presented a paper to the
Royal Society in London explaining the experiments
of Tom Wedgwood. Courtesy George Eastman House.*

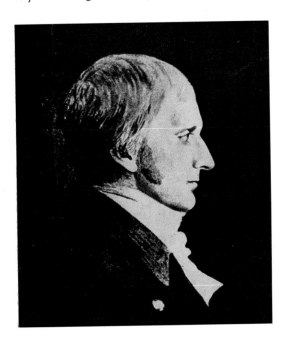

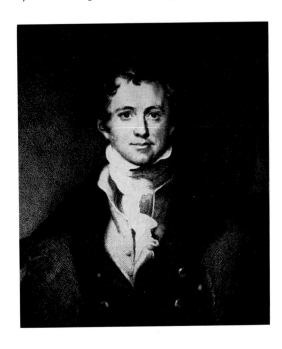

CHAPTER 2
Niepce: The World's First Photographer

IT IS GRATIFYING TO FIND Joseph Nicéphore Niepce, eclipsed for more than a hundred years by his one-time partner, Louis J. M. Daguerre, now once again being honored as the world's first photographer. Niepce not only produced a picture in a camera obscura; he invented an iris diaphragm to correct defects he observed in the full lens (an invention forgotten for more than fifty years; it had to be reinvented). Above all, Niepce was the first to make the image permanent.

He called these images caught in the camera obscura *"points de vue"* to distinguish them from his *"copies de gravure."* In the latter, he made a sandwich consisting of an engraving (made transparent with oil) placed between a sensitized plate and a sheet of clear glass; the glass kept the engraving flat while he exposed the array to the sun.

The images produced by both processes were referred to as "heliographs." The plates on which they were made were coated with bitumen of Judaea, a substance soluble in ethereal oils, such as oil of turpentine, oil of lavender, petroleum, and ether.

Niepce in 1813 had already been interested for several years in improving the process of lithography, which Alois Senefelder had invented in 1796. For Senefelder's heavy Bavarian limestone Niepce substituted a sheet of tin, upon which he had his young son draw designs with a greasy crayon. When the boy was called to the army in 1814, Niepce, unable to draw, found himself handicapped. He then began a series of experiments with various silver salts, intending to eliminate the need for an artist's talent by making light itself draw for him. He achieved the most satisfactory results with a varnish made of bitumen of Judaea dissolved in Dippel's animal oil. This solution he coated on a sheet of glass, copper, or pewter, exposing the sheet to the light from 2 to 4 hours to make a *copie de gravure* or fully 8 hours to produce a *point de vue*.

When the image on the varnish (or asphaltum, as it was also called) was hardened and the picture became visible to the eye, he brought the plate into a darkroom for treatment. First he subjected the plate to an acid bath which dissolved the varnish under the lines of the engraving. This varnish had been protected from the action of light during the exposure, and, accordingly, had remained soft and soluble. Niepce then sent the plate to his friend the artist-engraver, Lemaître (1797–1870), who incised the lines, inked the plate, and pulled an edition of prints as he would have done from any etched or engraved plate. Niepce's most successful heliograph was of Cardinal d'Amboise early in 1827.

According to the historian, Georges Potoniée, it can be proved that Niepce obtained a permanent impression in the camera obscura during the year 1822. However, only one of his *points de vue* that still exist can be dated definitely from the year 1826. This is in the collection of Helmut and Alison Gernsheim, who found it after a piece of research lasting years and involving trailing that would have pleased even the incomparable Sherlock Holmes. This picture seems certain to have been taken in 1826, because that was the year that Niepce turned to pewter instead of copper and zinc plates. Exposure took 8 hours, and this caused the sun to light both sides of the view, a building, taken from his room. Niepce wrote his son Isidore explaining that he preferred pewter, since it was darker than copper and bright when polished, so that the contrast of black and white lines remained much sharper.

His friend Lemaître suggested the perfect metal, silver plating on copper, which Daguerre was later to make universally popular in the daguerreotype. Niepce considered Lemaître's suggestion the perfect solution, for he intended to etch the best of his camera views, making incisions with a burin through the thin silver plate to the sturdier plate of copper below, which would enable him to pull an edition of prints.

Niepce continued to improve his heliogravure method, making the image a bit sharper by exposing the metal plate to the fumes of a few grains of iodine, then removing all the bitumen varnish to disclose the bare metal. The result was an image composed by the iodine vapors which had blackened the silver, contrasted to the shiny polished silver which had been under the hardened bitumen and which became visible when alcohol dissolved the varnish.

Niepce treated a glass plate as he did metal, with this distinguishing difference, that when the asphaltum was dissolved in oil of lavender, the plate was then washed and dried and viewed as a transparency. It is strange that Niepce, who was working toward a solution of the problem of making multiple reproductions, never seems to have used the transparency as a negative, to make prints from it on paper sensitized with silver salts. This negative-positive principle—from which all modern photography stems—was to be the invention of Fox Talbot several years later in England.

In 1829 the sixty-four-year-old Niepce was ill and badly in need of money. He and his brother Claude, who had died in England the previous year, had spent their patrimony on all kinds of inventions, prospering from none. There had never been a need to make money, for the Niepce family was rich and well-educated, and lived in a luxurious home at Châlons-sur-Sàone when Joseph was born in 1765. His father was a Councillor of the King, his mother the daughter of a noted lawyer. Joseph showed interest in inventions even while in his teens but studied to become a cleric, doffing the collar in 1792 to become an officer in the army, seeing active service in Sardinia and Italy. Ill health made him resign his commission, and for the next seven years he was in Nice as a member of the government administration.

He returned to his ancestral home in 1801 to devote himself immediately with his brother Claude to all kinds of scientific investigations, but it was heliography that was his major interest until he died in 1833.

Scientific research was costly even then. Niepce needed money desperately, but, even so, he didn't answer a letter from Daguerre, the successful entrepreneur of the Diorama in Paris, until a year had passed. And then he answered warily, giving no facts, but rather trying to ascertain the extent of Daguerre's experiments which, according to Daguerre, had been quite successful because of his invention of a new camera.

Returning from England later in that year, 1827, after visiting his sick brother, Niepce met with the affluent, prosperous Daguerre, twenty years his junior. They became partners in 1829, after Daguerre convinced Niepce not to publish his process even though he felt he couldn't

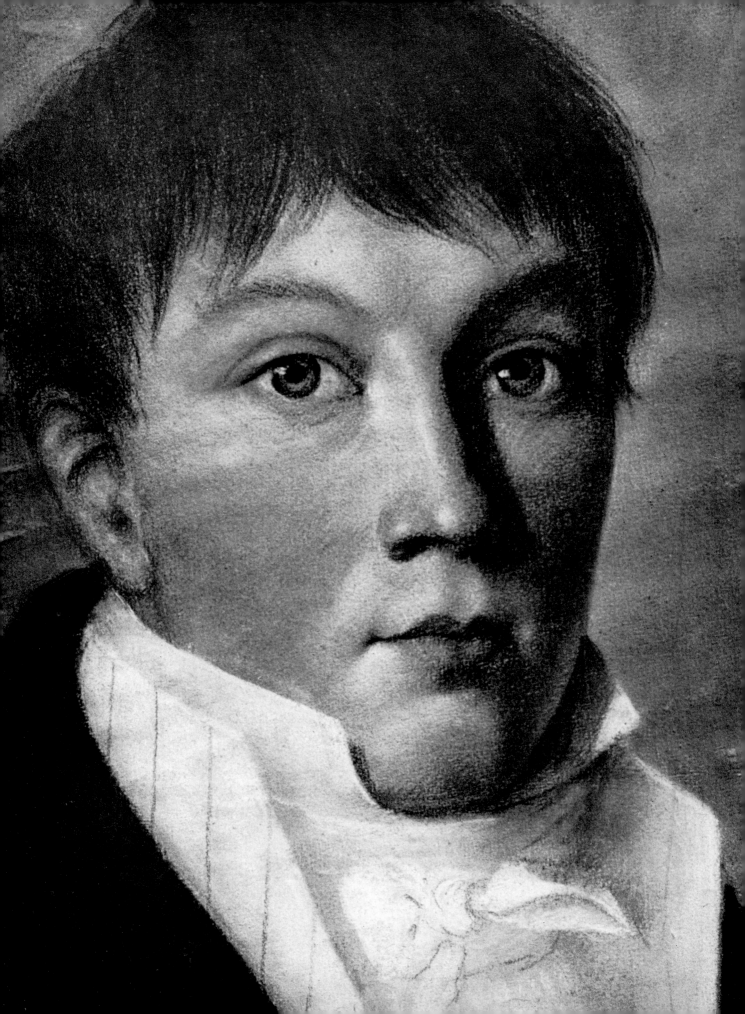

improve it any further. Daguerre's letter reads, ". . . there should be found a way to get a large profit out of the invention before publication, apart from the honors you will receive."

In October, 1829, Niepce wrote Daguerre, offering to cooperate with him "for the purpose of perfecting the heliographic process and to combine the advantages which might result in a complete success." A ten-year partnership contract was signed by both parties on December 14, 1829, which reads in part, "M. Daguerre invites M. Niepce to join him in order to obtain the perfection of a new method discovered by M. Niepce, for fixing the images of nature without having recourse to an artist."

Niepce contributed his invention, Daguerre contributed "a new adaptation of the camera obscura, his talents, and his labor."

It appears to have been an uneven bargain, for to the Niepce-Daguerre partnership the camera of Daguerre was still an uncertain, untried asset and, actually, all that was known of photography was the contribution of Niepce. But Daguerre was a vital half of the partnership; the aged and ill Niepce was discouraged about the future of his experiments and badly in need of Daguerre's youth and self-confidence. Above all Niepce had faith in Daguerre's abiding interest in photography, his conviction that the process would be perfected and become a commercial success. Niepce included in the contract the proviso that his son Isidore would succeed to the partnership in case he died before the contract expired.

Niepce sent Daguerre a detailed description of his process, a note on heliography, completely explaining the preparation of silver, copper, or glass plates, the proportions of the various mixtures, the solvents used in developing the image, the washing and fixing procedures, and the application of his latest experiments in the heliograph—using iodine vapors to blacken the image.

Niepce also demonstrated his techniques to Daguerre, who went to Châlons for this purpose. Daguerre left for Paris several days later and never saw Niepce again. Each man worked on the invention; little is known of their progress other than that Daguerre wrote in 1831, asking Niepce to experiment with iodine in combination with silver salts as a light-sensitive substance. Niepce did not respond enthusiastically. He had not been too successful in previous experiments with silver iodide—a silver halide which only when mixed in exactly the proper proportions can be made sensitive to light.

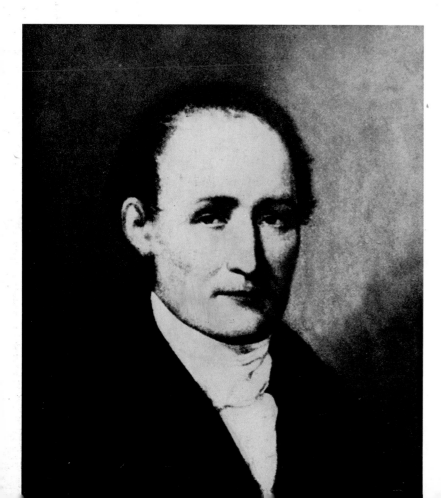

opposite page: Portrait of Nicéphore Niepce as a young man, *about 1785. Artist unknown. Courtesy Janine Niepce, Paris.*
left: Portrait of Nicéphore Niepce, *inventor of photography, painted by Leonard Berger 20 years after Niepce's death. Courtesy George Eastman House, Rochester.*

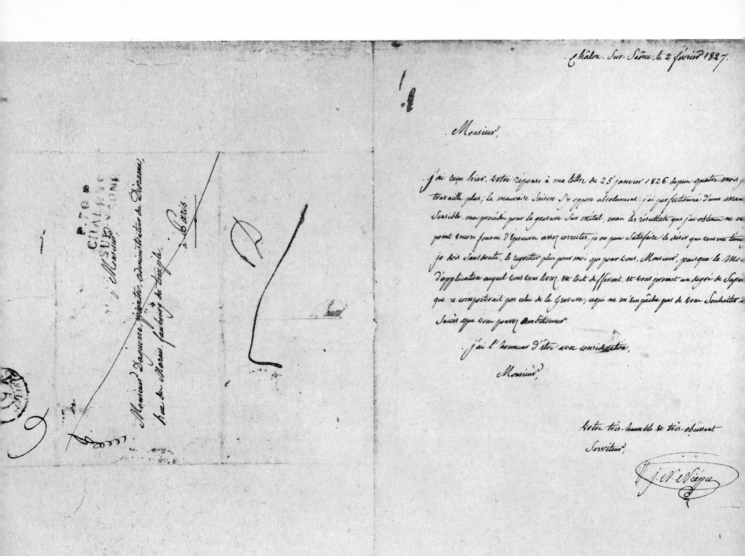

Letter dated February 2, 1827, from Niepce in which
he discourages Daguerre from continuing negotiations.
Taken from Anales del museo La Plata documentos
historicos relativos descobrimiento de la fotografia, Buenos
Aires, 1892. Courtesy the John Crerar Library, Chicago.

The letter reads:

Châlons-sur-Saône
2 February 1827

I received your reply yesterday answering my letter of
25 January 1826. The last four months I have not
worked; the winter months are not too favorable.
I have considerably improved my process of engraving
on metal, but the results I have obtained are not yet
good enough, and so I cannot satisfy the desire which
you express. I ought doubtless to regret this more
for my sake than for yours, sir, since your mode of
application is quite different and promises you a degree
of superiority over my engraving method. This does
not prevent me from wishing you all the success which
you could hope for.

I remain your humble servant
Niepce

ci-après.

article 12. Les comptes du caissier et l'état de Situation seront arrêtés, Signés et paraphés chaque Semestre par les deux associés.

art. 13. Les améliorations et perfectionnemens apportés à la dite découverte, ainsi que les perfectionnemens apportés à la chambre noire, Seront et demeureront acquis au profit des deux associés qui, lorsqu'ils Seront parvenus au but qu'ils Se proposent, feront un traité définitif entre Eux, Sur la base du présent.

Art. 14. Les bénéfices des associés dans les produits nets de la Société, Seront répartis par moitié entre Eux. Niepce en Sa qualité d'inventeur, et Mr. Daguerre, pour Sa perfectionnement.

Art. 15. Les contestations qui pourraient S'élever entre les associés, à raison de l'exécution du présent, Seront jugées définitivement Sans appel ni recours en cassation, par des Arbitres nommés par chacune des parties, à l'amiable, conformément à l'article 51 du Code de Commerce.

art. 16. En cas de dissolution de cette Société, la liquidation S'en fera par le caissier, à l'amiable, ou par les associés ensemble, ou enfin, par une personne tierce qu'ils nommeront à l'amiable, ou qui Sera nommée par le tribunal compétent à la diligence du plus actif des Associés.

Le tout a été ainsi réglé provisoirement entre les parties qui, pour l'exécution du présent, font élection de domicile en leurs demeures respectives, ci-devant désignées.

fait double et Signé à Châlon-Sur-Saône, le 14 Décembre 1829.

J'approuve quoique non écrit de ma main.

Je Soussigné, en ma qualité de Seul et unique héritier de mon père, Déclare avoir pris parfait connaissance du présent traité, et m'engage à en remplir Scrupuleusement toutes les Clauses Sous peine de Dommages et intérêts, ainsi qu'il est Stipulé dans l'article 6.

fait à Paris, le Neuf Mai mil huit cent trente Cinq.

Signatures of Joseph Nicéphore Niepce and Louis-Jacques-Mandé Daguerre on their contract of December 14, 1829. This contract, two letters from Niepce to Daguerre, and the contracts of Daguerre and Isidore Niepce were in the possession of Arago. Courtesy the John Crerar Library.

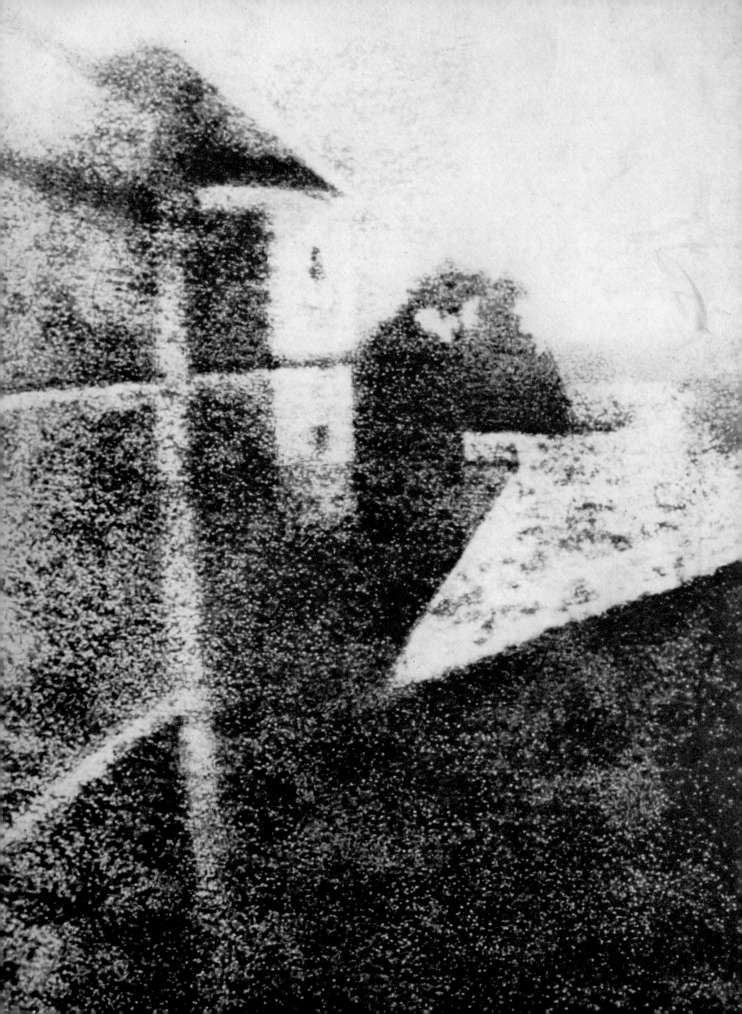

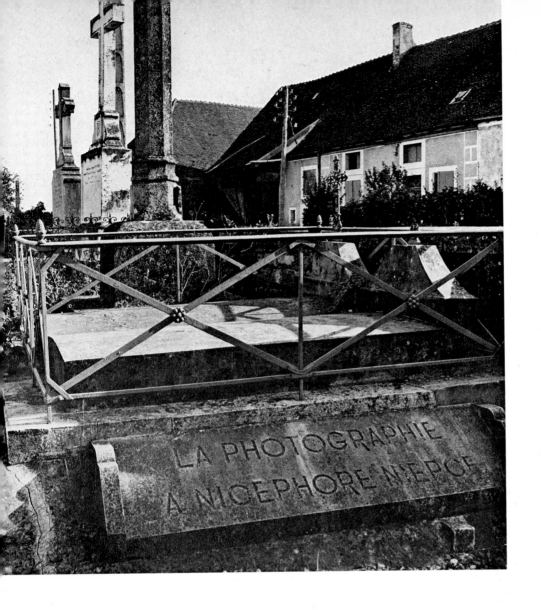

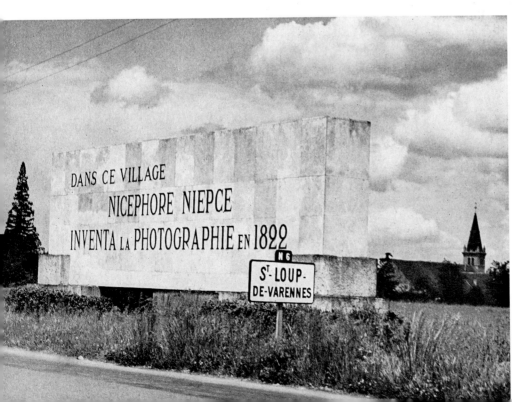

CHAPTER 3
Daguerre
and the Daguerreotype

LOUIS-JACQUES-MANDÉ DAGUERRE (1787–1851) did not invent photography, but he made it work, made it popular, and made it his own.

Within a year after its announcement in 1839 his name and his process were known in all parts of the world. Honors were showered on him and wealth and security were his. The name of Joseph Nicéphore Niepce was practically forgotten.

It was Daguerre, however, who actually made the Niepce invention work, using chemicals that Niepce never hit upon. His ingenious idea was to bring out the image by the vapor of mercury. He experimented first with bichloride of mercury, which just barely brought out the image; improved it by using sweet or subchloride of mercury; and, finally, in 1837, after eleven years of experimentation, hit upon the heating of mercury, letting the vapors develop the image. He then fixed the image perfectly and permanently by using a strong solution of common salt and hot water to dissolve away the particles of silver iodine not affected by the light.

Daguerre's principle of development by mercury vapor was original, a workable process based undoubtedly on knowledge he gained from Niepce. Niepce, however, contributed nothing to further the invention after 1829, nor did his son Isidore. Isidore became Daguerre's partner after Niepce died impoverished at the age of sixty-nine in the year 1833. The son, badly in need of money, signed a new contract several years later, stating that Daguerre was the inventor of the daguerreotype; and he permitted the original name of the firm, Niepce-Daguerre, to be reversed.

These were the steps of Daguerre's process:

1. Thin sheet of silver soldered onto a thicker sheet of copper.
2. Silver surface polished to a perfect finish.
3. Silver plate iodized by fumes of iodine making it sensitive to the light.
4. Prepared plate put in light-tight holder in the dark; plate holder placed in camera.
5. Camera placed on tripod, set in landscape, and pointed to any object in direct sunlight.
6. Lens uncovered 15 to 30 minutes (the best time for a picture by Niepce was 8 hours).
7. Latent image developed and made permanent by the following steps:

   a. Plate placed in a cabinet on a 45° angle above a container under which a spirit lamp heated the mercury to 150°F.
   b. Plate watched carefully until picture was made quite visible by the mercury particles adhering to the exposed silver.
   c. Plate plunged into cold water to harden surface.
   d. Plate submerged in a solution of common salt (after 1839 replaced by hyposulphite of soda, the fixing agent discovered by Sir John Herschel and immediately adopted by Daguerre).
   e. Plate then thoroughly washed to stop the action of the fixing agent.

The result was an individual picture, a positive. It could be seen only in certain lights; in direct rays of the sun it became a shiny sheet of metal. The image was reversed as in a mirror. It could not be multiplied or printed in unlimited numbers, as positives can be from a single negative—the negative-positive principle of photography was the invention of Fox Talbot. Both discoveries were announced in the same year.

To make the most of his invention Daguerre first tried to organize a corporation by public subscription. When this was unsuccessful, he attempted to sell it for a quarter of a million francs, but to cautious speculators this appeared too much of a gamble.

Daguerre created considerable interest, for he took pictures with his heavy camera and equipment along the boulevards of Paris. But he did not explain the operation and businessmen remained cold to its possibilities.

Daguerre then interested scientists in the invention, particularly the influential astronomer, Dominique-François Arago (1786–1853). Arago, believing a rumor that Russia and England were offering to buy the daguerreotype, reported Daguerre's achievement on January 7, 1839, to the Academy of Sciences, and proposed that the French government purchase the process.

The announcement of the daguerreotype produced a sensation. Scientific journals printed Arago's report. Daguerre became better known for this invention than for his well-established Diorama. He showed views of Paris taken by the daguerreotype process to newspaper editors, writers, and artists, who acclaimed him and his invention. Daguerre asked 200,000 francs for it and told Isidore Niepce he would split this with him if it were sold, deducting the amount Isidore had borrowed from him since his father's death.

Arago convinced Daguerre that a pension by the French government would be more of an honor, a national award of recognition for his invention, and he wrote Daguerre, "You will not suffer that we shall allow foreign nations the glory of presenting to the scientific and artistic world one of the most marvelous discoveries that honor our country."

A pension was agreed upon—6,000 francs annually for life to Daguerre and 4,000 for Isidore Niepce, with half pension for their widows. The proposal was presented to the Chamber of Deputies on June 15, 1839 and passed by King Louis Philippe a month later. On August 19 Arago made public Daguerre's startling method of obtaining a pictorial image from nature in all its details, unaided by the hand of an artist, a picture entirely drawn by the sun.

Arago's report was brilliant. He dazzled the audience with superb daguerreotypes taken by Daguerre. The members of the Academy of Sciences and the equally revered Academy of Fine Arts were entranced. Some of the finest intellects of France and of all Europe were present. Arago described the history of photography—making a number of errors, such as attributing the invention of the camera obscura to Della Porta and slighting Niepce's contribution—but he explained the daguerreotype process in scientific terms and in some detail. With clear insight he predicted its importance for the future, the consequences it would have in recording history. He closed his impassioned speech with the words, "France has adopted this discovery and from the first has shown her pride in being able to donate it generously to the whole world." Arago was apparently unaware that, just five days before, on August 14, Daguerre had secured a patent in England. The future looked rewarding.

Daguerre was again secure financially. Only several months before, on March 8, when his famous Diorama was burned to the ground, he had seemed destitute.

It was the Diorama, a huge, special structure with enormous 72-by-46-foot canvases, that, apparently, had brought Daguerre to experiment with photography. He was well acquainted with the camera obscura, and had made sketches from nature in his attempts to create an illusion of reality. In the Diorama he painted tremendous canvases so astonishingly realistic that visitors believed they were three-dimensional constructions in the building. He introduced the innovation of painting pictures on both sides of this canvas. The demands of the Diorama taxed his ingenuity, but he met its challenge by creating gigantic pictures with translucent and opaque paints, inventing shutters and screens to control the natural light that entered through the windows; and he developed spectacular effects in some scenes by manipulating oil lamps as spots and, in the last five years of the Diorama's existence, by using gaslight for even more novel illusionary effects. When he opened the Diorama in 1822 in Paris he was already well known as a painter of panoramas 350 feet long and 50 feet high and as a stage designer. He had received some acclaim for his easel paintings in *trompe-l'oeil* (pictures so realistic as to "fool the eye"). One of these paintings, undoubtedly his best, *Ruin of Holyrood Chapel*, earned him the red ribbon of the Legion of Honor when it was exhibited in 1824. He was to receive the rank of *officier* fifteen years later when the daguerreotype was announced.

This resourceful, colorful showman, who was his own greatest creation, came from a *petit-bourgeois* family. He was the son of a clerk employed on the royal estate in Orléans. The young Louis' formal education ended at fourteen. He was apprenticed for three years to an architect where he learned perspective and accurate architectural drafting. This experience, added to his natural gift for drawing, prepared him for another term of apprenticeship, this time for three years, to Degotti, the celebrated designer for stage and opera. After this term he became assistant to Prevost, a noted stage designer of the period with whom he remained for nine years, until 1813. Daguerre's work was singled out for praise by the critics —he was mentioned among actors, singers, composers, and conductors. The public applauded his elaborate productions and ingenious stage devices.

The Diorama was his crowning achievement as the creator of imposing spectacles. It was as popular as the movies are in our day and met about the same need for entertainment, travel, and illusion. In 1823, a year after they opened the Paris Diorama, Daguerre and his partner Bouton, also a painter of huge canvases, built a similar structure in London. Most of the thirty-one dioramas they painted for Paris were given an average showing of seven months and were then sent for viewing in the London Diorama. The exhibitions included such elaborate paintings as *The Valley of Sarnen in Switzerland, Interior of Chartres Cathedral, Effect of Fog and Snow Seen through a Ruined Gothic Colonnade, The Beginning of the Deluge, The Tomb of Napoleon at St. Helena,* the *Grand Canal of Venice,* and the *Solomon's Temple,* which burned with the Diorama in Paris but for which a sketch remains.

Interest in the Diorama had been waning; it had been operating at a loss when, in 1838, Daguerre tried to gain government support for it as an attraction that brought visitors to Paris. No funds were forthcoming. Daguerre threatened to close the Diorama and move to London, where the Diorama was still popular and profitable.

First official recognition of his contribution as a painter and creator of the diorama came when Arago had him include details of his diorama technique in the agreement with the government in which he disclosed the steps for making a daguerreotype. This was a ruse to obtain for Daguerre the greater share of the pension granted by the government, 6,000 francs for Daguerre and 4,000 for Isidore Niepce. How advantageous, when Daguerre had no plans to reopen the Diorama!

He concentrated on explaining the daguerreotype process, giving demonstrations to scientists and artists, simplifying the complicated scientific account given by Arago and exhibiting his own examples of the art. Daguerre started to manufacture apparatus for the daguerreotype with his brother-in-law, Giroux. Giroux, a stationer, quickly gave up his other business to devote himself exclusively to production of the Giroux camera. Chevalier ground the lenses; and each camera was stamped with a serial number, and signed by Daguerre, who thus made it official. Half the profits of this partnership were to go to Daguerre, who generously gave Isidore Niepce 50 per cent of his share.

The day after Arago made his report Giroux published Daguerre's seventy-nine-page manual. All the cameras he had on hand as well as the manual were sold out in a few days. The pamphlet went through thirty editions in French. Before the year was out it was translated into all languages and printed in all the capitals of Europe and in the city of New York.

Artists, scientists, and the general public quickly improved and modified Daguerre's process, shortening the

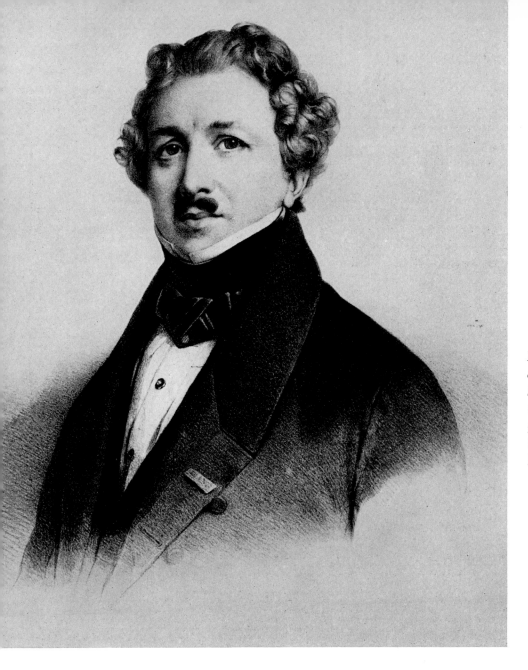

Daguerre was often a subject for artist friends. This lithograph by Henri Grevedon was drawn in 1837, two years before Daguerre published the daguerreotype process. Courtesy George Eastman House, Rochester.

exposure to several minutes, so that portraits seemed feasible and in one month became an actuality.

Samuel F. B. Morse, the artist and inventor of the telegraph, met Daguerre in Paris. Morse had written soon after the Diorama had burned down to inform Daguerre that he had been elected an honorary member of the National Academy of Design in New York; that the description of the daguerreotype Morse had sent home had been published in many American papers; and that, if Daguerre could prevail upon the French government to permit an exhibition of daguerreotypes to be shown in the United States six months before the process would be demonstrated in France, Daguerre would derive a "pecuniary advantage." There was no reply by Daguerre to this letter.

By September 20, 1839, Morse had his wife and daughter "sit from 10 to 20 minutes, out of doors, on the roof of a building, in the full sunlight and with the eyes closed." This is believed to be the first daguerreotype *portrait* taken in the world.

These long exposures were torture. It became obvious that the full-size 6½-by-8½-inch plate was too big for portraiture. This was remedied immediately by reducing its size to a quarter plate, bringing the required time

45

down to 2 minutes. Improved lenses, especially one invented by Joseph Max Petzval in 1840, a fast achromatic lens with large aperture, were decisive factors in making portraits possible. The conclusive discovery was that of faster chemicals. Mercury speeded up with bromine and chlorine vapors made the plate more sensitive, cutting quarter-plate exposure time down to 30 seconds.

Portraiture became a reality for the multitudes.

A prism turned the image around from its left-to-right-reversed attitude, so that the portrait was seen normally, as one is seen by people, not as one sees oneself in a mirror. A decided step forward was the construction, by 1841, of smaller apparatus that reduced Daguerre's 110 pounds of equipment to less than 10 pounds. Still further improvement was protection for the daguerreotype surface which was fragile and easily scratched or damaged. Hippolyte Fizeau, in 1840, had the thought of toning the image with chloride of gold. This not only increased the contrast of the image; it produced the beautiful deep, silvery-gray tone that oxidized into a rich, purplish brown.

Daguerre received honors and acclaim as his invention conquered the imagination of people everywhere. He himself, however, made no further contribution to photography after publication of his process. Until he died in 1851, he lived in retirement at Bry-sur-Marne about 6 miles from Paris. In 1843 he claimed to have perfected instantaneous photography, to have taken a bird in flight; but he could not prove his claim.

His last work was a return to his first and abiding love, a *trompe-l'oeil* painting representing soaring columns, deep vaulting, and stained-glass windows. He placed it behind the altar of a simple church in Bry, transforming the small church by his "magical" art into a great Gothic cathedral.

The inventor of the daguerreotype lies buried in a tomb, donated by his fellow citizens of Bry, where he was interred July 10, 1851, soon after his death.

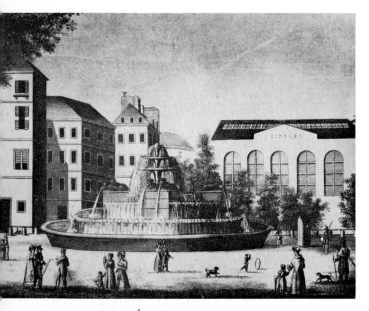

The Diorama in Paris, *about 1830, in which enormous paintings by Daguerre, 72 x 46 feet, were displayed. Wood engraving. Artist unknown. Courtesy George Eastman House.*

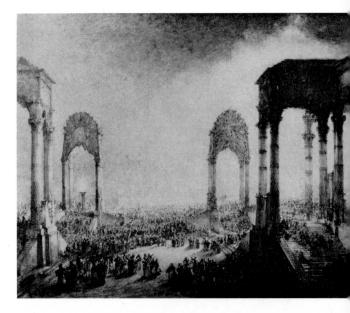

Solomon's Temple, *a sketch in color for the last Paris Diorama presentation, on view September 15, 1836, to March 8, 1839, when the Diorama burned to the ground. Courtesy George Eastman House.*

Diorama ticket, good for two, signed by
Daguerre, 1830. Courtesy George Eastman House.

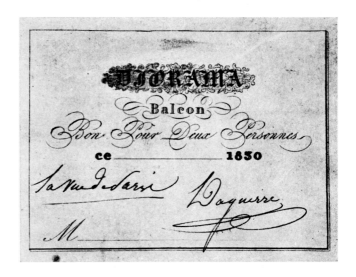

Holyrood Chapel, Edinburgh, *oil painting by Daguerre, 1824. Considered*
Daguerre's best easel painting. He was awarded the Legion of Honor
when it was exhibited. Courtesy Walker Art Gallery, Liverpool.

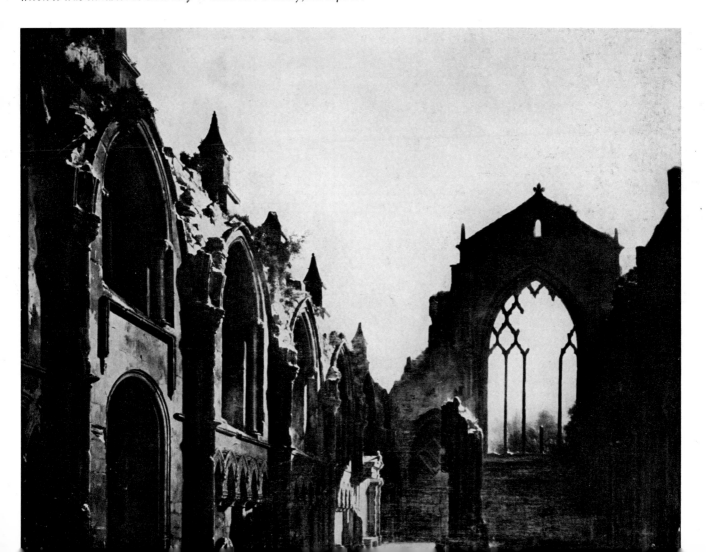

LOUIS-JACQUES-MANDE DAGUERRE, *The earliest surviving daguerreotype. Taken in the artist's studio, 1837. Courtesy Société française de photographie, Paris.*

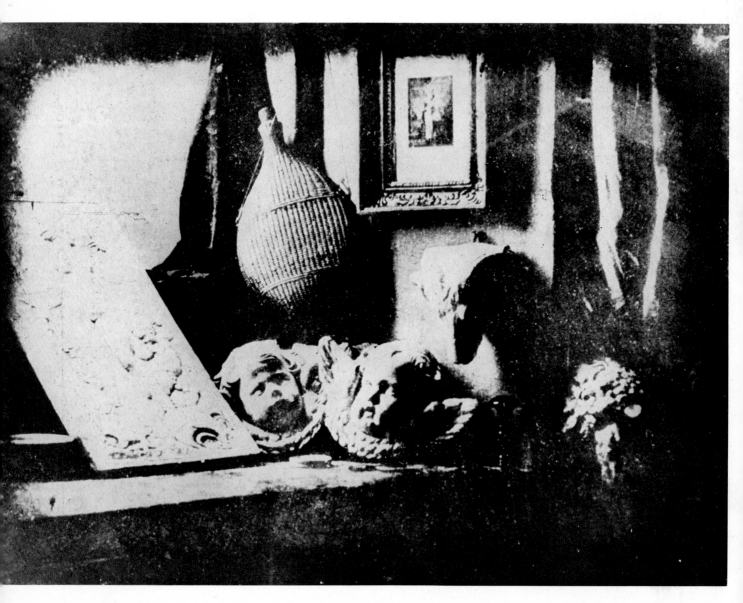

HISTORIQUE ET DESCRIPTION

DES PROCÉDÉS DU

DAGUERRÉOTYPE

ET DU DIORAMA,

PAR DAGUERRE,

Inventeur du Diorama, officier de la Légion-d'Honneur, membre de plusieurs Académies, etc., etc.

PARIS.

ALPHONSE GIROUX ET Cᵉ,
RUE DU COQ-SAINT-HONORÉ, 7,
Où se fabriquent les Appareils.
DELLOYE, LIBRAIRE,
PLACE DE LA BOURSE, 13.

. 1839.

The title page of the rare first edition of Daguerre's instruction manual, with imprint by Alphonse Giroux. Written in longhand on its face by M. Mentienne, son of Daguerre's closest friend, the mayor of Bry, is the inscription, "Given to my father by Daguerre in 1840." Courtesy George Eastman House.

Talent Through Sleep. *The press caricatured the daguerreotype from the very beginning. In the periodical* Today, *March 15, 1840, less than a year after Daguerre's process was announced, Gérard Fontallard satirized the long exposure necessary. Courtesy Gernsheim Collection, University of Texas.*

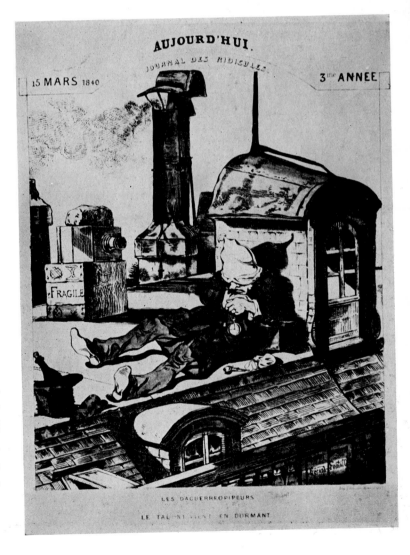

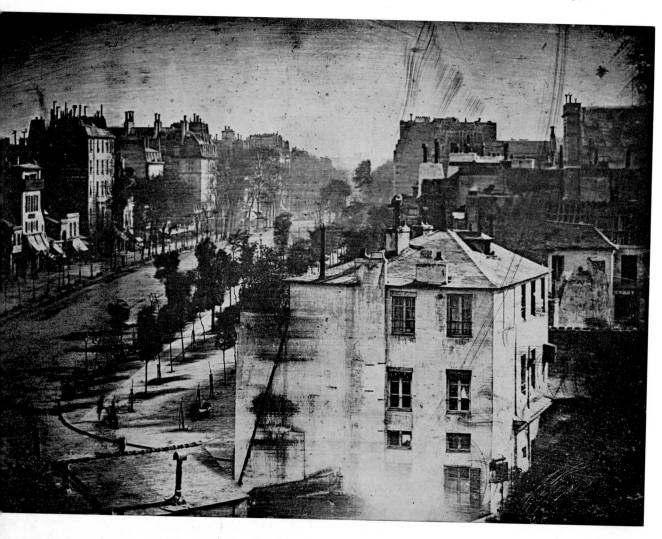

LOUIS-JACQUES-MANDE DAGUERRE, Paris Boulevard. *Daguerreotype, 1839. Sent by Daguerre to the King of Bavaria. This photograph (see detail on the facing page) is the first taken of a human being. The original, formerly in the National Museum, Munich, was destroyed during World War II. Samuel F. B. Morse wrote when he saw this daguerreotype, "The boulevard, so constantly filled with a moving throng of pedestrians and carriages, was perfectly solitary, except for an individual who was having his boots brushed." Courtesy George Eastman House.*

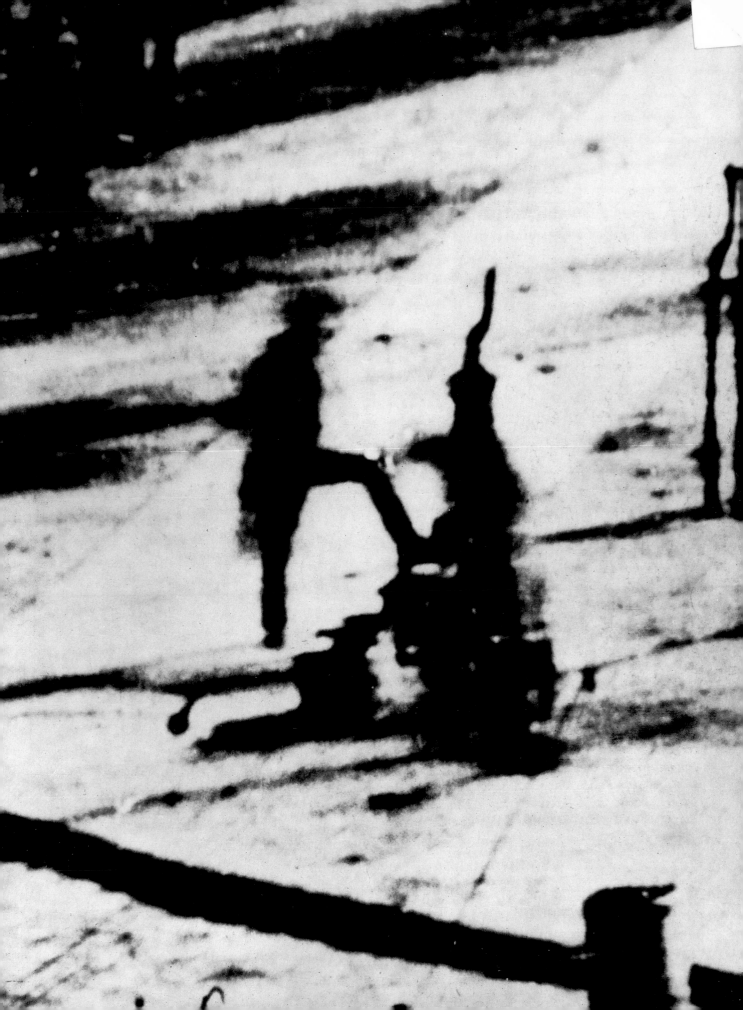

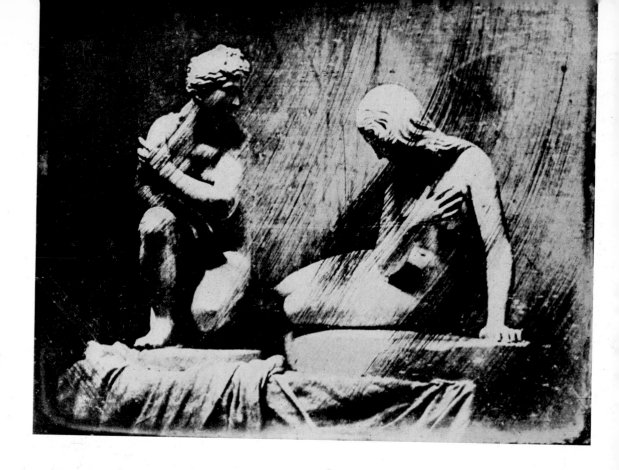

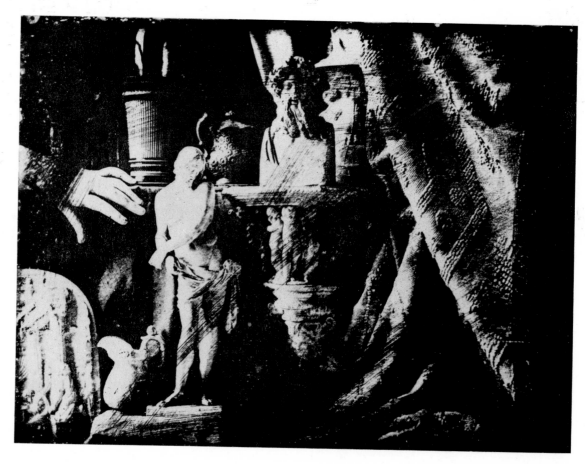

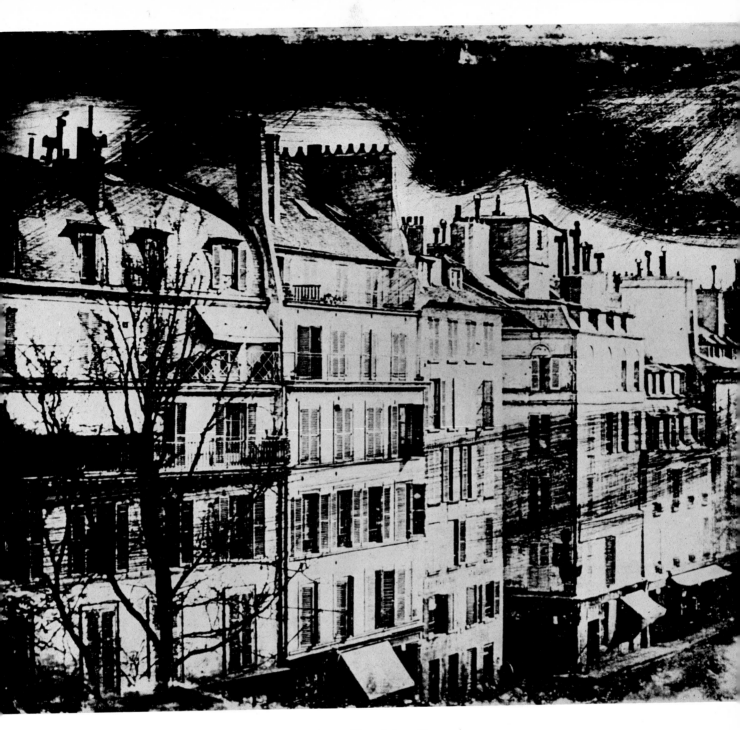

*Daguerreotypes by Daguerre, made 1839, rediscovered 1955. Dominique-François
Arago showed the following three of a group that Daguerre furnished to him in
August, 1839, at the meeting of the Academy of Sciences in which he made Daguerre's
process known. Two years later he presented the Perpignan Museum with these
daguerreotypes. On the back of each is written, "Picture which served to prove
the discovery of the Daguerreotype, given to M. Arago by his very humble servant
Daguerre." above: View of Paris. opposite page, above: Sculpture. left: Still Life.*

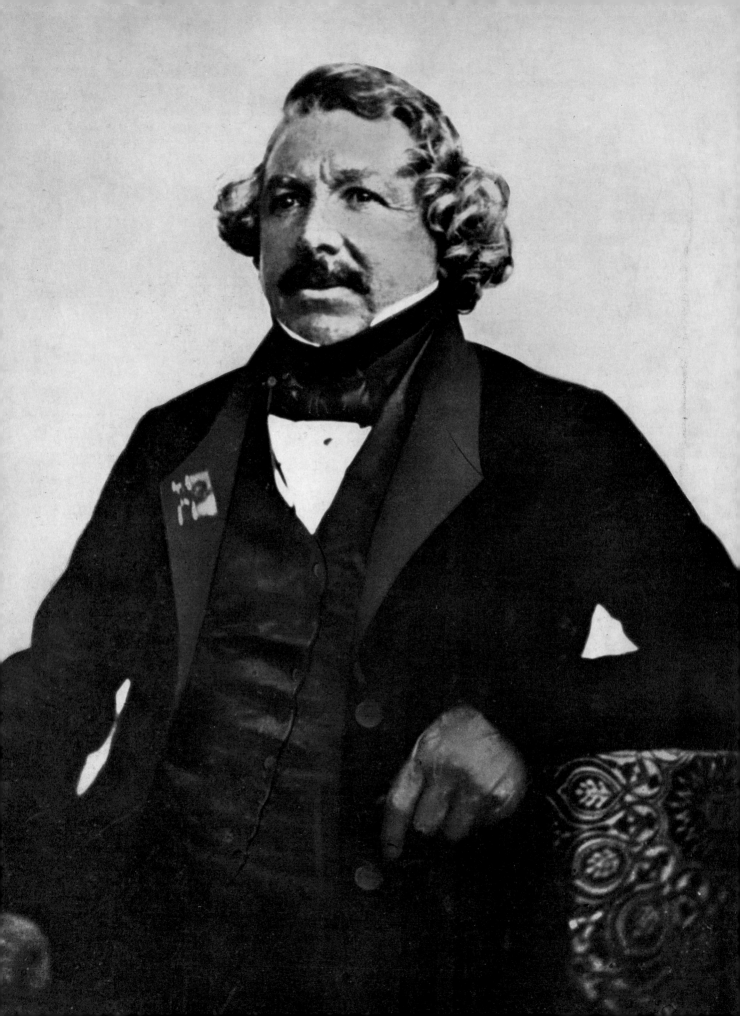

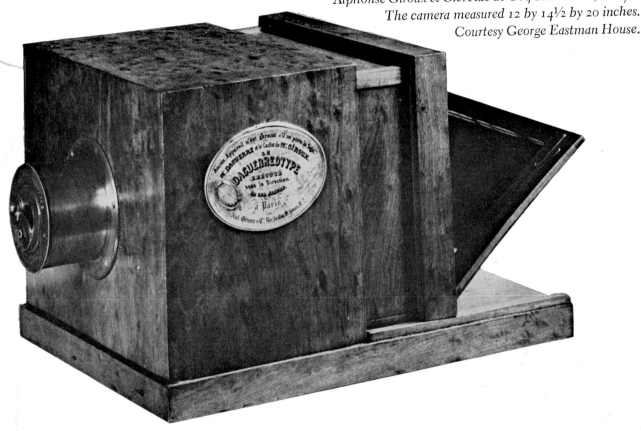

The official Daguerre camera produced by Daguerre's brother-in-law, Alphonse Giroux, with close-up of label which reads, "No apparatus guaranteed if it does not bear the signature of M. Daguerre and the seal of M. Giroux. The Daguerreotype, made under the direction of the inventor in Paris by Alphonse Giroux et Cie. Rue de Coq St. Honoré, No. 7." The camera measured 12 by 14½ by 20 inches. Courtesy George Eastman House.

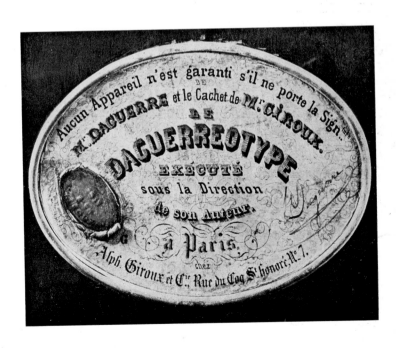

JEAN-BAPTISTE SABATIER BLOT
Daguerre. *Daguerreotype, 1844.*
Courtesy George Eastman House.

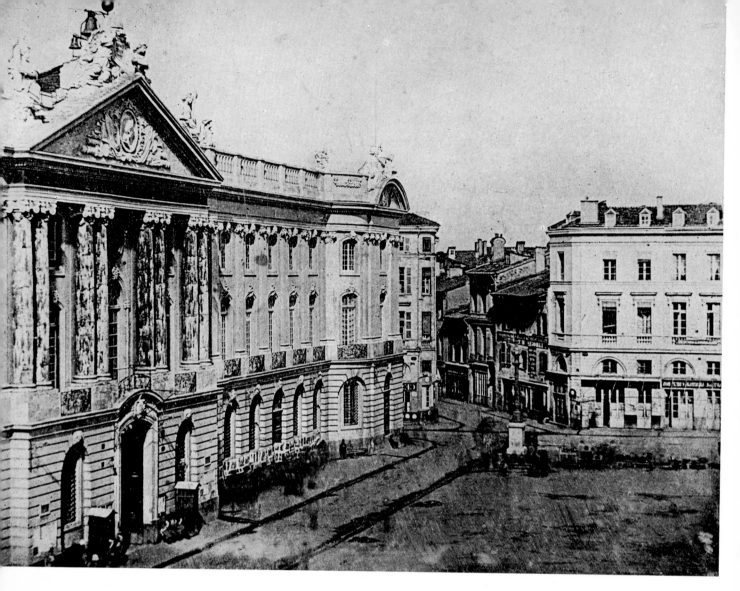

The official Daguerreotype camera was used on February 27, 1840, by Barthelmy-Urbain Bianchi, a Toulouse optical-instrument maker, who exposed 10 minutes to take the city hall of his home town and the Place du Capitole. An art exhibition, the first ever photographed, hangs on the wall of the city hall. The blob of black beneath the paintings is from active spectators attending the exhibition who left only "ghost" images although the sun bathers and seated sentries left their permanent mark. The image is reversed, as in all early daguerreotypes. Courtesy George Eastman House.

Camera and equipment designed by Gaudin and manufactured by Lerebours in 1841 for taking and processing daguerreotypes of 1/6 size. Outer wooden box serves both as camera and as carrying case for following accessories: glass lined coating box, mercury bath with sliding support, two single plate holders, slotted box to hold twelve plates. In little more than a year Daguerre's 110 pounds of equipment had been reduced to less than 10. Courtesy George Eastman House.

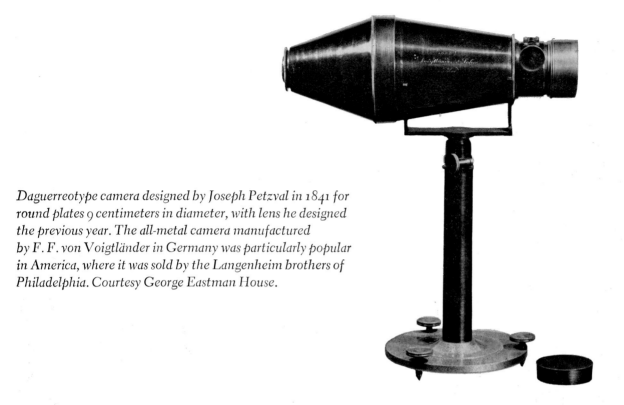

Daguerreotype camera designed by Joseph Petzval in 1841 for round plates 9 centimeters in diameter, with lens he designed the previous year. The all-metal camera manufactured by F. F. von Voigtländer in Germany was particularly popular in America, where it was sold by the Langenheim brothers of Philadelphia. Courtesy George Eastman House.

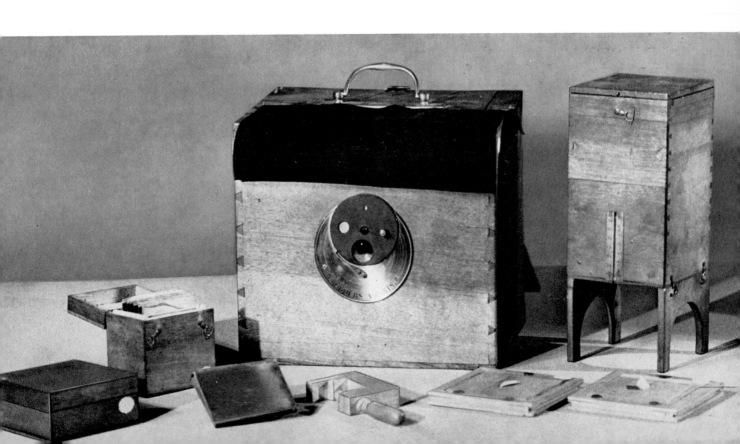

CHAPTER 4

The Daguerreotype in Europe

THE VERY FIRST YEAR of Daguerre's invention, enterprising publishers already saw great possibilities for profit from the travel books with reproductions of daguerreotype views. N. P. Lerebours of Paris, an optician who manufactured daguerreotype cameras closely resembling the official Giroux camera, hired artists and cameramen, equipped them with his outfits, and sent them to Italy, Greece, North Africa, Egypt, Damascus, Sweden, England, and as far west as Niagara Falls in the United States. Few of the daguerreotypists he commissioned are known by name today, and most of their original daguerreotypes have been lost.

Horace Vernet, romantic painter of battle scenes, accompanied by his nephew, Charles Bouton, and another artist photographer, Frederic Goupil-Fesquet, traveled for Lerebours in Egypt; on November 6, 1839, he wrote from Alexandria, "We keep Daguerreotyping like lions." Between 1840 and 1842 Lerebours published, from the thousands of daguerreotypes he had commissioned, 114 plates in aquatint as "Excursions Daguerriennes."

These aquatints and etchings were reproductions of daguerreotypes. Some images were traced directly, a procedure which scratched or irreparably ruined the silver plates. Aquatints were preferred to lithographs or woodcuts, for it was believed that they retained more of the daguerreotype's original subtleties of tonality and light. To his business in daguerreotype apparatus, lenses, and publications, Lerebours added the sale of original daguerreotypes of travel views.

Tourists, writers, and artists took daguerreotype cameras with them on trips, not only to secure records but to provide illustrations for future publications. Théophile Gautier wrote that he went to Spain with daguerreotype apparatus, but his success was negligible, for he had not mastered the technical problems of taking pictures. Joseph P. Girault de Prangy went to the Middle East, returning in 1844, after a two-year sojourn, with perfect daguerreotypes that he used to make illustrations for his book *Arabian Architecture and Monuments of Egypt, Syria, and Asia Minor.* An impressive selection of his original daguerreotypes, recently found in perfect condition, has been acquired by Helmut and Alison Gernsheim, for their famous collection.

Photographers often invented cameras for specific pictures. Friedrich von Martens constructed a camera that allowed the silvered plate to be curved, permitting him to take an exceptionally beautiful two-part panorama of Paris from the Louvre in 1846.

Artists and tourists continued to pursue the will-o'-the-wisp—perfect pictorial landscape. The lucrative end of the daguerreotype business was in the thousands of camera outfits and millions of silvered plates sold throughout Europe. Two thousand cameras and half a million plates were sold in Paris alone during 1847, mostly for portraiture. Daguerreotype parlors in France and England took portraits, charging $2 to $5 for plates ranging in size from 1½ by 2 to 6½ by 8½ inches, which were then set in *papier-mâché* frames or imitation gilt boxes.

Fortunes were reaped by the better-known parlors in the first years of the daguerreotype craze. Richebourg in Paris not only conducted a profitable studio but manufactured and handled apparatus for the trade.

Antoine Claudet, a fancy glass dealer in London, bought from Daguerre for $1,000 the first license to practice in England. He learned the process from Daguerre himself, whom he visited soon after Daguerre publicly demonstrated his invention. By the following year Claudet was selling daguerreotypes of famous views, daguerreotype apparatus, and lenses supplied him by his friend Lerebours.

Early in 1841 an ex–coal merchant named Richard Beard opened the first portrait studio in London, purchasing the right to use the mirror camera invented by Alexander Wolcott in New York the previous year. This enabled him to take pictures with exposures of 5 seconds to 5 minutes, depending on the size of the plates and the amount of sunlight. Beard also paid Daguerre for permis-

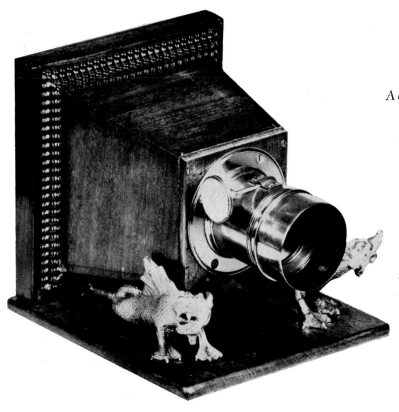

A camera in the shape of a truncated pyramid made in Paris by Bourguin, about 1844, with Petzval-type lens set in a focusing mount. The bronze dragons serve only to make it heavier and more ornate. Quarter plates used: 3¼ x 4¼ inches. Courtesy George Eastman House, Rochester.

sion to take daguerreotype portraits even though he did not use the official camera.

When Claudet discovered a faster combination of chemicals that enabled him to take daguerreotypes with the Giroux camera in 2 seconds to 2 minutes, he also opened a professional studio for portraiture in London.

Both studios were busy all day while the light lasted. Everyone in London wanted to have his picture taken and gladly paid for the privilege. Beard realized that a fortune was to be made if a monopoly of the process could be secured; quite inexplicably, he was able to purchase from Daguerre full patent rights for all England for less than $5,000. The following year, through the sale of license fees alone, he realized more than thirty times his investment.

Beard secured an injunction to restrict Claudet from

taking daguerreotypes, but the courts found in favor of Claudet, who was not compelled to relinquish his license. Claudet was devoted to developing the artistry and the technique of photography. He invented the darkroom red light, which did not affect the sensitive plate; and he conceived the idea of using painted backdrops in the studio to provide a pleasing change from the monotony of plain backgrounds behind the subject. Claudet photographed both inventors of photography—Daguerre and Fox Talbot—royalty, and other celebrities, and in 1853 he was appointed "Photographer in Ordinary to Queen Victoria."

Meanwhile, Richard Beard, who seemed to enjoy lawsuits, sued once too often for infringement of patent rights, in an action which took five years to result in a decision; although he won this case, he was soon after

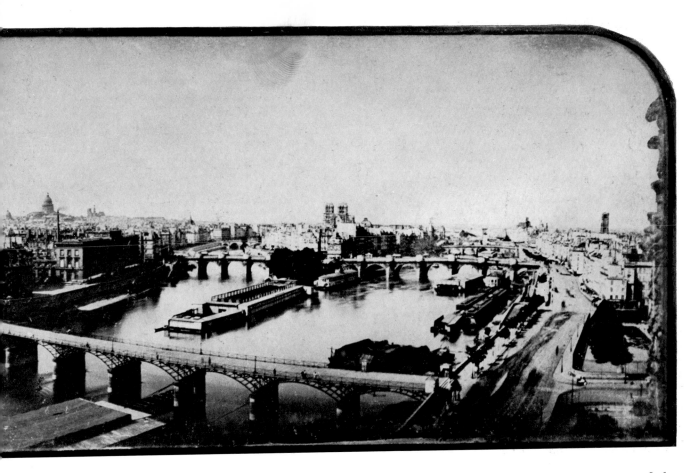

FRIEDRICH VON MARTENS, Panorama of Paris. *Daguerreotype, 1846.*
View from the Louvre. Taken with a camera that curved the
plates, invented by Von Martens. Courtesy George Eastman House.

declared bankrupt. During the years he held the patent for England, Beard had licensed many daguerreotypists, several of whom became famous, particularly the American, John E. Mayall, who had conducted a studio in his home town of Philadelphia before he came to London, as "Professor Highschool," and who had created ten daguerreotypes to illustrate the Lord's Prayer. Mayall made other allegorical pictures which brought him acclaim, but it was the high polish of the American daguerreotypes and dramatic, oversize plates that were singled out for praise. He took pictures of the Prince Consort, who was avidly interested in photography; and soon Mayall had in London two very fashionable studios which made him independently wealthy.

The art dealer Louis Sachse brought to Berlin, in 1839, the first camera made by Giroux, Daguerre's brother-in-law. Within less than two years Voigtländer had introduced an all-metal, conical-shaped camera with the Petzval lens that enabled him to take circular pictures about 3 inches in diameter. With the Voigtländer-Petzval lens began Germany's high reputation for high-quality optical goods and camera equipment.

Some of the finest early daguerreotype portraits were made by two artists-turned-photographer, Carl F. Stelzner and Herman Biow of Hamburg. Stelzner's training as a painter of miniature portraits is evident in his delicately delineated daguerreotypes, which he often colored by hand to simulate sensitively drawn miniatures on ivory. Both men made daguerreotypes of a terrible three-day fire that demolished an entire section of Hamburg in 1842. A Stelzner daguerreotype of the holocaust—the world's first news photograph—fortunately survives.

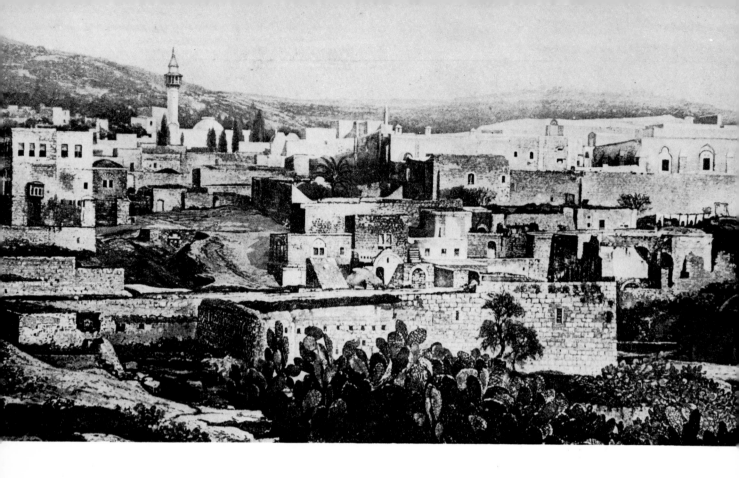

*Four aquatints by unknown
photographers, published in 1840-42 by
Lerebours in* Excursions Daguerriennes.
Courtesy George Eastman House.
above: Nazareth
below: Arch of Titus in Rome
upper right: Luxor, Egypt
lower right: Great Mosque in Algiers

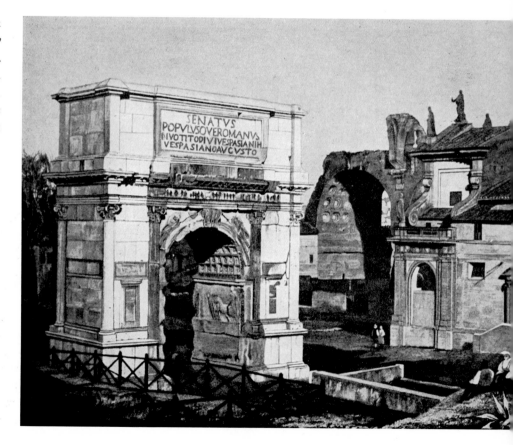

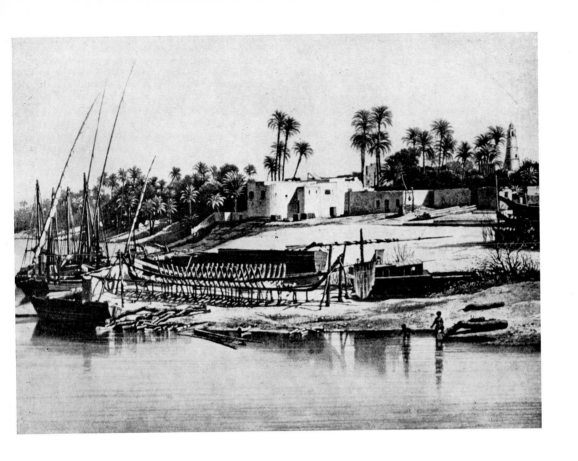

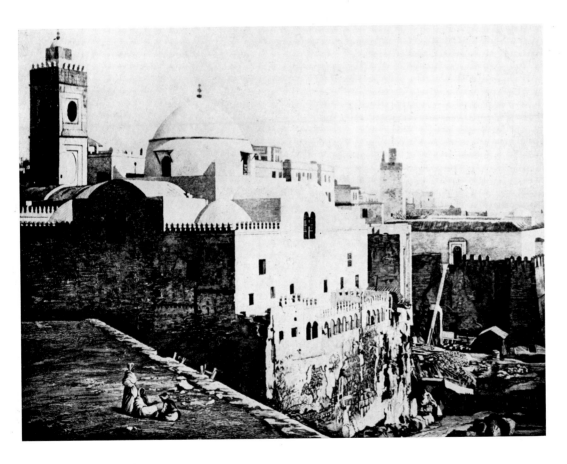

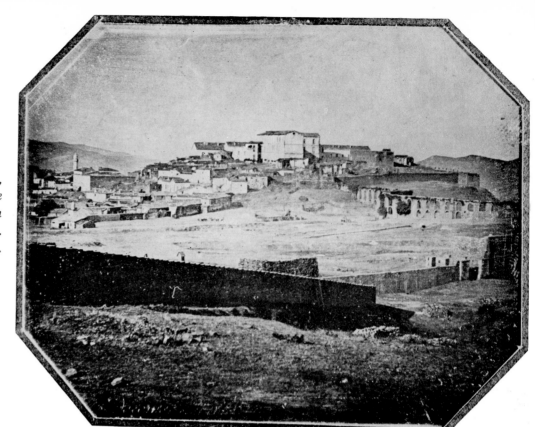

Medea, Algeria. *Daguerreotype, about 1850. The names Delemotte et Alary are scratched on plate in lower left corner. Courtesy George Eastman House.*

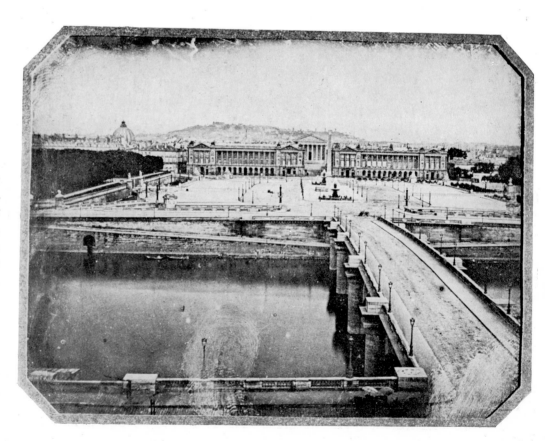

View of the Place de la Concorde, Paris. *Daguerreotype, about 1850. Daguerreotypist unknown. In the distance, Montmartre and its windmills. The image is reversed. Courtesy George Eastman House.*

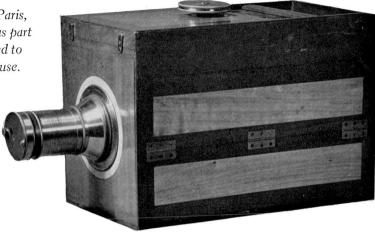

A collapsible camera made by Charles Chevalier in Paris, 1840, for whole plate, 6½ x 8½ inches. Furnished as part of a complete daguerreotype outfit; could also be used to take paper negatives. Courtesy George Eastman House.

Return of French Troops from Italy. *Daguerreotype, about 1858. Daguerreotypist unknown. An extremely rare example, with crowds of people, taken when process had been practically supplanted by collodion negative. Courtesy George Eastman House.*

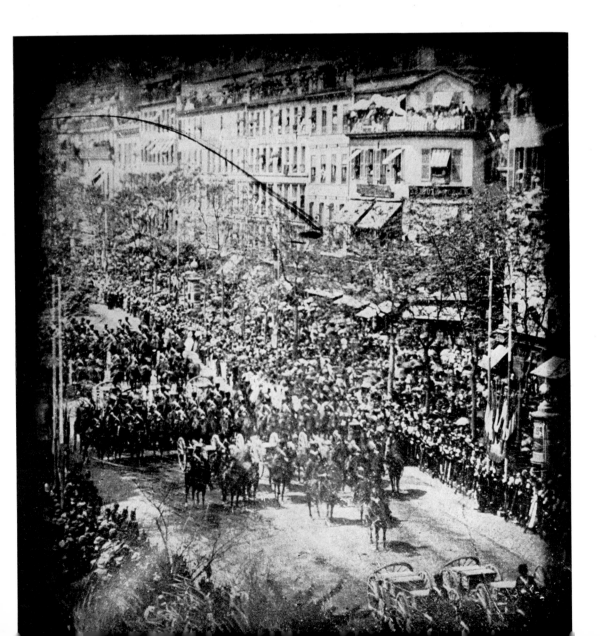

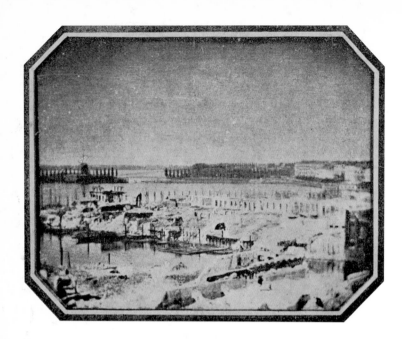

C. F. STELZNER, Hamburg Fire. *Daguerreotype,*
1842. The world's first news photograph.
Courtesy Museum für
Hamburgische Geschichte, Hamburg.

STELZNER, Oberleutnant H. N. Beseler.
Daguerreotype. Hamburg, 1843. Courtesy
Staatliche Landesbildstelle, Hamburg.

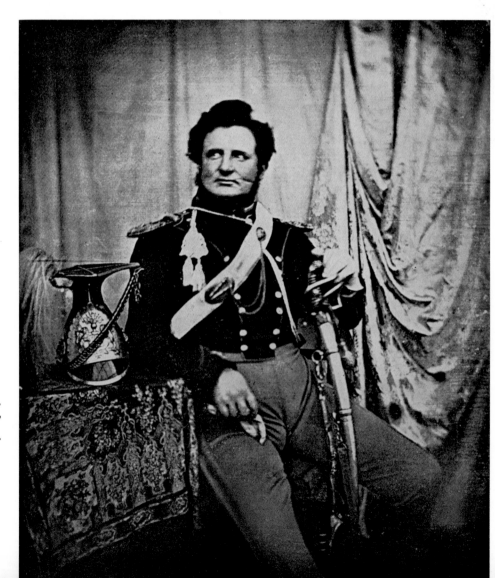

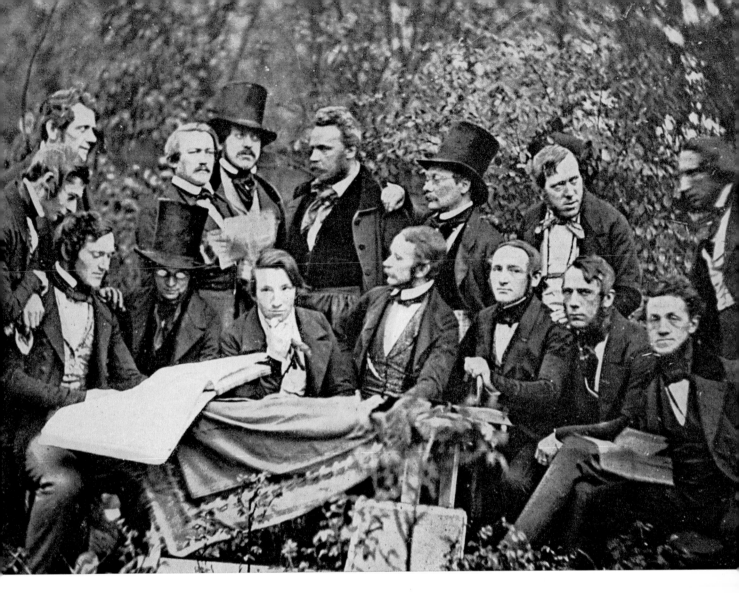

STELZNER, Outing of the Hamburg Art Club.
Daguerreotype, 1843.
Courtesy Staatliche Landesbildstelle.

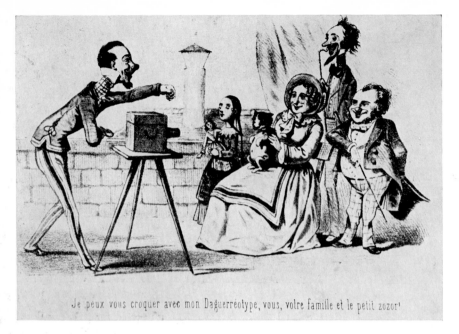

Je peux vous croquer avec mon Daguerréotype, vous, votre famille et le petit zozor'

A clinching argument of the daguerreo-typist was that he would "draw" the entire family for the same price as one member. In this lithograph by an unknown artist, about 1850, the caption shows the daguerreotypist saying, "I can sketch you with my daguerreotype, you, your family, and the little Zozor." Courtesy George Eastman House.

Oh Clarise, take a look at that big machine, it's as though a great big eye was looking at us.

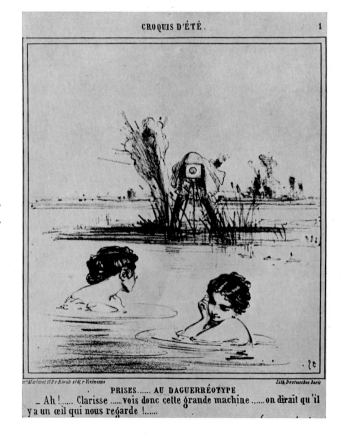

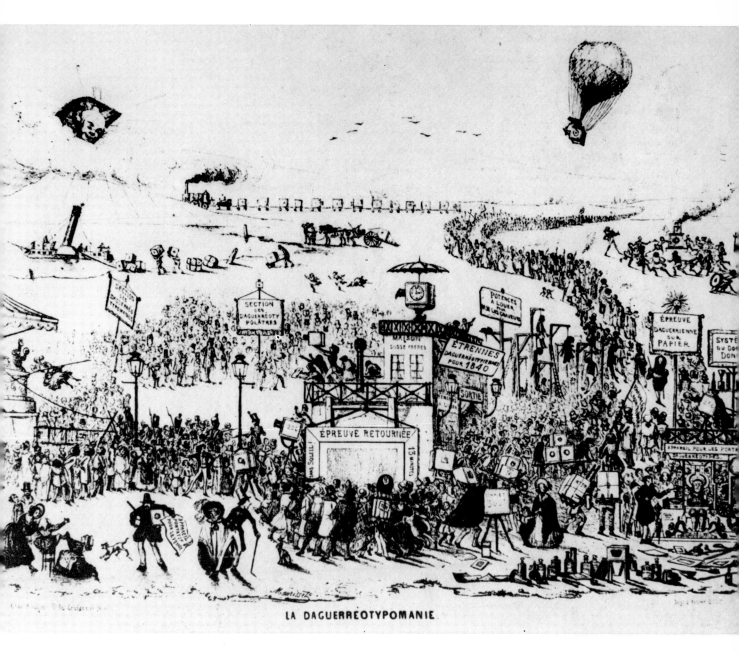

LA DAGUERRÉOTYPOMANIE

The Daguerreotype Craze. *Lithograph drawn by A. Maurisset for New Year's Day, 1840. Camera fans dance. Gallows for rent to engravers. A man struggles with an unwieldly camera marked "Apparatus for Travelers." A studio advertises portraits for New Year's presents. A man has his portrait made. Dr. Donne, who made the first engravings from daguerreotypes, is at work with his plates and presses. Moving in the distance is a freight train formed by cameras; a camera is suspended from a balloon; a ship is being loaded with camera supplies; and over all the sun shines and smiles. Courtesy George Eastman House.*

CHAPTER 5

The Daguerreotype in America

THE FIRST PORTRAITS taken by daguerreotype took so long that the subjects got sunburned. Portraiture was a terrible ordeal, suffered by sitting perfectly still in the direct sunlight for as much as 20 minutes. It was permissible to wink; the process was so slow that it did not matter.

To enable the sitter to keep his eyes open in the sun a blue sheet of glass was interposed; this did not lengthen the exposure very much, and soon all studios were equipped with blue skylights.

Daguerreotypes were hand-colored like miniatures, often by artists of some standing. The earliest attempts to color the fragile image came after experiments with painting on the protective glass proved unsuccessful. Dusting colored powders on a gum brushed onto the image also proved too harsh for the easily damaged daguerreotype. The only solution was for trained miniature painters laboriously to tint the face of the daguerreotype with as much caution and artistry as was necessary to do a miniature on ivory.

Dr. John William Draper, in 1839 in New York, said that he had to pose his models for 20 minutes in the open sunlight, the face whitened with powder and the eyes closed, to secure full-size daguerreotypes. Draper, who was a professor of chemistry at New York University, had learned of Daguerre's process by reading the first English translation to reach New York in October of 1839, but he had already experimented unsuccessfully for two years with the photograph as applied to science. He made himself a cigar-box camera and with it took a picture of a Unitarian Church from a university window. A month earlier his colleague, Professor Samuel F. B. Morse, had taken a picture of the same church from his window in the university. On April 19, 1840, Samuel Bemis in Boston took a daguerreotype of King's Chapel burying ground in an exposure lasting 40 minutes. By mid-1840, with better equipment, smaller-size plates, and faster chemicals at their disposal, the professors were ready to become partners in a portrait studio, which they built on the roof of the university.

At about the same time, Alexander S. Wolcott was issued the first patent in the United States for photography. This was for a camera with a concave mirror that reflected the sun's rays to the plate rather than with a lens that refracted rays to the plate. The new invention permitted more light to fall on the plate. The image was not reversed, but neither was it so sharp as the daguerreotype made in the usual lens camera. Wolcott and his partner John Johnson opened the world's first portrait studio in New York on March 4, 1840.

Daguerreotypists could operate only on sunny days, which occurred in New York more often than in London —a contributing factor to making American daguerreotype portraits universally acclaimed as the best.

On dull, overcast days Morse taught the process to a number of interested students, many of whom were to become leading daguerreotypists in the United States, among them Edward Anthony, Mathew B. Brady, and Albert S. Southworth. Using a regular daguerreotype camera, they were able to take studio portraits in sittings of 30 seconds to 2 minutes, and could cut this time in half by posing the subject directly in the sun.

After only six months Professor Draper dissolved the partnership; he was to utilize photography for scientific purposes the rest of his life. Professor Morse moved to another roof-top studio in the *Observer* building.

Morse's purpose in pursuing the perfection of the daguerreotype was to accumulate portraits of models he could use in painting. He was the first to take a class picture, at the thirtieth reunion, in August, 1840, of his Yale University class. Morse needed to realize some profit from his daguerreotype researches, for in the depression years of 1839–1840 he was spending much more than he could afford from his small salary as professor of literature and design at New York University. This salary was supplemented by the little tuition he received from his students in the daguerreotype process and by the portrait commissions he received intermittently. All the while he was seeking government support to perfect his invention of the magnetic telegraph.

All sorts of people turned to the daguerreotype to make an extra dollar. Some learned the craft well enough to open daguerreotype galleries. Others became professors of hocus pocus, making pictures in the mystifying darkroom, passing off the faint results as the best procurable; to many daguerreotyping was a form of advertising or a sideline to attract customers to their regular business.

In addition to the charlatans there were fine workmen, practicing daguerreotypists whose studios took superb portraits of illustrious citizens and charming pictures of a bygone day in a peaceful America.

One of these was John Plumbe, who, besides being a pioneer in chain-studio photography, was the first to write and pressure Congress for a railroad connecting the Atlantic with the Pacific. Soon after he learned the process in Washington in the summer of 1840, he opened a series of Daguerrean Galleries. During the next five years, thirteen Plumbe National Daguerrean Galleries were established in such widely separated cities as Boston, New York, Washington, and Philadelphia in the east, and Louisville, St. Louis, Cincinnati, and Dubuque in the west. He developed the "Plumbeotype," and hired artists to copy daguerreotype likenesses onto lithograph stones so that the prints could be pulled and sold in editions of any number desired by the customer.

The galleries made money, but unfortunately Plumbe was too busy pushing for a national railway, and permitted his managers to plunder the proceeds. By 1847 he was declared bankrupt, the galleries were closed, and he was on his way to California. It would be a fitting climax if we could report that this intrepid man found another fortune in the gold fields, but the truth is far more sad; he returned to Iowa and died by his own hand at the early age of forty-six.

Edward Anthony, trained as a civil engineer and graduated from Columbia at the age of twenty in 1838, learned the daguerreotype process as soon as it was introduced the next year. As there was little work to be found in his professional field, he accepted a commission to take daguerreotypes of disputed territory at the Canadian-American northeast boundary. These were the first pictures taken for a government survey.

A short time after this, Anthony and a partner, J. M. Edwards, were permitted by Anthony's friend and patron, Senator Thomas Hart Benton, chairman of the Senate Committee on Military Affairs, to use the committee room in Washington to take daguerreotypes of distinguished political figures. Among these was John Quincy Adams, who recorded in his diary, April 12, 1844, that he sat for three likenesses and that, as he walked out, "President Tyler and his son John came in, but I did not notice them."

Anthony took pictures of everybody of consequence, and formed a National Daguerrean Gallery which was on exhibition in New York City. This enterprise was supposedly entirely destroyed by fire in 1852 except for a single full figure portrait of John Quincy Adams.

A collection of daguerreotypes of prominent national politicians who were in Washington during the nine years Anthony and his partner had their gallery is now in the Chicago Historical Society. Though these cannot be positively identified as Anthony's, the consistent quality of the portrait, the dramatic posing of the subject, and the search to interpret the character of each person carry the mark of someone well trained, as Anthony was. Further evidence about dates and age of subjects depicted leads me to believe that these may be some of Anthony's lost daguerreotypes.

The collection includes Thomas Hart Benton, senator from Missouri; Lewis Cass, senator from Michigan and in 1848 Democratic candidate for the presidency; Presidents Martin Van Buren, John Tyler, Millard Fillmore, and Franklin Pierce; Louis Kossuth, Hungarian patriot who was in the United States 1851–1852, and the Span-ish-American revolutionary Narciso Lopez who was in Washington for three years until 1851.

The most notable name in American photography is Mathew B. Brady (he always spelled it with one "t" and never told anyone what the "B" stood for). A later chapter will be devoted to this exceptional man, historian documenter of the Civil War, publisher, and altogether the greatest recorder of American life in his day.

The first decade of the daguerreotype saw a thousand practitioners in the United States. There were seventy galleries in New York City alone, among them that of Jeremiah Gurney, a jeweler turned cameraman. His famous gallery, later conducted by his son Benjamin, moved ahead with photography as it developed, and survived for more than half a century.

Oliver Wendell Holmes called the daguerreotype "the mirror with a memory." His native Boston competed with New York in refining the silver image. Yankee ingenuity made possible the excellence of American daguerreotypes. John Whipple utilized a steam engine to run the buffing wheels to give the plates the highest possible polish, to heat the mercury, to prepare the distilled water for washing the plates, to cool the clients by running fans in the waiting rooms, and also to revolve a sign on the facade of the gallery.

One of the justifiably famous galleries in Boston was the establishment of Southworth and Hawes. This gal-

SAMUEL A. BEMIS, King's Chapel, Boston. *Daguerreotype, 1840. One of the earliest American daguerreotypes. Label on back reads: "April 19, 1840 Samuel A. Bemis first daguerreotype experiment. Iodizing process 25 minutes (apparatus new) Camera process 40 minutes, Wind N. W. sky clear air dry—very cold for season. Lens meniscus. Time 4:50 to 5:30 p.m. Daguerre's apparatus. N.Y. Plate ordinary." Courtesy George Eastman House, Rochester.*

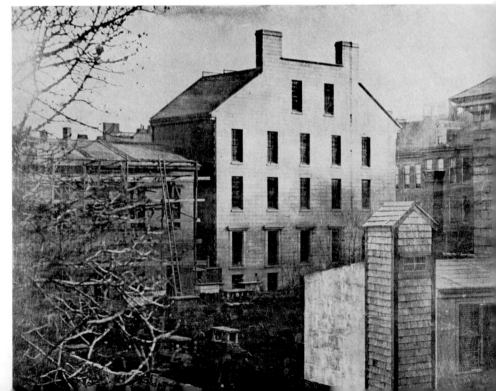

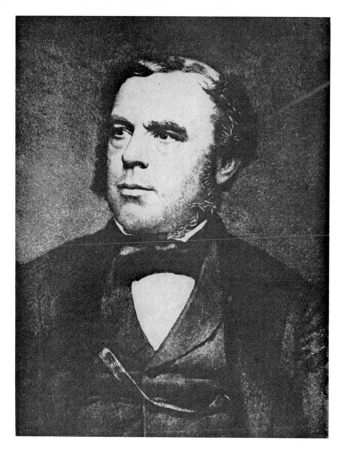

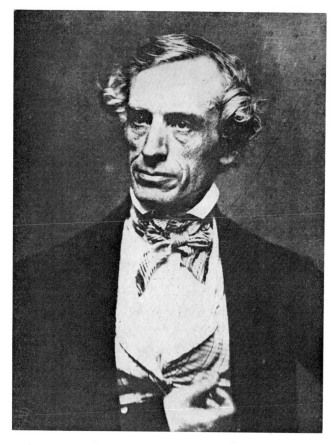

JOHN SARTAIN, Portrait of John William Draper. *After an engraving from M. A. Root, The Camera and the Pencil, Philadelphia, 1864. Two years before the daguerreotype was announced, Professor Draper was experimenting with photography; he made one of the first photographic portraits in 1839 and the first successful photograph of the moon the following year. Courtesy George Eastman House.*

Portrait of Samuel F. B. Morse. *Daguerreotype, about 1845. Photographer unknown. Painter, professor, inventor of the telegraph, Morse is believed to be the first American to learn the daguerreotype process. With his colleague, Professor Draper, he established a photographic studio on the roof of New York University. Courtesy George Eastman House.*

lery's portraits of celebrities are lifelike, free from the usual stiffness resulting from the rigid forked headrests and from the fixed pose often induced by filling out the subjects' hollow cheeks with wads of cotton or by fastening their jug ears to their skulls with sticking wax.

Albert S. Southworth learned the process from Morse in New York, and returned to Boston in 1843 to enter into partnership with Josiah Johnson Hawes, who remained a photographer until his death in 1901. The daguerrotypes made by Southworth and Hawes during the eighteen years of their partnership are today celebrated and sought as some of the finest examples of the art. These portraits were most often taken on whole plates

8½ by 6½ inches, and cost $5 or more. Competitors' prices were $1 for a quarter plate, with a free case.

The fine daguerreotype was doomed. It had lasted longer in America than anywhere else. At the Great Exhibition in the London Crystal Palace of 1851, Americans received three of the five medals awarded for daguerreotypes. The French by then excelled in photography on paper.

America soon turned to the cheaper process of the glass negative, from which a dozen or more positives could be made at the price of one good daguerreotype. It was the end of an era; a beautiful and unique art had died. The daguerreotype would never be revived.

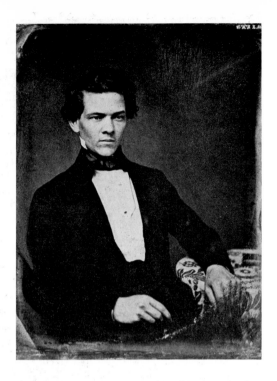

Portrait of John V. Farwell, *Chicago merchant.*
Daguerreotype, 1845-47. Photographer unknown.
Courtesy Chicago Historical Society.

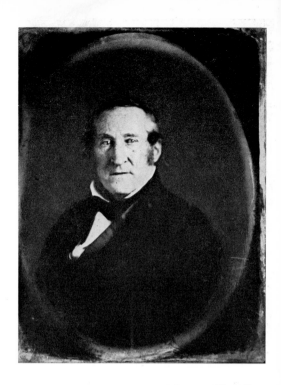

EDWARD ANTHONY, Senator Thomas Hart Bento
Daguerreotype, about 1848. Taken in Washing
Courtesy Chicago Historical Society.

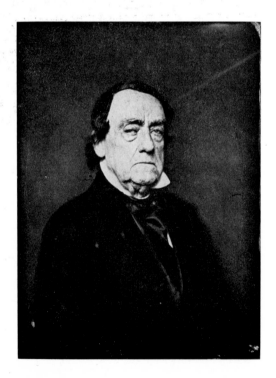

ANTHONY, Lewis Cass, *senator from Michigan and in*
1848 Democratic candidate for President. Courtesy
Chicago Historical Society.

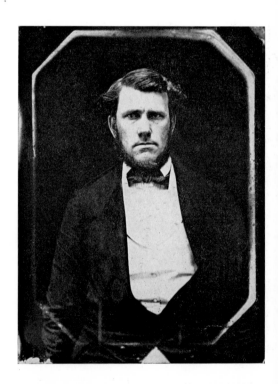

Portrait of John Wentworth. *Daguerreotype, 1*
Photographer unknown. Taken in Chicago
before Wentworth became Mayor. Courtesy
Chicago Historical Society.

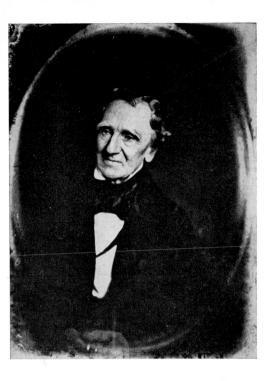

Portrait of Thomas Sully (1783-1872). *Daguerreotype, about 1848. Photographer unknown. American portrait painter. Courtesy Chicago Historical Society.*

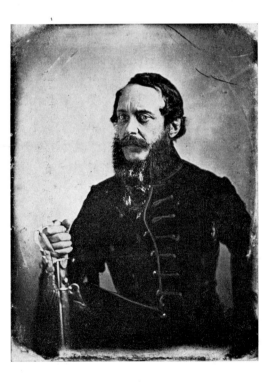

ANTHONY, Louis Kossuth, *Hungarian patriot. Daguerreotype, 1851, Washington. Courtesy Chicago Historical Society.*

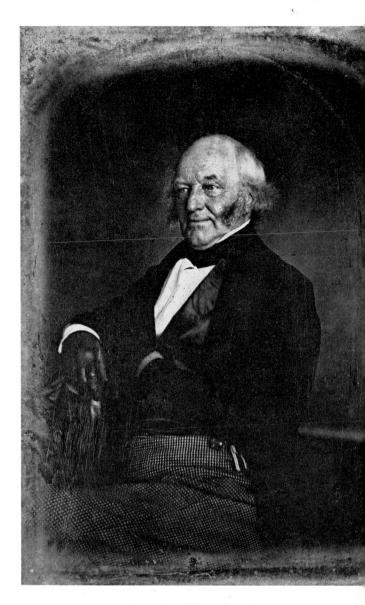

ANTHONY, Martin Van Buren. *Daguerreotype, about 1848. Van Buren left the presidency in 1841 but remained a political power for years. This daguerreotype appears to have been taken when he was about 66 years old. Though it is not certain, the picture seems to be one of the daguerreotypes which Anthony made for his National Daguerrean Gallery, which was destroyed by fire in 1852. Courtesy Chicago Historical Society.*

Unidentified Gold Miner in California. *Daguerreotype, about 1850. 2¾ x 3¼ inches. Daguerreotypist unknown. The leather pouch in which the miner sent the daguerreotype to a young lady in Illinois is at bottom. Courtesy George Eastman House.*

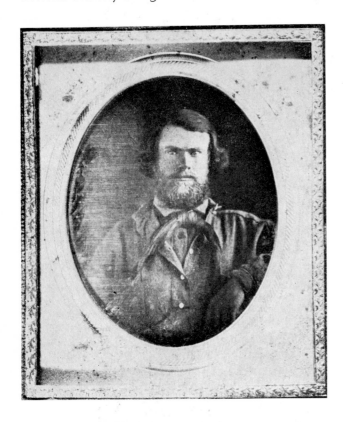

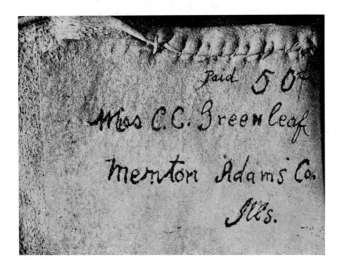

Portrait of Sam Houston. *Daguerreotype, about 1845. Photographer unknown. Toward the end of Houston's presidency of Texas, which was an independent republic from 1836 to 1845. Courtesy George Eastman House.*

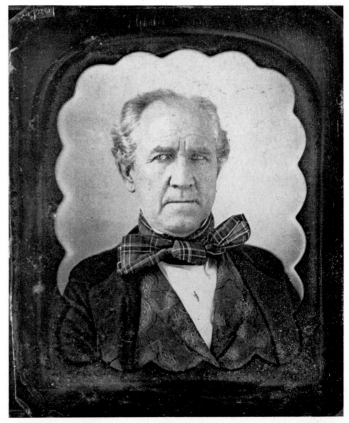

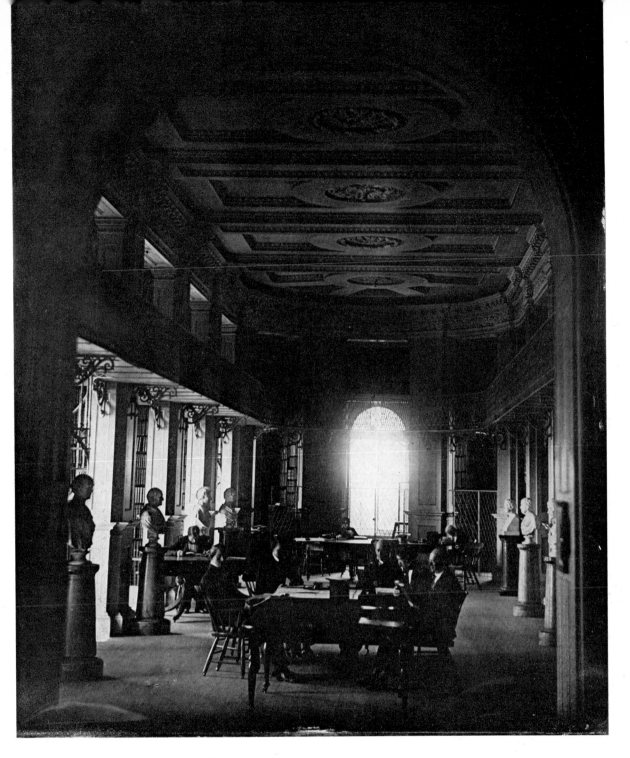

SOUTHWORTH AND HAWES, Interior of Boston Athenaeum.
About 1855. Courtesy George Eastman House.

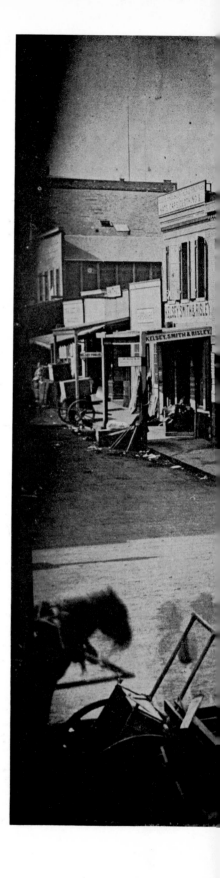

FRED COOMBS, San Francisco, corner of Clay and Montgomery Streets. *Daguerreotype, 1850. A sharp eye can see, on the druggist's signboard, "opium for sale" along with paints and varnishes. Courtesy George Eastman House.*

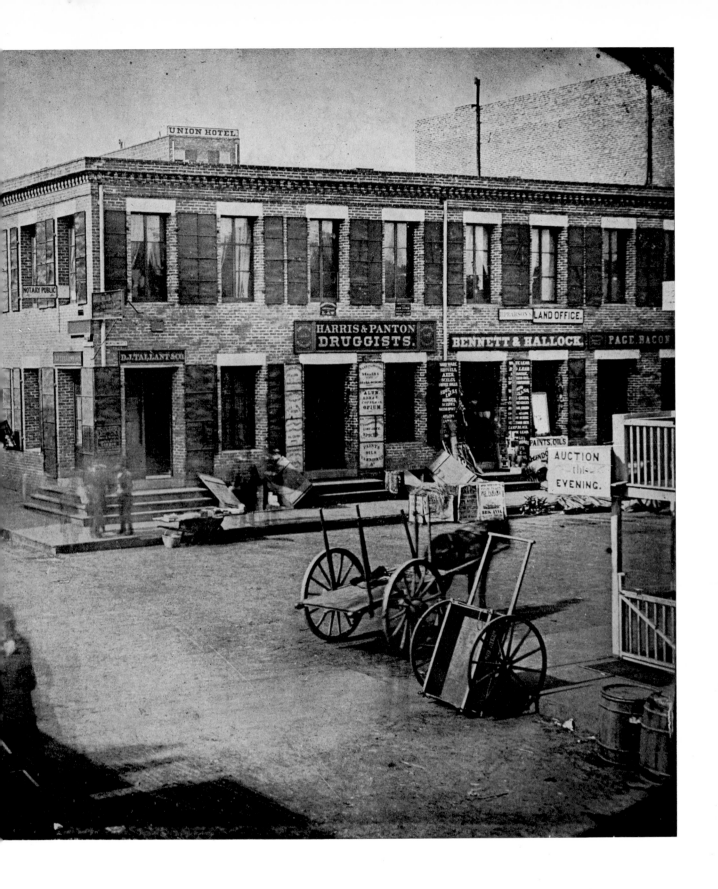

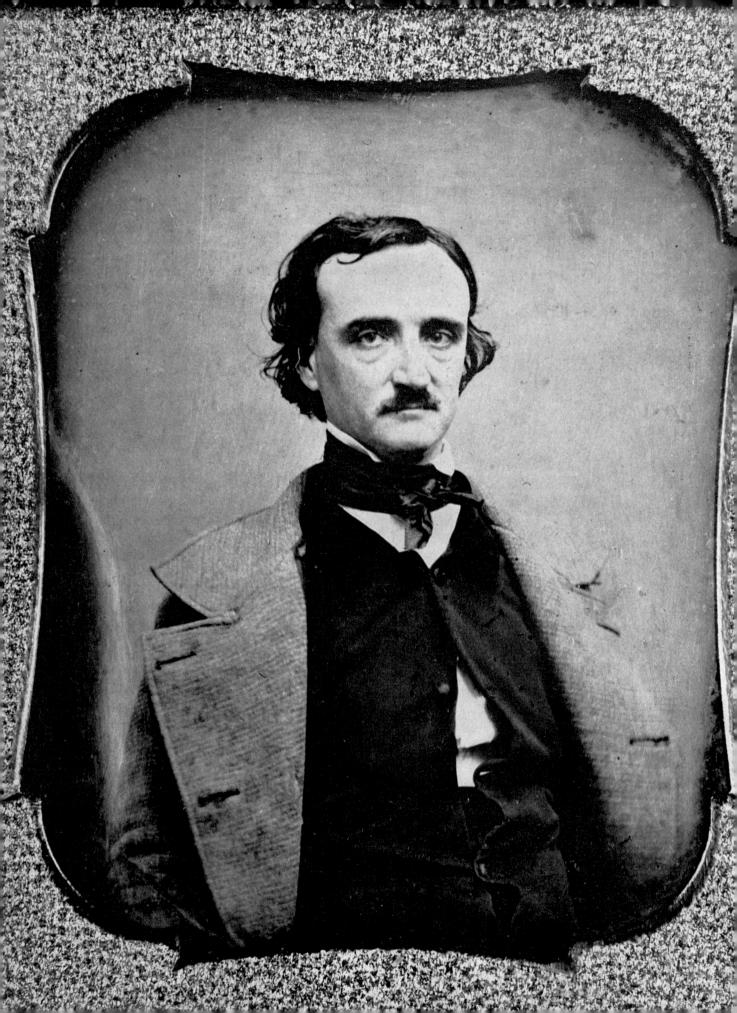

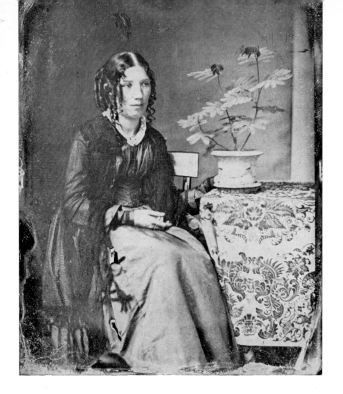

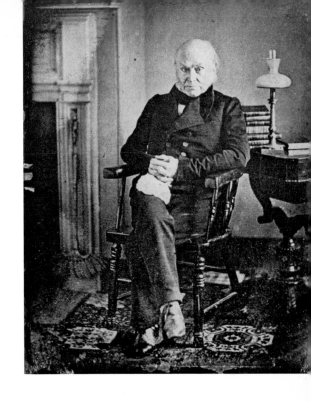

SOUTHWORTH AND HAWES STUDIO, BOSTON
above: Harriet Beecher Stowe. *Daguerreotype, about 1856.*
above, right: John Quincy Adams, President of the
United States. *Daguerreotype copy, about 1852. From an original*
daguerreotype made in 1848, the year when President Adams
died. Both, courtesy Metropolitan Museum of Art.

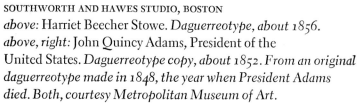

S. W. HARTSHORN, Edgar Allan Poe.
Daguerreotype, 1848. Taken a year before the
poet died. Poe was much enamored of the
daguerreotype. In 1840 he wrote, "In truth
the daguerreotyped plate is infinitely more
accurate in its presentation than any
painting by human hands." Courtesy
Brown University, Providence.

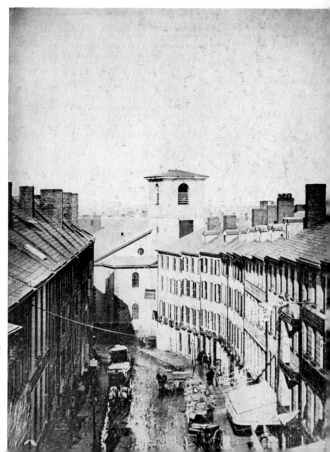

SOUTHWORTH AND HAWES STUDIO, BOSTON, Looking Down Brattle Street
Toward Brattle Square Church. *Daguerreotype, 1852. The silver*
image is reversed, as can be seen in Hudson & Company's awning.
Courtesy Metropolitan Museum of Art.

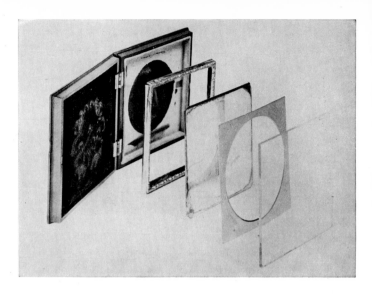

Assembling a daguerreotype. The first cases were made of tooled leather, but soon cheaper substitutes became popular, among them imitation leather and plastic cases made of sawdust and shellac with elaborate pressed-in designs. The glass, the oval frame, and the daguerreotype were assembled in a flexible gilded metal frame known in England as "pinchbeck" and in America as "preserver"; then the assembly was placed in the case. Courtesy George Eastman House.

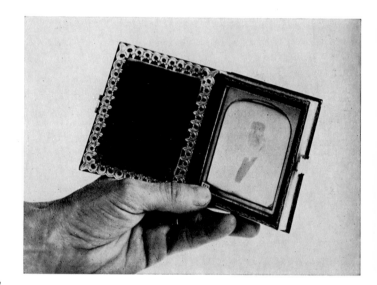

These two illustrations show that, when sunlight fell directly on a daguerreotype the silvered image became a negative—a turn of the wrist and the image became a fully recognizable positive. Courtesy George Eastman House.

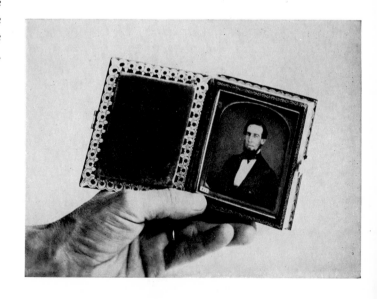

PART TWO

Masters of the Nineteenth Century

CHAPTER 6

Negatives and Positives

IN PART ONE of this book we saw photography grow like a baby inside the womb of painting and emerge into lusty infancy. Part Three will show how it ultimately became a medium of high artistic expression. Part Two, which you have now begun reading, deals with the time in between, with photography's vigorous adolescence, when it was a technical novelty and an industrial product serving pent-up graphic needs. Of the two processes announced almost simultaneously only one survived. Daguerreotype, so brilliantly launched, soon dropped away, like a used-up rocket stage. The negative-positive process, which is discussed at some length in the next chapters, proved more practical. It persisted, and underwent a complex evolution.

Photography's potential for full and accurate documentation was recognized early. Photographers, the *National Gazette* of Philadelphia predicted in the 1840s, "shall visit foreign parts, the courts of Europe, the palaces of the pashaws, the Red Sea and Holy Land, and the pyramids of Geza, and bring home exact representations of all the sublime and ridiculous objects which it now costs so much to see . . . it will be impossible for a tree to bud and blossom, a flower to go to seed, or a vegetable to sprout without executing at the same time an exact photograph of the wonderful process . . . a steam boiler cannot explode, or an ambitious river overflow its banks—a gardener cannot elope with an heiress, or a reverend bishop commit an indiscretion, but straightway, an officious daguerreotype will proclaim the whole affair to the world."

Pioneer photographers lost little time in fulfilling these predictions. Already photographic studio-factories were pouring out high-quality living human likenesses by the thousand. Before the ink of the *National Gazette* was fully dry, there were photographs of architectural European monuments and of the American frontier. Soon there would be others of the Arabian Desert, the Alps, the Pyramids of Gisa, Abu Simbel, and the Temples of Karnak; of the Mexican and Crimean war; of "Bloody Kansas" and the Sepoy Rebellion. Two photographic journals would start publishing in New York within ten months of each other. There would be photographic books, the forerunner of a mighty avalanche. A Bosto-

nian named Whipple would couple a camera to the telescope of the Harvard College Observatory to take a sharp, detailed likeness of the moon. In 1856 the University of London would add photography to its course of study. A few years later, Mathew B. Brady and his assistants would begin to document the American Civil War.

Although straightforward documentation was photography's major purpose and function a little more than a century ago, just as it is today, there was recognition on the highest levels of the communities of art and science that there were vast and various possibilities to be discovered and exploited. Thus, Sir Charles Eastlake, President of the Royal Academy, and Lord Rosse, President of the Royal Society, joined in a single plea to Fox Talbot, inventor of the negative-positive system, to relax some of his demands in the exercise of his patent rights.

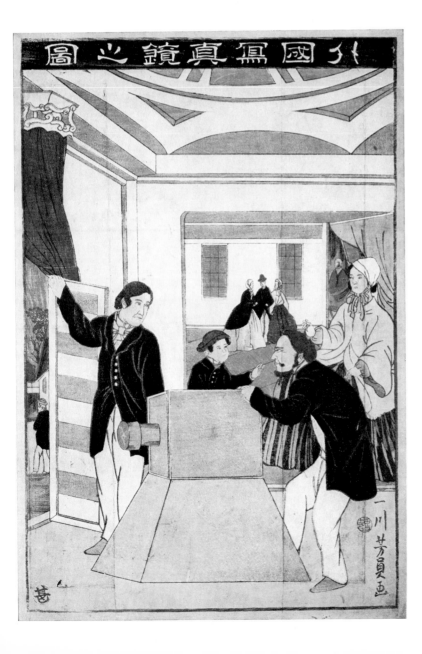

Japanese woodcut, 1851.
Dutch merchants with one of the
first cameras allowed into Japan.
Collection Peter Pollack.

Eastlake, moreover, accepted the presidency of the Photographic Society of London (now the Royal Photographic Society of Great Britain). In France, likewise, the first president of the Societé Héliographique was the great painter Baron Gros, and other founding members included Eugène Delacroix and the physicist Edouard Becquerel.

The mid-nineteenth century status of photography is revealed most clearly by the relationship that developed between photography and painting. The advent of the photographic process sent a shock wave reverberating through the world of art. At first a dangerous competitor was seen. Technological unemployment now threatened illustrators and graphic artists. The menace was the greater because the artistic ideal of detailed realism was so overpowering in those days. Partly in mourning, partly in pleasurable excitement, the painter Delaroche remarked that "from now on, painting is dead." He went on to say that photography satisfied "all the demands of art" and carried essential principles to "perfection." A number of painters, especially the less successful, abandoned their trade and mastered the new process. This development was of great benefit to photography, which was thereby provided with practitioners already skilled in the important business of fashioning well-ordered compositions. The most hostile reaction to photography came from the art critic Charles Baudelaire, who deplored the desertion of the secondary painters and predicted the corruption of art. Enough of an atmosphere of illegitimacy was thrown around photography so that, even today, many illustrators are reluctant to let it be known how much they depend on photos for information, study, and even inspiration. "It is admirable," J. A. D. Ingres said ruefully of photography, "but one must not admit it."

But photography was found immediately useful by some of the era's most distinguished painters, including Ingres himself. They saw it chiefly as an adjunct to painting, a labor-saving device that could provide instant substitutes for the sketches and detailed studies previously needed in the construction of finished paintings. It could also, on occasion, substitute for a live model—especially when provided by Nadar, who had as good an eye as any painter and lived by providing painters with outstandingly good source material. Delacroix not only posed models for study photographs but was an outspoken en-

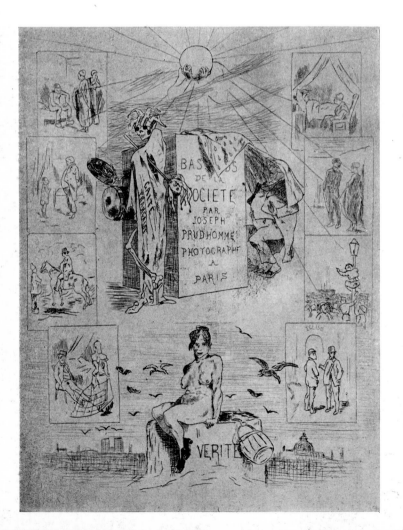

FELICIEN ROPS, *lithograph satirizing photography. About 1870. Collection Peter Pollack.*

EDGAR DEGAS, Self-Portrait with Mme. Zoë Halévy. *Photograph, 1895. Courtesy Metropolitan Museum of Art, New York.*

thusiast of photography and an exponent of its use in educating the artist's eye to qualities that might otherwise elude him. "How I regret," he wrote a friend, "that so wonderful an invention came so late. I mean as far as I am concerned."

From being a useful source of information, photography became much more. It was a source of inspiration: in composition, in form, in artists' conceptions of visual reality. The solidarity of Corot's early forms, for example, dissolved in his later work, especially in his foliage, which took on a misty, out-of-focus aspect. Degas (like Courbet and Manet, an amateur photographer himself) also used out-of-focus effects in distant detail. Degas, in addition (like the seventeenth-century artist Vermeer, whose vision was influenced by the camera obscura), telescoped and compressed perspective space in camera fashion, and (like the eighteenth-century artist Canaletto, another camera-obscura user) cut off edge detail in an arbitrary way.

The superrealism of the mid-nineteenth-century American *trompe-l'oeil* painters Harnett, Peto, and their imitators, in all probability, owed its exactitude to the influence of the daguerreotype, which it rivaled in mi-

nuteness of detail. It went the daguerreotype one better in mirroring nature, not only possessing the added dimension of truthful-looking color but also representing objects in their exact size. Like the daguerreotype, it struck wonder into those who saw it.

Photography had its effect on painting, and continues to have it. But the major impulse to new seeing that, beginning in the 1860s, transformed painting came from the previous researches of the French scientist Chevreul into the way the eye sees juxtaposed patches of color. Chevreul discovered an order of nature that became the theoretical basis of French Impressionism, which, in turn, provided the visual wonder and excitement that led to the development of modern photography as art. Modern photography as art owes something to the big-head portraits by Julia Margaret Cameron but little to the photography of Rejlander and Robinson, which was hopelessly mired in the stickiest depths of Victorian corn. It is fitting, therefore, that in paying homage to the grand old man Chevreul, to whom both photography and painting owed so much, Nadar should have opened a new pathway into visual communication—photojournalism (see pages 152-153).

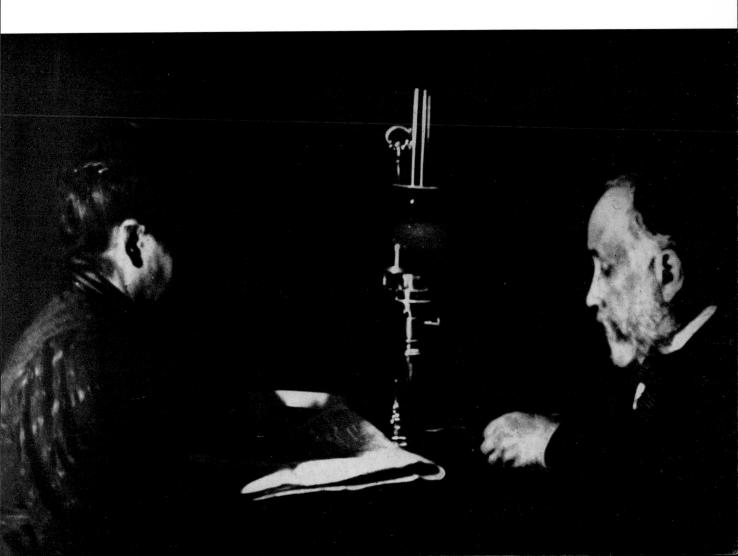

CHAPTER 7

Fox Talbot

THE DAGUERREOTYPE HELD EVERYONE ENTHRALLED—painter, engraver, etcher, lithographer, scientist. Its delicate tonality and immense detail, discernible by magnifying glass, seduced everyone away from the rougher picture on paper invented by Henry Fox Talbot and announced the same month.

Sir John Herschel, who named Talbot's invention "photography" and who also coined the words "negative" and "positive" to explain the process, considered the grainy paper print child's play compared with the silver image.

The beauty of the daguerreotype was unique, its impression on silver not to be compared with a photograph on paper or a print made by any of the graphic arts. Today we recognize its fineness and appreciate its gracefulness without expecting the photograph or etching to emulate its qualities.

It was Talbot's invention of a paper negative from which multiple prints could be made that became the foundation of modern photography. The daguerreotype, uniquely beautiful as it was, had had its day a little more than a decade after it was invented.

Arago's preliminary announcement of the daguerreotype on January 7, 1839, before the Academy of Sciences in Paris, goaded Fox Talbot to publish his process first. He feared that, if Daguerre's invention was similar to his own, all his years of work would go for naught. Before the end of January Talbot had the noted scientist Michael Faraday present at a meeting of the Royal Institution in London several of his pictures of flowers, leaves, and lace, figures from a painted glass, and a view of Venice, all made by superimposition of object or engraving on sensitized paper. In addition, Faraday exhibited a number of Talbot's "pictures representing the architecture of my home in the country . . . made with the camera obscura in the summer of 1835."

On the last day of January, 1839, Talbot read before the Royal Society his report, "Some Account of the Art of Photogenic Drawing, or the Process by Which Natural Objects May Be Made to Delineate Themselves without the Aid of the Artist's Pencil." In it he referred to the experiments conducted by Wedgwood and Davy, devoting a paragraph to "the art of fixing the shadow," which is what they admitted they were unable to do, but Talbot did not explain how he accomplished it. Three weeks later, on February 20, Talbot sent the Royal Society a second letter, in which he listed further discoveries in "photogenic drawing" and then gave full particulars of how he fixed the image—in a solution of common salt.

In *The Pencil of Nature*, published in 1844, the first book illustrated with photographs, Talbot describes what gave him the idea of making permanent the pictures that he saw through the camera obscura. He writes that it was in October, 1833, while he was at Lake Como in Italy and was trying to copy nature with the aid of Wollaston's camera lucida. "I came to the conclusion that the instrument required a previous knowledge of drawing which unfortunately I did not possess. I then thought of trying again a method which I had tried many years before. The method was to take a camera obscura and to throw the image of the objects on a piece of paper in its focus—fairy pictures, creations of a moment, and destined as rapidly to fade away. It was during these thoughts that the idea occurred to me, how charming it would be if it were possible to cause these natural images to imprint themselves durably, and remain fixed upon the paper!"

Talbot reasoned that, since light could effect changes in materials, all he had to do was to find the proper materials. Paper was the answer for him. He found that he could submerge a sheet of paper in a weak solution of salt and then, when it was dry, dip it in a solution of silver nitrate, thereby forming in the fibers of the paper the light-sensitive chemical, silver chloride. He first made copies of engravings, flowers, and lace, but, by the summer of 1835, he had experimented with both large and small cameras.

The small cameras his wife called "mousetraps." Talbot placed a number of them around his home, Lacock Abbey, near Chippenham, Wiltshire, and succeeded in securing in each, after only a 30-minute exposure, a perfect "miniature picture of the objects before which it had been placed." He fixed this inch-square image by washing the paper in a strong solution of common salt or with potassium iodide.

After Talbot's invention was announced, Sir John Herschel suggested to him that the unused silver chloride could be more effectively removed, so that the image would not change in sunlight, by using hyposulphite of soda, which Sir John had found twenty years before, in 1819, to be the best solvent of silver salts.

Talbot discovered, in 1840—as had Daguerre two years earlier—that he did not have to wait for the image to become visible. Development of the latent image enabled him to take a picture in minutes where it had formerly taken him hours. No longer was it necessary for him to peep through a hole cut in the camera to ascertain when the image was visible. Magically, the image appeared when the paper was developed in gallic acid. After development, Talbot used a hot solution of hypo to fix the image, washed the negative in pure water, dried it, and then made it transparent by waxing the paper. He contact-printed these negatives by sunlight on silver chloride paper, the simple paper that he had used from the beginning of his experiments.

These brilliantly improved negatives he called "calotypes," from the Greek meaning "beautiful pictures," but he later called them "Talbotypes."

Quite unexpectedly, in 1841, the wealthy Fox Talbot patented the process, limiting the number of photographers to those who would pay his license fee. The daguerreotype had been patented in England; international recognition and a substantial pension had been given Daguerre in France. Talbot had received little recognition in England for his paper process, which he had not patented when he had published it two years before and was deprecated as inferior to Daguerre's process.

Pique and the desire to reap some financial benefits—he had spent $35,000—seem to have moved him to patent his process. This was the first of many patents Talbot was to secure, exacting royalties from all and vigilantly prosecuting those who dared infringe.

Many patents he secured were for inventions that were already in existence, such as the method of development by means of gallic acid, which had been employed by the Reverend Joseph Bancroft Reade in 1837 but never published or patented.

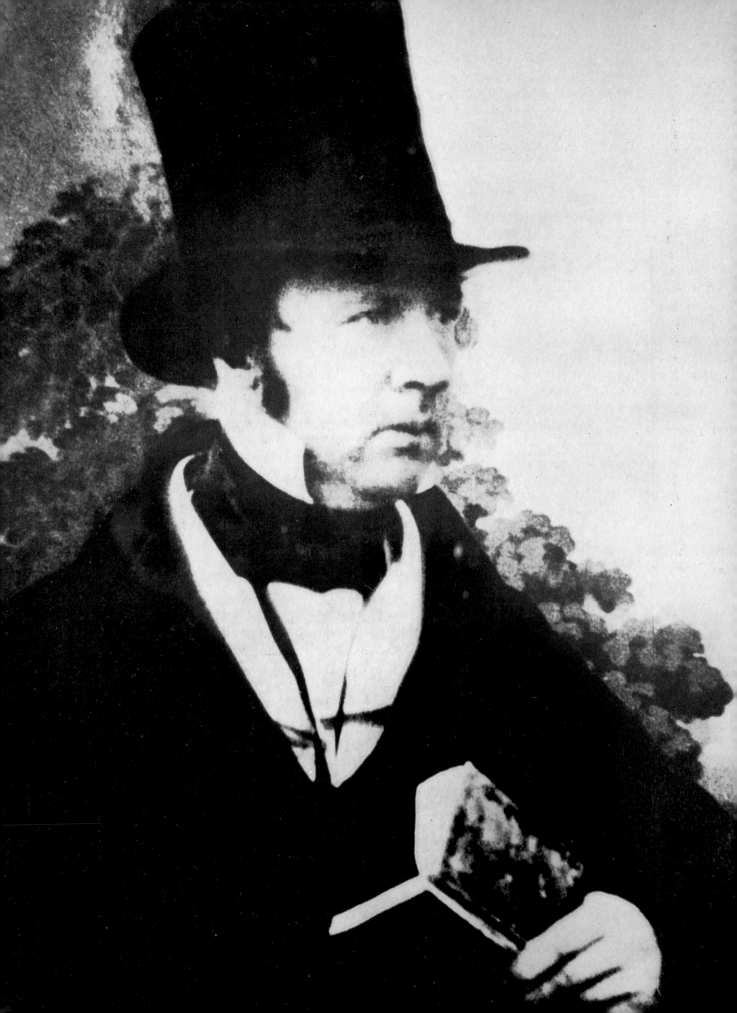

In his patent of June 1, 1843, Talbot included hyposulphite of soda as a fixing agent; this had been suggested to him four years earlier by its discoverer Sir John Herschel. He also included an enlarging process in this patent, the same procedure for which Alexander Wolcott had been given a patent a few months before.

There was no scientific board in England at that time to check on originality or to appraise the merit of a patent. In 1843 Talbot also patented books illustrated with photographs, for he was contemplating publication of his *Pencil of Nature*. This six-part book contains, as well as an explanatory text by the author, the history of his invention and 24 actual photographs of architecture, still lifes, sculpture, and scenes around Talbot's house. During 1845 Talbot published his second illustrated book, containing 23 photographs, entitled *Sun Pictures in Scotland*.

Talbot was rebuked and criticized by indignant writers who demanded that he relax his monopoly on discoveries that others had given freely to the world. This did not deter him. He continued to prosecute and would not abandon any of his patent rights. The president of the Royal Academy and the president of the Photographic Society appealed to him to relinquish his stifling controls. At long last, in the summer of 1852, he freed the process for artists, scientists, and amateurs, but retained the right to license photographers taking portraits for profit. Fortunes had been made in this field: Richard Beard in London had realized $200,000 in one year, and huge sums had been made by Claudet, Mayall, Collen, and others, and by many photographers in Europe and America.

Portraiture by Talbotype and daguerreotype was already doomed. The collodion process on glass had been invented in 1851 by Scott Archer, who had given it freely to the world. Talbot claimed that the new process was a variation of his patent and basically the same—the negative-positive principle applied to glass instead of paper.

The celebrated case that broke Fox Talbot's monopoly was brought to court in 1854. A professional portraitist named Silvester LaRoche refused to pay license fees Talbot sued. The jury heard arguments regarding photochemistry which gave the perplexed judge a hard time as he summed up the case for their benefit: "Is pyrogallic acid, though it may differ in shape, in its actions with reagents, in its composition, is it or is it not a chemical equivalent with gallonitrate of silver? If it is, the defendant is guilty; if it is not, he is not guilty."

The jury found LaRoche not guilty. They also found Talbot to be the first and true inventor of the Talbotype; this they explained as meaning the first to publish or disclose the process to the public.

Talbot's hold could have been broken earlier. Sir John

NTOINE CLAUDET, Portrait of Fox Talbot. *Daguerreotype 844. Courtesy George Eastman House, Rochester.*

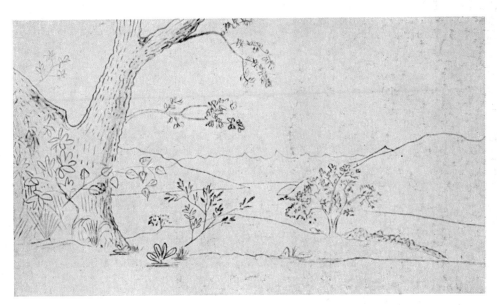

Sketch by Fox Talbot made with Wollaston's camera lucida, October 6, 1833. Courtesy Royal Photographic Society, London.

91

Herschel in 1839 made photographs on glass and had published his findings. Talbot's patents applied only to paper.

Sir John Herschel was one of the greatest inventors of photographic processes. A most important invention of his that is still in use is the cheapest, simplest permanent process for copying drawings or maps, the common blueprint.

Talbot did strange things. He patented the Talbotype in the United States six years after he patented the process in England. He sold the patent rights to the professional daguerreotypists William and Frederick Langenheim of Philadelphia for $6,000. The Langenheims never sold a single license in the States, where the daguerreotype remained unpatented, was faster and preferable, and where the little demand created for multiple prints could be satisfied by lithographing copies of photographs or by rephotographing the subject or the daguerreotype.

It is nevertheless to Fox Talbot that the entire world is indebted for the invention of the negative-positive process, from which all modern photography stems.

FOX TALBOT, Wilton House. *Calotype, about 1844.*
Courtesy Metropolitan Museum of Art, New York.

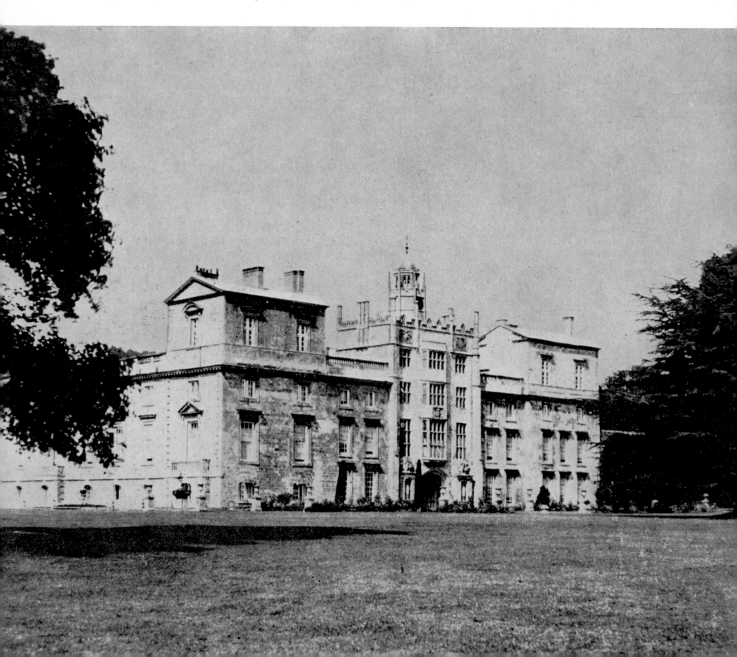

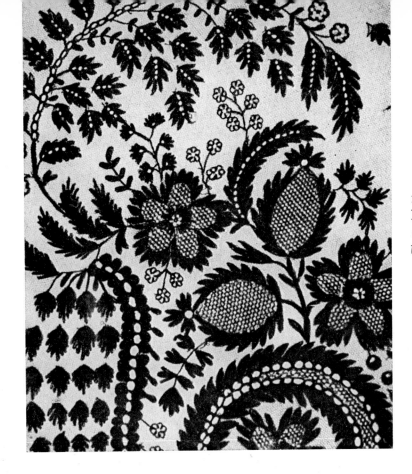

FOX TALBOT,
Lace. *"Photogenic drawing,"* 1843.
*Courtesy Gernsheim Collection,
University of Texas.*

FOX TALBOT, *first paper negative, one inch square. Lacock
Abbey, August, 1835. Courtesy Science Museum, London.*

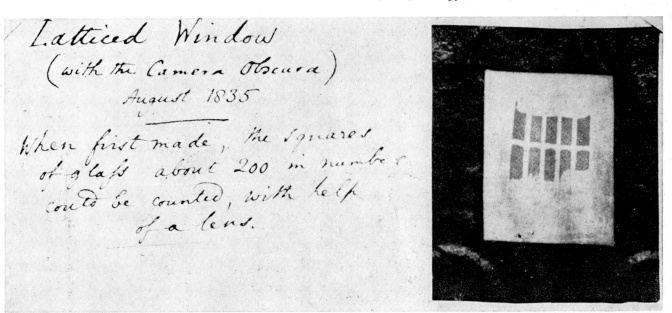

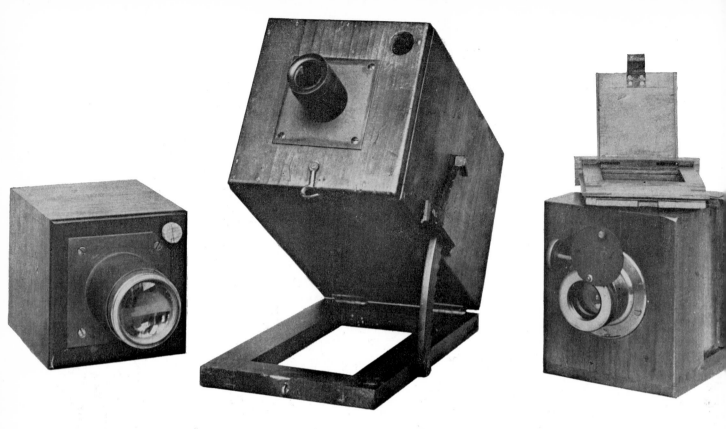

Fox Talbot's two earliest cameras with peep holes, and a
third designed for the later calotype process. Before development
of the "latent image," peep holes permitted photographers
to see when image was fully exposed on negatives.

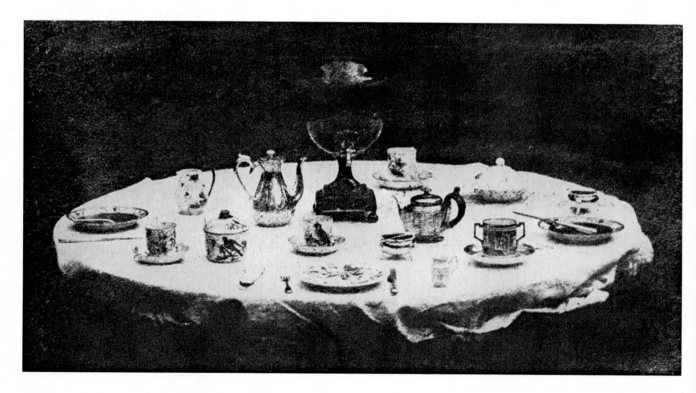

FOX TALBOT, Breakfast Table. *Photograph, 1840. Technique,
using paper negative, called "photogenic drawing" by inventor.*

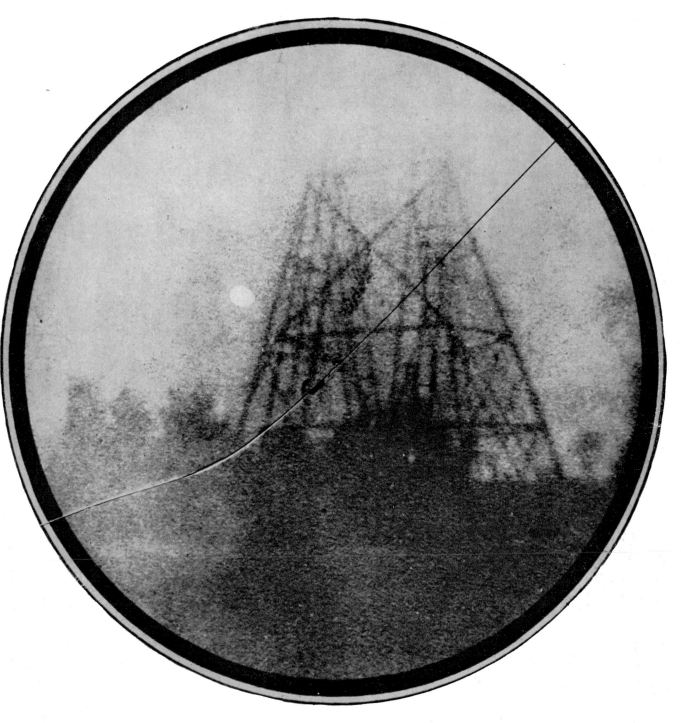

*Sir John F. W. Herschel's photograph on glass, of his
father's observatory, 1839. Courtesy Science Museum,
London, for all three pictures.*

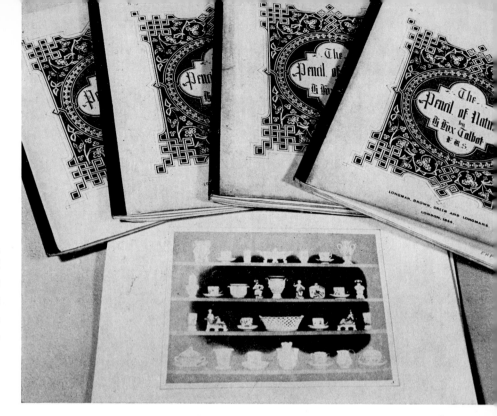

Fox Talbot's Pencil of Nature, *first book published with original photographs. Issued in six parts between 1844 and 1846, with pictures pasted in by hand. Courtesy George Eastman House.*

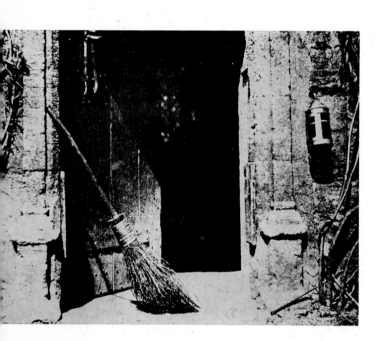

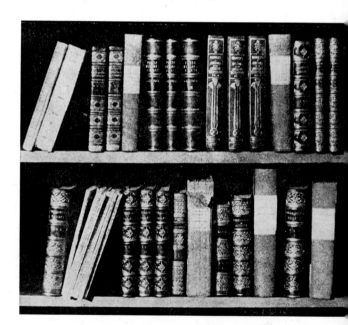

FOX TALBOT, The Broom *(left)* and Books *(above).*
From Pencil of Nature. *Calotype, 1844-46. Courtesy The Harold White Collection, Bromley, Kent, England.*

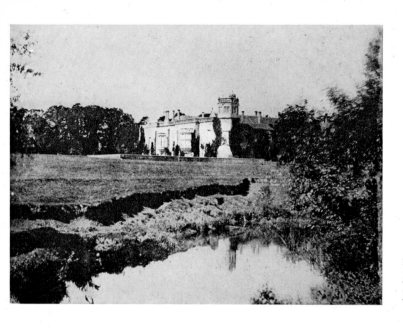

FOX TALBOT, Lacock Abbey *(left) and* The Ladder *(below).
From* Pencil of Nature. *Calotype, 1844-46. Courtesy The
Harold White Collection, Bromley, Kent, England.*

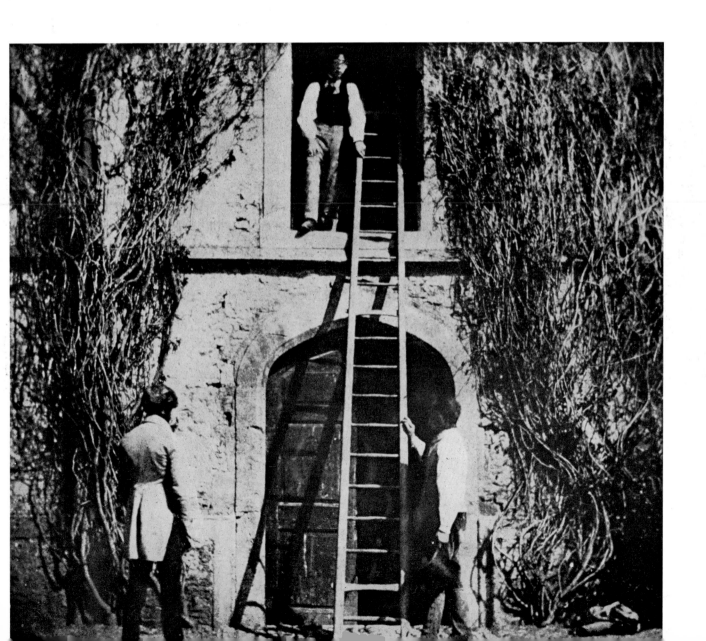

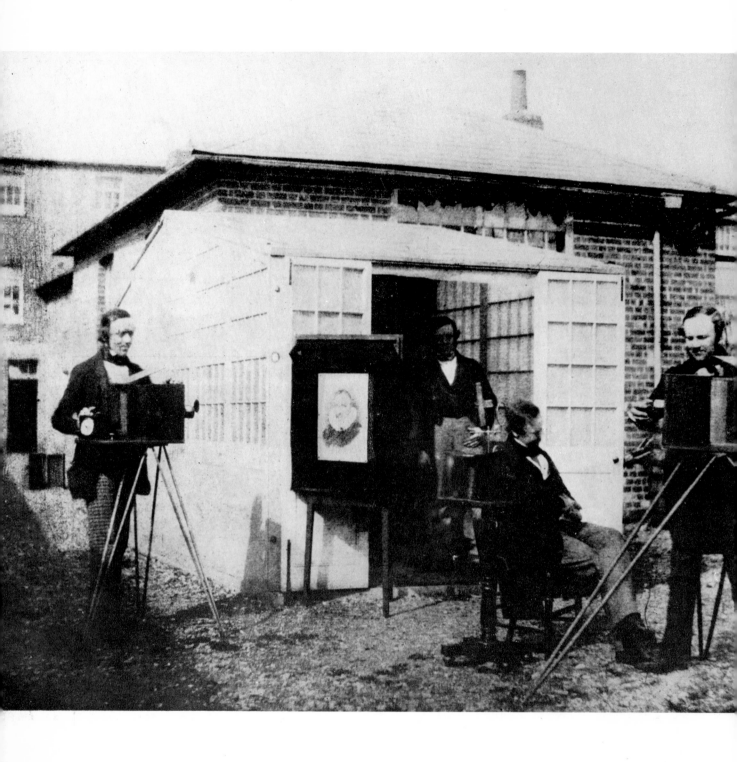

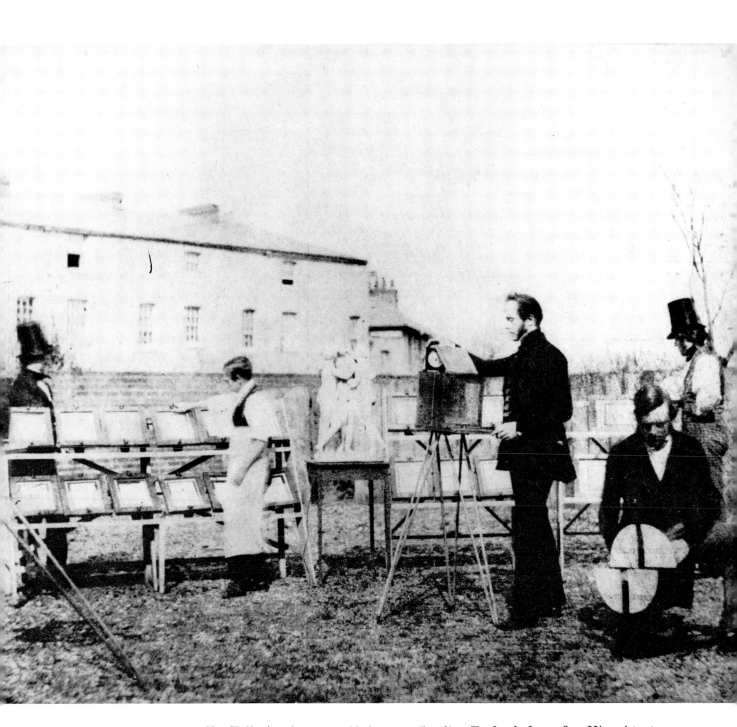

Fox Talbot's calotype establishment at Reading, England, about 1845. His assistants, seen from left to right in two separate exposures, are copying a painting, taking a portrait from life, printing by sunlight, and photographing a piece of sculpture. What the man kneeling at the right is doing is a mystery. Courtesy Science Museum.

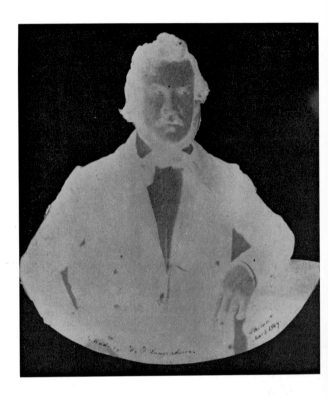

Paper envelope of the firm W. & F. Langenheim of Philadelphia, 1848, to whom Talbot sold patent rights for the United States. Courtesy George Eastman House.

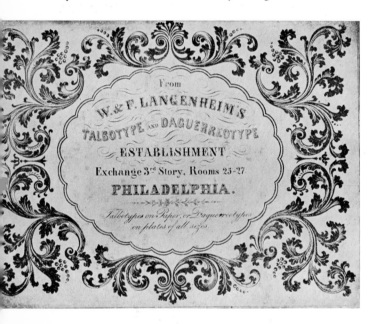

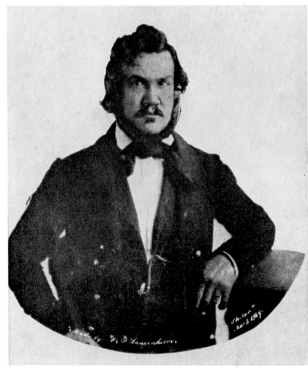

Paper negative and print signed "Made by W. & F. Langenheim, March 5, 1849." Courtesy George Eastman House.

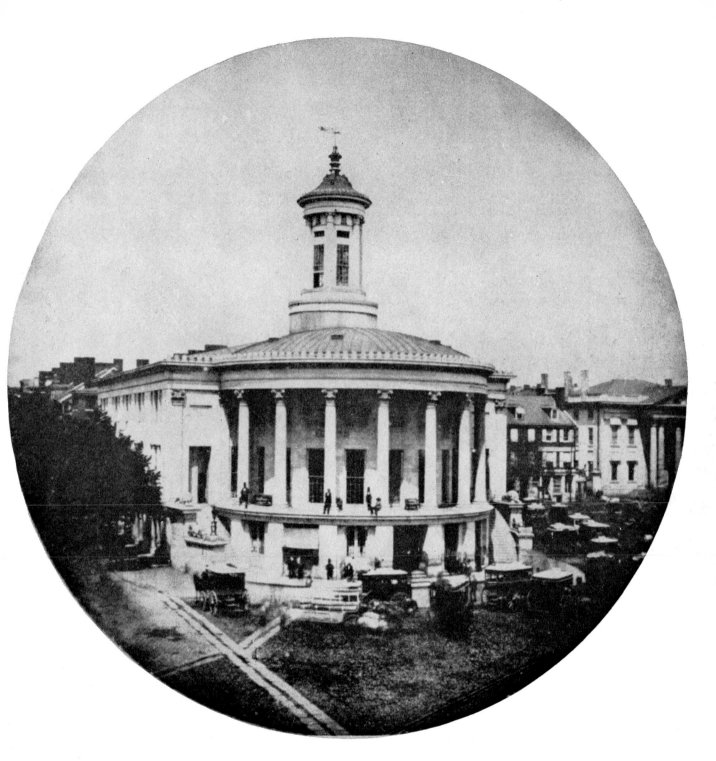

W. & F. LANGENHEIM, The Merchant's Exchange, Philadelphia. *Calotype, 1849.*
Signed and sent to Fox Talbot as a sample. Gift of Miss M. T. Talbot,
Lacock Abbey, England, through Harold White, to George Eastman House.

CHAPTER 8

Hill and Adamson: The Great Collaboration

THE GREATEST EXPONENTS of the calotype process were two men of Edinburgh, Scotland (where Fox Talbot's patent restrictions did not extend), a painter, David Octavius Hill, and a chemist-photographer, Robert Adamson. Collaborators for only five years—Adamson died at the age of twenty-seven in the year 1848—they took more than 1,500 pictures, including some of the finest portraits in the history of photography.

How necessary the young technician Adamson was to the association is evident from the fact that Hill produced few memorable photographs after Adamson's death, although he attempted to collaborate with other photographers whom he directed.

Together Hill and Adamson made some superb pictures, posing people singly, in pairs, or in groups in open sunlight, simulating interiors by placing chairs and other props and backdrops behind and around the figures. The subjects held head in hand or posed leaning body against a prop and assuming a relaxed, natural pose for exposures lasting 1 to 3 minutes.

Character is boldly expressed in each portrait. No attempt is made to hide lined features. Often deep shadows are left to emphasize the black and white masses of the face, repeated dramatically throughout all parts of the picture, in the hands, in the garments, as well as in the backgrounds. Detail was sacrificed, for the paper negative could never compete with the daguerreotype in securing seductive detail. Areas of light and dark were handled like the chiaroscuro in a drawing by Rembrandt.

It was in 1843 that Hill turned to the use of the camera when he was commissioned by the Free Church of Scotland to paint an enormous picture, 11'4" by 5'0", *Signing the Act of Separation and Deed of Demission*. On this monumental canvas Hill was to portray all 470 minister-delegates who resigned from the Church of Scotland, on the grounds that the congregation had the right to choose its own ministers, and then met in general assembly to commemorate their freedom from Queen and landed gentry.

Hill and Adamson secured likenesses and character studies of practically all the delegates in the few short years of their partnership. Besides these photographs, they took pictures of celebrated men and women, people of nobility, sailors, fishermen, and women, as well as landscapes of their native Scotland. Each of their pictures was marked with the unique artistry of their collaborative seeing. They devised a perfect way of using creatively the imperfect paper negative.

Hill was an accomplished lithographer; before he was nineteen he had published a portfolio of thirty lithographs depicting scenery in Perthshire, Scotland. He later became a painter of moody, literary, romantic landscapes. He painted a series of canvases interpreting the poems of Robert Burns; these were engraved and published as *The Land of Burns*.

In 1866, four years before his death, Hill's culminating work to which he had devoted twenty-two years of his life was at long last finished, and the huge canvas was accepted by the sponsor, The Scottish Free Church. All the ministers can be identified, as can Hill himself, his wife, and the lamented Adamson with his camera. The picture still hangs in the Presbytery Hall in Edinburgh.

Hill's paintings are not often remembered in discussions of nineteenth-century art. His work, with some few exceptions, pieces like the small painting *Leith Pier* now in the National Gallery of Scotland, would perhaps be entirely forgotten if it had not been for his collaboration with Adamson in photography.

It is to the everlasting credit of J. Craig Annan, a photographer in the 1890s who made prints from their old paper negatives, that interest was revived in these two pioneering Scotsmen, whose penetrating portraits are now conceded to be some of the finest ever made in the field of photography.

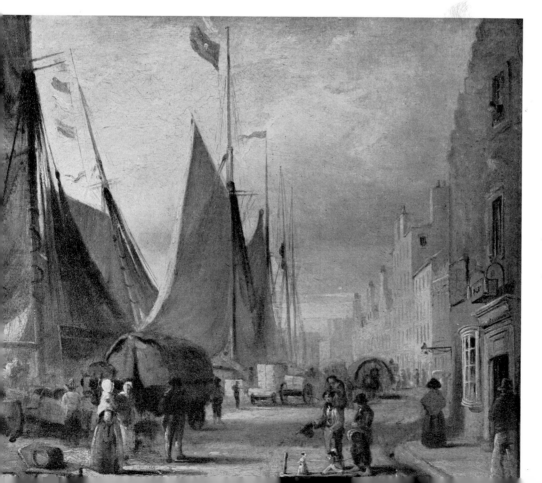

DAVID OCTAVIUS HILL, Leith Pier. *Oil painting on wood panel, 1840, 11¾ x 13½ inches. Courtesy The National Gallery of Scotland, Edinburgh.*

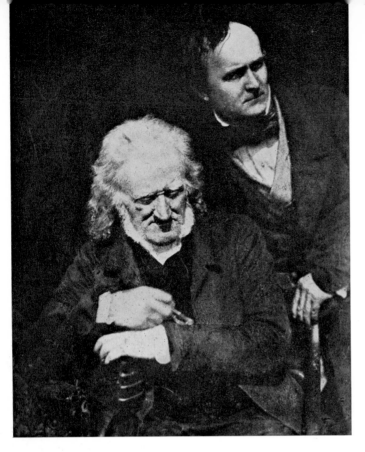

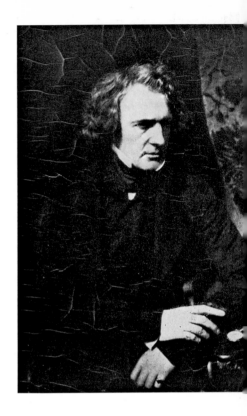

DAVID OCTAVIUS HILL AND ROBERT ADAMSON
above: John Henning and Alexander Handyside Ritchie.
Calotype, about 1845. The two noted sculptors, friends of Hill,
were his associates in the Royal Scottish Academy.
above right: Photograph of a Man. *Calotype, about 1846. Both,*
courtesy The Art Institute of Chicago, Stieglitz Collection.

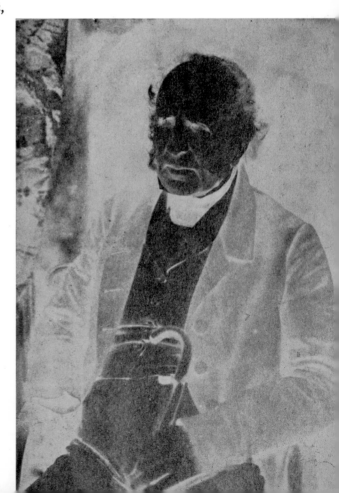

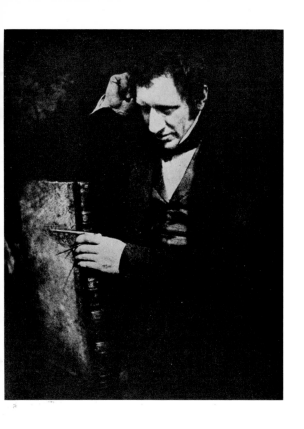

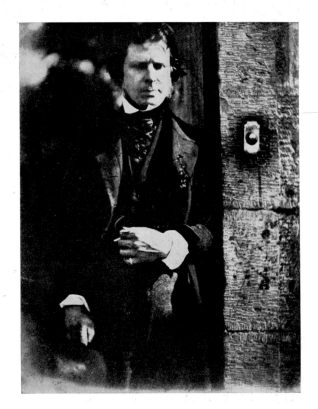

above: HILL AND ADAMSON, James Nasmyth.
*Calotype, 1845. Portrait of the engineer
and inventor of the steam hammer.
Courtesy The Art Institute of Chicago,
Stieglitz Collection.*
above left: ROBERT ADAMSON, David Octavius
Hill. *Calotype, about 1843. Courtesy
George Eastman House, Rochester.*

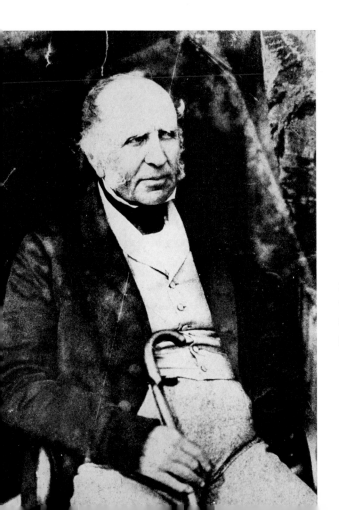

HILL AND ADAMSON, Portrait of a Minister.
*Calotype negative and print, about 1845;
contemporary print made from the original
paper negative. Courtesy George Eastman House.*

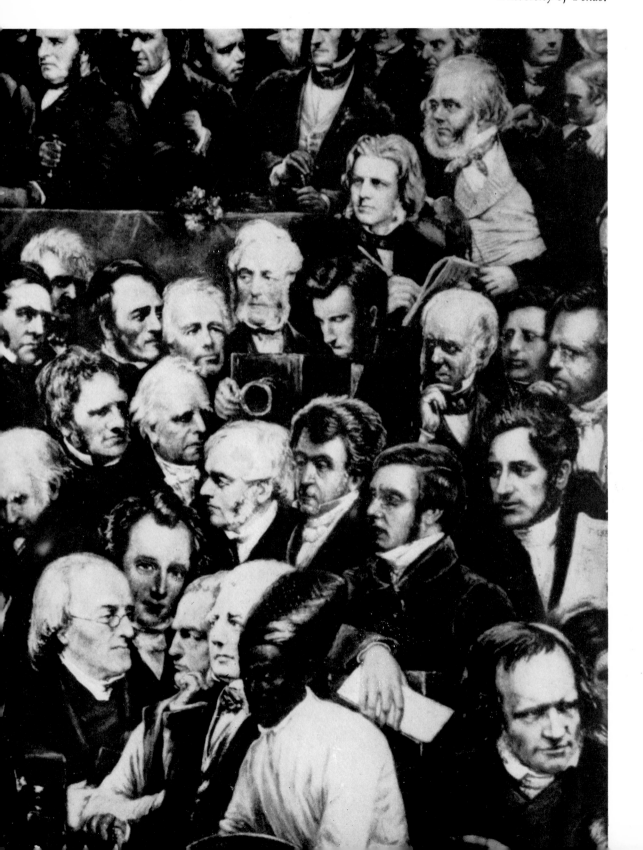

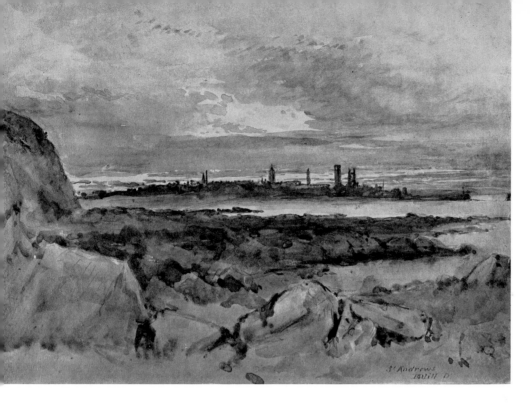

above: HILL. St. Andrews,
Ruins of Castle and Sea.
Watercolor, about 1845.
below: HILL AND ADAMSON.
*Rare calotype photograph
of same scene.
Both courtesy
George Eastman House.*

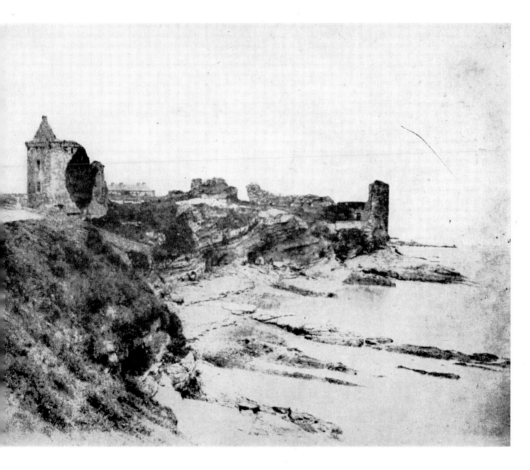

CHAPTER 9

Early Wet-plate Photography

Sir John Herschel experimented, none too successfully, with glass instead of paper or metal as a backing for sensitive silver salts. Niepce de St. Victor, a cousin of Nicéphore Niepce, perceived in 1847, upon studying Sir John's report published in the *Journal* of the Royal Society, that Sir John had failed to coat the glass with a suitable organic substance to serve as a binder for the sensitive silver.

A soldier by profession but an amateur scientist by avocation, Niepce de St. Victor lost his laboratory in the Revolution of 1848 when the barracks in which he resided were destroyed. He nevertheless continued his studies, experimenting first with starch and gelatin and then more satisfactorily with whites of eggs. To the white of egg he added a few drops of iodide of potassium and bromide of potassium plus a few grains of common salt, thoroughly whipped it into a froth, and then strained it through fine muslin.

This solution of iodized albumen he used to coat a sheet of glass and, when it was thoroughly dry, sensitized it by immersing it in nitrate of silver. The plate could be used wet or dry in the camera, but when dry it required a much longer exposure than did a daguerreotype or calotype. Convinced that his invention would have some importance in the world of photography, Niepce de St. Victor communicated his albumen process in June, 1848, to the Academy of Sciences in Paris.

Immediately after publication of the process, modifications and improvements were suggested for speeding up the sensitized albumen so that it could be used for taking portraits and figures, as well as architecture and landscape.

To eliminate the grain and other imperfections in paper, L. D. Blanquart-Evrard conceived the idea of coating paper with albumen for positives. After development, he dipped the print in a solution of chloride of gold, to achieve a range of cold pleasing tones in browns and grays as well as to make the image more permanent.

The consumption of eggs for albumen paper, which lasted as the most popular paper for more than forty years, was astronomical. All over the world hundreds of millions of eggs were broken open annually for the whites, the yolks either being wasted or sold to tanneries and bakeries.

Blanquart-Evrard, who had improved the calotype process but who never mentioned Talbot as its original inventor, established in Lille, France, the first mass-production, assembly-line method of printing. He employed about 40 girls, each of whom was trained to perform a specific operation. Blanquart-Evrard published in 1851 in France the first album of views with original photographs, and in the following year was the first to publish a book, *Egypte, Nubie, Palestine et Syrie*, illustrated with original photographs. This was an exceptionally attractive volume consisting of 125 brilliant prints from paper negatives taken by Maxime Du Camp, a noted writer turned photographer, who toured the mid-East for two years with the brilliant author and critic, Gustave Flaubert.

The paper negative experienced one further major improvement before it, like the daguerreotype and all other early processes, fell into limbo with the advent of Scott Archer's invention of the wet-collodion process. Gustave Le Gray, in 1851, immersed the paper negative in wax until it was completely impregnated, and then dried and sensitized the paper. The negative was now transparent; imperfections of the paper were now eliminated; and, above all, the negative could now be kept up to two weeks and then used dry. In addition to inventing the waxed-paper process, Gustave Le Gray experimented with collodion on glass and claimed to have invented the collodion process—but this was several months after Scott Archer in London had announced the substitution of collodion for albumen on glass and had published his formula in *The Chemist*, March, 1851.

Scott Archer, a British sculptor and photographer, dissolved guncotton, ether, and alcohol to make collodion (this formula had already been known to medicine for several years) and blended this with a solution of silver iodide and iodide of iron. This mixture was coated on a clean glass plate, which was then immersed in a solution of distilled water and silver nitrate, and exposed wet in the camera. The plate had to be developed while the collodion was still moist. The new process was faster than albumen or any of the other photographic methods. It required only 2 or 3 seconds exposure in direct sunlight, and the resulting subtleties of tonality were unequaled by any existing processes.

How generous was Scott Archer! He could have patented his invention and made untold fortunes for himself and his heirs, for the wet-collodion process was not to be superseded until more than thirty years later when the gelatin dry plate was marketed commercially. Archer announced his invention without restrictions and died impoverished at the age of forty-four in 1857. His name today is hardly known even by the innumerable commercial photoengravers all over the world who still use his invention of the wet-collodion process.

Since the ether in the collodion evaporated quickly, it was necessary to develop the plate directly after exposure. In extreme climates of desert or mountain this caused considerable difficulty, particularly since all preparations of the plate had to be done in total or semi-darkness. Not only was it necessary for the photographer to move with cameras, tripods, lenses, chemicals, glass plates of various sizes to fit his cameras, distilled water, measuring pots and trays, he had to lug along also a darkroom; all of this paraphernalia weighed about 120 pounds. A tent was invariably used for developing, although wicker baskets, boats, railway cars, wagons, and handcarts were at times transformed to serve this purpose.

The wet-collodion process was immediately applied to portraiture. In America, where the daguerreotype held in fashion and demand longer than anywhere in Europe, a patent was issued for "ambrotype" portraits made in the same sizes as daguerreotypes and advertised as having the advantage of being visible at all times, not, like the mirror-like surface of the silver image, only in certain lights.

Ambrotypes (from the Greek for "imperishable") were negative portraits on glass deliberately underexposed to make a faint image. These were backed up with black paper or velvet or sometimes painted black. As the image was reversed, it was often the practice to lay the glass negative face-down on the paper or velvet to make it appear as a positive. With a sheet of glass as a protecting cover, the entire assembly was then placed in an elaborate designed "union" case, which made it resemble even more closely the costlier daguerreotype.

Three photographers who took superb pictures with the collodion process, one in the deserts of Egypt and the other two in the Alps of Switzerland, were Francis Frith of England and the Bisson brothers of France.

The Middle East was part of the Grand Tour during the latter part of the nineteeth century, creating a constant demand for photographs of Egyptian antiquities and views of the Nile River and of the Holy Land. Publishers in Europe and England sent expeditions of photographers to appease this public demand from which they reaped considerable profit. A publisher who was also a talented photographer, Francis Frith of London, in 1856 traveled up the Nile taking pictures with various-sized cameras, one for tremendous plates measuring 16 by 20 inches. Starting from the Delta, he went up the river more than 800 miles to the Fifth Cataract, beyond the present border of Egypt and the Sudan. He took magnificent pictures of the Pyramids and the Great Sphinx at Gizeh, the Temples at Karnak and Luxor, the monumental sculpture submerged in the sands at Thebes, and fragments of architecture peering through the backed up waters of the Nile at Philae.

How spectacular a series of pictures! What fortitude and resourcefulness it required of Francis Frith to get them! In the dry heat of Egypt the wet-collodion dried much faster than the usual 10 minutes it took on a hot summer day in England. Every movement in the stifling darkroom tent had to be carefully husbanded. The fumes evaporating from the ether, held inside the airless tent, were suffocating. The heat of the desert outside the tent would often reach 110 degrees, and inside, at temperatures of 130, the collodion boiled. At times the sudden sandstorms would pockmark the plates or ruin them entirely. Despite all these hardships Frith secured sufficient negatives to make a selection of extraordinary pictures for publication the following year in a book on Egypt containing original photographs and descriptions of his experiences. From his three trips to Egypt and the Holy Land Frith published a total of seven books.

Though he assembled many more portfolios of photographs covering his extensive travels throughout western Europe and also made twenty-four photographs illustrating Longfellow's *Hyperion*, his finest photographs are those he took the first years with his camera on his trips

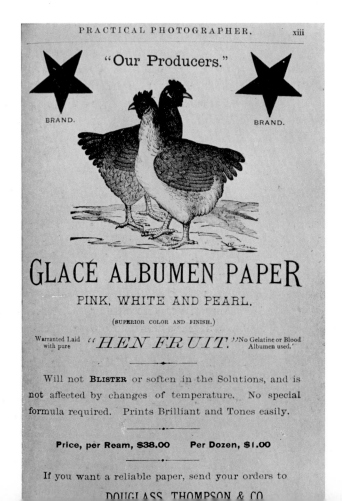

Advertisement for albumen paper, about 1860. Courtesy George Eastman House, Rochester.

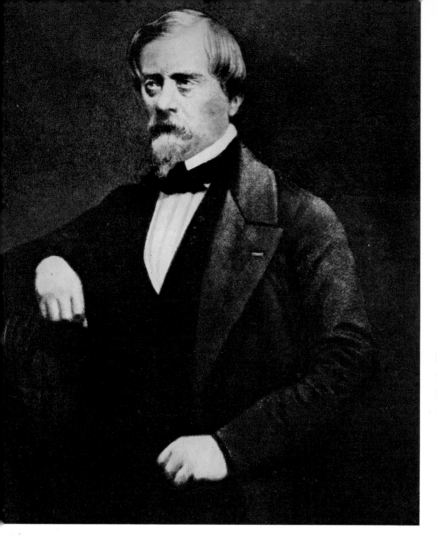

Portrait of Niepce de St. Victor. *Photographer unknown. The inventor of the albumen process, from a photocopy of an albumen original, about 1848. Courtesy George Eastman House.*

to the Middle East. Frith lived to be seventy-six years old, dying in 1898.

To some photographers using the collodion process, the hot light and hardships of the desert were not comparable to the cold light and hardships of the mountains. It became a feat of endurance to take pictures in the intense cold of ice and snow on windswept peaks at approximately 16,000 feet, in the heady atmosphere of the Alps. Some of the finest photographs of mountain scenes ever taken are the work of Louis Auguste Bisson and his brother, Auguste Rosalie. In an album owned by Eastman House the pictures contained are all marked with a stamp in red ink on the lower right corner, "Bisson Frères." Entitled *Mont Blanc and Its Glaciers*, the twenty-four photographs range in size from 9 inches by 15 inches to 12 inches by 17 inches. They were made by the brothers Bisson in 1860 on a mountain-climbing expedition when they accompanied Emperor Napoleon III and Empress Eugénie to Switzerland. The plates were coated with collodion which barely flowed in the below-

zero cold of the Alps and, after development, were washed with melted snow. Despite the imperfect coating of the plates, which accounts for the uneven quality in the skies, the photographs of the mountains are superbly designed and dramatically composed in bold areas of black and white. The brothers repeated the ascent the following year, setting out from Chamonix with guide and a band of porters to carry their photographic gear. They reached the summit in the early morning, broke out the equipment, heated the collodion over weak lamps in the bitter cold, sensitized the plates, took the pictures, developed them before the collodion hardened or froze, then washed the developed negatives in ice-cold water. From the top of the mountain they managed to get three pictures, repacked their gear, and started down the dangerous descent. Lower down the dedicated men again assembled the camera and equipment for several more excellent views on the open glacier.

Louis Auguste Bisson was known to have made daguerreotypes as early as 1840, portraying a smiling infant,

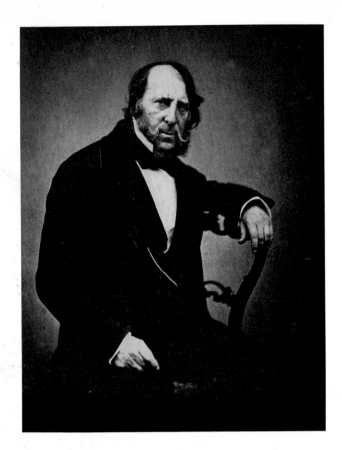

Portrait of George Cruikshank. *Wet-collodion process, 1854. Photographer unknown. The English caricaturist and wit. Courtesy George Eastman House.*

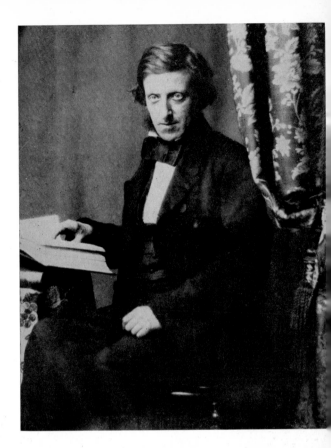

Portrait of Frederick Scott Archer. *Ambrotype, 1855. The inventor of the wet-collodion process, which revolutionized photography. Courtesy Science Museum, London.*

a mourning procession, and the bridges of Paris. In the first daguerreotype exhibition held in Paris in 1844, François Arago singled out one of Auguste's daguerreotypes for an award.

The Bisson brothers were the sons of an artist who specialized in heraldic painting. Louis Auguste studied architecture and chemistry, but became a pupil of Daguerre the year the process was announced and in less than a year opened a studio with his brother.

It is not for their daguerreotypes, however, that the Bisson brothers are remembered, nor for their landscapes, architectural subjects, and copies of paintings that they used to illustrate books, but rather for their fearless assaults on Mont Blanc when they secured a mere handful of exceptionally beautiful pictures.

Another courageous photographer, the first to cover a war under fire, was Roger Fenton, who photographed the Crimean War in 1855. Equipped with a darkroom wagon

boldly emblazoned "Photographic Van," he took pictures of the fortifications, ships and stores, installations, battlefields, officers, and men, and some of the most attractive behind-the-lines canteen operators seen in any war, who doubled as nurses for Florence Nightingale. The heat of the Russian peninsula in the Black Sea, coupled with the necessary long exposures, created hardships in preparing the short-lived collodion glass plates, which often kept Fenton from taking photographs during the several hottest hours of the day. Despite all discomforts and the sicknesses epidemic in the area, Fenton succeeded in securing more than 300 negatives in less than four months. A trained painter, Fenton overcame the obstacle of his big cameras, which prohibited instantaneous pictures, by encompassing in his ground glass vast subjects and wide vistas creating engaging compositions. These are often dramatically theatrical, resembling the romantic painting of the period in mood.

Equally theatrical are his posed portraits of the fashionably apparelled generals.

Photographers the world over turned to the use of the wet-plate process. The Indian Mutiny of 1857 was recorded by F. Beato, a photographer whom Sir John Campbell (later to become Lord Clyde) included in his command when he stormed and subdued Lucknow and other centers of the massacre.

William Notman in the 1860s became internationally famous for his wet-plate pictures of Canadian pioneers.

He took a series of moose and buffalo hunters in "the bush" seated around a tent, trappers and guides wearing snowshoes in snow made of salt and white-fox fur, an Indian boy with a loaded toboggan, all held rigid in most complicated poses inside his Montreal studio, where he created elaborate settings praised as more realistic than those actually found in nature. The faster and versatile wet-collodion process freed the artistry and imagination of photographers, who left astounding records of their day throughout the entire world.

GUSTAVE LE GRAY, Seascape. *Wet-collodion photograph, 1856. For the first time, clouds, rolling waves, and a ship in motion have been stopped with "instantaneous" photography. Le Gray was an artist, photographer, and inventor of the waxed-paper process. Courtesy George Eastman House.*

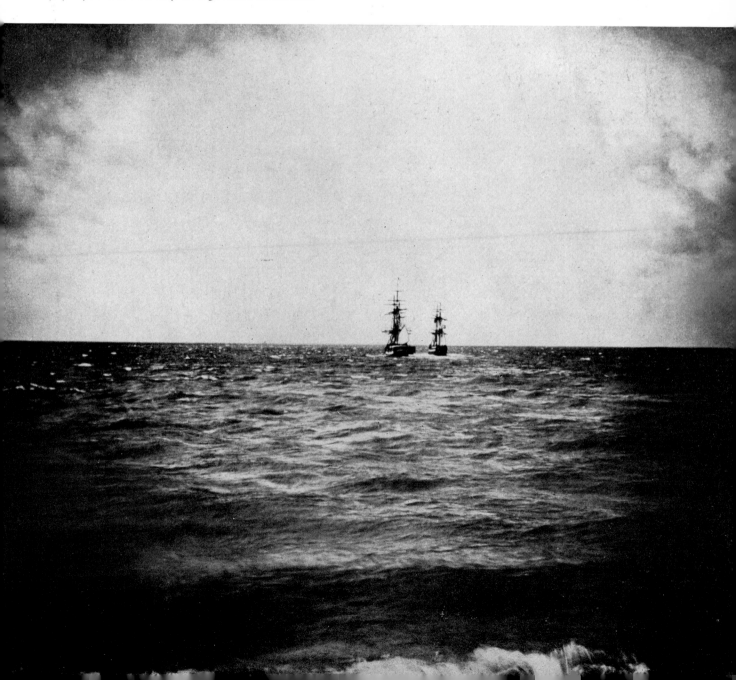

A. MACGLASHON, Bullock Wagon in Melbourne, Australia. *Wet-collodion photograph, 1856. One of the earliest photographs taken in Australia. MacGlashon later collaborated briefly with David Octavius Hill in Edinburgh in 1862. Courtesy George Eastman House.*

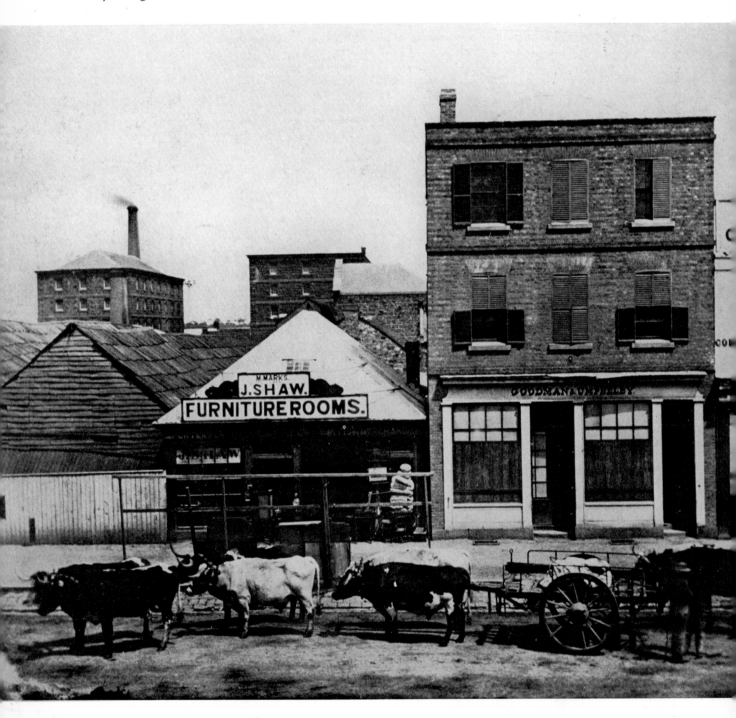

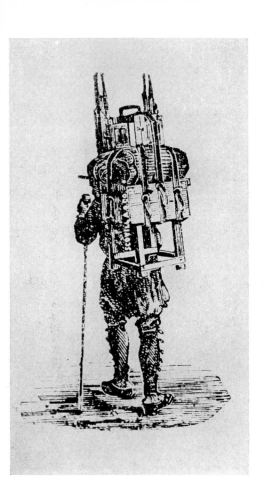

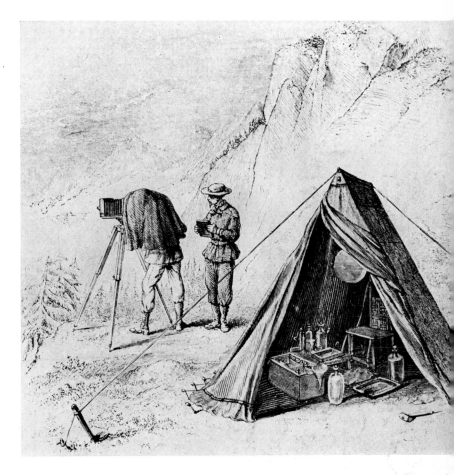

Two wood engravings of the photographer's pack, 70 to 120 pounds of equipment, during the wet-collodion period. In the 1870s the Scoville trademark was overprinted on the engraving made earlier in France. Courtesy George Eastman House.

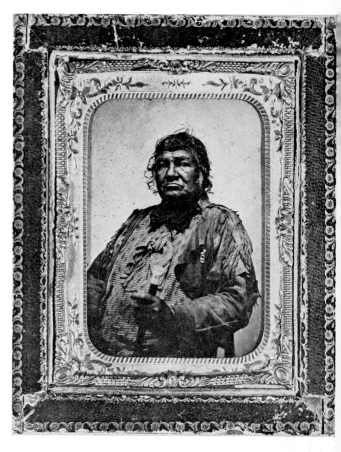

H. B. FIELD, Shabbona. *Ambrotype, 1857.*
Portrait of the eighty-two-year-old Indian chief.
Courtesy Chicago Historical Society.

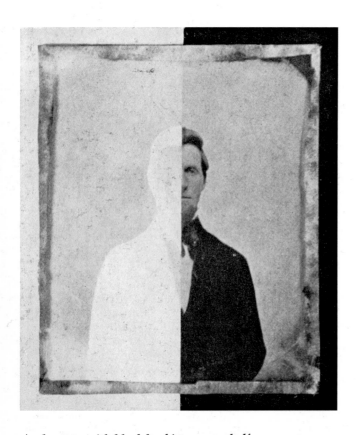

Ambrotype with black backing on one half
to show its negative-positive character.
Courtesy George Eastman House.

MAXIME DU CAMP, Colossus of Abu Simbel, Egyp
Calotype, 1850. Printed by Blanquart-Evrar
Courtesy George Eastman Hous

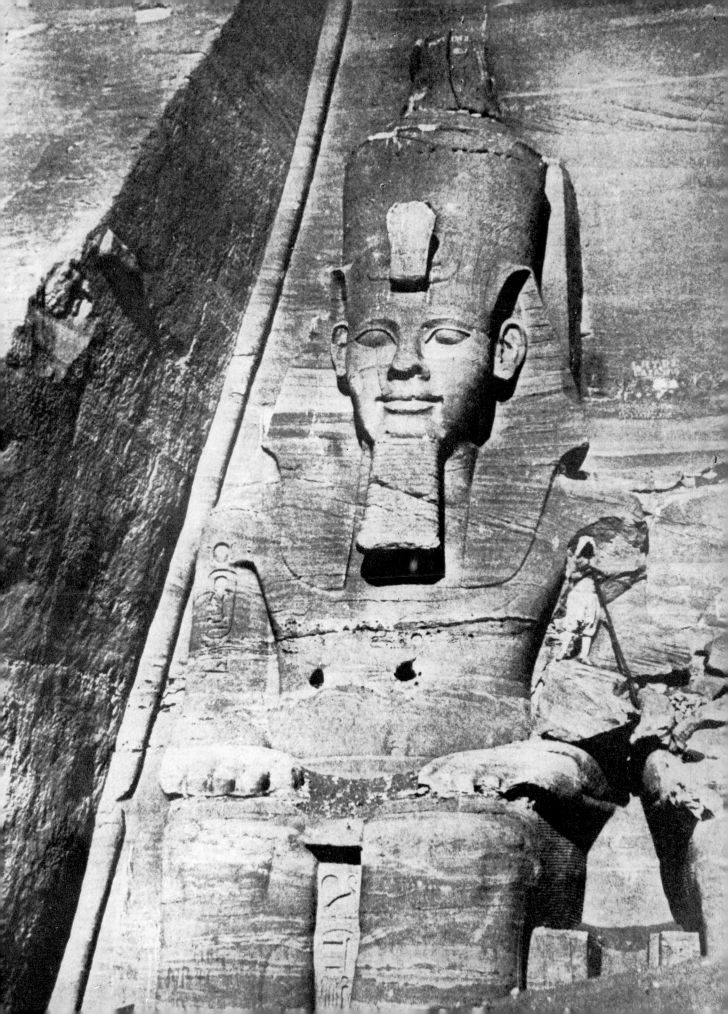

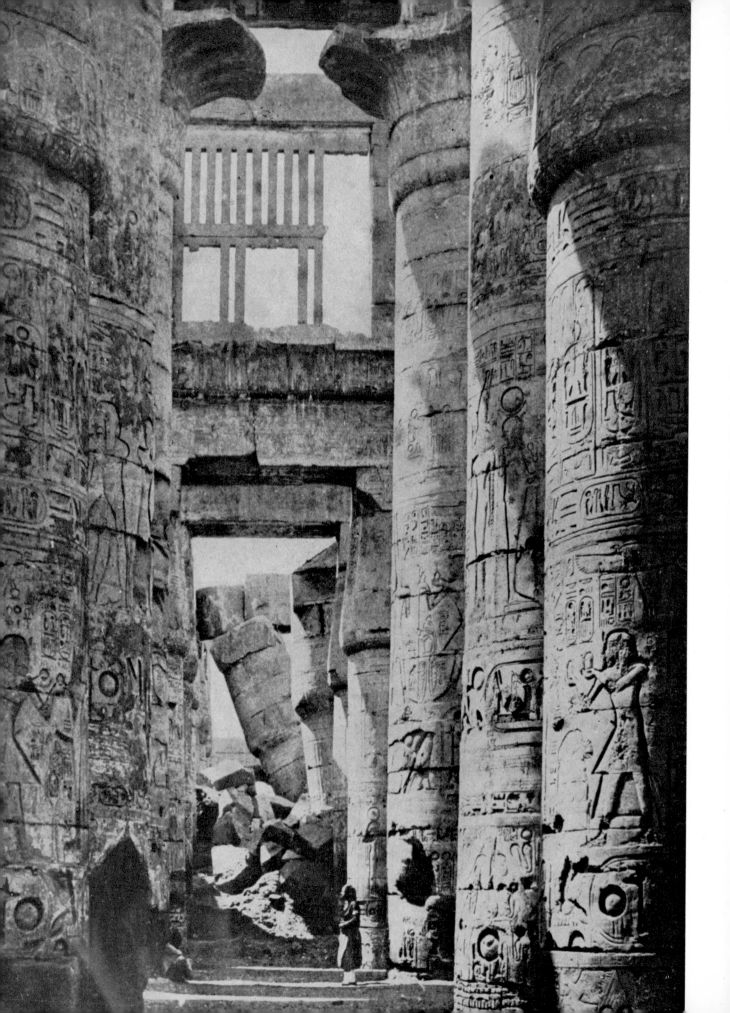

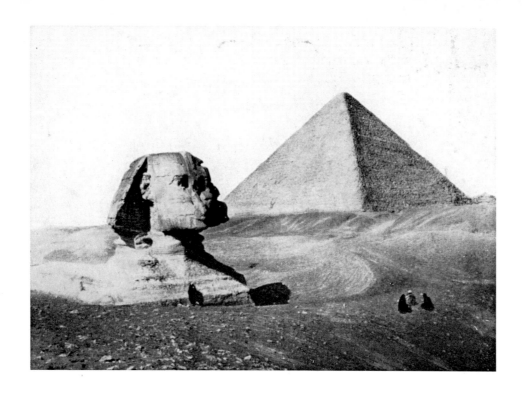

FRANCIS FRITH, *Wet-plate photographs.*
above: Pyramid of Cheops and the Sphinx,
Gizeh, Egypt. *1858. Courtesy George Eastman House.*
left: Hypostyle Hall, Luxor, Egypt.
below: Approach to Philae, Egypt.
Both, courtesy The Art Institute of Chicago.

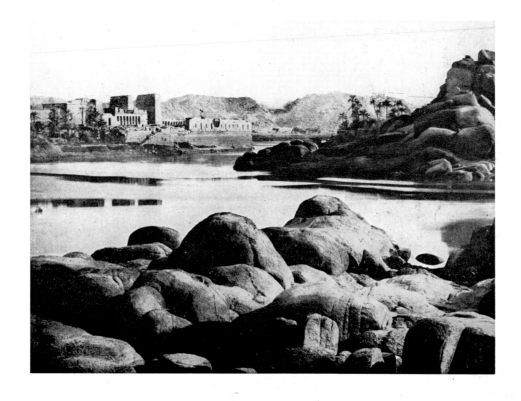

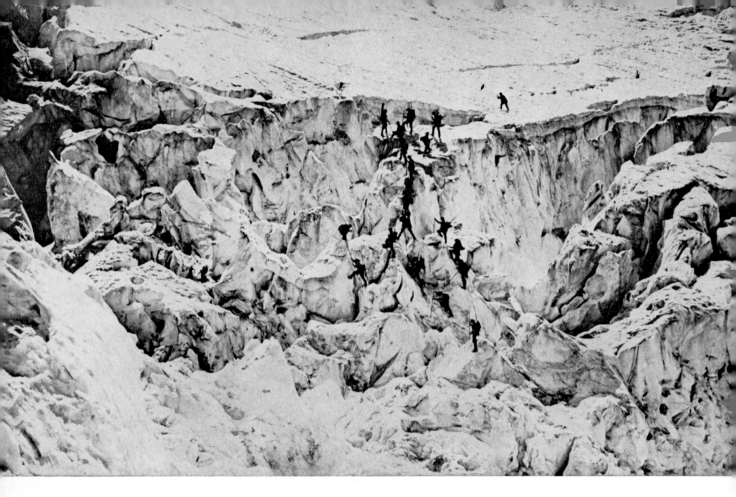

BISSON FRERES. *Five photographs of the Alps. Wet-plate process, 1860.*
Taken by the Bisson brothers when they ascended Mont Blanc, accompanying
Emperor Napoleon III and the Empress Eugénie. Courtesy George Eastman House.
above: Halfway Point.
right: Entrance to the
Valley of Chamonix.

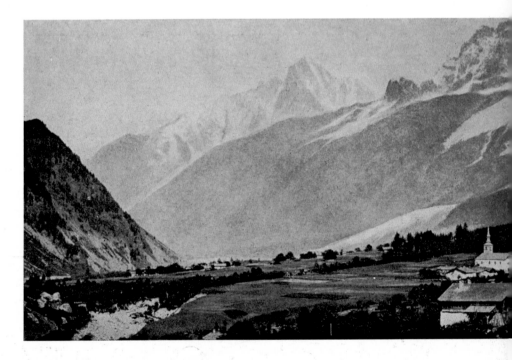

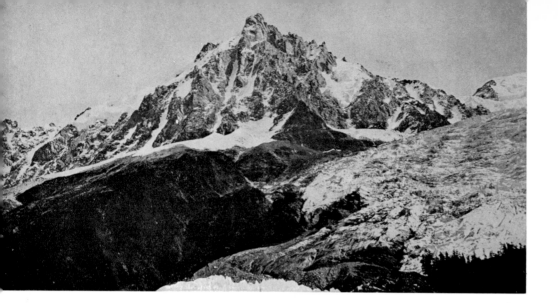

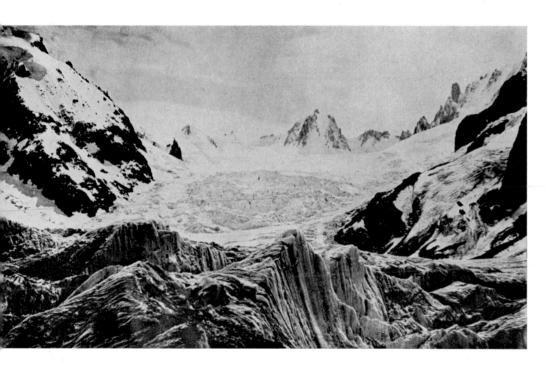

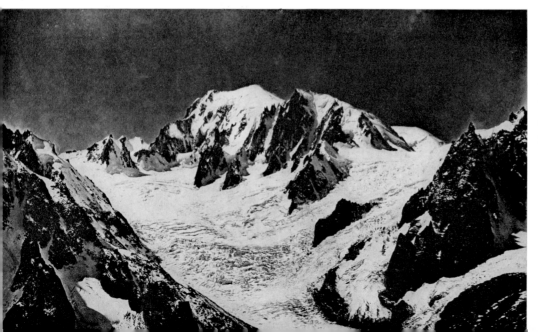

top: Ascension of Mont Blanc.
middle: The Range of Mont Blanc
bottom: View of the "Garden"
from Mont Blanc.

121

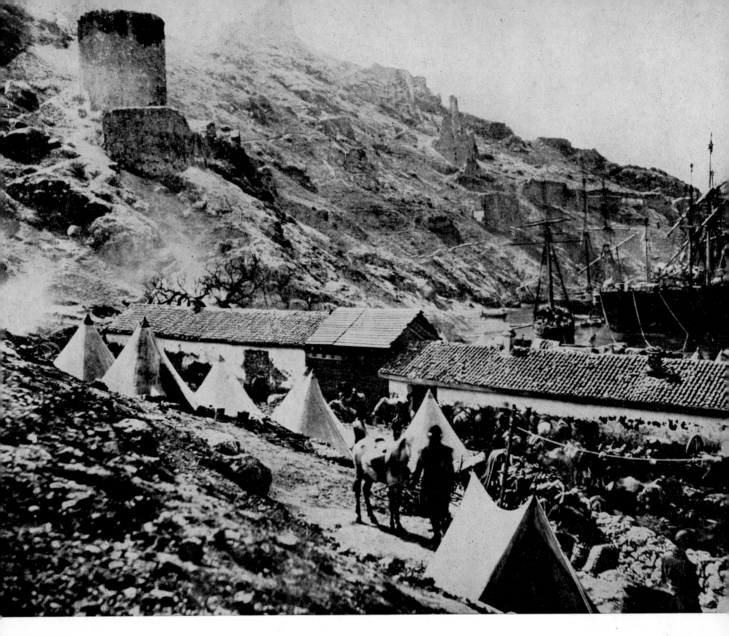

ROGER FENTON
Wet-plate photographs of the Crimean War, 1855.
above: The Fort at the Entrance to Balaclava Harbor.
right: A "Cantinière" in the Crimean War,
who doubled as nurse for Florence Nightingale.
All courtesy George Eastman House.

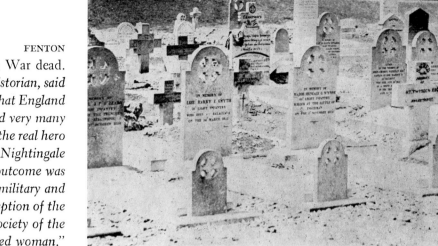

FENTON

Graves of Crimean War dead. *G. M. Trevelyan, the historian, said that "The 25,000 lives that England lost in the Crimea saved very many more in years to come. For the real hero of the war was Florence Nightingale and its most indubitable outcome was modern nursing, both military and civil, and a new conception of the potentiality and place in society of the trained and educated woman."*

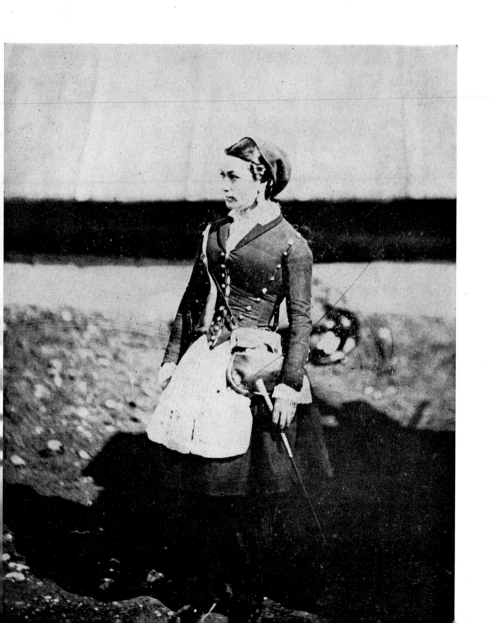

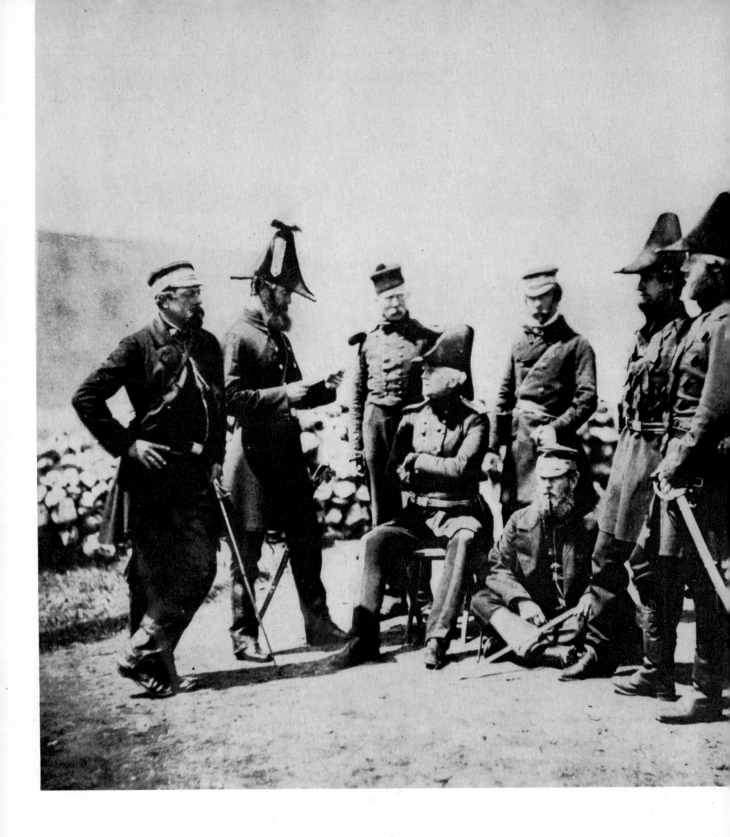

FENTON. *Wet-plate photographs, 1855.*
below: Balaclava Harbor during the Crimean War.
opposite page: Portrait Group of Crimean War Officers.
Both, courtesy George Eastman House.

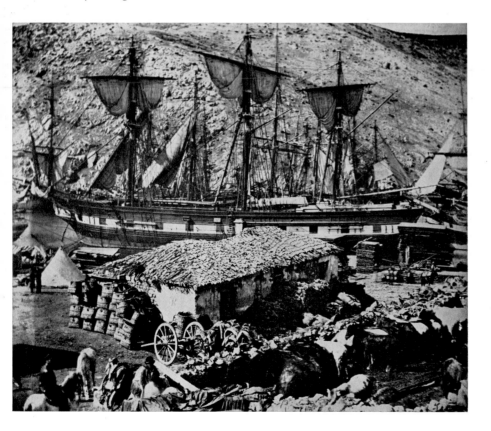

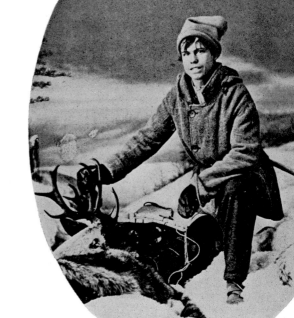

WILLIAM NOTMAN
Four photographs of the early 1860's. Montreal, Canada.
right: Colonel Rhodes' Indian Boy.
below: Trapping the Carcajou.
opposite page, above: Moose Hunting.
opposite page, below: The Hunters' Camp.
Courtesy George Eastman House.

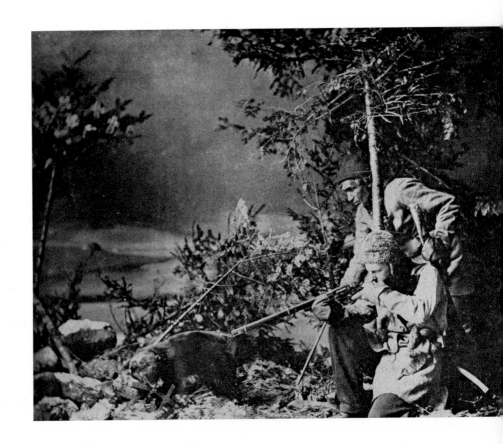

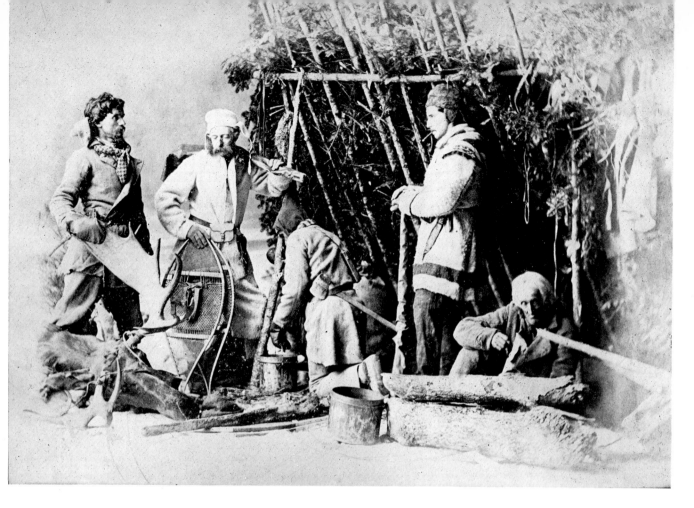

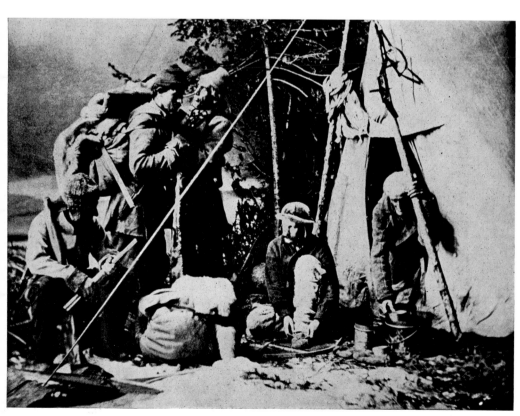

CHAPTER 10
Hesler: Chicago Pioneer

ALEXANDER HESLER, a pioneer photographer of Chicago, was considered in the 1850s "one of America's greatest daguerreotypists." In 1851 he was photographing the frontier on the upper Mississippi in the Minnesota Territory where he took full-size daguerreotype plates of the Falls of St. Anthony, Fort Snelling, and Minnehaha Falls. It was in connection with this last picture, which he exhibited in his Chicago studio two years later, that his early reputation as a sensitive photographer was established nationally. Henry Wadsworth Longfellow, in a letter as well as in an autographed first edition of *Hiawatha* which he sent to Hesler, acknowledged that the daguerreotype of Minnehaha Falls given him by his friend Senator Charles Sumner of Massachusetts was the inspiration for his poem *Hiawatha*. The daguerreotype was bought by the Senator's brother from Hesler either in Chicago or, as one story has it, while they both happened to meet in Minnesota.

In his journal dated June 22, 1854, Longfellow records, "I have at length hit upon a plan for a poem on the American Indian which seems to be the right one and the only. It is to weave together their beautiful traditions into a whole." On June 29 Longfellow decided to call it *Hiawatha*.

What seems possible is that Longfellow had been considering a poem on the Indian for some time and that Hesler's captivating daguerreotype of the poetically named Minnehaha Falls gave him the impetus to begin and complete what was to become one of his most celebrated works.

In 1852 the twenty-nine-year-old Hesler was using his daguerreotype apparatus in Galena, Illinois. It had been five years since learning the art in Buffalo, practicing it for a couple of years in Madison, and taking portraits of the Wisconsin legislature in session before his trip to the Minnesota Territory. Though born in Montreal, he was but a boy when his family moved to Racine, Wisconsin, and for the rest of his life (he died in 1895) he was considered a midwestern photographer, conducting studios at various addresses in Chicago. The first of these he established in late 1853 on La Salle Street. He prospered. He opened another. He added a miniature painter to his staff. He learned paper photography, the wet-collodion process, and the stereograph, which enabled him to advertise that he could take any kind of photographic commission from a portrait in miniature to one more than life size.

In 1855 he won an award at the American Institute Annual Fair held in New York. This was the first of many prizes and awards he was subsequently to receive for his photographs, particularly for his portraits of children. He learned child photography by personal experience, for he was the father of eight, four of whom lived to maturity. In 1857 he took the famous ruffled-hair portrait of Abraham Lincoln later used as the frontispiece of the book by Nicolay and Hay. He photographed Lincoln in Springfield and in Chicago. His gallery was a rendezvous for politicians and celebrities. Hesler's two wet-plate photographs in 1860 of a well-dressed, combed, and unbearded Lincoln were both badly damaged in 1933 when sent through the mails. The fragmented glass plates were deposited in the Smithsonian Institution. In 1958 discovery was made of two copy negatives that Hesler, for his own protection, had made from the finest prints. The copy negatives were acquired from the Chicago Historical Society, by whose permission they are here reproduced for the first time in any book.

In later years Hesler was to win fame for such photographs as *Picturesque Evanston*, but this was in the days of art photography and carbon prints, which by then had lost the intrinsic beauty and honesty that Hesler had instilled into his early works. His best photographs were taken before the Chicago Fire of 1871. Many of these early efforts survived, but unfortunately the original letter sent by Longfellow is believed to have been burned in the great holocaust.

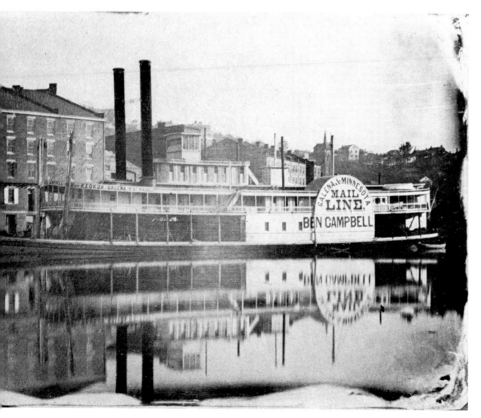

ALEXANDER HESLER, The Mississippi River Packet, Ben Campbell, Galena, Illinois. *Daguerreotype, 1852. The daguerreotype has been printed in reverse so that the name can be read. The Ben Campbell was built in 1851 and burned the summer of 1860. Courtesy Chicago Historical Society.*

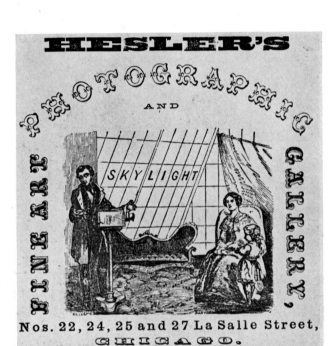

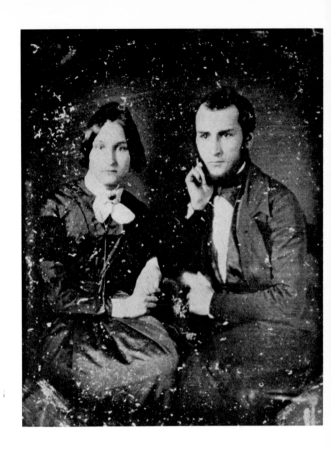

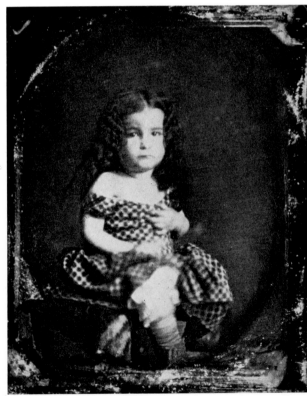

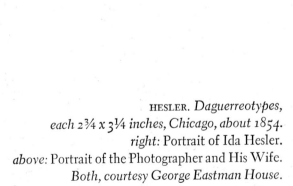

HESLER. *Daguerreotypes,*
each 2¾ x 3¼ inches, Chicago, about 1854.
right: Portrait of Ida Hesler.
above: Portrait of the Photographer and His Wife.
Both, courtesy George Eastman House.

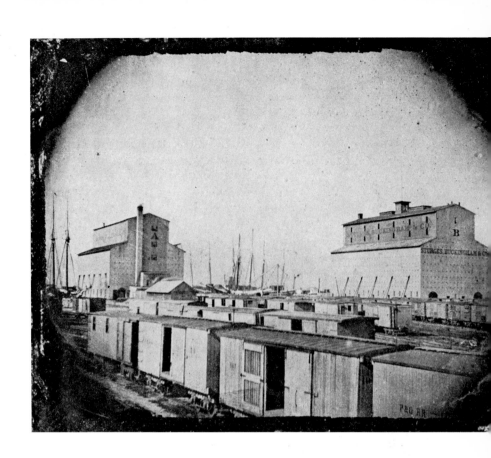

HESLER, *Ambrotypes*, 1855-58.
above: Grain Elevator and Freight Cars.
*At mouth of Chicago
River, Chicago, Illinois.*
right: Levee at Galena, Illinois.
*Daguerreotype, 1852. The U.S. mail and
passenger packet New St. Paul was built
at New Albany, Indiana, in 1852. The
packet Nominee, built in 1848, sank in the
upper Mississippi in 1854.
Courtesy Chicago Historical Society.*

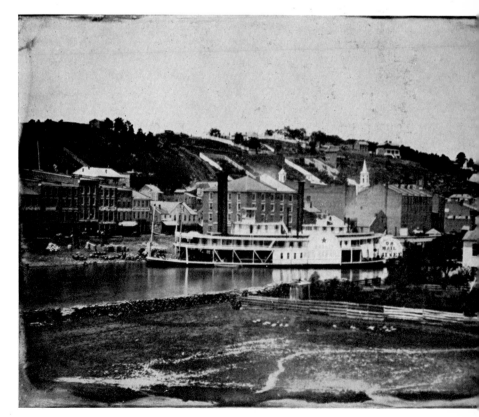

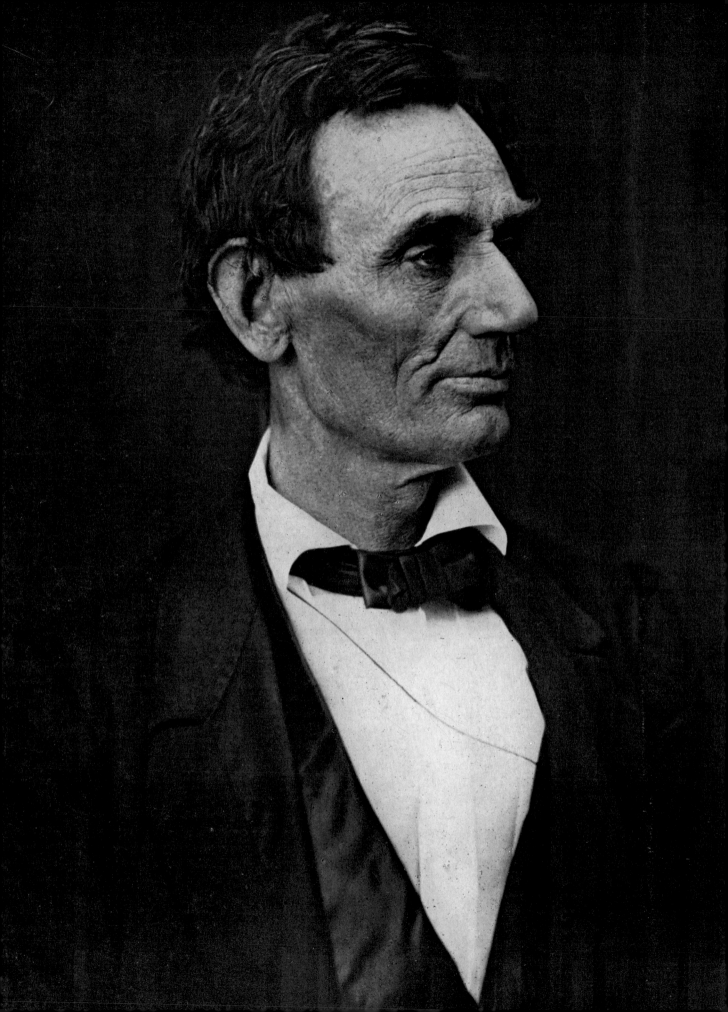

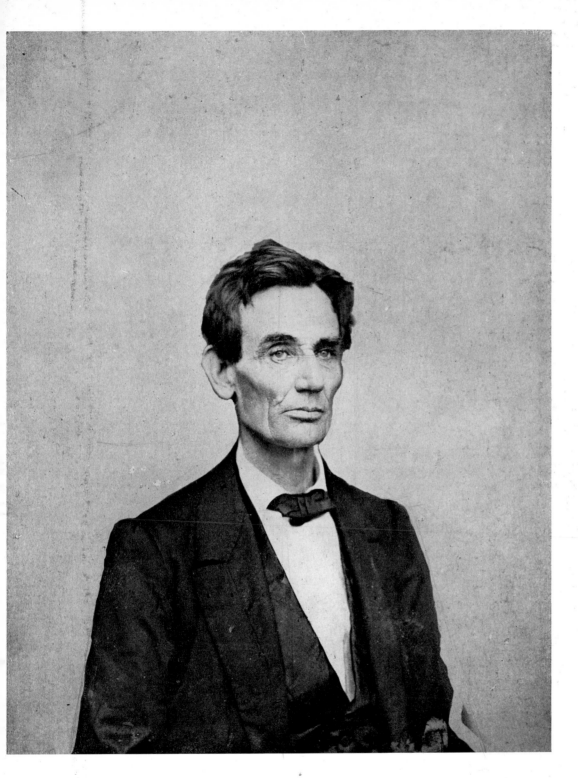

HESLER, Two portraits of Abraham Lincoln.
*Springfield, Illinois, 1860. Courtesy Chicago
Historical Society.*

CHAPTER 11

The Stereoscope: Pictures in Pairs

SIR CHARLES WHEATSTONE, in 1838, described the stereoscope, which he had invented in an attempt to re-create mechanically the natural phenomenon of binocular vision. In binocular vision each of our eyes receives a different image. This is important to our perception of depth because, although our brain combines both images into one, that one unified image conveys three-dimensionality and distance as neither of the two flat images could by itself. In a viewing device Sir Charles offered the eyes two flat drawings of solid objects, each in perspective, each as it might have been seen by a different eye, expecting to create the illusion of the third dimension. It worked none too satisfactorily. With the announcement of photography the perfect solution to successful stereoscopy seemed at hand. Fox Talbot made calotypes of still lifes for Sir Charles' invention, when the shiny surfaces of the daguerreotype were found to be unsatisfactory.

It was in 1849 that Sir David Brewster invented a stereoscope with two magnifying lenses separated by 2½ inches, the usual distance between the eyes in human beings; he limited the height to 3 inches, making it easy to handle. Brewster showed a number of pictures including a binocular portrait of his good friend Dr. John Adamson, but could get no English optician or photography house to manufacture and market his stereoscope.

Jules Duboscq in Paris the following year undertook the construction of Brewster's stereoscope and the preparation of daguerreotypes to fit.

In the Crystal Palace Exhibition of 1851 in London the Duboscq and Soleil (Duboscq's father-in-law) stereoscope was exhibited with a fine collection of daguerreotype stereo images. The stereoscope became tremendously popular when Queen Victoria and Prince Albert admired the display and evinced interest in this new form of photography. Not only did Duboscq and Soleil in Paris manufacture the stereoscope; the demand was met by photographic houses all over Europe and the United States. In Philadelphia J. F. Mascher early in 1853 received a patent for a simple folding stereoscope made of a leather box holding two images and two lenses. More than a million prism stereoscopes of the Brewster type were sold by 1856 in England alone. The London Stereoscope Company, which offered a wide selection of stereo slides to choose from at about a quarter each, advertised, "No home without a stereoscope," and offered a viewer for sale at less than a dollar.

Sir David Brewster, by 1849, had also invented the binocular camera but had not had it produced. Until 1853 either an ordinary camera set in a groove moved sideways for the second exposure or two single cameras were used to make stereo pictures. The two-lens camera with the lenses separated by 2½ inches taking two small pictures simultaneously was produced in 1853 by an English optician who was followed immediately by many European manufacturers.

Duboscq and Soleil took stereoscopic daguerreotypes with their new camera, among them a still life of optical equipment consisting of an hourglass, binoculars, lens, telescope, globe, planetary system, telegraph instrument, an alphabet in the round and, in the lower right-hand corner, their Brewster stereoscope.

In 1855 Warren Thompson, an American, had already been in Paris at least six years while working in photography. He had received an award in 1849 at the exhibition held at the Academy of Sciences and in 1851 his daguerreotype of an eclipse of the sun had been officially praised. Using the new binocular camera in 1855 he made a series of stereoscopic daguerreotypes of which three magnificent, penetrating portraits survive: a lady china painter, a hunter with flower in buttonhole holding a dead hare, and a pensive man with head in hand.

By 1860 the London Stereographic Company slogan was practically a reality; few homes were without a stereoscope and a batch of slides. Hundreds of thousands of stereographic slides depicting nearly every corner of the globe were available in shops or by mail at the nominal prices of today's picture postcards ranging from a nickel to a quarter. The studio of John Mayall continued to prosper by offering for sale cartes de visite of Queen Victoria and Prince Albert.

Oliver Wendell Holmes was entranced with the travel pictures. The details, evoking the illusion of reality, enabled him, he said, to be "a spectator to the best views the world had to offer." He wrote three articles in two years for the Atlantic Monthly, the first in 1859 entitled "The Stereoscope and the Stereograph,"—the latter word coined to describe the stereopicture. Holmes urged his readers to travel with him, by stereoscope and the imagination, to the remotest parts of the world "to view the wonders of the Nile, the ruins of Baalbeck, Ann Hathaway's cottage, the rawest Western settlement and the Shanties of Pike's Peak" (photographers with their stereoscope cameras had penetrated the frontier for photography supply houses in the East). Holmes then called attention to such a universal thing as a clothesline, which appears in pictures taken all over the world, and he writes, "The very things which an artist would leave out or render imperfectly, the photographer takes infinite care with and so makes its illusions perfect."

Holmes predicted that the stereoscope would be used to record "the next European War" and that the time would come when there would be "imperial, national and city stereographic libraries," and operation of exchange depots for slides, and he concludes, "we are looking into stereoscopes as pretty toys . . . but before another generation has passed away, it will be recognized that a new epoch in the history of human progress dates from the time when 'He Who never but in uncreated light, Dwelt from eternity . . . Took a pencil of fire from the hand of the angel standing in the sun and placed it in the hand of a mortal'."

Holmes by 1861 said that he had viewed a hundred thousand slides and it took only twenty-five to give one a headache. He designed and made a more practical stereoscope instrument, a hand viewer consisting of a light, portable horizontal board slotted to receive the stereograph slides and a small handle below to hold the device up to the eyes. Some few small modifications were made in the history of the stereoscope—such as the sliding carrier—but the basic design for the most practical stereoscope Holmes gave to the world.

E. & H. T. Anthony Company of New York and Langenheim Brothers of Philadelphia commissioned photographers to take not only views but pictures of events of the day, which they then sold along with those they imported from Europe. Untold numbers were bought. Holmes's suggestion to develop public stereo libraries was never acted on. It is in our generation that these stereoscopic cards are considered of historic importance and are now being collected.

Interest in the stereoscope went through several waves. The first popularity of the later fifties was superseded by the *carte de visite*, a fabulous fashion of the sixties. In the next two decades it was again revived for several years. The Holmes stereoscope was now made of aluminum and, again after the turn of the century until World War I, the stereo was popular at various times. All photographic processes as they developed were turned to the making of stereographs. This is true today, with the foolproof special stereo cameras, electric viewers, and the latest of fast color film.

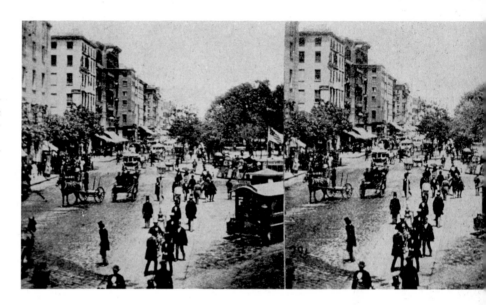

EDWARD ANTHONY, Broadway, New York. *Stereograph card, 1859. From the series: "Anthony's Instantaneous Views." Courtesy George Eastman House.*

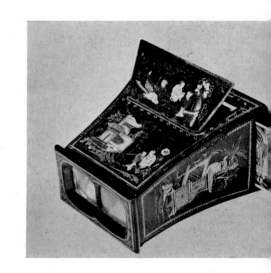

right: A fancy Brewster-type stereoscope, made in England about 1850. The lid was opened to view stereo on metal plates. The bottom was opened and the top lid closed to view stereo transparencies on glass; the stereoscope was then held up to the light. center: Daguerreotype case with lenses for viewing stereo pair. Patented by Stull, Philadelphia, 1855. Both, courtesy George Eastman House. far right: Folding pocket stereoscope, 1853, made in England by W. E. Kilburn. J. F. Mascher, Philadelphia, patented the identical construction early in 1853. Courtesy Gernsheim Collection, University of Texas.

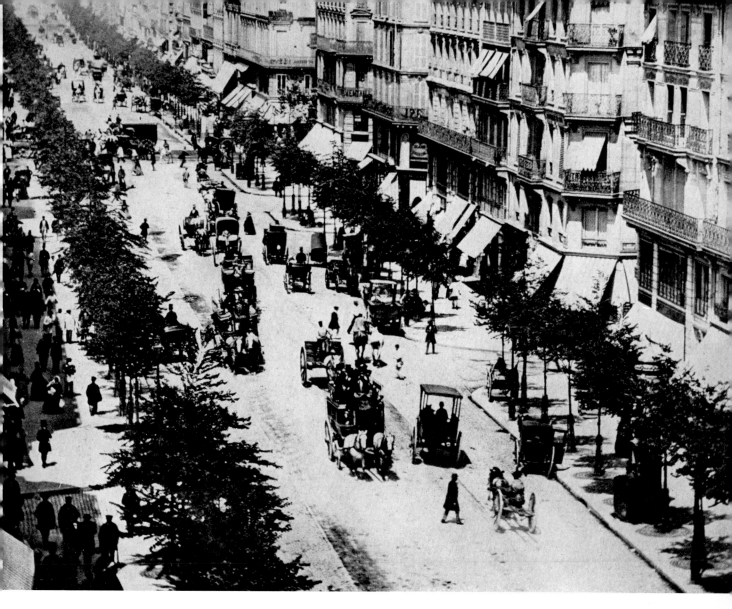

FERRIER AND SULIER, Paris Boulevard. *Detail of one part of a positive stereographic pair on glass, 1860. An extraordinary early instantaneous photograph. Courtesy George Eastman House.*

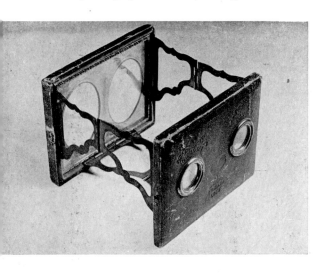

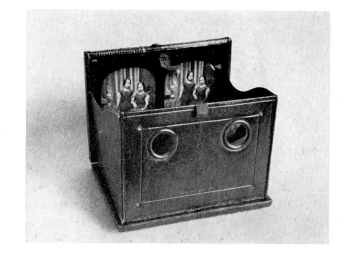

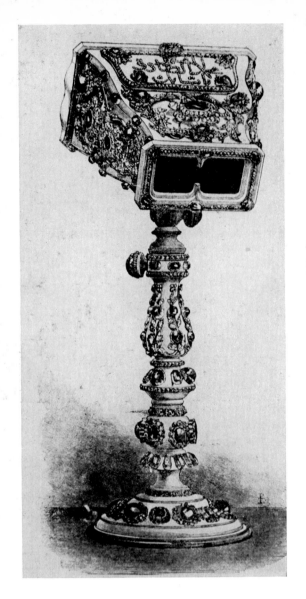

A jeweled stereoscope with Arabic inscription set in lid, made by Emmanuel London, 1862. Courtesy Gernsheim Collection, University of Texas.

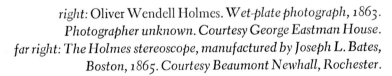

right: Oliver Wendell Holmes. Wet-plate photograph, 1863. Photographer unknown. Courtesy George Eastman House. far right: The Holmes stereoscope, manufactured by Joseph L. Bates, Boston, 1865. Courtesy Beaumont Newhall, Rochester.

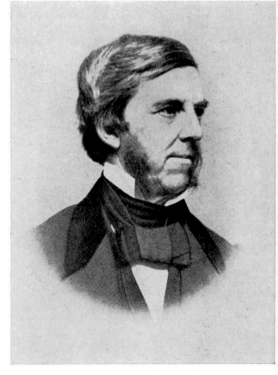

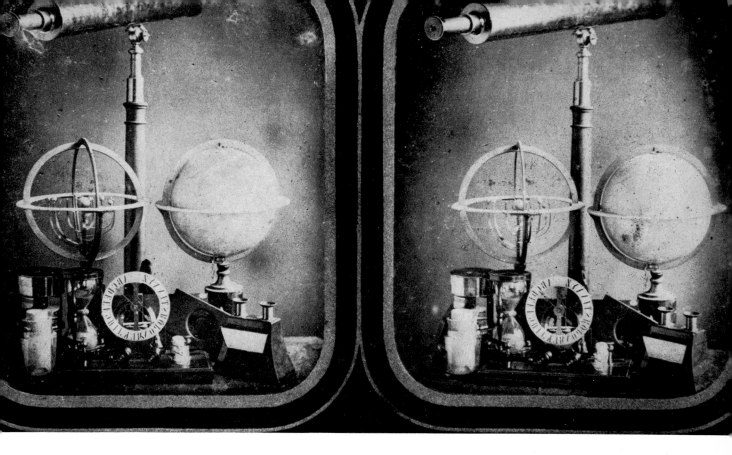

Stereoscopic daguerreotype made by Duboscq and Soleil, Paris optical firm that first manufactured and marketed the stereoscope invented by Sir David Brewster (one is shown below, left). Their product, purchased by Queen Victoria at London Crystal Palace, 1851, started world-wide interest in stereophotography. Courtesy George Eastman House.

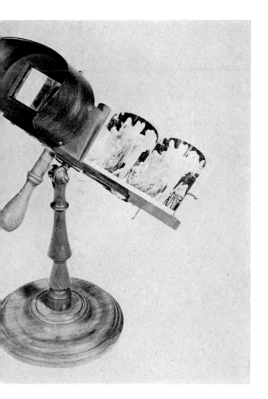

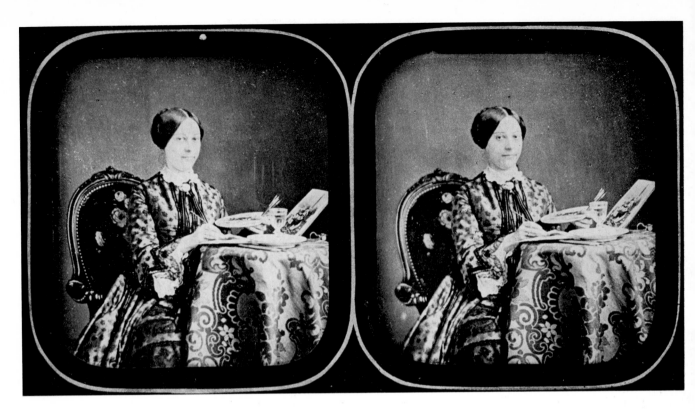

WARREN THOMPSON, *American.*
Stereoscopic daguerreotype, Paris, 1855.
Lady China Painter.
Courtesy George Eastman House.

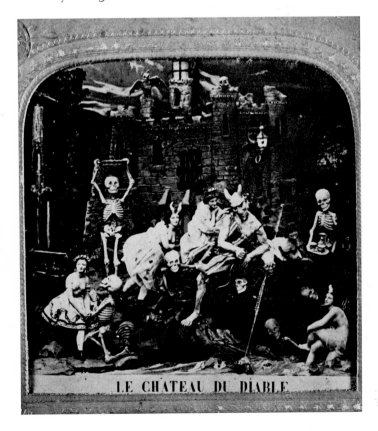

LE CHATEAU DU DIABLE

One part of a comic stereographic pair.
About 1860, France. Photographer unknown.
Courtesy George Eastman House.

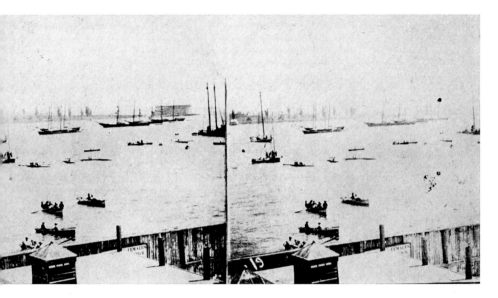

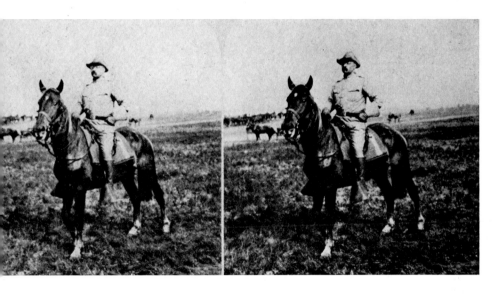

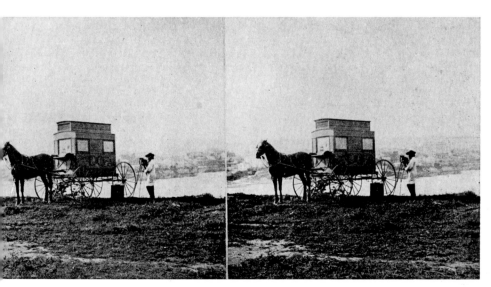

ANTHONY. *Stereograph, 1859-70.*
From the series:
"Anthony's Instantaneous Views."
top: Fourth of July Regatta,
Preparing for the Start.
Collection Dr. G. L. Howe,
Rochester, and courtesy
George Eastman House.
center: UNDERWOOD AND UNDERWOOD,
publishers, Colonel Theodore Roosevelt
of the Rough Riders. *Stereograph,*
about 1898. Photographer unknown.
Courtesy George Eastman House.
bottom: W. E. Bowman of Ottawa,
Illinois, and his Photographic
Wagon. *About 1870.*
Collection Dr. G. L. Howe.
Courtesy George Eastman House.

CHAPTER 12

Nadar: The 'Titian of Photography'

MANY PAINTERS, printmakers, and sculptors in France reacted violently against photography and its incredible popularity. Condemnations were showered upon it in press articles and caricatures. Not only had it become an economic threat to the artist; its claims as an art form were resented.

Baudelaire in the *Revue Francaise*, 1859, wrote "We must see that photography is again confined to its sole task, which consists in being the servant of science and art, but the very humble servant like typography and stenography which have neither created nor improved literature."

The camera was a threat. The purpose of art was being changed by the public's demands for more exact likenesses, more perfect rendition of detail. The camera supplied the people with what they wanted.

Good artists domesticated the camera. Corot said that the lens made him view nature differently. He used the new technique, combining it with his work in the graphic arts to create a new kind of print, the *cliché verre*. He covered a sheet of glass either with black paint or with albumen, which he exposed to sunlight to make opaque. With a stylus he then scratched a design on the coated surface of the glass and used the finished state as a negative. He then printed an entire edition on sensitized photographic paper, respecting the finished product as he would his etchings. The *cliché-verre* process was practiced also by Delacroix, Daubigny, Rousseau, Millet, and others, but Corot seems to have been more attuned to the process than the others; he finished his sixty-sixth plate on his seventy-eighth birthday, though none were sold during his lifetime.

It was the unimaginative artists, who painted the superficial appearances of things rather than their emotional responses and interpretations of nature, who found in the camera a crutch and aid, often abandoning pencil and brush for the heavily detailed pictures they could make with chemicals and lens. These inept artists left little memorable work in either medium.

Too few good artists turned to photography and used it creatively. Those who did are remembered as artists with the camera. "Nadar," pseudonym for Gaspard Felix Tournachon, was such an artist. Daumier caricatured photography in his lithographs, ridiculing it as spiritless and satirizing the *bourgeoisie* for their attitude toward the new invention. Nadar, however, he respected as a man and as an artist, for, despite the mechanical quality of the camera, Nadar concentrated on face and gesture and emphasized the psychological characteristics of his subjects. He made the pose express the character of a subject as much as did the face, and he made every salient feature of body and face stand out by permitting no props or backgrounds to interfere with the person.

How extraordinary were the photographs of Nadar is attested to by the fact that the great French classicist painter, Ingres, sent to Nadar every person whose likeness he wanted. According to Ingres's biographer, E. de Mirecourt, Ingres painted his remarkable portraits from these photographs without having a need for the subject to be present. Artists called Nadar "the Titian of Photography."

Nadar came to the camera by way of the theatre; he was a playwright. As an artist he was a well-respected painter of portraits. As a journalist he worked with Daumier as a caricaturist for *Charivari*. At the age of thirty, in 1850, Nadar was the darling of the boulevards, celebrated for his wit; but neither theatre, salon, nor journal offered him sufficient livelihood. Though prejudiced against photography, like most artists, he joined his brother Adrien's studio in 1852, but the partnership soon ended in the law courts. In 1854 Nadar published *Le Panthéon Nadar*, a huge lithograph composed of 280 caricatures; this was the first in a proposed set of four.

He had hit upon the same idea as had David Octavius Hill: to photograph his subjects before drawing their caricatures. Nadar's great portraits of the literati and the celebrated appeared not as caricatures but as perfect reproductions of his original photographs, in the expressive volumes of *Galerie contemporaine*.

Nadar opened his own photography studio on the Boulevard des Capucines. Writers, artists, and composers of note found the atmosphere so cordial that they met there regularly. Nadar photographed them all: Manet, Corot, Dumas, Monet, Baudelaire, George Sand, Delacroix, Sarah Bernhardt, Daumier, Doré, Berlioz, Wagner, and an uncountable number of others. He invariably signed his prints, as an artist would his etchings or lithographs.

It was the realistic, sharply delineated daguerreotype of an earlier day that he emulated rather than the work of later photographers who were striving for the fuzzy, hazy effects dear to the Impressionists. The Impressionist painters were as much obsessed with sunlight and the out-of-doors as the most enthusiastic photographer. The solid objects occupying seen reality the painters transformed with their palette of misty color into a hazy, created unreality of shimmering beauty. The public rejected their work, as did the academic painters and their coterie of critics.

Nadar turned over his studio for the first Impressionist Exhibition in 1874. It took daring and courage to flaunt the official Salon and the press, but this action was typical of the Radical Republican, Nadar, who fifteen years earlier had refused to follow Napoleon III with his balloon photography because he had not believed in the Emperor's campaign against Austria.

Nadar was the first aerial photographer, taking pictures successfully from a balloon in 1856. His first efforts failed, for the gas seeping out of the balloon caked the collodion on his plates. Nadar had to coat and develop the wet-collodion plates, crouching in a little darkroom set up in the swinging, lurching basket of the balloon. He took a dozen views of Paris. In 1863 he built the world's largest balloon, which measured 90 feet in diameter and was named "The Giant." He tried to initiate aerial passenger service within France, but on its second ascent The Giant went out of control and came down in Germany; the passengers were dragged for miles before the basket caught and held.

The siege of Paris was an ideal opportunity for Nadar and aerial photography to play an important role. On September 18, 1870, the capital was left without any means of communication with the outside world.

Through Nadar's instigation the balloon Neptune was aloft within less than a week. Prussian guns could not reach the heights at which the balloon soared. During the 131-day siege, fifty-five balloons left Paris with passengers, mail, and carrier pigeons. The birds returned with microscopically photographed messages on thin collodion film—a special process conceived by M. Dagron—rolled into minute tubes and affixed to their tails. When the pigeons arrived in their Paris dovecots, the cylinders were opened and the film was placed between two sheets of glass and projected onto a screen. This process of enlarging a picture by projection worked on the same principle as the eighteenth century's magic lantern. The carrier pigeon–balloon post kept Paris in contact with the world all during the siege.

Nadar was also one of the first photographers to take pictures with artificial light. He took electric-light photographs of the catacombs and sewers of Paris in about 20-minute exposures as early as 1860.

Nadar lived to be ninety years old, dying in 1910. Thirty years earlier he turned over his studio to his son Paul, who continued to use his father's pseudonym and made it officially his own. Together they created for *Le Journal Illustré* a feature which has since become standard in photojournalism. Paul, acting as cameraman with a stenographer to record the ensuing conversation verbatim and with Nadar as questioner, interviewed the French scientist Michel Eugène Chevreul on the eve of his hundredth birthday in 1886. The photographs showed the enthusiastic response of the aged man to Nadar's queries on "The Art of Living." The stenographer's notes served as captions for the original pictures.

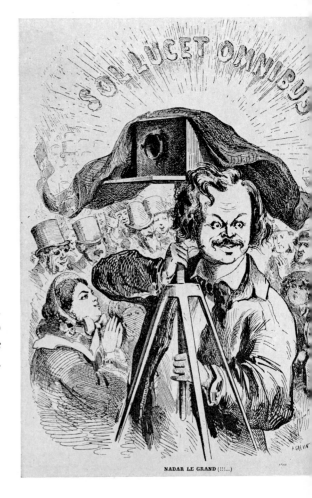

A. GRÉVIN, Nadar the Great. *Wood engraving, about 1870. Friend of artists,* boulevardier, *popular with the many who came to his studio for portraits, Nadar was a subject for cartoons and caricatures in the press of his day. Courtesy George Eastman House, Rochester.*

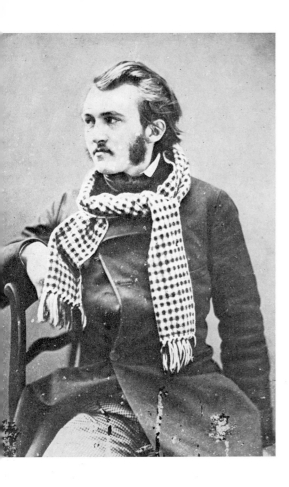

NADAR, Portrait of Gustave Doré. *Wet-plate photograph, about 1855. Nadar's real name was Gaspard Félix Tournachon. A contemporary said to him: "Your name isn't Tournachon—it's 'tour-nadar.' You stick in a stiletto and turn it." Tournachon liked the word, and took its latter half for a pseudonym.*

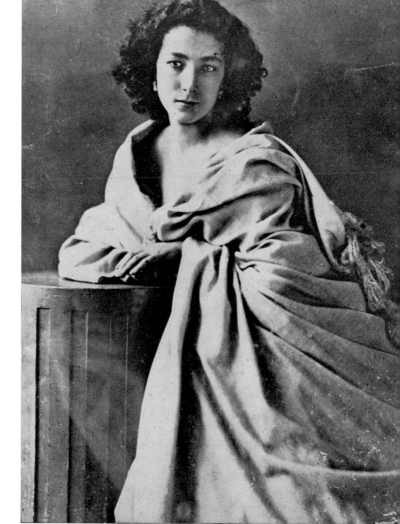

NADAR, Portrait of Sarah Bernhardt. 1859. *Both photos this page, courtesy George Eastman House.*

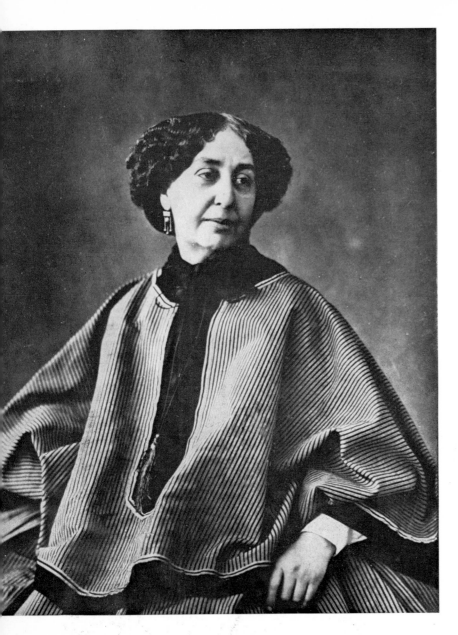

NADAR. *Four photographs, all courtesy George Eastman House.*
Portrait of George Sand. After a Woodburytype reproduction
of a wet-plate photograph. From Galerie contemporaine, 1870.

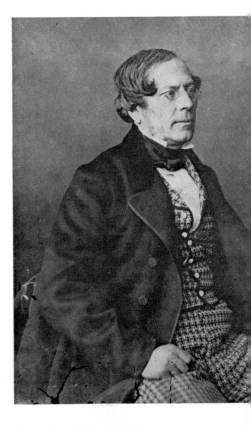

Portrait of Charles de Lesseps.
Wet-plate photograph, 1860.

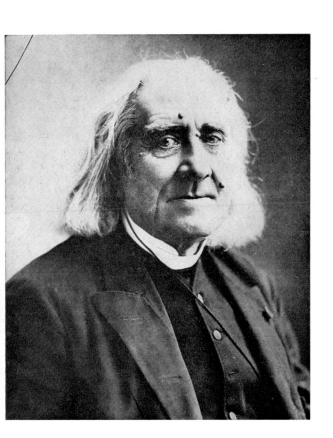

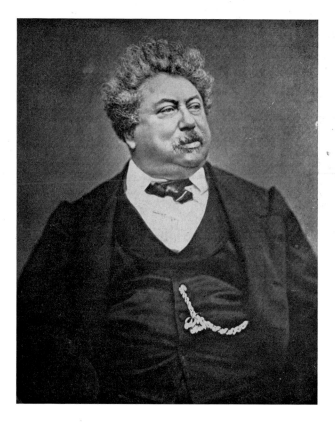

Portrait of Franz Liszt, 1886.

Portrait of Alexandre Dumas.
*After a Woodburytype reproduction
of a wet-plate photograph.*
From Galerie contemporaine, 1870.

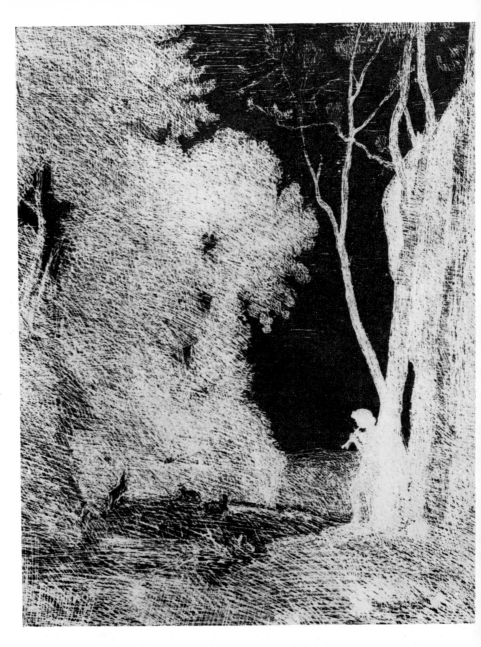

COROT, Le Petit Berger. *Negative and positive of* cliché
verre, *about 1858. One of the sixty-six he made in this
medium. Glass was coated with paint or albumen; the drawing
was scratched in with a stylus; the design formed in the emulsion was
used as a negative; an entire edition was then printed on photographic
paper. Courtesy Metropolitan Museum of Art, New York.*

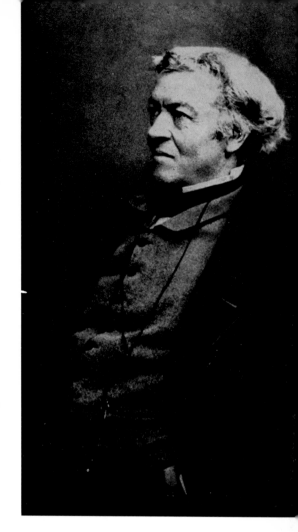

NADAR, Portrait of Jean-Baptiste-Camille Corot. *Wet-plate photograph, about 1860. Courtesy George Eastman House.*

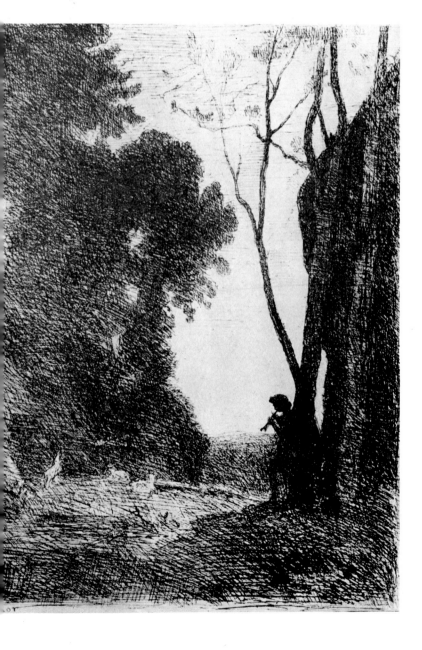

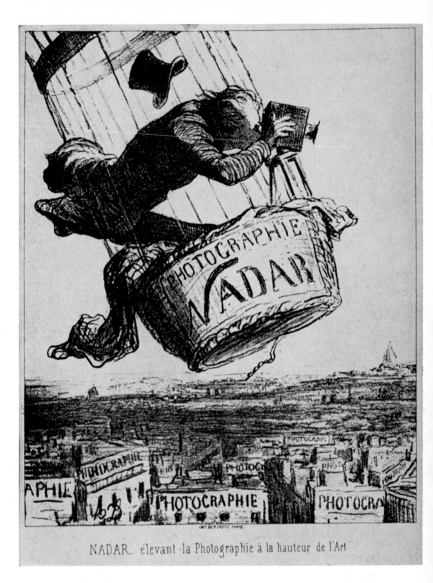

NADAR élevant la Photographie à la hauteur de l'Art

HONORE DAUMIER, *Nadar Elevating Photography to a High Art. Lithograph, May, 1862. Shows Nadar as an aerial photographer, and suggests how free Nadar was from the usual earthbound photography studios spreading all over Paris. Nadar did not take his pictures from a tripod as shown; he either attached the camera to the side of the basket or put the lens through the bottom.*

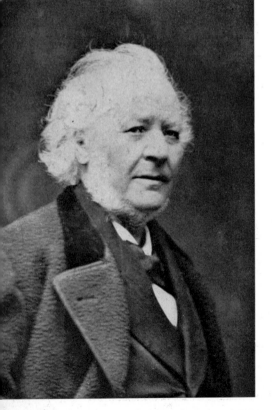

NADAR, *Portrait of Honoré Daumier.* 1877. *After a Woodburytype reproduction of wet-plate photograph. From Galerie contemporaine. Both photos this page courtesy George Eastman House.*

NADAR, Aerial View of Paris. *Print from wet-plate negative, 1859. Taken from the swinging basket of a balloon over Paris. Courtesy Gernsheim Collection, University of Texas.*

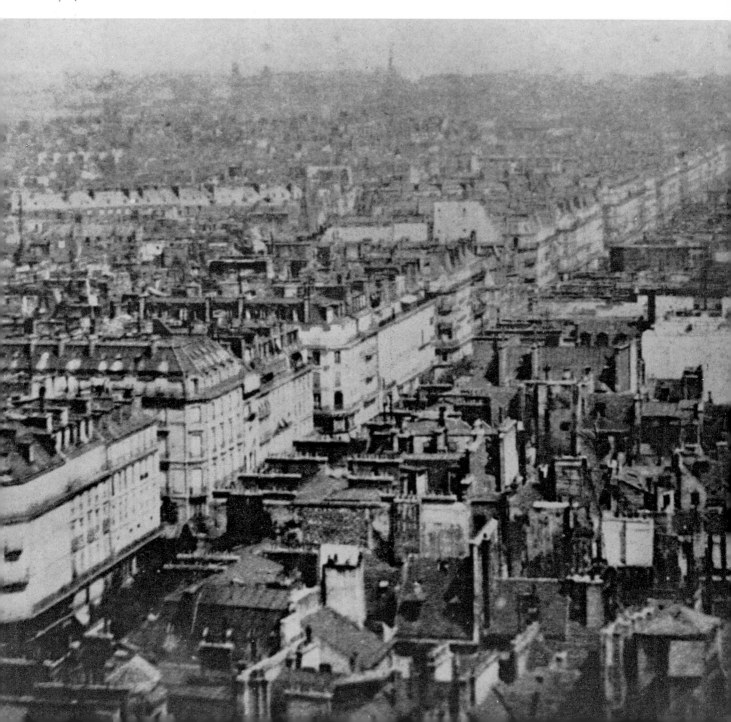

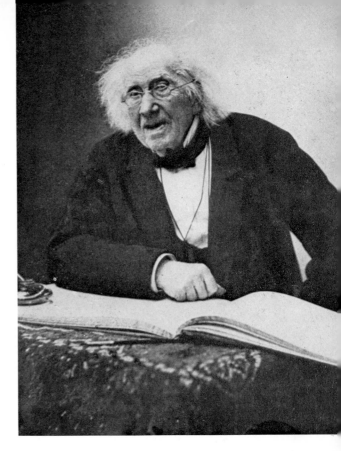

PAUL NADAR, Nadar interviews Chevreul.
Wet-plate photographs, 1886.
The birth of photojournalism.
Michel Eugène Chevreul tells about the art
of living a hundred years, talking to Nadar
while Nadar's son Paul works the camera.
Chevreul was an early investigator of the
role of the eye in color perception. His
theories were a direct influence on all
important French painters from Delacroix
to Seurat. Courtesy George Eastman House.

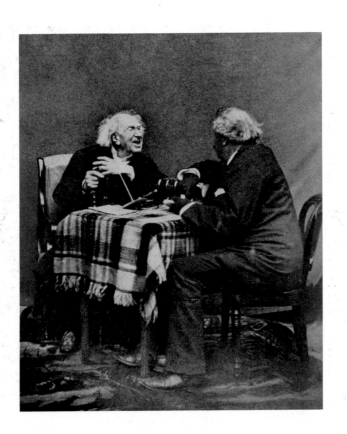

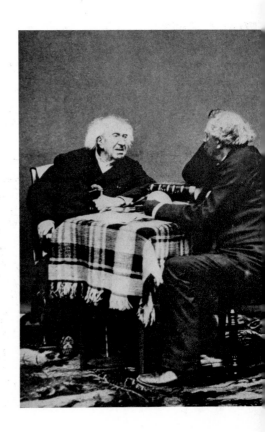

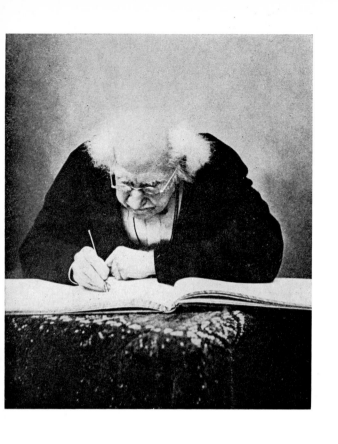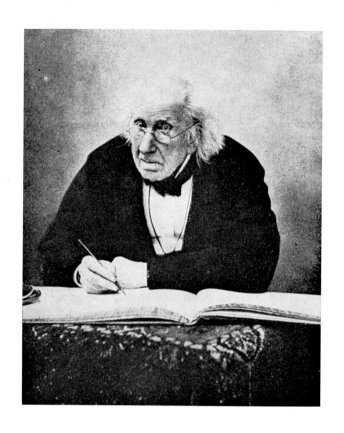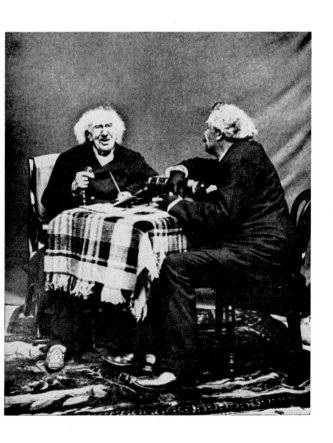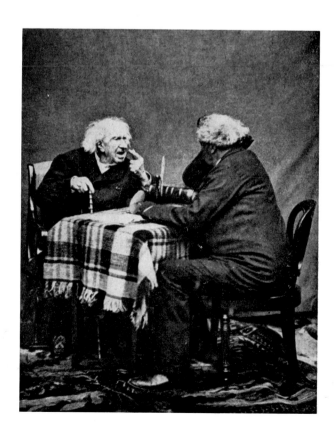

CHAPTER 13

The Ubiquitous Carte de Visite

THE CAREER OF ETIENNE CARJAT (1828–1906) ran strangely parallel with Nadar's. Carjat was also an artist, a caricaturist, and a writer as well as the editor of the journal *Le Boulevard*, which flourished for several years in the 1860s. In 1862 Daumier's caricature of Nadar taking aerial views of Paris from a balloon appeared in Carjat's publication.

Carjat ran a photostudio as a hobby, taking time from his other interests to photograph celebrities—famous men and women he met in his role as editor and distinguished people who were his personal friends. Like Nadar, he attracted people in all walks of life through the warmth of his personality. Unlike Nadar, he had no assistants in his studio. He therefore produced fewer portraits, but many of these are considered finer expressions of the sitter's character than any others.

Another figure who enjoyed a considerable reputation in the Second Empire as photographer and sculptor was Adam-Salomon (1811–1881). Photography was part-time work with him also; he used the camera for extra income and always charged the highest prices. His photographs were remarkable for their lighting, which he used to model the planes of the face, creating deep shadows and highlighted ridges to echo the effect of modeling in clay.

Adam-Salomon also made photographs that deliberately resembled seventeenth-century Dutch portraits. These chiaroscuro photographs, in which the head and hands compose the white areas, patently emulate another form of art. The closer his approximation the more praise his photographs received from critics of both art and photography. The highest praise a photograph could receive was that it resembled a painting. With Salomon photography went off on a tangent. It took more than fifty years to bring the art of photography, a graphic art in its own right, back to the honest purpose in which the camera does its best work.

A little-known photographer of high caliber was Pierre Petit, in the 1860s considered with Nadar and Carjat in the front rank of his profession. Petit was born in 1823; by the time he was seventeen he was an accomplished daguerreotypist and, by 1860, in partnership with a man named Trinquart, he was conducting a studio titled "Photographie de Deux-Mondes." It was said that he stored there 229,000 negatives he had taken in less than twenty years. Petit was appointed official photographer of the Paris World's Fair of 1867, and he was commissioned to photograph the raising of the Statue of Liberty.

Portrait photographers, in order to compete with lithographers and etchers, tried to make ever larger and more imposing photographs. In 1854 Adolphe Eugène Disdéri (1819–1890?) patented in Paris the "carte de visite," a camera with four lenses that made eight small photographs measuring 3¼ by 2⅛ inches on a full-size plate of 6½ by 8½ inches. These eight photographs, each on an average-size 4-by-2½-inch visiting card, sold for about $4, less than half the price a portrait photographer usually charged for a single full-size print.

Disdéri was a colorful, self-confident, publicity-conscious salesman who, though uneducated, did things with a flourish that captivated commoner and king. The Emperor Napoleon III, marching at the head of his troops to Italy for another of his "prestige wars" with Austria, stopped his army, which waited on the street while he and his staff walked into Disdéri's studio to sit for carte-de-visite portraits. The story spread. Immediately every person in Paris had to have carte-de-visite photographs made by Disdéri. What a showman! Disdéri rose to the occasion. He dressed extravagantly. His wide full beard he draped over satin blouses of shrieking colors which he bound at the waist with enormous belts; below, he wore short hussar trousers. Dressed in this outlandish costume, Disdéri took pictures in his studio with dramatic, imperious gestures. The crowds loved it; they flocked to his studio. He opened a second studio in southern France and still others in London and Madrid.

Emperor Napoleon III and the Empress appointed him official court photographer.

Disdéri earned millions and he spent millions. He bought houses and horses, elegant mansions, and stables of thoroughbreds. He was a lavish host; he acquired princely habits. In 1866 the insatiable demand for cartes de visite ceased as suddenly as it began. Disdéri thought up novelties to revive his flagging business or touted tricks in photography which already existed, such as pictures on silk and ceramics. Nothing worked. He could not compete with the cheap competition that he had created; the price of the carte de visite had been driven down to $1 a dozen.

Four years later the Franco-Prussian War caused the dethronement of the Emperor. The Second Empire collapsed and so did Disdéri's entire fortune. He was bankrupt. He went to the Riviera. He walked the beach at Nice, it was said, with a camera, taking pictures of tourists for a pittance. Through the lens he saw visions of his astounding days in Paris. He died with his dreams, a pauper, forgotten; it must have been in the summer of 1890, for he was not seen on the beach again.

The carte de visite revolutionized photography. Millions of people, as the craze swept England and America, went to have their portraits taken. Studios also sold cards of the royal family and of the famous. Tens of thousands of cards were sold of the pictures of Queen Victoria and the Prince Consort taken by Mayall in 1861. Cartes of celebrities enjoyed the same kind of popular sale in the United States.

The carte de visite was a standardized, stereotyped kind of picture. Most often a full figure, the picture showed a person standing next to a column, or a table piled high with books, in front of a heavy, velvet drapery. The head was so small in relation to the card, about ¼ inch to the 3½ or 4 inches of the total length of card, that it required but a second to hold the pose and was therefore most often a likeness in focus. The photograph, however, usually revealed little of the subject's character through lighting or pose. At the prices charged no individual attention could be given the small carte de visite.

There had to be some way to save the untold thousands of cards which piled up from family and friends who either called and left cards or exchanged them on birthdays and holidays. The answer was the carte-de-visite album. Some albums sold at nominal prices and others were very elaborate, bound in fine, tooled, expensive leather. The album became a required feature, the perfect conversation piece for every Victorian parlor and drawing room.

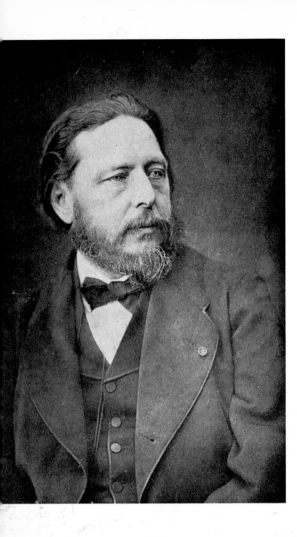

MULNIER, Jules Breton, French Painter. *From Woodburytype reproduction of wet-plate photograph, 1882. From* Galerie contemporaine. *Courtesy George Eastman House, Rochester.*

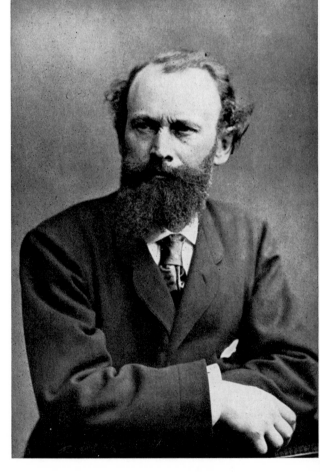

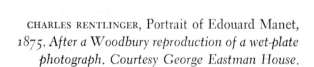

CHARLES RENTLINGER, Portrait of Edouard Manet, *1875. After a Woodbury reproduction of a wet-plate photograph. Courtesy George Eastman House.*

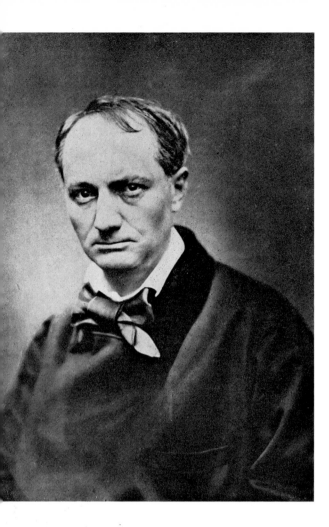

ETIENNE CARJAT, Portrait of Charles Baudelaire. *From Woodburytype of wet-plate photograph, 1863. From Nadar, Galerie contemporaine, 1870. Courtesy George Eastman House.*

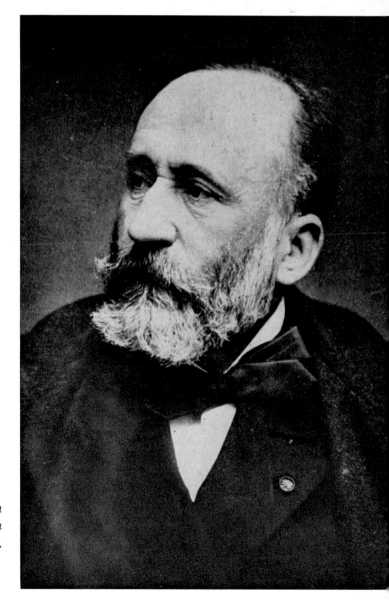

CARJAT, Puvis de Chavannes, French Painter. *From oodburytype reproduction of wet-plate photograph, 1878. From Galerie contemporaine. Courtesy George Eastman House.*

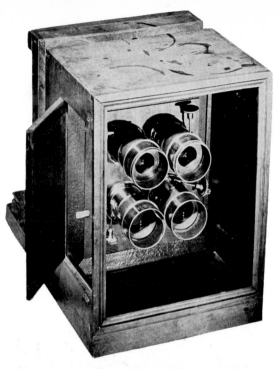

The carte-de-visite camera patented by Disdéri in 1854. Eight exposures were obtained on a 6½ x 8½ inch plate. The print was then cut up and mounted on cards approximately 4 x 2½ inches, the size of a visiting card. Courtesy George Eastman House.

DISDERI. Sheets of uncut carte-de-visite photographs of Martha Muravieva. Courtesy George Eastman House.

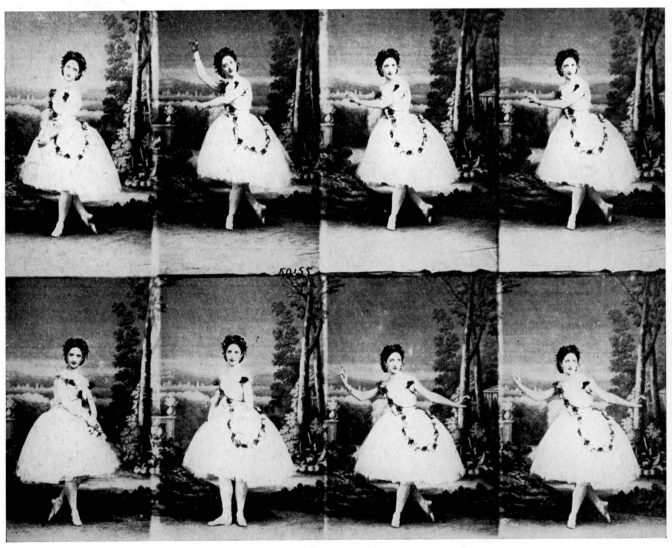

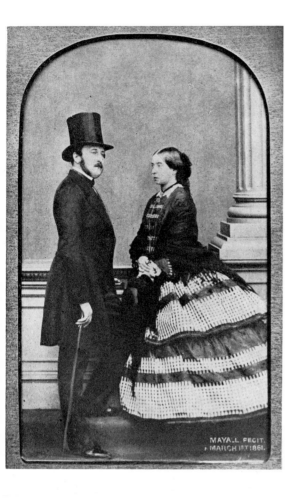

left: JOHN MAYALL, Queen Victoria and the Prince Consort. *London, 1861. Carte-de-visite. Courtesy Gernsheim Collection, University of Texas.*
below: Portrait of Queen Victoria. *Photograph on silk, about 1866. By Downey. Courtesy George Eastman House.*

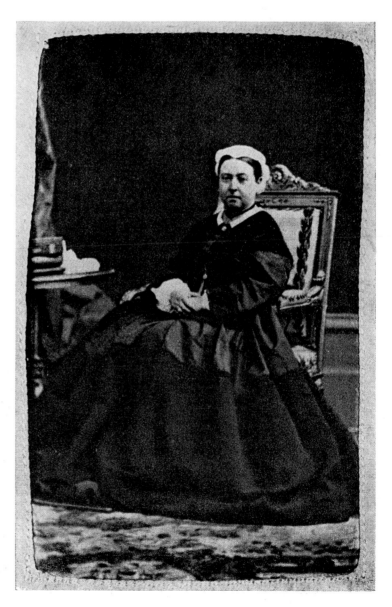

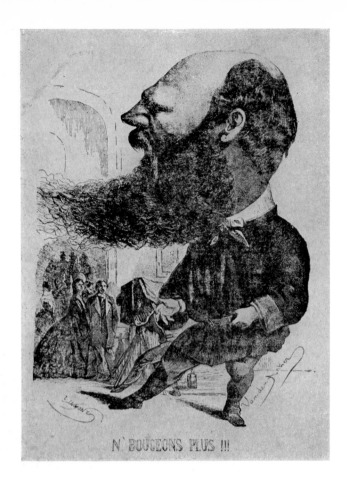

N' BOUGEONS PLUS !!!

Disdéri and the strange garb he affected. Wood engraving caricature by Van den Acter, which Disdéri used as an advertisement in the Paris journals of 1861. Courtesy Gernsheim Collection, University of Texas.

A rare carte-de-visite *album by various photographers of the late 1850s and early 1860s in France. Opposite is the page to which the album is opened, with four photographs of the Emperor Napoleon III. The two at top are by Disdéri, bottom left is by Mayer and Pierson, and bottom right by Appert. Courtesy George Eastman House*

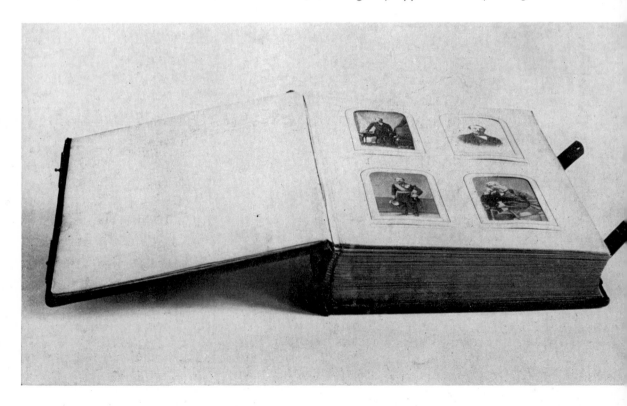

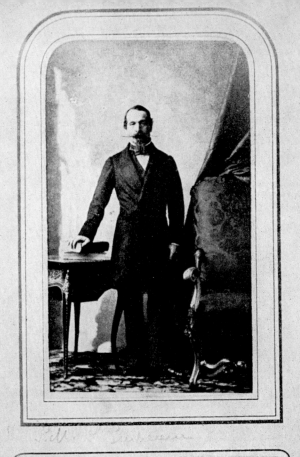

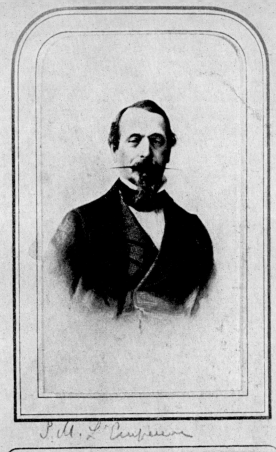

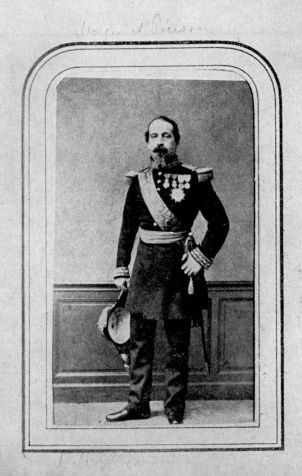

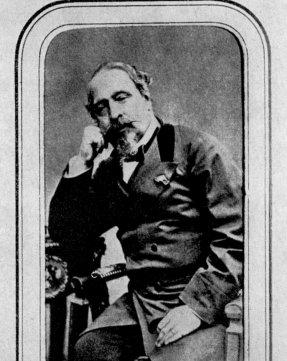

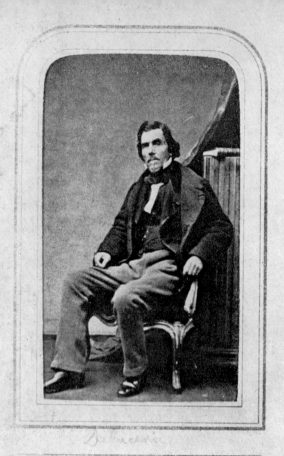

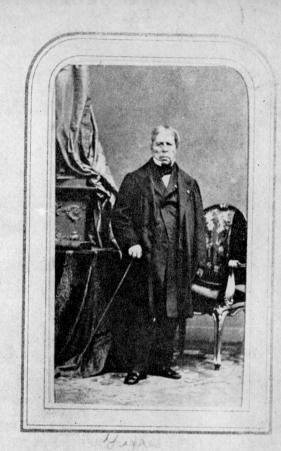

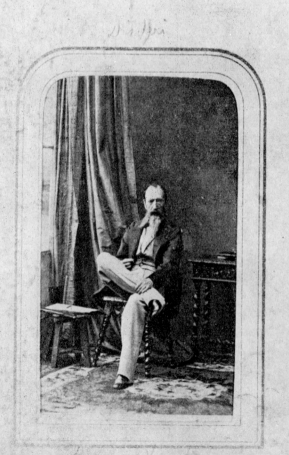

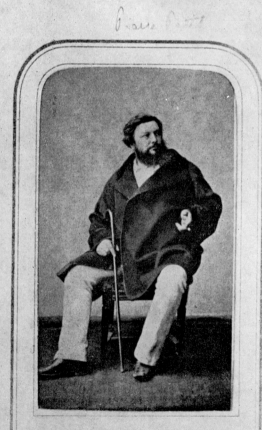

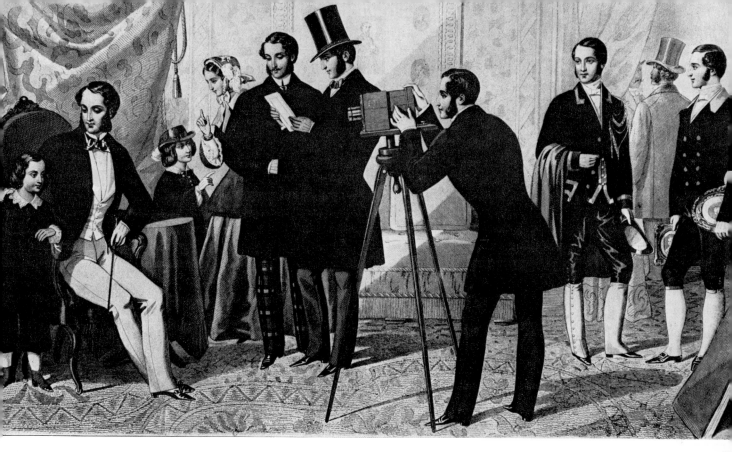

A French fashion plate of 1857, featuring a camera. Lack of character in the models and the proportion of head to body shown here became the ideal of the carte de visite. Courtesy George Eastman House.

Another page from the carte-de-visite *album.*
upper left: Delacroix, *by* PIERRE PETIT
upper right: Ingres, *by* DISDERI
lower left: Horace Vernet, *by* DISDERI
lower right: Courbet, *by* PIERRE PETIT
Courtesy George Eastman House.

Lithograph by R. de Moraine, which photographers used in attempting to revive business after the carte-de-visite *craze suddenly stopped. Courtesy George Eastman House.*

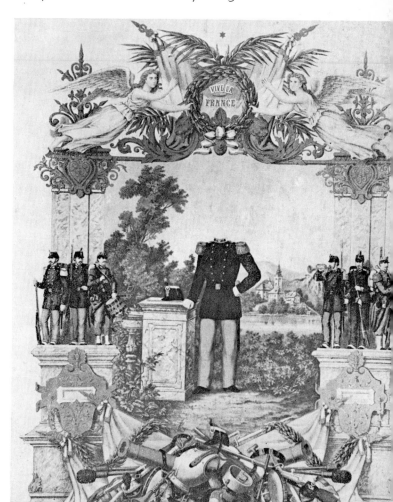

CHAPTER 14

Julia Margaret Cameron: Portraits Out of Focus

JULIA MARGARET CAMERON (1815–1879) was endowed with a combination of eccentricities, energy, and inspiration that prompted her to photograph great Victorian personalities and enabled her to reflect their spirit, power, and character better than any portraitist. She concentrated on their heads, revealing their depths of mind as she revealed her own depth of feeling about them. Titans of their day they were—among them Tennyson, Darwin, Browning, Longfellow, Sir John Herschel, George Frederick Watts, Anthony Trollope, and Thomas Carlyle.

It seemed ludicrous; her "head hunting" was without parallel and was not confined to celebrities. She would pursue perfect strangers, "kidnap" them, make them pose stock still, without a head rest, for as long as 7 minutes, and repeat the torture again and again until she was satisfied. Once Robert Browning, admonished to wait for her return and overwhelmed by her commanding personality, sat for three hours while she busied herself in the darkroom.

It was the soul of the subject she was after. The camera provided her with the ideal instrument to record the facial characteristics of her intellectual heroes. Her studio was her gallery of the sanctified; she created ikons to worship. Her photographs of plain people were comparatively uninteresting, merely records containing little more than fuzzy likenesses of persons she obviously did not worship.

Mrs. Cameron was never known to photograph a landscape. The forms of the land and of growing things did not satisfy her as did portrait subjects as a vehicle for expression of her feelings. However, her illustrations of Tennyson's romantic poems and of her own complex allegories pleased her artistic sensibilities. She learned illustration from her mentor, George Frederick Watts; her allegorical photographs, like Watts's allegorical paintings, were tasteless and sentimental.

Her forte, as we see it today, was the direct, close-up portrait. She permitted no retouching, no enlarging; only contact prints were made from her enormous wet plates which measured 8 by 10 or 12 by 15 inches. A Herculean task, hardly a proper one for a strange, wealthy woman not too particular about her dress and habits—often there were thumbprints, dust spots, cracked glass negatives, and editions of uneven prints.

She was a dedicated artistic "primitive" with a camera. Her photographs are out of focus, not deliberately soft focus—this was later to become the vogue in photography —but literally not sharp because the lenses she used could not be made to photograph sharp details. Had she compromised with the size of the camera and substituted a smaller one, had she pulled back from the subject so that his every movement and tremor would not have registered, or had she concentrated all the light possible on the subject rather than the small amount of top light she permitted to enter her small glass studio, the photographs would have been sharper and the sitter would not have been subjected to the misery of such lengthy exposures. But, had she had any consideration either for subject or herself, she would not have been Julia Margaret Cameron.

Her lavish idolatry of eminent poets, painters, and writers she disclosed in her portraits. She presented what she felt were their finest attributes. In each the face is unsmiling; it fills the plate. She was intent on securing a lasting expression that she considered beautiful—by which she also meant spiritual. She rarely photographed the body or hands of these men. She followed no one's style. She was attacked persistently for her bad technique by critics and members of the London Photographic Society. Nothing fazed her. She persisted in taking immortal photographs of men's heads.

Her philosophy, akin to Carlyle's hero worship, seems to coincide with the early aims of George Frederick Watts, the celebrated Victorian painter. In his early portraits, many of them sensitive, Watts attempted to paint the soul. Mrs. Cameron knew paintings and painter well, years before she took up the camera. She met him regu-

larly at Little Holland House in London, where Watts lived with Mrs. Cameron's sister and brother-in-law, Mr. and Mrs. Thoby Prinsep. Watts was the original "man who came to dinner": invited for two weeks, he stayed more than twenty years. Then, to prove how much he enjoyed their company, he built a house on the Isle of Wight, near Mr. and Mrs. Cameron; the Prinseps stayed there with him for an additional several years. Watts sought protection against loneliness and melancholia in the family life of others. Mrs. Cameron's sister, Mrs. Prinsep, conducted in Little Holland House a literary and artistic salon around the painter, whose affairs she managed, and made a red-doored studio available to him in her house. She arranged the marriage of the forty-seven-year-old Watts to the sixteen-year-old Ellen Terry, a marriage which lasted long enough for Mrs. Cameron to take one of her most beautiful photographs.

Watts was the major influence on Mrs. Cameron as a photographer. Aspiring to become England's Michelangelo, he had become a philosopher with a paint brush; he moralized in frescoes on public walls and in tremendous romantic canvases. These paintings were really bad literature. Like the Pre-Raphaelites, Watts believed "a picture after all is but an open book where those who have eyes to see can read strange matters." Watts was considered to be not only a painter but a prophet and teacher who painted the ultimate truth.

The Victorians revered him for lengthy literary messages on such themes as *Death Crowning Innocence*, and *When Poverty Comes in at the Door, Love Flies out at the Window*—small ideas and puny emotions, blown up through saccharine sentimentalism.

Literary ideas replaced plastic ideas for Watts; and he instilled this conception in Mrs. Cameron. Her photographic allegories are no more respected or remembered today than those painted by Watts. She posed and photographed such allegorical subjects as *Faith, Hope and Charity, Peace, Love and Faith*. Watts praised these efforts, not her portraits.

Mrs. Cameron photographed her children (she had six), her grandchildren, her maids, her sisters, and her nephews whenever celebrities or strangers were not available, and she used them as subjects for her photographic illustrations of Tennyson's poetry. In 1860 she moved to the Isle of Wight, in Freshwater Bay to be near Tennyson, the Poet Laureate. Her friendship with him and his family had started in the same way as many friendships she had sought. She would begin with a gift of an Indian shawl, then several days later another shawl, then carved ivories, jewelry, and bric-a-brac—all this from India where she had been born and where she had married a well-to-do jurist and plantation owner; she had come to England with an inexhaustible supply of silks and artifacts from the East. Though her gifts may have embarrassed the recipients, even the most irritated eventually gave in, sat for his portrait, and counted on the friendship of the ebullient Mrs. Cameron. Tennyson and his poems were her inspiration for allegoric and illustrative photography. Mrs. Cameron's first volume, containing twelve photographs illustrating Tennyson's *Idylls of the King and Other Poems*, appeared in 1875; a little later a second volume with an additional twelve photographs was published. Both received critical acclaim in the press "as they had been executed at the Laureate's own request and dedicated by gracious permission to the Crown Prin-

cess of Germany and the Princess Royal of England." Photography was competing with the brush and using motivation detrimental to both.

In the latter part of 1875 Mr. Cameron suddenly decided to return to Ceylon. The story goes that one day he borrowed a son's overcoat and strolled down to the sea, the first time he had left the grounds of his house in twelve years, and the sight of the ocean filled him with a yearning to see Ceylon again and to be with his two sons who were managing his plantations.

It was a perfect departure for Mrs. Cameron. Quite incongruously she tipped the railroad-station porters with portraits of Carlyle and Tennyson, saying that she had no more money. Some of these pictures are still to be seen on the station walls.

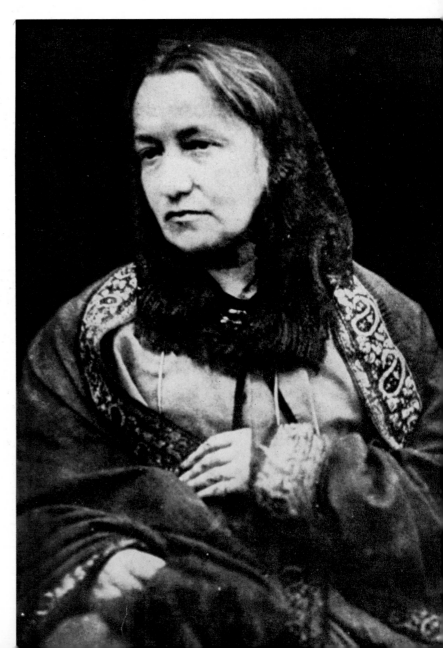

HENRY HERSCHEL HAY CAMERON, *Portrait of Julia Margaret Cameron, 1870. Taken by Mrs. Cameron's son. Courtesy Gernsheim Collection, University of Texas.*

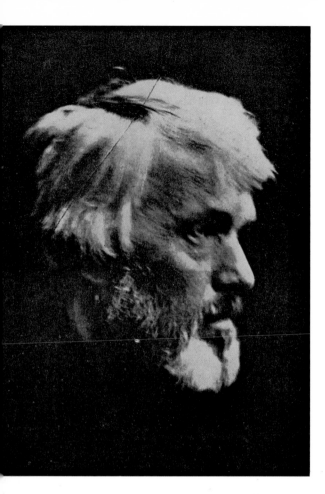

JULIA MARGARET CAMERON
above: Portrait of Thomas Carlyle,
*about 1867. Out of focus, plate cracked
and spotted. Characteristic of Mrs.
Cameron's equipment and technique.*
right: Portrait of Charles Darwin, *1869.
Both, courtesy The Art Institute
of Chicago, Stieglitz Collection.*

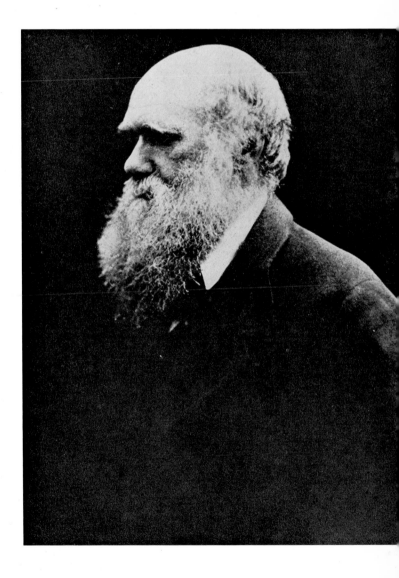

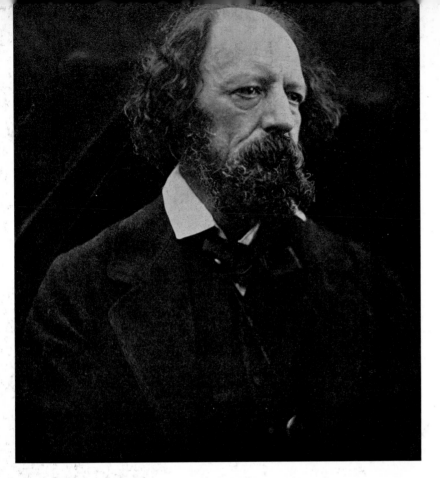

JULIA MARGARET CAMERON
above: Portrait of Alfred, Lord Tennyson.
June 3, 1868.
right: Portrait of Henry Wadsworth Longfellow,
*1868. Longfellow visited Tennyson on
the Isle of Wight, and was prevailed upon by
the insistent Mrs. Cameron to sit for his
portrait. One of the rare portraits in which
she included more than the head.*
opposite page: Portrait of Sir John Herschel.
*Wet-plate photograph, 1867. The pioneer in
photography and noted astronomer at the age of
seventy-five. One of Mrs. Cameron's
greatest photographs.*
*All, courtesy The Art Institute
of Chicago, Stieglitz Collection.*

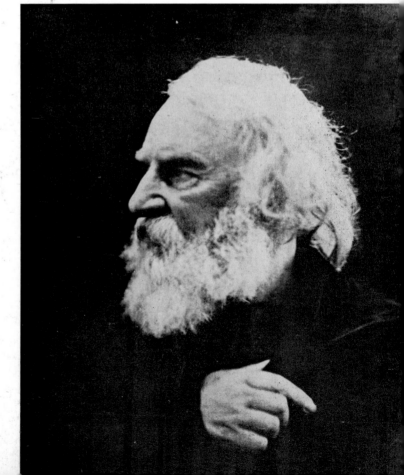

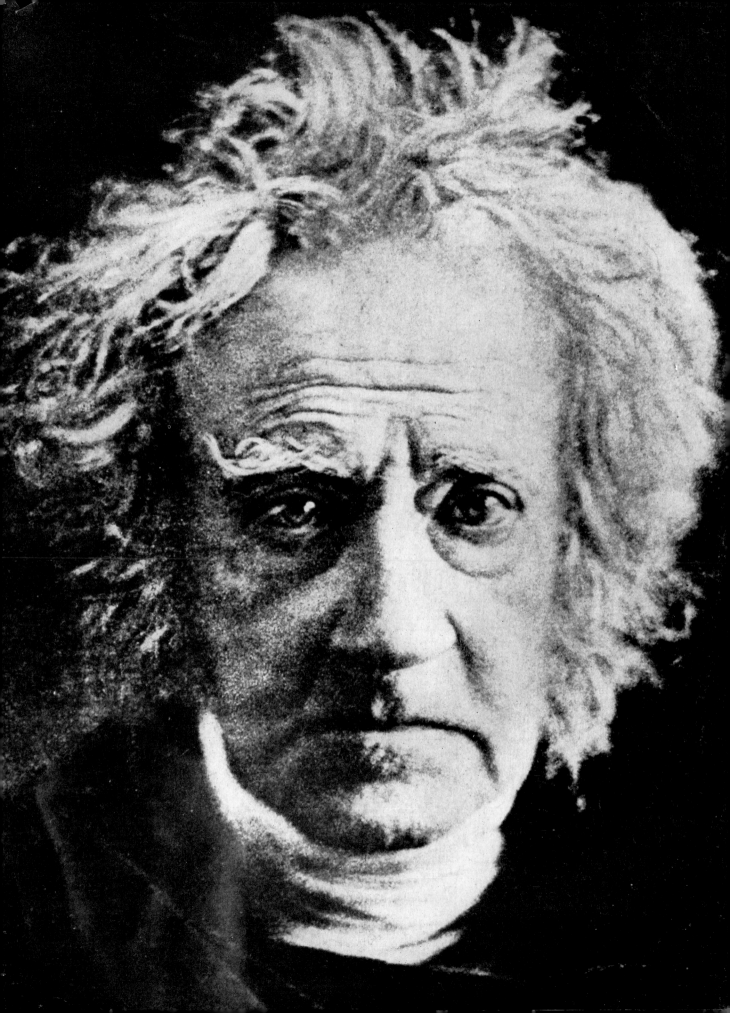

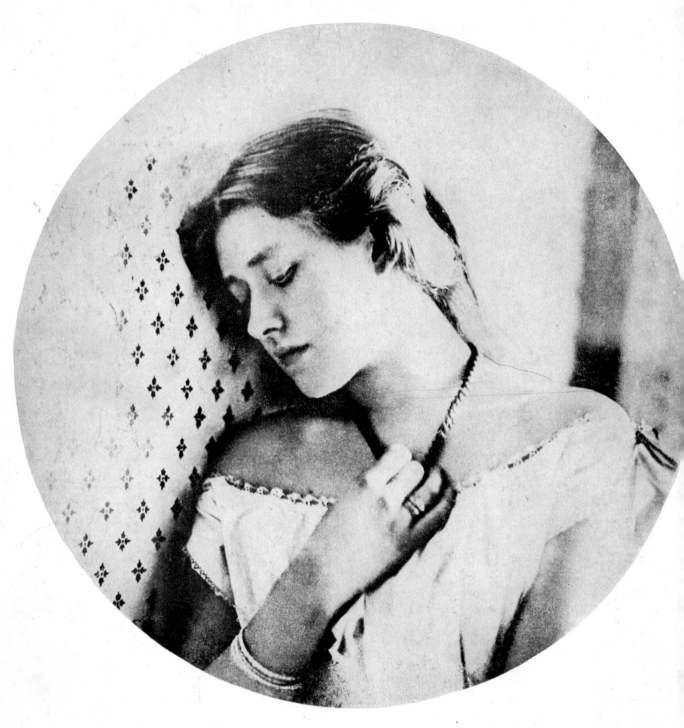

JULIA MARGARET CAMERON, Portrait of Ellen Terry, 1864.
*The famous actress at age sixteen, then recently married
to the painter G. F. Watts, more than thirty years her
senior. Courtesy Metropolitan Museum of Art.*

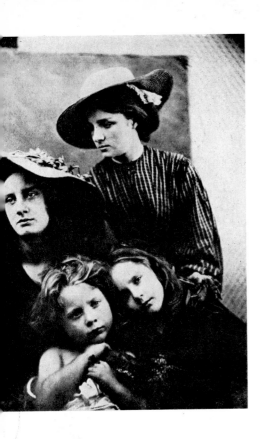

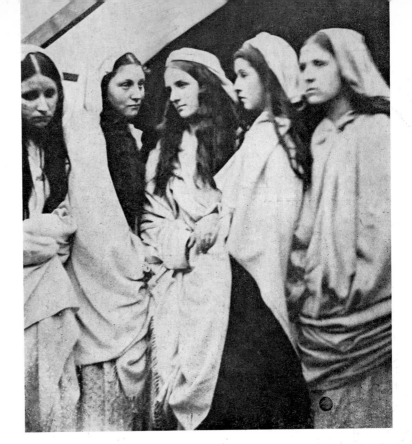

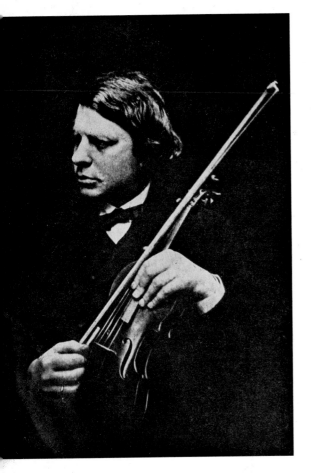

JULIA MARGARET CAMERON
above: The Foolish Virgins. *Allegorical photograph, about 1865.*
above left: Summer Days. *About 1865. An early photograph of
servants and friends' children. Both, courtesy George Eastman House.*
left: Portrait of Joseph Joachim, 1868. *The famous
violinist, to whom Brahms dedicated his violin concerto.
Courtesy The Art Institute of Chicago, Stieglitz Collection.*

CHAPTER 15
Rejlander, Robinson, and 'Art' Photography

The art of the sentimental Victorian age was the idealized storytelling genre or allegorical painting, as beloved in the academies of the Continent as it was in England.

Thoroughly grounded in this literary atmosphere of art was Oscar G. Rejlander (1813–1875) of Sweden, who studied painting and sculpture at the Academy in Rome. His subsequent stay in Paris served to confirm his approach to painting; his portraits glorified the sitter extravagantly and his complicated allegories became ever more involved.

He went to England when he married an Englishwoman and decided to pursue photography for a livelihood; but he continued to paint portraits sporadically and several of these were exhibited at the Royal Academy over the years.

Telling about his conversion to photography, Rejlander writes that he took all five lessons in one afternoon, the calotype, the waxed-paper process, and a half-hour on the collodion process. He then writes, "It would have saved me a year or more of trouble and expense had I attended carefully to the rudiments of the art for a month."

Despite this inadequate training in technique, Rejlander opened a studio. What he had learned of art and particularly the keen eye he had developed in observing nique facets of character in people benefited him greatly in photography when he emulated with the camera the last theatrical and literary allegories he had made with the brush.

In 1856 he made a composite print, 31 by 16 inches, from thirty different negatives. It was an immediate sensation. This allegorical picture, *The Two Paths of Life*, represents a venerable sage introducing two young men into life. The serene, philosophical one turns to religion, charity, industry, and the other virtues, while the second young man rushes madly into the pleasures of the world, typified by various figures representing "Gambling, Wine, Licentiousness and other Vices, ending in Suicide, Insanity and Death." In the front center of the picture is a figure of "Repentance with the Emblem of Hope." Thus was this allegory described when it was first shown.

Praise was heaped on the print, although in Scotland it was refused admittance in an exhibition for being too nude. Shown the same year at the Art Treasures exhibition in Manchester, it was purchased by Queen Victoria.

Neither sensual, natural, nor moral, the allegory appealed to the Victorian romantic, who was literary-minded. Had Hogarth been alive and painting his epic *Marriage à la Mode*, or his *Harlot's Progress*, his work would not have been stomached.

Rejlander's combination photographs made up of artificial poses and contrived scenes from retouched negatives, with desired effects painted in and undesired effects painted out, were loved in their day and still hold the "arty" photographer enthralled.

The Impressionists were rediscovering nature and the effect of changing light on form and color while the artist-photographer lost himself in the false art prevailing in the Victorian studio.

If Rejlander had had fast film and a candid camera in his hands, he might have left a penetrating and valid record of his day. His artistic training caused him to seek and register the intensity of emotional feeling he observed in the swarming streets of London. The slower collodion process caused him to direct people to assume and re-enact the emotions he observed and mimicked for them. Charles Darwin, seeing these posed but nonetheless emotionally charged portraits, approached Rejlander to collaborate on a book, *The Expression of the Emotions in Man and Animals*. Rejlander made twenty-eight photographs of men, women, and children, whom he directed in displaying various emotions; for several of these he posed himself. His plates were too slow or else he was not interested in animals—no pictures of emotions of nonhumans appear in the book.

Rejlander continued with combination printing, but never again attempted such a complex picture as *The Two Paths of Life*. *The Head of St. John the Baptist* he made from only two negatives and *The Dream* (1860) from one straight negative. This was a strange allegory charged with Freudian meanings.

Five years later he was still enmeshed in the pictorial aims of "high-art" photography. Ever the experimenter, however, he developed the double exposure and the photomontage, superimposing one negative on another to make a modern-appearing multiple-exposure photograph entitled *Hard Times*. From these experiments he realized considerable recognition but little profit. His main source of income for the rest of his life was from making portraits and from supplying artists with nude and clothed studies of adults and children. These pictures of children, convincingly enacting his poses and embodying the emotion he tried to convey, found praise from the Reverend Charles L. Dodgson—Lewis Carroll—who came to study with Rejlander. The creator of *Alice in Wonderland* took some unforgettable pictures of artists, fellow professors, and particularly of children. Rejlander made a sensitive photograph of Dodgson holding a big lens and a focusing cloth.

It was a long time before photography stopped looking to painting for guidance. Henry Peach Robinson (1830–1901), a talented painter who turned photographer in the year 1858, followed Rejlander into the vehement controversy over combination printing by exhibiting a picture, *Fading Away*, made from five negatives. This was a picture of a dying girl seated in a chair and sadly watched by sister and mother while father looks out of an open window; it had printed on its mat a verse from Shelley's *Queen Mab*:

Must then that peerless form
Which love and admiration cannot view
Without a beating heart; those azure veins,
Which steal like streams along a field of snow;
That lovely outline, which is fair
As breathing marble, perish?

The "art photograph," as Robinson described these elaborately fabricated pictures, was severely criticized for misrepresenting the truth, but the Royal House was impressed with combination prints and purchased *Fading Away*. The Prince Consort gave Robinson a standing order for one print of each such photograph that he would make. Robinson became not only the leading pictorial photographer of England but a prolific writer of manuals and treatises on photography. His first book,

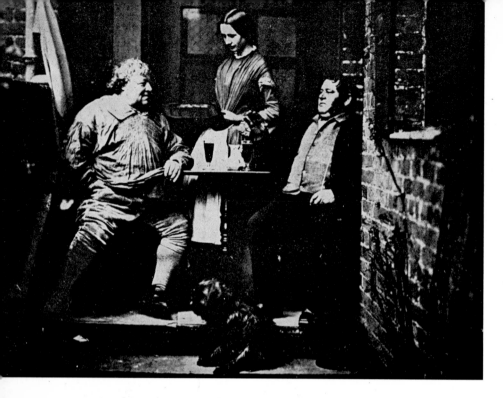

OSCAR G. REJLANDER, Two Gentlemen Taking Wine. *Composite photograph, about 1860. Courtesy George Eastman House, Rochester.*

REJLANDER, Two Paths of Life. *Composite picture, 31 x 16 inches, 1856. Made from thirty negatives. Courtesy George Eastman House.*

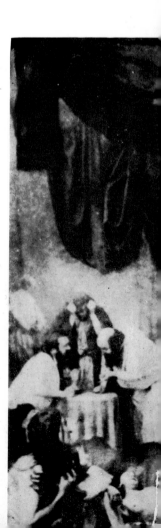

Pictorial Effects in Photography, was published in 1869; toward the end of his life he published *Picture Making by Photography* and *Art Photography*; all three were translated into many languages and printed in many editions.

Robinson became the most bemedaled photographer of his day. His hidebound, academic rules of balanced composition and his pedantic preachments to photographers to "avoid the mean and ugly"—"correct the unpicturesque"—"mix photography with drawing," and to prefer the artificial atmosphere constructed inside the studio to the world outside have had a stultifying effect on pictorialists to this day, as have his sentimentally poetic titles.

Robinson continued to write and lecture on photography, always stressing the making of a photograph instead of the honest taking of one. His influence was felt in photographic circles everywhere, especially after his retirement in 1888, when he became vice-president of the Royal Photographic Society. He discontinued his advocacy of composite pictures, suggesting the use of multiple negatives only in emergencies when single negatives could not accomplish the desired results pictorially.

He produced some charming single-negative pictures neither sentimental nor "high art." These were realistic pictures posed but not obviously so, unretouched, and with an honest intent to portray the character of the subject. In his later writings Robinson derides the soft-focus exponents and he is offended by receiving the commendation that one of his prints did not look like a photograph. He writes, "Why should we try to make our pictures look like the results of other arts?" and he concludes, contradicting his earlier writing in which he favored the mixing of the artificial with the realistic, by writing, "What the photographer has to do is to make pictures with the means at his disposal, and to present them as having been done with those means and no other." He closes with these words, "The limitations of photography as an art have not been definitely fixed."

Robinson's later admonitions, however, seem never to have been read by his followers. Contradictions served only to confuse the pictorialists, who work by rote and rule. It was the rare photographer who read Robinson and then used his tools creatively.

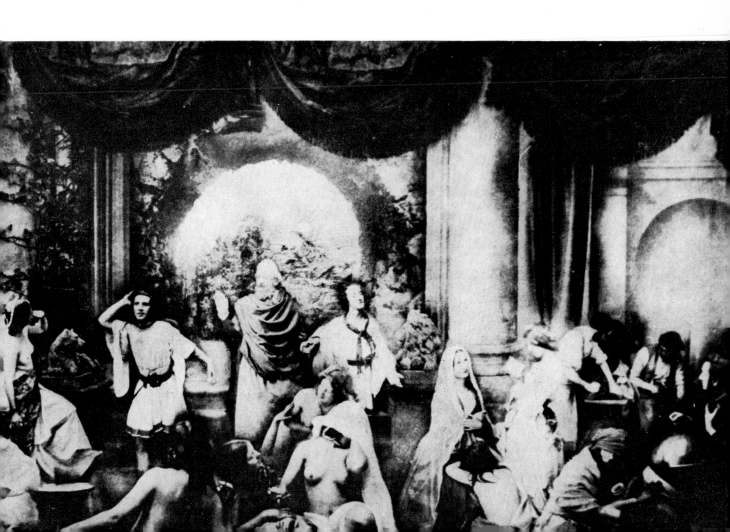

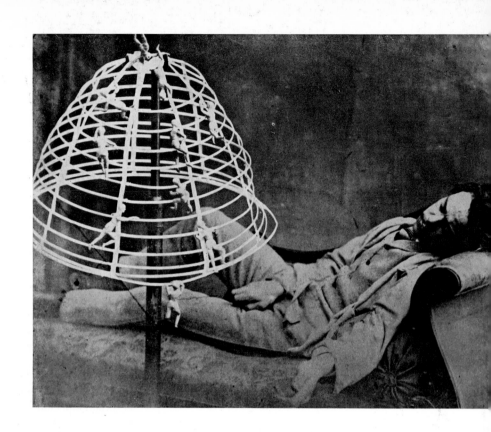

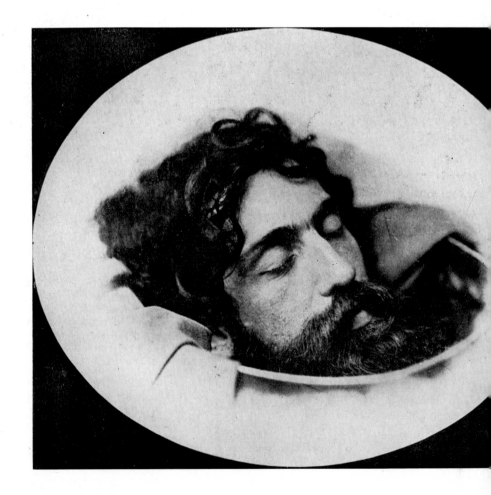

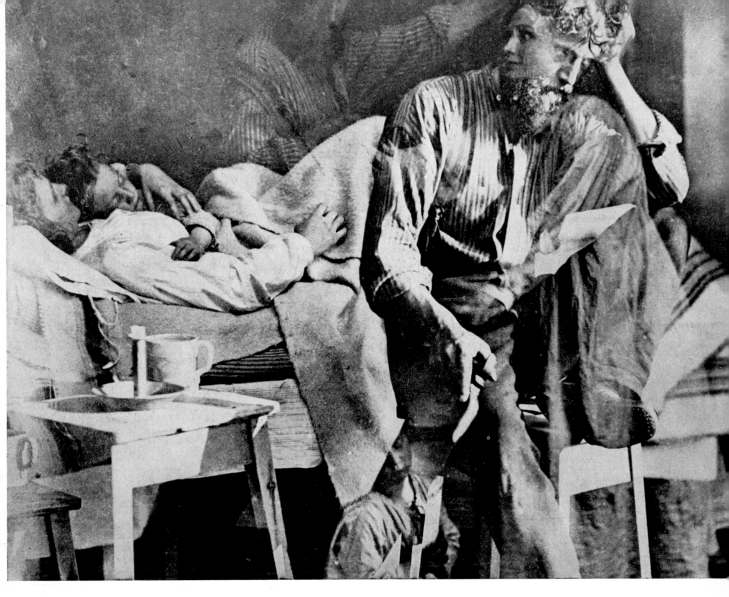

REJLANDER
above: Hard Times. *"Spiritistical photo" printed from several*
superimposed plates, 1860.
opposite page, above: The Dream. 1860. *A crinoline hoop,*
an artist's mannikin, and a troubled dreamer.
opposite page, below: Head of St. John the Baptist.
Composite photograph from two negatives, about 1860.
All, courtesy George Eastman House.

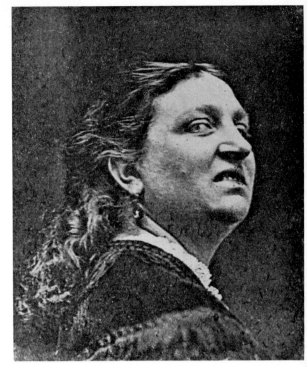

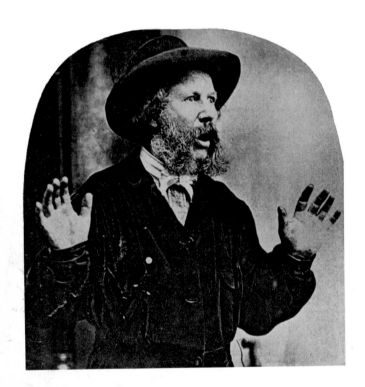

REJLANDER. *Three photographs,*
1873, for Charles Darwin's book,
Expression of the Emotions.
Courtesy The Art Institute of Chicago.
above: Sneering and Defiance.
left: Fear *(Self-portrait).*
below: Grief.

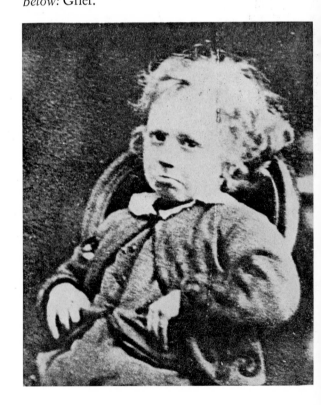

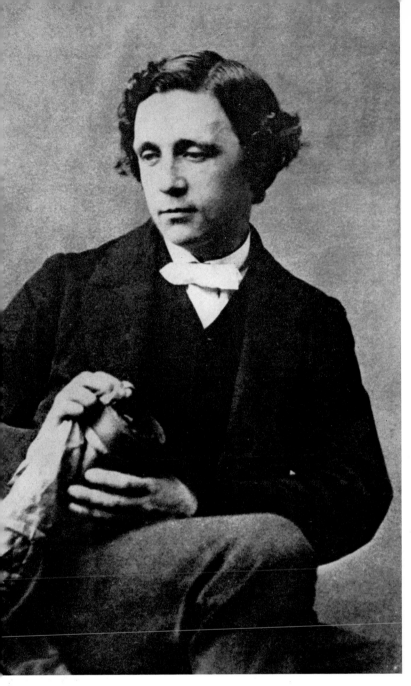

REJLANDER, Portrait of The Reverend Charles L. Dodgson (Lewis Carroll). 1863. *Courtesy Gernsheim Collection, University of Texas.*

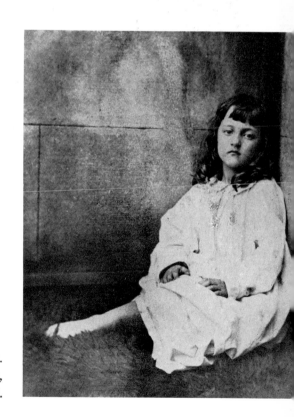

LEWIS CARROLL, Portrait of Mary Millais. 1865. *Courtesy Gernsheim Collection, University of Texas.*

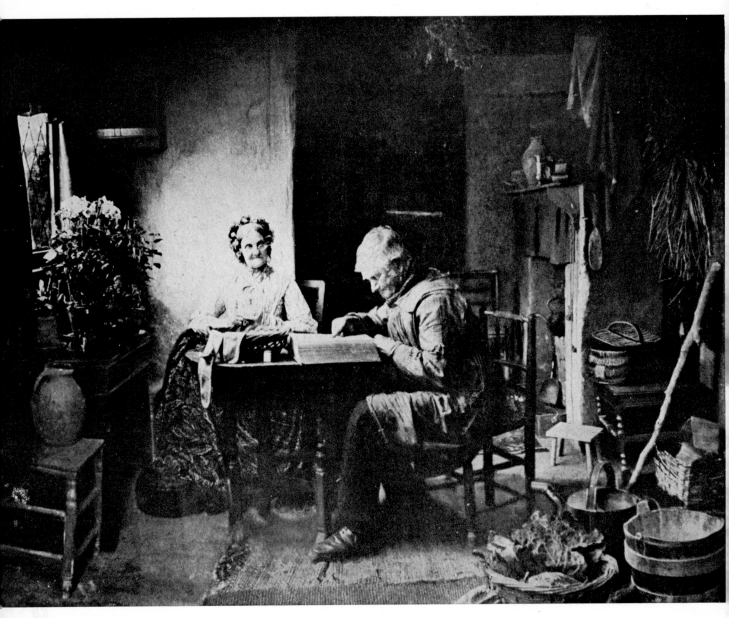

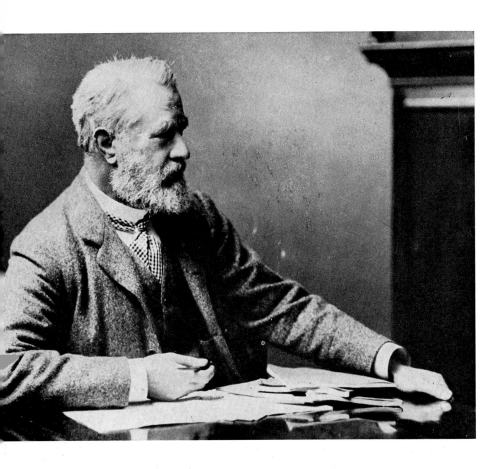

RALPH W. ROBINSON
Portrait of Henry Peach Robinson. 1897.
A *portrait of the photographer's father.*
Courtesy Gernsheim Collection,
University of Texas.

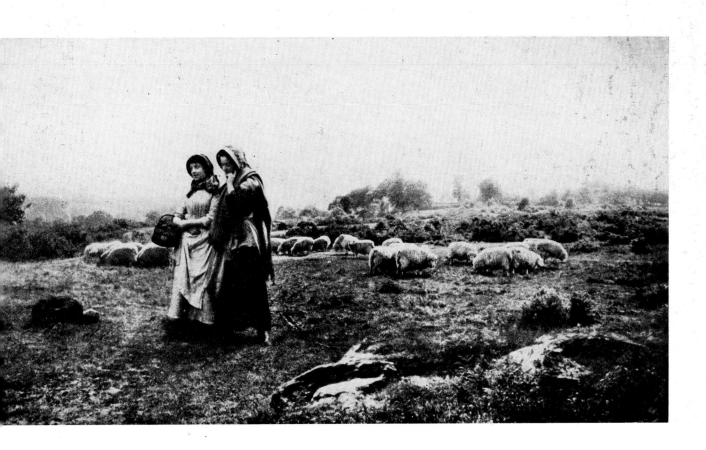

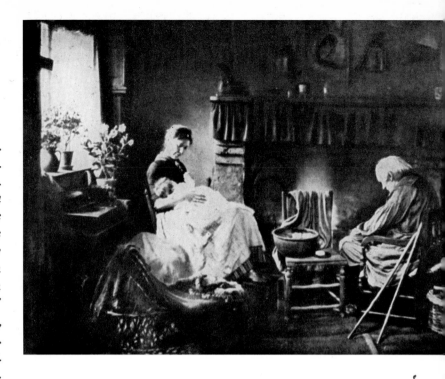

ROBINSON, *right:* Dawn and Sunset.
Composite photograph, about 1885.
Courtesy George Eastman House.
below: Pencil sketch, about 1860, for a
composite picture. One photographic
figure is already pasted in. The three
or four other photographs necessary
to complete the picture would have been
joined and rephotographed; such
prints were sold as works of "high art."
Courtesy Gernsheim Collection,
University of Texas.
opposite page, top: Fading Away.
Composite photograph, 1858.
Made from five negatives, the joints
subtly hidden. The Prince Consort
was so impressed with such photographs
that Robinson was given a standing
order for a copy of every composite
print he made. Courtesy Royal
Photographic Society, London.

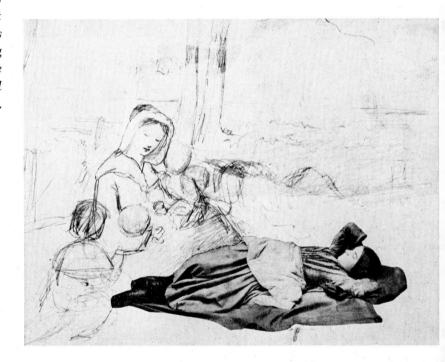

ROBINS
Women and Children in Count
Composite photograph, June, 18
Courtesy George Eastman Hou

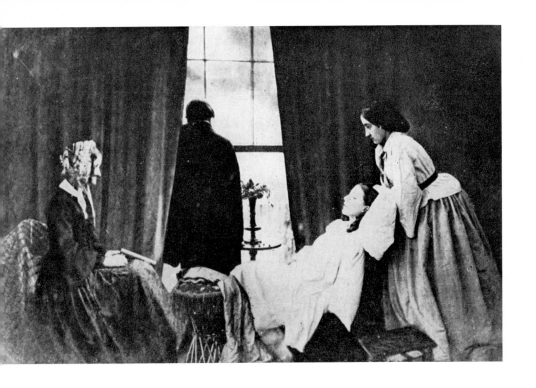

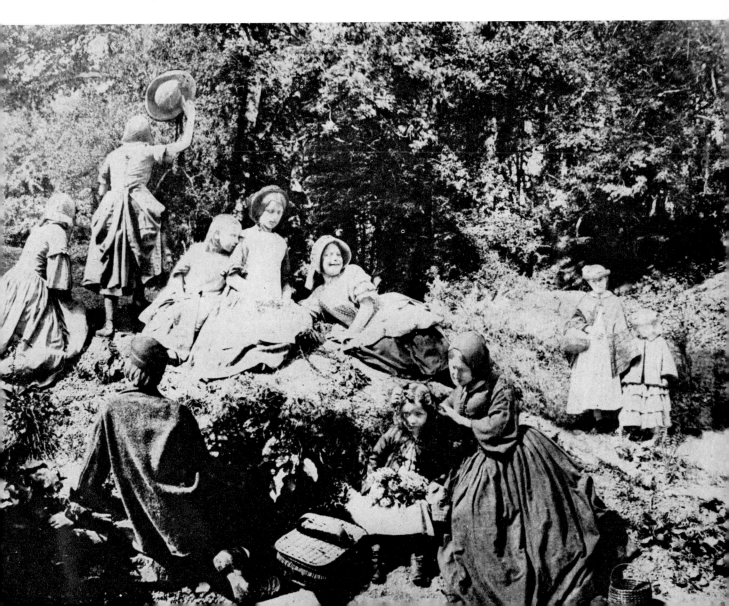

CHAPTER 16

Brady: Cameraman of the Civil War

IT IS OFTEN FORGOTTEN that Mathew B. Brady, the most representative photographer of his day, took his portraits of the mighty and the famed with a sensitivity and artistry that he had first learned to put into pictures with a brush. His teacher was William Page, twelve years his senior, whom Brady met when he was only sixteen years old in 1839. He had just left his birthplace of Lake George, Warren County, New York. Brady painted portraits under the guidance of Page while they traveled as itinerant limners from Saratoga to New York City. Early the next year Page took Brady, still encouraging him to be a painter, to meet and perhaps study with his former instructor, Samuel F. B. Morse. Instead of signing up for courses in art, Brady enrolled in a class which Professors Morse and Draper were conducting on the daguerreotype process.

Brady's energy was boundless; he experimented with the lenses and the chemicals and made himself thoroughly proficient in all of the many delicate operations. He had to learn daguerreotypy completely for although his slight, 5-foot-6, square-shouldered, trim figure was endowed with inexhaustible energy and initiative, Brady was cursed with exceptionally weak and ever-failing eyes. There are no pictures extant showing Brady without glasses; year by year he was fitted with ever-thicker lenses.

In 1841 and for the following three years, to make money not only to pay his tuition at the university but also to accumulate capital so that he could open a gallery, Brady owned a factory which manufactured cases for jewelers and daguerreotypists. A letter dated June 17, 1843, in the Boyer Collection of Eastman House, addressed to A. S. Southworth in Boston, describes a new case he is manufacturing and offers for sale. The letter is undoubtedly written and signed by Brady. Mr. James D. Horan in his recently published, highly readable biography of Brady, *Historian with a Camera*, asks whether Brady was able to read but not write or whether, perhaps, it was his bad eyesight that kept him from writing. Mr. Horan's conclusions are that no truly ascertainable signature of Brady has been isolated, though what must necessarily have been his signature Mr. Horan calls attention to as appearing on a bill of sale of a piece of land in 1869, on a paper of his bankruptcy proceedings in 1873 and below the lithograph which was made of Brady by François d'Avignon in 1851; all are quite different. What now seems to be a positive signature of Brady of 1843 should prove that Brady could both read and write. However, he favored his ailing eyes and practically never wrote to anyone himself once he could afford to hire secretaries.

Following the practice of Samuel F. B. Morse, Brady opened a skylight-roofed studio on Broadway and Fulton Street in 1844. He had just reached his majority. That first year he was awarded a prize at the American Institute in New York for a daguerreotype; the following year he reaped more recognition by winning a gold medal; and the top award was his a year later. Brady then began to accumulate the most historically important pictorial record of the nation's statesmen and celebrities for a period of nearly fifty years, from President John Quincy Adams to President William McKinley.

Just a few days before Andrew Jackson died on June 8, 1845, Brady dispatched a photographer to the Hermitage in Nashville to take several daguerreotypes of Old Hickory, seventh President of the United States. One of these was donated to Eastman House by A. Conger Goodyear.

Brady conceived the idea of publishing books of likenesses of the notables who sat for his camera. In 1850 Brady published *The Gallery of Illustrious Americans* with twelve lithographed reproductions, eleven made from his daguerreotypes by François d'Avignon, whom he paid $100 a stone. The text he commissioned C. E. Lester to write, but it is not stated how much he paid for the writing. The impressive volume received critical acclaim and, though it was a financial failure, Brady considered it money well spent for a prestige piece and contemplated issuing another volume.

He continued to gather daguerreotypes not only of statesmen and soldiers but of practically all people in the public eye, including actors and actresses, doctors and professors, engineers and architects, opera stars and chess players. The people who made news in their day were recorded for posterity in elusive quicksilver made permanent through its vapors. Brady and his assistants took thousands of portraits which were used for wood engravings and lithographs to illustrate pages of the pictorial journals, newspapers, and books, until the nation's best known by-line was "From a Daguerreotype by Brady."

In 1847 Brady opened a branch gallery in Washington where it became the practice for the President and his cabinet and members of Congress, at one time or another, to entrust their heads to Brady's "immobilizer," as the torturous head clamp was called.

Both galleries thrived with business. Brady never displayed more energy, working every moment while there was light, despite his weak eyesight. Though he colored and tinted daguerreotypes, some on sensitized ivory, he sent forty-eight black-and-white images on silver to the London Crystal Palace Exhibition in 1851. His work was awarded a medal and singled out by critics as "noble examples of this style of art."

By 1853 Brady had almost forsaken the daguerreotype for ambrotype photographs made by the wet-plate process. He relied more and more on his assistants to man the cameras—the strain on his eyes was too tiring. He started to specialize in "imperials," enlargements of 17 by 20 inches, often life-size heads tinted or painted by artists on Brady's staff. This process made a photograph more costly than the usual oil painting procurable in the days before the Civil War. Orders for imperials by the wealthy and powerful were balanced by the mass business during the *carte-de-visite* craze as hordes of customers crowded his two establishments. As another source of income he and his assistants operated a school of photography.

In 1853 Brady opened a new gallery two flights above Thompson's saloon on Broadway. It was decorated at enormous expense with "satin and gold paper on the walls, embroidered draperies over the windows, an enameled chandelier hanging from the ceiling and the floors carpeted with superior velvet tapestry," according to the editor of *Humphrey's Journal*, who concludes, after describing the "superb rosewood furniture," by writing: "On the wall we find the Daguerreotypes of Presidents, Generals, Kings, Queens, Noblemen—*and more nobler men*—men and women of all nations and professions."

In 1856 Brady paid the fare to bring Alexander Gardner from Scotland to New York. From then until 1863, when Gardner left Brady to cover the Civil War as a free-lance photographer, the two men made an ideal working team. An experienced photographer, especially in the wet-plate process and in enlarging, Gardner organized Brady's establishments to make impressive, delicately retouched and profitable monumental portraits. In 1858 Brady made Gardner manager of his Washington gallery. Brady's business flourished. Early in 1860 he moved his New York gallery for the third and last time. Always located on Broadway, this time he moved to Tenth Street, opening the most ornate, elegant, and fashionable gallery of the day. The imperials of the mighty covered the reception-room walls. The fashionable came to add their pictures to the roster of the distinguished, and all flocked to Brady's after the visit of the Prince of Wales.

One photograph that Brady himself took on February 27, 1860, changed the entire course of his life. Abraham Lincoln said of this picture two years later, "Brady and the Cooper Union speech made me President of the United States." Brady's portrait of the tall, unbearded lawyer introduced Lincoln, through the illustrated press and Currier and Ives prints, as a man of profound dignity and inner strength. This was only the first of many sittings Lincoln was to give Brady.

It was with Lincoln's election and the beginning of the war that Brady lost interest in collecting a gallery of the illustrious and determined to document through photography the entire Civil War. His historic pictures enabled people to follow the course of battle, to be witness to scenes of actual conflict, and to feel the devastations of war.

Brady visited Lincoln, who wrote "Pass Brady" on a piece of paper, gave him his blessing but no money, and cautioned him that there would be no money forthcoming for such a project. Brady did not need money when the war started. By the time it was over he had spent his fortune of more than $100,000, and owed $25,000

FRANÇOIS D'AVIGNON, Portrait of Mathew B. Brady. *Lithograph, 1850. First published in* The Photographic Art Journal, *January, 1851. Courtesy George Eastman House.*

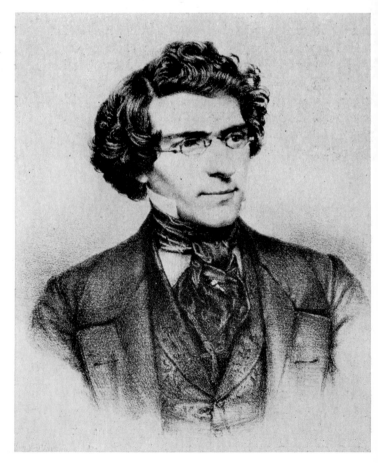

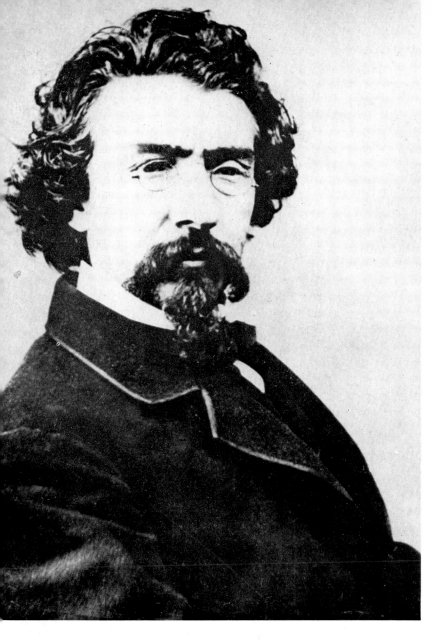

BRADY STAFF, Portrait of Mathew B. Brady.
About 1863. By one of Brady's assistants.
Courtesy Gernsheim Collection,
University of Texas.

more to Anthony's for photographic materials. But, in the beginning, every man from buck private to general had to have his picture taken and ordered *cartes de visite* by the dozen; the entire day there were lines before Brady's establishments. The cheap and popular tintype Brady left to others, who took literally millions in army camps and bivouac areas.

Brady took many of his best men with him into the field; by war's end he had financed twenty teams which had covered practically every major engagement in every theater of war. Each was equipped with a wagon of photographic material which the soldiers dubbed a "What-Is-It?" wagon. Alexander Gardner and his son James were with the Army of the Potomac; Timothy H. O'Sullivan

was at Gettysburg and Richmond; and others whose names are known, remembered by a credit line given below pictures in albums published after the war, were J. F. Coonley, C. N. Barnard, Louis H. Landy, T. C. Roche, William R. Pywell, David Knox, Samuel C. Chester, and D. B. Woodbury. The Confederate Army's most prominent photographer, George F. Cook of Charleston, was one of Brady's helpers.

Brady himself took the first pictures of the war, the rout at Bull Run. He returned with his wagon and a number of negatives which the press hailed as "reliable records," buying them for wood engravings and lithograph illustrations. Again beneath most pictures, this time of war, appeared the credit line "From a photograph by

Brady." He had organized the first newspicture agency.

The War Department suddenly saw the value of photography and assigned George M. Barnard to the Engineers to take pictures of army installations and the terrain. Barnard's best war pictures were made as he accompanied General Sherman on his march to the sea.

It took strength of purpose and disregard of danger to coop oneself up in a wagon which invited a marksman's bullet, and prepare glass plates in the semi-darkness for cumbersome cameras like the popular stereo and the 8-by-10-inch view camera. Too slow to stop action, Brady and his men trained themselves to see and take grim still lifes which reflected the action frozen in death. The battlefield, littered like an upturned wastebasket, showering papers and pictures amidst the ungraceful, sprawling dead, made for poignant pictures of readily imagined fierce action.

Oliver Wendell Holmes saw Brady's own pictures that he took at Antietam and wrote in the *Atlantic*, "These terrible mementoes of one of the most sanguinary conflicts of the war, we owe to the enterprise of Mr. Brady of New York. . . . Who wishes to know what war is, look at this series of illustrations."

It was the sale of stereo cards which Gardner hoped

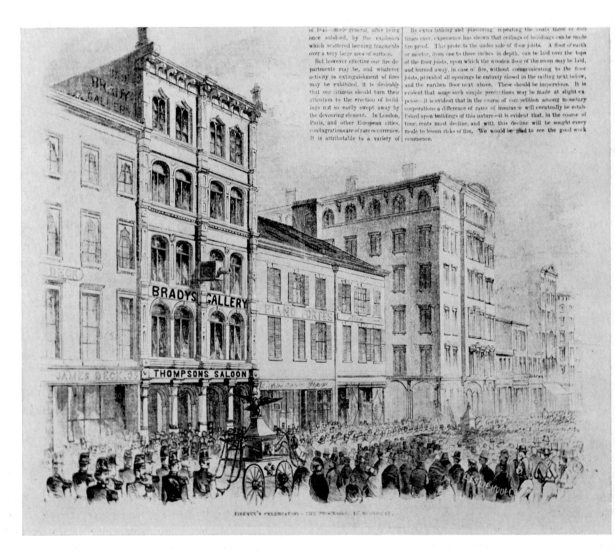

BRADY STAFF, Brady's Gallery. *Wood engraving from a photograph, about 1853.*
Brady's ornate and elegant establishment was opened on Broadway above
Thompson's Saloon, 1853, where he placed his own sign and a huge camera.
Engraving made from "A photograph by Brady." From Gleason's Pictorial Magazine.
Courtesy George Eastman House.

A letter definitely by Brady and signed by him, dated June 17, 1843, when he was making jewelry and daguerreotype cases in New York. Courtesy George Eastman House, Boyer Collection.

would be a source of income when he opened his gallery in Washington a year after he left Brady. What caused them to separate is not definitely known, but money matters could well have been behind it. Brady owed Gardner money for services as he owed Anthony for supplies. Some of the prints Gardner took for Brady during the war Brady must have given him when they parted in lieu of salary owed. These photographs appeared in albums along with pictures identifiable as Gardner's or his son's taken after they left Brady.

No matter what happened, Brady's resolve never lessened; he persisted in recording the nation's greatest conflict. His galleries in New York, without him, made portraits of visiting celebrities; this income supported Brady's war pictures. He and his teams took thousands of grave and penetrating documents. Grant's march on Richmond was a nine-month campaign. T. C. Roche and Tim O'Sullivan were along most of the time, exposing themselves again and again in the midst of bombardment to get a picture. Brady came to Richmond immediately after the surrender. He called on General Robert E. Lee, whom he had photographed in Washington, and convinced the revered leader of the Confederate Army to pose with his son and his aide, Colonel Taylor; they sat on the back porch of Lee's home on Franklin Street. This is one of Brady's greatest historic photographs.

In Washington the returning armies again lined up at Brady's for pictures to compare their war-lined faces

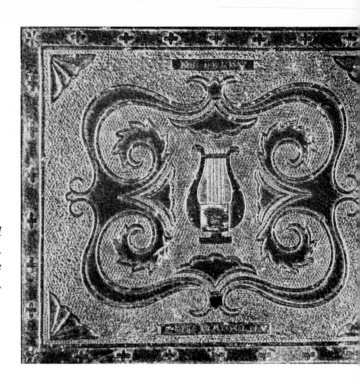

Rare daguerreotype case, made in New York, and signed M. B. Brady. On opposite page is a detail of the name. Brady was in this business from 1841 to 1844, when he opened his first gallery. Courtesy George Eastman House.

with the proud face of youth Brady had captured when they sat for him the day they donned their uniforms. General Sherman and his staff came for a group picture but without General Blair. Brady or one of his assistants took the general at a later date, and pasted the deliberately posed and perfectly proportioned picture onto the board already imprinted with his name.

The excitement of the postwar period in Washington and in New York died down; business at Brady's stood still. His wife, Julia, was ill; Brady was broke. People wanted to forget the war; there was no market for war pictures. To pay Anthony's bill for supplies Brady relinquished a duplicate set of his war negatives; he sold his New York studio and some real estate he owned.

The War Department, in July, 1874, paid a storage bill Brady owed amounting to $2,840, for which they secured a large number of photographic negatives of war views as well as pictures of prominent men. General Benjamin F. Butler questioned the War Department's title to this property. He and General James A. Garfield (later President) evaluated the collection at $150,000 and succeeded in getting an appropriation of $25,000 paid to Mathew B. Brady on April 15, 1875. How many pieces were in the collection? For twenty-two years no

once took the time to find out; meanwhile an untold number of glass plates were broken, irreparably scratched, or lost. The first catalogue in 1897 disclosed 6,000 plates still in good condition.

A third representative group of negatives, the Brady-Handy collection, was recently purchased by the Library of Congress for $25,000, paid to the two daughters of Levin C. Handy, Brady's nephew-in-law. Handy had come to Washington in 1866 at the age of twelve seeking work, and within two years Brady had made him into a fine portrait photographer. Handy ran the gallery in Washington, continuing Brady's practice of securing the distinguished and the fashionable to sit for portraits.

After the death of his wife, Brady made his home with his nephew. One day in 1895 Brady, now practically blind, was run over by a vehicle. He recovered and went to New York City, where he was planning an exhibition of his war photographs, but on January 15, 1896, two weeks before the show opened, he died.

Mathew B. Brady lies buried in Arlington Cemetery with the great Civil War heroes whom he photographed and whom the nation knows as living men primarily because of one man whose most honorable medal was a by-line "Photograph by Brady."

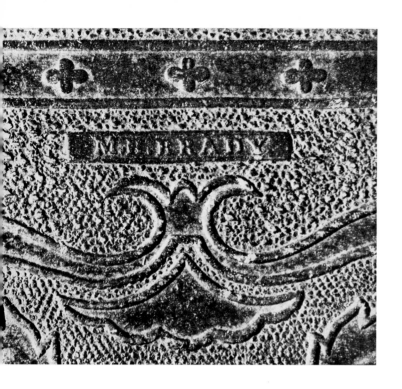

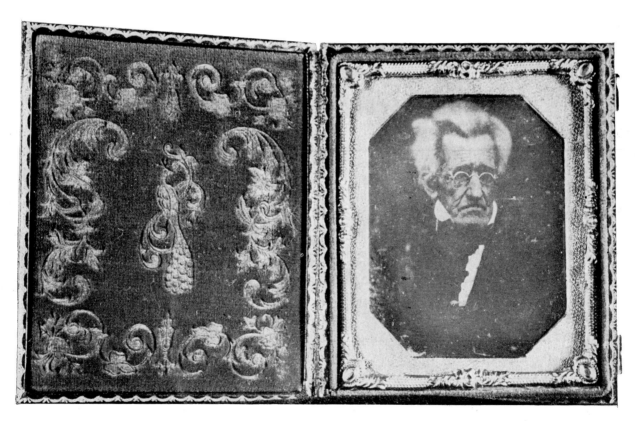

BRADY STAFF, Portrait of Andrew Jackson. *Daguerreotype, 1845. The seventh President, in the year of his death. Taken at The Hermitage in Nashville, where Brady had sent a team to make sure that Old Hickory would be included in his proposed Gallery of Illustrious Americans. Courtesy George Eastman House, a gift of A. Conger Goodyear.*

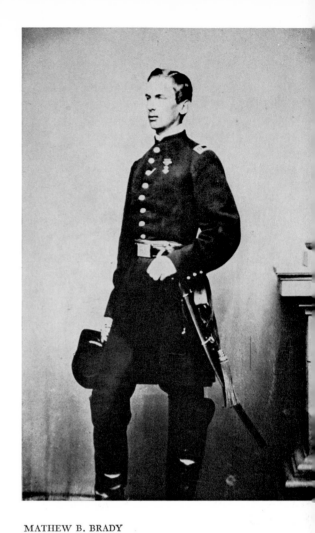

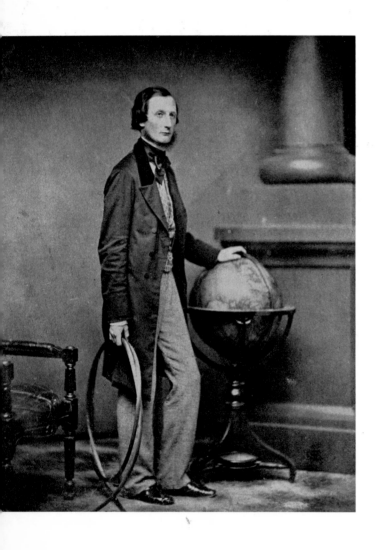

MATHEW B. BRADY
above: Portrait of the Duc de Chartres. *1861.*
Robert d'Orléans, Duc de Chartres, grandson of King
Louis-Philippe of France, Captain in the United State
Army 1861-62. He took the oath of allegiance
but served without pay.
left: Portrait of Cyrus West Field. *1858. Taken*
in the year when Field laid the transatlantic cable
between the United States and England.
opposite page, left: Portrait of Jefferson Davis. *1860.*
Taken in Washington the year before Davis became
president of the Confederate States.
opposite page, right: General Robert E. Lee and Staff
1865. At left is Major General George Washington
Custis Lee, son of General Lee; at right Colonel
Walter Taylor. One of five photographs Brady took
of Lee on the back porch of his house
on Franklin Street in Richmond.
All four, courtesy Chicago Historical Society.

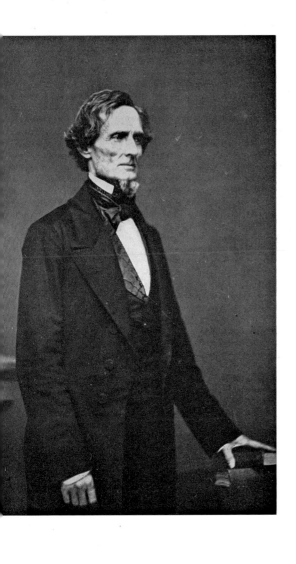

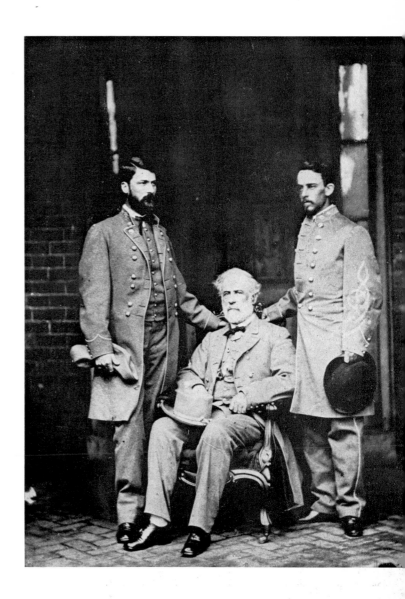

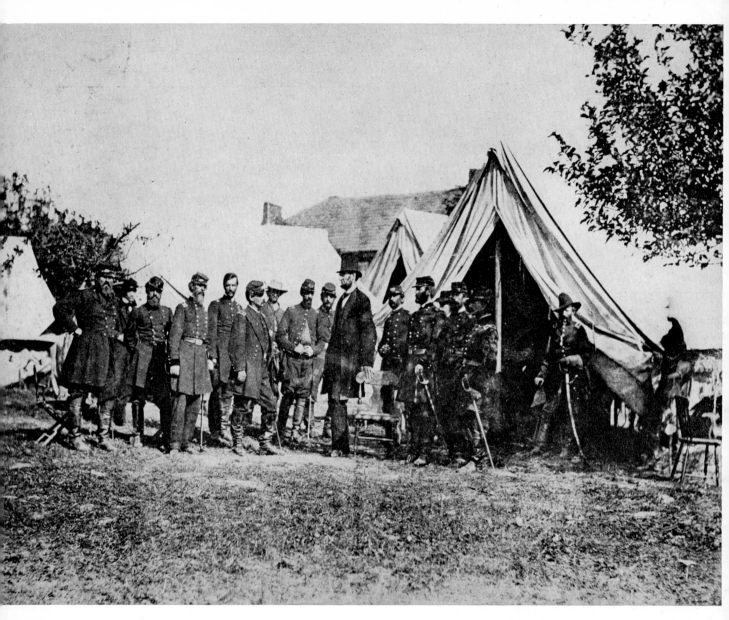

ALEXANDER GARDNER, President Lincoln and General McClellan
on the Battlefield of Antietam. *Wet-plate photograph, October 1862.*
Courtesy George Eastman House.

Two tintypes, one of an unknown corporal in the uniform of the Union Army,
the other of the only identifiable Negro soldier of the 200,000 who served—
Sgt. J. L. Baldwin of Company G, 56th U. S. Colored Infantry, organized August, 1863.
Photographer unknown. Courtesy Chicago Historical Society.

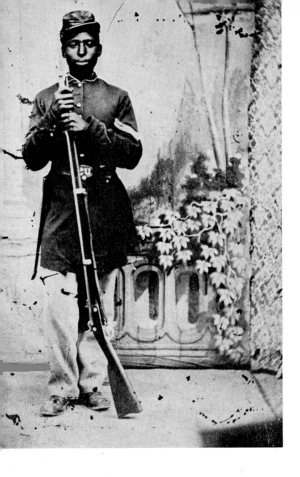

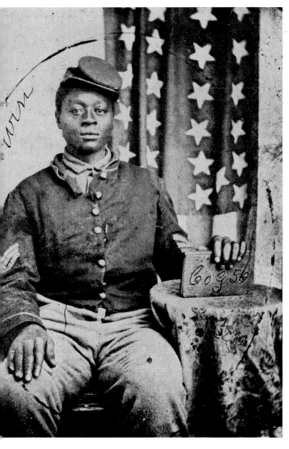

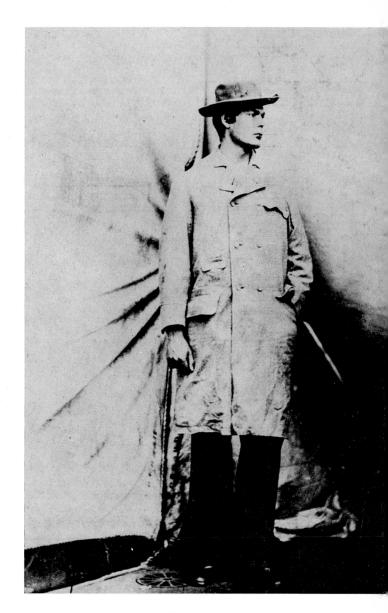

GARDNER, Portrait of Lewis Payne. *Wet-plate photograph, about 1865. Conspirator in the assassination of President Lincoln. On the night of April 14, 1865, he attacked Secretary of State William H. Seward with a knife. Courtesy George Eastman House.*

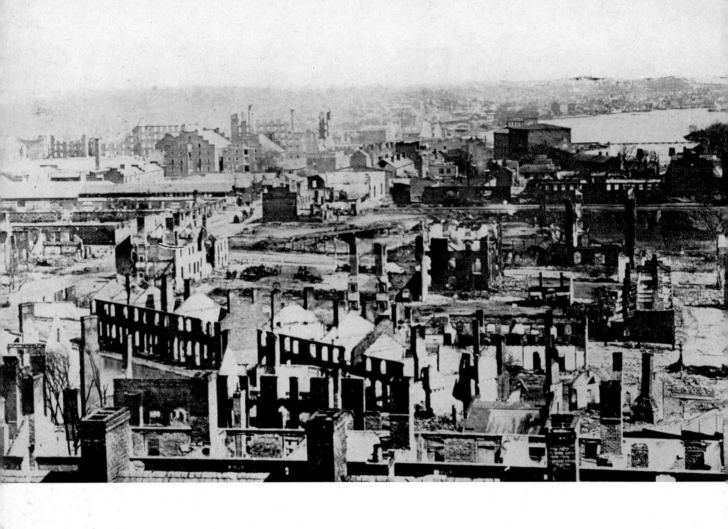

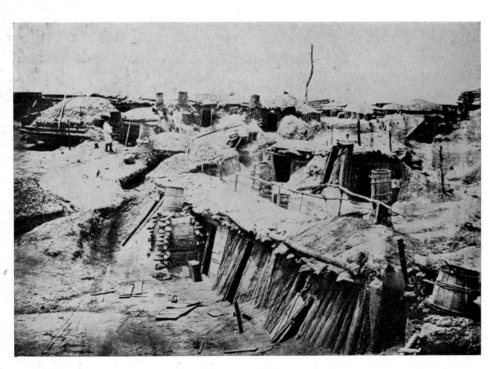

left: BRADY STAFF, Ruins of Richmond, Virginia. *April 12, 1865,*
by an unidentified Brady team. Courtesy George Eastman House.
below, left: TIMOTHY H. O'SULLIVAN, Quarters of Men in Fort Sedgwick,
Generally Known as Fort Hell. *May, 1865. Print by Alexander Gardner.*
below: GARDNER, Home of a Rebel Sharpshooter, Gettysburg.
Wet-plate photograph, 1863. Both, courtesy Chicago Historical Society.

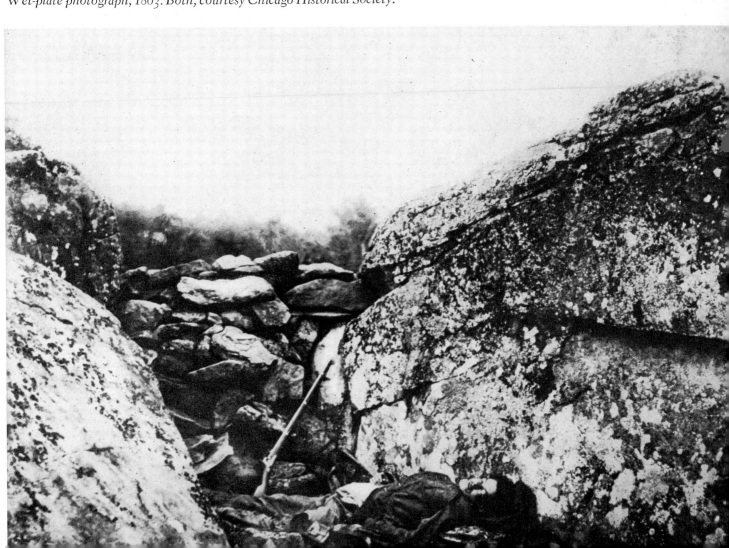

CHAPTER 17
Pioneers of the West

WITH THE CRY OF GOLD IN 1849 and the race for it across the country, a daguerreotypist, Robert H. Vance, trundled along with his equipment in the wake of the miners with their tools. It is evident that Vance was in California during 1849 and 1850, for in 1851 he brought to New York three hundred whole-plate daguerreotypes of miners panning gold and a number of magnificent views of California's scenery. A contemporary account describes and praises the daguerreotypes and then reports that he sold the collection to Jeremiah Gurney for much less than the $3,700 he spent in securing the silver images and their fitted plush cases.

The collection's next owner was J. W. Fitzgibbon of St. Louis, himself a daguerreotypist of the expanding frontier, who showed Vance's work in his gallery. The final disposition of the collection remains a mystery; no trace has existed for more than seventy-five years.

Vance learned the wet-collodion process while he was in the East, substituting an 11-by-14-inch camera for the smaller daguerreotype and returning to California to open a studio in San Francisco. An album of sharp prints taken in 1859 on 11-by-14-inch plates, attributed to Vance and recently acquired by Eastman House, depict temporary camps along the sand and rock bars and mining operations in dried river beds.

Another album of original photographs published in

1856–1857 by Herre and Bauer at the office of the *San Francisco Journal* are pictures by George R. Farden of the wooden streets, intimate parks, views of the sea, and the tall four-story buildings of the lively city on the Pacific.

One of the really gifted cameramen who photographed the West was Timothy H. O'Sullivan, who had been with Brady at Gettysburg and Richmond and who had seen three full years of misery through his ground glass. He had survived, but not even Brady himself could have lured him back into the sophisticated atmosphere of the studio. Celebrities and cities, though he had been born in New York, held no more fascination for him.

He sought continued adventure through his camera: the sight of unexplored lands and out-of-the-way places. The government, in 1867, sponsored a geological exploration of the fortieth parallel, to be directed by Clarence King. O'Sullivan was official photographer for the three years of the expedition. He took pictures of nature's grandeur in the falls, lakes, rivers, and mountain ranges of the towering Rockies, and he went down hundreds of feet inside mines to take pictures by magnesium flares. What an impression they made as the nation saw them reproduced in the illustrated press!

In 1870 O'Sullivan came down from the mountains to take his cameras into the steaming jungles of Panama. For a year he was with the Commander Selfridge expedition, which the government had sent out to survey and map a possible ship canal across the Isthmus of Darien, as the Isthmus of Panama was then called. Insects, swamp fevers, impenetrable jungle, and wild beasts were among the hardships that he encountered, and often made it as difficult to secure pictures as it had been during the war. O'Sullivan endured it all and was not deterred from his purpose. Using an 11-by-14-inch camera as well as a stereo, he made hundreds of negatives, turning them over to Commander Selfridge who four years later incorporated them into his official report.

The next year O'Sullivan was again in the West. Thoroughly trained in the rough life required by expedition photography, he was immediately signed up by Lieutenant George M. Wheeler, who was directing a series of surveys in the Southwest. O'Sullivan was to make two subsequent annual expeditions with Lieutenant Wheeler, skipping 1872, when he went East. The very first year O'Sullivan made more than three hundred negatives, using large cameras to retain all the detail possible in contact prints of the majestic scenery of the canyons of the Colorado River.

In 1873 the Wheeler survey explored Arizona, where O'Sullivan photographed the White House ruins at Canyon de Chelly, one of his most superb pictures. The name is a distortion from the Navaho, *Tse-Yee*, meaning "within the rocks." The drying up of the wells because of a drought which lasted for most of the later thirteenth century made the Indians abandon their hallowed cliff dwellings.

In the O'Sullivan picture the overhanging cliff is given prominence and the texture emphasized by the striking sidelight cutting across the striated wall. It is a brilliantly envisioned wall seen floating above the ancient dwellings, which are set in a semicircular cave on a ridge seventy feet above the canyon bed. Below, two barely discernible men hold a rope attached to two other men standing on the roof of the ruins.

Not much is known of O'Sullivan after the 1874 expedition conducted by the now-promoted Captain Wheeler. It is believed that he worked off and on for Alexander Gardner in Washington. It is definitely known that both Brady and Gardner recommended him for a job as chief photographer in the Treasury Department, for which he was hired. He worked in Washington about six months, fell ill, and resigned. Two years later the scant record lists O'Sullivan's death, January 14, 1882, age forty-two, perhaps forty-three. His exact birth date was never certain. What is certain is that in his sick body, suffering with tuberculosis, was a courageous spirit, an alertness to the art of the camera, and an indomitable will to leave a living record of the terrors of war and the splendors of nature.

A contemporary of O'Sullivan who lived a year less than a century, from 1843 to 1942, was William Henry Jackson. He served the year 1862 in the Civil War. His enlistment over, he resumed work in a Vermont photographer's studio. He left in 1866 for St. Louis, where he become a bullwhacker of an ox train crossing the plains. He sketched, worked as a hired hand, tried prospecting when he was in California early the next year, and then hired on to drive wild horses back east as far as Omaha. Here, in late 1867, his career as a photographer really began in partnership with his brother Edward, who came out from their home town of Peru, New York. They opened a studio, but Edward soon tired of photography and returned to farming.

In 1869 Jackson took a series of pictures along the Union Pacific railroad, trading photographs for bunk and board with the section hands. He roamed the country with his camera, going to Salt Lake City and the Black Hills of Wyoming, taking side trips, and returning to some out-of-the-way station where he caught a train for

Omaha and his gallery. Dr. Ferdinand V. Hayden of the United States Geological Survey of the Territories hired Jackson in 1870 to join a three-month expedition from August to November, at no pay but expenses and permission to keep the negatives with the proviso that prints be made available to Hayden when he requested them.

Jackson photographed along the Oregon-Mormon trail, the North Platte River where a dry gorge was named Jackson Canyon in his honor, along the badlands of Wyoming, the Uinta Mountains, down the Green River through Bridger's Pass, then on to Pike's Peak and Denver in the cold and snow of an early winter. Jackson liked the life. He deliberately went to Washington to sign up with Dr. Hayden as official photographer for the following year. He closed his studio in Omaha.

Yellowstone was the expedition's field of operations in 1871. Jackson took an 8-by-10-inch and a stereo camera plus 200 pounds of equipment, mostly packed on his mule "Hypo." Jackson, who sketched and painted water colors when he did not photograph, was pleased to find the famous New York artist, Thomas Moran, accompanying the expedition to paint Yellowstone's scenic marvels. Other members of the party were divers scientists, geologists, topographers, and naturalists, who recorded in cold reports what Jackson photographed so beautifully. Nine of his photographs saved Yellowstone for the people of America, making an area of 3,578 square miles into the country's first national park.

Dr. Hayden bound nine of Jackson's best photographs including Mammoth Hot Springs, Tower Falls, Grand Canyon of the Yellowstone, The Great Falls, and the Crater of the Grotto Geyser, into individually gold embossed volumes for each member of the House and Senate. The bill passed by a good margin, and President Grant signed it March 1, 1872, removing one of the nation's wonders forever from commercial exploitation for private gain.

The third expedition of Dr. Hayden extended exploration of Yellowstone, but Jackson took off with one assis

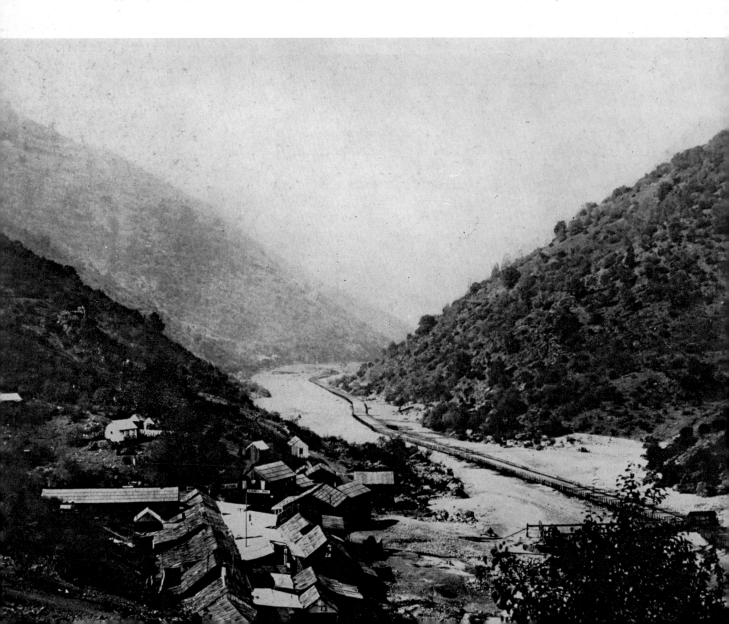

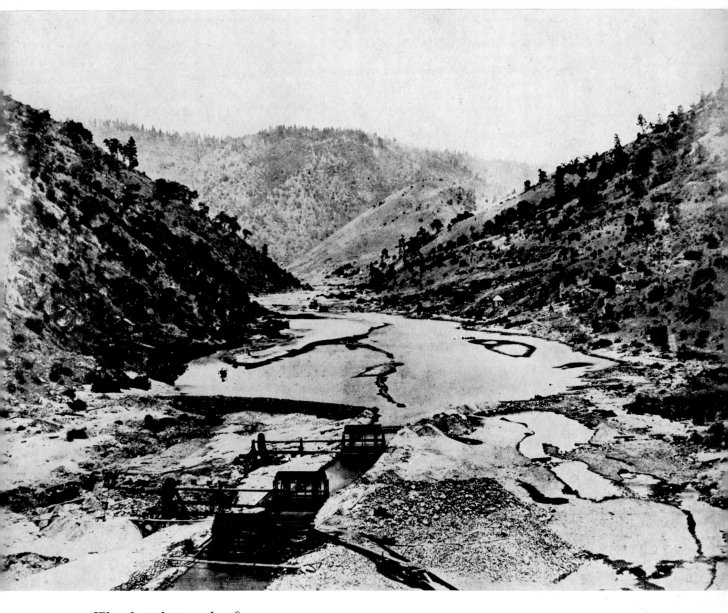

ROBERT H. VANCE, *Wet-plate photographs, 1859.*
Left: View of Maine Bar from the East.
Above: View of Poverty Bar to Oregon Bar.
River-Bed Mining in California.
Both, courtesy George Eastman House, Rochester.

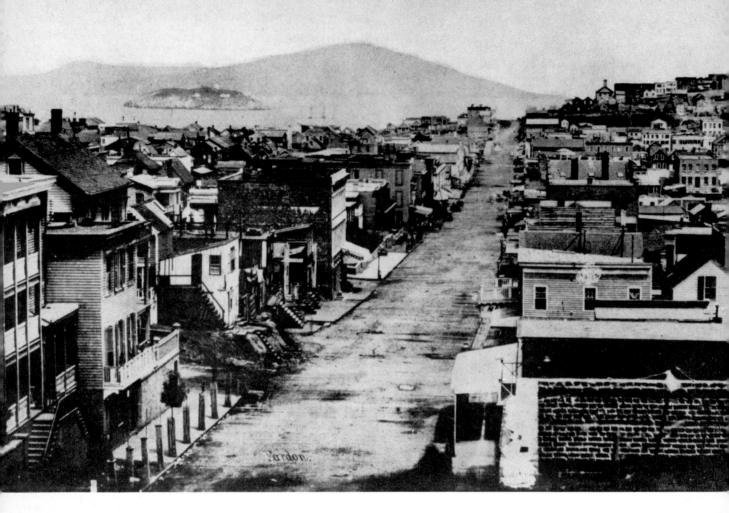

above: GEORGE R. FARDON, View of San Francisco
Wet-plate photograph, 1856. Courtesy George Eastman House

right: O'SULLIVAN
Sand Springs, Nevada. *Wet-plate photograph, 1867*
Courtesy George Eastman House

tant and three different-sized cameras for the Great Teton Range near the head of Snake River. In the snow and cold at 11,000 feet he took some superb panoramic views of the Three Tetons as they towered above him. The highest, 13,858, named after Dr. Hayden, was 7,000 feet above Jackson's Lake, the second natural site named after the dedicated photographer.

In the 1873 expedition Jackson directed a botanist, an entomologist, a cook, and two assistants as a unit. Starting from Long's Peak in Estes Park, Jackson took a series of connected views, panoramas, and close-ups of Gray's Peak, Pike's Peak and Torrey's Peak, the icy front-range summits of the Rocky Mountains. At the foot of the mountains Jackson photographed the eroded sandstone shapes of Monument Park and the Garden of the Gods. On August 24, Jackson photographed for the first time

The Mount of the Holy Cross, located in the Red Table Mountains of Colorado at 14,176 feet. The snow here lies permanently frozen in a hundred-foot crevice in the shape of a cross 1,500 feet in length and 700 feet in width.

On the same expedition Jackson photographed the weathered and deserted cliff dwellings of the Mesa Verde, now also a national park, in the San Juan Mountains of Colorado. Jackson Butte of the Mesa Verde was named after him on that trip. The following year, 1875, he again visited the region; this time, in addition to his usual cameras, he hauled along on an extra mule a camera capable of taking negatives 20-by-24 inches. What skill it required to coat evenly a glass plate two feet wide, expose, and develop, all in a maximum of 15 minutes while the collodion was still moist!

Jackson's impressive record, according to a catalogue

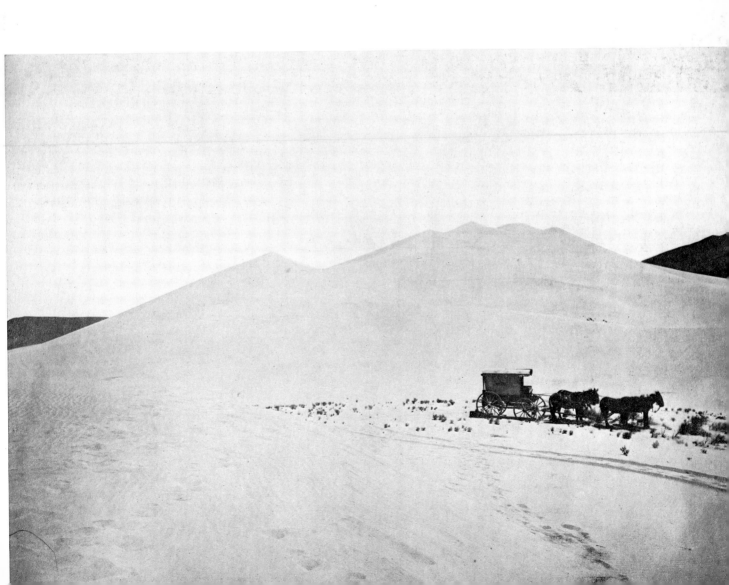

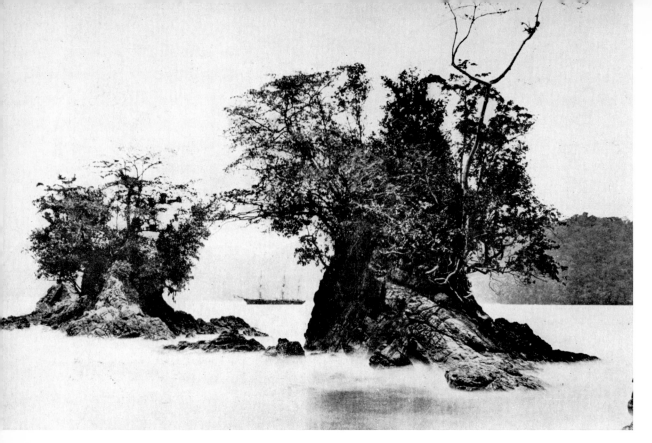

TIMOTHY H. O'SULLIVAN, *Three wet-plate photographs.*
above: Panama-Limon Bay at High Tide. 1870.
right: Self-Portrait. *From a stereograph, 1870. Taken*
during the Selfridge Darien (Panama) expedition.
opposite page: Black Canyon, Colorado River. 1871.
The photographer's boat and equipment.
All three, courtesy George Eastman House.

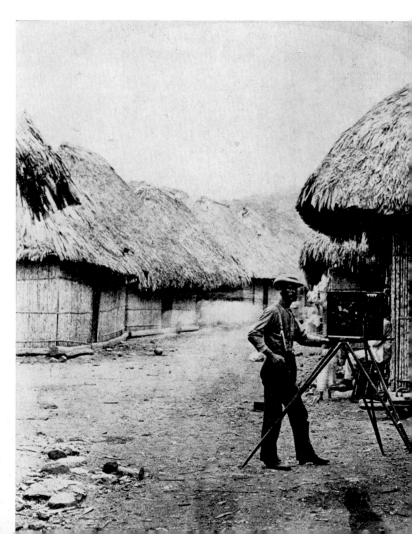

of his photographs published in 1875 which covers his seven expeditions with Dr. Hayden, consists of 973 stereos, 308 negatives 5-by-8 inches, 107 11-by-14, 526 8-by-10, and 12 20-by-24. The best day he could expose only thirty-two negatives. Exposure was by hand cap, the smallest of openings used to gain the sharpest of definition demanding 15 seconds exposures.

The year 1876 Jackson devoted to the construction of a model based on his photographs of the cliff dwellings for the Philadelphia Centennial. The next year was a lost one. Exploring the Pueblos of New Mexico, again for Dr. Hayden, he used the new dry plates manufactured commercially for the first time. What a heartbreaking experience to see a year's results all come out black from the developer! The manufacturer's guaranty did replace the defective plates free of charge.

Jackson opened a studio in Denver three years later. All over the world he sold famous views of nature on stereoscope cards, large prints suitable for framing, and smaller sizes to book publishers for illustrations. The rail-roads of the west bought many of his old prints and commissioned him to take new pictures for promotional purposes. His photographs made people aware of the breathtaking beauty to be seen in America; and trips to the national parks became one of the country's grand tours. The millions of photographs of Old Faithful and the other wonders of Yellowstone taken with advanced equipment have never surpassed the pictures taken by Jackson with his messy wet plates and unwieldy cameras.

Not the wonders of nature but rather soldiers, buffalo, and the landscape of the "Big Open," as he called the prairie and badlands between the Yellowstone and Missouri Rivers, were the subjects for the unique pictures of the frontier taken by Laton Alton Huffman. Huffman became post photographer at Fort Keogh, Montana Territory, in 1878.

In below-zero temperatures Huffman followed the soldiers dressed in their indispensable buffalo coats as they drilled in knee-high snowdrifts. He photographed the officers, men, scouts, trappers, and famous Indian chiefs

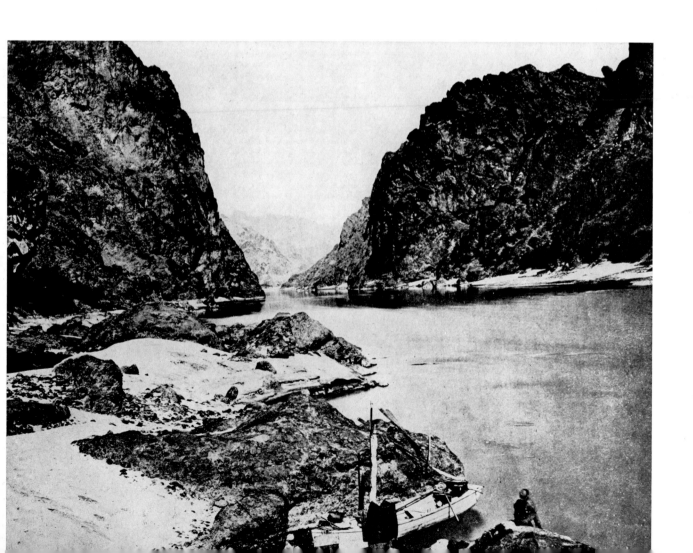

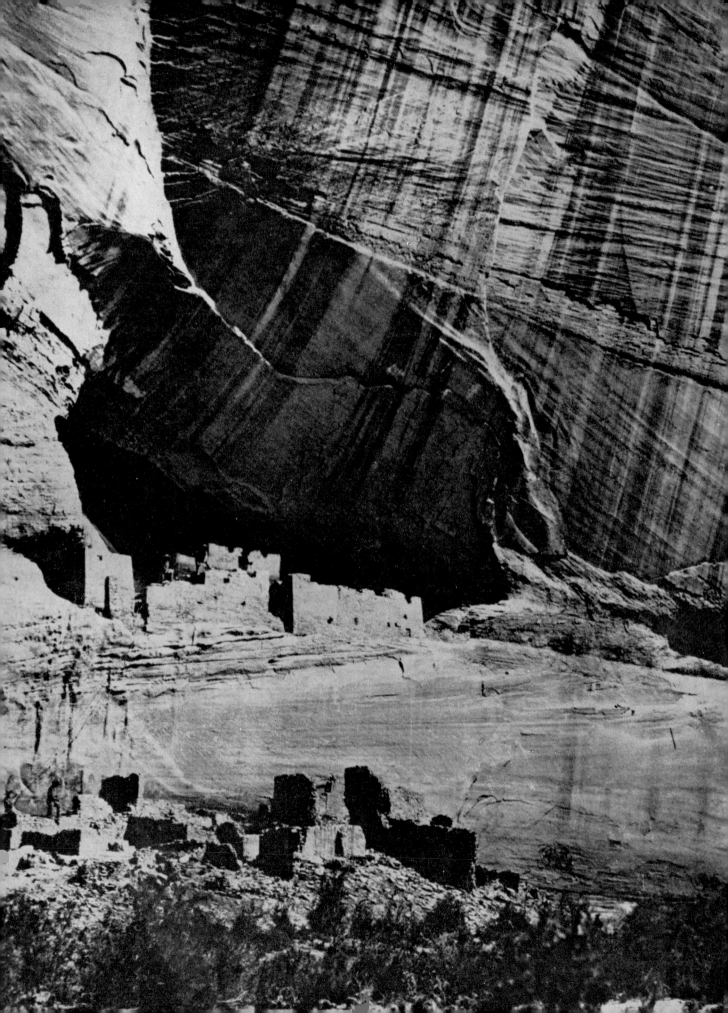

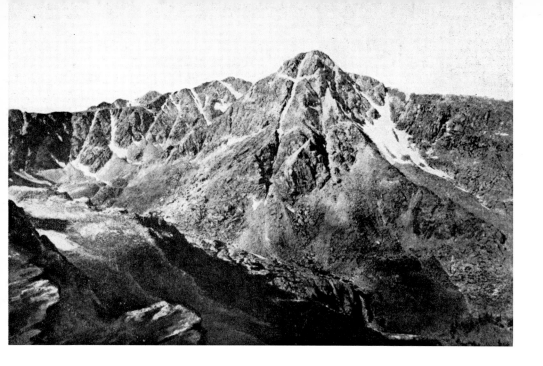

above: JACKSON, Mount of the Holy Cross.
Wet-plate photograph, 1874.
Courtesy George Eastman House.

opposite page:
O'SULLIVAN, Ruins of White House,
Canyon de Chelly, Arizona.
Cliff dwellings abandoned in the thirteenth century.
Two explorers in the bed of the canyon
attached by rope to two others standing
on the roof of the ruined house.
Wheeler expedition.
Courtesy George Eastman House.

right: W. H. Jackson in Yosemite Valley,
Observation Point.
Wet-plate photograph, 1873.
Photographer unknown.
Courtesy Denver Public Library,
Western Collection.

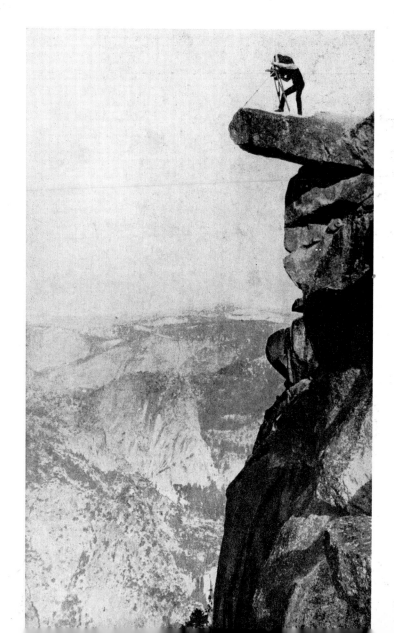

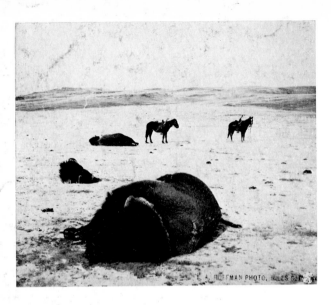

HUFFMAN, After the Buffalo Run. *North Montana, 1879.*
Courtesy Mrs. Ruth Huffman Scott.

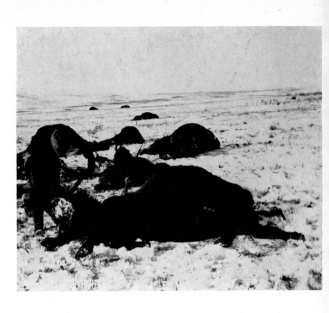

HUFFMAN, Taking the Tongues of Buffaloes. *Montana,*
1878. Courtesy Mrs. Ruth Huffman Scott.

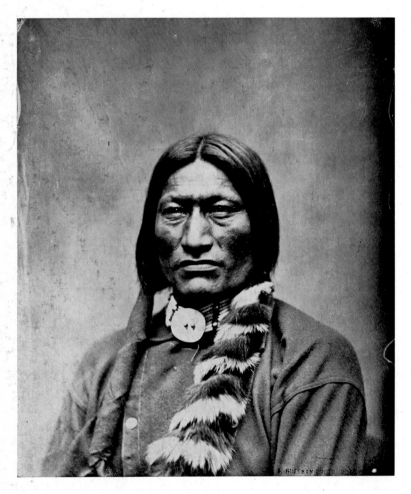

HUFFMAN
Red-Armed Panther, a Cheyenne
Indian Scout. *Fort Keogh, Montana, 1879.*
Courtesy Mrs. Ruth Huffman Scott.

JACKSON
Old Faithful, Yellowstone National Park.
Wet-plate photograph, 1870.
First picture taken of the geyser.
Courtesy George Eastman House.

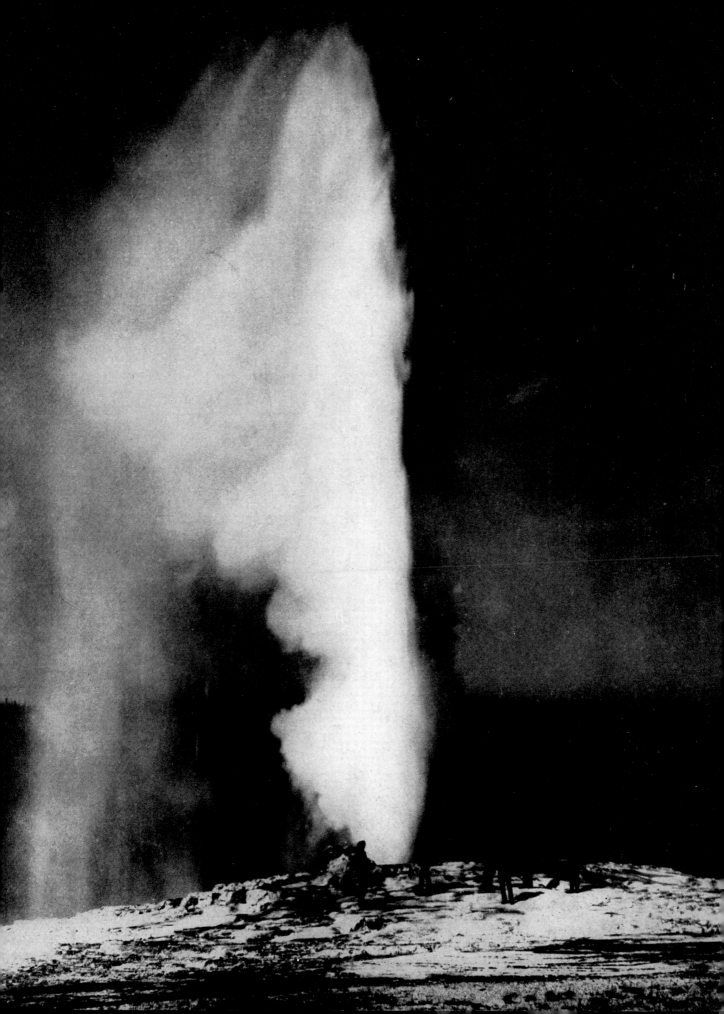

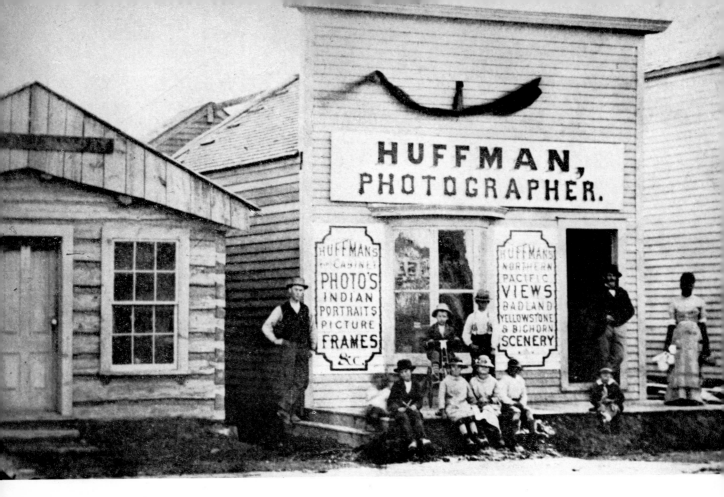

Laton Alton Huffman's studio, in Miles City, Montana, about 1880.
Courtesy W. R. Felton, Sioux City, Iowa.

with nostalgic names, Sitting Bull, Spotted Eagle, Two Moon, and Rain in the Face, either in his studio in the fort or in their buffalo-hide tepees surrounded by their squaws and children.

In 1880 Huffman opened a studio in Miles City, Montana, but for days the camera was with him photographing "buffalo by the thousands in every direction," as he recorded on May 12. Three years later the hide hunters with their heavy rifles had killed off hundreds of thousands in just one corner of Montana alone, for hides which brought around $2.50 each. Huffman photographed the willful destruction of the prairie-lording buffalo. Later he photographed hunting parties shooting elk, antelope, bear, and other game, but by 1883 the loping bison killed for hide and tongue was only a topic for conversation around the fire.

In his Miles City studio Huffman photographed such celebrities as Calamity Jane, Teddy Roosevelt, noblemen from Europe already pursuing the legend of the red man and unnamed colorful visitors to the wide open cow town. Cattlemen and cow punchers sat for his camera mostly in the open. He roamed with them on roundup to secure an honest and impressive graphic record of the straight-backed, pigeon-breasted, unglamorized cowboy who were fighting a losing battle with the sheep herder for the land. Huffman saw the changing frontier, and photographed it honestly and with insight—the homesteader in his sod hut, the barbed wire and the plow, and the closing of the open prairie forever.

Geographical memorials should be named in honor of L. A. Huffman and T. H. O'Sullivan to rank along with Mt. Watkins in Yosemite National Park, Mt. Millers in the Henry Mountains of Utah, Mt. Haynes in Yellowstone National Park, and the Canyon, Butte, and Lake named in honor of W. H. Jackson, all commemorating photographers of historic and artistic prominence.

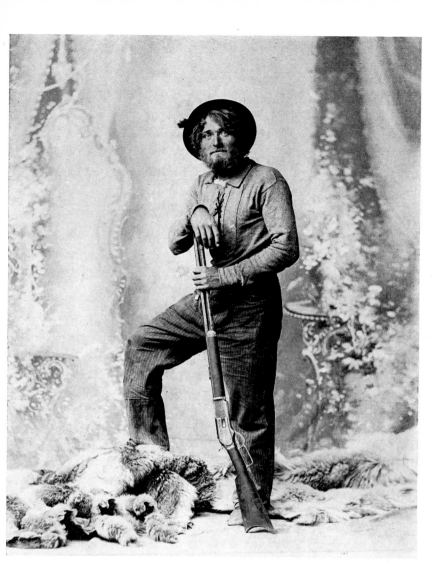

LATON ALTON HUFFMAN
left: Typical Sheep Herder.
Taken in Miles City, Montana,
photo studio, about 1880.
below: Guard Mounts in Buffalo
Coats. *Wet-plate photograph,*
Fort Keogh, Montana.
Both, courtesy Mrs. Ruth Huffman
Scott, Miles City, Montana.

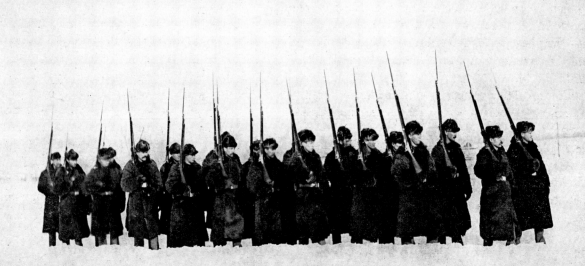

CHAPTER 18

Muybridge and Eakins: Photography of Motion

ONE OF THE GREAT CONTRIBUTORS to the invention of the motion picture was born in England as Edward James Muggeridge, but changed his name early in life to what he believed was its true Saxon spelling, Eadweard Muybridge (1830–1904). In 1852 he migrated to America and is first mentioned for a series of large photographs he took in Yosemite in 1867. The superb cloud effects printed in from a second negative received praise from admiring critics awarding medals in International Exhibitions; and twenty of these composite photographs were in the first guidebook to Yosemite's wonders.

In 1868, less than a year after the United States government purchased Alaska from the Russians, Muybridge was sent along as official photograher with the military force empowered to take over the newly acquired territory formally.

Ex-Governor Leland Stanford in 1872, according to the traditional story, bet a friend $25,000 that a race horse had all four feet off the ground at one time during its running gait. Muybridge, who had an established reputation as a photographer, was hired to photograph Occident, a famous trotting horse in Stanford's stable. Despite a fast shutter that Muybridge had invented and white sheets covering the track to give extra light, the wet-plate process of that time was too slow to give proof, but there was sufficient indication that the ex-Governor was correct, and Muybridge was asked to continue.

He was not to resume his experiments, however, for five years. In 1873 he photographed the guerrilla fighting amidst the lava beds in the Modoc Indian War at the California-Oregon border. The next postponement was caused not by an assignment but by a scandal and a murder that sent him to Panama and Guatemala for several years until he felt safe to return to California. In 1874 Muybridge shot and killed his wife's lover. He was acquitted by a jury, which accepted as evidence of Muybridge's temporary insanity testimony given by his former employer who said, "He was most eccentric. In his work he would not take a picture unless the view suited him." Within the California code of honor Muybridge was justified, but it was wiser not to tempt fate and he left the country.

Late in 1877 the truthfulness of a wood engraving based on a Muybridge photograph of the trotter Occident was questioned, since the photograph was admittedly retouched. In June 1878 ex-Governor Leland Stanford invited the San Francisco press to witness Muybridge photographing a trotting horse and a racing mare.

Twelve cameras were set up, each fitted with a drop shutter triggered by a spring or rubber band. From each camera a fine wire was stretched across the track, activated by the iron rim of the wheel of the sulky, which closed an electrical circuit, thereby releasing the shutters one after another.

The track was prepared to concentrate the maximum amount of light for the fastest exposures. The ground was sprinkled with powdered lime; the background screen was intensely white, covered with rock salt; everything was in the brightest sunshine; and, though Muybridge still used wet plates, the collodion had been speeded up by "ripening" or aging.

For photographing the handsome mare Sallie Gardner twelve fine black threads were placed across the track, striking her breast high and releasing the shutters. The resulting photographs proved conclusively that the four feet of a galloping horse are all off the ground only when they are bunched together under the belly.

The English mezzotints depicting pink-coated riders astride galloping hobby horses, with the front feet stretching straight ahead and the hind feet extended behind, were now seen as quaint and the representations of centuries were refuted. Artists all over the world recognized that personal observations, no matter how keen, could not compare with the instantaneous vision obtainable by camera. Frederic Remington and Charles Russell, famous painters of cowboys and horses, were influenced by these revelations of Muybridge's *Horse in Mo-*

tion, as was the celebrated French painter of cavalry and battle scenes, Ernest Meissonier.

On May 14, 1880, the San Francisco Art Association presented the first photographs of a galloping horse projected on a large screen by a special magic lantern. It was so realistic, a reporter covering the program wrote, that the only thing missing was the clatter of hoofs. Animated cartoons and the movements of a dance (the sequence photographed in frozen poses so that the music could be played in perfect time to it) had been projected on a screen a decade earlier, but Muybridge had actually presented the first motion picture.

This "zoogyroscope," or "zoopraxiscope" as he later called it, worked on the principle of an old toy, the zoetrope. The Muybridge projector used two glass disks, one containing twelve images revolving in one direction and a second slotted disk, caused to revolve in the opposite direction, which served as a shutter.

Muybridge did not pursue motion-picture photography. Improved machines were to be developed by Professor E. J. Marey, G. Demeney, and the Lumière Brothers in France, and by Thomas A. Edison in the United States, all of whom acknowledged their debt to Muybridge.

Photographing animal and human locomotion was Muybridge's main interest, and for this he received a grant from the University of Pennsylvania, where he stayed for three years until 1887. The eleven volumes published that year under the auspices of the university, *Animal Locomotion: Electro Photographic Investigations of Consecutive Phases of Animal Movements*, cover Muybridge's photographic experiments from 1872 to 1885 and consist of more than 100,000 photographs. The animals shown are not only the domestic dog, cat, and horse, but also moose, elk, bear, raccoon, lion, tiger, monkey, and birds.

Most of his photographs of humans are nudes, a number depicting cripples in abnormal movements, anticipating a great demand by artists who would substitute photographs for live models.

Muybridge retired to England, but returned briefly in 1893 to lecture on animal locomotion at the Columbian Exposition's "Zoopraxographical Hall" in Chicago. He published the *Human Figure in Motion* in 1901, but he never left England again and did little in photography the rest of his days; he died at his birthplace, Kingston-on-Thames, in 1904.

It is not generally known that Thomas Eakins (1844–1916), today accepted as one of America's great nineteenth-century painters, was also an ardent photographer. The stark realism and honesty with which, in his painted portraits, he brought out the inherent strength and character of the subject, Eakins tried to achieve as well when he photographed. His strong will and his rejection of clever and fashionable likeness kept him from copying photographs when painting portraits.

He photographed and painted his favorite younger sister in 1882 (the year she died) and painted their childhood friend, Miss Mary Adeline Williams, "Addie," more than a decade later. Both portraits he made correspond to what he conceived as artistic truth. The blunt, realistic, detailed photograph is an artistic end in itself; the painting constructed stroke by stroke reflects his expert knowledge of anatomy and his skillful draftsmanship. What is inherent in both the painting and the photograph of his sister is Eakins's realistic, humanistic approach to art, stressing within the limitations of each medium the dignity and spirit of the subject.

A friend of Eakins once said that he would not pose for him, for "he would bring out all those traits of character that I have been trying to conceal for years."

Eakins's keen interest in photography prompted him to correspond with Muybridge. In 1879 he recommended a more accurate method of measuring the horse's gait which, however, Muybridge did not adopt. In 1884 Eakins, as head of the Pennsylvania Academy of Fine Arts, the oldest art school in America, invited Muybridge to lecture. He also helped interest people in raising funds for Muybridge to continue his experiments at the University of Pennsylvania. Eakins was appointed a member of the supervising committee.

A brilliant anatomist, Eakins had studied human and animal anatomy for several years at Jefferson Medical College; he embraced enthusiastically the opportunity to collaborate with Muybridge. They soon differed. Eakins's scientifically trained mind readily observed that twelve or twenty-four separate cameras could not follow the speed of a subject exactly. He preferred a simpler and more accurate method, using a single camera. In front of its lens revolved a disc with a hole in it which permitted a series of superimposed distinguishable images to be taken on one plate. It was Eakins's contention that the sequence of movement relating one shape to another throughout an entire action could be followed more easily than the separate actions photographed by Muybridge's multiple cameras.

A man walking, pole-vaulting, running, a woman model jumping or lifting an object, all became fit subjects

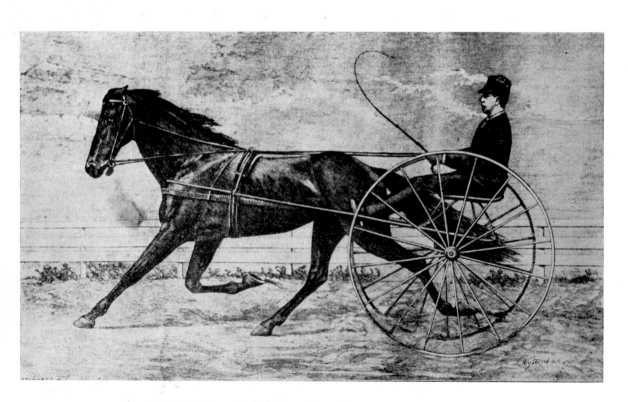

EADWEARD MUYBRIDGE, Horse Trotting at 36 Feet per Second.
From a wood engraving after a wet-plate photograph of 1877.
Exposure: 1/1000 second. Courtesy George Eastman House, Rochester.

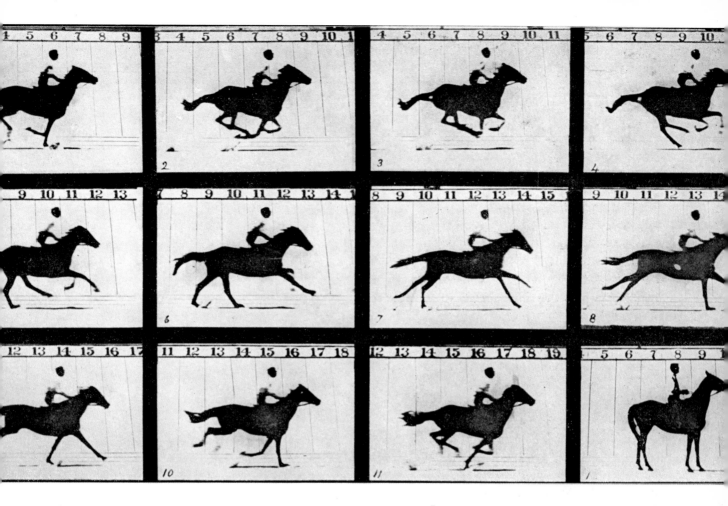

UYBRIDGE, Horse in Motion. *Wet-plate photographs, 1878. The horse illie Gardner, owned by Leland Stanford, running at a 1.40 gait over alo Alto track, San Francisco, June 19, 1878. First successful photographs moving horse. The negatives were made at intervals of 27 inches to lustrate consecutive positions assumed during a single stride of the mare. he vertical lines are 27 inches apart; the horizontal lines represent evation of 4 inches each. Exposure of each negative, less than /2000 second; twelve cameras used. Courtesy George Eastman House.*

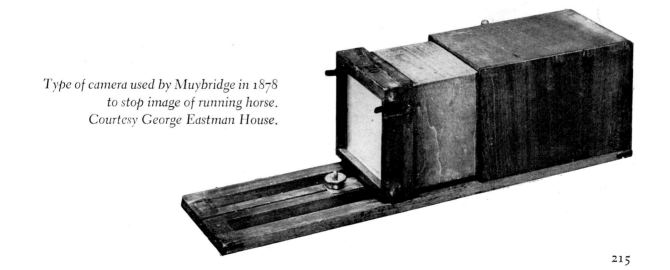

Type of camera used by Muybridge in 1878 to stop image of running horse. Courtesy George Eastman House.

215

for Eakins in 1884. He did not publish his photographs. Professor E. J. Marey of France, whose camera principle of revolving discs for fast photographs Eakins modified and used, did publish similar experiments with the multiple shapes of a nude figure superimposed on a single plate. None of the photographs published created a stir of protest. In 1912 Marcel Duchamp translated similar experiments into an oil painting, *Nude Descending a Staircase*, which created a furor of protest and, strangely enough, is still often vilified.

Eakins continued his experiments with nude athletes and models as well as with horses in motion. In 1885 he lectured at the university with a projector he either invented or borrowed from Muybridge. Having succeeded in establishing the principle that a single camera taking pictures of a subject in motion from a single viewpoint

was a preferable way, he gave up his experiments. His purpose, like Muybridge's, was to analyze motion, and in this they were both successful; both contributed through their experiments to the development of the motion picture.

Eakins, the artist, continued to use the still camera for graphic art. A photograph was to be respected and retained as a fine-art print, such as an etching or lithograph. A master draftsman, he compared a fine photograph to a master drawing and felt therefore that it deserved the best of paper. Accordingly, he printed on costly platinum paper capable of retaining the most subtle and delicate tones.

As an artist Eakins was neglected until the latter years of his life; as a photographer he is only now coming into his own.

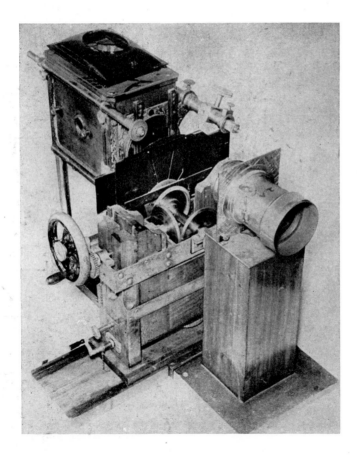

Zoogyroscope. Motion-picture projector invented 1880 by Muybridge for showing sequence photographs made on glass discs. Courtesy George Eastman House.

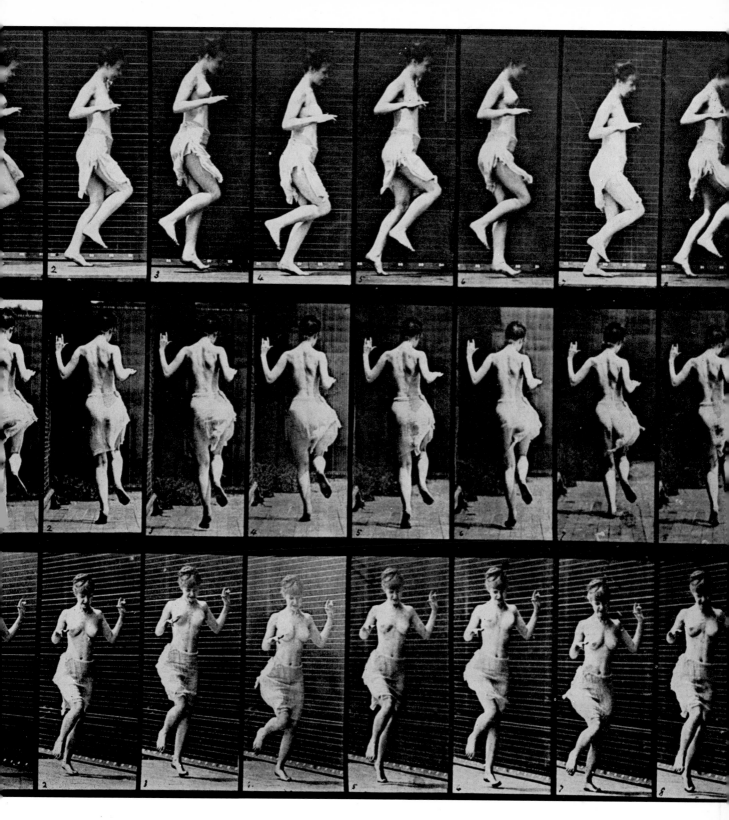

MUYBRIDGE, Figure Hopping. 1887. *Sequence of eight stages of movement, simultaneously photographed by multiple cameras at three different positions. Courtesy Cooper Union Museum Library, New York.*

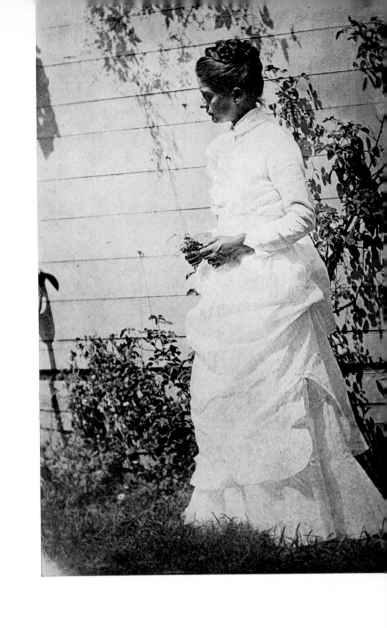
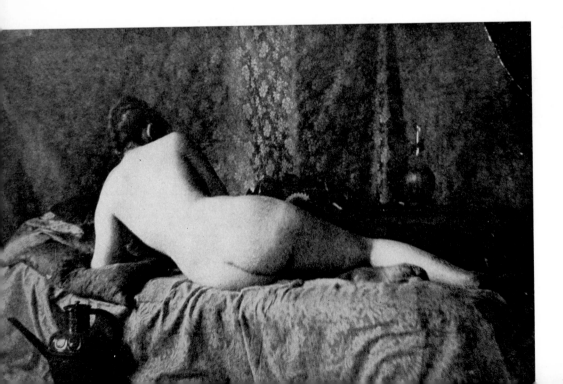

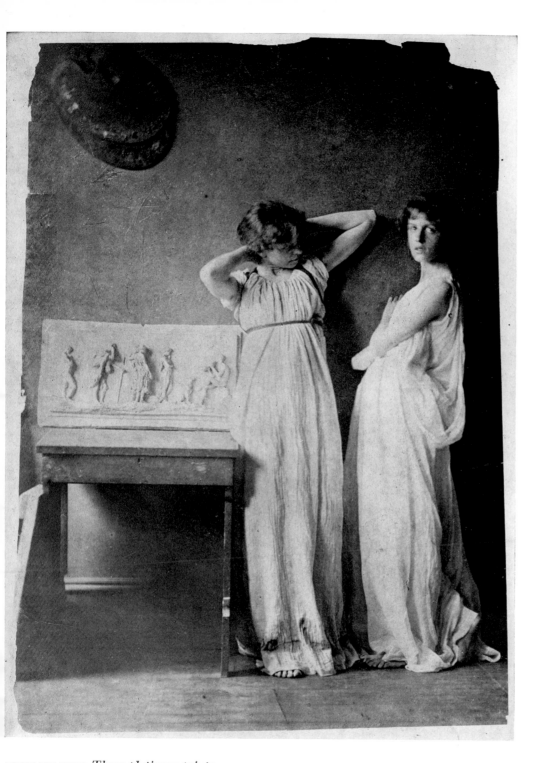

THOMAS EAKINS. *Three platinum prints.*
Courtesy Metropolitan Museum of Art, New York.
above: Two Girls in Greek Dress. *About 1880.*
opposite page, above: Portrait of Mary Macdowell.
About 1886. Sister of Mrs. Eakins.
left: Nude Model. *About 1880.*

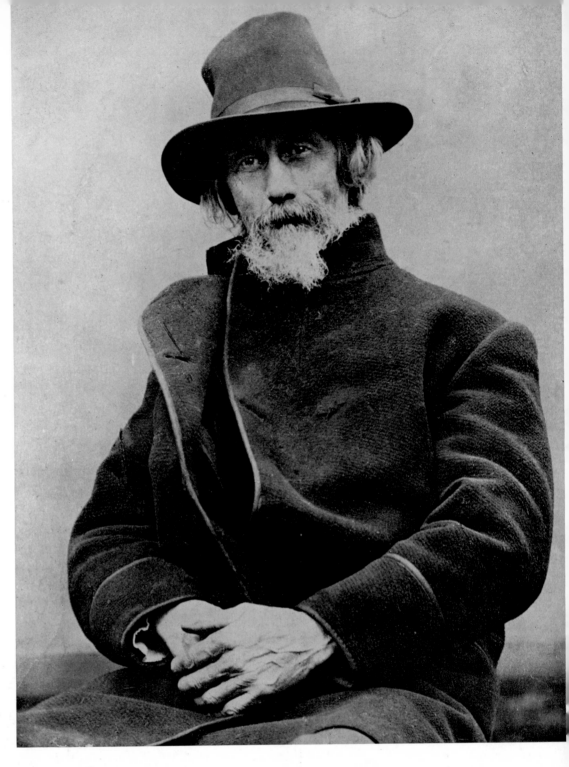

EAKINS
above: Portrait of William H. Macdowell. *Albumen
print. About 1890. Macdowell, an engraver, was father-in-law
of the artist. Courtesy Metropolitan Museum of Art.
opposite page, above:* Portrait of William H. Macdowell.
*Oil painting, 1891. Courtesy Randolph-Macon Woman's
College, Lynchburg, Virginia.*

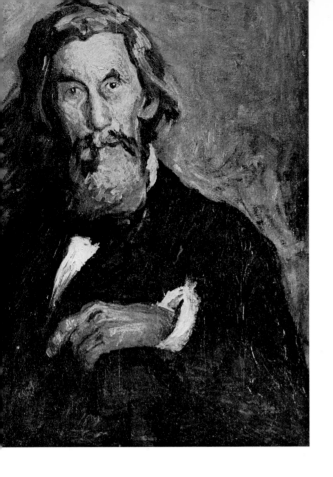

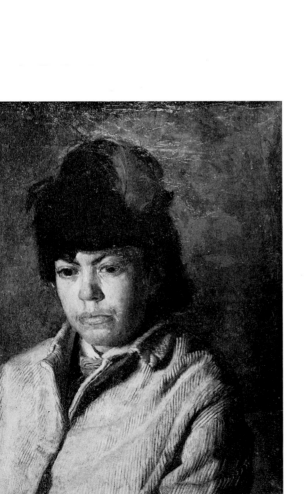

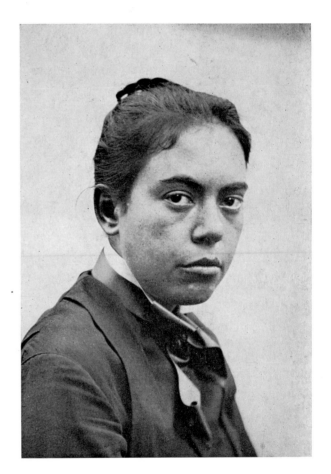

EAKINS

above: Portrait of Margaret Eakins. *Glass positive,*
1882. Courtesy Metropolitan Museum of Art.
left: Margaret in Skating Costume. *Oil painting,*
1871. Courtesy Philadelphia Museum of Art.

221

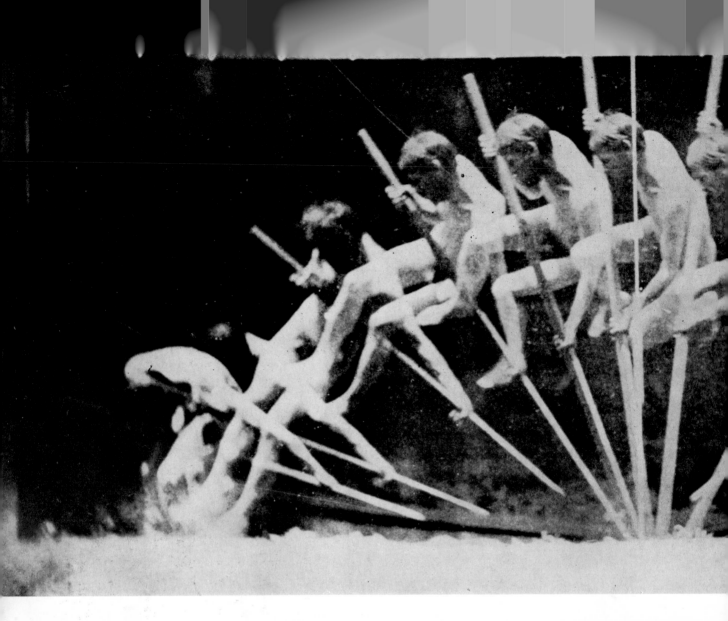

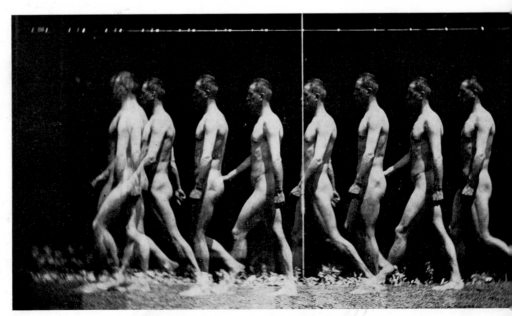

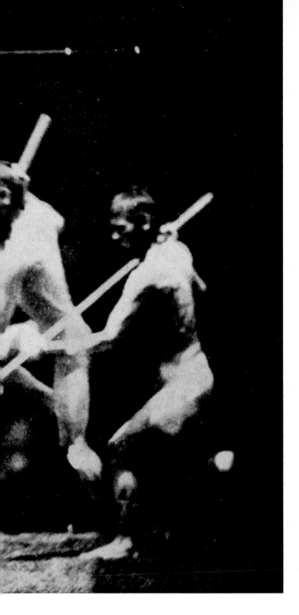

EAKINS
left: Pole Vaulter. *Wet-plate photograph, 1884.*
Courtesy Metropolitan Museum of Art.
below, left: Man Walking. *Wet-plate photograph,*
1884. Courtesy George Eastman House.

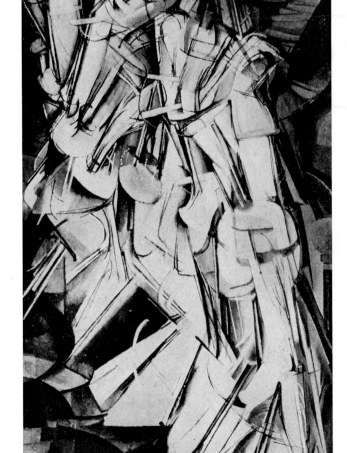

MARCEL DUCHAMP, Nude Descending a Staircase.
Oil painting, 1912. Philadelphia Museum of Art.
The Louise and Walter Arensberg Collection.

CHAPTER 19

Footlights, Skylights, and Tintypes

THERE WERE MORE THAN THREE HUNDRED photographers' galleries in New York City alone by 1870. Brady was still there, though he was soon to close his establishment on Broadway in order to concentrate on his Washington practice; Gurney's widely known gallery flourished, and that of Frederick, his former partner; but the three most elegant galleries in New York operating in the seventies were those of Napoleon Sarony, William Kurtz, and José Maria Mora.

All three—like Falk, who opened his gallery a decade later—specialized in photographing celebrated actors and actresses. Their pictures of the glamorous and beautiful in turn attracted society women and first-nighters to their studios. A considerable profit was enjoyed by all galleries in the sale of cabinet-size (4-by-5½-inch) and *carte-de-visite* (3¾-by-2¼-inch) portraits of the nation's prominent theatrical personalities, dressed in the costumes of their most popular roles. Each gallery accumulated thousands of negatives and sold innumerable pictures through the theater, hotels, the mail, and various other channels, paying a small royalty, if any, to the pictured actor or actress. The photographs were considered such good advertising by management and performer that a commission for posing was rarely exacted.

Of the three galleries, Sarony's was the best known, Mora's the most profitable, and Kurtz's the most artistic.

William Kurtz, born in Germany in 1834, was an artist-adventurer who had served his time as a boy with the German army and had fought with the English army during the Crimean War and with the Union Army in America's Civil War. In London he had been trained as a lithographic artist and had also taught art. Upon opening his New York gallery soon after the close of the Civil War, he introduced a method of lighting, modeling the subject's entire face through an arrangement of tinfoil reflectors, which became known as "Rembrandt" photography. A sensitive portrait photographer, Kurtz dispensed with elaborate or painted backgrounds, eliminated incongruous costumes, and used contrasty, simple backgrounds in order to secure as wide a range of tonality as possible with the wet-collodion process. The subtle Rembrandt photograph became enormously respected and popular among competent photographers, who were able to control and capture the nuances of lighting and modeling demanded by this style. Kurtz received many prizes for portrait photography, including the highest award of the International Exhibition, Vienna, in 1873.

José Maria Mora, born in Cuba in 1849, studied art and photography in Madrid, but received two years' additional training in the intricacies of the camera from Sarony before he opened his own gallery in 1870. Immediately he prospered, and became famous for his pictures of renowned actresses whom he posed with rich accessories in front of painted scenic backgrounds. Mora's reputation grew with his designs for his painted backgrounds. Soon he had hundreds of them standing one behind another ready to be used for any kind of effect from drawing room to log cabin, from desert to mountain top, with appropriate props to complete the picture.

L. W. Seavey introduced painted backgrounds for photographers; these quickly became standardized as accessories for the trade, along with automatic head supports, retouching machines, false pianos, balustrades, stairs, and chairs.

Photography's most famous chair was Napoleon Sarony's, in which consummate actors and actresses sat and played to his camera as to an immense audience. When the exact pose, the precise expression, was struck, the imperious five-foot-one-inch Napoleon, the same size as the Little Corporal and just as indomitable, hollered "Hold it," and for the 15 seconds to the 1 minute required, they all held it. Where other photographers forced the subject's head and body into vise-like clamps, asking them at the same time to "smile and look pleasant" (a cartoon of the period was captioned "You may resume your natural glum look in just a moment"), Sarony caught the actor in a pose best portraying a role without forced effects or awkward stiffness.

The warm, dramatic, and excitable personality of Sarony made a profound impression on his sitters. Those who did not respond or fall under his spell he refused to take at all or turned over to one of his assistants. Thomas Nast wrote, "He made everyone he photographed look like Sarony . . . the same feeling was in every picture . . . all his sitters seemed to catch the Sarony trick of expression and pose."

He worked hard to get a picture that satisfied him. He dressed up in a hussar's uniform. (His father had been an officer in the Black Hussars of the Austrian Army and had migrated after the battle of Waterloo to Quebec. There the future photographer had been born and named after Napoleon, whose death had taken place the same year, 1821.)

When Sarony photographed Jim Mace, the English pugilist, he sparred with the delighted champion until he had found a pose acceptable for the camera.

Sarony always complained that Sarah Bernhardt never arrived early enough to take advantage of the best light. He photographed her as the dying Camille—a representative pose, since, on her first American tour, in the eight plays she performed she was dead by the final curtain in six.

A few days after Oscar Wilde made his famous quip to the customs officer at New York's port of entry, "I have nothing to declare except my genius," he was standing in his get-up of knee breeches, although without the gilded lily he was wont to carry, in front of Sarony's camera.

Sarony photographed the elder Sothern as Lord Dundreary in *Our American Cousin*, the role he was performing at Ford's Theater the night Lincoln was shot. The ever-remembered Joe Jefferson, who played Rip Van Winkle off and on from 1859 to 1904, Sarony photographed posed before and after his long nap.

The many-times-married Adah Isaacs Menken, who loved dogs and "fed them cubes of sugar soaked in brandy and champagne," according to Mark Twain who watched her do it, came to Sarony's in London in 1864 when Napoleon worked there for his prosperous brother, Oliver, who ran a successful gallery and photograph supply house. In New York Sarony again photographed Adah Menken the year he opened his gallery in 1866. She posed in the elaborate costume she wore in *Mazeppa*, daringly exposing her legs and limbs in tights. At the climax of the play she was bound "naked" to the back of a wild horse "which galloped up a succession of runways to the top of the theater while audiences roared their tribute."

Showman and picturesque figure, Sarony printed his flowing signature in red ink on every size photograph that left his gallery, and across the facade of the five-story structure he painted his name in huge script. He stocked the building with a fantastic assortment of curios and antiques including stuffed birds, tattered tapestries, sleighs, sleds, altars, Buddhas, armor, and sculpture, over which an Egyptian mummy stood guard at the head of the slow-ascending hydraulic elevator just big enough to accommodate him and one customer. He picked from this theatrical treasure house the props he needed for his pictures.

In May 1896 Sarony sold at auction this tremendous hodge-podge curio collection. Six months later he was dead. Pall bearers were fellow members of the Tile Club, the reputable painters William M. Chase and Edward Moran, and the writer, F. Hopkinson Smith. Smith wrote a novel, *The Fortunes of Oliver Horn*, in which Sarony figured as the character Julius Bianchi; in it an artist-lithographer known to his fellow "skylarkers" as "the Pole" brings to the club a countess—obviously a takeoff inspired by Sarah Bernhardt.

Trained as an artist in Paris for six years before he turned to photography, Sarony continued to make lithographs and paint canvases all his life, puerile efforts resembling the commercial hack work of the period. Of his years spent in photography he complained, "all day long I must pose and arrange for these eternal photographs They will have me. Nobody but me will do . . . [but] all my art in the photograph I value as nothing."

If Sarony underestimated his life's work and displayed little pride in the art of his camera, the itinerant tintype "professor," the ever-present man with the black box at beach, carnivals, and congested streets, or located in

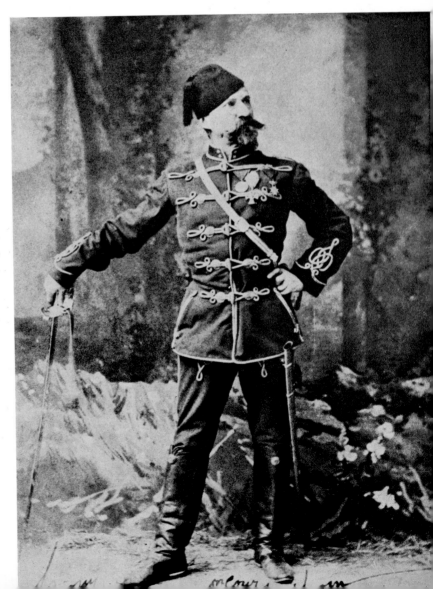

Napoleon Sarony in Hussar's Uniform.
Taken by Sarony's assistant, about 1870.
Courtesy George Eastman House, Rochester.

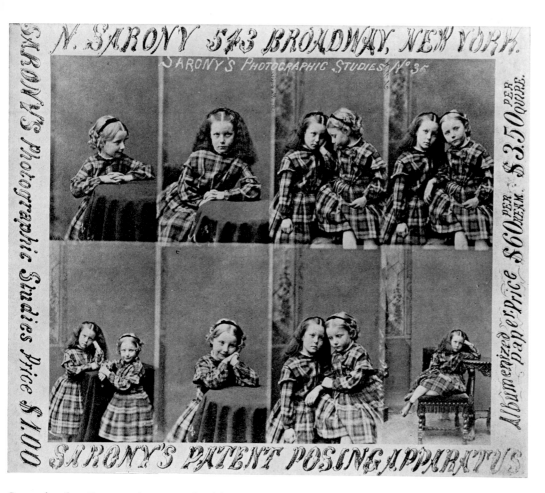

Sarony's advertisement for cartes de visite.
Courtesy Museum of the City of New York.

special tintype galleries near the board walks of the country, knew that the pictures he took on thin sheets of iron, lacquered and sensitized, had no artistic value at all. The whites came out a dull gray and, though black patent leather, oilcloth, and enameled papers were tried as substitutes, the cheap single positive picture on "tin" never lost its popularity. The results could be seen in a few minutes; the pictures were permanent; and, though easily scratched, they were less fragile than the more costly ambrotypes on glass. Assembled in a union case, the tintype became a family heirloom along with the earlier daguerreotypes.

Tintypes in miniature appeared on rings, brooches, tie pins, cufflinks, and were the first political buttons containing pictures of the candidates. A patent was granted for tintype photographs to be attached to tombstones.

The poor and lowly tintype was invented by Adolphe Alexandre Mestin, a Frenchman, in 1853, and patented two years later by an American, Hamilton L. Smith, who called them "melainotypes" from the prefix meaning black. They were also called "ferrotypes" meaning iron. They were introduced to Europe in the 1870s, and were advertised as American ferrotypes, mounted on a paper cutout, and sold more cheaply than any other existing photographic image. The distinctive tintype was fortunately preserved in a fancy, tooled album; so also were the enormously popular "gems," which measured less than an inch. Not considered art, tintypes preserved for our day the honest and untouched face of the unsophisticated who posed for this picture and not for public or posterity. The ingratiating, unique, and unidentified tintype image often captivates the spectator.

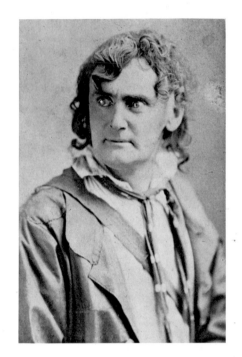

SARONY
Joe Jefferson as Rip van Winkle.
Before and after his long nap.
Cartes de visite, 1869. Courtesy
Cornelia Otis Skinner, New York.

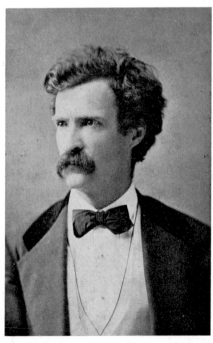

GURNEY. *Cartes de visite, 1870.*
right: Mark Twain.
far right: Edwin Booth.
Courtesy Cornelia Otis Skinner.

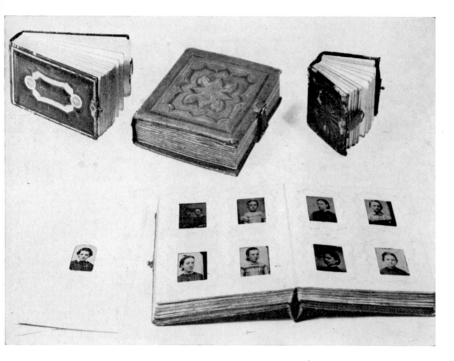

Miniature albums for the "gem" tintypes,
measuring 7/8 x 3/4 inches, about 1880.
Courtesy George Eastman House.

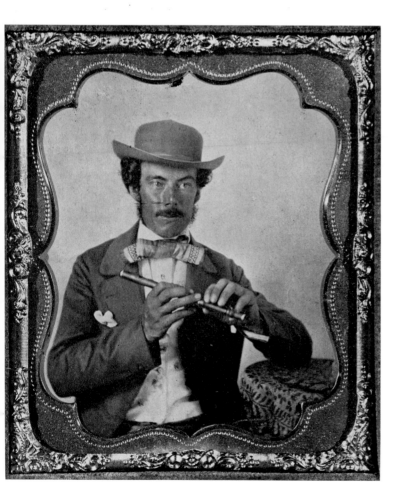

Two tintypes, about 1880. Photographers unknown,
Courtesy Metropolitan Museum of Art, New York.

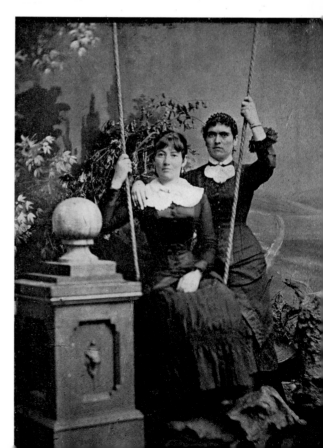

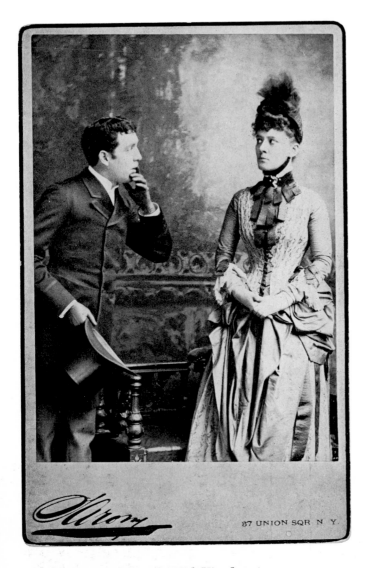

SARONY, Otis Skinner with Edith Kingdon
in a Daly Company Performance. 1885.
Courtesy Cornelia Otis Skinner.

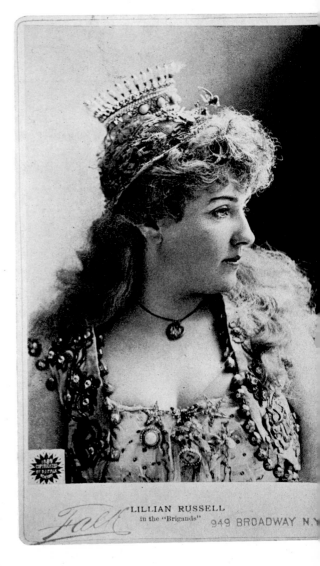

FALK, Lillian Russell.
Cabinet-size photograph, 1889
Courtesy George Eastman House.

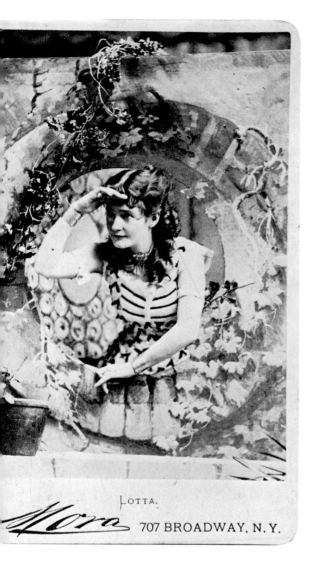

LOTTA.

Mora   707 BROADWAY, N.Y.

, Lotta Crabtree.
...et-size photograph, about 1885.
...tesy George Eastman House.

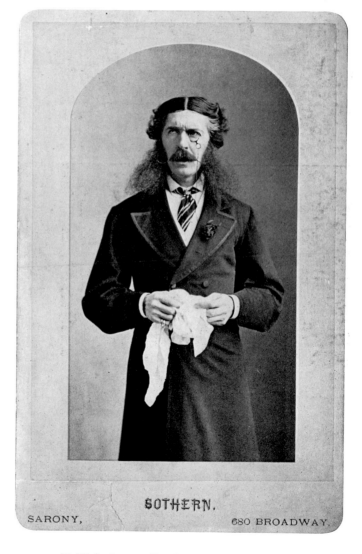

SOTHERN.

SARONY,   680 BROADWAY.

SARONY, E. H. Sothern as Lord Dundreary.
About 1885.
Courtesy Cornelia Otis Skinner.

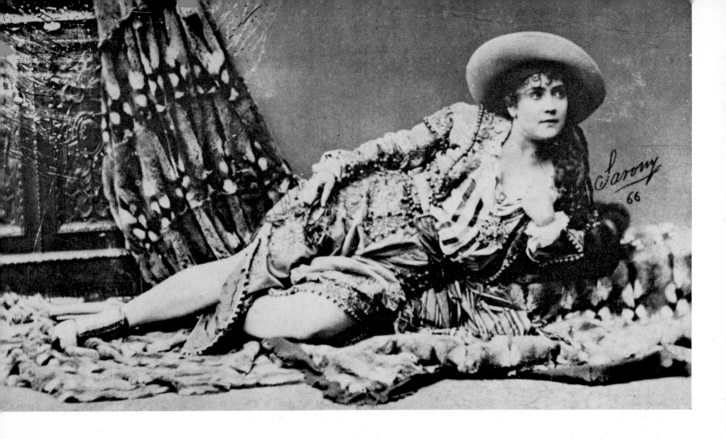

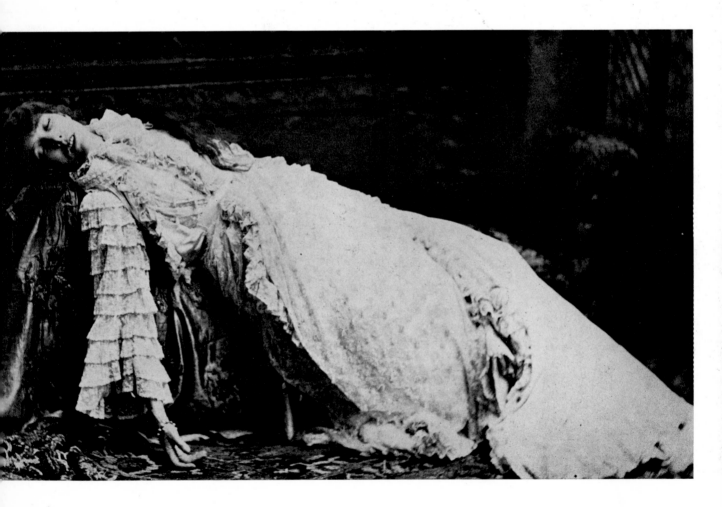

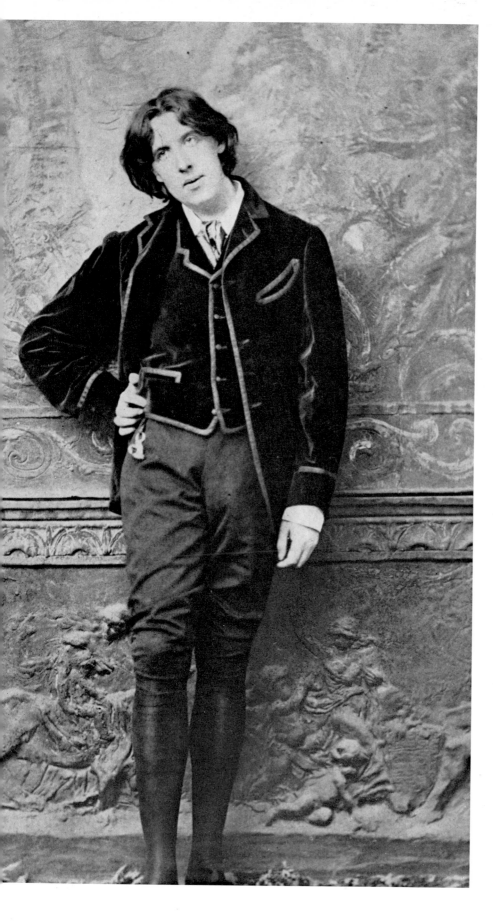

SARONY
left: Oscar Wilde. *1882*.
opposite page, above: Adah Isaacs
Menken in "Mazeppa." *1866*.
opposite page, below: Sarah
Bernhardt in "Camille." *1880*.
All three, courtesy
George Eastman House.

CHAPTER 20

The 'Detective' Camera and the Kodak

IN 1871 DR. RICHARD LEACH MADDOX, an English physician and amateur photographer, substituted gelatin for collodion. This new process, the gelatin-bromide dry plate, published on September 8 in the *British Journal of Photography*, permitted free use to all interested.

Unfortunately the first dry plates were slower than wet plates. The new invention was not generally adopted until 1878, when the improved, ready-made plates, by then faster than any other process, could be bought commercially, stored, exposed at will, and developed at leisure. Before 1880 most amateurs and practically all professional photographers had abandoned the unwieldy, messy, demanding collodion process in favor of the costlier but more advantageous dry plate.

A pioneer maker of gelatin dry plates in America was George Eastman, who worked during the day in a Rochester, New York, bank and at night coated glass plates by hand with the liquefied, sensitized gelatin. Eastman soon improved the uniformity of the plate by inventing a machine to do the coating. In 1879 he patented the machine in England and the following year secured a patent for the same invention in the United States. That same year E. and H. T. Anthony, the largest dealer of photographic materials in the country, were handling Eastman dry plates. Prices of cameras were cut as Anthony's advertised "dry-plate photography for the millions." A small 4-by-5 camera with a lens, a tripod, and a dozen Eastman dry plates, could be bought for as little as $12.25.

In 1881 Eastman left the bank to devote full time to his expanding dry-plate factory, which, throughout the previous winter, had been sending the packaged dry plates to Anthony's in anticipation of the spring and summer business. All these plates went bad. They quickly lost their sensitivity. Complaints poured in to Anthony, who sent them on to Eastman. His next move made him friends and staunch supporters among camera-men everywhere. First he located the cause of the trouble; then he replaced all defective plates with corrected ones.

During the next two years Eastman improved the plates, increasing the sensitivity of the emulsion and its stability in any kind of climate. Professional photographers swore by his products. He prospered. He built a larger plant and Anthony's looked forward to greater sales of Eastman's rapid gelatin plates.

Eastman continued his experiments, searching for a new system of photography to supersede the gelatin dry plate. He went back to using paper as a base and invented a machine to prepare and coat a roll of paper. After exposure and processing, the paper negatives were treated with castor oil to make them transparent—just as Fox Talbot's calotypes had been dipped in oil back in the early forties. These negatives did not compare with glass plates for clarity. Eastman then tried coating the paper with two layers of gelatin. After developing and fixing the bottom layer was dissolved in warm water, leaving the image on the sensitized upper layer of gelatin, which was then dried in contact with a sheet of heavier gelatin.

The greatest virtue of this new "American film," as Eastman called it, was its flexibility. A roll holder could be fitted to any existing camera, even one hand-held.

The fast dry plate of several years earlier had made possible the hand-held camera, thereby eliminating the tripod. Instantaneous photography was an actuality. The snapshot had come into its own. No longer was photography the field of the professional and the dedicated amateur willing to undergo the hardships demanded by the wet plate. Box cameras held in the hands of gumshoe amateurs trying to catch candid pictures gave the name

"detective cameras" to the strange box without bellows. Most of these were manufactured by the Scovill Manufacturing Company and by Anthony, companies which later merged to become Ansco. Some of this sleuthing was necessary if one wanted to be a candid-camera man. Social etiquette of the 1880s and 1890s would hardly sanction a stranger's approaching a person and asking him to pose; a formal introduction was obligatory just to ask for permission to photograph. Efforts to circumvent these difficulties led to strange solutions: detective cameras were disguised in a number of ways. Hidden in a derby hat one camera was advertised as a "practical secret camera that defies detection" and sold for 42 shillings in London. A Frenchman marketed a "detective camera" in the form of a pistol, strangely believing that the operator would go unnoticed pointing at a person what obviously appeared to be a gun. More discreet hidden camera instruments were fitted into binoculars, books, ready-for-mailing packages, coin boxes, canes, and cravats—the lens in the cravat camera masqueraded as a

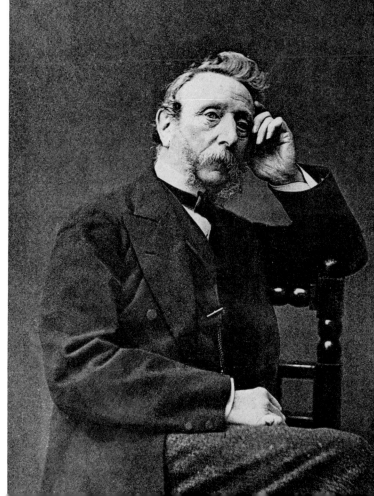

F. DEBENHAM, Dr. Richard L. Maddox. *Portrait, about 1880, of man who invented the gelatine dry plate in London, 1871. Courtesy George Eastman House, Rochester.*

stick pin, and the shutter was operated by a string or bulb held in the pocket.

Eastman in 1886 designed and patented a box camera with a standard roll holder for forty-eight 4″-by-5″ negatives, a focusing lens, and what he termed an "alligator shutter," but it did not work too well. Two years later he developed the perfect amateur camera of its day and coined a word which has been synonymous with "camera" ever since, "Kodak." The Kodak was a small box, a little over 6 inches long, 3½ inches wide, and less than 4 inches high. Anyone could operate it who, according to the Kodak Manual, was able to: 1. Point the camera. 2. Press the button. 3. Turn the key. 4. Pull the cord.

The No. 1 Kodak was not a pinhole camera. It was fitted with a lens and masked to take a circle negative 2¼ inches in diameter. One hundred negatives were on the roll. When the roll was fully exposed the entire camera was mailed back to Eastman, who returned the camera reloaded plus the negatives and one hundred mounted prints (or as many as were not blanks) from the first roll, all for the sum of $10. The original outlay was $25 for the first loaded camera. Every purchaser became an avid amateur.

It was George Eastman's slogan, "You press the button, we do the rest," that accounted for what was to become the first world-wide folk art.

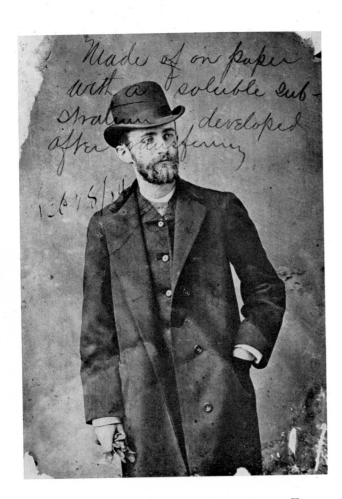

George Eastman. 1884. *Photographer unknown. Eastman made this print on his new film, February 8, 1884, and wrote "Made on paper with a soluble substratum developed after transferring." Signed across the lapels. Courtesy George Eastman House.*

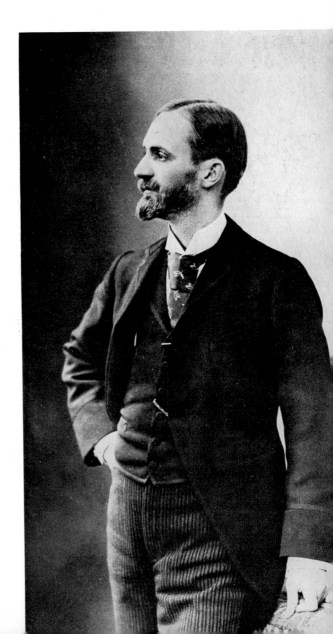

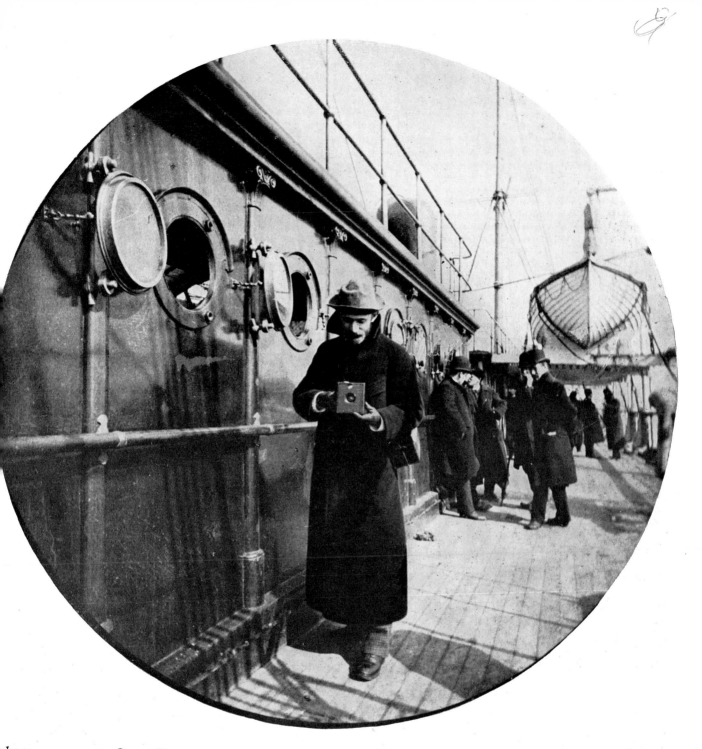

above: FRED CHURCH, George Eastman on Board Ship.
Taken 1890 with No. 1 Kodak identical with one Eastman holds in his hands.
left: PAUL NADAR, George Eastman. Paris, 1890.
Both, courtesy George Eastman House.

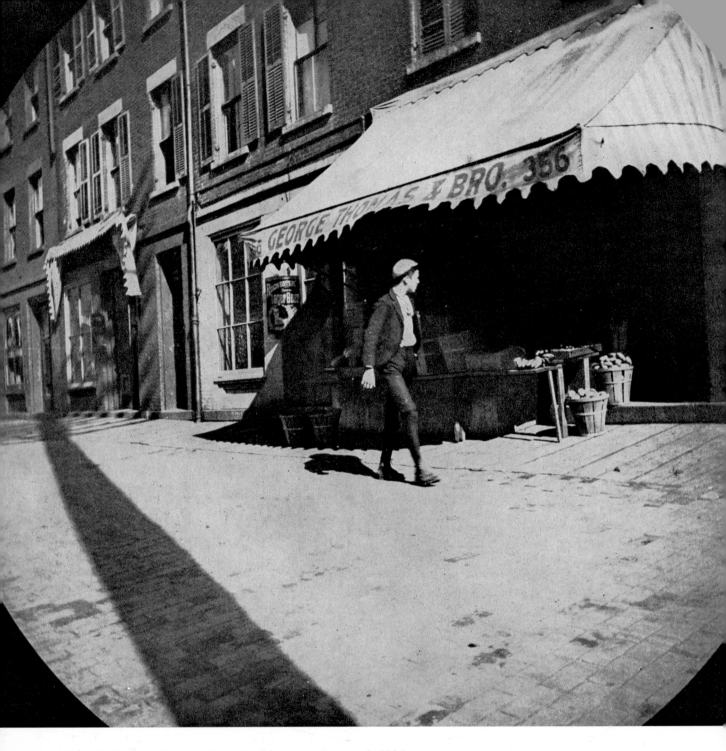

*above: Enlarged print from No. 1 Kodak camera, invented 1888 by
George Eastman, original size 2½ inches diameter. Photographer unknown.*

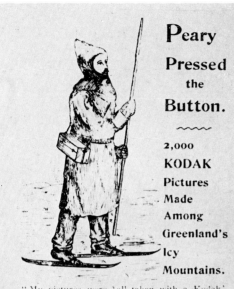

P
Pressed
the
Button.

~~~

2,000
KODAK
Pictures
Made
Among
Greenland's
Icy
Mountains.

" My pictures were 'all taken with a Kodak'
and I regard the Kodak as responsible for my
having obtained a series of pictures which in
quality and quantity exceed any that have been
brought back from Greenland and the Smith
Sound region.

R. E. PEARY, U. S. N.

EASTMAN KODAK CO.,
Rochester, N.Y.

left: Eastman Kodak Company advertisement, 1892.
below, left: Model No. 1, Kodak camera, 1888.
A circular negative on roll film was used.
below: "Hat" detective camera, about 1889,
for sale in London at two guineas, with fitting.
All, courtesy George Eastman House.

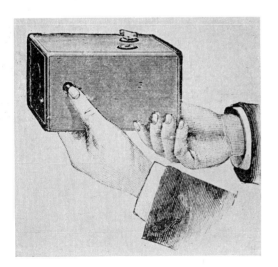

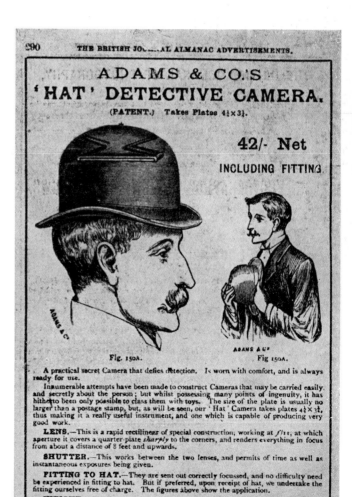

290   THE BRITISH JOURNAL ALMANAC ADVERTISEMENTS.

ADAMS & CO.'S
'HAT' DETECTIVE CAMERA.
(PATENT.) Takes Plates 4¼×3¼.

42/- Net
INCLUDING FITTING

Fig. 150A.   Fig 150A.

A practical secret Camera that defies detection. Is worn with comfort, and is always
ready for use.

Innumerable attempts have been made to construct Cameras that may be carried easily
and secretly about the person; but whilst possessing many points of ingenuity, it has
hitherto been only possible to class them with toys. The size of the plate is usually no
larger than a postage stamp, but, as will be seen, our 'Hat' Camera takes plates 4¼×3¼,
thus making it a really useful instrument, and one which is capable of producing very
good work.

LENS.—This is a rapid rectilinear of special construction, working at $f/11$, at which
aperture it covers a quarter-plate *sharply* to the corners, and renders everything in focus
from about a distance of 8 feet and upwards.

SHUTTER.—This works between the two lenses, and permits of time as well as
instantaneous exposures being given.

FITTING TO HAT.—They are sent out correctly focussed, and no difficulty need
be experienced in fitting to hat. But if preferred, upon receipt of hat, we undertake the
fitting ourselves free of charge. The figures above show the application.

WEIGHT.—The Camera alone weighs 2½ ozs. only. It is not necessary to carry
the lens and shutter, as this may be immediately placed in position by a bayonet joint.
Even with lens and shutter, the weight is only 3½ ozs. A Focussing Screen is also
supplied, and one Dark Slide.

Price £2 2s. net, including fitting.

Extra Dark Slides, 4/- each. A neat leather case is supplied for the lens and shutter.

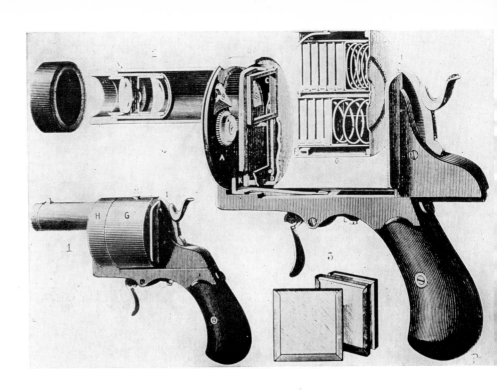

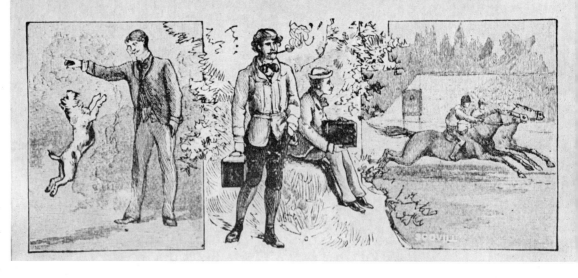

above: Detective cameras for sale in 1886
by the Scovill Manufacturing Company.
top: A pistol camera for candid photographs,
about 1888. Both, courtesy George Eastman House.

PART THREE

Masters of the Modern Era

CHAPTER 21
Photography Comes of Age

"FROM NOW ON, painting is dead!" exclaimed Paul Delaroche, painter of portraits and historical subjects, when Daguerre's new process bursts upon an astonished world.

Delaroche's shock tells us a great deal about why French artists invented photography. They invented it to satisfy a driving inner need. They had been trying to do something in painting—almost succeeding, moreover —that the camera was better fitted for.

Let us take a first-class painted portrait of the few years just before Daguerre's invention, deprive it of its colors, and shrink its scale to that of a daguerreotype. The result is the illustration opposite these words. And then let us compare this picture with another just below: an illustration of a first-class early daguerreotype portrait. These two pictures look very much alike. What do they have in common? An ideal that can be summed up in the phrase "truth to nature." Unvarnished truth: a precise, detailed, and accurate description. And naturalness: the record of a patterning born, not made; the chance result of a movement in nature rather than the artificial product of human calculation. Neither image, of course, realized this intention completely. The painter could not turn himself into a machine; and the machine could not refuse to obey the will of its master. Ingres's portrait of Monsieur Bertin has more personality and psychological insight than the portrait of Daguerre by Monsieur Blot. But the

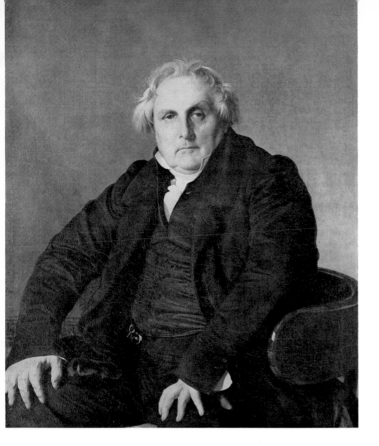

J.-A.-D. INGRES, Louis Bertin.
Oil Painting, 1832.
Courtesy The Louvre.

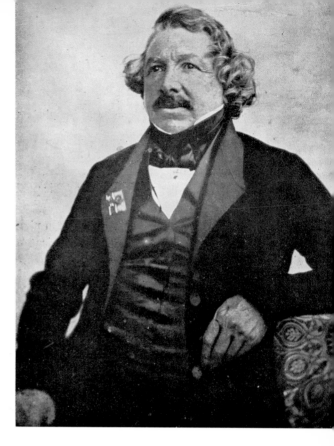

JEAN-BAPTISTE SABATIER BLOT
Daguerre. *Daguerreotype, 1844.*
Courtesy George Eastman House.

same cannot be said for portraits in the same basic style by some of Ingres's very skillful but also very literal and rather unimaginative followers. Except for having color, such work had no advantage over the daguerreotype. In time, portrait painting became a vestigial art and professional portrait painters little more than fashionable hacks. There were great portraits by great painters, let it be said. But they were no longer portraits in the traditional sense, and certainly not precise, detailed, and accurate descriptions. Portraits by Van Gogh and Cézanne were, on the one hand, records of the artist's inner, personal feelings about his sitter, and, on the other, structures built of harmony, form, and color. The intentions of these artists in making portraits were as far from Ingres's as from Daguerre's.

The art of painting did not die when a machine satisfied some of the painters' needs—far from it. But it did take a new turning. The art of photography proved more conservative. Born of painting, it remained tied to its mother art for half a century and longer, depending upon painting for its avowed aesthetic standards even while its own were beginning to develop and grow. It took time for photographers to discover the natural vocabulary and grammar of the new system of image making; and meanwhile the traditional aesthetic standards inherited from painting bore down upon them heavily. Thus, the major photographers of the Victorian era did not see photography as a basic medium of art and did not explore their medium to its limits. Or, if they did explore it in this way, as Muybridge and Eakins did in their studies of motion (see page 216) they were taken up by its scientific aspects, and were unaware of the fact that they had come upon a new world of forms. Photography, thus, was not to emerge as a full-fledged independent art until shortly before 1900. It then developed at an ever-mounting rate, spinning off new modes of visual communication and new ways of creative seeing.

Photography as conscious art, in the Europe of 1860 to 1890, was the "art photography" concocted by Rejlander and Robinson at mid-century. In style and in spirit, as

243

we have seen, it was enmeshed in the stubborn conservatism and heavy sentimentality of the academic painting that its practitioners imitated and revered. In America at that time there was no interest in photography as art. American photographers were far too engrossed in making likenesses of our great-grandfathers and recording the wonders of the American West. They were exposed to the ideas and images of the European pictorialists through the wistful efforts of photographic publications, but responded to them not at all.

A new questing spirit entered European photography in the 1880s on the heels of the convenient "dry-plate process for the millions." The entrenched and conservative professional photographers, who followed Henry Peach Robinson's rules of "art photography" as though they had been laid down by heaven to endure for all time, were now challenged by an army of forward-looking amateurs eager to experiment with their new-found medium. Rejecting the sterile academism of the professionals, the new men of photography found artistic kinship in contemporary Impressionism. The energies of the movement were to carry photography beyond the point where it was necessary to depend upon the vision of another medium; and photography would soon begin to speak in its own voice.

Peter Henry Emerson, an American physician living in London, was the initiator of the bold new movement. The camera had its own rules, Emerson said, and it was the photographer's glorious task to discover them. At first he was a champion of soft-focus photography. It corresponded to natural vision, he wrote in his *Naturalistic Photography*, and was surpassed as an art only by painting. He reversed himself after becoming convinced by Whistler that he was confusing art with nature. Emerson then published a black-bordered pamphlet entitled *Death of Naturalistic Photography, a Renunciation*. A master of vituperation, he defined "photographic Impressionist" as "a term consecrate to charlatans and especially to photographic impostors, pickpockets, parasites and vanity-intoxicated amateurs." He called attention to the limitations of photography. "The individuality of the photographer is cramped . . . ," he wrote. "Control of the picture is possible to a slight degree . . . the powers of selection and rejection are fatally limited . . . it is impossible in most subjects to alter your values as you wish...." In discussing the issue of sharpness versus diffusion, he wrote: "If the work is for scientific purposes work sharply, if for amusement please yourself, if for business do what will pay."

It is unnecessary either to agree or disagree with what Emerson was saying in order to realize that he was launching a great photographic revolution. He was doing nothing less than initiating straight photography, if only in the realm of ideas. But it was not only in the realm of ideas. This man practiced what he preached. Turning away from second-hand images, he scanned his surroundings for patterns and structures that evoked a sense of peaceful commerce between man and nature. Learning how to see, he let the camera do the talking. The impressive results can be seen here in three serene, delicate, and firmly composed man-and-nature scenes from the beautiful lagoons of the Norfolk Broads, all taken in the 1880s.

In 1892, in company with other earnest amateurs, Emerson formed the Linked Ring, an international group dedicated to photography as art. One of its members was Frank Sutcliffe, whose *Water Rats* of 1896 was a marvelous revelation of what could be done with a camera. Evoking the poetry in modern urban-industrial life, this photo prefigured the paintings of Luks, Sloan, and other American painters of the Ashcan School a decade or two later. Another member of the Linked Ring was the extremely talented Frederick H. Evans, who took up photography rather late in life. Evans made large-format views of English and French cathedrals impressive for clean sense of space and texture and grasp of architectural forms. He also made straight-forward and unsentimental but extremely sensitive portraits of his friends and admirers Aubrey Beardsley and George Bernard Shaw. (Shaw himself was an enthusiastic amateur photographer—of the soft-focus school—and a brilliant writer on the subject of photography.) In 1900 Edward Steichen called Evans's work "the most beautiful rendering of architecture we have ever known," and in 1903 Alfred Stieglitz wrote, "He stands alone in architectural photography." In 1967 Eastman House organized a traveling exhibition of 41 of Evans's original platinum prints, including portraits, architectural subjects, and scenes of the English countryside. Evans loved platinum paper for its great delicacy and permanence. The star print of the show, perhaps, was *Sea of Steps*, 1903, an interior view of the chapter house of Wells Cathedral. "The beautiful curve of the steps," Evans wrote of it, ". . . is for all the world like the surge of a great wave. . . . It is one of the most imaginative lines it has been my good fortune to try and depict. . . ." In calling his own purposes "the straightest of straight photography," Evans gave a name to the great mainstream of the photographic currents of the past seventy-five years.

Around 1900, the center of gravity of photography as

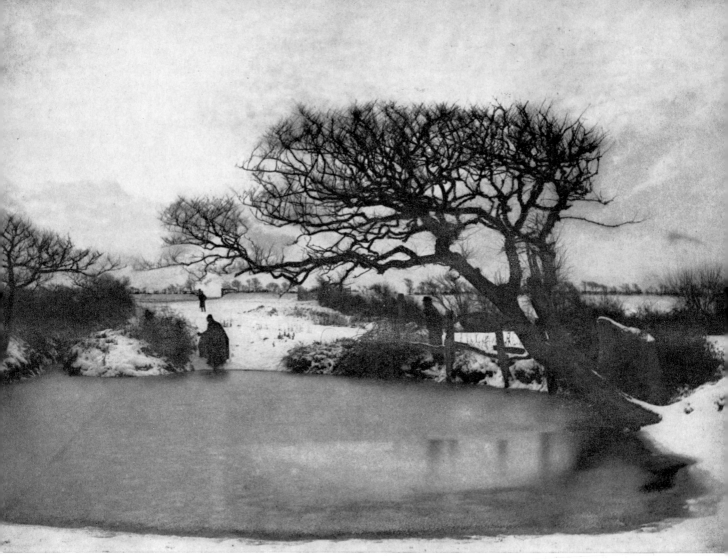

PETER HENRY EMERSON, Pond in Winter. 1888.
Courtesy George Eastman House.

art traveled westward to the United States, where Alfred Stieglitz became the leading figure in photography's coming of age. There were at least two greatly gifted photographers in America when Stieglitz returned there in 1890 after eight years of European training: Eakins and Riis. But Eakins' photographs were to all intents and purposes unknown, and Riis's artistry was unrecognized, least of all by Riis himself.

Many young men, most notably Edward Steichen, Clarence White, and Alvin L. White, joined Stieglitz in what eventually became the Photo-Secession group, a New York counterpart of London's Linked Ring. Their struggles to break with the past began well behind the advanced position of the Linked Ring, however. Like Emerson, they took inspiration from Whistler, but, un-

like Emerson, from Whistler's paintings and etchings rather than from his ideas about photography. They found Whistler's Japanese-print-derived "arrangements" and misty nocturnes thoroughly irresistible and these qualities sometimes became more important in their work than the subjects they were photographing. Their ideals took shape in soft focusing, intense whites, and deep, velvety black shadows on strongly textured papers. Whistler's butterfly monogram was emulated; so were his pastel-colored mounts and distinctive Art Nouveau gold frame.

The new gum-bichromate process enabled the photographer to become a painter of a kind, for he could apply sensitized silver salts with a brush, build up weak areas, or wash away undesired details. Photographs came to

245

resemble charcoal drawings, mezzotints, and water-colors. A Frenchman who adopted the gum-bichromate process, Robert Demachy, claimed in an article published in Stieglitz's quarterly magazine *Camera Work* that there was "no limit to what the photographer can do to make a photograph a work of art. . . . Meddling with a gum print may or may not add the vital spark, though without the meddling there will surely be no spark whatever."

Edward Steichen and Clarence White produced gum prints of such splendor between 1900 and the outbreak of World War I as almost to confirm the correctness of Demachy's judgment; and Stieglitz was to say in 1902 that it was "justifiable to use any means upon a negative or paper to attain the desired end." Stieglitz's statement was by no means the equivalent of Demachy's. Stieglitz did not wish to limit photography as art to manipulated images. He wished it to flex its muscles, to burst its chains, to find out what the limits of photography were and then to exceed those limits. The task of the photographer, he felt, was to experiment and explore. He himself experimented with various types of manipulation, the gum process included. But almost all the photos he made up to the last minute of his life were straight as straight could be: the subject itself, unmannered, unmanipulated, not even cropped, and seemingly live and breathing. And, through his ceaseless experimentation, he left his touch on almost every phase of modern photography: the incisive psychological portrait, the revealing social document, the aspect of nature not grasped by the unaided eye, and the poetry of the urban-industrial environment.

The key to how the Photo-Secessionists shaped and were to shape the course of the art of photography was not their early infatuation with a soft-focus aesthetic but rather their questing spirit and the reaffirmation of the goal of "truth to nature" that gave photography its original impulse. The aesthetic changed but the questing spirit did not. The first half of the twentieth century became the great classic era of photography; and men whom we first meet as painting-bound pictorialists led the way in bringing it to an astonishing height of technical perfection, to a sweeping variety of visual image and visual idiom, to a great depth of penetration and unprecedented communicative power.

Alvin L. Coburn, a founding member of Photo-Secession, began as early as 1913 to go beyond the familiar world of forms to which photographers had limited themselves and enter the extended world of large-scale forms available to the camera. One of his pictures made in that year is *The Octopus* (see page 341), a view of New York's Central Park and also a revelation of the abstract pattern that the camera, through a sharply angled bird's-eye perspective, could discover in such a place. This picture antedates Moholy-Nagy's *Radio Tower* (see page 340) by fifteen years. An equally extraordinary spatial effect is produced by *Roofs of Paris*. Here Alvin Coburn has anticipated Andreas Feininger (compare page 601). His image not only reveals abstract pattern and expressively compressed space but warns us that not too long hence cities will begin to strangle on buildings, traffic, and humanity.

Steichen, another original Photo-Secessionist, split precise technical control of tonal and sharpness values into a thousand calibrated intervals, photographing a white cup and saucer more than a thousand times.

Stieglitz explored the camera's capability of isolating details in nature and thereby exposing abstract patterns.

During the fertile decade defaced by the outbreak of World War I, these developers and expanders of human vision were joined by outstanding recruits to their cause of photography as art. Among them was Paul Strand, whose honesty and intensity of vision was no less than theirs. His sense of poetry in the immediate environment was also a good match for that of his elders and his sense of the poetic values latent in machine civilization was, if anything, greater. Strand was, and is, a superb craftsman—linked with the platinum-paper enthusiasts of the turn of the century through his insistence upon that extremely flexible printing medium so long as it remained on the market. He used platinum paper to achieve tonal delicacy and fully described detail. But, in spite of his concern for *matière*—the material quality of the print aside from what was being photographed—Strand looked to the subject itself for the poetic vision he wished to evoke.

Strand's vision of photography as subject-rooted exploration of reality was adopted around 1915 by his exact contemporary Charles Sheeler, who was influenced in the new direction by the example of modern art, especially Cubism. Sheeler, a photographer of architecture for his bread and butter, in 1913 rented a Bucks County farmhouse where, on weekends, he could follow the career of painting for which he had been trained. He was fascinated by the strong forms of Bucks County barns, which he saw as patterns of cleanly defined intersecting planes, photographing and painting them with the precision of a scientist and the sensibility of a poet. He made photographs of African primitive sculptures and of industrial scenes, and, in 1921, collaborated with Paul

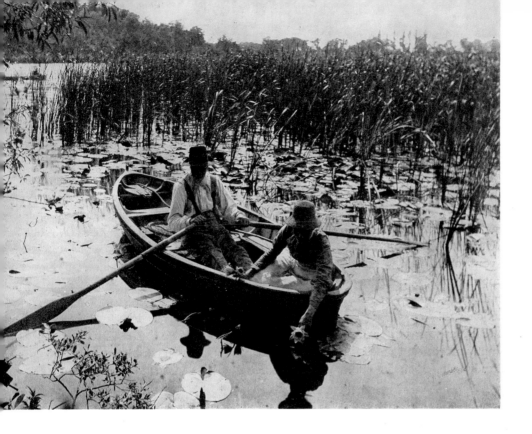

EMERSON
above: Gathering Water Lilies. 1866.
below: Gunner Working up to Fowl. 1886.
Both Courtesy George Eastman House.

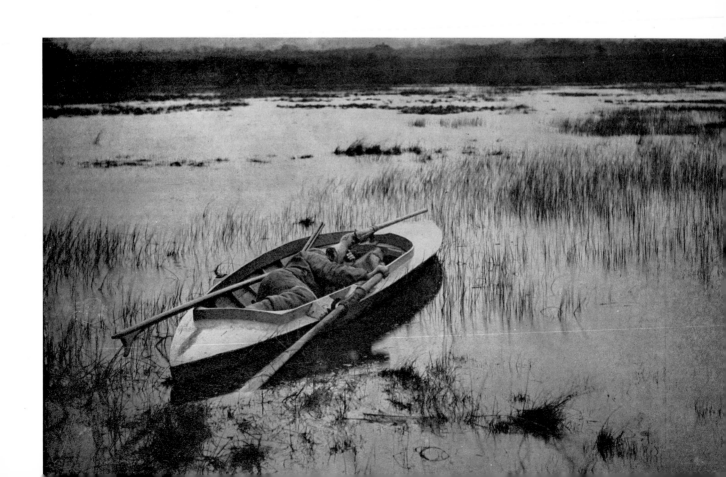

Strand in creating the film *Manhatta*, which proclaimed the pride, energy, scale, and geometric order of the modern urban metropolis. This joint effort was instrumental in securing Sheeler a Ford Motor Company assignment to photograph the huge River Rouge plant and its workings. Few images of the industrial scene can match Sheeler's River Rouge images for majesty and power.

Few new talents appeared in Europe during the years that marked the advent of Strand and Sheeler; the young men of the Old World were again at war. The novel spirit in photography continued to be represented by such veterans as Emerson and Evans. Unheralded and unsung, Eugène Atget (q.v.) — two years older than Emerson—was making a vast and uncompromisingly real report on Paris's streets, streetwalkers, windows, courtyards, street hawkers, and corner circuses.

New European talents, however, appeared in vast numbers in the 1920s and promptly proceeded to make up for lost time. The spirit already manifest in Strand and Sheeler began to appear in Germany in the photographs of the *Neue Sachlichkeit*—the New Realism movement—notably in the straightforward, unretouched, aggressively close-up views of objects of our common perception. Some of the best of these were taken by Albert Renger-Patsch and August Sander.

The German Christian Schad, the Hungarian Laszlo Moholy-Nagy, and the American expatriate Man Ray carried abstract photography into new creative realms and developed a means for making complex images on photographic papers and other sensitized materials without the use of a camera. The scope of photography was further extended by the advent of the 35-millimeter Leica camera in 1925, with its big, fast lens, high-speed shutter, and fine-grain film, which could withstand considerable enlargement and still retain its clarity. Dr. Erich Salomon made split-second use of his miniature camera (he first used little glass plates, not film) to catch statesmen and celebrities with their guard down. The excitement

FRANK SUTCLIFFE, Water Rats. *1896. Courtesy George Eastman House.*

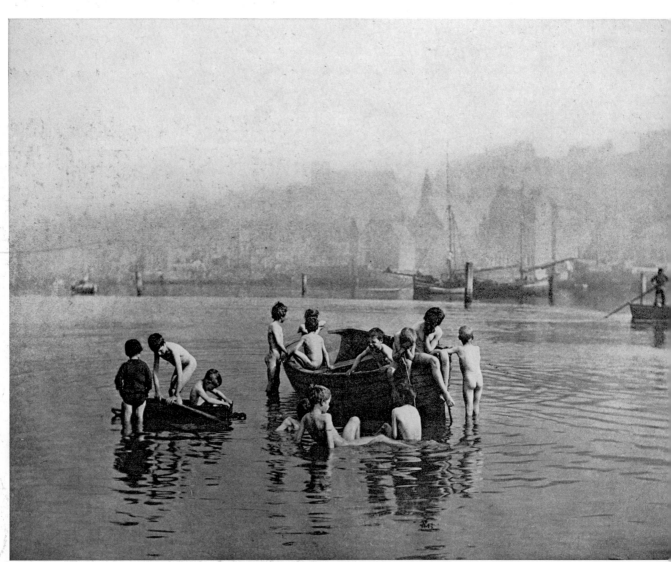

and immediacy of unposed "candid" photography thus became a new and prized quality of magazine photography; and the picture-viewing public delighted in plain-as-day evidence that the great and powerful were only human beings after all. A pioneer photojournalist and master of photography as art appeared in the person of André Kertesz. His work inspired Brassai and Cartier-Bresson, to whom, somehow, he communicated his own gift for grasping that special micromoment in which some human action revealed significance. In spite of the richness, breadth, and high achievement of European photography of the 1920s, however, the star exhibits of the tradition-shattering *Film und Foto* show held in Stuttgart, 1929, under the sponsorship of the Deutsche Werkbund, were the "straight" photographs of an American group. Among its members were Steichen, Sheeler, Imogen Cunningham, Berenice Abbott, and Edward Weston. The sharply defined and classically composed photographs of the Americans created a profound impression. In the face of such accomplishment it took a very brave or very stubborn man to deny that photography was now an art of the highest order.

The aesthetic beliefs of the Americans exhibiting at *Film und Foto* were written up for the official catalogue by Edward Weston. Those beliefs were stark honesty in the use of materials and equipment, absolute control over composition and tonal range, and reality so keenly sensed and so meticulously re-created that it was like seeing the world for the first time. Some of Weston's followers and a newcomer, Ansel Adams, who later gave these artistic imperatives detailed, quantitative expression, formed "Group f/64" to promote Weston's vision of photography. The vision represented by Group f/64 dominated serious photography during the 1930s, which, years of economic depression though they were, were also years of opportunity and challenge for photographers. The photographer's newly revealed power to make the grim facts of the political and social scene come to memorable life gave rise to the "documentary" photograph. The documentary became an extremely effective means of mass communications under Roy Stryker of the Farm Security Administration. All photographs are documents, of course, but the special and persistent meaning acquired by the word in the days of the New Deal has to do with the eloquent, imaginative interpretation of society in crisis. The FSA group of no more than a dozen photographers were equally dedicated to Roy Stryker's ideal, which might be described as Group f/64 vision in the service of revealing the human condition. The expressive extremes of this artistic fellowship were repre-

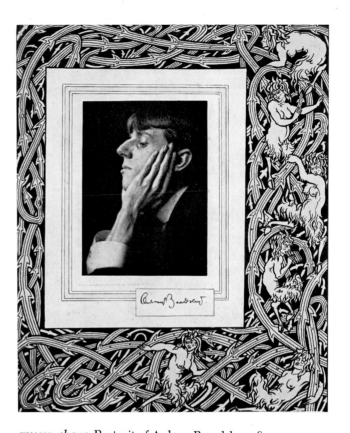

EVANS, *above:* Portrait of Aubrey Beardsley. 1894.
Courtesy Worcester Museum of Art.
below: Sea of Steps. 1903. *Chapter-house interior. Wells Cathedra*
Courtesy George Eastman House.

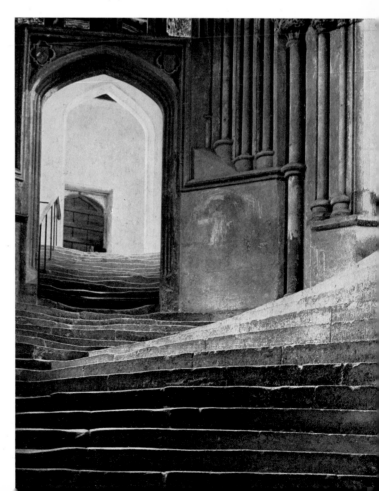

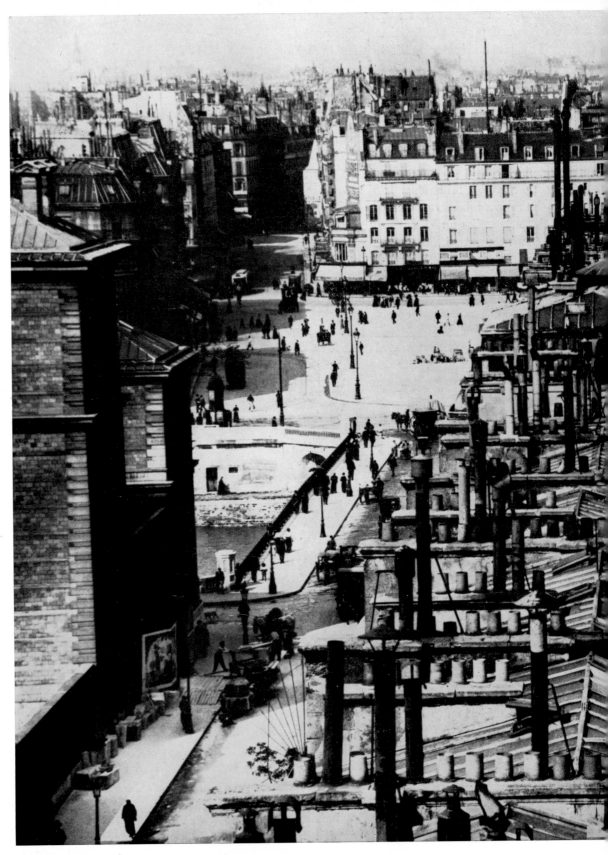

ALVIN L. COBURN,
Roofs of Paris. 1917.
Courtesy George Eastman House.

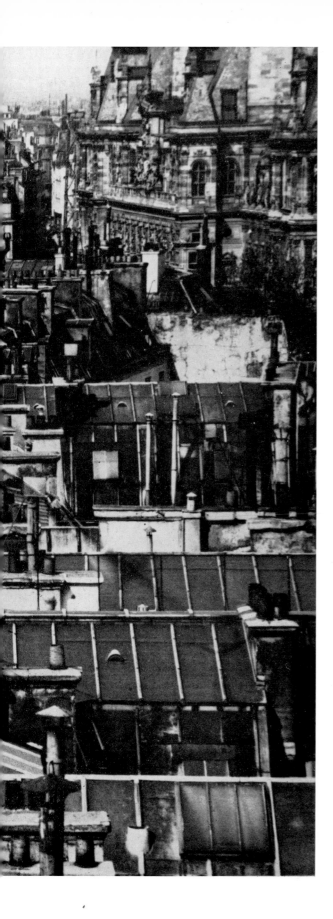

sented by the work of the recently deceased Dorothea Lange, on the one hand, and Walker Evans, on the other. Lange's warmth and human sympathy guided her camera toward the bewildered faces of migrant workers and their families; those faces tell us their stories with utter directness. The documentary photograph is no longer a novelty, but a major exhibition of Lange's work held by the Museum of Modern Art in New York a few years ago shows us that her great documentaries have lost none of their emotional impact during the past thirty years. Evans was a photographer of things and places, rather than people, and he photographed cities, shacks, cemeteries, and eroded land with almost clinical detachment and thoroughly brilliant technique. Of Walker Evans' photographs combined with James Agee's text into a book *Let Us Now Praise Famous Men*, the critic Lincoln Kirstein wrote, "The facts sing for themselves."

Other meritorious work was performed for the United States Government, particularly the Federal Art Project of the Works Progress Administration, for which Berenice Abbott interpreted New York City in depth with her camera. She was well prepared for this task, for she had been Man Ray's assistant and had also steeped herself in Atget's top-to-bottom depiction of Paris. The jewel-like images of Berenice Abbott's *Changing New York*, published in 1939, were a multileveled evocation of the heart and soul of this greatest of American cities. They were also an invaluable record of New York as it was before its postwar transformation at the hands of building wreckers and builders. Abbott moved on from interpretation of the urban scene to interpretation of the technical and scientific landscape, for which she has anatomized the bouncing of balls, the motion of machines, and the flight of birds.

The appearance of a new type of picture magazine in 1936 brought photography's prewar development to its final phase. *Life* magazine and the American public were made for each other, it seemed. Three of the infant publication's four staff photographers—Alfred Eisenstaedt, Thomas McEvoy, and Peter Stackpole—swept readers off their feet with brilliant displays of unposed candid camerawork, the most prized quality in press photography at that time. The remaining staff photographer, Margaret Bourke-White, realizing that the picture magazine would revolutionize mass communication, reached out for the idioms of a new visual language in her cover story of a dam-building colony for *Life's* first issue. She brought the photo essay to maturity in a single stroke; and, thus, modern photojournalism was born.

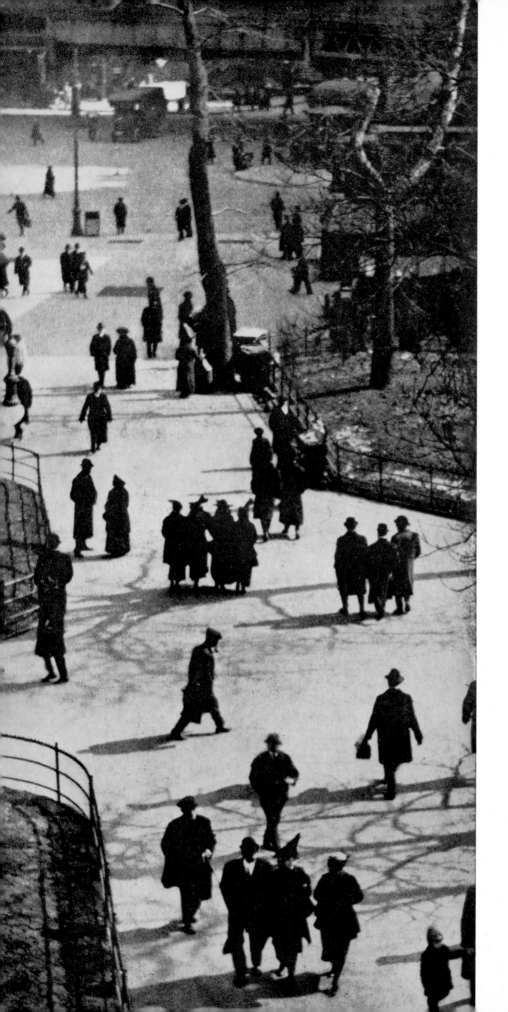

PAUL STRAND,
left: Morningside Heights. 1915.
opposite page:
above left: Blind. 1913.
above right: Christos. 1933.
below: The Family. 1953.
*All courtesy Museum
of Modern Art, New York.*

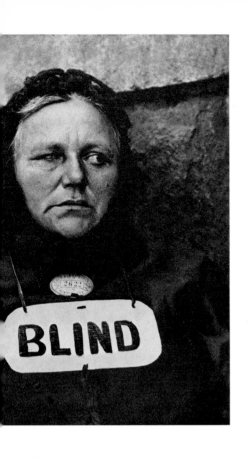
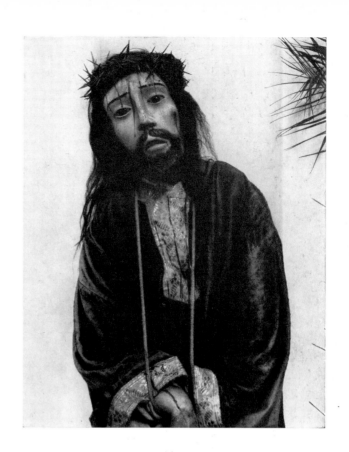
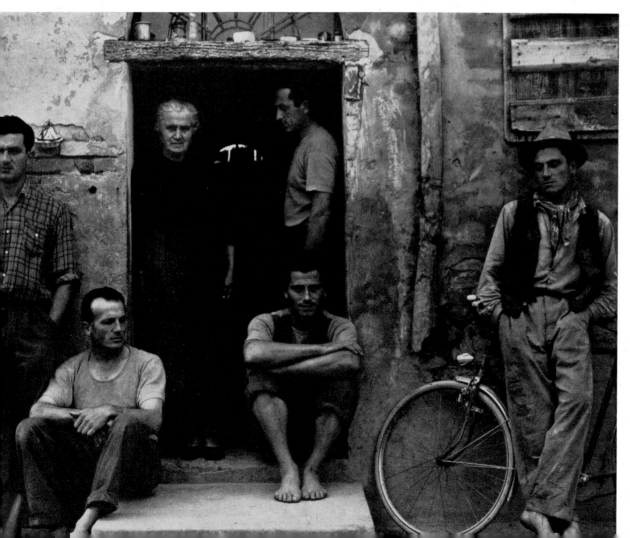

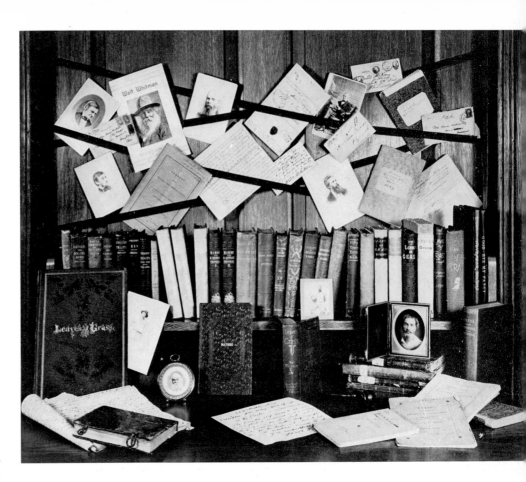

CHARLES SHEELER,
above: Whitmaniana. *About 1921.*
below: La Marseillaise. *About 1926.*
All courtesy Mrs. Sheeler and
the Downtown Gallery

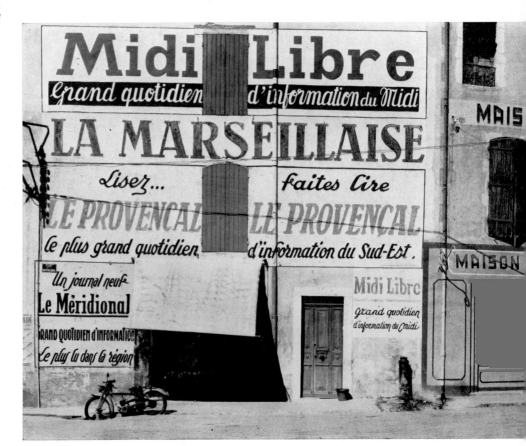

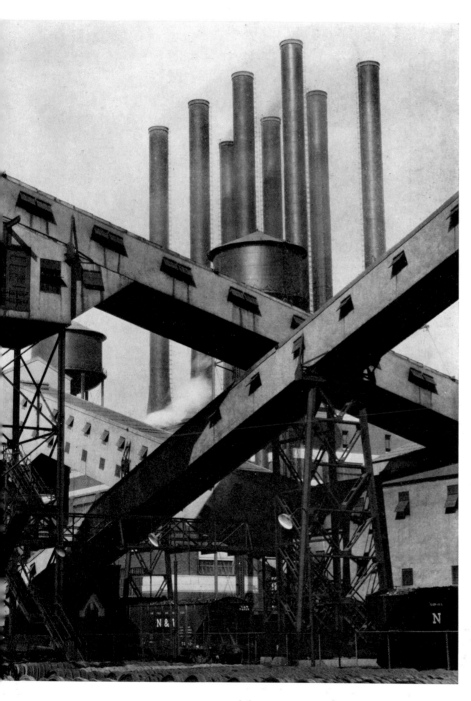

CHARLES SHEELER
Ford Plant, River Rouge. *1927*.

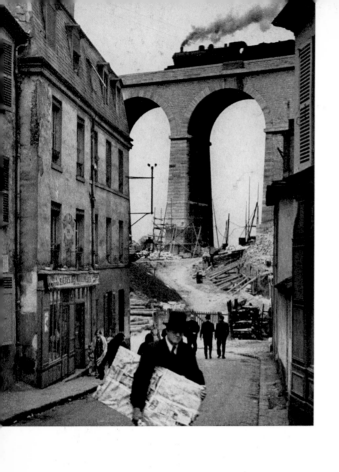
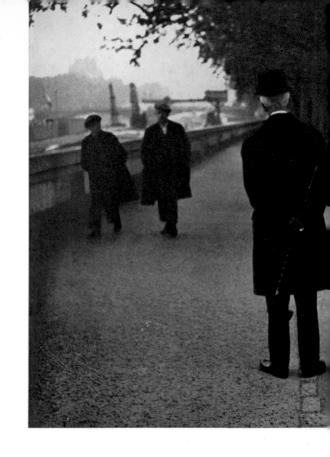
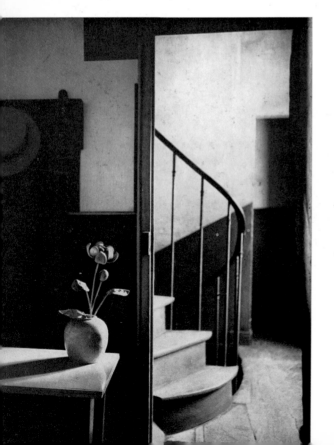
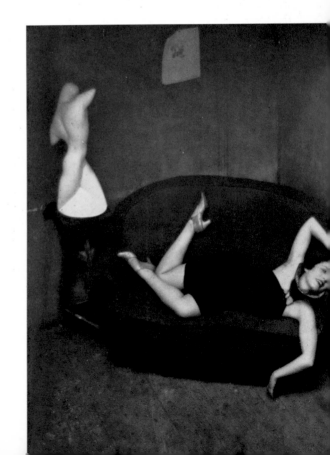

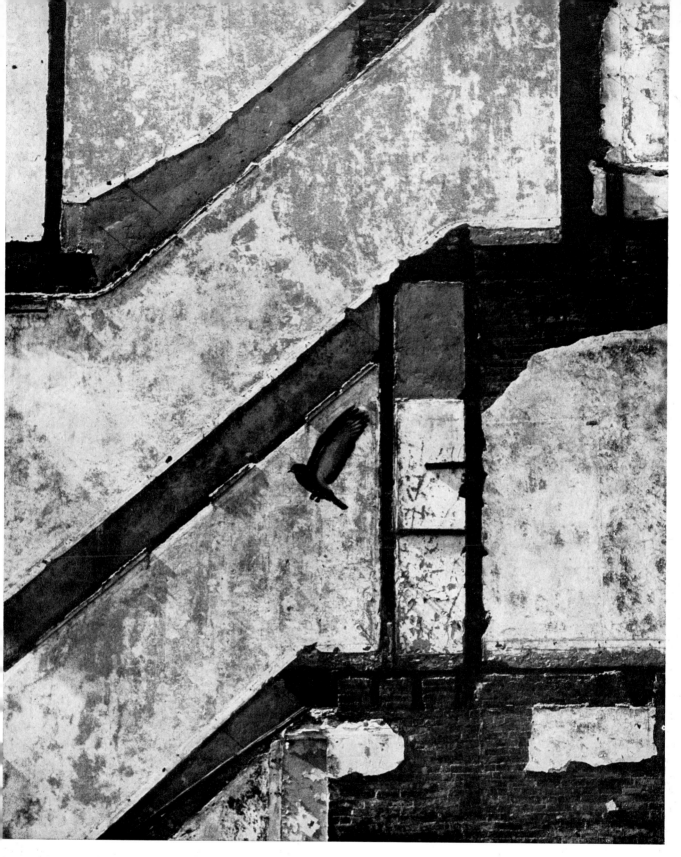

ANDRE KERTESZ, *above:* Building and Bird. *New York. 1966.*
opposite page, above left: Meudon. *1928.*
above right: Man with Cane. *Paris. 1926.*
below left: Mondrian's Studio. *Paris. 1926.*
below right: Satiric Dancer. *Paris. 1926.*
All Courtesy Magnum Photos.

CHAPTER 22
Stieglitz: An American Legend

THERE ARE SOME EARLY PHOTOGRAPHS by Alfred Stieglitz (1864–1946) that are poetic gems, superb pictures which, more than fifty years later, hold their own as works of graphic art. Repeated viewings do not dull their esthetic impact—barren trees bordering a Munich road in November, 1885; Paula intently writing a letter in Berlin, the summer of 1889; a Fifth Avenue horse car at the terminal in the snowstorm of 1893; sparkling wet streets at night taken in 1896 in front of New York's Plaza; delicate, budding leaves of a young tree, and an unconcerned sweeper on a soft street in *Spring Showers* of 1902; and, closing this portfolio of everlasting appealing photographs, *The Steerage* of 1907.

It was not that Stieglitz did not continue to take memorable pictures. All his long life he saw the world in terms of the camera. Photography was his basic medium as an artist though he let his personality expand by becoming editor and writer, pioneer art dealer for *avant-garde* artists of two continents, and champion of constantly changing photographic-art movements.

In the beginning, in 1890, when he had just returned to his native land after eight years in Germany where he had forsaken the study of engineering for photography, New York first exerted its power over him. He then revealed through his pictures his imaginative response to such exciting visual stimuli. It was not reportage that he created with his camera, although his work was strikingly honest; through his cultivated eye and comprehensive technique it went beyond the limited validity of a mere record.

Stieglitz was to say in later years, "I have found my subjects within sixty yards of my door," and he spoke of the "exploration of the familiar." In 1890 these thoughts were revolutionary. Those were the days of sentimental genre pictures, composite and "high art" photographs, which Dr. P. H. Emerson, the author of *Naturalistic Photography* had attacked in London but which were still the criteria of excellence in New York's camera clubs, where their artificial images hung on the line in every annual arty salon.

During these years, 1890–1895, Stieglitz tried to make himself financially independent by conducting a photo-engraving business. The photogravure process was always to intrigue him; he considered this mechanical reproduction process second only to an original platinum print.

Every free moment Stieglitz stalked the streets with his hand-held "detective camera." He took straight pictures; he did not retouch, enlarge, or indulge in any camera tricks. In this he followed Dr. P. H. Emerson, who in 1887 had given Stieglitz his first bit of encouragement by awarding him two guineas and a silver medal. This was the first of 150 medals Stieglitz was to win in the

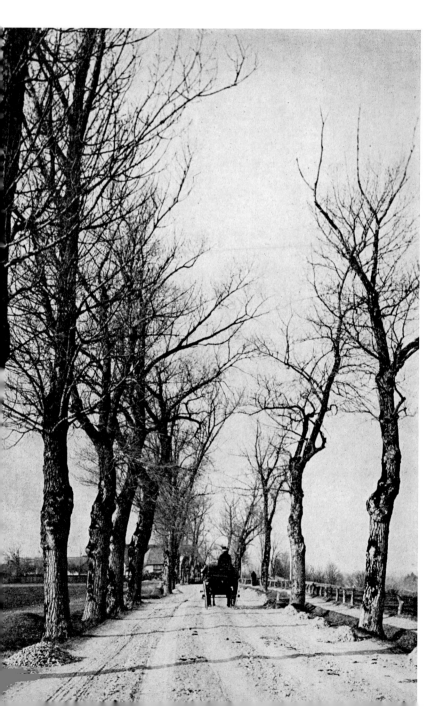

ALFRED STIEGLITZ, November Days. *Munich, 1885.*

259

early 1890s, at a time when he was advocating the abolition of the medal system.

Stieglitz joined the Society of Amateur Photographers and became editor of their publication, *The American Amateur Photographer*. He advocated pictorial photography and recommended a new annual photographic salon without prizes or medals. The Society and the New York Camera Club combined in 1897 to form The Camera Club; Stieglitz was elected vice-president and editor of its publication, *Camera Notes*. That year he saw published his first portfolio of photographs, *Picturesque Bits of New York*.

Losing patience with the stubborn conservatism of the Camera Club, Stieglitz resigned the editorship of *Camera Notes* and founded Photo-Secession along with John G. Bullock, William B. Dyer, Frank Eugene, Dallett Fuguet, Gertrude Kasebier, Joseph T. Keiley, Robert S. Redfield, Eva Watson Schutze, Edward J. Steichen, Edmund Stirling, John Francis Strauss, and Clarence H. White. The official organ of the group was *Camera Work* with Stieglitz as editor and publisher and Keiley, Fuguet, and Strauss as associate editors. The purpose as outlined in the prospectus of Photo Secession was "to hold together those Americans devoted to pictorial photography . . . to exhibit the best that has been accomplished by its members or other photographers and above all to dignify that profession until recently looked upon as a trade."

Its purposes were similar to the Linked Ring in London. In 1905 Photo Secession opened the Little Gallery, designed by Steichen, at 291 Fifth Avenue in New York. Stieglitz was the director. For the next twelve years photographs by the members vied with paintings and drawings by Matisse, Marin, Hartley, Weber, Rousseau, Renoir, Cézanne, Manet, Picasso, Braque, Picabia, Dove, and O'Keeffe, sculpture by Rodin and Brancusi, Japanese prints and African Negro carvings. Many of these artists were shown for the first time in America, years before the shattering Armory Show of 1913 and long before any American museum purchased a sculpture by Brancusi or a painting by Picasso.

The first Matisse exhibition, held at 291 in April, 1908, had been arranged through Steichen in Paris. Critics reviled the "wild man." "His idea is that you should in painting get as far away from nature as possible," wrote Chamberlain of the *Evening Mail*, and Elizabeth Cary of *The New York Times* said of paintings by the Fauve Matisse, "ugly and distorted, many of them amounting to caricatures without significance."

The Camera Club, of which Stieglitz was a founder, expelled him because he exhibited Matisse, whom they

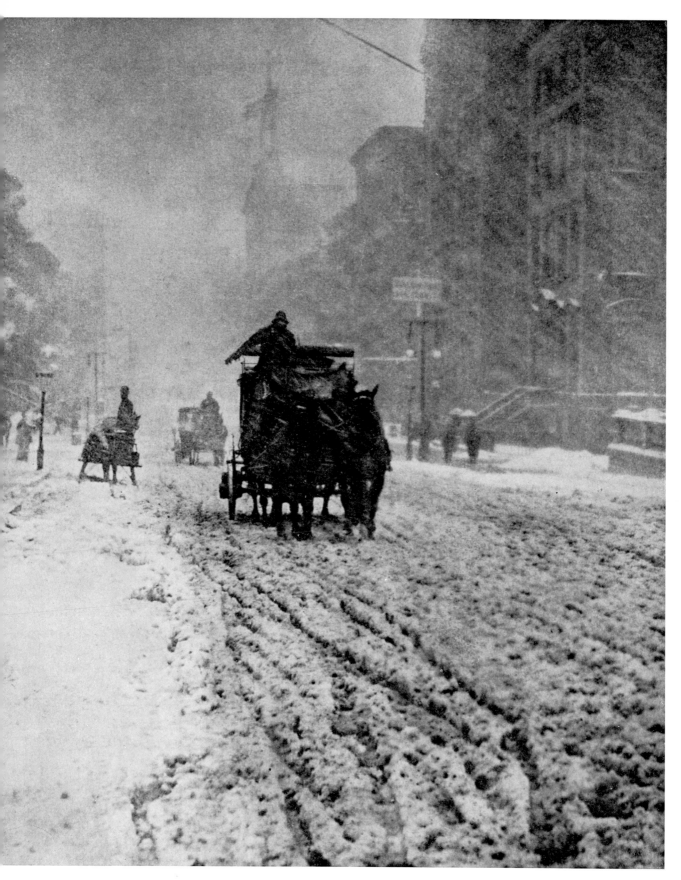

STIEGLITZ, Winter on Fifth Avenue. *1893. Courtesy George Eastman House, Rochester.*

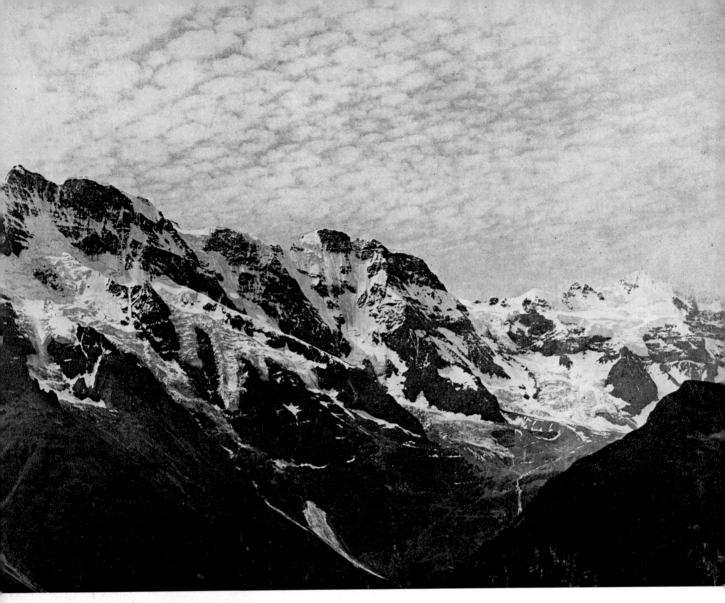

STIEGLITZ, Snow-Capped Mountains. *About 1887.*

regarded as an "arch Satanist" and a "menace to artistic morals." Stieglitz never let the club reinstate him, although they made several overtures.

In 1910 the Albright Art Gallery in Buffalo, New York, fell to the persuasive blandishments of Stieglitz, turning the Museum over to Photo Secession for an international exhibition of pictorial photography. Five hundred photographs ranging in treatment from pictorial realism to imitation painting were installed on specially prepared walls. Fifteen were purchased for the museum's permanent collection. An important battle had been won, for official and dignified recognition. Photographers rejoiced, but under Stieglitz, who footed all its bills and found himself short of funds, 291, the Little Gallery, devoted more time to art exhibitions that helped defray expenses.

Camera Work also devoted more space to reproductions of artists' works plus articles and a box-score reprint of all that the newspaper art critics wrote about any art exhibition at 291. Reproductions by photogravure of paintings and photographs appeared regularly. Some photographers, particularly Stieglitz in America and Emerson in England, preferred this commercial form of printing for any large edition of prints. It was a short-lived contention of Stieglitz at this time that only one perfect print could be got from a negative, thereby claiming uniqueness for a photograph as for a painting.

The fifty uniformly printed issues of *Camera Work* contained special articles by George Bernard Shaw,

Maurice Maeterlinck, Sadakichi Hartmann (whose first pieces were signed Sidney Allan), Robert Demachy, Benjamin De Casseres, Frederick H. Evans, J. B. Kerfoot, Gertrude Stein, and a host of other writers on modern art or photography. Shaw, writing an appreciation of A. L. Coburn, compares his efforts to Bellini, Hals, and Holbein, whose "styles he can emulate at will," and he closes with, "he is free of that clumsy tool, the human hand, which will always go its own single way and no other." Exaggerated claims for photography, even by Shaw, did not lessen the photographic artistry of Coburn whose portraits remain rich and delicate examples of the platinotype and gum-print processes.

Arguments about what constitutes an artist appeared in the pages of *Camera Work*; "Pros and Cons" was a page title for Frederick H. Evans. J. B. Kerfoot wrote "The Rubaiyat of Kodak McFilm." Shaw in "The Unmechanicalism of Photography" cautioned the exhibitors of the London Photographic Exhibition (for which he had originally written the article as a foreword to the catalogue) as follows: "Let nobody suppose that the critics who stood for Sargent against Bouguereau, for Monet against Vicat Cole, nearly twenty years ago, are now going to stand for the photographers who imitate Sargent and Monet against original photographers."

What and who was original was aired in every issue, and Stieglitz, brilliant editor that he was, gave each writer, photographer, and artist the right to discover new and personal paths. It was a costly publication. The finest of paper and type faces, hand-pulled gravure reproduc-

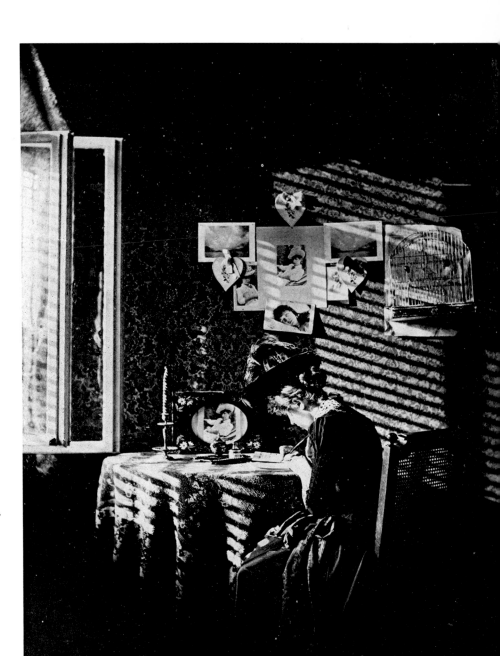

STIEGLITZ, Paula. *Berlin, 1889.*

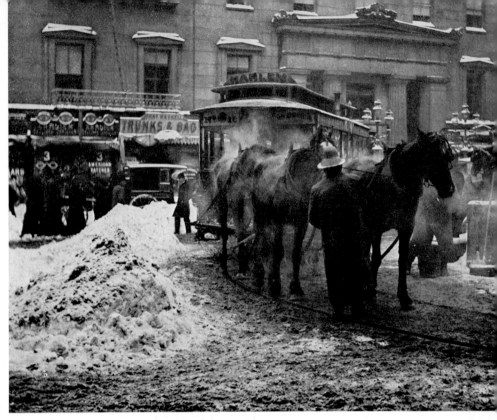

STIEGLITZ, The Terminal. 1893

tions on "rice silk" paper tipped into each issue, and expensive individual designing of each page, made it hardly profitable to publish. The original price was $4 for an annual subscription of four issues. Toward the end it was $8 a year, but, by 1917, when publication was suspended, there were less than forty subscribers. One of the country's most distinguished magazines had folded, and soon 291 closed its doors.

Stieglitz photographed his friends: the artists of his gallery, John Marin, Arthur Dove, Marsden Hartley, Georgia O'Keeffe, Charles Demuth—clear and incisive pictures, brilliant characterizations. For the eight-year interval between the closing of 291 and the opening of the "Intimate Gallery" in room 303 of the Anderson Gallery in 1925, Stieglitz arranged exhibitions of his artists' works in various New York galleries and held three retrospective exhibitions of his own photographs. The contributions of his career were impressively clear to all who attended Mitchell Kennerly's Gallery, where there were exhibited 145 of Stieglitz's prints from 1886 to 1921. The press extolled their virtues. In the catalogue Stieglitz's statement read in part, "My ideal is to achieve the ability to produce numberless prints from each negative, prints all significantly alive, yet indistinguishably alike."

Stieglitz photographed parts of the human body: hands, feet, breasts, buttocks, torso. These portraits without faces were followed with photographs of clouds which Stieglitz called "equivalents." He started out to prove that the merit of his photographs was not dependent on the sitter's personality and appearance or upon the influence Stieglitz exerted over him. In photographing clouds by sunlight and moonlight or shimmering leaves and blades of grass, he endowed these with the equivalent emotion and excitement he had instilled in the portaits of artists or in the buildings of New York.

Stieglitz continued to extend his concepts of photography, re-evaluating his work according to the contemporary requirement of using the full negative sharply. In the new Intimate Gallery he sponsored and exhibited the work of Paul Strand, a photographer of brilliant promise he had added to his roster. In 1924 Stieglitz married Georgia O'Keeffe. That same year the Boston Museum of Fine Arts acquired twenty-seven of his photographs and the Royal Photographic Society awarded him the Progress Medal.

In 1930 he opened An American Place at 509 Madison Avenue in room 1710. His camera lay idle most of the time; he had suffered a heart attack and rarely left the gallery. He saw the artists whom he had handled become accepted internationally and their work enter the na-

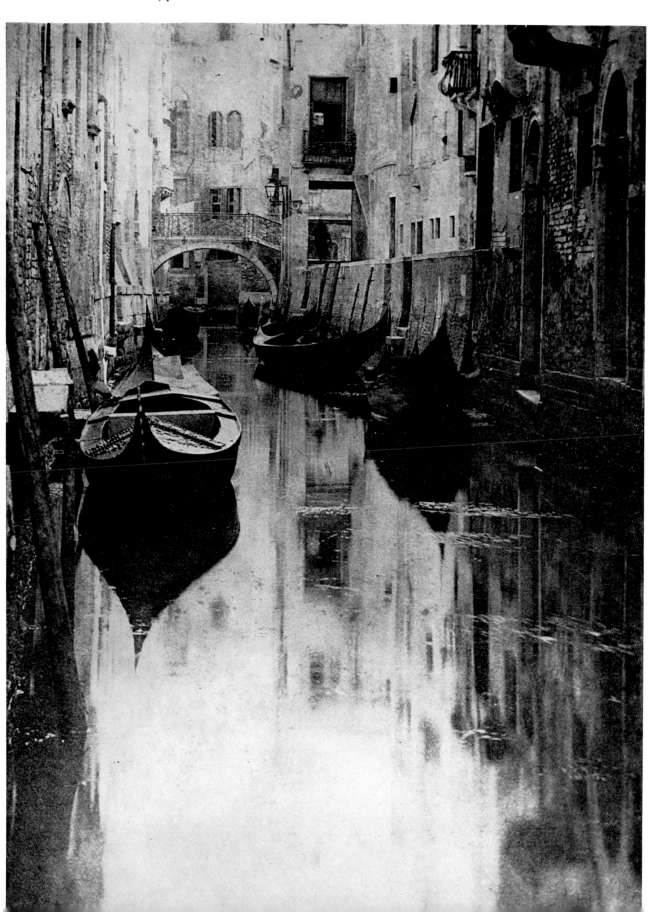

STIEGLITZ, Venice Canal. 1894.

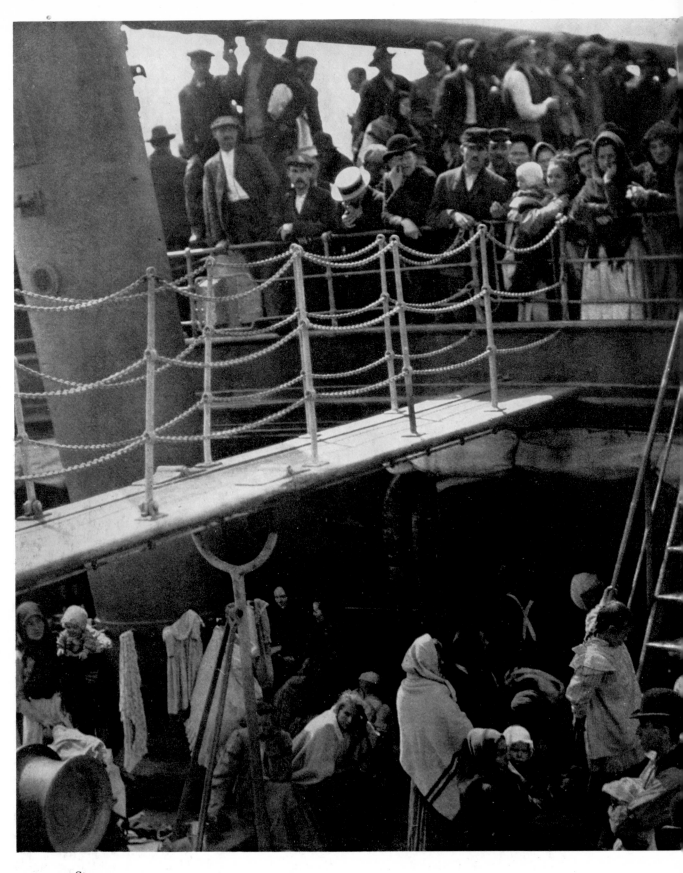

STIEGLITZ, Steerage. 1907.

tion's major museums. Stieglitz never ceased his efforts to demonstrate the genius of his artists, but his sales methods were decidedly untraditional. He put a possible client out of his gallery and explained, "I am not in business, I am not interested in exhibitions and pictures, I am not a salesman, nor are the pictures here for sale, although under certain circumstances certain pictures may be acquired."

Stieglitz was a powerful and positive personality in the annals of American art. In his lifetime he became a legendary character of whom a collective panegyric portrait, a eulogy, was published twelve years before his death. Today myriads of people recognize him as one of America's pre-eminent photographers, as all over the country they view his prints in museums to which Georgia O'Keeffe donated for posterity the life production of Alfred Stieglitz.

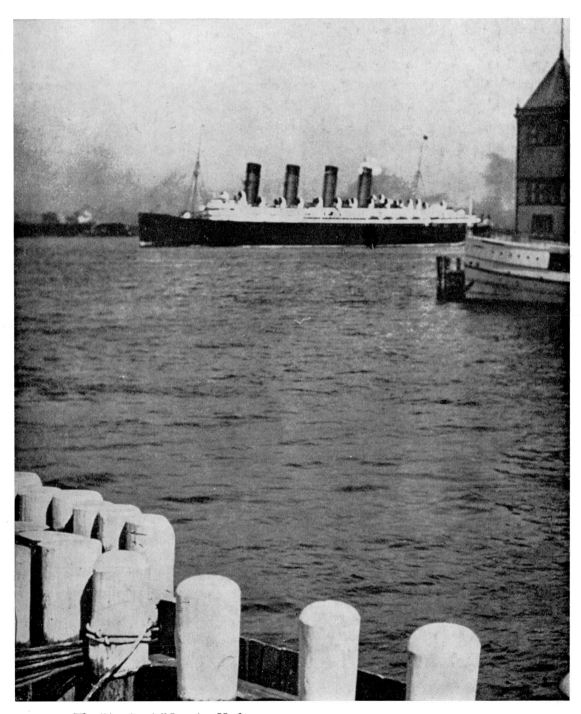

STIEGLITZ, The "Aquitania" Leaving Harbor. 1910.

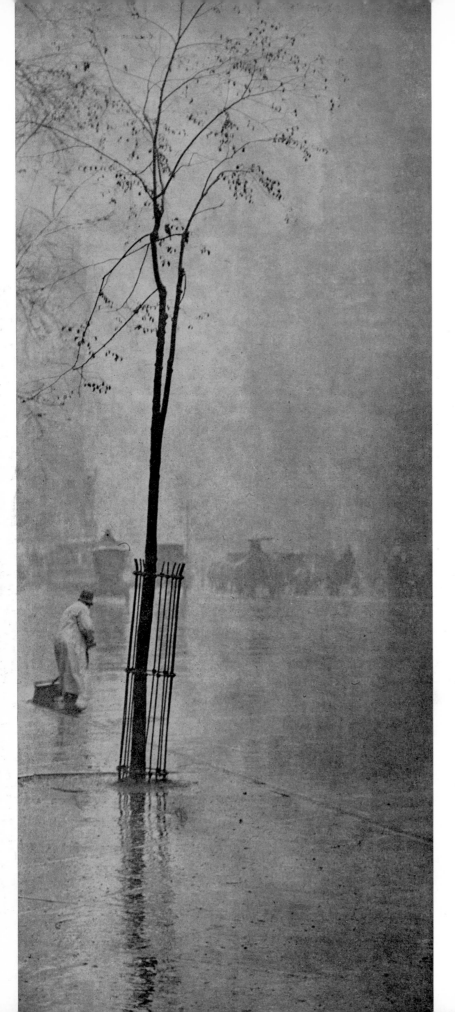

STIEGLITZ, Spring Showers. *1902.*

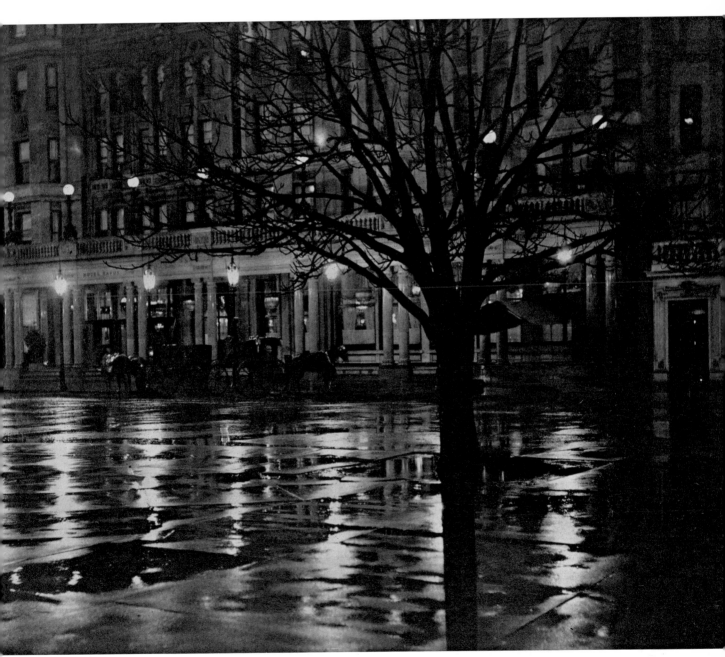

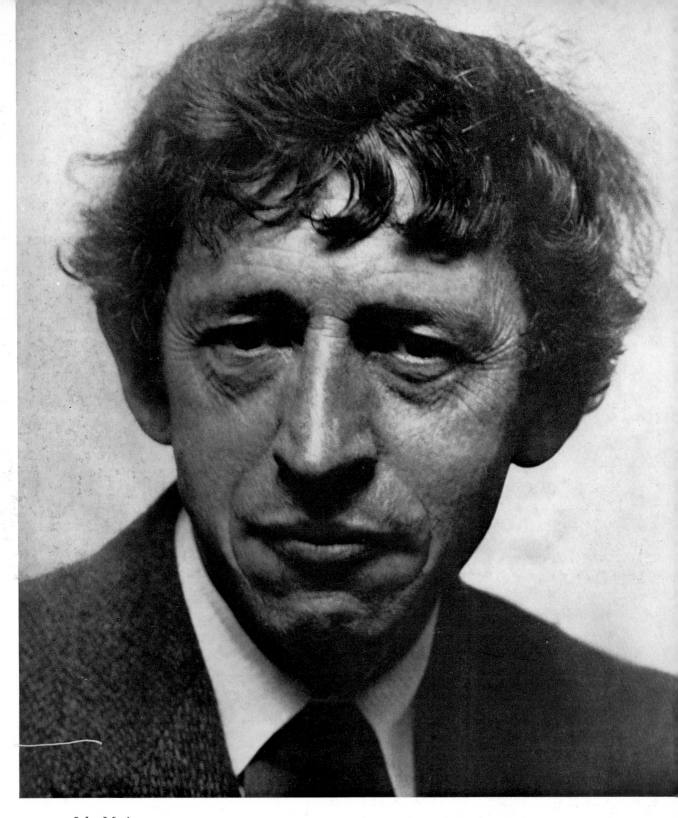

STIEGLITZ, John Marin. *1920.*

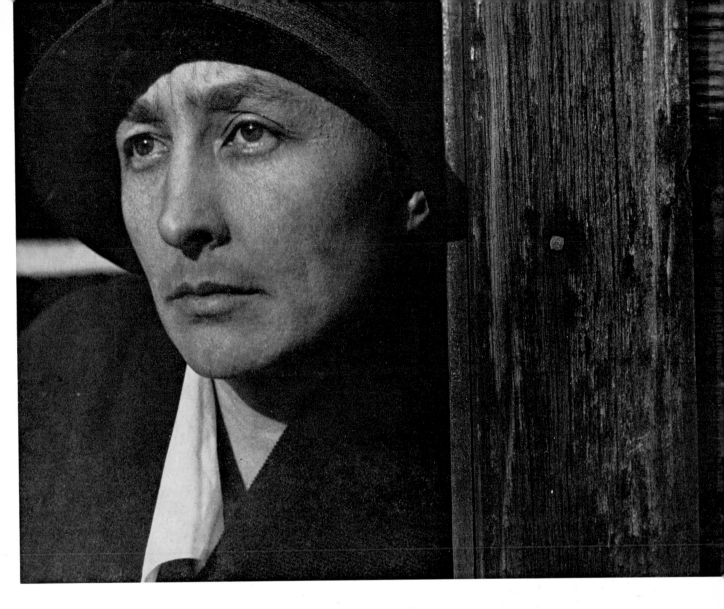

STIEGLITZ, *above*: Georgia O'Keeffe Wearing Hat. 1930.
below: Georgia O'Keeffe's Hands. *About 1919.*

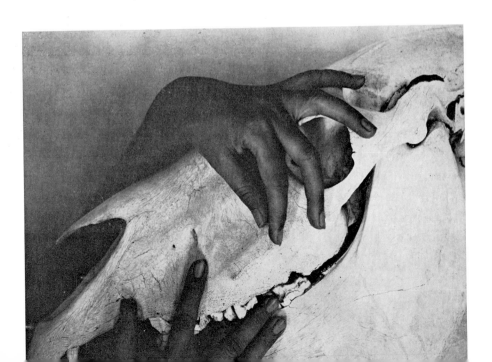

CHAPTER 23

Steichen: Painter, Photographer, Curator

EDWARD STEICHEN was born in Luxembourg in 1879, and raised in Wisconsin, for the family soon moved to Milwaukee. At the age of fourteen he came to Chicago to see the art and photography exhibitions at the World's Columbian Exposition. He was going to be a painter. During the next several years he sent canvases to the Art Institute's annual exhibitions, but not one was accepted. He took a job as illustrator in a lithography plant. He made snapshots of people and photographs for advertising. One sold. Again he submitted pictures to the Art Institute of Chicago. This time they were photographs and they were accepted by a jury that included Alfred Stieglitz and Clarence White. Stieglitz and White were impressed with a photograph entitled *The Pool,* which Stieglitz bought two years later and called a "masterpiece" (a term art critics accused photographers of using quite casually).

Milwaukee could not hold Steichen much longer after this bit of encouragement. He went to see Stieglitz in New York soon after the turn of the century. The following year he was in London photographing George Bernard Shaw, preceded by his friend Alvin Langdon Coburn. Shaw was an amateur photographer of three years standing. Why had he taken up the camera? In 1949 he wrote Helmut Gernsheim, in answer to this question, "I always wanted to draw and paint. I had no literary ambition: I aspired to be a Michael Angelo, not a Shakespear. But I could not draw well enough to satisfy myself; and the instruction I could get was worse than useless. So when dry plates and push buttons came into the market I bought a box camera and began pushing the button. This was in 1898."

Then Steichen was in Paris. In 1902 he entered two paintings in the Paris Salon and sent also a bunch of photographs labeled drawings, but the jury rejected these just before the opening—not, they explained, because they were not so good as the paintings but because they feared an avalanche of photo entries.

Steichen photographed Rodin flanked by his sculptures of Victor Hugo and *The Thinker*. He became fast friends with the dynamic sculptor and his family. He photographed all Rodin's work, including the monolithic Balzac which, fifty years later, he was to photograph again when the Museum of Modern Art acquired a bronze cast and installed it in the sculpture garden.

Steichen returned to the United States in 1902. He designed the Photo-Secession Gallery at 291. Stieglitz bought prints from him, paying him $50 to $100 each. Stieglitz demanded respect for photography and he demanded a price for photographs. Advertisers not only paid handsomely for the use of photographs; they had to insure the print against the slightest smudge of the printer's thumb.

Stieglitz exhibited and sold Steichen's paintings and photographs. The usual price was $50 or $60 per print,

but for the portraits of Theodore Roosevelt and William Howard Taft a national magazine paid $500 each for the privilege to reproduce. In the first issue of *Camera Work*, January, 1903, Steichen wrote a statement on "ye fakers," claiming that all artists take liberties with reality and "fake" or make a picture. In the second issue of *Camera Work*, three months later, eight of Steichen's photographs were reproduced plus a tribute to him and his work written by the Japanese-Irish-American art critic, Sadakichi Hartmann. Stieglitz published a Steichen supplement in the April, 1906, issue, reproducing sixteen photographs by photogravure, one in two colors, and in the following issue published a three-color reproduction of a powerful portrait of G. B. Shaw by Steichen.

In 1905 the London Salon reviewer, A. C. R. Carter, wrote on seeing the Steichen show, "Is photography an art? Let the answer be, 'Yes, if it's Steichen.' And, some day doubtless another man will spring forth and be to Steichen as Steichen is to Stieglitz. The services rendered to the cause of pictorial photography by Alfred Stieglitz must not be forgotten, for it was his pioneership which cleared the tangled ground and made a Steichen possible."

Robert Demachy wrote, "The best results I have ever seen in the gum process are Steichen's, Puyo's, Watzek's and Kuhn's . . . they have always reminded me forcibly of fine engravings, fine etchings, fine lithographs and fine wash drawings."

An American art critic, Fitzgerald of the *New York*

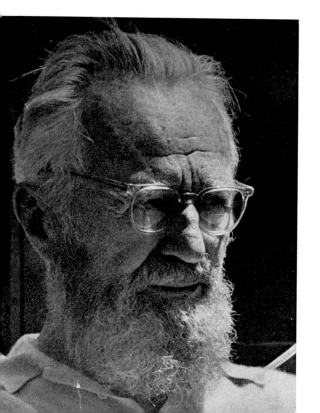

JOAN MILLER, Edward Steichen. 1963.
Courtesy Museum of Modern Art, New York.

Evening Sun, seeing a similar show a bit later, wrote, "I am ignorant whether Eduard [he spelt it with a "u" until after World War I] Steichen is more painter or photographer."

In 1908 Steichen was again in France, this time for a sojourn of six years. Not content to be painter and photographer, he became immersed in the study of plants, not only photographing them but actually breeding flowers for which he was awarded a gold medal by the Horticultural Society of France.

World War I changed his life. He returned to the States. During the Second Battle of the Marne he was appointed technical adviser of the army's aerial photographic services. Here was the end of the gum prints; the arty, fuzzy photograph was a thing of the past. Sharp and brilliant detail was required; photographs had to be so clearly defined that everything could be recognized from aerial views. Lives depended on it. The Army taught Colonel Steichen a new way of photography.

He took a year out after his discharge to experiment with straight photography. He photographed a white cup and saucer against a black velvet background more than a thousand times. He sought perfect control to achieve maximum realism and the faintest, most subtle grada-tions in white, gray, and black. He put away his brushes, burned his paintings. What he knew of art and design, the keen eye he had developed in painting portraits, now combined with a masterful technique, enabled him to portray forcefully the diverse personalities, the intellectuals and the socially prominent who came to pose.

Elegant fashions and industrial advertising became his forte in photography. He made commercial photographic art pay. In 1923 Frank Crowninshield induced him to join Condé Nast's staff as photographer for *Vogue* and *Vanity Fair*. Wedding gowns and silver, toothpaste and cold cream, matches and watches, a rich variety of the nation's most highly touted products sat for his camera and appeared in the slick magazines along with his portraits of the lettered and the celebrated from all walks of life. His photographs of the twenties and thirties form a pictorial record, like Nadar's and Brady's in their day.

The United States Navy in the early days of World War II waived age limitations for Captain Edward Steichen, USNR. His "Road to Victory" photography exhibition, which was shown in Grand Central Station soon after Pearl Harbor, was a powerful force in unifying the nation's will. There was no one better qualified to organize a department with an avowed purpose to photo-

All photographs in this chapter are courtesy The Art Institute of Chicago, Stieglitz Collection, unless otherwise noted.

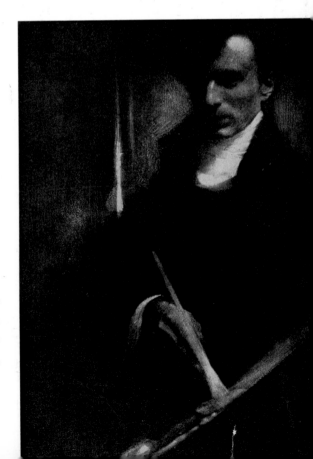

EDWARD STEICHEN, *right:* Self-Portrait. *Gum print, 1902.*
opposite page: J. P. Morgan. *About 1903. Steichen's most famous portrait, commissioned by the artist Carlos Baca-Flor, whose portrait, painted from this photograph, lies forgotten in a storage bin. The highlight on the arm of the chair resembles a poised dagger held in the financier's hand. Courtesy Metropolitan Museum of Art, New York.*

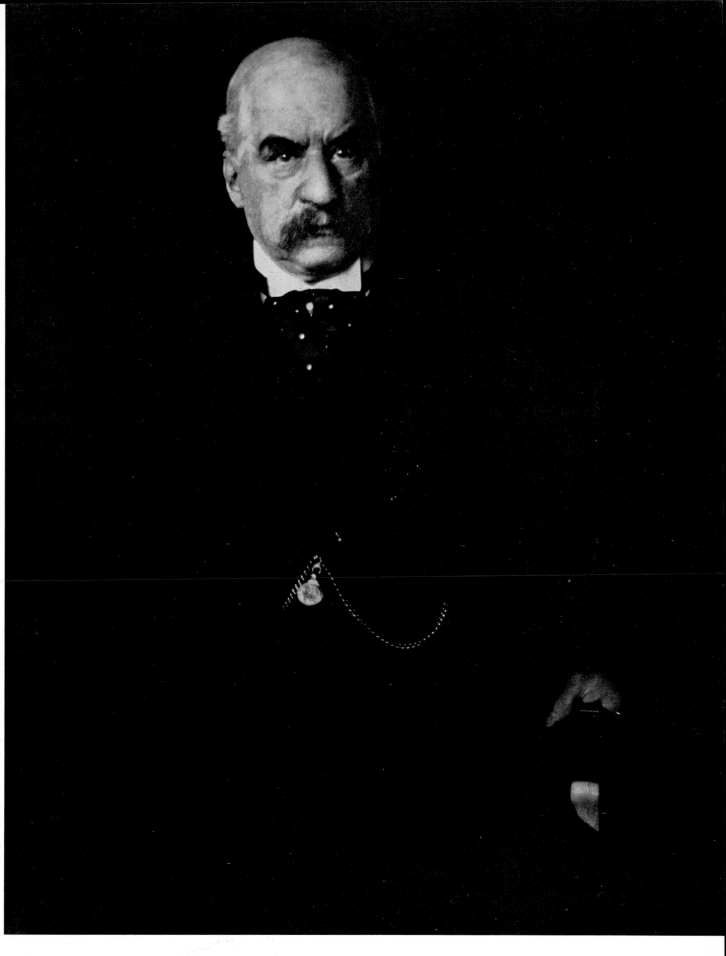

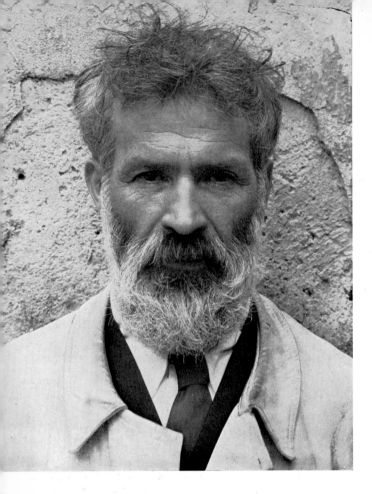

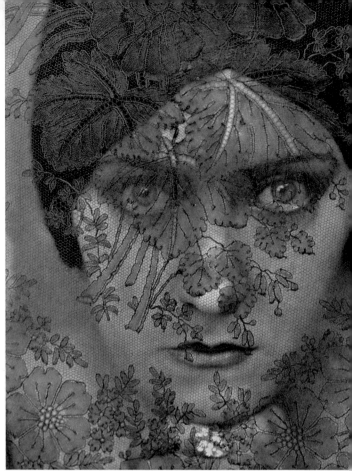

graph the entire war at sea, no matter how long it would take. The record of the men he commanded adds up to a remarkable pictorial account of every engagement of the Navy that will be a boon for all future historians.

An army colonel in World War I and a navy captain in World War II, the high-ranking officer Edward Steichen fought his valiant battles with film carried by some of the nation's prized magazine and press photographers. He doffed his uniform to serve as director of photography for the Museum of Modern Art, New York.

He arranged photography exhibitions by **creative photographers** who used any camera or style they chose. Through his efforts photography as an art form found acceptance among critics and visitors along with paintings and prints. No excessive claims were made for photography; no academic form was insisted upon. Only "good" photographs were eligible for exhibition. This example in free expression for creative photography inaugurated by Beaumont and Nancy Newhall, Steichen's predecessors at the Museum of Modern Art, and carried

forward by him is now followed by progressive museums all over the country.

"The Family of Man," the most popular photography exhibition ever assembled, was selected by Steichen from among two million prints sent in by photographers from all over the world, and was on tour for five years.

Steichen, at 90, maintains his love affair with photography. For the past decade, a shad-blow tree has posed for him, season after season, in all its changing grandeur—in rain, sleet, wind and snow, in full flowering, in full leaf and bare—and he has made an unusual and sensitive record in both color and black-and-white.

The Museum of Modern Art (which established the Edward Steichen Photography Center in 1964, and with which he holds the title of Director Emeritus) maintains regular contact with him and discusses plans for the future. It is always the future for great artists: like the aged Hokusai, "the old man mad for drawing," Steichen needs more time and pleads that he is just now learning to see.

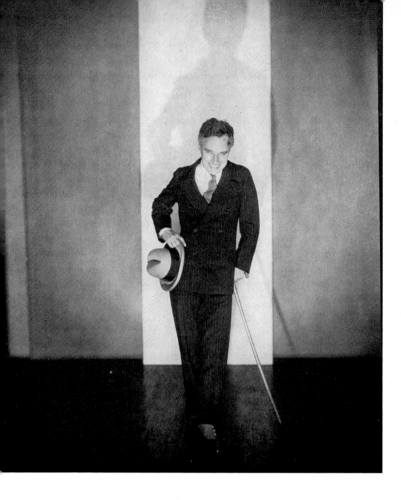

EDWARD STEICHEN, *opposite page, left:* Brancusi. 1922.
opposite page, right: Swanson. For Vanity Fair, 1925.
left, above: Chaplin. For Vanity Fair, 1925.
left, below: Garbo. For Vanity Fair, 1928.
All courtesy Museum of Modern Art, New York.

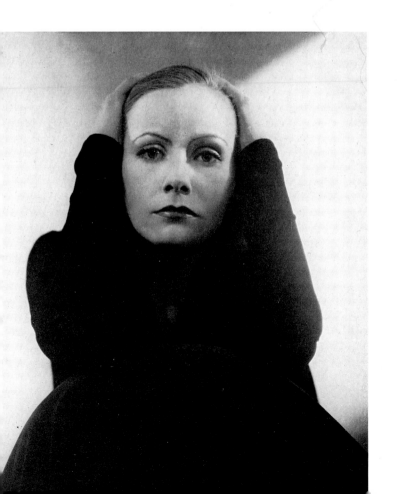

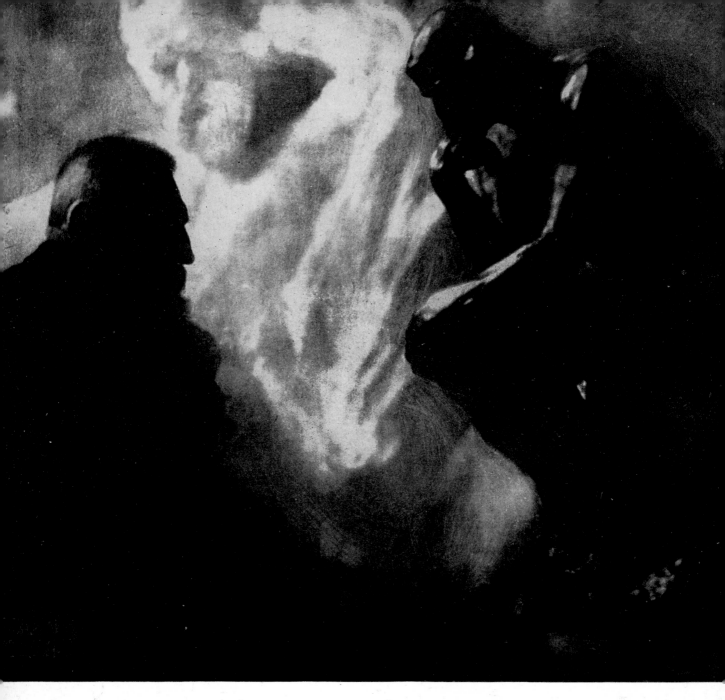

STEICHEN, *above:* Rodin with His Sculptures
"Victor Hugo" and "The Thinker." *Gum print,* 1902.

opposite page: Matches and Match Boxes. *For a fabric design,*
Shad-blow Tree.
Heavy Roses.
Hellcat Landing on USS Lexington. *U.S. Navy Photo,*
All courtesy Museum of Modern Art, New

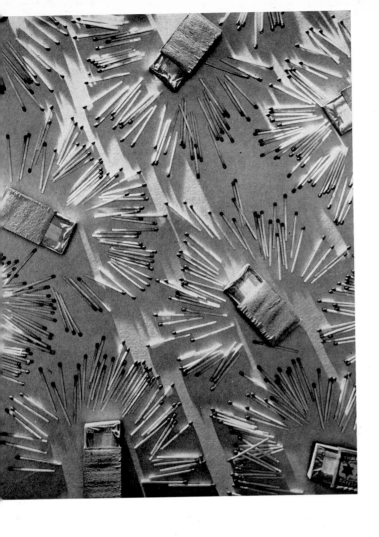
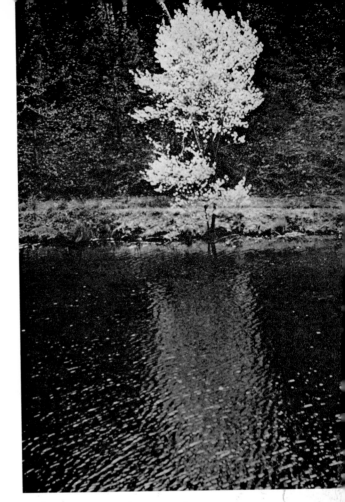
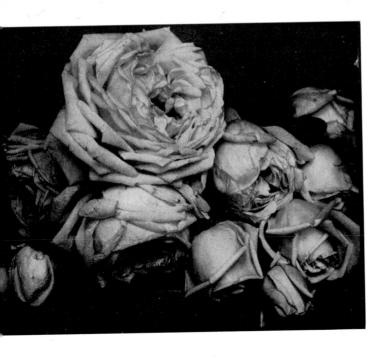
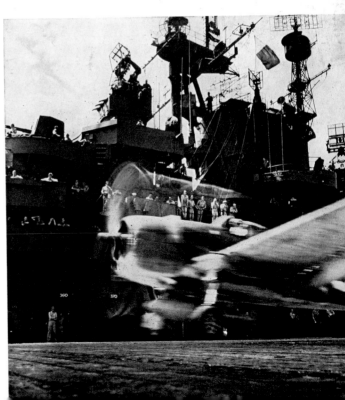

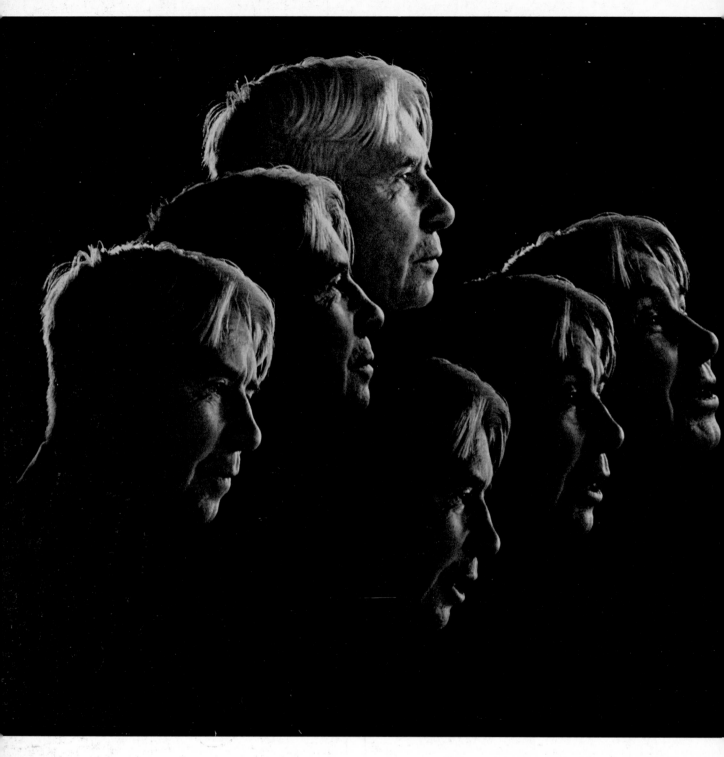

STEICHEN, Carl Sandburg. *Montage.* 193[
Courtesy Museum of Modern Art, New Yor[

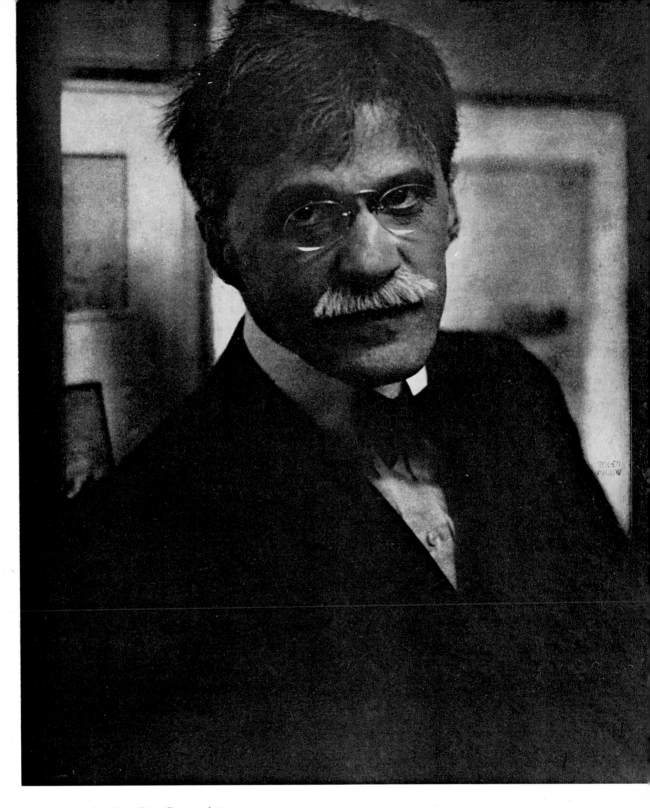

STEICHEN, Alfred Stieglitz. *Gum print, 1915.*

CHAPTER 24

Lartigue: Boy Photographer of La Belle Epoque

THE CLEAR, UNWAVERING VISION of childhood is one of the qualities most longed for by mature artists. Lartigue, as a photographer, had this vision—he shared it with children, for he *was* a child. His technique was precociously accomplished and mature, and, happily, was used not in aping the photographer's elders but in recording the innocent, miraculous seeing of childhood. In consequence, the world was rewarded with a unique set of images, unsurpassed for authenticity and freshness.

There is a lesson here, and let us hope that some educators, somewhere, will not overlook it. Put a camera and a roll of film in the hands of school children—the younger the better—and send them out into their world to use it. Do this in a sustained and systematic way, month by month and year by year, and their ability to perceive and understand both themselves and their environment will be raised to an unprecedented level.

Jacques-Henri Lartigue was born in the 1890s, that elegant decade which saw the flowering of the *Art Nouveau* style in the arts and decoration. Its impulses had still not subsided in 1903, when the seven-year-old Lartigue was given his first camera, and were not to disappear until the disastrous reality of World War I would close the prewar world forever. Meanwhile, some of the finest photographs recording the wit and sense-bound happiness of the period were to come from the camera of that little boy.

He was much too young to take the aging "grand horizontals" at Maxims, but the exquisite gowns of the women in his family hint at the colorful décolleté that the couturiers of Paris conceived for the fine ladies of prewar Europe.

Ladies in their finery, at the beach, in the Bois de Boulogne, at the races, along the avenues—how splendid they looked to the little boy. Growing into young manhood by 1910, he was still invisible to those ravishing women, who went on being themselves, oblivious to the record they were leaving in his hands. His incredible ability to observe, to recognize the mystery and excitement of the moment, to see the sinuous, serpentine lines of their smoothly flowing figures produced photographs that fill us with nostalgic yearning for the secure and luxuriously beautiful period of *Art Nouveau*.

Lartigue's photographs re-create, again and again, a living ornamental symbol of the period: a woman swathed in yards of transparent cloth. A lacy veil over her face, a lorgnette in her gloved hand, an egret-feathered hat on her head, she glows with the iridescence of a Tiffany lamp, to the wonderment of the little boy with a camera.

The ladies were but one of Lartigue's interests. The activities of his exuberant family were the center of his life—his brothers and cousins cavorting on homemade aquatic vehicles or playing in the pond on his father's large estate in Corbevoie. There were two- and three-seat bobsleds mounted on four bicycle wheels; there were automobiles, gliders, airplanes, kites, and skis. Everything he and his family did at home or on vacations, accompanied by swarms of relatives and servants, he took with the ever-better cameras and equipment that he acquired between his eighth and twenty-first year, when he gave up photography for easel painting. The keenness of his insight and brilliance of his observation of people, things, and places seemed to come to an end when he started to work out his aesthetic problems on canvas.

One hundred and sixty photographs taken by Lartigue between 1904 and 1914, together with his comments, were published in 1966 as the book *Boyhood Photographs of J.-H. Lartigue: The Family Album of the Gilded Age*. Three years earlier, 42 of the photographs were shown at the Museum of Modern Art, New York, after having been left forgotten in a closet for half a century.

The fanciful spirit of *La Belle Epoque*, as revealed in Lartigue's delightful photographs, amused the many spectators who flocked to see the exhibition. The woes and perils endured by the world in the past five decades were dissolved for a time by a revelation of the wonderful days before World War I. Lartigue's genius as a photographer was immediately recognized by critics and visitors alike. His unique perceptive powers and feeling for the immediate qualities of the subject surprised everyone who realized that he took some of the finest pictures in the exhibition when only ten years old.

Lartigue's innate talent for the camera was asserted the moment that his father (himself an amateur photographer and the boy's teacher in darkroom techniques) gave him a large camera on a tripod and a stool so he could climb up to see the image on the ground glass. It is hard to believe that in 1905 Jacques-Henri could photograph the last *Gordon Bennett Cup Race* with its complex diagonal composition, its forceful rendition of the mud-caked, weary, oil-smeared drivers, and its unposed timekeepers derided by spectators suspicious of the official time. A year earlier he had photographed France's first successful public flight: a glider, piloted by Gabriel Voisin, taking off from the top of a sand dune and covering the unbelievable distance of twenty yards. Under the direction of Jacques' older brother, gliders were made by the chambermaids, cooks, housekeepers, valet, and gardener of the Lartigue household.

The elder brother flew one of the contraptions for enough seconds to enable Jacques-Henri to record the formidable event. Jacques-Henri also recorded flights that ended in utter collapse of the homemade aircraft.

By 1908, Lartigue was a dedicated "action photographer." He used the newest cameras to stop action, getting thrilling pictures of aviation's pioneers. He ran after strange winged vehicles resembling bats and birds and powered by human leg muscles operating sprocket-and-chain drives. He hoped to catch them in flight, but instead got impressive and charming pictures of their inevitable crash on the hillside.

The removal of the Lartigue family in 1911 to Paris, near the Avenue du Bois, gave Jacques-Henri his chance to photograph the fashionable women taking their daily promenade in the Bois de Boulogne. Stationing himself on a bench along the so-called "Path of Virtue," he would click his noisy shutter as the ladies and their escorts sailed by.

Jacques-Henri continued to alternate photographs of smiling ladies in rustling silk and photographs of winter sports and auto racing, but the great period for him and for the world was coming to an end. He turned away from the camera to enter art school; the world turned away from the pursuits of peace and *La Belle Epoque* became a historic and literary legend.

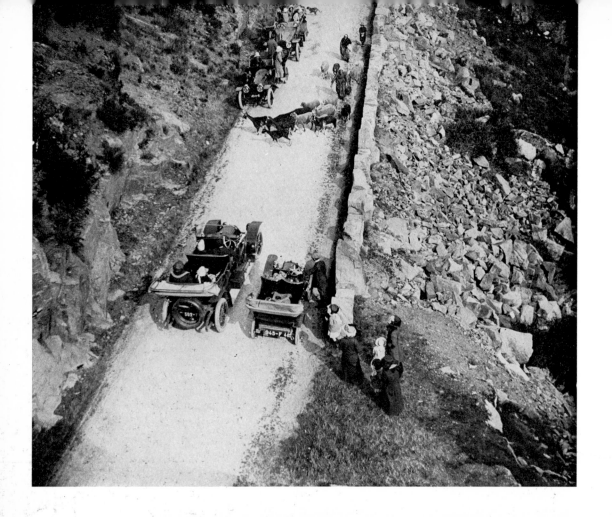

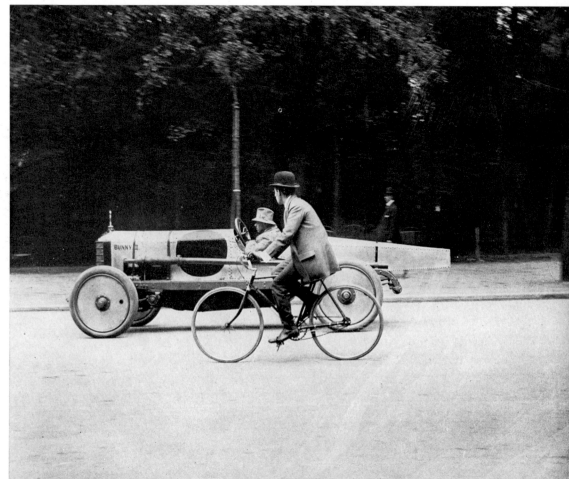

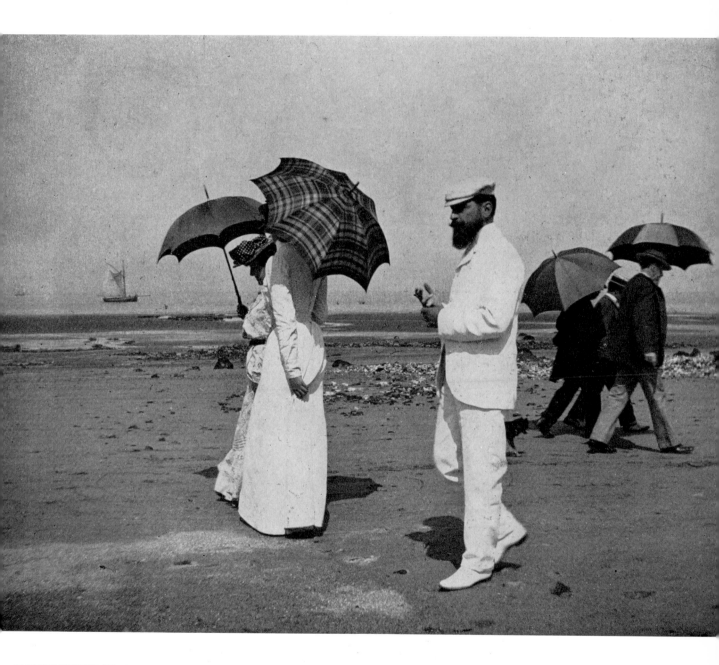

JACQUES-HENRI LARTIGUE
above: The Beach at Villerville. *1908*.
opposite page, above: The Lartigue Family on Tour in Their New Peugeot. *1912*.
below: Paris. *1912*.

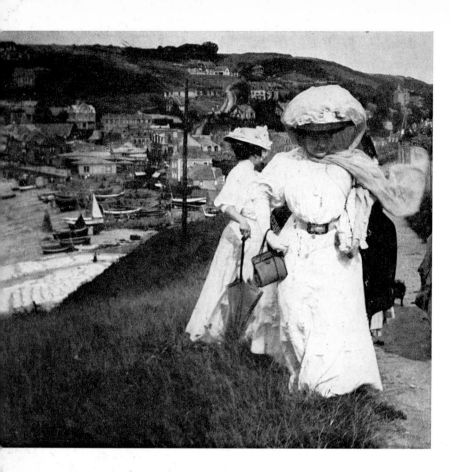

LARTIGUE
The Beach at Pourville. *1908.*
below: The Lartigue Family
Invents a Glider. *1908.*

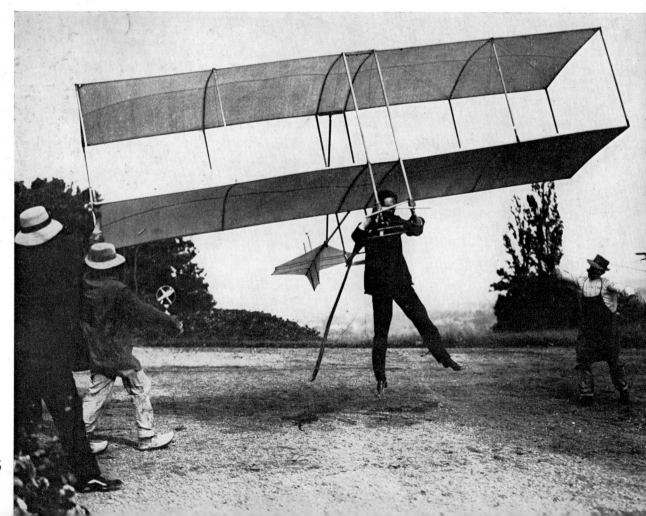

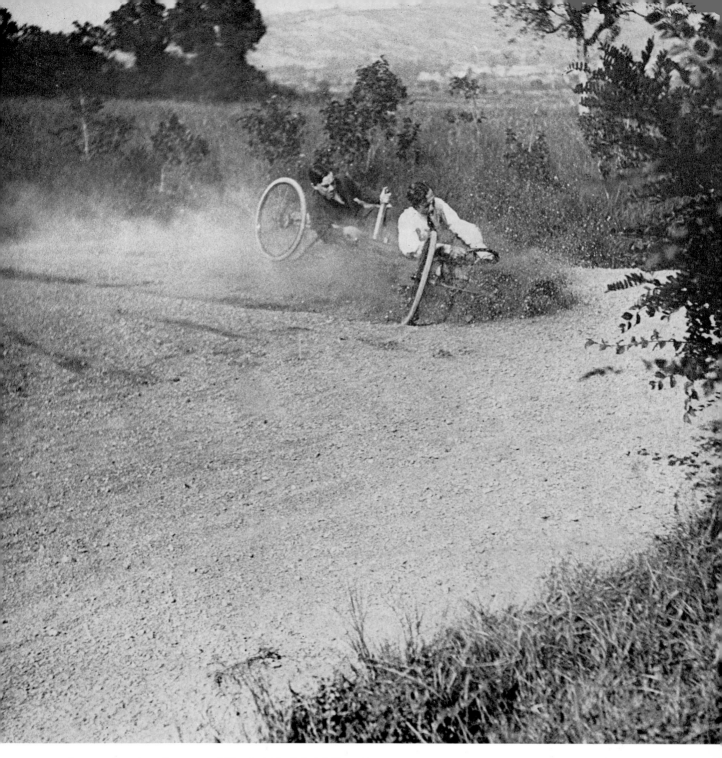

LARTIGUE, Jacques Lartigue Invents a Wheeled "Bobsleigh." 1908.

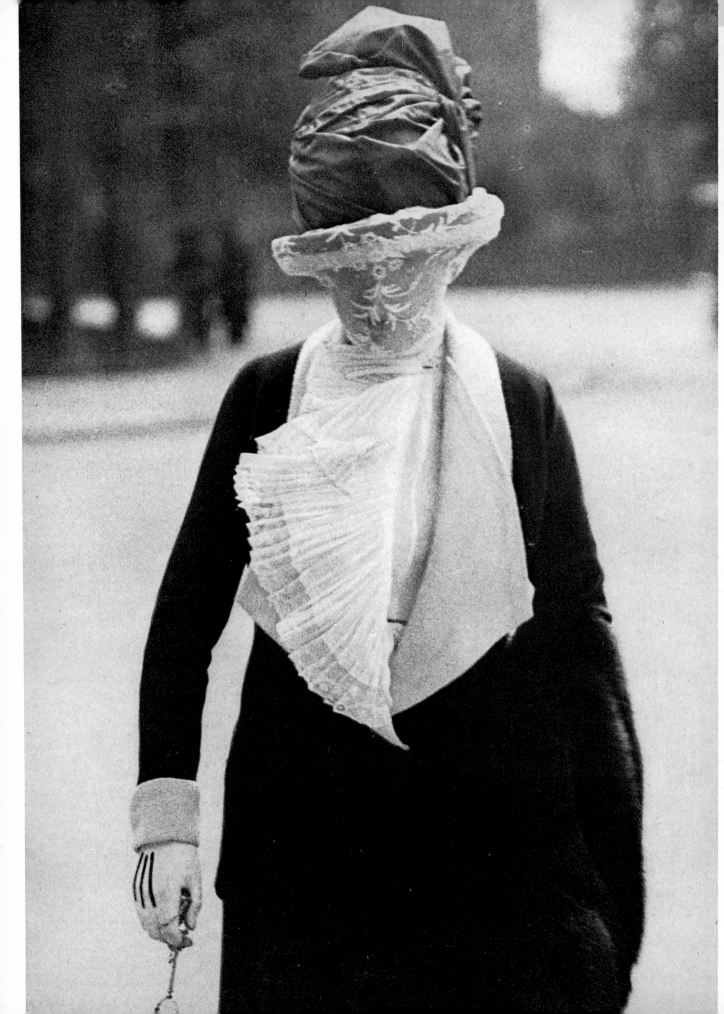

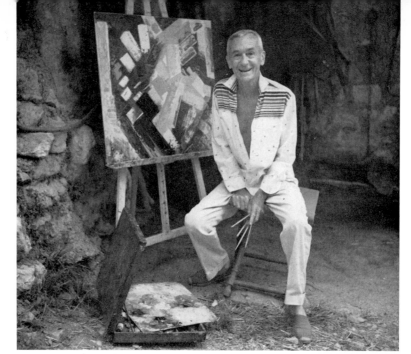

TIGUE, Self-portrait with Brushes,
Paints, and Easel. *1965*.
below: The Airplane Meet at
Combegrasse. *1922*,
opposite page:
L'Avenue des Acacias.
1911.

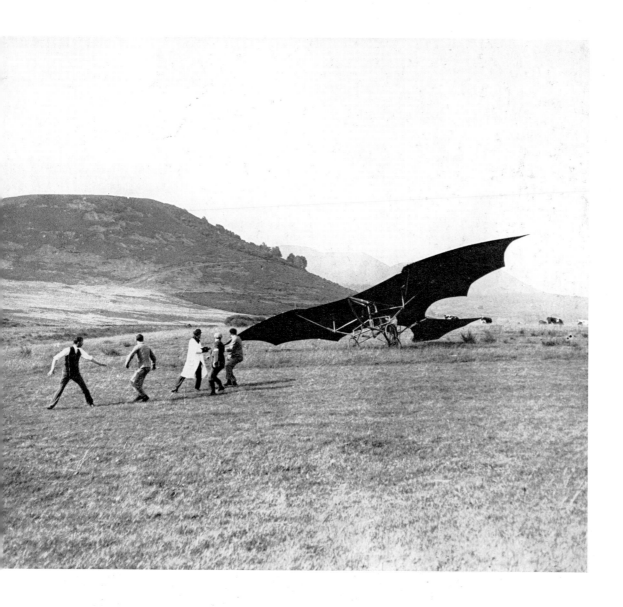

CHAPTER 25

Atget and the Streets of Paris

Two years before the turn of the twentieth century, at a time when the woolly, the soft-focus, the arty, the polished, and the overpictorial were the styles most likely to receive recognition in the journals of the day, Alfred Stieglitz in New York, Paul Martin in London, and Eugène Atget in Paris set their cameras to capture authentic photographs of what they saw in the places where they lived. Atget brought honesty into focus for an intimate and direct record of the many-sided Paris that he explored. This record has since become the inspiration for straight, documentary photographers everywhere.

Atget turned to the camera in 1898, when he was forty-two years old. For a decade he had tried to be an actor, playing bit parts in the provinces of France and the suburbs of Paris. He seems hardly the matinée-idol type, this taciturn man who had shipped out as a cabin boy at thirteen and had followed the sea for more than fifteen years before putting on grease paint.

With the decision to leave the stage came the necessity of finding work to support himself and an ailing wife ten years his senior. He tried painting for a year; this was not the answer. He wanted to record everything that he felt was of importance in Paris; for this the brush was inadequate. He acquired a bulky, heavy, view camera with a simple and not very sharp lens; it never left the tripod on which he mounted it. For the next twenty-nine years, until he died in 1927, Atget recorded as realistically as possible whatever appealed to him in his beloved Paris. He would carry this cumbersome equipment, traveling by bus in all seasons of the year, often before dawn, to capture the morning light on the silent streets. All districts knew this wizened man, hands and especially fingernails permanently blackened by photographer's chemicals, who was seen standing in a long, stained overcoat, pockets bulging with plate holders for his big 7¼-by-9¼-inch negatives.

His camera was little suited to stop action. He photographed architecture steeped in the atmosphere of the nineteenth century during the first quarter of the twentieth. Decaying châteaux and miserable shacks were his subjects, monuments and markets, staircases, facades, iron grilles, balconies and circus fronts in the flowering style of *Art Nouveau*, cobblestones and curbstones of empty streets, reflections in store windows and dressed mannikins. All these he photographed with remarkable clarity of detail, making a graphic historical record of his personal and often poetic vision. Critics have since referred to him as "the Walt Whitman of the camera."

He asked people to pose; for with his camera even the slightest movement would cause a blurred image—though he didn't mind ghost images in his pictures of architectural or inanimate subjects. He photographed hawkers of the streets, umbrella men, ragpickers, and streetwalkers. In one photograph a streetwalker stands

EUGENE ATGET, Street Circus. *Paris, about 1910.*

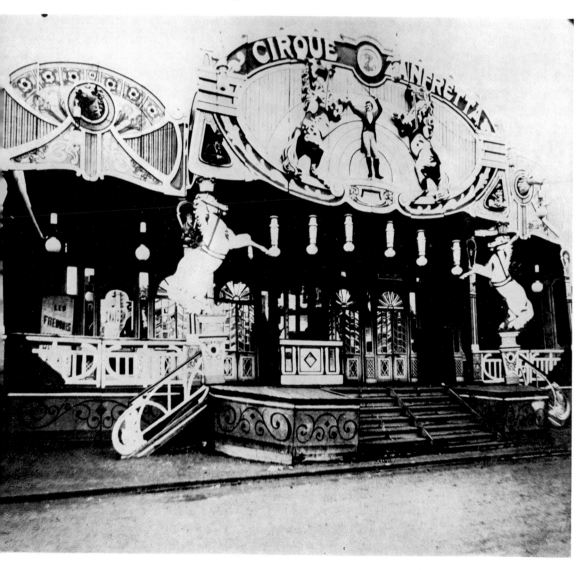

in the doorway of a house, obviously pleased to pose in her new fox-fur neckpiece, high lace boots, and the pert short skirt of her profession. Atget saw beauty in all manner of things, places, and people.

He made a precarious livelihood by taking commissions from authors; for one author of a book on prostitution he made photographs of brothels in Paris; for the French Archives he made a documentary series of photographs of historical buildings and medieval statuary; and to the artists of Paris he made available photographs of a thousand subjects. On the ground floor of the building where he had a fifth-floor apartment and darkroom was a sign, "Atget—Documents for Artists." Braque and Utrillo were the first to walk up and buy some of his prints at the most reasonable prices; he was so proud to see his photographs being used by the artists. His photographs served as the artists' memory, substitutes for detail drawings or pictures of mood and atmosphere of a given scene that the artist was painting.

Atget had that incredible quality of character inherent in some great artists who willingly spend a lifetime happily working without bothering about fame; men like Henri Rousseau, Van Gogh, Modigliani, and Soutine. Atget was honored by the artists as was Rousseau; Picasso, Marcel Duchamp, and especially Man Ray joined his circle of admirers. He served the Surrealist painters with authentic documents related to their conception of painting incongruous elements in juxtaposition. They honored him in 1926, when he was seventy years old, by reproducing two of his photographs in *La Révolution Surréaliste*, their official organ.

Atget's vision affected painting, but his photographs were not influenced by the paintings of his contemporaries or of the past. He imitated no artist or photographer, but his direct use of the camera is in the tradition of Fenton, Nadar, and Brady. He continued photographing one subject until he was satisfied that he had said something original about some overlooked aspect of Paris or until he was commissioned to do something else. His work grows out of the subject; it is not something derived from the art of painting. That may well be why his work was never exhibited in any photographic salon nor given any official recognition.

Man Ray, painter and photographer, introduced Atget to the Surrealists. And Berenice Abbott, in 1927 while working for Man Ray in Paris, photographed Atget (still in his long coat but quite unexpectedly with face washed and hair slicked down for the occasion) shortly before he died. After his death she rescued most of the 8,000 or so negatives that constituted his life's work. She bought a superb collection of about 2,000 negatives from Atget's landlord, brought them back to New York, made perfect prints, wrote enthusiastic articles and a book about his life, and arranged international shows of his photographs.

All contemporary documentary photographers are indebted to Berenice Abbott for preserving the vital contribution Atget made to photography. His pictures are so inspiring and powerfully honest that they have the quality of transporting the viewer to the time, place, and mood of the image. Atget reveals the perfect instant that best expresses the image he felt so deeply; it is that inborn emotional capacity that is Atget's impact on the seeing of our day. He is the spirtual ancestor of today's best documentary photographers, who carry forward with faster and better equipment his passion for honest, straight photography, endowing the image with explicit fullness composed from accidental arrangements of visual elements.

*All photographs in this chapter are
courtesy George Eastman House, Rochester.*

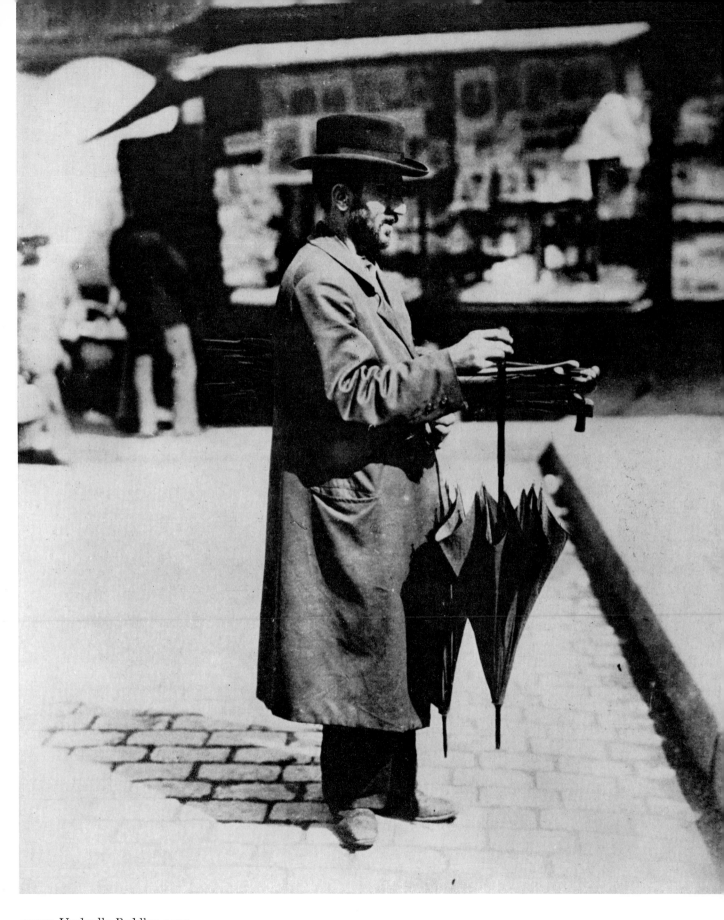

ATGET, Umbrella Peddler. *1910.*

ATGET
below: Wellhead. *Paris, about 1910.*
right: Paris Scene. 1905.

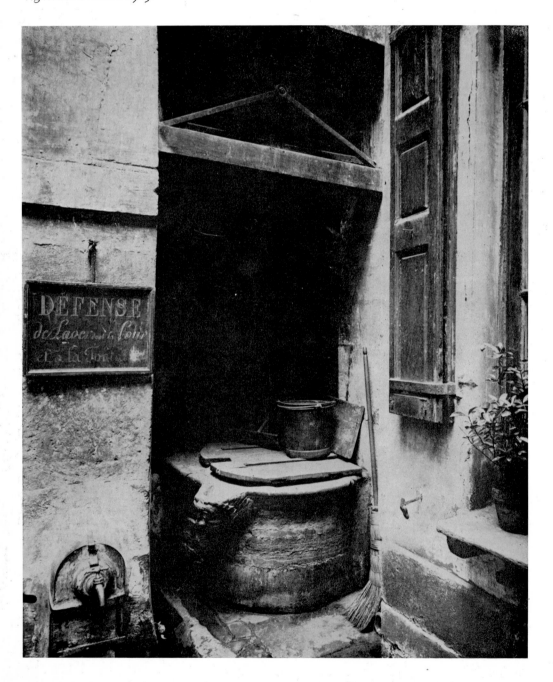

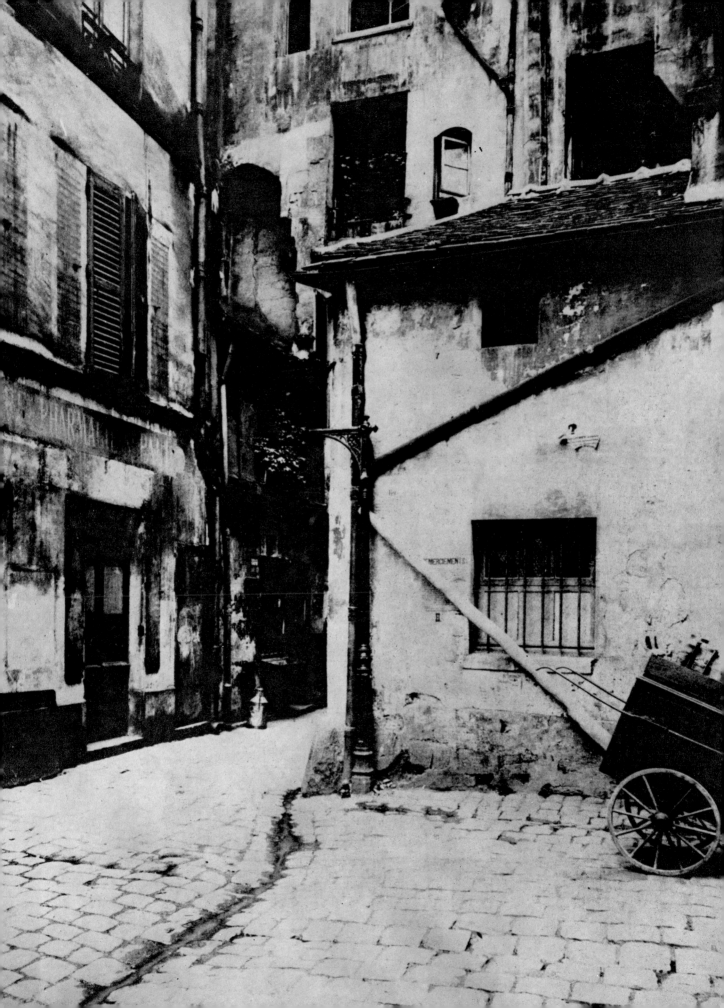

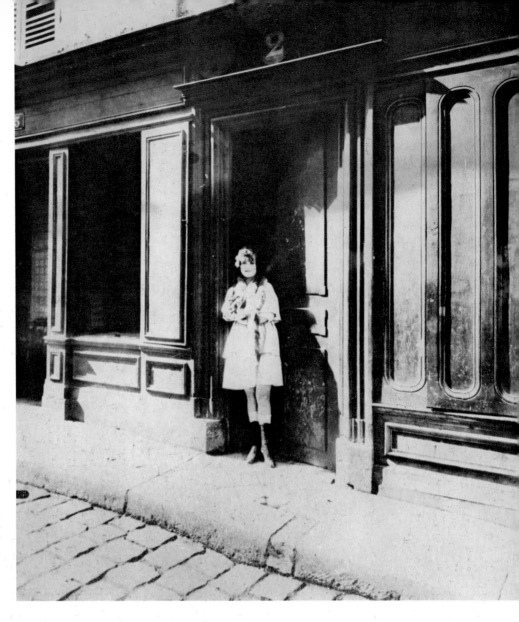

ATGET

above: Girl in Doorway of Brothel. *About 1920.*
right: Shop Window. *Paris, about 1910.*

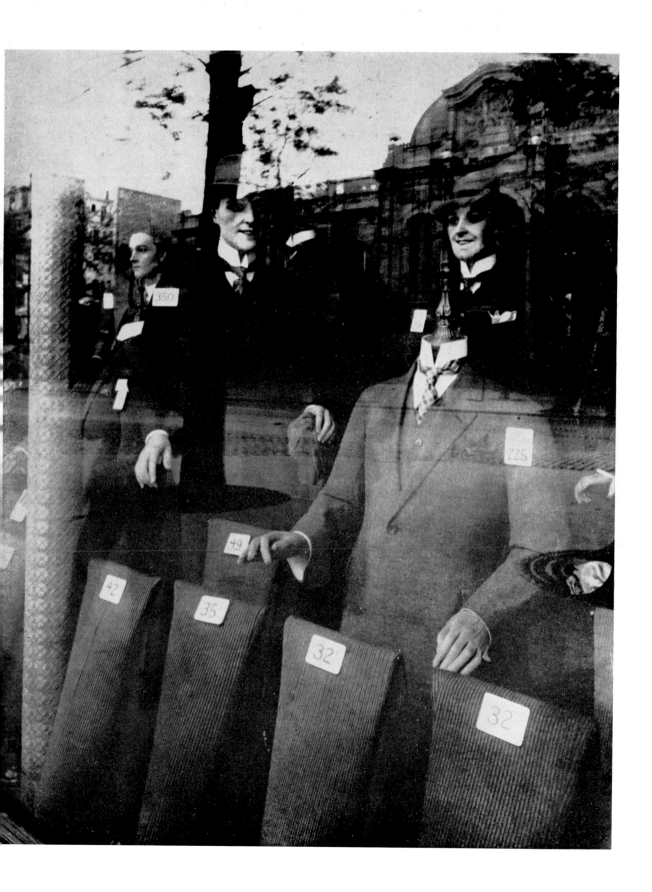

CHAPTER 26
Riis and Hine: Social Idealists with the Camera

LIKE THE PAMPHLETS OF VOLTAIRE, the photographs of Jacob A. Riis (1849–1914) helped to start a revolution. The revolt was in New York in 1887 against the wretched slums, the degrading tenements, and the venal corruption that permitted this misery to exist. Riis was a police reporter for *The Evening Sun*, America's first journalist-photographer. His writing was convincing, but his camera was decisive in making his work an incontrovertible, powerful weapon. Riis knew the underprivileged. In 1890 he wrote *How the Other Half Lives*, a book about his observations in the overcrowded, diseased, and criminally dark tenements which Lord Bryce in his *American Commonwealth* had called "the conspicuous failure of the city."

Riis was one of the first to use flash when it was introduced in the United States. This consisted of a mixture of powdered magnesium and potassium chlorate; it was first manufactured as cartridges to be used in what appeared to be a pistol. Because it brought out many a concealed weapon of those he would photograph, Riis soon substituted a frying pan to hold the powder which he ignited by hand. It burned in a blinding flash and exploded in the air; Riis photographed and, amid the resulting dense smoke, grabbed camera and tripod and ran. In this way he photographed the *Mulberry Bend Hideout* under a bridge, *Lodgings in Pell Street*, and *The East Side Growler Gang*.

He continued to gather evidence, in words and pictures, of the monstrous horrors in the tenements. Some of these five- and six-story wooden firetraps were without light and ventilation except for twilight air shafts. A typical block housed 2,781 people and had one bathtub. A half million people lived in the slums, nine or more to a room. Sweatshops abounded in the tenements, where no child-labor law could protect the children who worked an average of twelve hours a day in permanent semi-darkness for an average of 5 cents an hour.

Riis poked his camera into every unsavory street, into the most unattractive, unglamorous facets of the great city. His pictures and stories appeared in *The Sun*; of his photographs he made slides which he used in lectures; he wrote magazine articles and books. He was to see nine books published altogether, including *Children of the Poor*, 1892; *Out of Mulberry Street*, 1898; *Battle with the Slums*, 1902; *Children of the Tenements* and *Theodore Roosevelt, the Citizen* in 1904.

Theodore Roosevelt, as police commissioner of New York City, abolished the noisome horror of police lodging houses when Riis called his attention to them. Twenty-five years earlier, in 1870, when Riis had arrived in New York from his native Denmark, he had spent nights in the reeking jails. They had grown grimier since that day; the few pennies charge remained the same. Trained as a carpenter and writer, he wandered America's eastern cities from one job to another for the next seven years, until in 1877 he found work as a reporter on *The New York Tribune*.

JACOB A. RIIS, The Street, The Childrens' Only Playground. 1892.

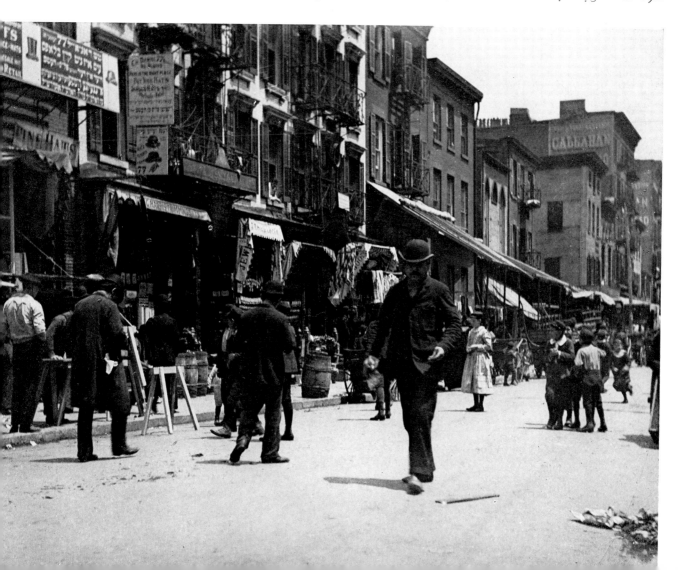

It was as a journalist with pen and camera that Riis made his tremendous pioneer reforms. Through his untiring efforts rear tenements were destroyed, child-labor laws were amended and enforced, a truant school was established, and desks became compulsory equipment for children in the schools. One of his greatest triumphs was the elimination of Mulberry Bend, a hangout for a bunch of toughs. A year later an appreciative city built a park and settlement house on this site, naming it in his honor. Today housing projects, schools, parks, and playgrounds all over the country are named to commemorate Jacob A. Riis.

It is Riis the photographer who concerns us. He used the camera only to illustrate his stories, to prove with documentary evidence the truth of what he was writing. He would never have considered his pictures works of art; he would not have indulged in such discussions. His interest would have extended to techniques that would guarantee a clearer, more detailed picture. Nevertheless, this dedicated man left a mighty series of pictures motivated by the depth of his humanitarian feelings. Their purpose accomplished, his photographs remain persuasive and moving pictures deeply appreciated every time they are exhibited. Riis's son, Dr. Roger William Riis, presented 412 of his father's glass negatives to the Museum of the City of New York, where exhibitions of Riis's photographs are often shown.

All photographs in this section are made by John H. Heffren from the
original Riis negatives, courtesy Museum of the City of New York.

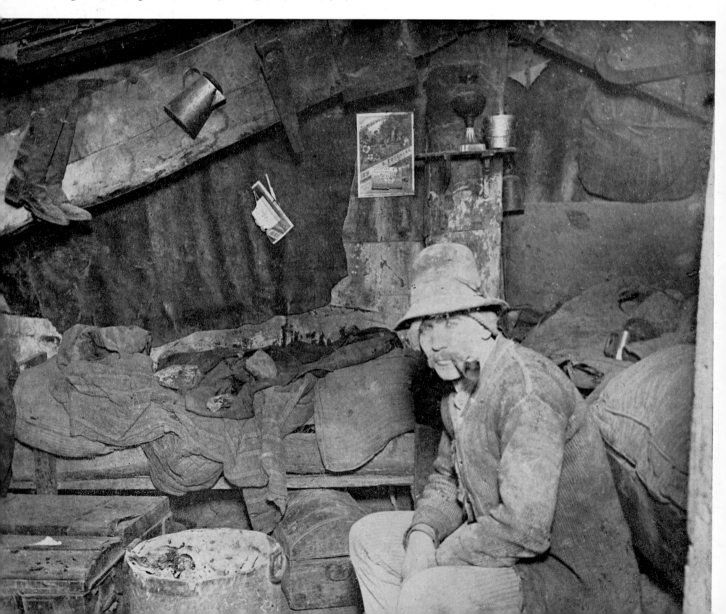

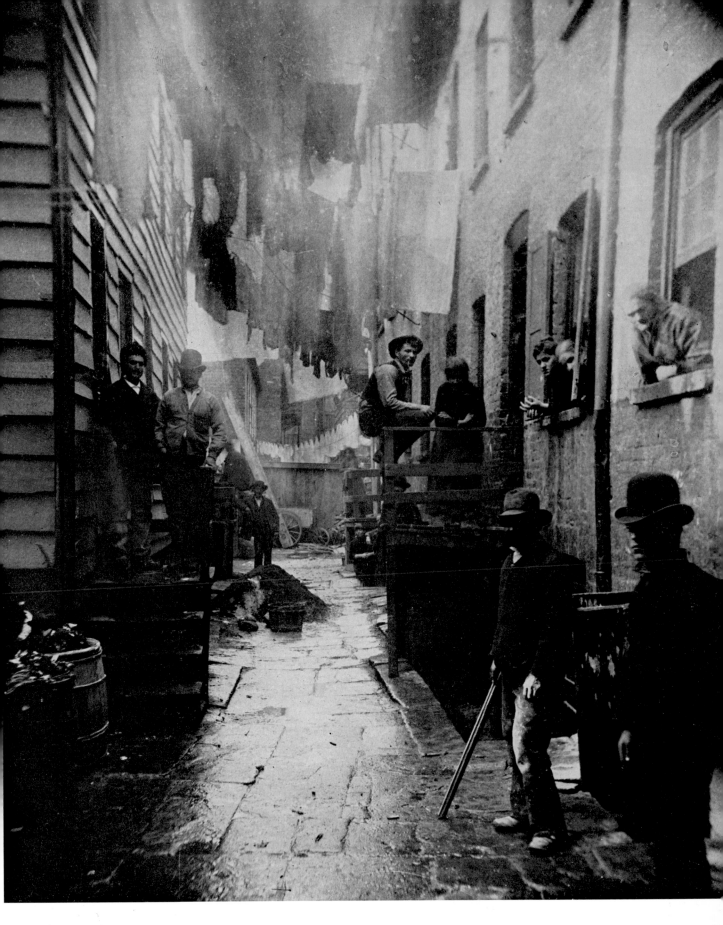

RIIS, *above*: Bandits' Roost, 59½ Mulberry Street. *1888.*
opposite page: In Sleeping Quarters. Rivington Street Dump. *About 1892.*

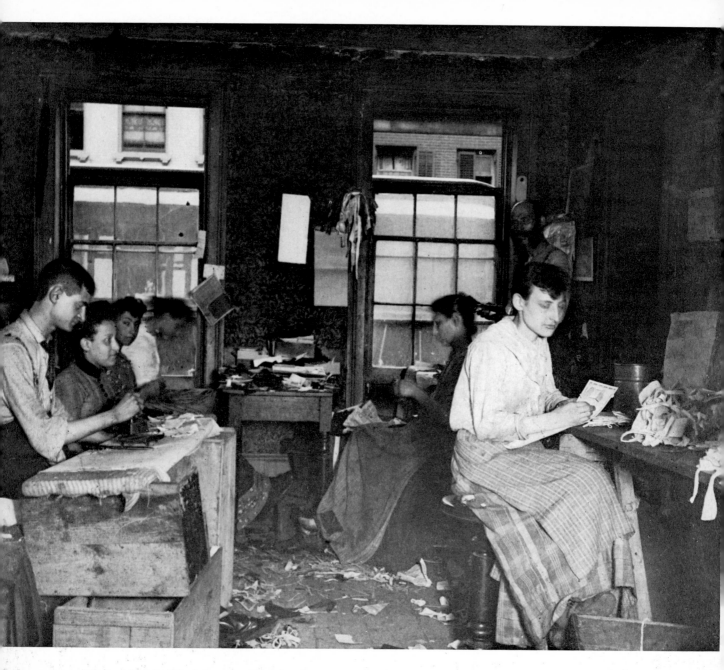

RIIS, *above:* Necktie Workshop in a Division Street Tenement. *1890.*
right: A Class in the Condemned Essex Market School with Gas Burning by Day. *1902.*

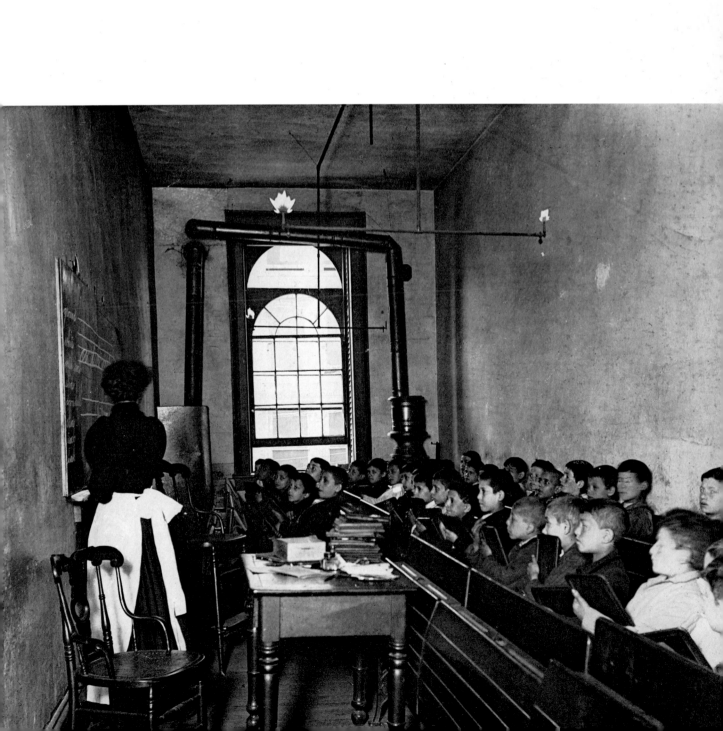

LEWIS W. HINE

THE UNENDING POLEMIC regarding art and photography that raged among the members of Photo-Secession and in the pages of *Camera Work* touched Lewis W. Hine (1874–1940) hardly more than it did Jacob A. Riis. Hine was a trained sociologist who learned how to use the camera in order to satisfy an urgent need to take honest pictures telling forceful truths about intolerable injustices which he saw all around him.

Lewis Wickes Hine was born in 1874 in Oshkosh, Wisconsin; as a boy he worked long hours a day in a factory, learning first-hand what he was to photograph later. He studied at the State Normal School in his home town, then attended the University of Chicago and New York University, from which he received a master's degree.

In 1901 Hine went to teach at the Ethical Culture School in New York. Two years later he acquired camera and flash gun. He learned control of his equipment through trial and error as he took photographs intended to dramatize the school's program.

He gave up teaching to become a full-time photographer. He became a free-lance conscience with a camera. Ellis Island, New York's port of entry where millions of immigrants first saw the "promised land," drew him to photograph sad-eyed "madonnas" surrounded by their bundles and children. He followed them through the gates into the overcrowded slums, the swarming streets and the impossible, enslaving jobs. All this he put into sharp focus as a social indictment against the conditions offered its new citizens by the nation's largest and richest city. The magazine *Charities and the Commons* published these pictures in 1908. The same year the magazine's editors hired him to make a complete, sociological study with his camera of miners' lives; a truthful and comprehensive portrayal of their housing, health, children, education, and death, which was published as *The*

All photographs in this section are courtesy George Eastman House, Rochester.

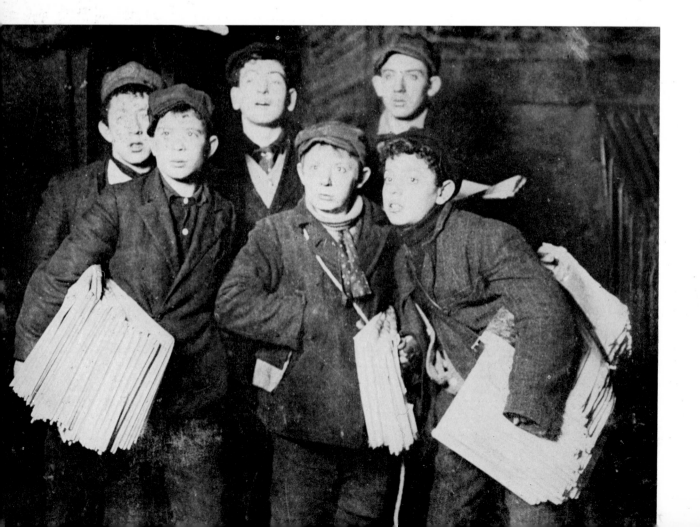

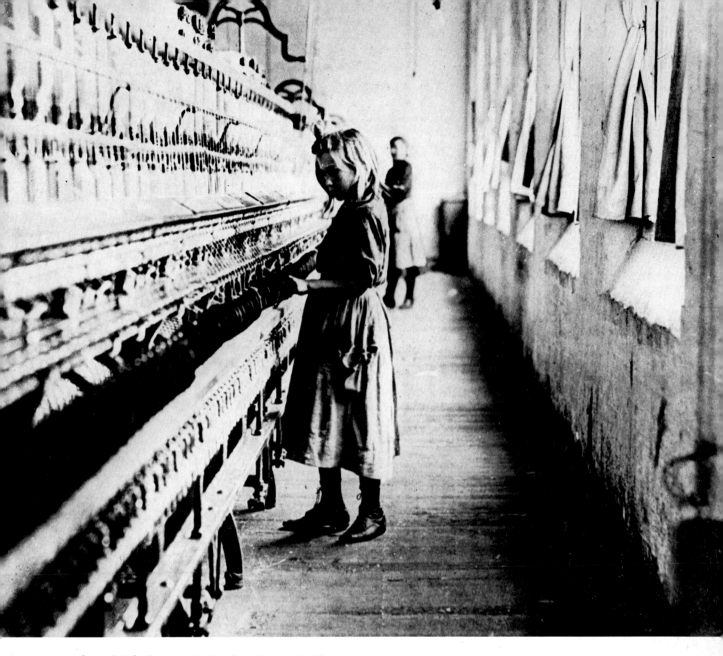

LEWIS W. HINE, *above:* Little Spinner in Carolina Cotton Mill. *1909.*
left: Group of Newsboys. *Taken with flash at midnight on Brooklyn Bridge, 1909.*

Pittsburgh Survey. Three years later he was appointed staff photographer for the National Child Labor Committee to investigate child-labor conditions existing in the United States. Hine returned with a series of appalling pictures that shocked the country. Children as young as eight years old worked in cotton mills tending machines, were hired as coal breakers in dangerous mines, and sold newspapers in freezing weather late at night. These starving, exploited children had little chance for an education or hope for the future. Hine took notes of what they said and estimated the children's size by marking his vest buttons. He kept a sociological record of

their health, their habits, and all he encountered. The nation reacted immediately. His vivid photographs, published as human documents, were strikingly clear. A protective child-labor law was passed. Hine had made the camera into a formidable weapon for social progress.

In World War I he was with the American Red Cross overseas as a photographer, and after the armistice he remained with Red Cross Relief to feed the desolate and help the wretched in the Balkans.

He returned to New York in 1920. He still lugged his big camera. He was a sociologist; not all America was sordid and slums, not all workers were exploited and

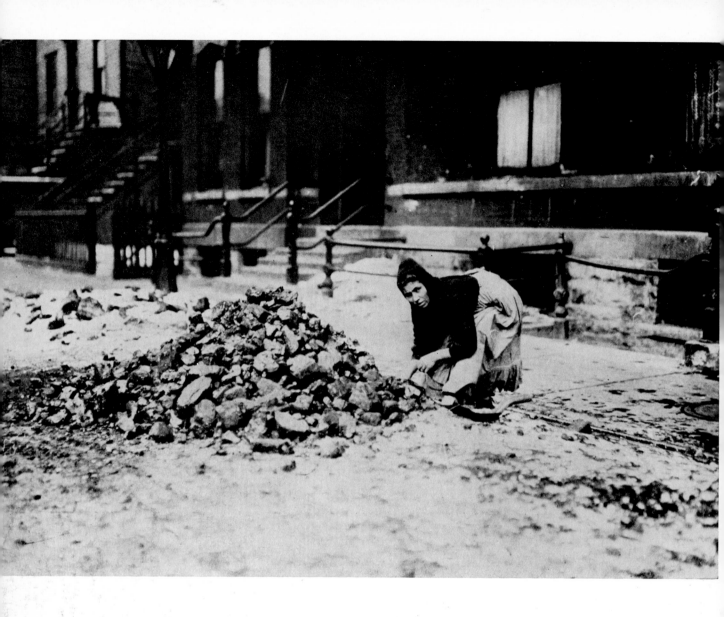

enslaved. He believed in his country; he believed in the people from all over the world who came to this land and built this country. He took hundreds of pictures of *Men at Work*, vigorous men with pride in themselves and in their work. A positive statement was to be made. What was more positive than the Empire State Building then being erected? He was hired as its official photographer. All the languages heard in the tenements were heard here also. Floor by floor Hine photographed the men building the nation's tallest skyscraper. He toasted his bread alongside them in the forge used to heat rivets. His photographs ingeniously reflect the men's attitude towards the work and the building. "Topping Out Day,"

when the last girder of the mooring mast was riveted, Hine had himself swung out on the end of a crane. His legs twined around the hook, a clumsy 4-by-5 camera in both hands, intent only upon capturing the historic moment on his film, he knew no fear. No one was there to take his picture hanging perilously over New York's streets. The men's job was done. Hine had a series of fine photographs, not a mere record glorifying labor.

Hine, humanitarian with a camera, wrote his own best explanation of his purposes: "There were two things I wanted to do. I wanted to show the things that had to be corrected. I wanted to show the things that had to be appreciated."

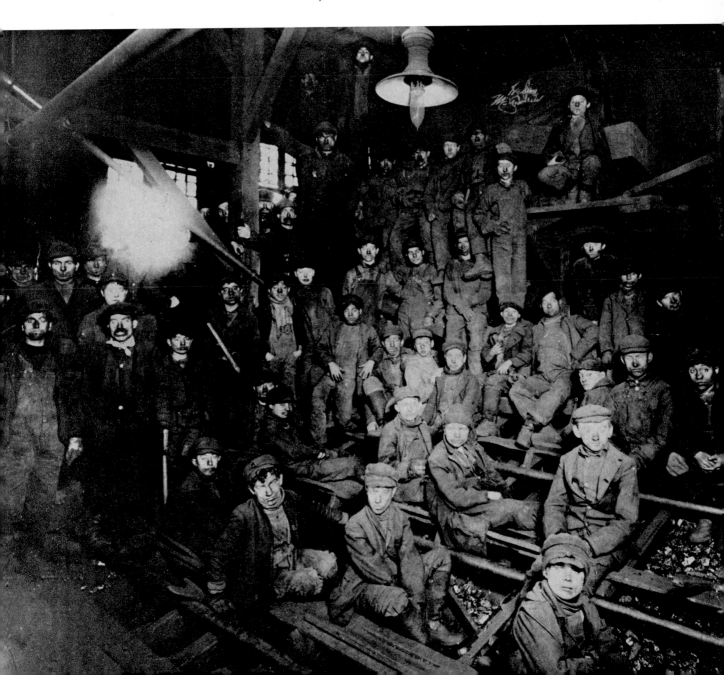

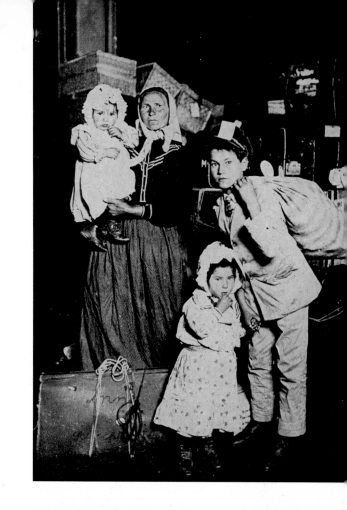

HINE, *below*: Sidewalks of New York. *1910*.
right: Italian Family Seeking Lost Baggage. *Ellis Island, 1905*.
opposite page: Madonna of Ellis Island. *1905*.

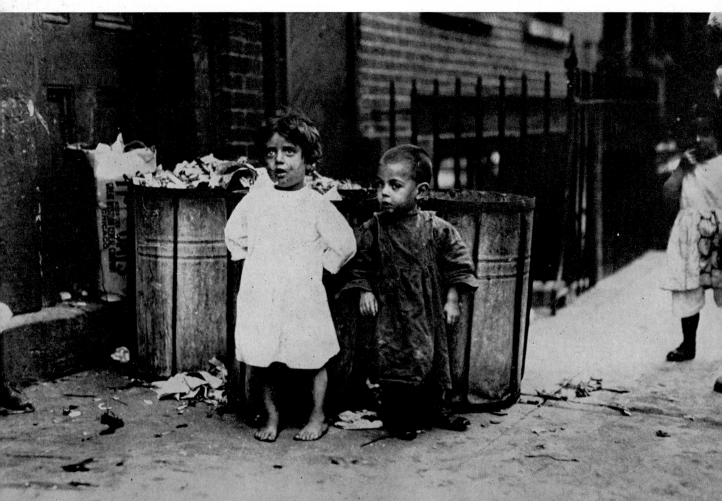

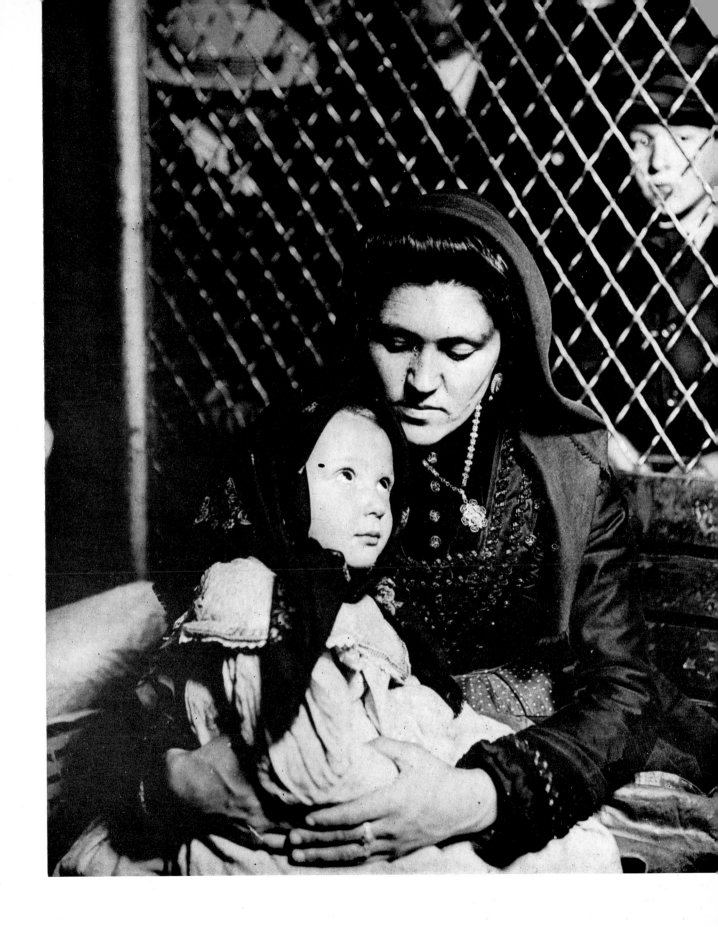

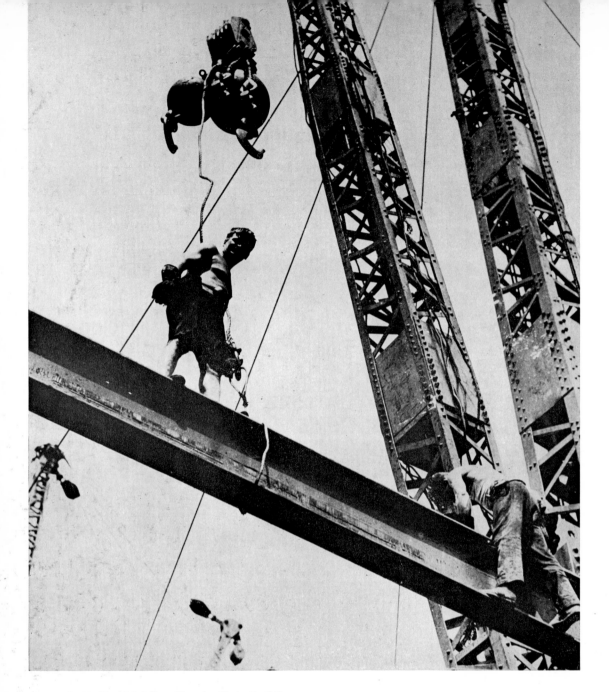

HINE, *above:* Derrick Men, Empire State Building. *1931.*
right: Riveting the Last Beam, Empire State Building. *1931.*

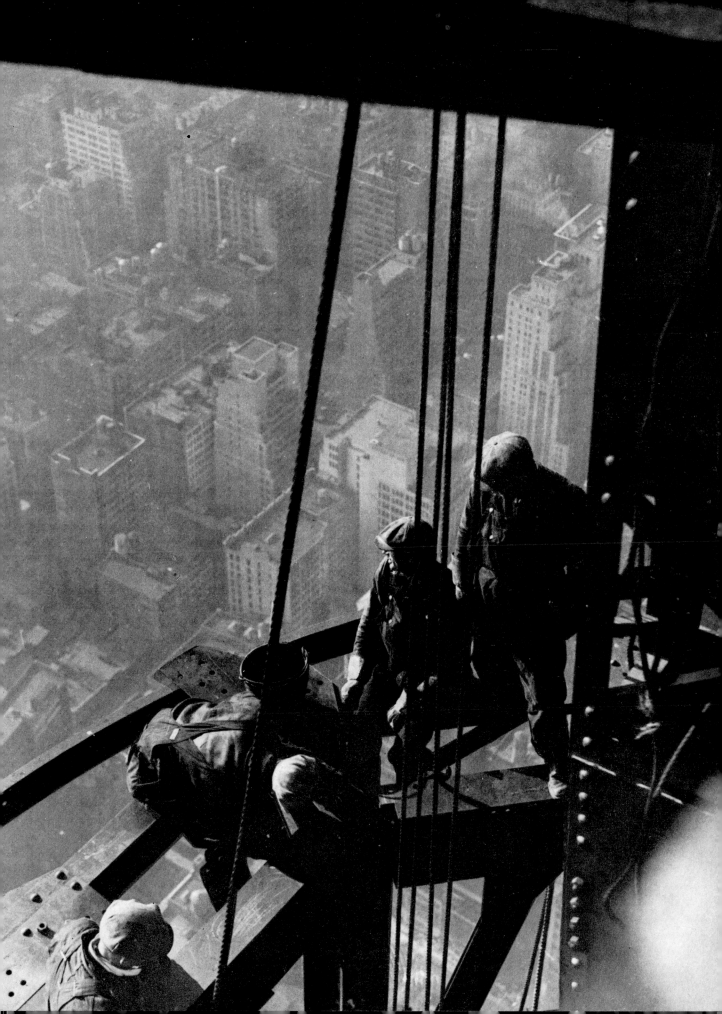

CHAPTER 27

Genthe: Celebrities and Anonymous Throngs

ARNOLD GENTHE (1869–1942) thought he had invented the candid photograph about a half century ago, but what he actually created is as formalized as the portrait technique he so valiantly fought.

For thirty years he took pictures of the world's great. Three Presidents sat for him: Theodore Roosevelt, William Howard Taft, and Woodrow Wilson; two of the nation's wealthiest men: John D. Rockefeller and Andrew Mellon; many international celebrities of the stage —Bernhardt, Pavlova, Isadora Duncan, Ellen Terry, Greta Garbo, Eleanora Duse; and the highborn everywhere. With his camera he traveled the entire world.

Dr. Genthe (it was not an honorary title; he received a doctorate from the University of Jena for work in philology in 1894, before he was twenty-five years old) was an urbane bachelor, six-foot-two, charming, and an accomplished linguist. With his beautiful head and courtly manners he was considered one of the most artistic candid photographers of his time.

But his was not candid photography as we see it today. The only thing candid about it was that he snapped the shutter when the sitter didn't expect him to. What Genthe tried for was "art" photography; his purpose was to make the photograph resemble one or another of the graphic arts.

A familiar nude was a copy of some ancient Greek

orso; he called it "living sculpture." A portrait of an American girl's profile was skillful when it was made to resemble that of the Venus de Milo. Portraits, no matter of whom, were most successful when they were mistaken for mezzotints. Pictures of dancers on the beach were deliberately made to resemble soft-ground etchings or charcoal drawings; landscapes in effect became muted water colors.

Emphasis was on soft focus with velvety blacks and brilliant whites, ideas he took from the chiaroscuro paintings of Rembrandt and Caravaggio or from lithographs by Toulouse-Lautrec; he created what became known as the "Genthe style."

Still, he was a radical with a camera, for he gave it the respect an artist has for his equipment, and he made it work for him creatively. He broke with the muscle-bound traditions, the uniform sharpness, the characterless stiff poses that were the characteristic of photographers of the day, especially in San Francisco, where he opened his first gallery around the turn of the century. Nor did Genthe indulge in the practice prevalent in commercial studios and arty photographic circles of retouching or drawing on a negative.

He was selective, a master in modeling with light, always attempting to capture the poetic mood, thereby creating his conception of a romantic picture. A soft moonglow suffuses all his important portraits. Through film, lens, lighting, and the use of mat paper for printing, the age lines of his sitters were eliminated.

In several portraits he indicated ideas which have been further developed in our day by magazine photographers who portray the subject set in the midst of his profession's symbols. In the twenties Genthe made a series of photographs in which the subject is surrounded by props: Henri Charpentier, the chef, is seen wearing a huge white cap, holding a pot lid open over a stove; Childe Hassam stands beside an etching press. These were made in the studio and bear the imprint of Genthe's academic romanticism—he strove, he said, "to show the mind and the spirit of the person."

His greatest pictures he took in 1894 when he first arrived, in San Francisco's Chinatown, and, a little more than a decade later, when he photographed the earthquake which destroyed San Francisco. It is for these exceptional, honest pictures, deeply charged with feeling, rather than for the Genthe style of art portraiture that he will be remembered.

San Francisco's Chinatown sixty years ago was a transplanted Canton; few changes were made when it was moved from the opposite shores of the Pacific. It was

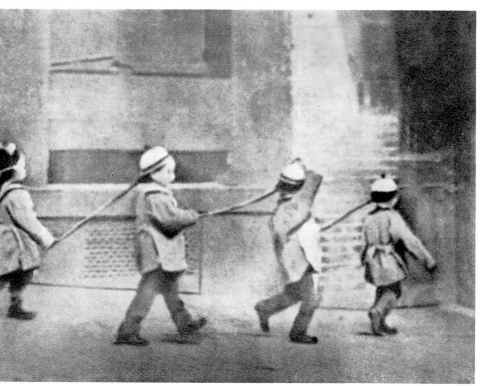

All photographs in this chapter courtesy The Art Institute of Chicago.

ARNOLD GENTHE, Pigtail Parade, San Francisco. *About 1897.*

313

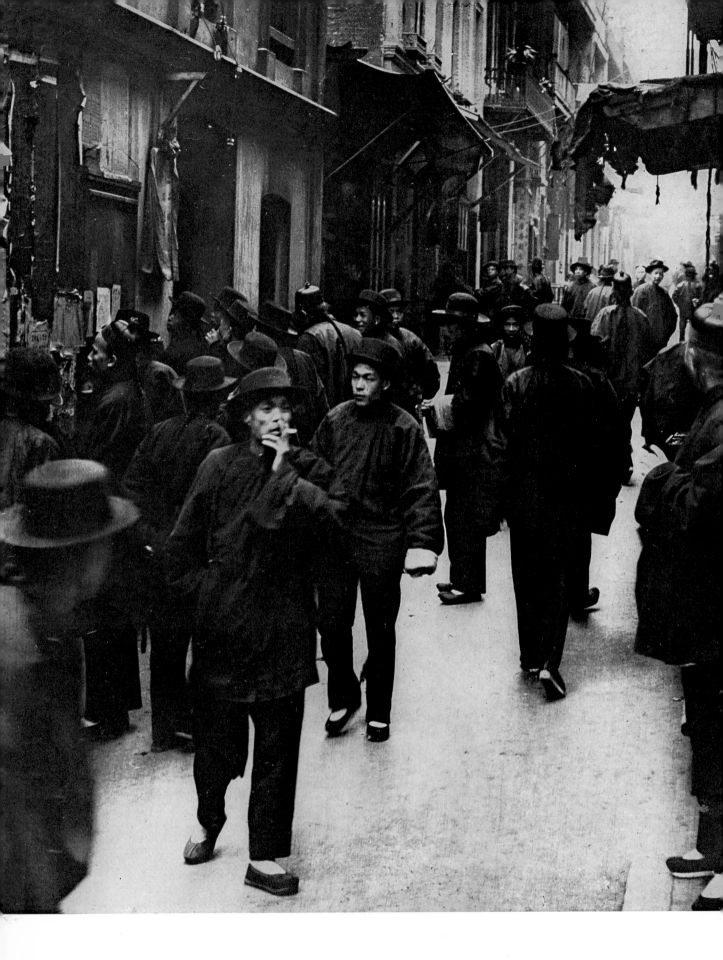

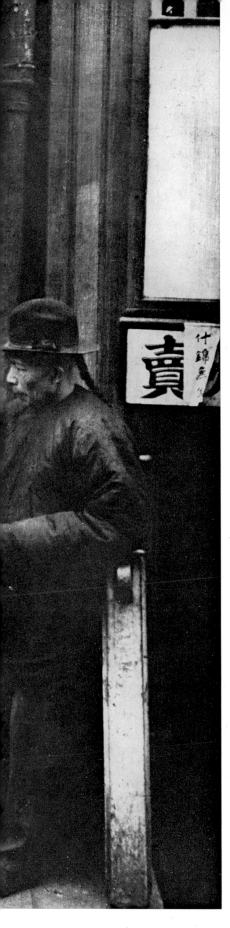

an Oriental city within the city of San Francisco. Ten thousand black-clad men shuffled silently in the sandal-wood-scented streets, streets with such descriptive names as the "Street of the Sing Song Girls," "The Street of the Gamblers," "The Street of the Butchers," and many others including the "Devil's Kitchen." Genthe shuffled along with the denizens of the district. He became a familiar figure. Unobtrusively he slipped a small camera with its fast Zeiss lens from his pocket.

To the superstitious Chinese, young and old, the camera was a "black devil box" which contained all the evils of the world ready to pounce out on them when the box clicked.

Genthe took the only complete record extant of China-town and the strange people and places that flourished with their Oriental flavor in the dissolute, beautiful city of the Pacific Coast. He took photographs of the derelict dope addicts and murderers, the rich, silken-embroidered costumes of the merchants and their children as they lived within painted frame buildings supporting bal-conies festooned with flower pots and gay, multicolored lanterns hanging in the cool courtyards.

It was all wiped out in one angry day, April 18, 1906, the day of the earthquake of San Francisco. Genthe's powerful pictorial record remains, a remarkable series of *documents* made years before the word was ever used in connection with photography in America.

The day it happened Genthe's studio fell apart at the first tremor. Fire wiped out everything a little later. By this time picture taking with him was automatic. He borrowed the first camera he laid hands on in a store he found open. It was a simple box, a 3A Kodak Special. He stuffed his pockets with film and he roamed the devas-tated city from Fisherman's Wharf to Nob Hill, shoot-ing pictures of the collapsing, dynamited buildings, the consuming fires, and the dazed, wandering people.

Genthe lost his studio, his equipment, his precious library of three thousand volumes, but he fortunately saved the negatives of his Chinatown pictures. Will Irwin, a writer with whom he later collaborated on a book, had prevailed upon Genthe to put his Chinese

GENTHE, Street of the Gamblers,
Chinatown, San Francisco. *About 1896.*

negatives in a vault. They came through the fire unscathed and now are in the Archives of the Library of Congress.

Genthe was to stay in San Francisco five more years. From 1911 to his death in 1942 at the age of seventy-three, his studio was in New York, on the top floor of a building in the heart of the shopping district. He roamed the world taking pictures of people and places, in his soft-focus Genthe style, not like the earlier sharper, profounder pictures he had made in San Francisco when he first took up the camera.

In New York Genthe gained an enviable reputation as a photographer of tycoons and celebrities in all fields; here he perfected his internationally popular technique. In his autobiography written late in life he commented, "Today I have only gratitude, untouched by regret, for my part as one of the pioneers in the development of an art which has done so much to spread the gospel of beauty . . ." [I helped] "lift photography from the mechanical, lifeless medium it had become to the dignity and status of a real art."

It is strange—a lifetime as a portrait photographer of great names, and Arnold Genthe's most memorable portraits were made in the first decade of his life as cameraman in San Francisco's Chinatown, where there were no names of importance, only anonymous throngs.

GENTHE, *below:* Chicken Vendor.
right: Street of the Balconies,
Chinatown, San Francisco. *About 1896.*

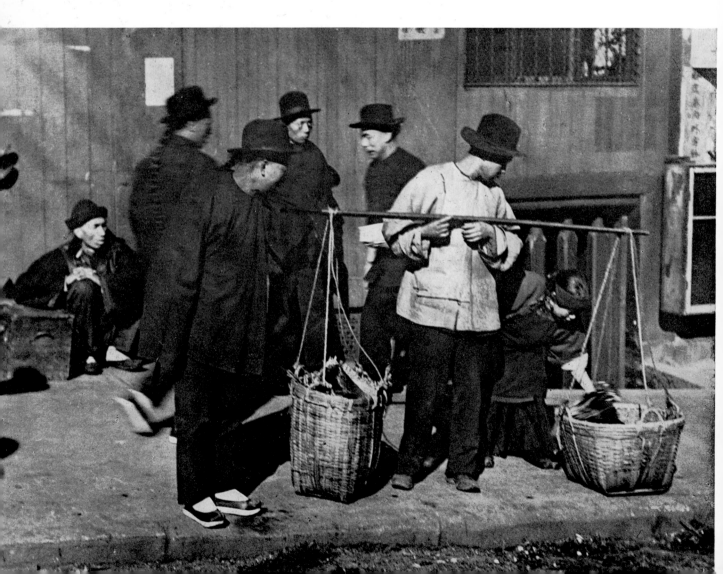

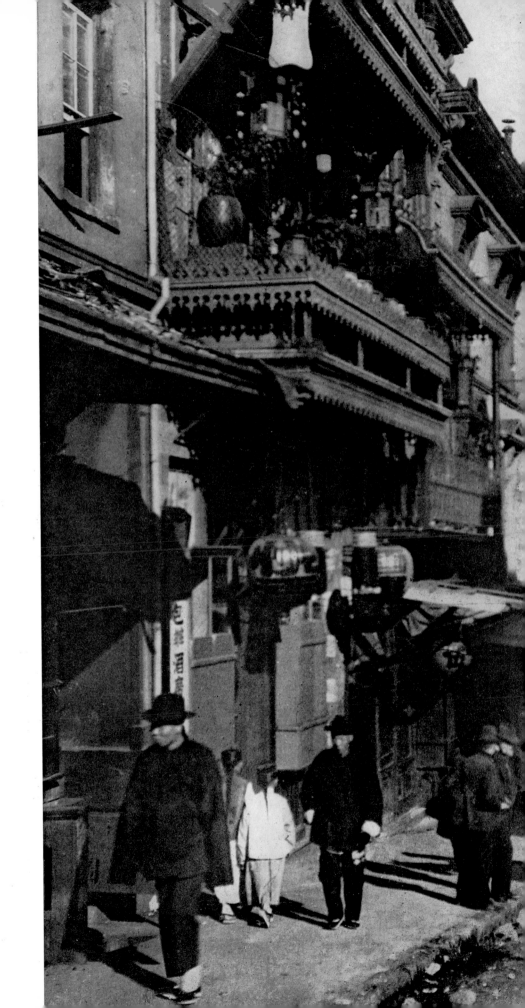

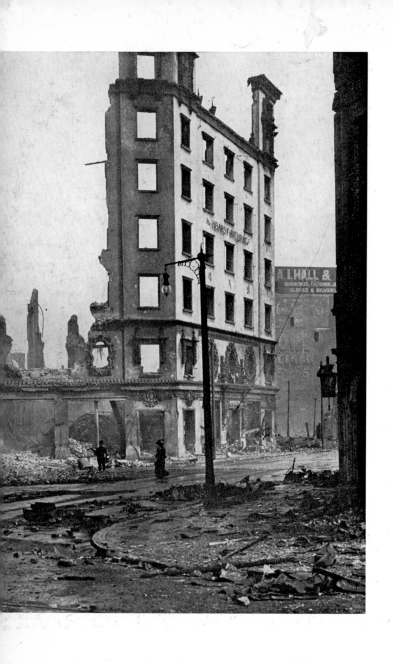

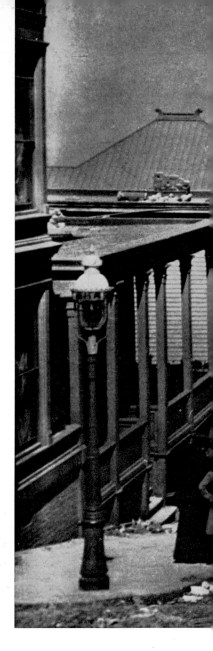

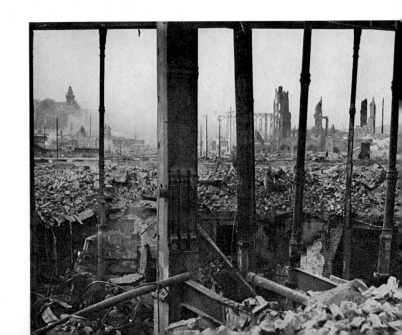

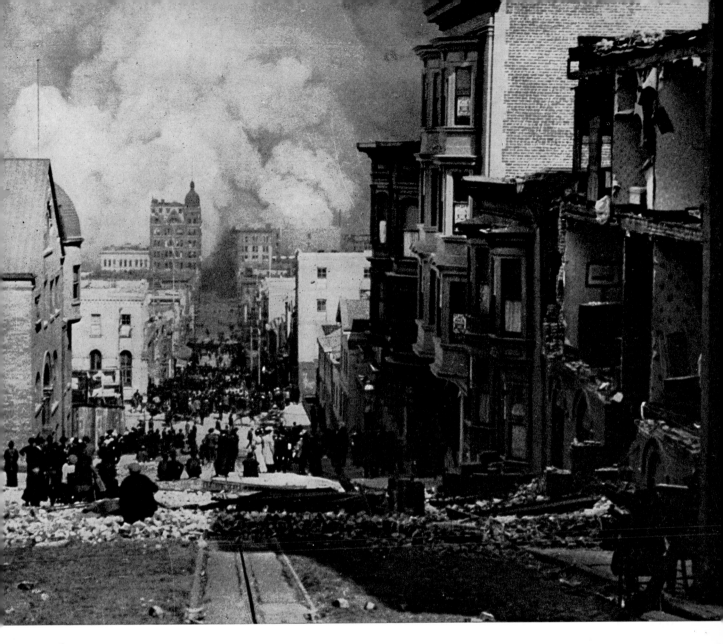

GENTHE, *Scenes of the San Francisco earthquake and fire, week of April, 1906. Prints made by Ansel Adams from original negatives.* *above:* View of Sacramento Street. *opposite page:* Two Views.

CHAPTER 28

Edward Weston: A New Vision

VERY FEW CREATIVE PHOTOGRAPHERS were trained as cameramen. Most were artists, others teachers, engineers, musicians, writers, sociologists, following professions which gave them little if any aesthetic satisfaction. Often as mature men they became photographers to experiment and explore a personal way of seeing, to create their kind of a picture.

Edward Weston is the exception, the rare creative photographer who as a boy definitely knew his destiny. He told me in his cabin near Carmel, California, in 1952, "I saw my first exhibition of photographs at the Art Institute of Chicago exactly fifty years ago when I was sixteen. It changed my whole life. I made father buy me a camera and from that moment on I was absorbed with it."

Three years later, in 1905, he was in California canvassing door to door, hauling a post-card camera, and taking pictures of babies, family groups, marriages, funerals; a dollar a dozen was the usual price. He worked in commercial studios, he studied and mastered the intricacies of the darkroom. Portrait photography was to be his livelihood.

He married in 1909 and in the next decade fathered four sons. In 1911 he opened a portrait studio in Tropico, California. He specialized in portraits of children and he started to use natural light inside his studio. Soon Weston became a name to reckon with in portrait and pictorial photography. Honors were heaped upon him; he was elected to the London Salon and, closer to home, he demonstrated and lectured on his techniques. One-man shows added to his reputation but his soft-focus "arty" photographs, so acclaimed by the amateur and the camera clubs, left him feeling empty and unsatisfied. He knew that the pictures were tricky, but what qualities he wanted to capture with his camera, he still did not know.

Had it not been for the San Francisco Fair of 1915, where Weston was introduced to modern art, creative music, and contemporary literature, he might have continued to photograph "exalted portraits" to meet the financial demands of his growing family. Under the stimulus of abstract art Weston generated a creative response within himself. He broke with his former successes; he no longer submitted his pictures to the salons. But he had no steady means of income; so his conservative friends and family frowned on these Bohemian antics.

Weston went back to his camera. He experimented constantly with the extreme close-up and the abstraction. He created heightened effects in shadows by mixing artificial and natural light and he photographed fragments of the figure rather than the entire human body. He found he could express himself as an artist with the camera; he was as original with his chosen medium as the artists he respected and he did not have to emulate their styles.

Beginning in 1922 in Ohio, he made the first of his dramatic compositions revealing the clear forms and rhythms inherent in the great manufacturing plants of American industry. The abstract designs to be found in the substantial reality of architecture which Weston disclosed in his photographs immediately influenced photographers who still exploit his conception.

August 2, 1923, on board ship from New York to Mexico, Weston makes a first entry in his Day Book. "Certainly it is not to escape myself that I am Mexico bound . . . I am good friends with myself. Nor do I hunt new subject matter, that is at hand out the back door—anywhere . . . I feel a battle ahead to avoid being swept away by the picturesque, the romantic."

Three weeks later in Mexico City he notes his exhibition is attended by "men—men—men—ten to one woman. I have never before heard such intense and understanding appreciation."

By January of next year he records, "I am now only approaching an attainment in photography that in my ego of several years ago I thought I had reached long ago. It will be necessary to destroy, unlearn and rebuild." He scrupulously scrutinizes all he had produced, comparing his former work with the portraits and the pictures of maguey plants he now photographs. He is not satisfied. He goes back to experiments, photographing still lifes of the toys and objects found in the house. He visits Mexico's pyramids and small towns, searches landscape, sky, and people for new visions with his camera, for photographs to perpetuate the peak of his emotional, artistic seeing. He is seeking the precise pinpoint in time before he snaps the shutter, and for his income he carefully tends a little portrait studio in Mexico City.

In September, 1925, after a brief visit to California he returns with his son Brett. He holds an exhibition of his photographs in the State Museum of Guadalajara. The powerful painter of protest, Alfaro Siqueiros wrote, "In Weston's photographs the texture, the physical quality of things is rendered with the utmost exactness, the rough is rough, the smooth is smooth, flesh is alive, stone is hard. The things have a definite proportion and weight, and are placed at a clearly defined distance one from another . . . the beauty which these photographs of Weston's possess, is *photographic beauty*."

His stimulating friend, Diego Rivera, wrote, "Few are the modern plastic expressions that have given me purer and more intense joy than the masterpieces that are frequently produced in the work of Edward Weston . . . There is not in Europe, by far, a photographer of such dimensions . . . Edward Weston is the American artist, one whose sensibility contains the extreme modernity of the plasticity of the North and the living tradition of the Land of the South, Mexico."

The third of the triumvirate who fathered the Mexican Renaissance, the one-handed José Clemente Orozco, did not write about Weston, but five years later he arranged and installed Weston's exhibition of photographs in New York City.

One entry in the 1926 day book Weston kept in Mexico, reads, "Give me peace and an hour's time and I create. Emotional heights are easily attained, peace and time are not," and a later entry the same year, "I have been slow developing, perhaps laying the stronger foundation. Almost forty and am now beginning to realize—to see."

Cézanne's old complaint in his exact word "realize." The cry of a creative artist used when he could not satisfactorily complete a painting as he sat in front of Mont St. Victoire in southern France, now, unawares, used in the same way by Weston trying to create his kind of a picture before the mountains of Mexico.

Weston loved the country, the landscape, the people, and the art world of which he had become a vital part, but Mexico couldn't keep him; his roots were to the north. In January, 1927, he writes, "During these three months since returning to California I have done nothing for myself . . . I am not yet an integral part of these surroundings, one foot is still in Mexico."

A fertile artist does not lie fallow long. By April he had photographed two nudes, "which go beyond those considered fine in Mexico" and a month later he records, "I have two new loves, bananas and shells." That summer he added radishes, eggplant, canteloupes, artichokes, cabbages, and peppers. Vegetables became vital to his artistic life. He saw sculpture in growing forms ever-changing in the light. New discoveries in seeing, surface textures, interrelated rhythms, movements in shapes, and designs which critics called erotic symbols. The selective power of Weston had conceived of a shell and a vegetable as something monumental just as he had reduced a mountain to the intimacy of a figure. He had created an artistic entity with his camera, willfully isolating his subject, deliberately selecting film, lens, paper, and chemicals to complete a photographic image he envisioned before he exposed.

The following summer he and his son Brett closed a portrait studio they had tried in San Francisco and moved south to Carmel in the mountains near Monterey. With his 8-by-10-inch view camera he was soon out taking pictures of tangled tree stumps, eroded rocks, and the sea at Point Lobos which his poet friend, Robinson Jeffers, had described as "strange, introverted and storm-twisted." It had a beauty that stamped itself on his emotions, resulting in a series of his most exciting photographs of nature.

In 1932 Ansel Adams, then a pianist with an amateur's portfolio of pictures, Willard Van Dyke, Imogen Cunningham, several other young independent photographers interested in sharp focus, and Edward Weston, formed a group they named "f/64" after one of the small shutter stops which allow for straight, clear detailed pictures. It was a stand in the mountains of the West against the plague of the pictorial salon rolling across the country. The group held its first exhibition of straight photography in the De Young Museum in San Francisco. The exhibition won the respect of photographers everywhere.

Within a year Weston withdrew from the group to live at Carmel a free, Thoreau kind of life. He took his camera into the huge ranches of southern California shooting orchards and fields, geometric patterns of growing things, monumental vistas instead of close-ups, but with as much attention paid to the forms and the composition as he had to a single pepper or to a nude figure.

In 1936 he discovered the sand dunes at Oceano with their long undulating shapes, soft rounded forms, deep black shadows, and myriads of textured sands; here he made what many consider to be his greatest pictures.

In 1937 he became the first photographer to receive a Guggenheim Fellowship. $2,000! He was free for a year —no portraits, no pictures for anyone but himself and his new wife, Charis. They bought a car, a tarpaulin to convert it into a darkroom, sleeping bags, some canned goods, and they were off for Death Valley. Most of their money went for photography. They carried twelve holders which could take twenty-four pieces of cut film for his 8-by-10-inch camera. There would be no enlarging, only contact printing. Big camera, small shutter stops, and contact printing for the finest details possible. Each piece of film he made count. Nothing was left to chance. "When I look on my ground glass before exposure I must know and see exactly how my finished print will look," Weston wrote.

He didn't wait for a picture, for the light to change, or for animals or people to come into or go out of a scene. He explains, "If I must wait an hour, I put up my camera and go on, knowing I am likely to find three subjects just as good in the same hour."

For the purposeful Westons the money went far; $2,000 took them 35,000 miles. Weston was "realizing," creating pictures in the vastness of nature through his ground glass—a profound artistic emotion instantaneously captured. The following year he saw the results; it took him all of 1938 to print his 1,500 negatives; the Guggenheim Fellowship had been extended to make this possible. His wife, Charis Wilson Weston, had kept a log. It was published along with ninety-six of his photographs two years later as *California and the West*. The photographs he took are for the most part spontaneous and direct translations of nature portraying his sensitive reactions to desert, mountain, and sea. He does not describe or record what he sees; he makes pictures of his sensuous contact with nature.

The Fellowship over, back he went to his kind of honest, unretouched portraits for which by this time he had a few customers. Often he would take the subject near his shack or on the rocks near the sea close by.

In 1941 he was commissioned to make photographic interpretations all over the nation to illustrate a new edition of Walt Whitman's *Leaves of Grass* which when published contained fifty of his photographs.

The war years he spent at his cabin in Carmel photographing with his big camera the graceful, living sculptural forms of his many cats as they entered and left

˙ EDWARD WESTON, Halved Cabbage. 1930.

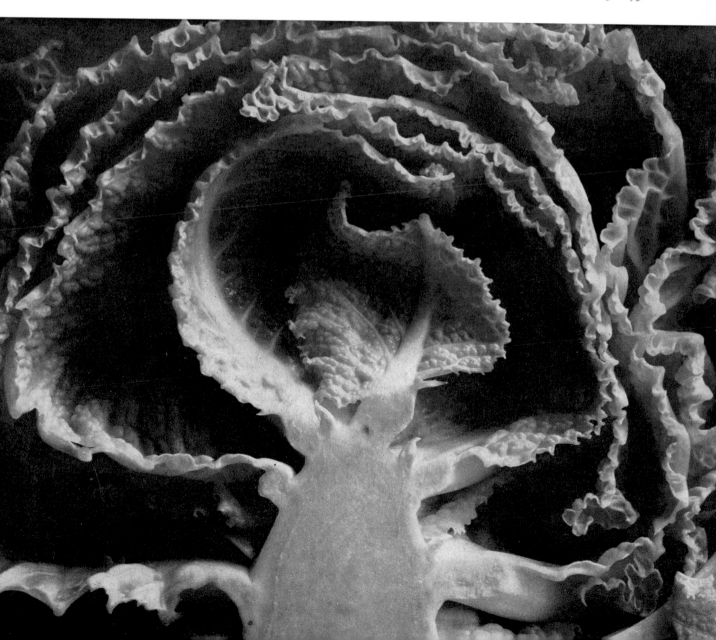

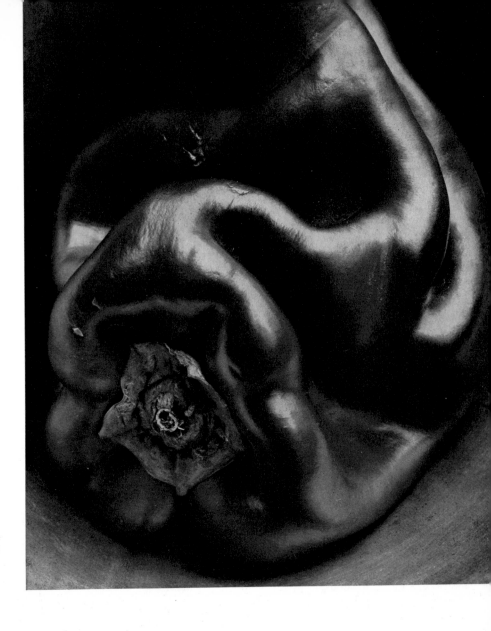

through their own little door he had cut for them. His four sons were in service. One of his favorite views, Point Lobos, was under Army jurisdiction. Restricted, the prolific photographer worked with objects, animals, people. He had once written, "Limitations need not interfere with full creative expression."

Health, never one of his problems, suddenly became his major concern when he fell ill with crippling Parkinson's disease. Unable to hold a camera in his trembling hands, the undaunted Weston directed his sons Brett and Cole to print editions of prints from his original negatives resulting in albums of his superb photographs.

On January 1, 1958 (while this chapter was being written) Edward Weston died, aged 71. As a photographer he has done much for our day, shaping the ideal and purposes of photography. His best works are profoundly spiritual interpretations of nature, photograph in his own distinct style.

WESTON
below: Nude on Beach. *California, 1936.*
left: Pepper. 1930.

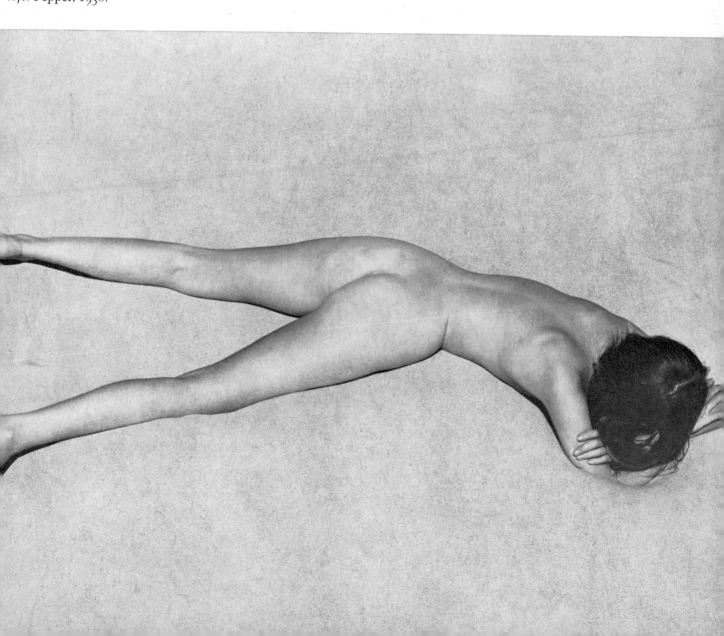

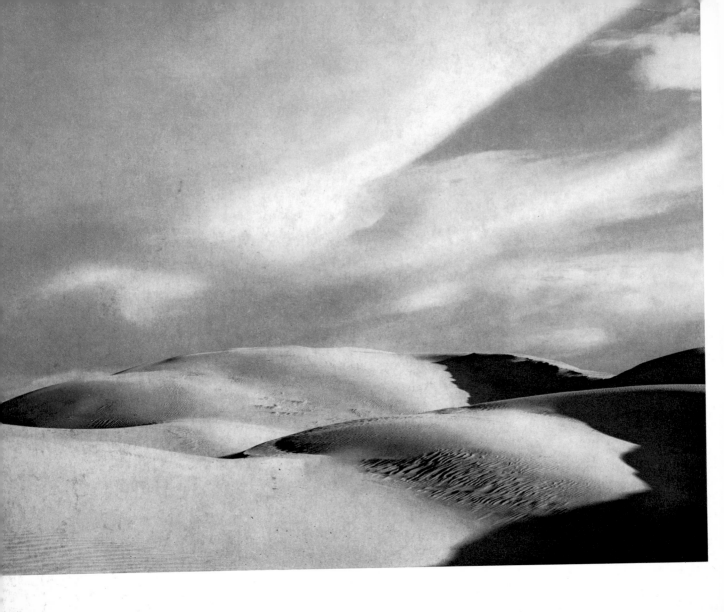

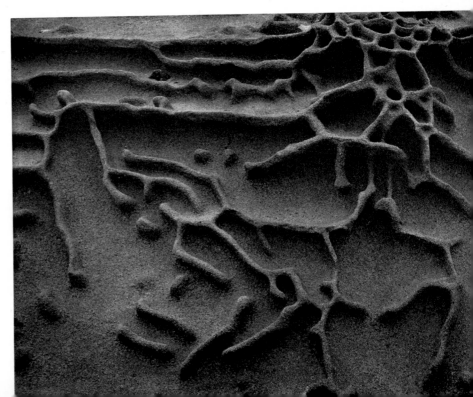

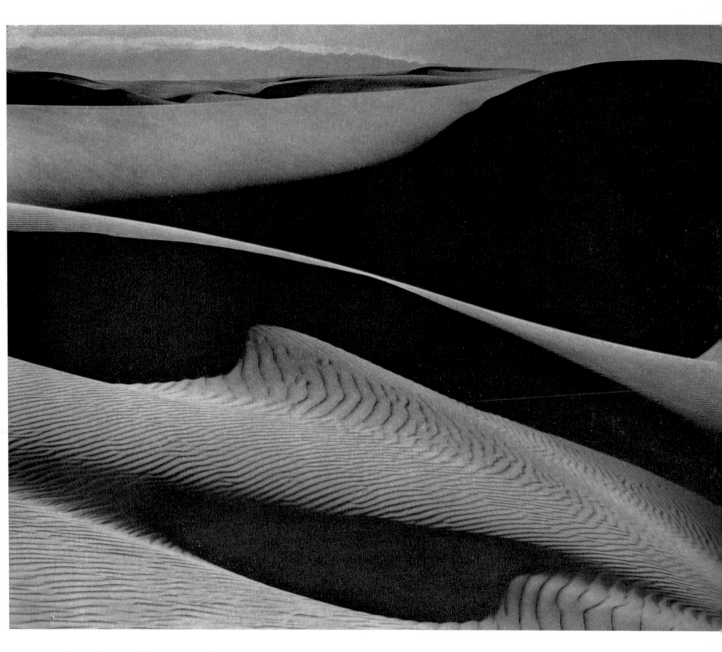

WESTON, *above*: Dunes. *Oceano, 1936.*
opposite page, above: Dunes. *Oceano, 1936.*
left: Rock Erosion. *1942.*

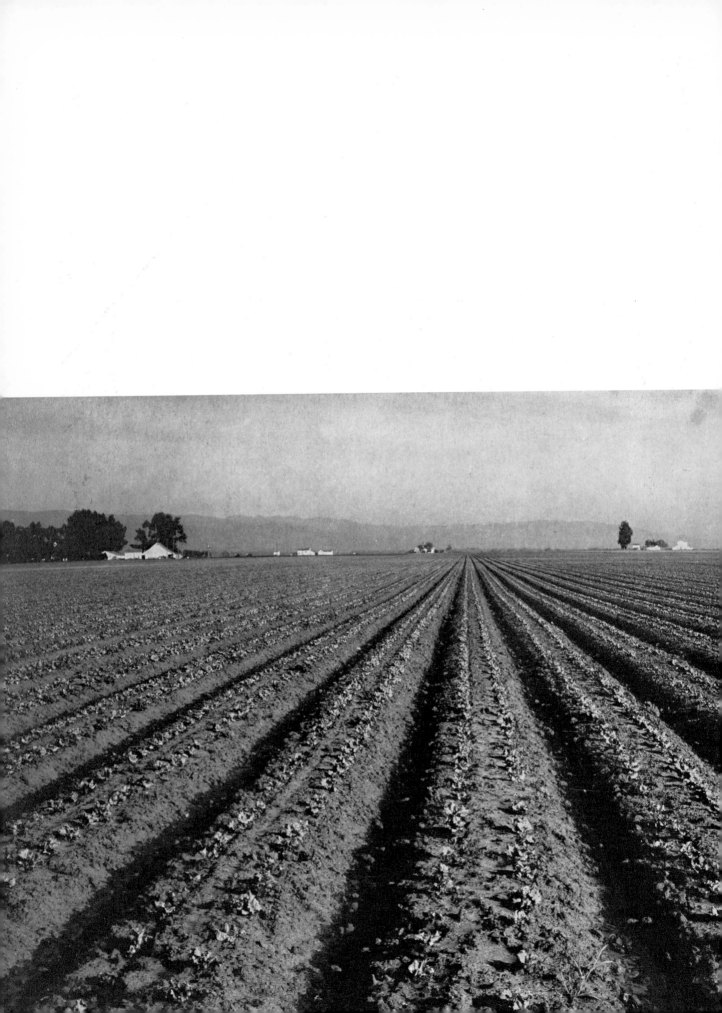

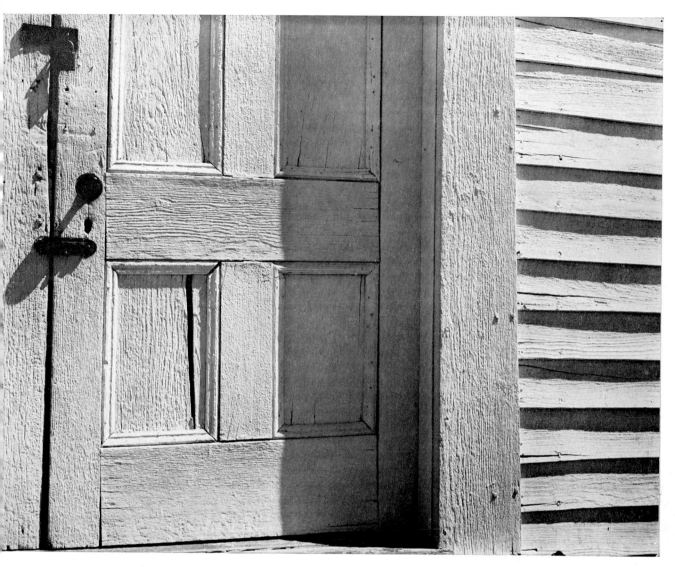

WESTON, *above:* Church Door. *Hornitos, 1940.*
left: Field of Lettuce. *Salinas, California, 1934.*

CHAPTER 29
Lensless Photography

ABSTRACT PHOTOGRAPHY took on importance when men of creative vision began to focus on relations between things rather than on the things themselves—not people, trees, flowers, animals, clouds, and rivers, but pattern and form, line and volume, texture and shape. The pioneers of this shift in seeing were the advanced painters of the 1880s and 1890s. The great liberating movements in photography during the next decades made similar experimentation in the photographic medium inevitable.

Do we see "reality" when we see things and "unreality" when we see structural relations? No, each way of seeing is just as real as the other. But the first is the ordinary, familiar way we see in the ordinary context of our ordinary life. It is so deeply rooted in us that our ordinary context of seeing must be altered somehow if we are to see relations before we see recognizable things. Abstract photographers give us unfamiliar views of the world —an extreme close-up charged with detail, an unusually angled perspective, a multiple exposure—thus transforming familiar reality into something new, different, and strange, hardly recognizable as things. There was something paradoxical half a century ago about breaking down familiar reality by photographic means, for the camera, after all, had been invented for faithful documentation of familiar reality with a detailed accuracy impossible to the human hand and pigment-laden brush. Even today this paradox weighs heavily upon the thinking of leading photographic spirits, a number of whom feel strongly that photographers have no right to interfere with "natural" photographic processes by darkroom manipulations, or to put the lens aside and create designs by placing objects upon photosensitive materials. But there are no absolutes to which artists can be held today.

In the 1910s Sheeler and Strand (see pp. 252-255) with their geometric conception of landscape and the city scene, took major steps toward abstract photographic vision, although neither man went so far as to detach the formal relations of the seen world from the subjects that he photographed. One of the earliest men to do so was Francis Bruguière, a painter turned photographer and a member of Photo-Secession after meeting Alfred Stieglitz. His interest in photography could be defined as the poetry of light rather than investigation of structural realities. After experimenting with multiple exposures as early as 1912, he turned in the following decade, first to photographing the theater stage by its own light and then to experimenting with stage lighting, which he gave a new dramatic dimension. He turned light into an actor with an important role to play in enabling the theater to deliver its messages. In the late 1920s he took motion pictures of forms created by light and motion. In reaching beyond the graphic aspects of photography at that early time, he was singularly prophetic of our own day, when artists and designers of all kinds are finding light the newest and most exciting of creative mediums and are making use of photographic means to shape a new world of light-created forms.

Alvin Langdon Coburn was another early exponent and practitioner of abstract photography. "If it is not possible to be 'modern' with the newest of all the arts," he wrote in 1916, "we had better bury our black boxes and go back to scratching with a sharp bone in the manner of our remote Darwinian ancestors. I do not think that we have even begun to realize the possibilities of the camera. The beauty of design displayed by the microscope seems to me a wonderful field to explore . . . the use of prisms for the splitting of images into segments has been very slightly experimented with, and multiple exposures on the same plate . . . neglected almost entirely."

Coburn's *Paris Rooftops* (see page 250) and *Octopus, New York*, both 1913, are astonishingly early examples of fully mature photographic abstractionism. *Octopus* is a prophecy of Moholy-Nagy's *From The Radio Tower* of fifteen years later. Coburn's "Vortographs," kaleidoscopic patterns produced as early as 1917, may well have

been the first completely nonobjective photographic images. The painter-photographer Christian Schad, in 1918, imposed scraps of paper and other flat shapes on photosensitive paper, producing Cubist compositions by this means and anticipating by several years the more complicated lensless images of Moholy-Nagy and Man Ray. There were nineteenth-century precedents for Schad's techniques—if not for its Cubist aesthetic vision —notably Fox Talbot's "photogenic drawings" (see page 93) and the *cliché verre* glass prints made by Corot, Millet, Daubigny and various other French painters of the Barbizon School (see pages 148-149).

Shortly after World War I, Man Ray, an American artist living in Paris, began to explore the manipulative aspects of darkroom technique and artificial-light control, in some instances achieving interesting transformations of the normal photographic image and in others creating light paintings, as it were, along the lines of Christian Schad's "Schadograph." Man Ray's "Rayographs" were richer and more complex than Schad's experimental images, for Ray's system added beams and moving pencils of light to Schad's simpler technique of spreading objects on photographic papers. In addition Ray made effective use of solarization, which is to say that he gave a latent image a momentary second exposure to light before developing his film; prints produced from negatives treated in this way exhibited strong black lines along the major contours. The phenomenon of solarization had long been known; Ray was the first to see a creative potential in it rather than a technical defect.

In Germany, during the 1920s, the boundaries of photographs were boldly extended to take in vast new areas of abstract and applied photography. In the Bauhaus at Dessau, the great school for artists and designers and the center for basic experiments in every field of the visual arts, the camera was valued as an instrument for creative imagery. These images were used as elements in constructing designs for exhibitions, photomurals, posters, advertising, layout, and typography; they became a new photographic vocabulary used to communicate ideas. Such uses, commonplace today, were first conceived by the Bauhaus group before 1930. Since then, applied photography has become firmly woven into our daily life.

The moving spirit in Bauhaus photography was Laszlo Moholy-Nagy, born in Hungary, 1895. Moholy taught at the Bauhaus during the years 1923–28. He came to the United States in 1937, and from that time until his death in 1946 was director of the New Bauhaus, Chicago, later called The Institute of Design and now a division

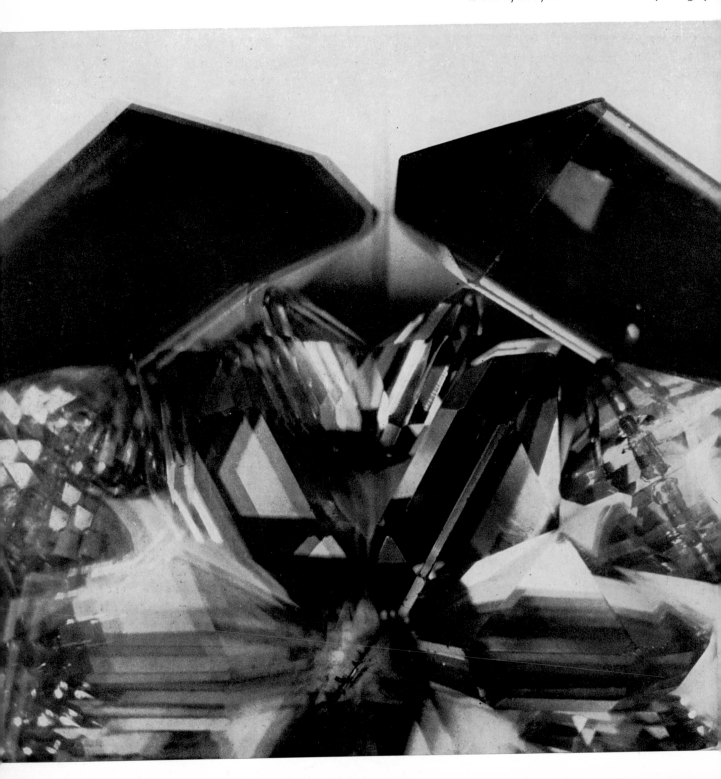

of the Illinois Institute of Technology. Wherever he was, Moholy taught that the photographic image should be a fresh, original interpretation of visual experience. He stressed photography without regard for story or landscape, and advocated the use of mixed techniques and manipulations: distortion, enlargement, blanking out, montage, double exposure, double printing, negative effects, bird's-eye and worm's-eye views. He reawakened artistic interest in photomontage, often adding fanciful touches and Surrealist incongruities. He produced other startling effects through negative images and multiple overprintings, frequently employing forms taken from radiography and microscopy. Through his experiments with light and the photographic image in Germany and America, he became one of the greatest influences on modern design all over the world.

Moholy himself created many abstract photographs, inspired by—and in turn inspiring—abstract painting. He was among the first to create the kind of image, made without using the camera, known as the photogram: an abstract photographic print made by placing opaque objects and those of varying degrees of transparency on a sheet of sensitive paper, "painting" the subject with a flashlight, and developing to secure a single print. The cast shadows created by the flashlight enriched and unified the pattern and added the illusion of a third dimension.

Gyorgy Kepes, simultaneously with Man Ray and Moholy-Nagy, experimented with the photogram in the late 1920s shortly after his graduation from the Royal Academy Of Art, Budapest. He worked with Moholy in Berlin, went to London, and in 1936, came to America.

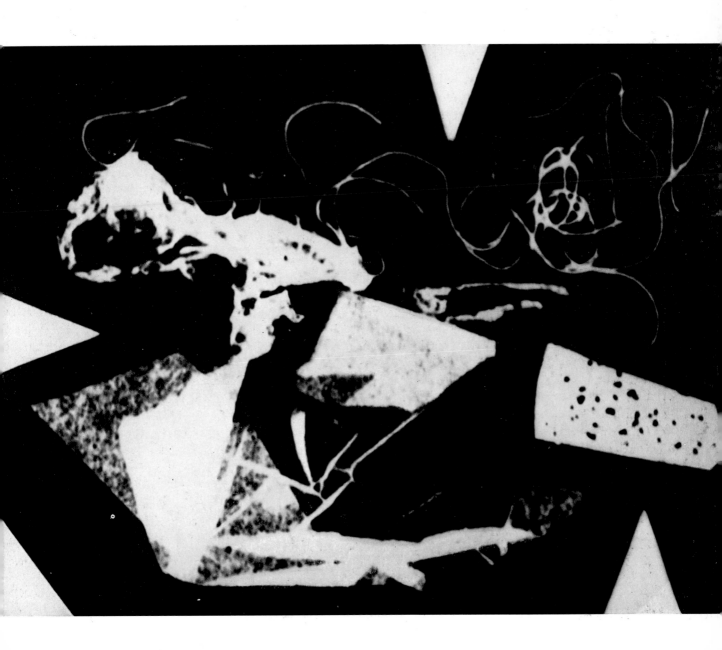

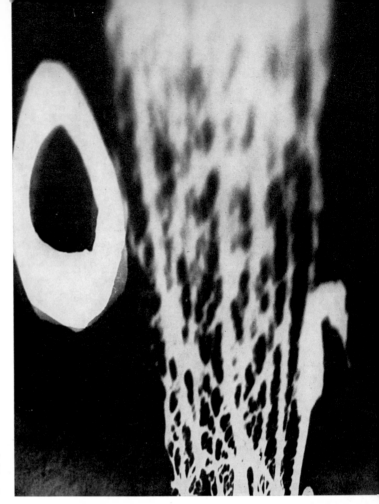

SCHAD, Schadograph 52. *1919.*
Schad soon dropped titles and
merely numbered his compositions.

He was cofounder with Moholy of the New Bauhaus, Chicago. At present he is director of the Center for Advanced Visual Design at Massachusetts Institute of Technology. A versatile and wide-ranging designer, artist, and writer, he is also one of the most influential teachers of his generation in many areas of design. Both as artist and as teacher, he has contributed greatly to understanding of light and color as means of evoking emotional response, despite the elimination of representational images.

The coming of age of abstract photography was proclaimed by the tradition-shattering *Film und Foto* international exhibition of more than a thousand photographs, which was held in Stuttgart, 1929, under the sponsorship of the Deutsche Werkbund, an arts-and-crafts organization led chiefly by the Bauhaus group. This exhibition included the photograms of Moholy-Nagy, the similar "Rayographs" of Man Ray, and the new photographic visions of the Bauhaus: aerial views, X-ray, news, advertising, and scientific photographs notable for form and movement.

Abstract photography, in its development, became a kind of borderland between straight photography and abstract painting. In 1956 the Belgian photographer Pierre Cordier began to obtain marvelously rich images both in color and in black-and-white, through the direct action of chemicals on photosensitive paper. No objects are interposed between the paper and a light source, so that the "chimmigramme," so-called, is not photographic even in the sense of Moholy's photograms, Kepes's photodrawings, or Man Ray's Rayographs. Thoroughly alive and sensuously rich, Cordier's chimmigrammes make bold use of both intended and chance effects. They are controlled accidents in much the same sense as the "action painting" of Cordier's exact contemporary the late Jackson Pollock.

Cordier is not alone in his experiments; and it would appear that no foreseeable limits can be set to further developments in "photographic" abstraction. Special mention may be made of Don Snyder's "lumographs," which are brilliantly colored abstractly patterned 2 x 2 lantern slides of inks and dyes baked onto optical glass. Dr. Timothy Leary makes effective use of Snyder lumographs in his elaborate "psychedelic" slide presentations in which a battery of projectors combines, superimposes, flickers, and fades the primary images.

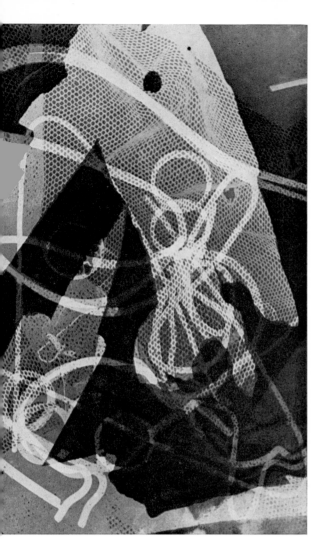

above: SCHAD, Shadograph 21. 1919.
right: Schadograph 60. 1920.

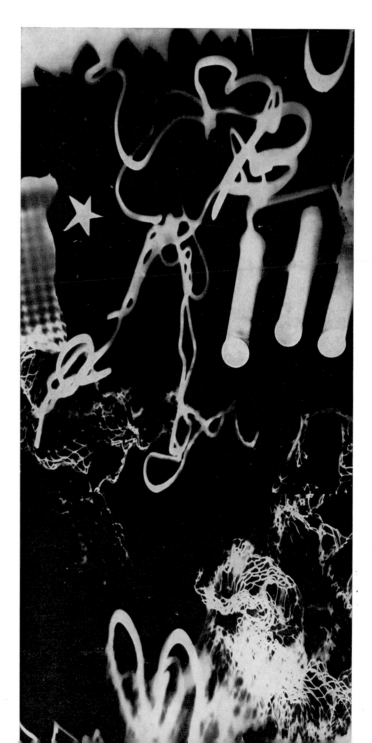

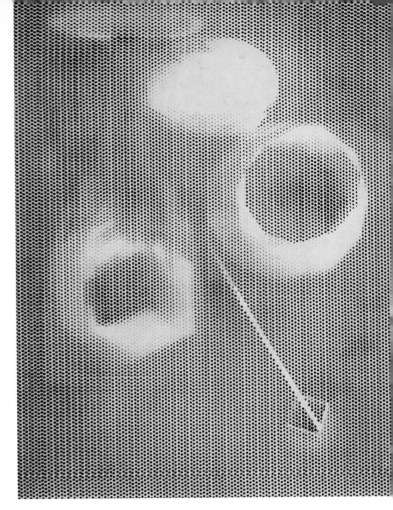

MAN RAY,
Rayograph. *1922.*
Rayograph. *1922.*
opposite page:
Rayograph. *1923.*
Rayograph. *1926.*

All Man Ray photographs
courtesy Museum of Modern Art, New York,
gift of James Thrall Soby.

336

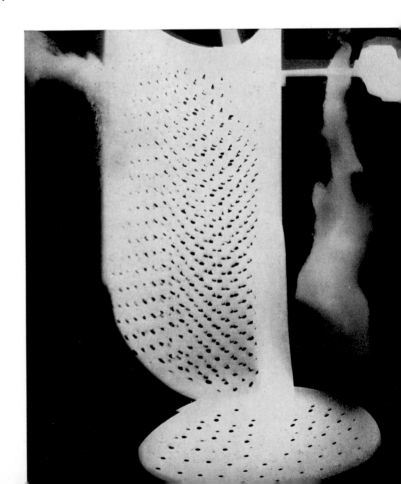

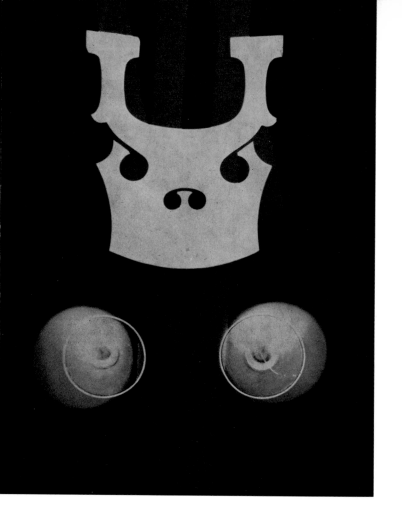

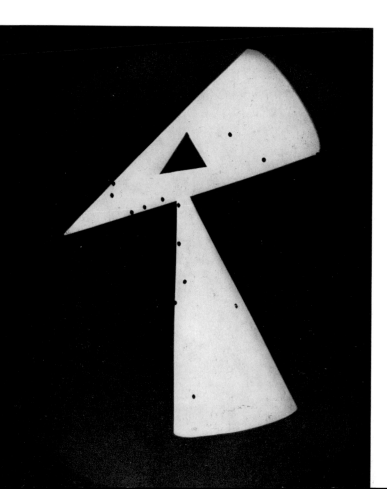

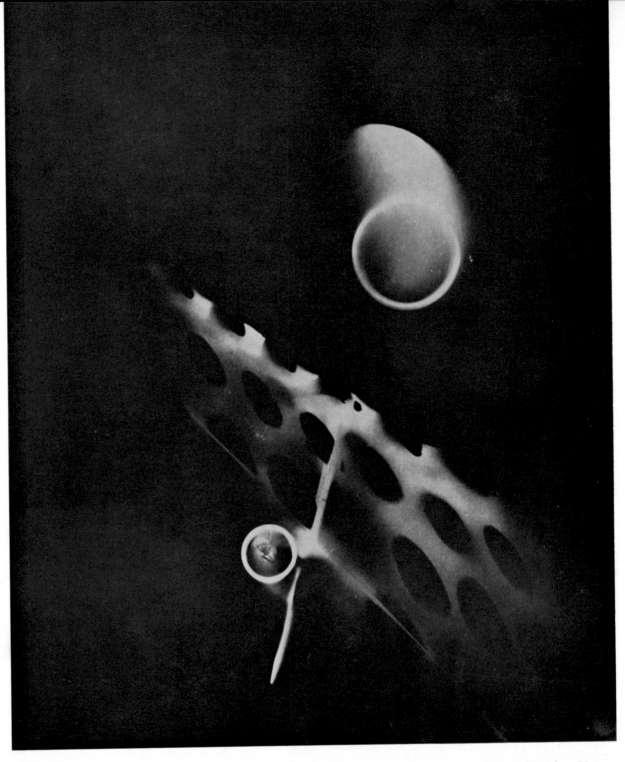

LASZLO MOHOLY-NAGY, *above:* Photogram. *1926. Courtesy George Eastman House.*
right: Nude. *Negative print, 1929. Courtesy Museum of Modern Art, New York.*

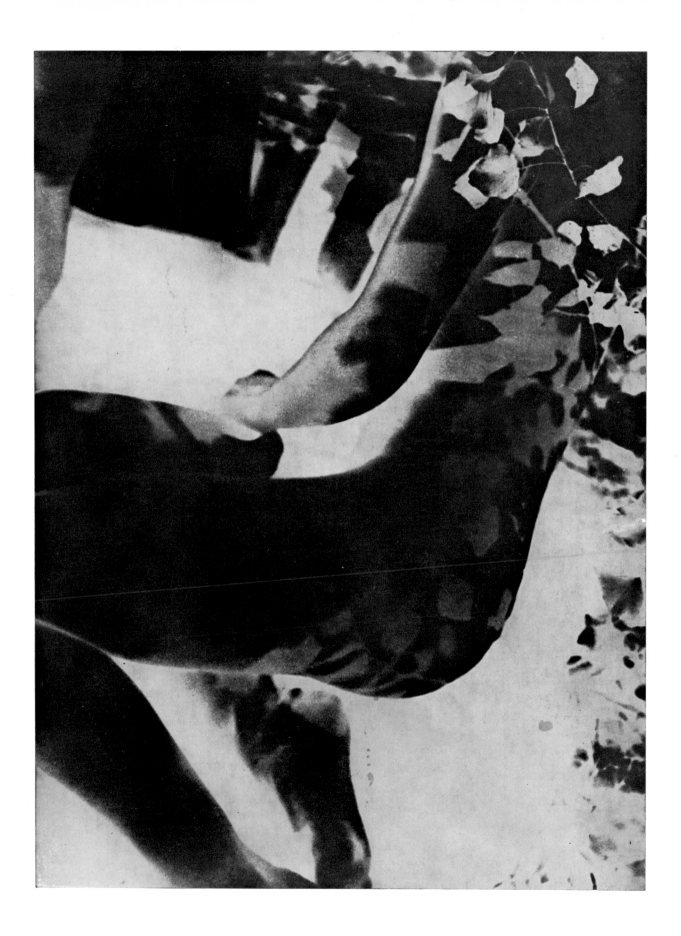

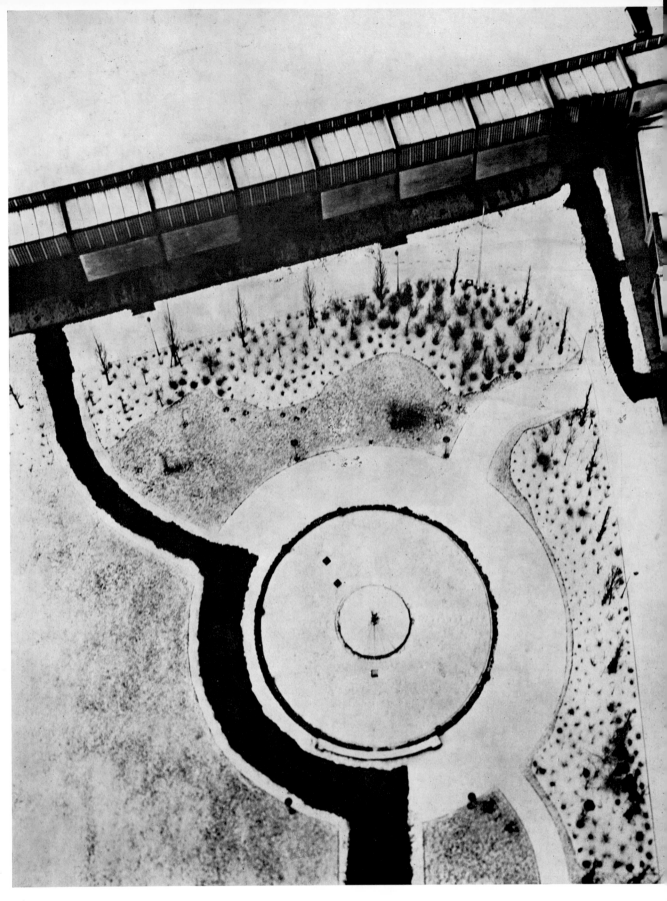

MOHOLY-NAGY, From the Radio Tower. *Berlin, 1928.*
Courtesy Museum of Modern Art.

340

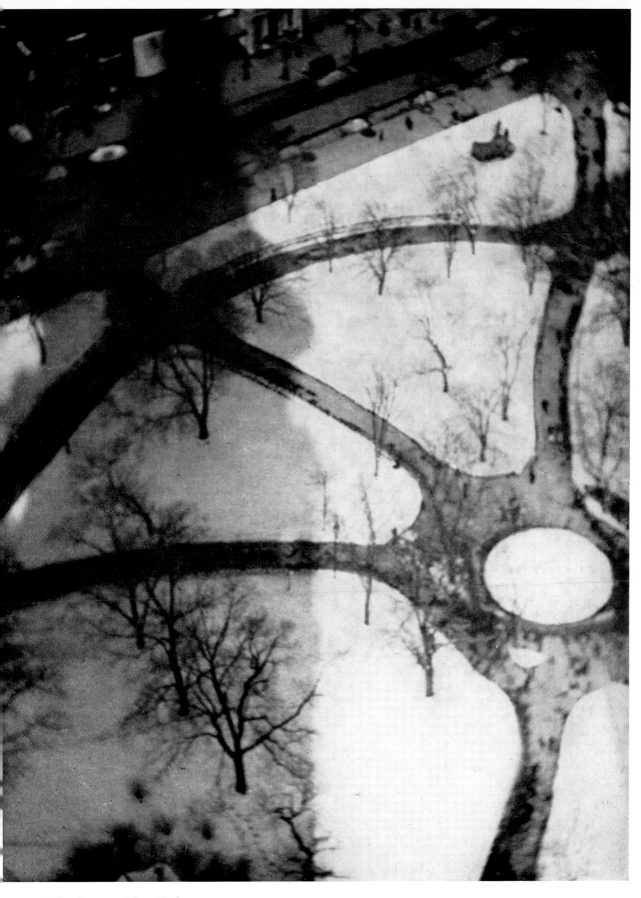

COBURN, The Octopus, New York. 1913.
Courtesy George Eastman House.

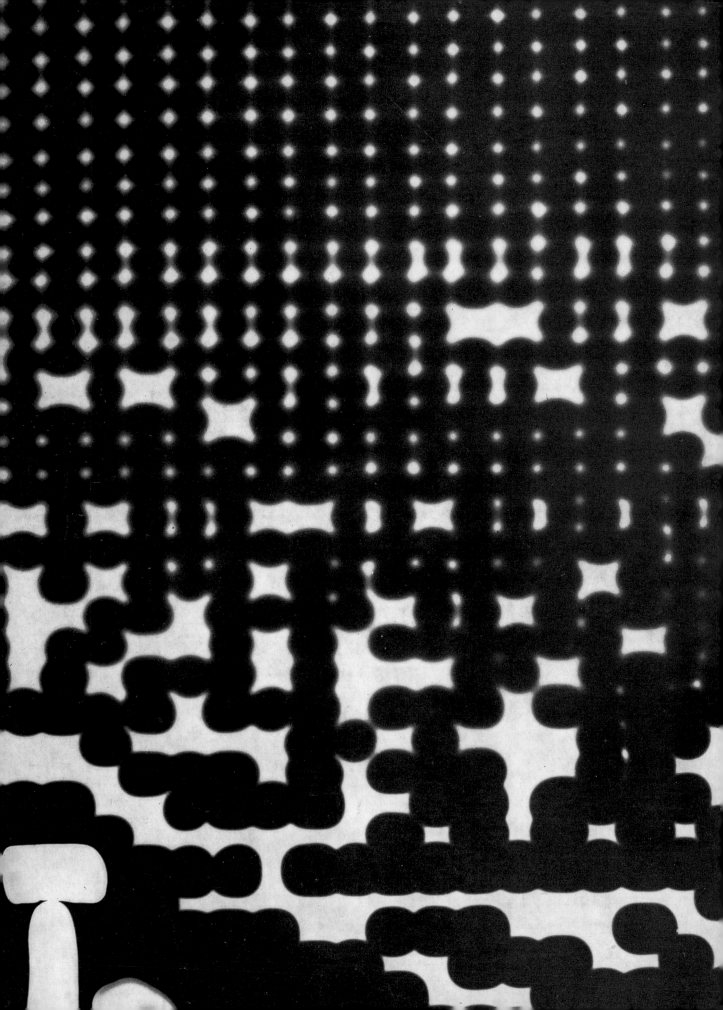

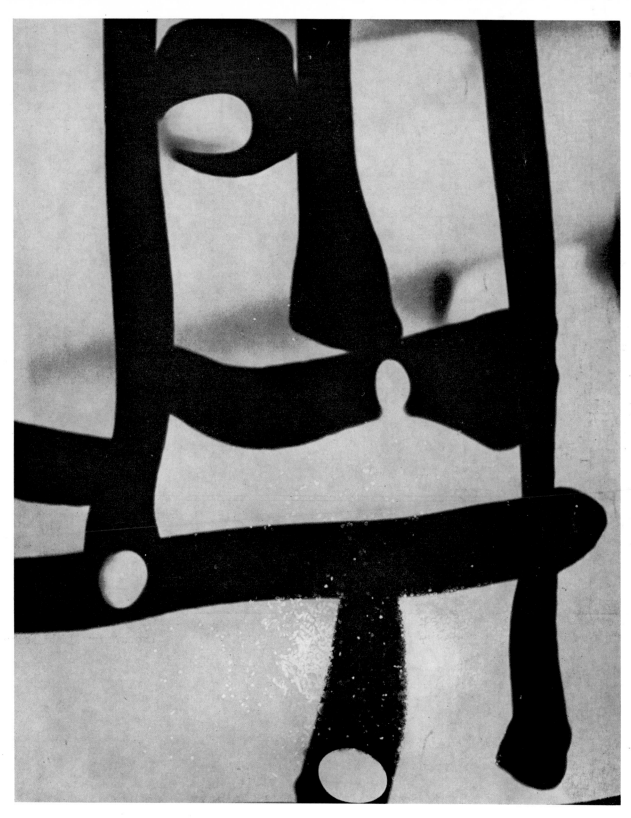

KEPES, *above*: Photodrawing. 1958.
left: Photodrawing. 1958.

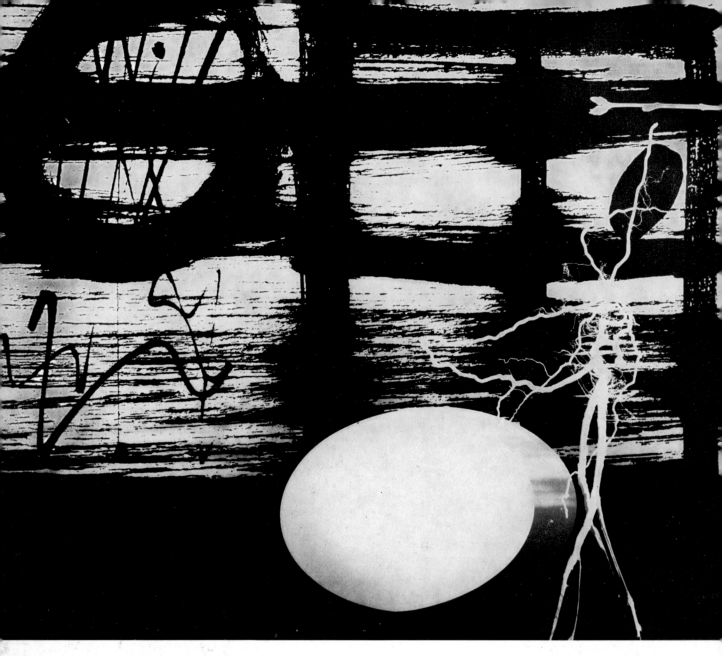

GYORGY KEPES. Light Texture. 1950.

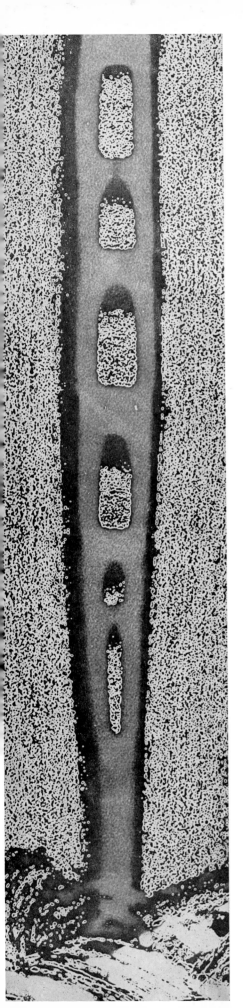

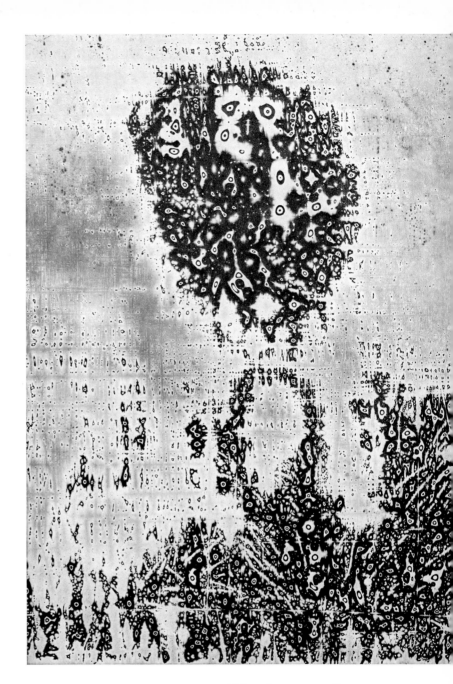

PIERRE CORDIER, *above*: Generation. *Chimmigramme, 1960.*
left: Echelle. *Chimmigramme (detail), 1960.*

CHAPTER 30

Roy Stryker: Documentaries for Government and Industry

DURING THE DEPRESSION Roy E. Stryker, an inspired teacher, used photographs as visual aids for teaching the entire nation something about the somber, seamy existence endured by Americans residing in rural slums. In 1935, when Professor Rexford Tugwell was head of the Resettlement Administration (R.A.), he called on his former student, Roy Stryker, to head a new photography project intended for the Farm Security Administration (F.S.A.), the alphabetical successor to R.A. Mr. Stryker left the sheltered academic life of Columbia University, where he had been teaching, for the three ring circus of politicians, idealists, and brain-trusters then starring in the marble tents of Washington, D.C.

Stryker's objective was to investigate and record the human problems which beset millions of people living on impoverished, drought-stricken land. He turned the spotlight on the conditions of the lowest third, that third which President Roosevelt had referred to as "ill housed, ill clothed and ill fed."

F.S.A. became a vigorous factor in presenting the truth, creating indignation at the plight of the migrant worker, and propagandizing for a break in the destructive grip in which economics and the elements held the marginal farmer. In the early days Roy Stryker sacrificed quality in his desire to secure accurate photographs; too many pictures in F.S.A. files are mere documents with a much feeling for photographic beauty as a photostat. These are crowded with detail, insensitive, and harsh.

Fortunately, the sensitivity of the photographers whom Stryker hired, combined with his own sympathy for the farmer and his keen interest in providing effective pictures for the nation's press, produced in time a series of truly remarkable documentary photographs. These are dramatically organized around a central idea, they are penetrating interpretations of how people fared on the land. Stryker permitted no posed shots, no tricky angles, or darkroom manipulations. He talked with his photographers—six was the most F.S.A. employed at any time—suggested books to them on the geography, history, and economics of the proposed story. Only after thorough indoctrination did they go out to take their pictures.

Some of today's best known names in documentary and journalistic photography joined his staff—Ben Shahn (now more famous as a painter), Edwin Rosskam, Walker Evans, Dorothea Lange, Arthur Rothstein, Carl Mydans, Marjorie Collins, Russell Lee, John Vachon, Gordon Roger Parks, Marion Post Wolcott, and Jack Delano. They took a composite picture of the country that was a revelation to the nation of how the "submerged third" existed.

Stryker's photographers had their troubles. Rothstein photographed a cow's skull against scrub grass where he had found it; he then moved it several feet to photograph it on sun-parched soil that made for a better background. Both prints were sent to the papers. One editor spotted the discrepancy and Stryker was accused of deliberately making distorted propaganda pictures; the skull became the celebrated exposé of an election year, 1936. Stryker admitted that the photographer had moved the skull and said to an investigating committee, "What the hell, the point of the picture is that there's a drought. Cattle are dying; and don't tell me that the photographer got out of the drought area by moving 10 feet." John Vachon was pitchforked by an irascible, New Deal-hating farmer, and Jack Delano was jailed by a security-minded policeman in Pennsylvania who stopped him from photographing a steel mill.

Some F.S.A. photographs remain great pictures today, symbols of that terrible time in America; they become for today harbingers of what may beset the nation again if the people are not wary. Arthur Rothstein's photograph of an Oklahoma farmer and his children fighting their way through a gritty duststorm never fails to elicit an emotional response, nor does Walker Evans's child's grave, a picture of a saucer burial taken in Alabama, or Jack Delano's Negro family in a rural house in Georgia.

John Steinbeck credits Dorothea Lange's studies of the Okies and other migrants with inspiring his classic novel *Grapes of Wrath*.

It was Stryker's desire to secure a record of social significance, a vital picture of the hectic, harrowing days which the nation was enduring. Reproductions were used not only in the nation's newspapers and magazines, but also to illustrate such books as *Forty Acres and Steel Mules*, by Herman Nixon, *Washington Nerve Center*, by Edwin Rosskam, and *Land of the Free*, by Archibald MacLeish, who wrote in his preface, "The original purpose had been to write some sort of text to which these photographs might serve as commentary. But so great was the stubborn inward livingness of these vivid American documents that the result was a reversal of that plan."

American Photographs by Walker Evans, published by the Museum of Modern Art, included many pictures Evans took for the F.S.A. Richard Wright collaborated with Edwin Rosskam on 12 *Million Black Voices*.

Stryker did not overlook the positive facets of America. He sought for a full-rounded picture, and said to his photographers, "Do not forsake the country for a one-sided picture of its poor in rural slums." A representative of the German Embassy looking for photographs of "typical" Americans intended for the Nazi press was shown by Stryker only photographs of prosperous farms and full employment in industry.

In the eight years of the existence of F.S.A., more than 200,000 photographs entered F.S.A. files, ranging in subject matter from courthouses, crops, and culture to churches, criminals, and farm workers (all now in the Library of Congress). Roy Stryker inspired the photographers "to give their fraction of a second's exposure to the integrity of truth." He did not insist on a picture of squalor, of sickly, impoverished people. What he asked for was a document as opposed to the pictorial, romantic, false, or smug. He wanted a direct, honest record of a particular society and its environment, with an informative rather than a fanciful approach.

Stryker and F.S.A. went to the Office of War Information soon after the war started. Stryker recommended unsuccessfully that his realistic procedure in photography be applied to the war effort. The dull pictures required of him and his crew were too confining; he soon left to take the opportunity offered him by Standard Oil of New Jersey. He was to organize for Standard Oil a library of documentary photographs recording the essential role of oil in the life of America. It was to be a free picture file available to Standard Oil's house organ *The Lamp*

347

and to schools, libraries, publishers, editors—all for a courtesy credit line.

Stryker used the same method that he had used at F.S.A.; his work for Standard Oil became an extension of the pioneering program that he had developed for the government. He hired some of the best photographers who had worked for him on F.S.A. and sent them to Standard Oil installations all over the world, from the hot sands of the Persian Gulf to the permafrost of the Arctic Circle. The resultant photographs were of great technical efficacy and dramatic artistry, and again clearly revealed men's relation to their environment. A miser-

able climate, a lonely outpost, a man's relation to his home, his work, and his fellow men—every aspect of the oil industry and its operation was recorded.

Harold Corsini learned all he could in New York about weather conditions, geography, Eskimo mores and Eskimo history in anticipation of a ten-week stay in the far Northwest territory of Canada—Stryker always seeks resourcefulness in his photographers. Edwin Rosskam and his wife, Louise, portrayed the immense refineries in Louisiana with insight and artistry, purposefully selecting parts of pipes, tubes, tanks, and towers to capture moving compositions. John Vachon took a superb pic-

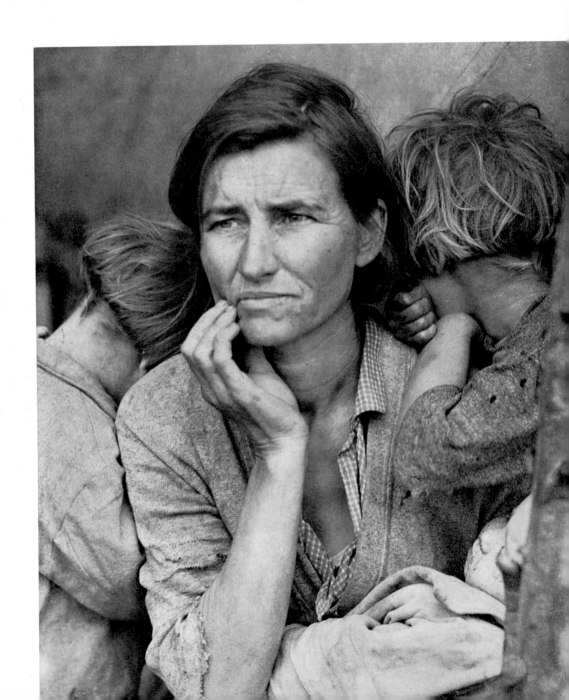

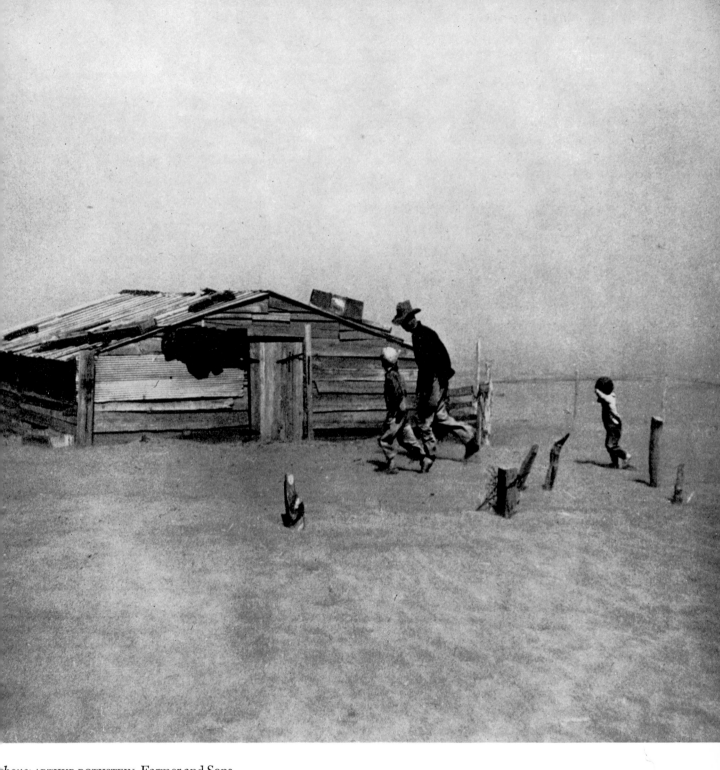

bove: ARTHUR ROTHSTEIN, Farmer and Sons
Walking in Dust Storm. Cimarron, Oklahoma, 1936.
eft: DOROTHEA LANGE, California. *1936.*

below: RUSSELL LEE, Southeast Missouri Farm, Son of Sharecropper Combing Hair. *May, 19*
right: BEN SHAHN, Rehabilitation of Clients, F.S.A. *October, 19*

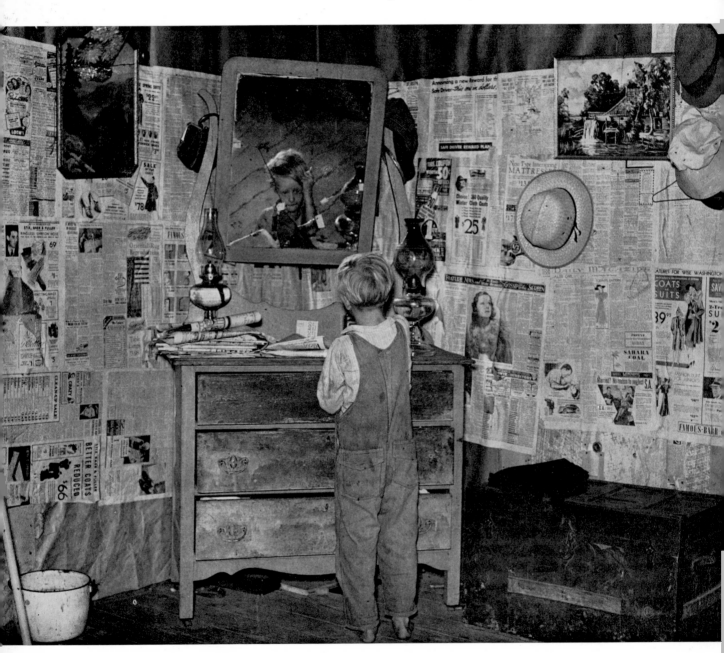

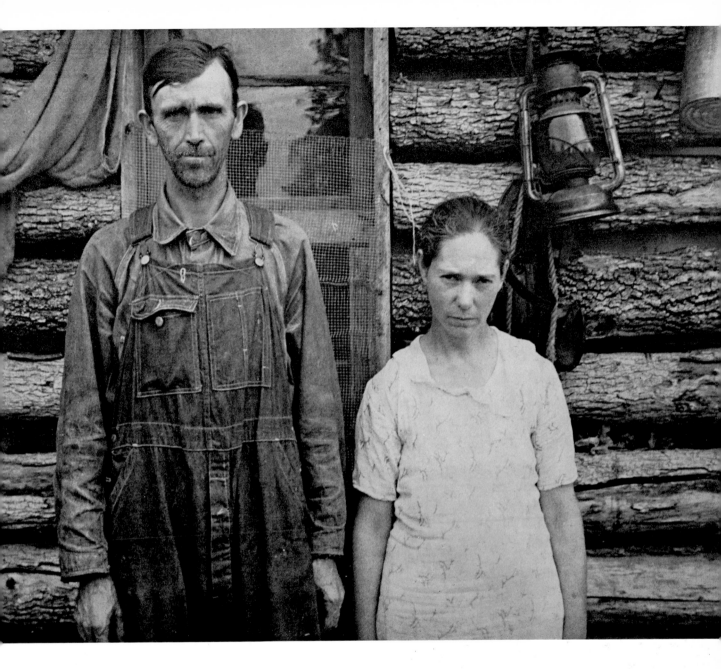

ire of derricks rising out of the sea in Venezuela, and
'odd Webb's picture of Pittsburgh spells a city's surging
ower.

There was now better equipment, more time for pre-
minary study, and better pay for the cameramen.
tryker enthusiastically directed them in securing a com-
rehensive picture of the tremendous oil industry that
veryone could understand. Their pictures of the vital
ple which oil plays in the economy record reality with
truth that is far removed from the one-sided muckrak-
ng of Ida Tarbell a generation earlier.

Public-relations purposes led to the financing of pro-
rams of positive photography for Standard Oil Co. of

New Jersey and the steel industry (Stryker was head of
Jones and Laughlin Steel Company's photo file), but in
photography for industry, as in photography for government, Roy Stryker continued his unique personal contribution of truth to history and of penetration in depth.

Stryker is now retired. He lives in Colorado, "looking
out at the mountains I loved even as a kid," he said to
me one day in 1966 when I phoned from New York for
advice about to how to build a photo library for a large
foundation. Typically, he advised that the foundation
"get the best photographers and see that each picture
tells the truth."

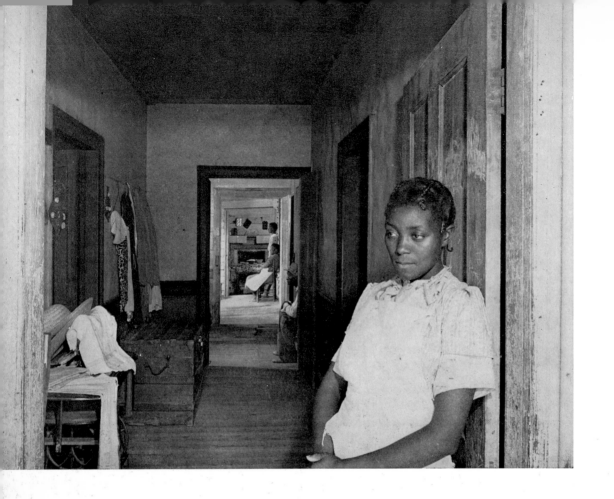

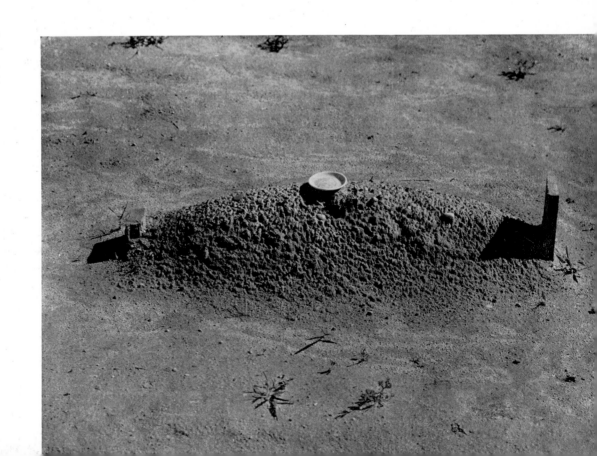

ow: WALKER EVANS, Graveyard in Easton, Pennsylvania. 1936.
: JACK DELANO, Interior of Rural House. *Greene County, Georgia, 1941.*
osite page, below: WALKER EVANS, Child's Grave. *Alabama, 1936.*

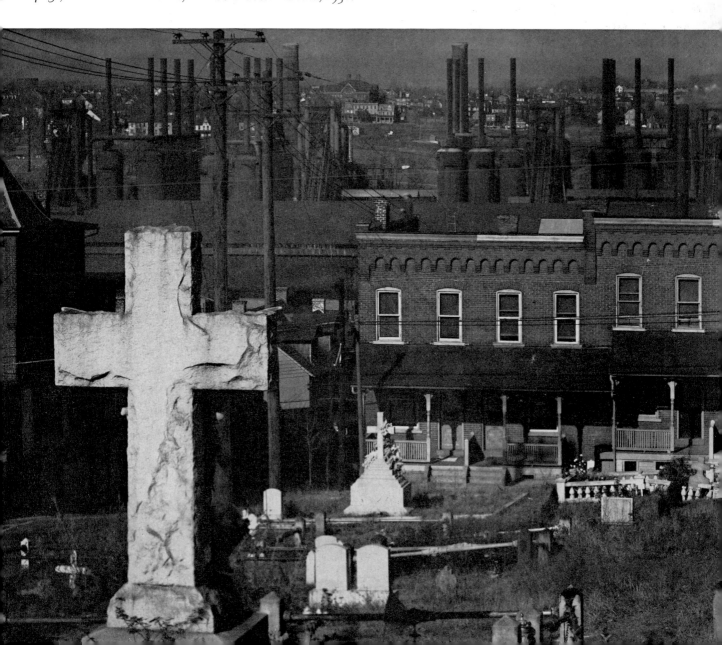

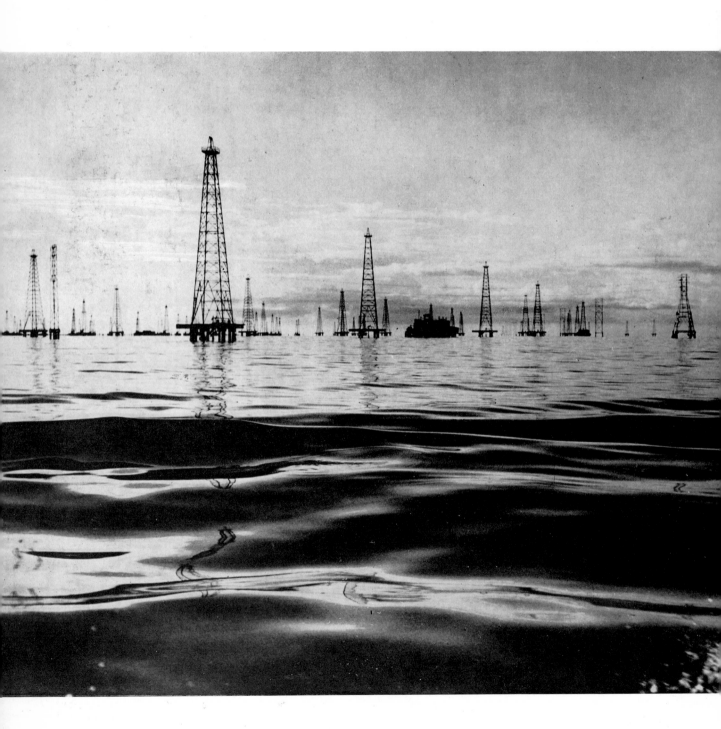

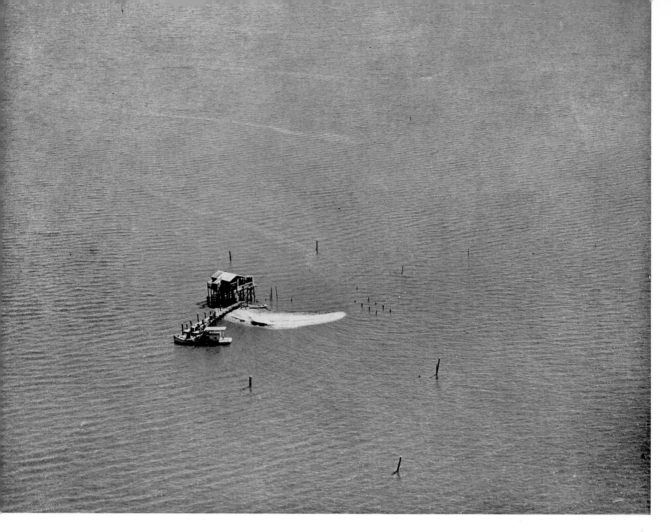

above: CHARLES ROTKIN, Reef in Barataria Bay, South of New Orleans. *1948.*
left: JOHN VACHON, Western Venezuela—Tia Juana Field. *1944.*

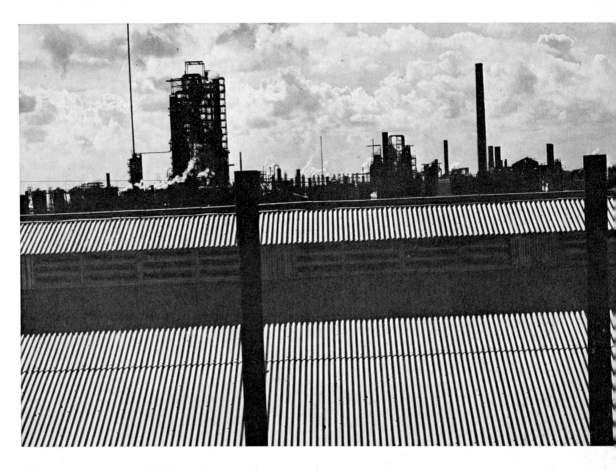

above: HAROLD CORSINI, Refinery. *Baytown, Texas, 1946.*
left: EDWIN AND LOUISE ROSSKAM, Oil Train on Prairie. *Cut Bank, Montana, 1944.*

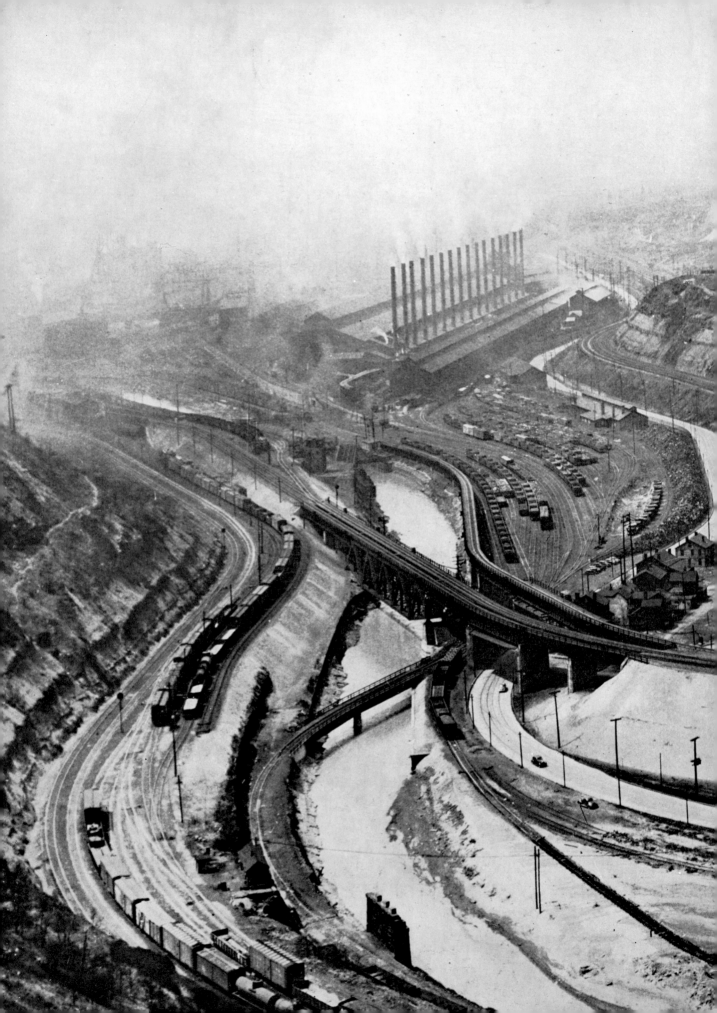

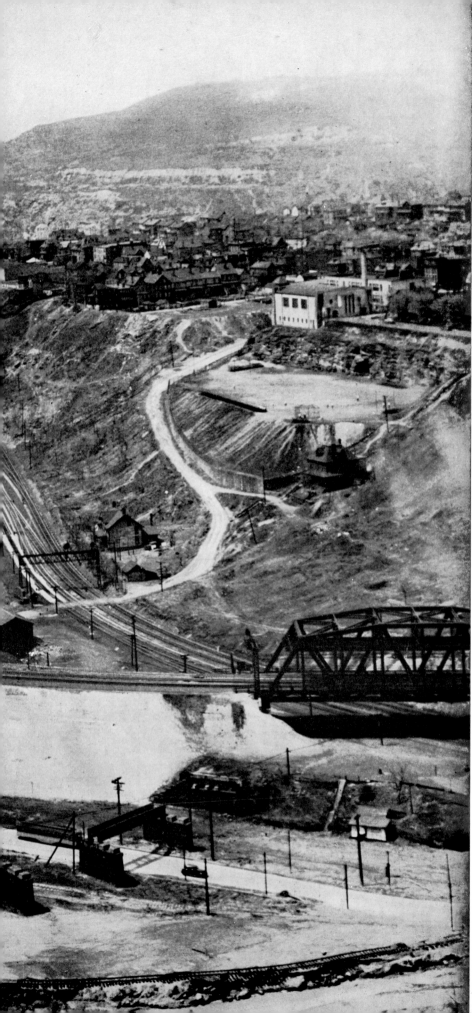

TODD WEBB
Pittsburgh, Pennsylvania.
1948.

CHAPTER 31

Ansel Adams: Interpreter of Nature

IN A TIME when so much in modern art escapes th understanding of the great majority of humanity, th incredibly skillful photographs of Ansel Adams exert tremendous appeal whenever they are exhibited in th nation's museums.

Adams's best photographs represent the aspiration held by innumerable pictorial cameramen of all th world, amateur and professional. Ansel Adams's distinc tion is in the sensitivity and poetry that he introduce into his photographs and in the control that he maintain over his medium through his formidable scientific knowl edge. He is the founder of a complex "zone system o planned photography." This system separates tona values of subjects according to "zones" or levels and after readings are taken with a light meter, provides th photographer with step-by-step guidance in exposure development, and printing, to achieve a predetermined structure of tones.

Adams, in addition, is ever alert to arrangements in nature that make for dramatic masses, counterbalance of forms, and subtle tones, as well as for stability of de sign to control the over-all image. In his best photograph each element is considered in relation to the whole pic ture, which shows his instantaneous interpretation of the ever-changing, accidental play of light on landscape.

Several of his finest photographs go far beyond the purely visual and the technically perfect. These are idealizations of nature that border on the profoundly spiritual. Were it not for his inherent deep feeling for the exalted landscape of the West, feeling that he instills into his works, his photographs would be merely the best obtainable in picture postcards. It is the sensitive, interpretive seeing of Ansel Adams, who constructs his photographs as pictorial architecture, that carries him far beyond photographers of ordinary vision. Copyists who attempt to follow him inevitably secure only superficial, over-dramatized imitations of his work, and miss the vision of the mysterious, living forces in nature that inspires Adams in all seasons of the year and at all times of day and night to compose pictures of specific landscapes and to transpose what he sees to sensitized plates at the peak moments of his perception.

To the geometry of composition Adams supplies mathematical patterns from music (he was a gifted pianist who gave up the concert stage for the camera in 1930 when he was twenty-eight years old). He composes photographs with a musical rationalism and repetition: slight variations on a theme in photography. There is a similarity in his compositions: foreground, mountain peaks, and sky, a harmonious balance of dark, light, and lighter shades of gray, with only rarely a deep impenetrable black. Adams is always mindful of perspective and horizon, of patterns in horizontal and diagonal lines, of strong verticals and repeated triangular forms.

Recognition of the object is always important in Ansel Adams's work organized though it is in decorative patterns with countless details. Abstraction and transformation of the object, the core of strikingness and power in modern art and photography, are alien to Adams's purpose. Adams's later photographs conceived in all-over textures and patterns of leaves, ferns, trees, stones, and boards can be compared to musical sonatas and fugues. They are less complex in composition than his earlier elaborate pictures of imposing mountainous landscapes inspired by soaring symphonies.

His deep response to nature is Ansel Adams's poetic lever, for without it he would be bogged down in his scientific system of photography. What enables artists like Seurat in the last century, with his belief that anyone could become an artist who learned his "Pointillist" science of applying color, and like Ansel Adams in our day, with his zone system of composition planning, to reach creative heights is their power to rise above their own self-imposed, confining formulas.

Adams has an unappeasable appetite for the grandeur of the Rockies; a nineteenth-century Romantic poet's attachment, a soul-searching affinity for nature's most impressive manifestations. Themes and conceptions that could be interpreted perhaps more readily in abstract music he attempts to interpret pictorially. A panorama that he has seen immediately in its entirety he feels to require a prolonged subsequent reading for the yielding of its full importance, like the sustained listening to a symphony. As the camera catches the landscape with its single eye, he freezes movement, relating diversified objects, textures, and tones with an almost musical point and counterpoint, and compressing deep space into a flat sheet of film, usually 8 by 10 inches. About his work Adams wrote, "Before exposure of the negative, I must visualize the final print. My creative concept is based on my response to the subject before me in space, and on the aggregate of emotional and intellectual experience back of me in time."

If communication were the only criterion in art, the beautiful, recognizable, and evocative photographs of Ansel Adams would be considered the most significant creations of our time. The enchanting, aesthetic power of Adams's finest photographs remains effective despite repeated viewing. Each photograph is a perfect rendition, to be seen as often as one would listen to a recording of a virtuoso musical performance.

To enable a wider audience to see his pictures than that which usually attends his exhibitions, Adams has developed a means of reproducing his prints in halftone engravings, using special inks, reminiscent of the quality demanded by Stieglitz and Emerson a generation ago. Nineteen books and extravagantly produced portfolios of his photographs have been published to date—*John Muir Trail, Four Seasons in Yosemite, My Camera in the National Parks*, and several "how to do it" books, for the most part excellent technical treatises illustrated with fine halftone reproductions of his own photographs.

In 1944 he made the photographs, wrote the text, and, at his own expense, prepared an exhibition of documentary pictures of the Japanese-Americans evacuated from the West Coast to the flat desert expanse of Manzanar Valley. The six-foot photographs, which were exhibited at New York's Museum of Modern Art, became a rallying force for all who, in the name of justice, wished to help loyal Japanese-Americans to regain their rightful positions as peaceful citizens.

Several years earlier Adams had been appointed photo-muralist for the U.S. Department of Interior, and, in the same year, had assisted Beaumont Newhall to found at the Museum of Modern Art the first department devoted to photography as a fine art. During World War II he served as a consultant in photography to the Armed Services.

At the war's end Adams started classes at the California School of Fine Arts in San Francisco for advanced amateurs and professionals, teaching his own scientific system of unmanipulated straight photography and his own aesthetic philosophy. This credo was based on thoughts of Stieglitz, who first showed Ansel's photographs in 1936, and of Edward Weston, who was an influence in the early days of their association in the group known as f/64.

Grants from the Guggenheim Memorial Foundation in 1946 and in 1948 permitted him to photograph the national parks and monuments in Hawaii, Alaska, and all over the United States. Today, with his teaching, he operates studios in San Francisco and in Yosemite and takes assignments from national magazines—*Life, Time, Fortune, Arizona Highways*, etc.—if the work appeals to him. Industrial firms have commissioned him to photograph and produce portfolios of considerable beauty and prestige. A series of his photographs with text by Nancy Newhall were issued as impressive pamphlets on Death Valley and the Mission of San Xavier. He has produced several books with her since then, notably *This is the American Earth*, the first of the Sierra Club's "exhibition format" publications. In 1963 the first volume of her biography of him, *The Eloquent Light*, was published by the Sierra Club. *Fiat Lux*, a word-and-picture book celebrating the centennial of the University of California, appeared in 1968.

A skilled musician, an erudite naturalist, a gifted writer and teacher, and an exuberant, warm personality, Ansel Adams willingly embraces the term "photographer" as belonging to a noble profession. This profession, he once wrote, "is deserving of attention and respect equal to that accorded painting, literature, music and architecture."

All photographs in this chapter courtesy Ansel Adams, San Francisco, unless otherwise noted.

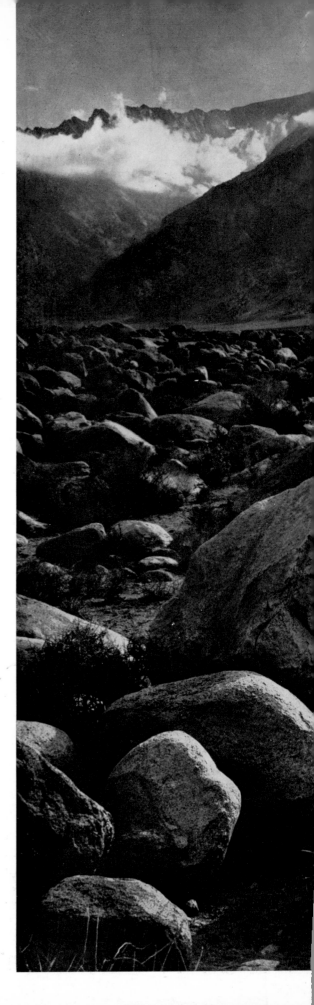

ANSEL ADAMS, Mount Williamson, from Manzanar, California. 1943.

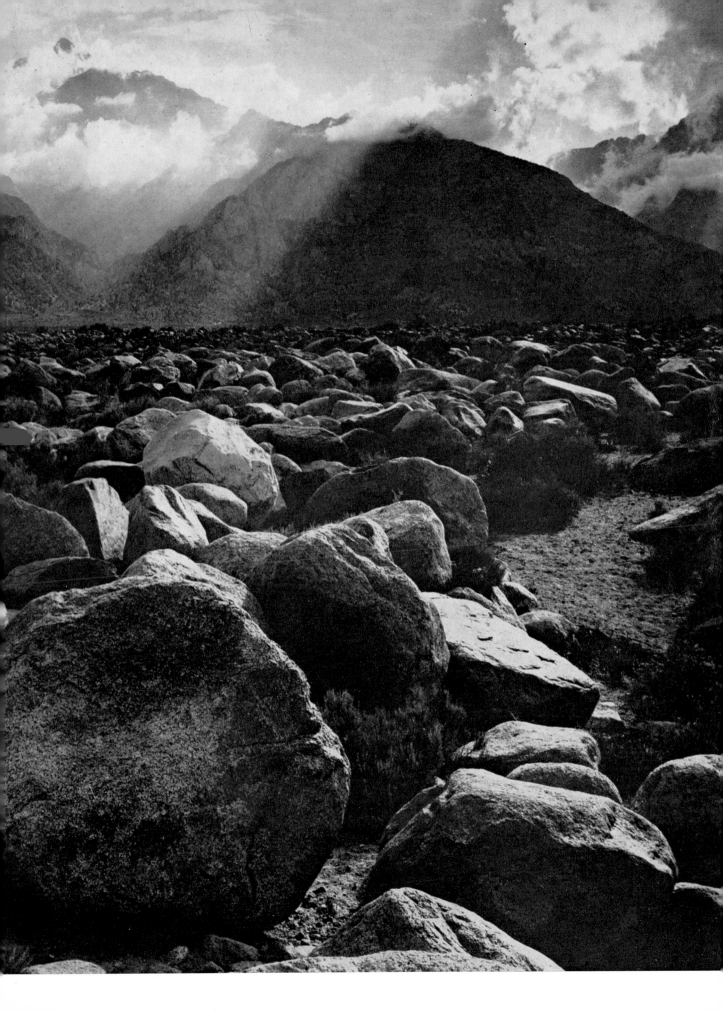

ADAMS, *below*: Roots. *Foster Gardens, Honolulu, Hawaii, 1948.*
right: Autumn. *Great Smoky Mountains National Park, Tennessee, 1948.*

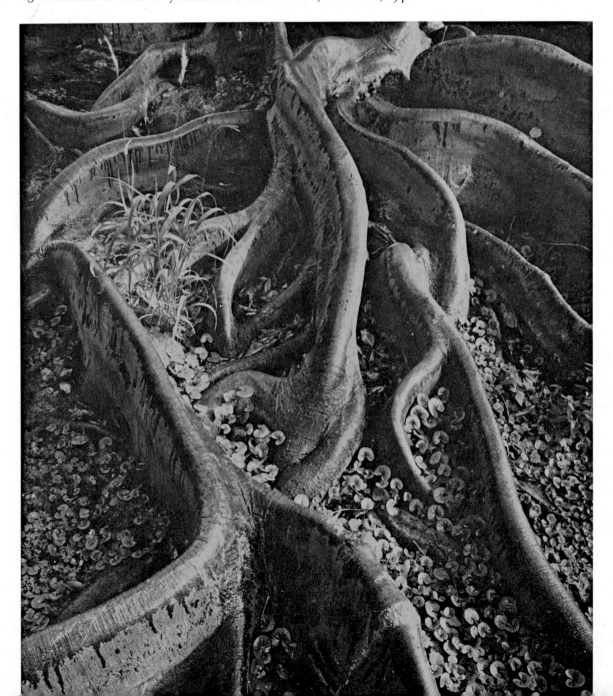

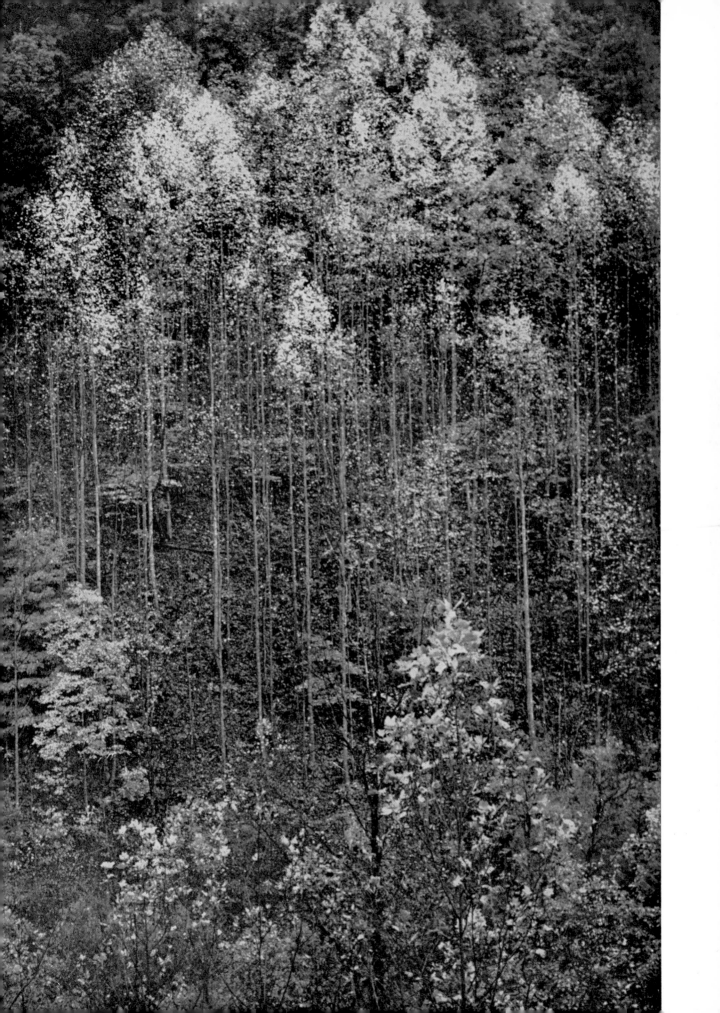

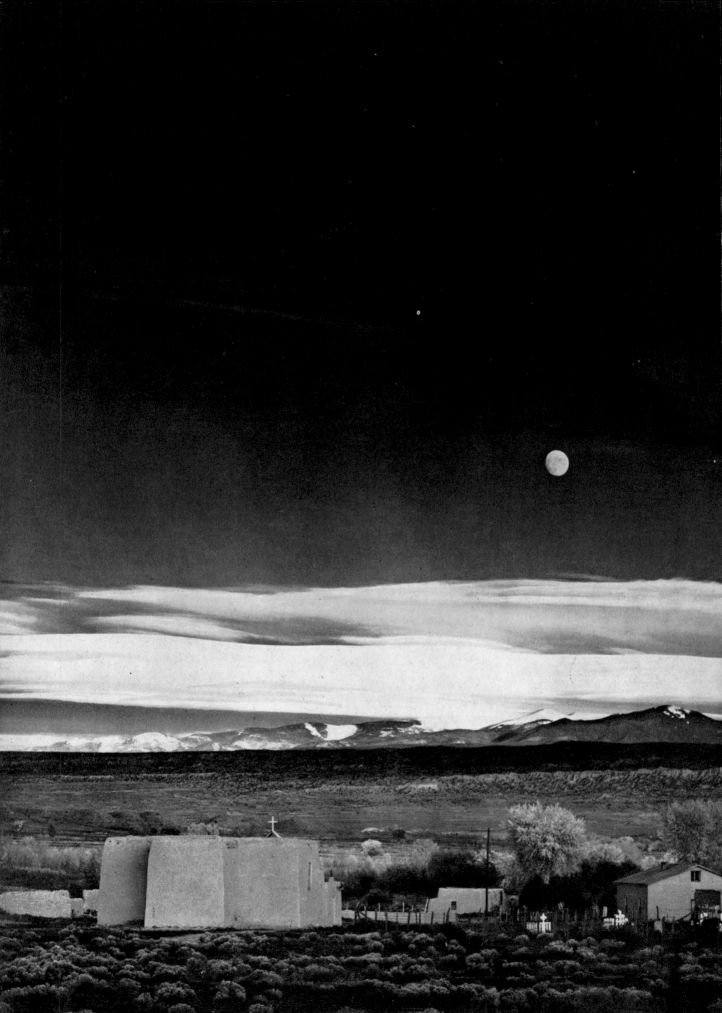

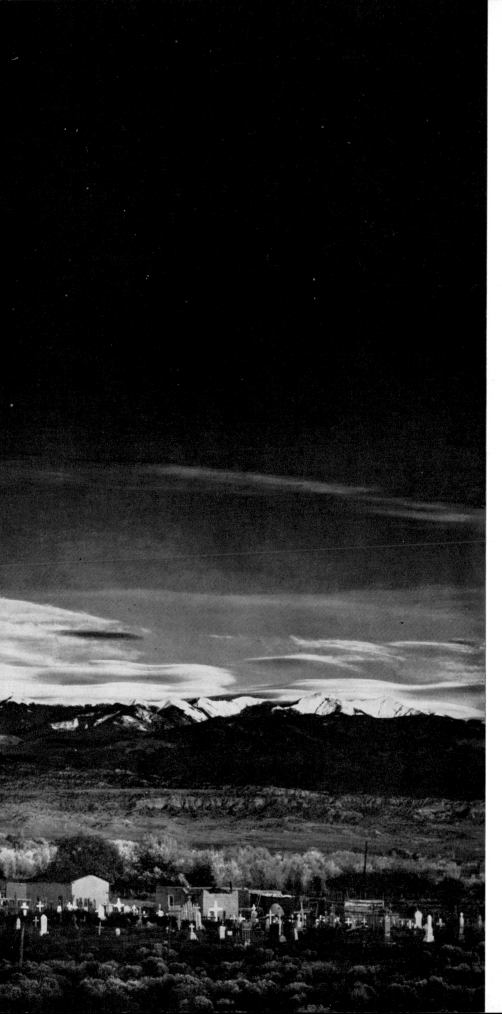

ADAMS, Moonrise.
Hernandez, New Mexico.
1941.

367

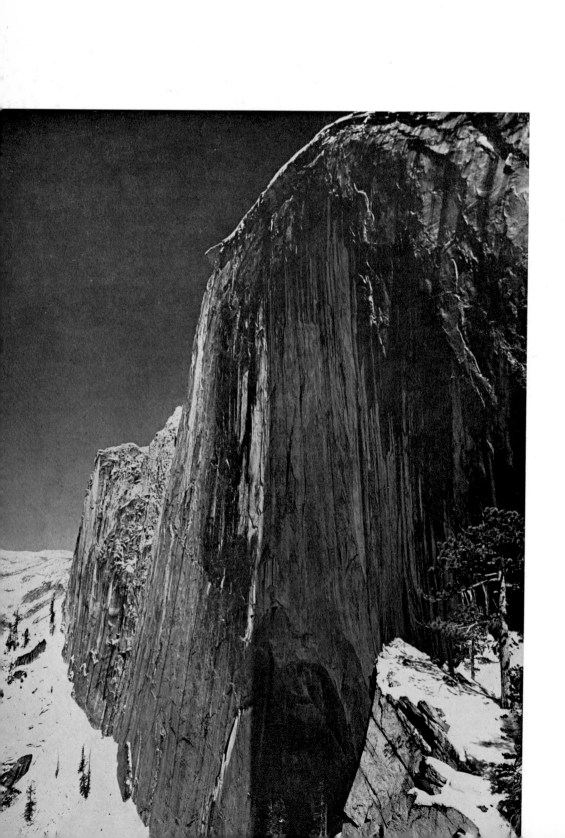
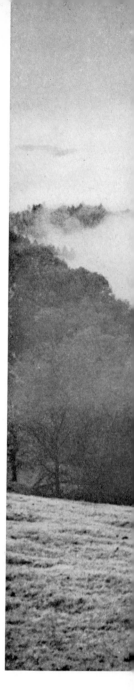

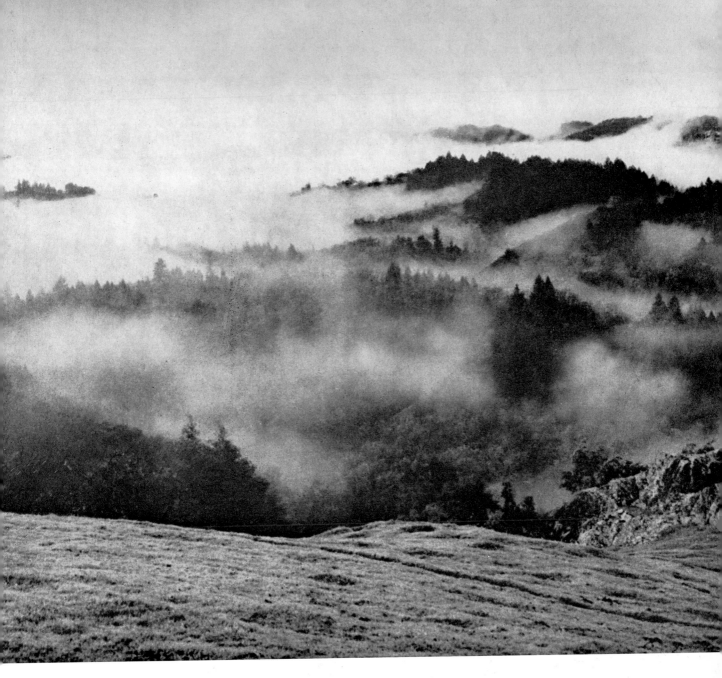

ADAMS, *above*: Rain. *Coast Range Hills, California*, 1950. *Courtesy Mr. Jack Stiball.*
left: The Face of Half Dome. *Yosemite Valley*, 1927.

CHAPTER 32
Masters of the Miniature Camera: Salomon and Eisenstaedt

MODERN PHOTOJOURNALISM became possible with the invention of the miniature camera. With the advent of the 35-millimeter Leica, invented in 1914 and placed on the market in Germany in 1925, 35-millimeter photography brought changes to every branch of photography. It enabled photographers to see commonplace, everyday objects in new and bolder perspectives and extended their ability to apprehend shapes and forms in space.

Dr. Paul Wolff, an early miniature-camera enthusiast, taught his students how to select the most effective angle, wait for the precise instant, stop movement at its peak, and see and compose simultaneously. His principles of miniature photography—minus his outmoded aesthetic of soft, salon-type photography—still guide leading photographers.

The great photographers in Germany during the 1920s were men of rare ability and intellectual breadth who taught that perception of form and beauty could be heightened by means of camera vision. They demanded that photographers as well as painters and designers be allowed the freedom to experiment in order to establish new identities for their art.

Behind-the-scenes glimpses of internationally famous political personalities at League of Nations conferences in the late 1920s were taken by the brilliant multilingual lawyer, Dr. Erich Salomon, one of the first to use a miniature camera for news pictures. It was said of him that there were "just three things necessary for a League of Nations conference: a few Foreign Secretaries, a table, and Dr. Erich Salomon." Magazine and press photographers ever since have followed his unposed candid-camera style as an ideal.

Dr. Salomon was an audacious as well as an ingenious photographer. He conceived a bagful of tricks to circumvent the "photographs forbidden" signs put up at all political meetings during the 1920s and 1930s. His many subterfuges included cutting a hole in his derby hat for a concealed lens or hiding his camera in a large armsling, hollowed-out books, or a flower pot, triggering the shutter by a remote cable release. Dr. Salomon's hunting grounds were not only the conference rooms of international politicians in Geneva, Paris, London, and Washington; he also covered nonpolitical activities, such as murder trials, society balls and concerts, catching princes, presidents, and chimney-sweeps off their guard. He was truly a photohistorian—photography's first—as well as an artist of rare integrity and skill.

Under Hitler, creative development in art and photography was interrupted in Germany. Neither experimentation nor free expression was permitted: leading teachers and practitioners in all branches of the arts left the country. Most of the important Bauhaus personalities—Walter Gropius, Mies van der Rohe, Laszlo Moholy-Nagy, Herbert Bayer, Lyonel Feininger—eventually came to the United States, where their influence on the visual arts remains a powerful force.

When the Nazis destroyed the great publishing house of Ullstein with its three picture magazines, for which men like Dr. Erich Salomon (who died with his family, except for one son, Peter Hunter-Salomon, in the gas chambers of Auschwitz), Alfred Eisenstaedt, Philippe Halsman, and Fritz Goro (all three came to work for *Life* magazine) took celebrated news pictures, an army of brilliant photographers and editors went to all parts of the free world to found magazines that have since become world-renowned.

Like Cartier-Bresson and other miniature-camera specialists, Eisenstaedt is a connoisseur of action patterns. He sees the flow of happenings around him as sequences with a beginning, a climax, and end—and he never fails to discern the image or the moment that carries the deepest significance. Many pictures serve their purpose as an illustration or technical experiment and are quickly forgotten. Very few photos by Eisenstaedt are in this class. Very many, on the contrary, become increasingly provocative with each viewing. His best works stir the senses and emotions as do the best prints in all the graphic arts; they haunt the memory and draw one to view them again and again in order to find fresh associations, new interpretations. Their strength lies in their simplicity of design. Eisenstaedt's portraits clearly reveal the spirit and character of his subjects, whether celebrated or unrenowned. His scenes likewise, in their intimacy, make a viewer a participant, giving him a feeling of being actually present beside the photographer, for example in a picture of 1932 showing a lovely dark-haired girl seated in an adjoining box of the beautiful five-tiered La Scala opera house in Milan. It is a suspended moment, just before the conductor lifts his baton and the lights are lowered on a most appealing, festive social scene.

There is authenticity, reality, and honesty in Eisenstaedt's photographs. He does not pose people; he takes them wherever they are, in whatever light exists, at whatever they are doing. They forget that he is there. Perhaps his small size—he is 5 feet 4 inches—and his small cameras—he uses Leicas exclusively—help make him unobtrusive; but it is his psychological approach that serves him best. People are ready to like him because he is ready to like them. He discerns their character quickly and reacts accordingly. He puts them at ease by the way he works. He knows his equipment thoroughly: he evaluates the light subconsciously, rarely consulting his light meter, instinctively works fast, and covers his camera with his body until he is ready to shoot. He talks softly, he is relaxed; the subject forgets him. When the precise instant is at hand Eisenstaedt becomes acutely sensitive to all the factors that he weighs. It is his moment of artistry and his decisive finger secures a photograph now indelibly marked with his unique style.

That brilliant, precise style of Eisenstaedt's grew out of his pioneering efforts with small cameras after he had mastered pictorial photography. There is still something of his early, soft, painterly feeling for dense shadows and soft whites to be found in his frank, realistic pictures of today. The blending of the pictorial and the candid makes him the towering photojournalist consciously working for the vertical page of *Life* magazine, and telling his story to its weekly readership of more than twenty million people.

Eisenstaedt, like most great photographers, entered the field as a mature man. The year was 1926—he was twenty-eight years old. Fifteen years before, while attend-

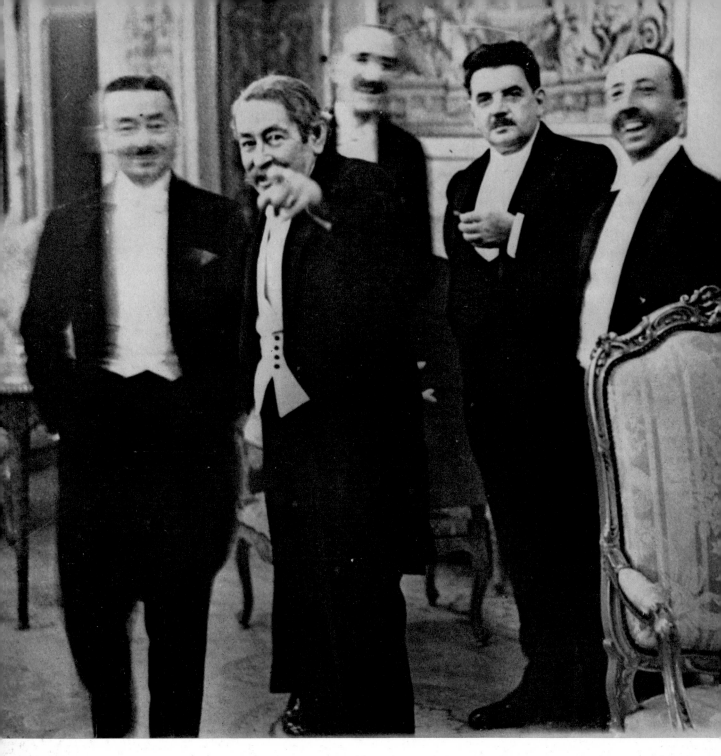

SALOMON, *above:* It's That Salomon Again! *Paris, 193*
Aristide Briand points to the photographer who, he had be
would get into a secret session of the French Foreign Offic

below: King Fuad of Egypt and Entourage in Berlin State Opera Box
of President Hindenburg. *1930. Both, courtesy Peter Hunter, Amsterdam.*

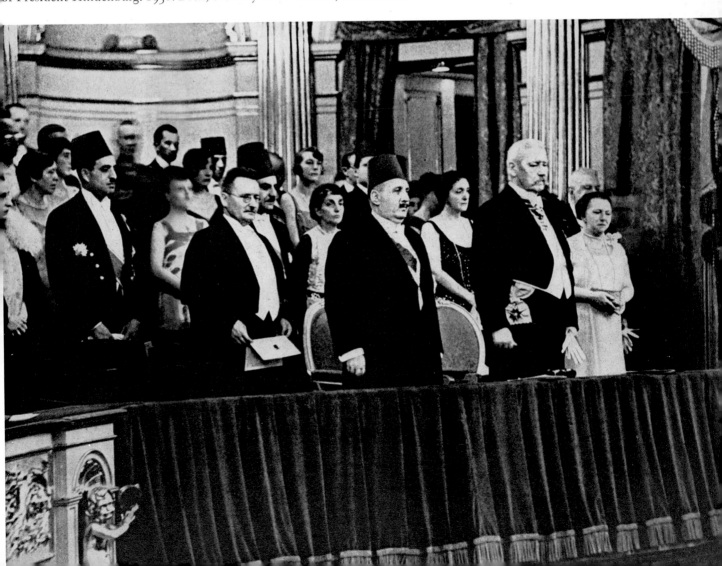

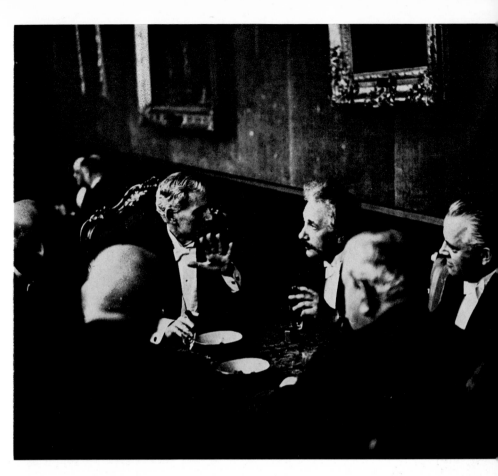

above and right:
Reception in Berlin. 1931. *British Prime Minister Ramsay
MacDonald explains the theory of relativity to Albert Einstein.
Einstein expounds on his hopes for the peace conference.
Both, courtesy Peter Hunter, Amsterdam.*

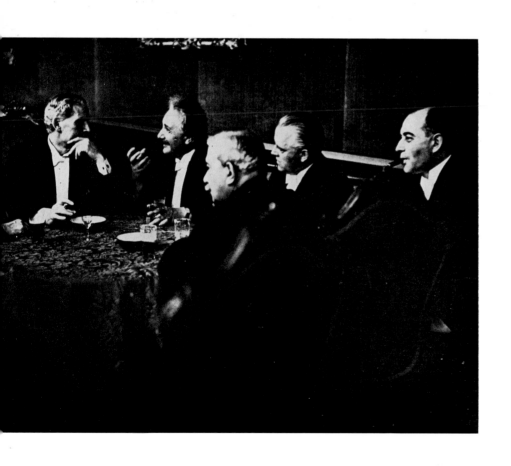

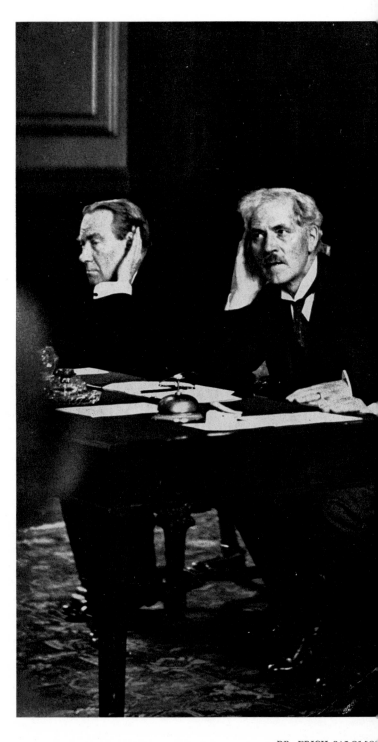

DR. ERICH SALOMON

Stanley Baldwin and Prime Minister Ramsay MacDonald
During a Press Conference. *London, September, 1931. One of the
first informal photographs taken at the Foreign Office*

g school, he had been given a Kodak, which he thereafter used intermittently without any purpose other than
to take snapshots. In 1916 he was drafted into the
German army. Badly wounded during the offensive in
Flanders, he was invalided out of the service, not to
again use of his legs for more than a year. The well-to-do
Eisenstaedt family was ruined during the postwar inflation, and the recently hospitalized veteran took a job .
selling buttons and belts to the wholesale trade. For
several years he carried his sample case, attended concert
hall and opera house, for he loved music, and talked
about philosophy and art at the cafés where, one evening,
a friend introduced him to pictorial photography. He
learned soft focus, bromoil, and all the darkroom tricks
to make photography resemble a painting or a charcoal
drawing. He sold his buttons only for income with which
to buy more equipment. He sold an "arty" print to an
editor of the *Berliner Tageblatt* who showed him several
candid portraits and suggested he try to emulate the style
of Dr. Erich Salomon, an early exponent of the miniature camera.

Eisenstaedt bought a small camera, forerunner of the
Leica. It had a fast lens but required focusing with a
magnifying glass on the ground glass. He took various
assignments, often wearing white tie and tails which he
had fitted up with pockets to hide the small plate holders
the camera demanded. It was during one of these assignments that he took the memorable picture of Marlene
Dietrich attired in male top hat and tails.

On December 3, 1929, Eisenstaedt quit buttons and
belts for good to become a professional photographer. A
week later he was in Stockholm to cover the Nobel Prize
ceremonies, securing an intimate informal picture of
Thomas Mann standing slender and assured at a podium;
a magnificent moment in the great novelist's life before
he was forced to flee the Nazi terror to preserve his intellectual integrity. Eisenstaedt became Europe's best
known press photographer during the next several years,
accepting all sorts of assignments, including a flight of
the Graf Zeppelin to Brazil, and then he too escaped
from the Nazis.

For the Associated Press in 1935 he covered the Ethiopian preparations for the Mussolini-manufactured war
with Italy. Eisenstaedt took more than 3,500 negatives
using three Leica cameras fitted with 35, 50, and 90 mm.
lenses. His pictures of the Queen of Sheba's descendants
enhanced his reputation internationally, particularly a
close-up picture of the calloused, mud-caked feet of a
prone Ethiopian soldier.

In December, 1935, he arrived in the United States

pleased but surprised to learn he was deeply respected
for his pioneer efforts in candid press photography.

In November, 1935, Time Inc., after considering calling their proposed new publication *Show Book*, named
it *Life* magazine and hired Alfred Eisenstaedt as one of
its first photographers. On the more than 1,300 assignments since then he has covered every conceivable kind
of a story both large and small in every corner of the
globe. More than eighty of his photographs have made
Life covers. In 1966 he published his overwhelming book
Witness to Our Time, with 48 color photos, 379 black-
and-whites, and his own incisive commentary. A retrospective exhibition of his photographs was held coinci-
dentally in the Time-Life Gallery.

People on a circular or square staircase have always
appealed to him. He repeatedly finds this composition or
variations of it, nurses, midshipmen, hotel employees.
Perfect spacing and proportion invariably result in a
series of diminishing concentric circles or squares.

Eistenstaedt has innately the photojournalist's most
important requisite; he is there when something is
happening. He takes the overall picture as well as the
salient detail; together they make the picture story. The
movers and shakers he takes, the personalities and the
place. Consciously he brings the viewer along with him
to be an eyewitness; his purpose is to make *Life's* readers
feel like participants. This ability to make people iden-
tify with a picture is the high standard of professional
photojournalism reserved for a rare few who have developed personal styles.

Always the perfectionist, Eisenstaedt goes to any
lengths to get his picture. He had himself tied for six
hours to the bridge of the Queen Mary to photograph
the height of a storm's fury. Once he was led blindfold
to a gambler's hideout in Tokyo. Another time his life
was endangered as he photographed the Mau Mau
Terror in Kenya. He endured the enervating rain forest
of Dutch Guiana, which he explored for weeks with his
camera. Tenacious and fearless when pursuing a story,
he exhausts every angle with infinite patience to achieve
his kind of picture.

In general coverage of news stories as in his portraits,
he is the complete master of his medium. His file is a
veritable *Who's Who* of the world in practically every
field of endeavor. Eisenstaedt once wrote about taking
portraits, "If I photograph a king and he is a king in his
own right, I am equally a photographer in my own right.
You will only be able to photograph people if you truly
like them and they respect you."

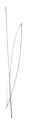

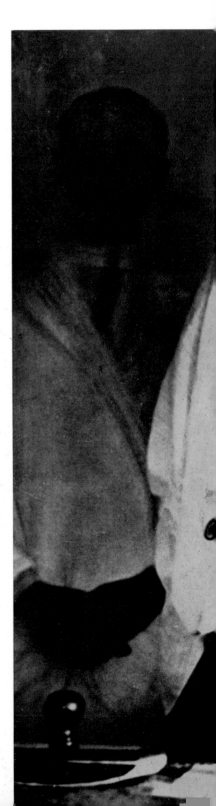

ALFRED EISENSTAEDT, Ethiopian Judge. 1935.

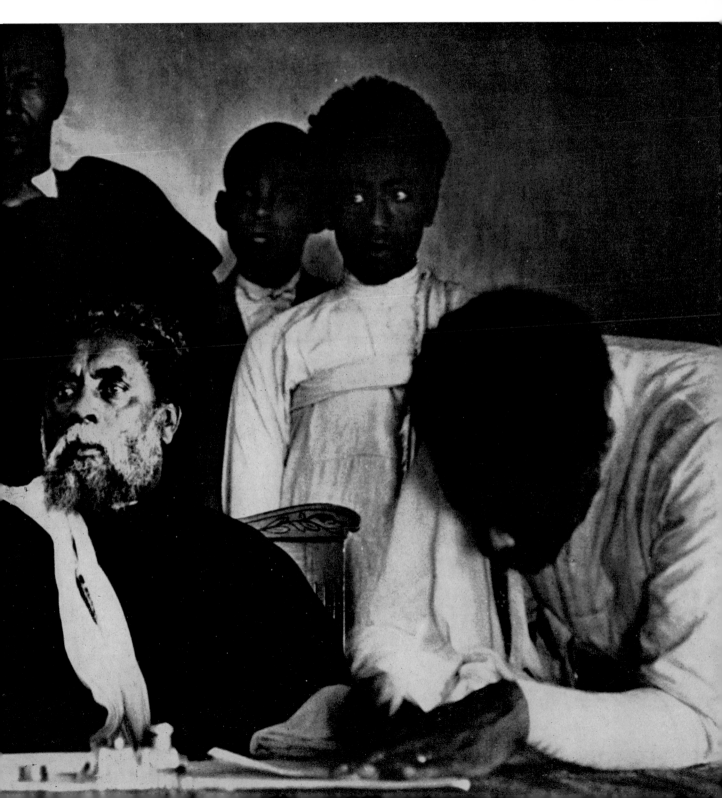

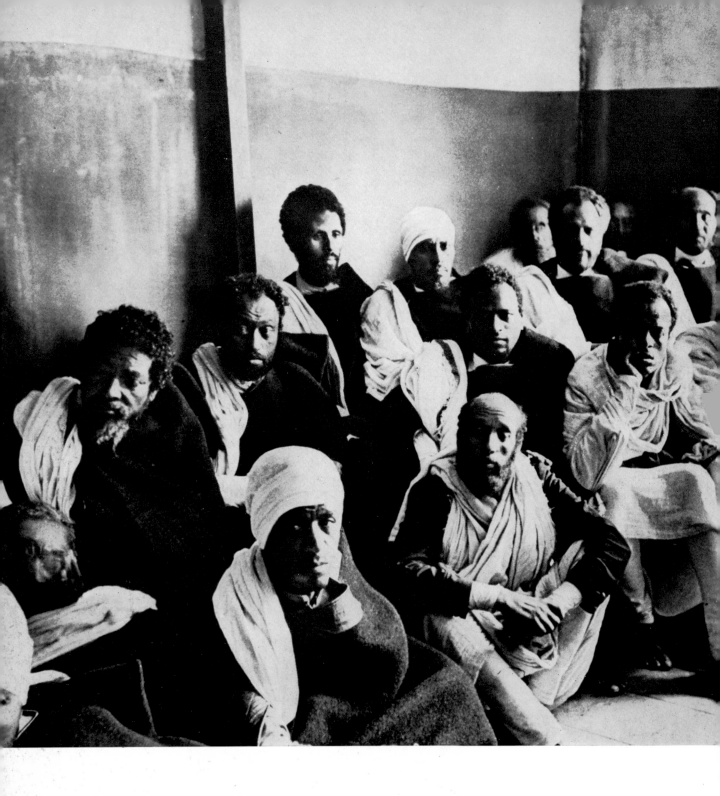

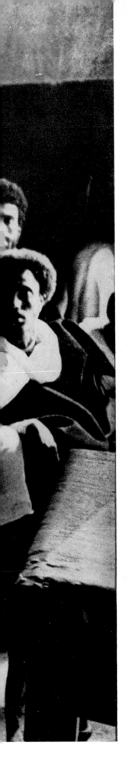

EISENSTAEDT, *below*: Feet of Ethiopian Soldier. 1935.
left: Spectators at Trial in Ethiopia. 1935.

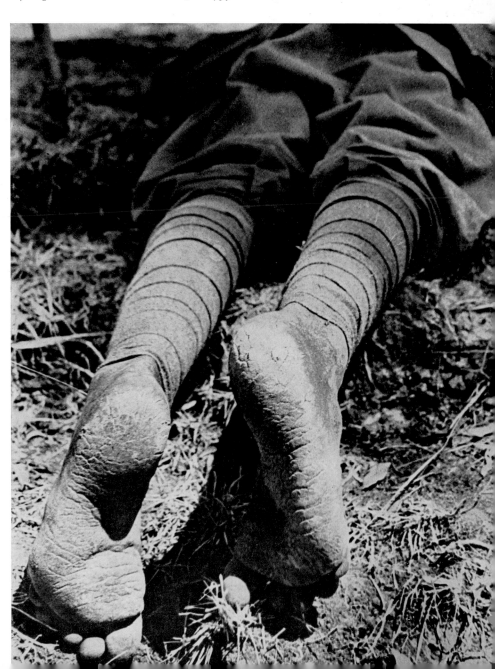

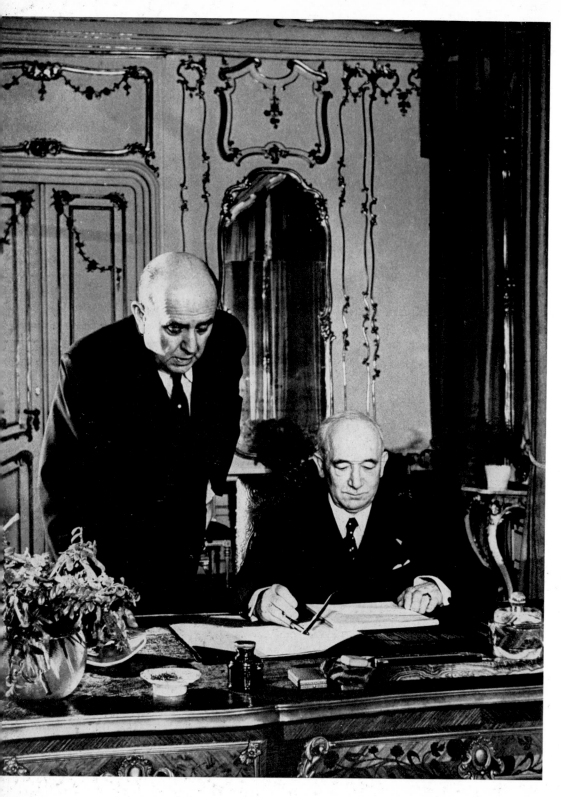

EISENSTAEDT
above: Jan Masaryk and Eduard Benes. *1947*.
right: Augustus John. *1951*.

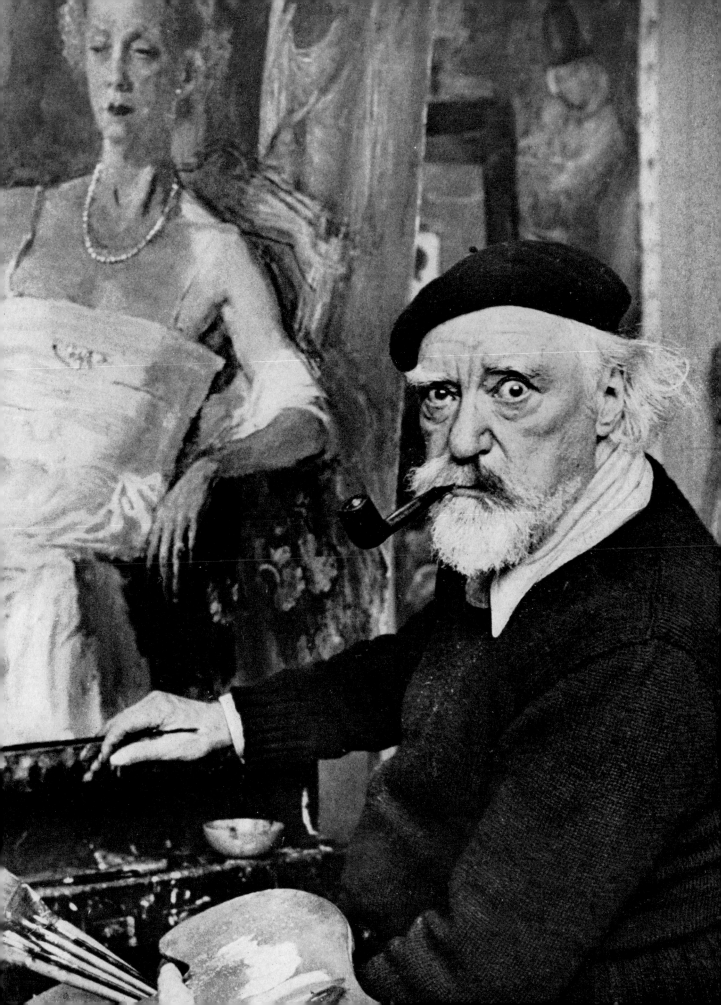

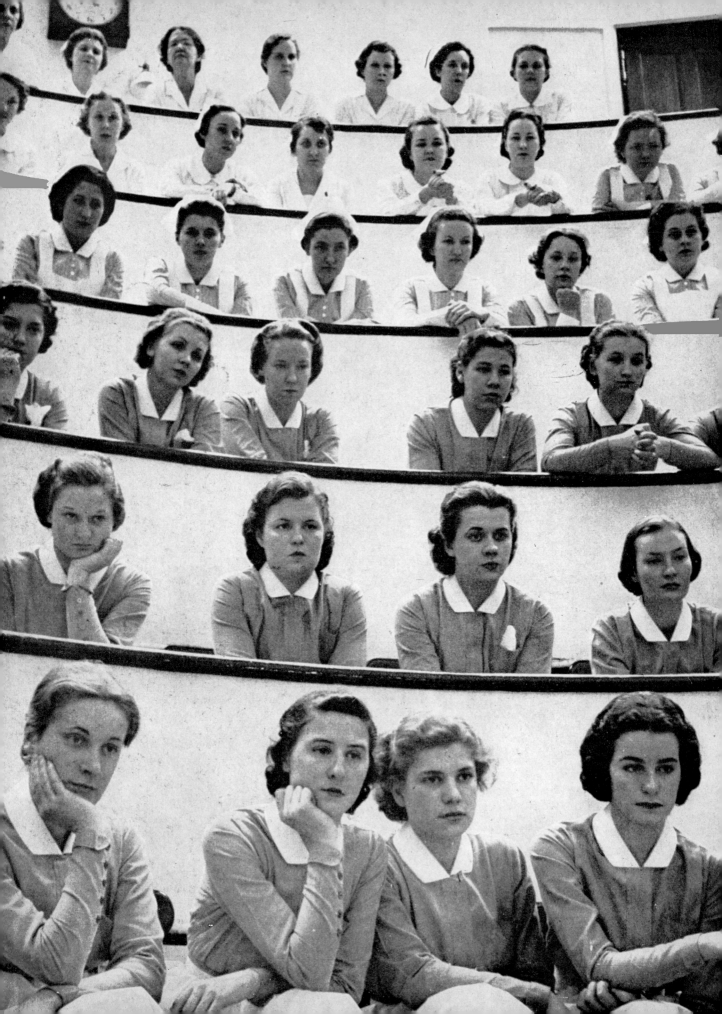

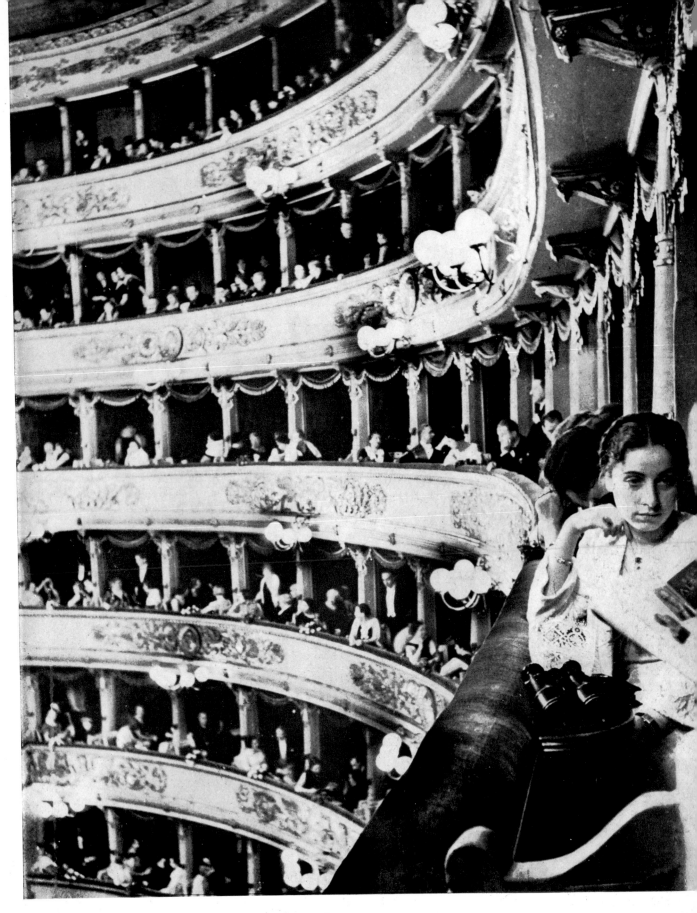

EISENSTAEDT, *above*: La Scala Opera House. *Milan, 1932.*
left: Nurses Attending Lecture, Roosevelt Hospital. *1937.*

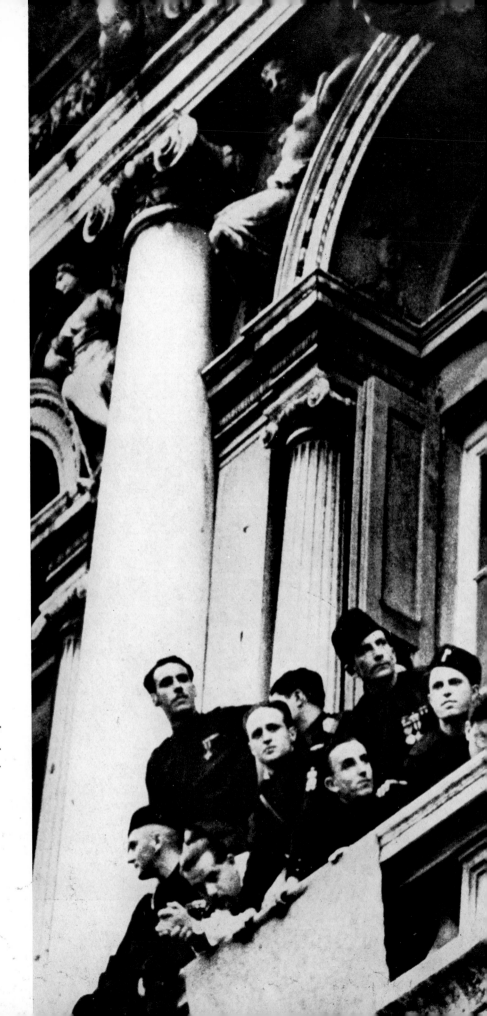

EISENSTAEDT
Mussolini.
1934.

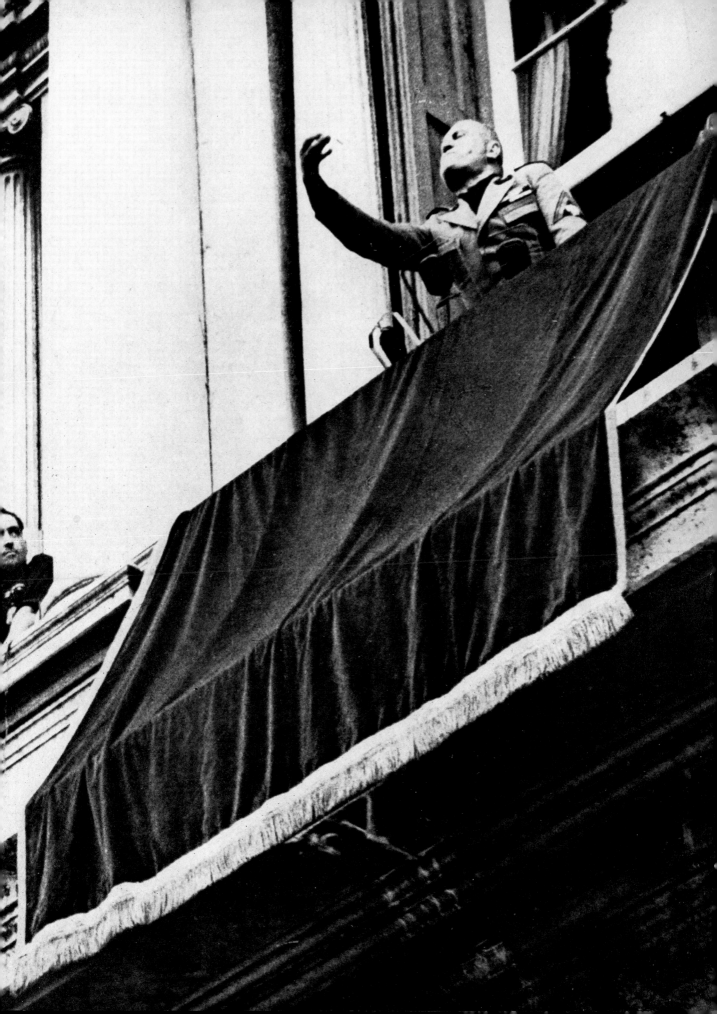

CHAPTER 33

Margaret Bourke-White: Roving Recorder

MARGARET BOURKE-WHITE discovers the objective reality of any given story, isolates it, and then relates each photograph to the totality of the story she envisions. She creates a dynamic journalistic photo-essay, a complete story communicating visual insights not only about how the subject looks but about what it says to her.

She seeks to picture the environment and the social background of her subjects, the work they do, the lives they live. She is aware of their appearance as she is aware of their personalities; the fraction of a second when the picture is taken is alive with meaning. Her purpose is visual communication for the great body of *Life*'s readers; immediate recognition for those who see superficially and deeper meanings for the more sagacious. Her way of capturing the image calls forth varying levels of emotional response; her essays are of complex dimensions, new experiences in journalistic photography. Her work is a sort of candid eavesdropping, consciously controlled by the shape of the 35mm film she uses. Both she and *Life*'s readers complete the picture; each feels a participant. Recently she wrote, "In some cases you feel you have stepped right into the lives of the people you are photographing."

It has been so since her first picture story for *Life* magazine. The original cover on November 23, 1936, was her photograph of the overpowering, repeated concrete orms of Fort Peck Dam; in the lead story of nine pages ... e depicted intimately the workers' lives in the boom- ... own atmosphere of the Montana construction project. ... his dynamic treatment was an important factor in ... etting *Life's* style of photographic essay. It was a new ... yle for her as well. Her reputation had been gained as ... n industrial photographer, taking unusual perspectives ... f skyscrapers and grain elevators, steel mills and smoke- ... acks, machine gears and dynamos. "She transformed ... he American factory into a Gothic cathedral and glori- ... ed the gears," wrote one critic.

A graduate of Cornell University, where she had ... tudied biology and philosophy, she found her life's in- ... erest in the camera, first as a commercial photographer ... or bankers, architects, and industrialists, making limited ... rogress, and then as a photojournalist for magazine pub- ... ishers, developing photojournalism to a high personal ... evel. Henry R. Luce hired her as a photographer for ... *ortune* eight months before the first issue appeared in ... 930. The following year she was sent to Germany to ... hotograph the Krupp Iron Works and then, on her ... wn, she went to Russia to take pictures of the Soviet's ... ive Year Plan. Without escort or assistance she photo- ... raphed factories far from the cities, securing a percep- ... ive record of the ruthless initial industrialization plan ... ttempted by the Bolshevik government.

Fortune and *Life* magazines have sent her everywhere ... n the globe, a million miles, she estimates, producing a ... quarter of a million negatives. A chic, soft-spoken, attrac- ... ive woman, danger stimulates her; she controls her fears ... hrough immersing herself in the sensitive seeing of ... hotography. A camera steadies her hands and purpose ... s a scalpel does a surgeon's.

In Moscow, which the Nazis bombed at first by the ... ight of parachuted magnesium flares, Margaret Bourke- ... White, the only American photographer in Russia, set ... p her cameras on the roof of the hotel opposite the ... Kremlin to take her pictures by this suspended eerie light.

In World War II she was the first woman photog- ... apher accredited to the United States Armed Forces and ... immediately felt the taste of war when the troopship she ... was aboard was torpedoed and sunk en route to North ... Africa. This was not the only time she was to lose her ... cameras; five fell into the sea when a helicopter from ... which she was doing a story on U.S. Navy rescue tech- ... niques crashed into Chesapeake Bay.

She covered the American infantry men's two-year ... war in Italy, risking her life to get pictures, as they fought ... their way up the boot into Germany. She barely escaped ... when Nazi flyers attacked an unarmed observation plane

from which she was photographing the bombed city of Cologne. She shocked the world into awareness of Nazi maniacal destructiveness with her pictures of human starvation in the concentration camps and of the dead in the grisly gas chambers.

Margaret Bourke-White writes crisply and brilliantly, perfectly complementing her photographs. She tells a story succinctly without editorializing. In *Dear Father-land, Rest Quietly* the pictures give graphic dimensions to the verbal descriptions of her feelings. Two other books of her war experiences illustrated with her pictures were published during the conflict, *Shooting the Russian War* and *Purple Heart Valley*; then in 1949 there was *Halfway to Freedom*.

The war over, she again began her travels; one of the first assignments she accepted was to photograph Gandhi in India. Gandhi's secretary made her learn patiently to spin before he permitted her to photograph the Mahatma at his wheel. She later wrote of this experience, "If you want to photograph a man spinning, give some thought to why he spins. Understanding for a photog-rapher is as important as the equipment he uses. . . . In the case of Gandhi, the spinning wheel was laden with meaning; for millions of Indians it was the symbol of the fight for independence which Gandhi successfully led."

She was on hand with her camera during the hectic, frenzied days of the "Great Migration," the exchange of the Hindu-Moslem population, and the birth of Paki-stan. Stark, contrasting pictures of the dead put out in the streets of Calcutta to be devoured by vultures; a rich moneylender's ostentatious house decorated with crystal chandeliers, gilt mirrors, and family portraits, and a lovely sensitive portrait of a girl wearing necklaces of beads and British coins.

For Margaret Bourke-White a return home to *Life's* office is but to ready herself for another assignment. Racial tensions and conflict about "apartheid" brought her to South Africa in 1950. In Johannesburg she went almost two miles into the earth to photograph sweating Negro miners in temperatures that registered 100 degrees despite air conditioning.

The following year over Kansas she flew 42,000 feet high in a jet plane to photograph another jet attempting to break the sound barrier, and took an exquisite abstract picture of white vapor trails in an illimitable black sky. Pursuing the Air Force story, she was the only woman accredited to fly on a mission in a B-47, the fastest bomber at that time.

Undeterred by the price that the Communists put on

her head to keep her from entering Korea, she went deep into the mountains held by the Red guerillas, photographing the bitter struggle in a series of decisively dramatic pictures.

Lectures, writing, and *Life* magazine assignments now make up her existence. Nothing daunts her zeal for the camera. She has taken pictures from every kind of a conveyance; on a recent assignment she went from Maine to Central America by canoe, plane, and muleback, to secure a photographic essay on American Jesuits, which was later published with a special text in collaboration with Father John La Farge, S.J. In former years she had collaborated with Erskine Caldwell (to whom she was once married); in 1937 they published *You Have Seen Their Faces*, two years later *North of the Danube*, and in 1941 *Say Is This the U.S.A.?*

In her thirty years with a camera Margaret Bourke-White has produced a tremendous variety of photographs, including industrial, war, and foreign reporting and photographic essays of world-famous leaders, among them Roosevelt, Churchill, Madame Chiang Kai-shek, Nehru, and Pope Pius XII. She has created a chronicle of our time, a personal interpretation through photography of vital days in contemporary history. Conscious an artist with the camera, Margaret Bourke-White explains her viewpoint, "Everything in the picture should contribute to the statement . . . good photography is pruning process, a matter of fastidious selection."

All photographs in this chapter courtesy Life Magazine, copyright Time, Inc.

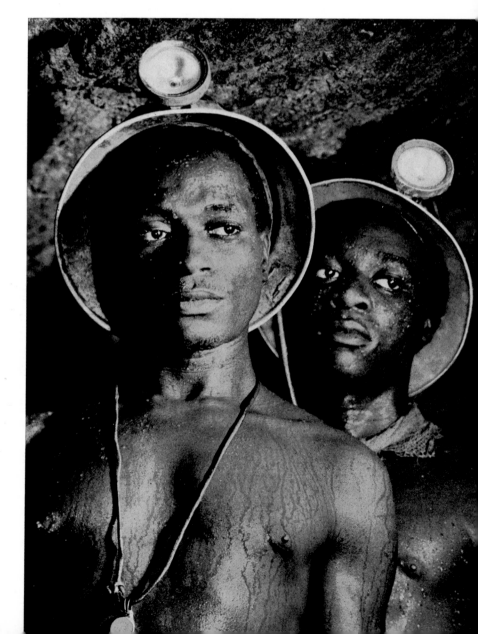

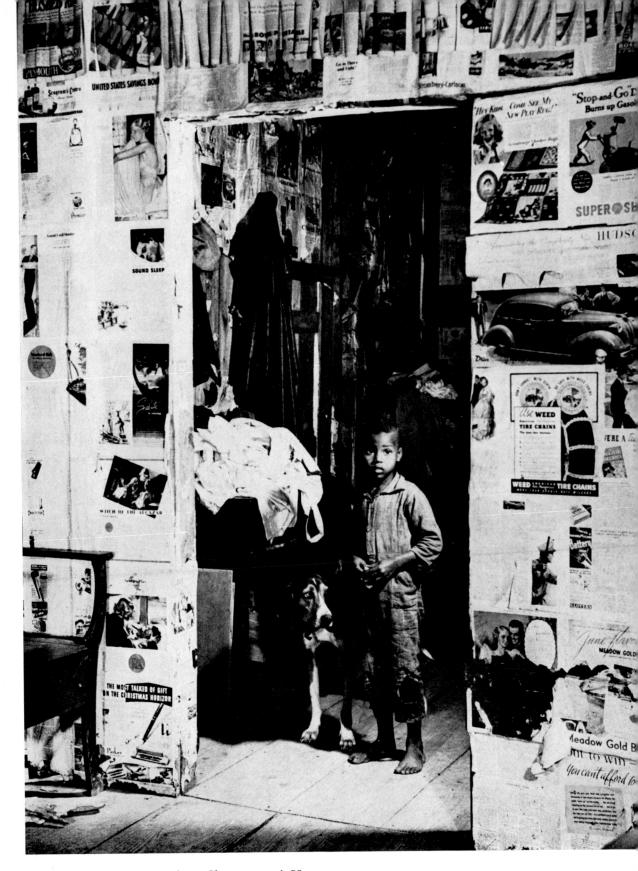

MARGARET BOURKE-WHITE, *above*: Sharecropper's Home. *1937*.
left: South African Gold Miners. Johannesburg, *1950*.

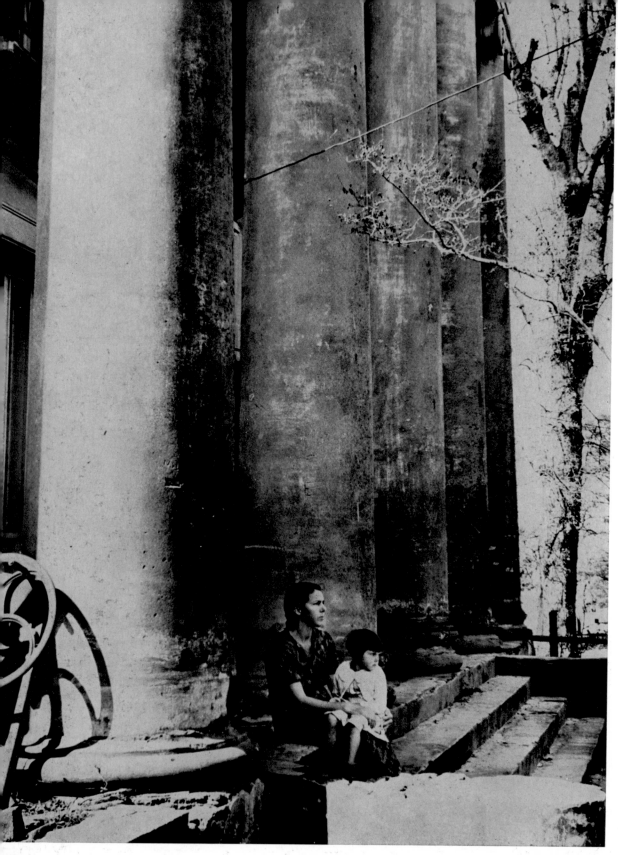

MARGARET BOURKE-WHITE
above: The Plantation. *1937.*
right: Indian Girl. *1948.*

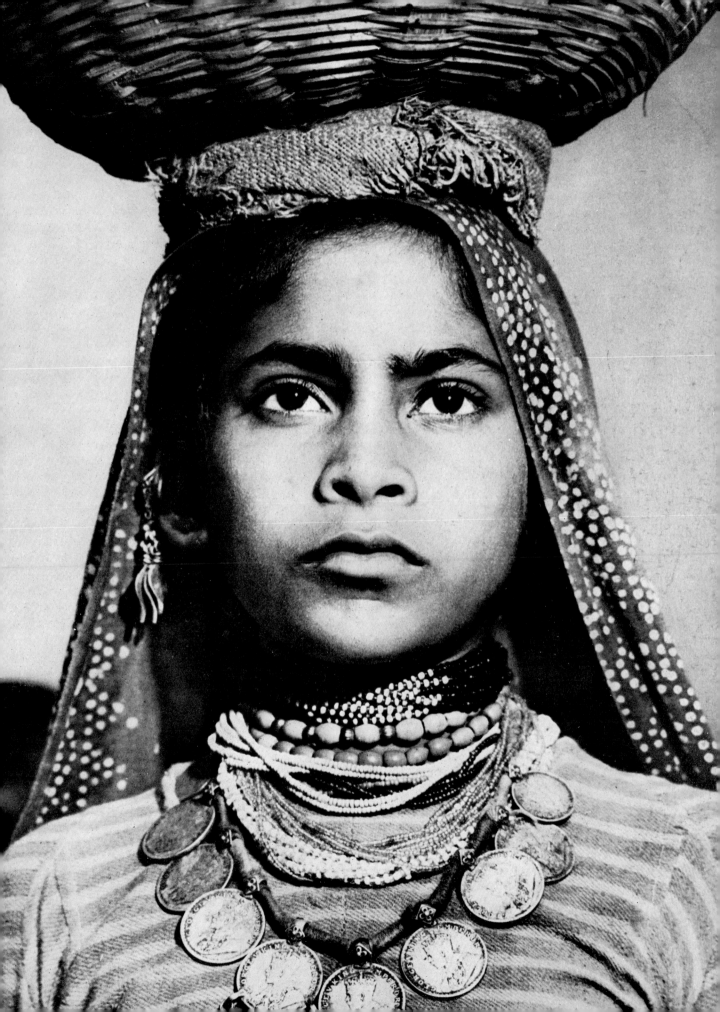

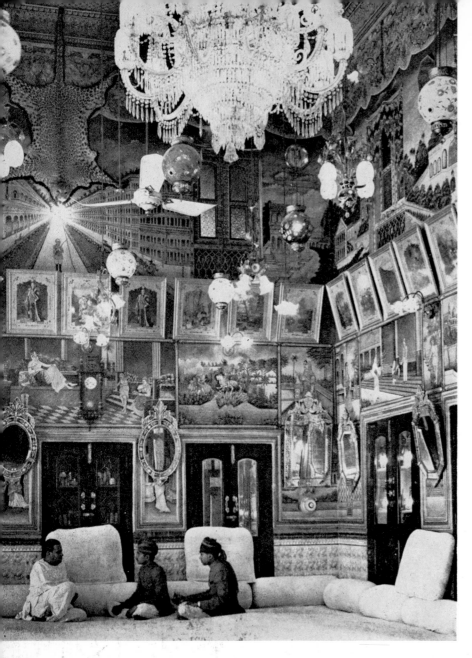

MARGARET BOURKE-WHITE
above: Moneylender's Home. *India, 1947.*
right: Vultures. *Calcutta, 1948.*

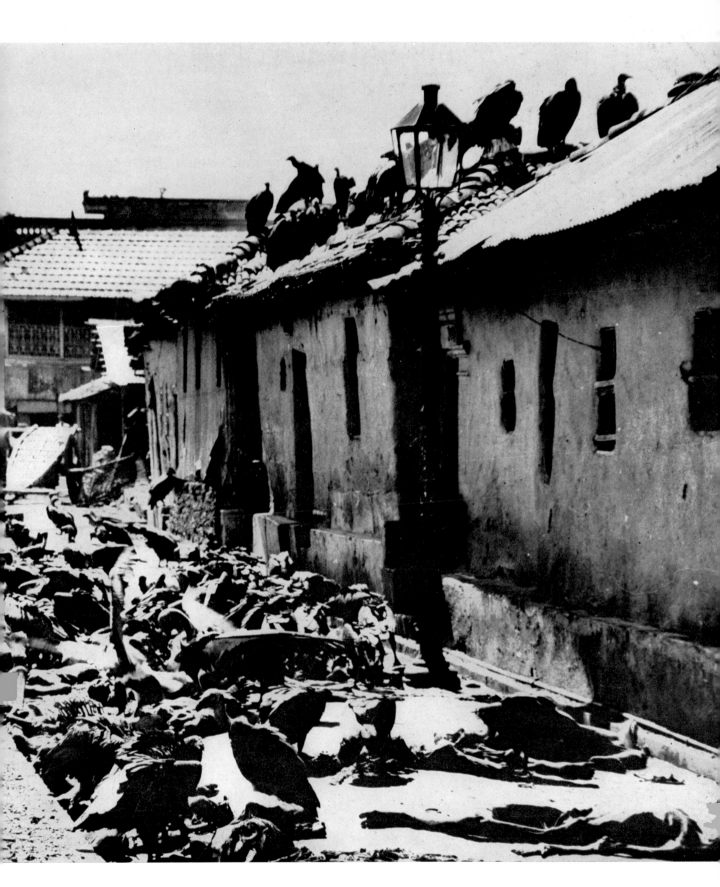

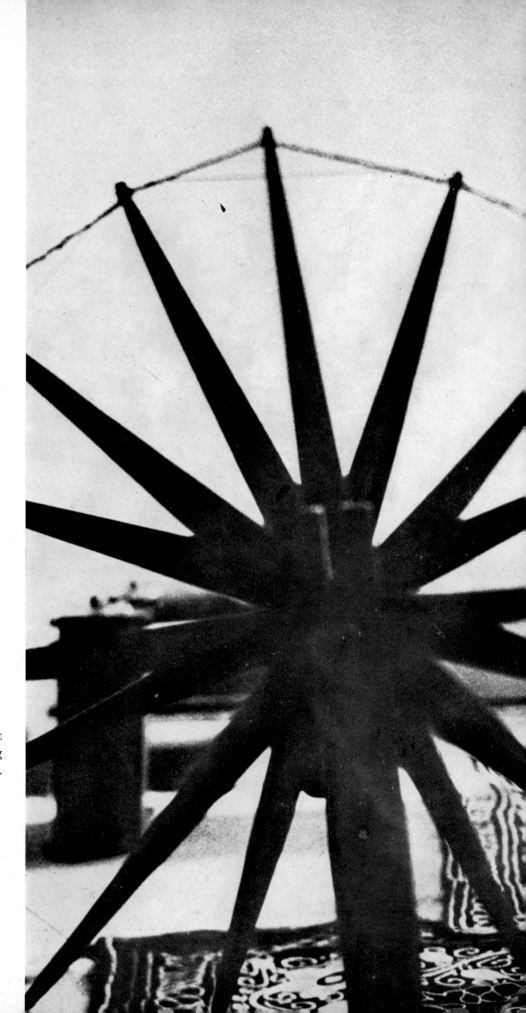

MARGARET BOURKE-WHITE
Mahatma Gandhi at a Spinning
Wheel. *Poona, India, 1946.*

396

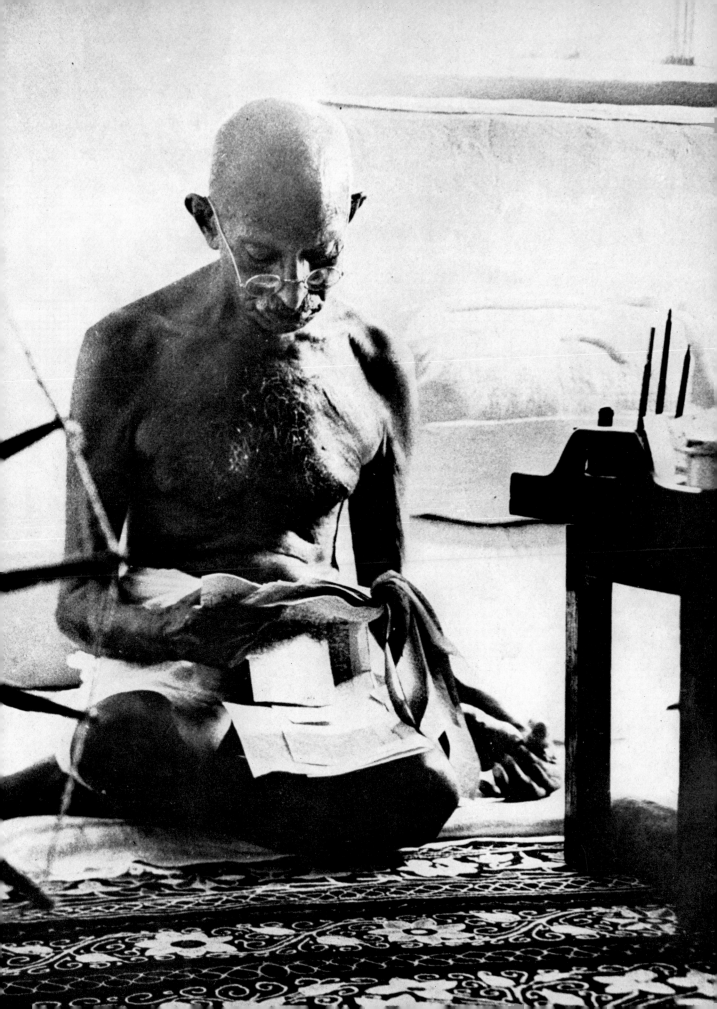

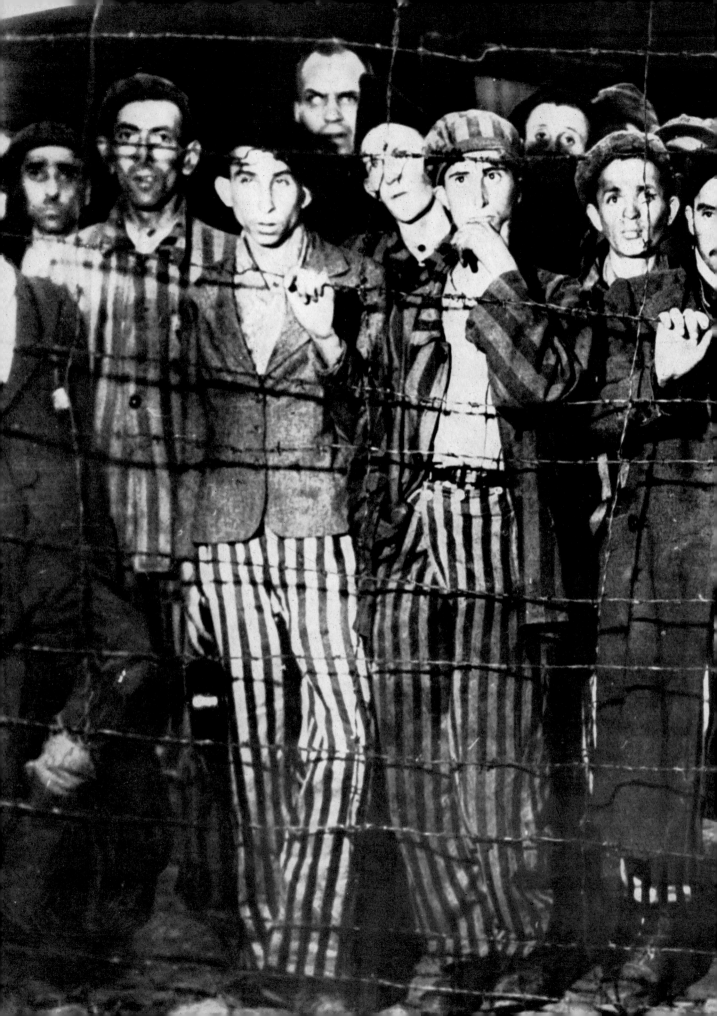

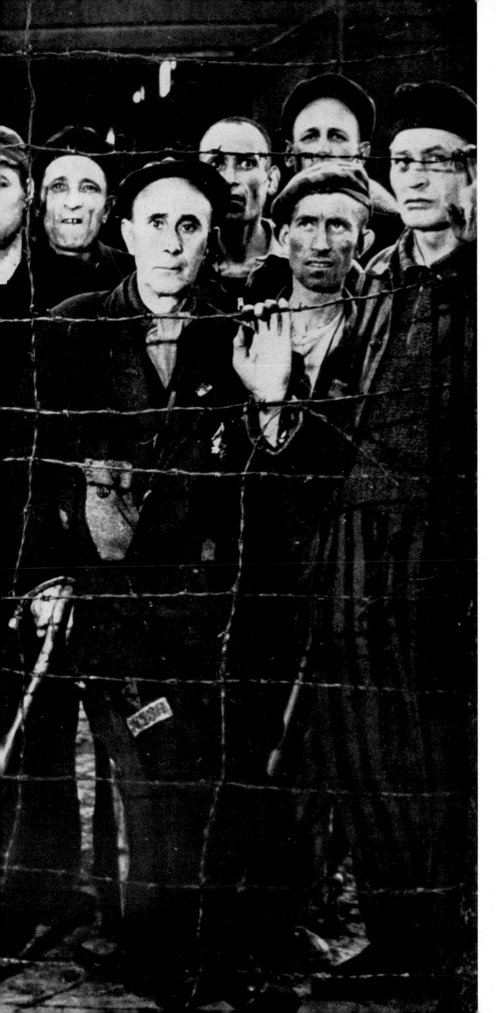

MARGARET BOURKE-WHITE
Buchenwald Victims. *1945.*

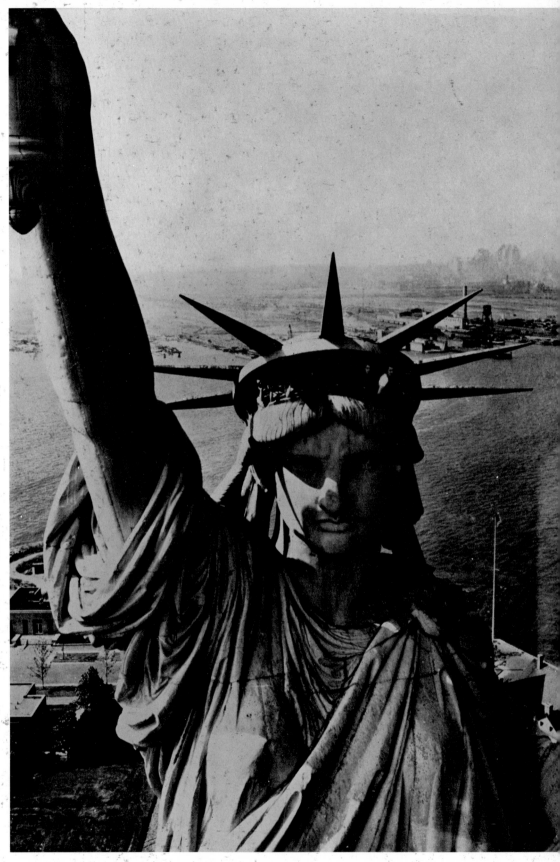

MARGARET BOURKE-WHITE. The Face of Liberty. 1954.

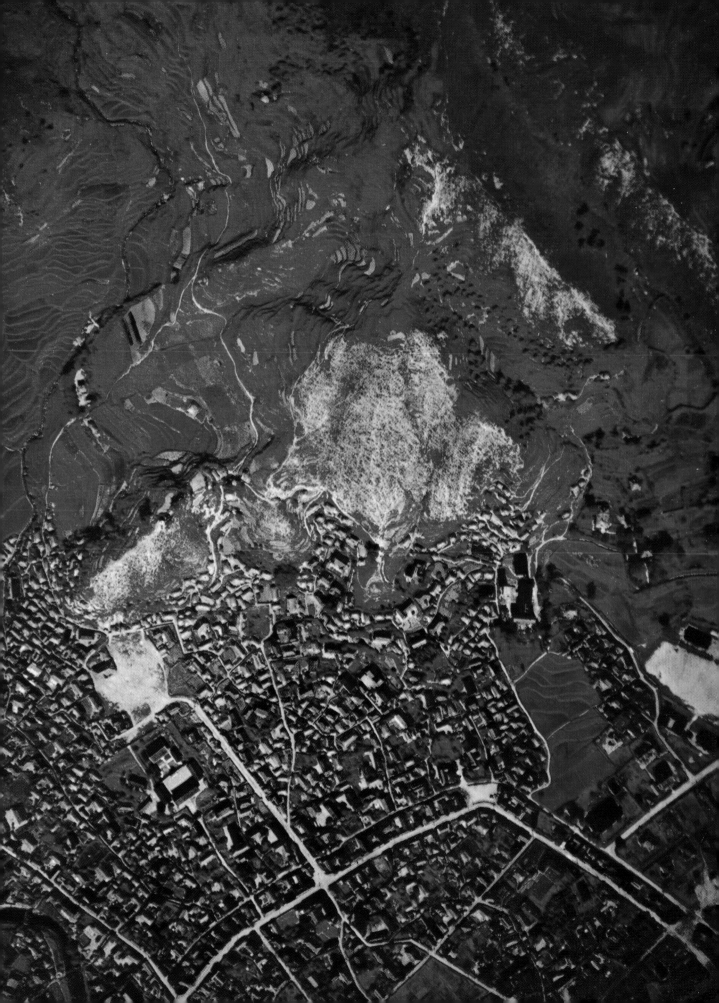

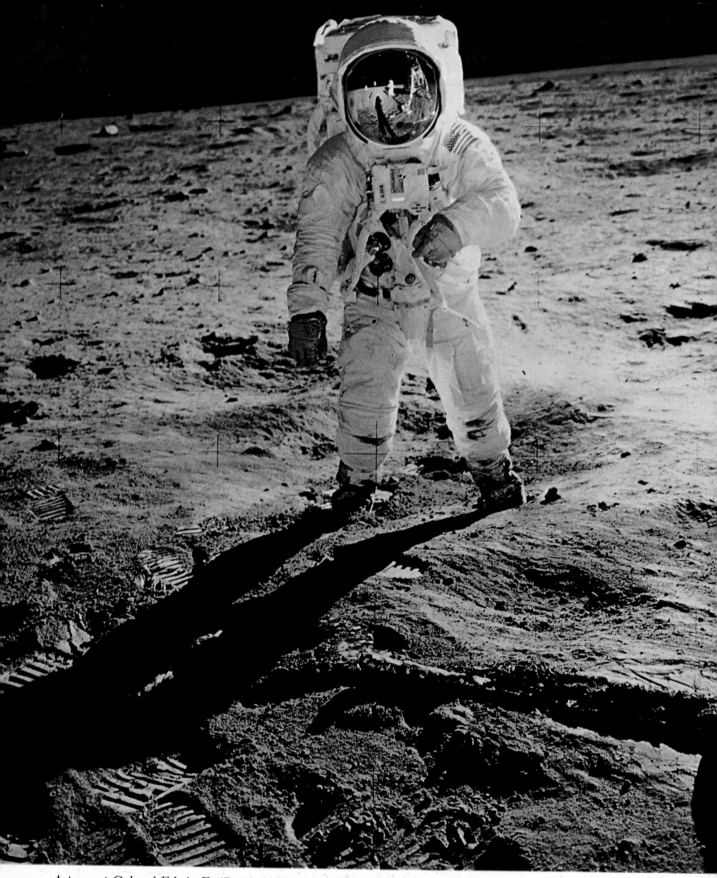

Astronaut Colonel Edwin E. (Buzz) Aldrin's visor mirrors the television camera, flag, lunar module, part of the scientific package, and Astronaut Neil Armstrong (the photographer) in this picture taken on the moon during the Apollo 11 mission, July 16, 1969. Ektachrome courtesy NASA.

Major William A. Anders, Apollo 8 astronaut, who along with Colonel Frank Borman and Captain James A. Lovell Jr. first circled the moon on December 24, 1968, said just before departure: "By having a camera connected to an eyeball connected to a brain up there, we can really do a job that cannot possibly be done with unmanned vehicles." This magnificent photograph, showing the blue-brown earth in a black sky along with the desolate "wet sand" landscape of the moon, supports the astronaut's contention. Ektachrome courtesy NASA.

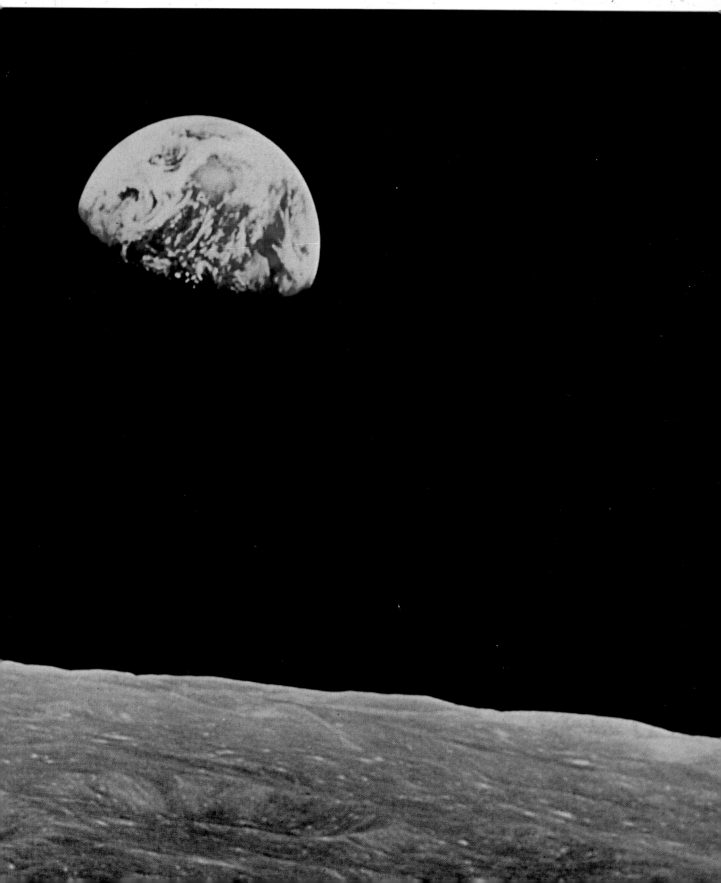

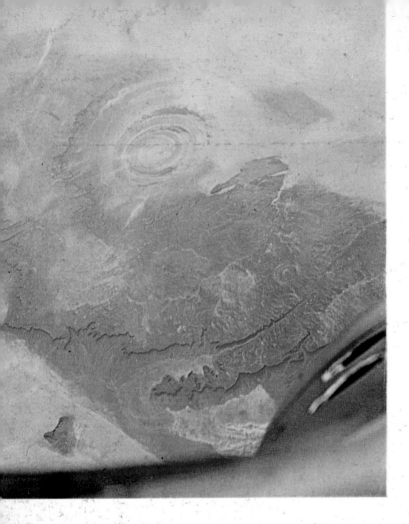

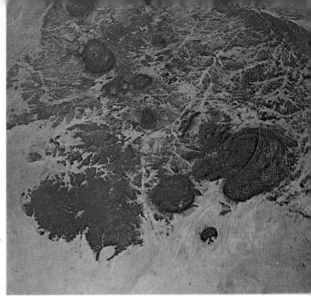

Burnt and Withered Face of African Deserts in the Blue Planet Earth. *Taken 130 miles in the air on June 1965 from Gemini 4 by Astronaut James A. McDivitt.*

left: Western Sahara, Mauretania. Richat Structure, which could have resulted from a meteorite impact. *above:* Northern Sahara. The Air Mountains of Niger. *below:* Northern Sahara Sand Dunes in Central Algeria. *Ektachromes courtesy NASA.*

facing page: GEORGE HOLTON, Penguins. 19

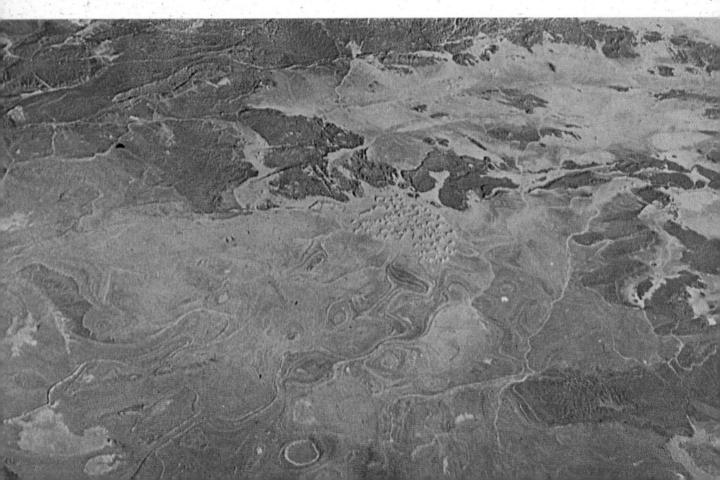

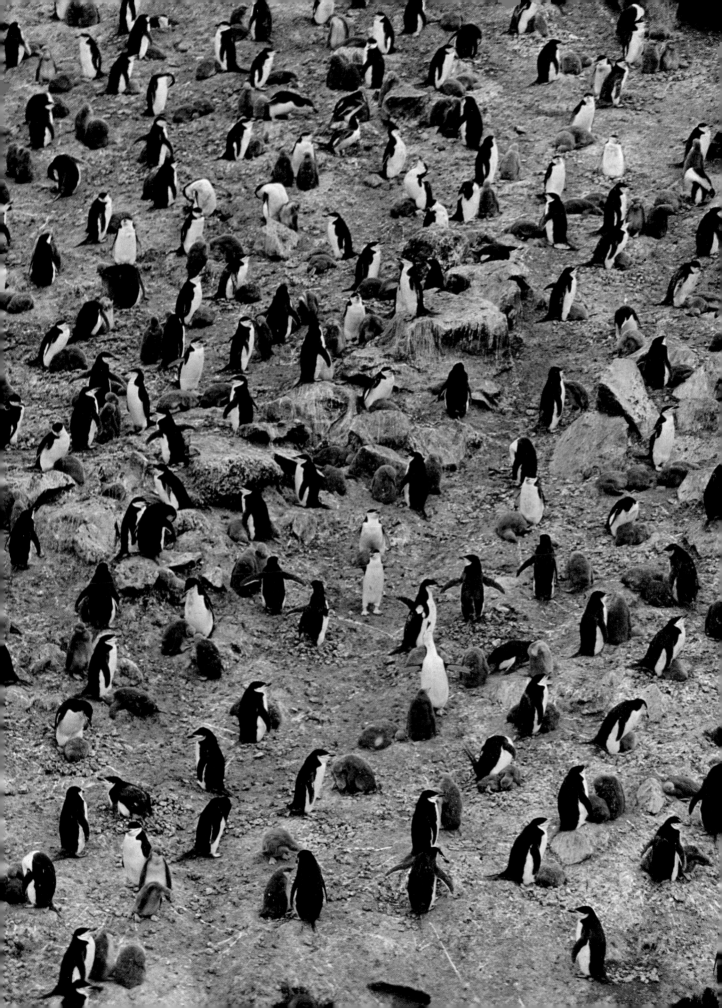

ELIOT ELISOFON, *below:* Decorated Man in New Guinea. 1957.
right: Bather in Tahitian Rapids. 1955.
Both, courtesy Life Magazine, copyright Time, Inc.

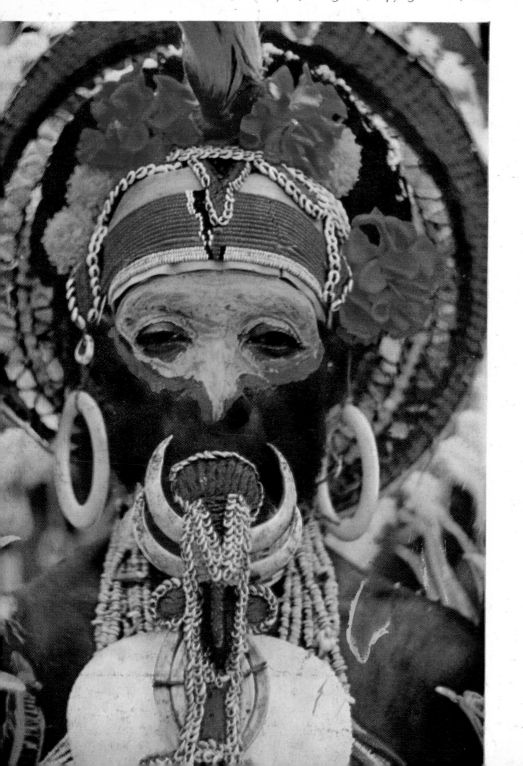

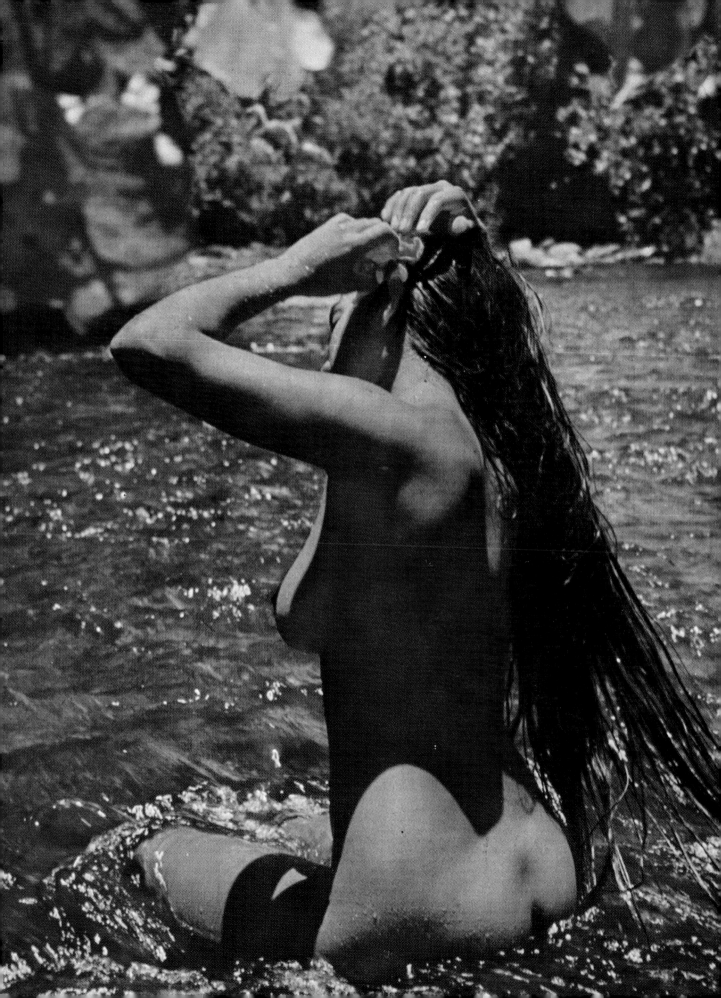

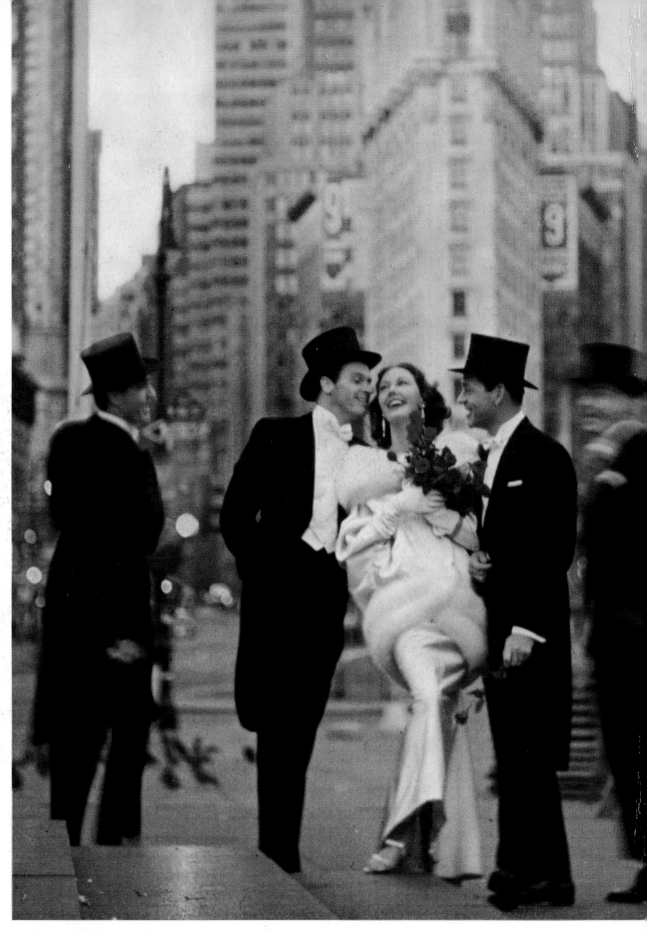

above: GORDON PARKS, Fashion in Times Square. 1956.
Courtesy Life Magazine, copyright Time, Inc.

PART FOUR
Color: Another Dimension

CHAPTER 34
Exploring the New Horizon

"I HAVE TRIED TO EXPRESS the terrible passions of humanity by means of red and green," wrote Van Gogh in discussing his *Night Café*. "The room is blood red and dark yellow. The color is not true from the realist point of view; it is a color suggesting some emotions of an ardent temperament."

Such an attitude toward color is coming to the fore among practitioners of the infant art of color photography. This art came into being a few years after the end of World War II when a new type of color film enabled still photographers, for the first time, to process their own color negatives and print their own color positives as quickly and simply as, previously, they had processed black-and-white. From then on, creative photographers could explore the possibilities of controlling images through using color in novel, imaginative, and often, non-realistic ways.

For three-quarters of a century before the advent of the new film, color processing was specialized and laborious. Taking a color photograph required three separate negatives, and making a color print on paper required the conversion of three black-and-white negatives into three layers of dyed gelatin, which were assembled in register. The bewildering mass of chemicals and methods kept the great masters of black-and-white photography from turning their talents toward color; they made only a few color photographs. Color photographs, accordingly, belonged almost entirely to the realm of technical and applied photography. They were used in scientific work, advertising, and color reproduction. And all color theory, practical color photography, and color printing had as their most important aim the reproduction of natural color literally and faithfully.

All color photography is based upon the principle that every hue can be rendered by a combination of only three "primary" colors. Practical use of this principle was made in the eighteenth century, when inexpensive color mezzotints, after well-known paintings, employed combinations of three basic colors. In 1855, James Clerk Maxwell anticipated color photography by pointing out that primary colors in light could be combined in this manner; in 1861 he projected an image of a tartan ribbon on a screen where three component color images were superimposed. In 1868 Louis Ducos du Hauron in Paris outlined a number of techniques for producing color photographs on paper. These formed the basis for color photography until 1930, when Mannes and Godowsky developed for the movies the Kodachrome method of producing a positive transparency on a single film. In 1938 Kodachrome film and the similar Agfacolor, invented almost simultaneously in Germany, became available to still photography. It was then that the use of color film became widespread, although both Kodachrome and Agfacolor had to be returned by the photographers to the film manufacturers for complicated processing, which involved development, re-exposure, dyeing, and bleaching of all three sensitive coatings on the film. It was Mannes and Godowsky again who invented the reversal film, Ektachrome, which permitted photographers to do their own color-processing, becoming generally available in 1950. Kodacolor and Ektacolor soon followed. These were nonreversal materials, which is to say that the exposed film, when developed, was in color, complementary to the colors of the subject photographed. The complementaries were reversed to become the colors of the subject in prints made from Kodacolor and Ektacolor films, just as black-and-white-negative values are reversed in their positive prints. In 1963 Edwin H. Land's 60-second Polacolor material was released by Polaroid. Four years earlier, Land had dethroned the classical three-color theory of color vision, showing that a full-color image is seen by the eye when only a pair of color-separation photos of a subject are superimposed, one of them illuminated by a longer wave length than the other. Polacolor now makes use of three primary-color dyes, but color film of the future may not do so.

Color photography brought a new impact to adver-

tising and made reproduction of the world's art universally available. In science, color extended the investigative range of photography: what in black-and-white might be identical grays, in a color photograph might resolve into a purple and a green, providing differentiation beyond the possibility of the more limited medium. Color photography in science has also produced effects that are pictorially startling, for example in the recording of the complicated color patterns created when crystals are subjected to polarized light. Color photography with infra-red filters transforms the familiar world into a glowing pattern of reds, yellows, browns, and blacks, revealing nature in unexpected ways, and especially useful in the detection of camouflage, buried archaeological sites, and images not visible inside the spectrum of "white light."

Some of these unusual visions of science may have provided inspiration to the creative photographer, to whom the chief value of color photography does not rest in the quality of literal accuracy but rather in the expressive qualities of the finished picture. This value is independent of the accurate reproduction of natural color although accurate reproduction may on occasion provide new and exciting insights. The colorist with a camera sees and feels a color combination as a play of tones and hues throughout the area encompassed. He relates the psychological and emotional forces of color to his subject, no matter whether the colors are seen in sunlight; controlled by artificial light; achieved through multiple exposures creating overlapping colors; displaced from sharp focus with lenses that change the normal color balance of the spectrum; fused and blurred by shutter speeds that are slow when action is fast; made bright and strong by underexposure or subdued and pale by overexposure.

Most professionals reduce their "palette" and limit themselves to dark tones accented by some few brilliant beams of colored light. The strong dyes of color photography are more insistent than the tempered colors mixed by the painter. A painting serves its purpose as a picture on a wall, whereas a photograph is intended primarily for the pages of a picture magazine. Camera color and the printed page are often, therefore, purposely more compelling in their demands for immediate attention. Ever more vivid color values are sought by magazine and advertising photographers, to catch the reader's eye.

Although the crisply brilliant results achieved by such accomplished photographers as Dan Budnick, George Holton, Eliot Porter, and Peter Fink are arguments for this point of view, some of the finest color photos, nevertheless, have been taken on gray, rainy, and foggy days. The questing spirit of today's photographers does not allow any branch of photography to remain the prisoner of a formula very long.

Confident control over end result, the following through of a final decision made at the snap of the shutter, has not been easy to attain. There was first the necessity to learn how to see color as film and lens see it rather than as eyes see it. For example, when the cameraman's purpose is to reproduce nature's colors exactly, he introduces compensations in exposing daylight film under conditions of diffused morning or evening light. He does this because such film is "balanced"—i.e., has been formulated chemically to produce the seen color combination after normal exposure and processing —for bright middle-of-the-day sunlight. Otherwise he may receive a surprise. Surprises, in color photography, often take such form as the appearance of blue-green where red was expected—a far more startling result than the unexpected shade of gray that may creep into a black-and-white picture.

Conscious control of color accidents, deliberate disobedience of the film manufacturer's traffic rules for the purpose of achieving colors contrary to usual human experience, has become part of the technique of a number of creative photographers, such as Ernst Haas, Marie Cosindas, Fred Lyon, Hamaya, and Nina Leen. The overbright color range of the new fast color film is the delight of the amateur seeking ever more realistic snapshots. The marvelous capabilities of the latest automatic cameras and films have deceived many photographers, both amateur and professional, into believing that literal reproduction is the color camera's major sphere of artistry. The artist-photographer knows this to be untrue.

The national picture magazines have provided an excellent training ground for color photographers, making available to them for experimentation a generous supply of expensive color material. Experience with the new negative-color film is gradually being built there; and it is there that color photography is gradually developing its own standards. The artistry and style of individual photographers are transforming the objects they "see" into a new type of richer visual expression within its own technical limitations and imitating no other medium. Photographers like Philippe Halsman, Eliot Elisofon, Dmitri Kessel, Fritz Goro, Gordon Parks, and Gjon Mili have by now attained their due measure of importance and appreciation for their color work along with the universal acclaim received by them and similarly talented photographers for their prints in black-and-white.

Infra-red black and white film penetrating haze shows hundreds of square miles from 20,000 feet. Black spot is a lake. Courtesy United States Air Force. opposite page: Camouflage detection with color film and infra-red filter, in Korea, 1955 Living greenery appears red, dead vegetation such as thatched roofs shows up dark Courtesy Life Magazine and United States Air Force

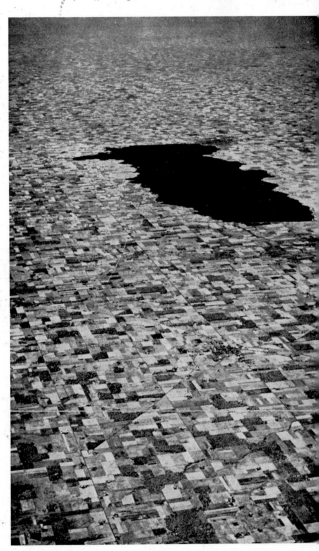

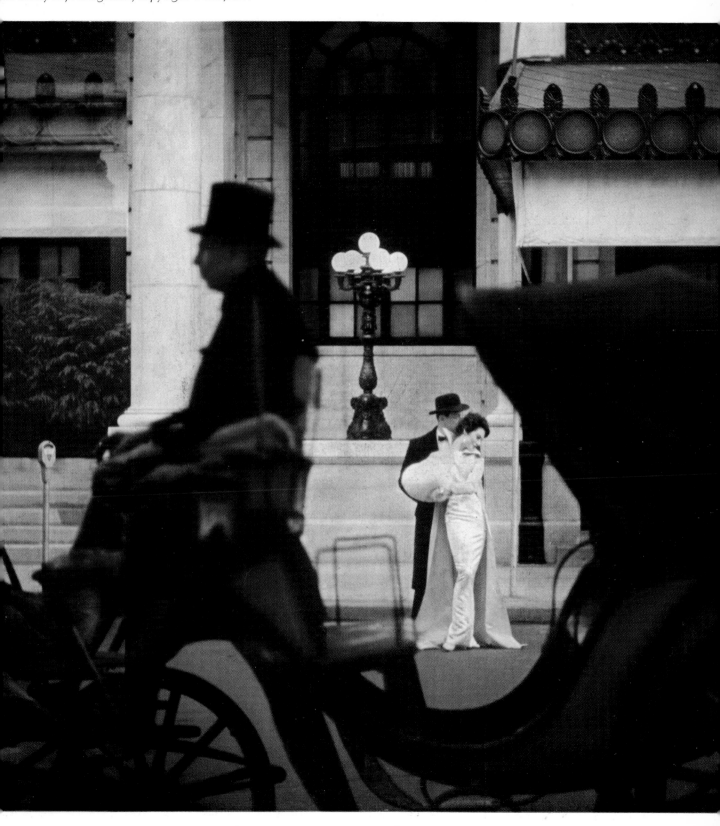

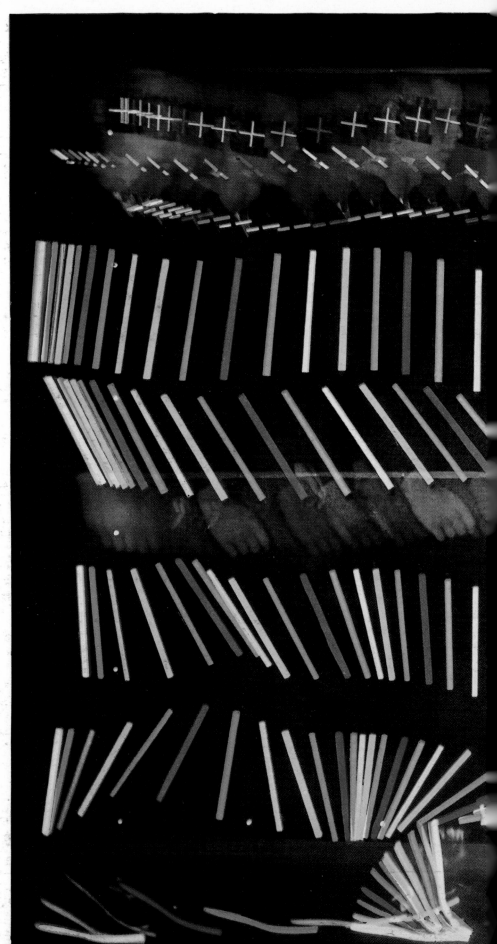

YALE JOEL, Flow of Muscular
Movement. 1958.
Courtesy Life Magazine,
copyright Time, Inc.

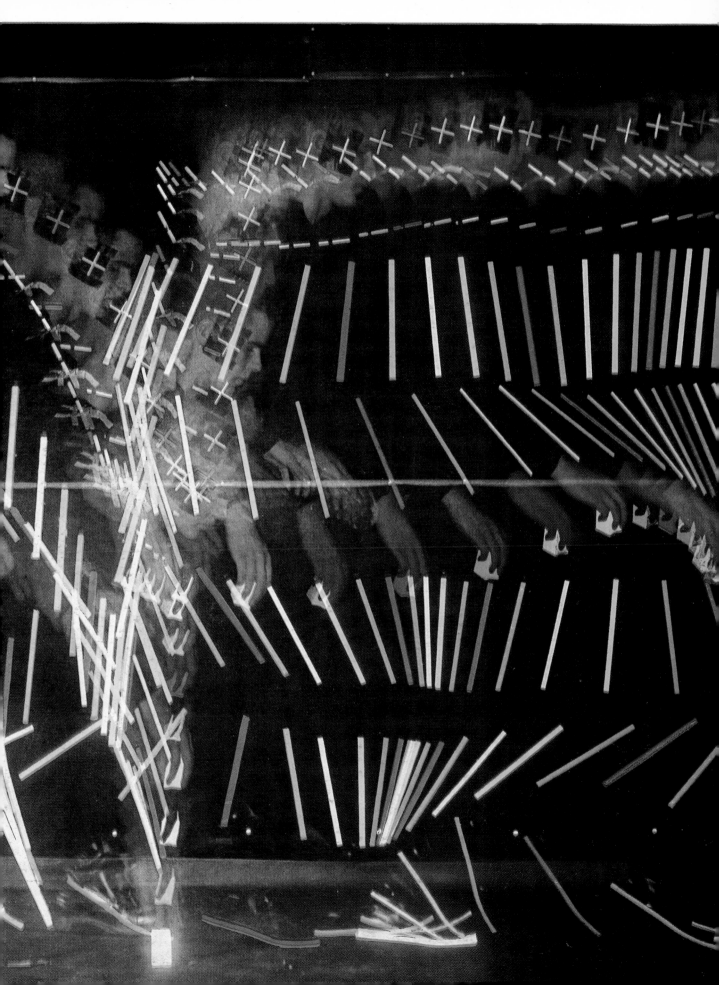

ERNST HAAS
below: Yellow Sulphur Landscape. 1966.
right: Broadway Sign Painter. 1953.
Courtesy Life Magazine and Magnum Photos, New York.

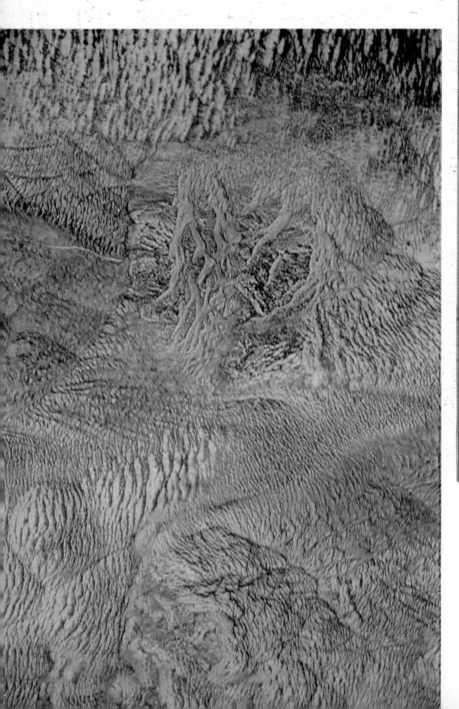

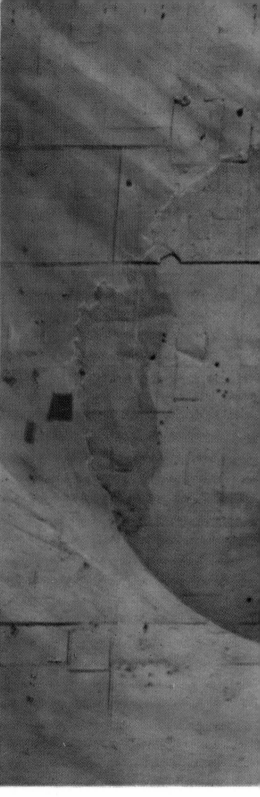

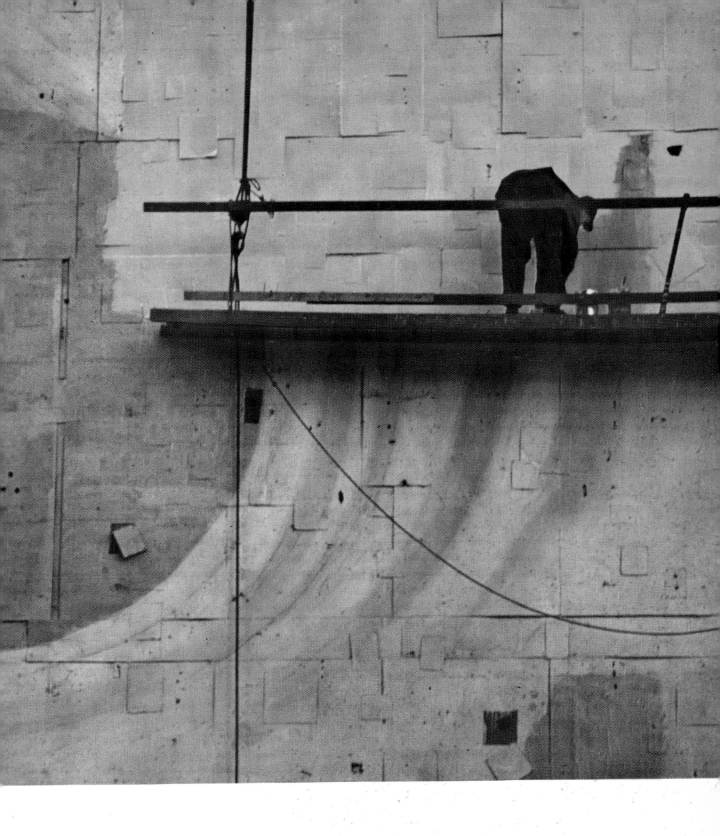

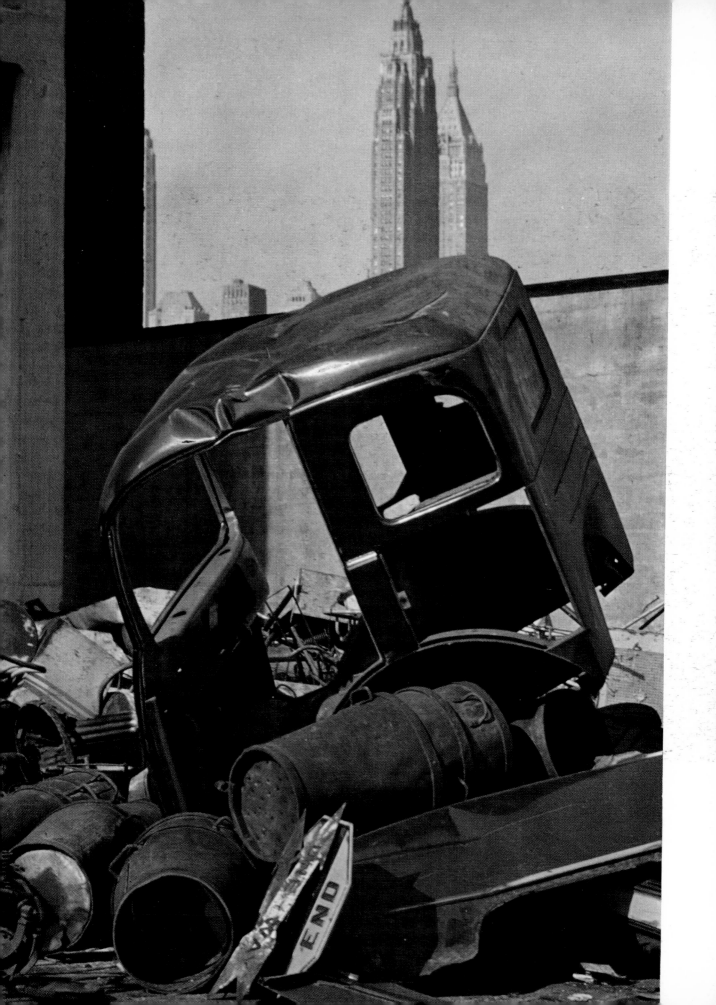

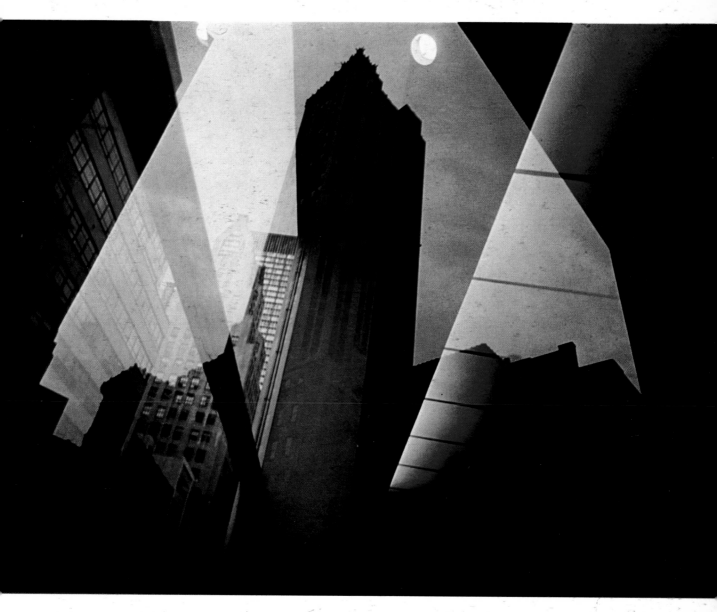

HAAS, *above:* New York Triangle. *1965.*
left: Manhattan Spires from Brooklyn Junkyard. *1953.*
Courtesy Life Magazine and Magnum Photos, New York.

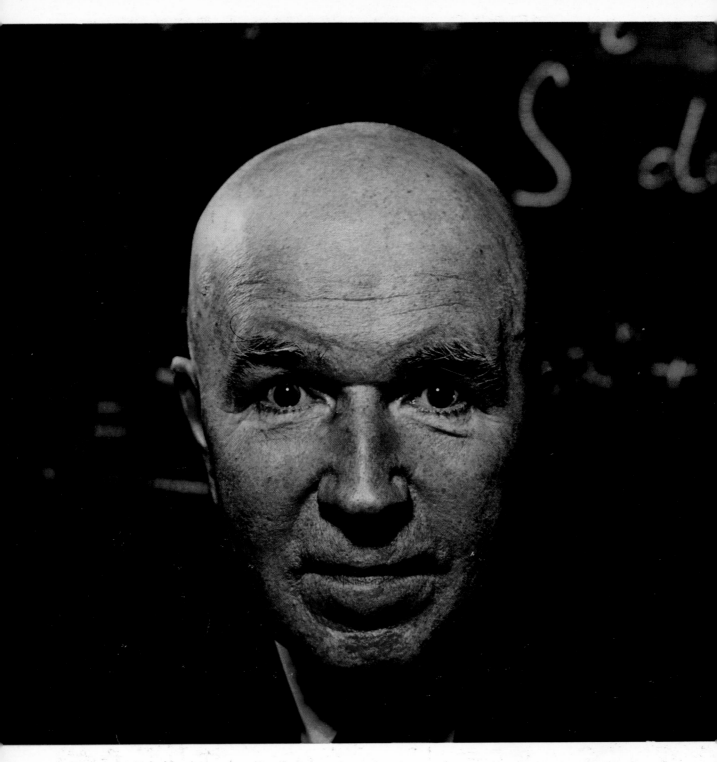

PHILIPPE HALSMAN
Ivan M. Vinogradov. *1961*.
facing page: Judge Learned Hand. *1957*.

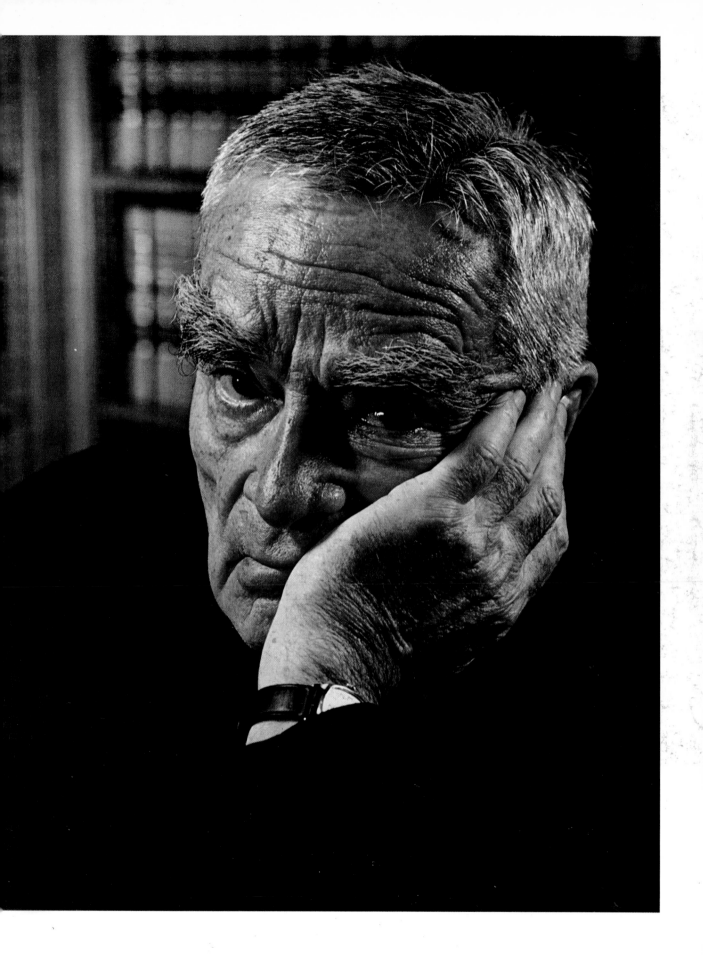

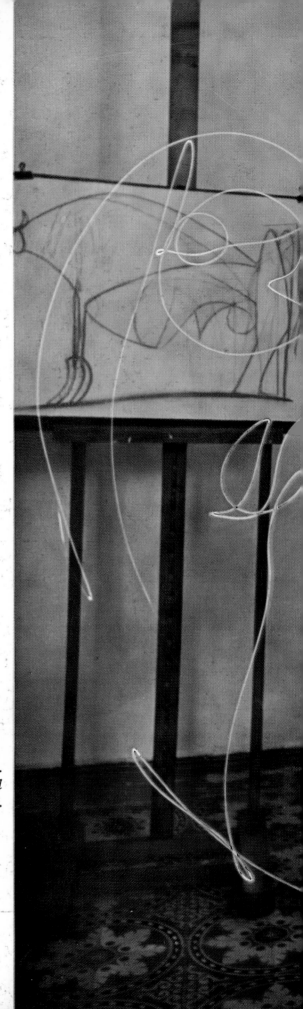

GJON MILI, Picasso Drawing With Light. 1951.
From The Art and Technique of Color Photography, *edited
by Alexander Liberman. Courtesy Condé Nast Publications, Inc.*

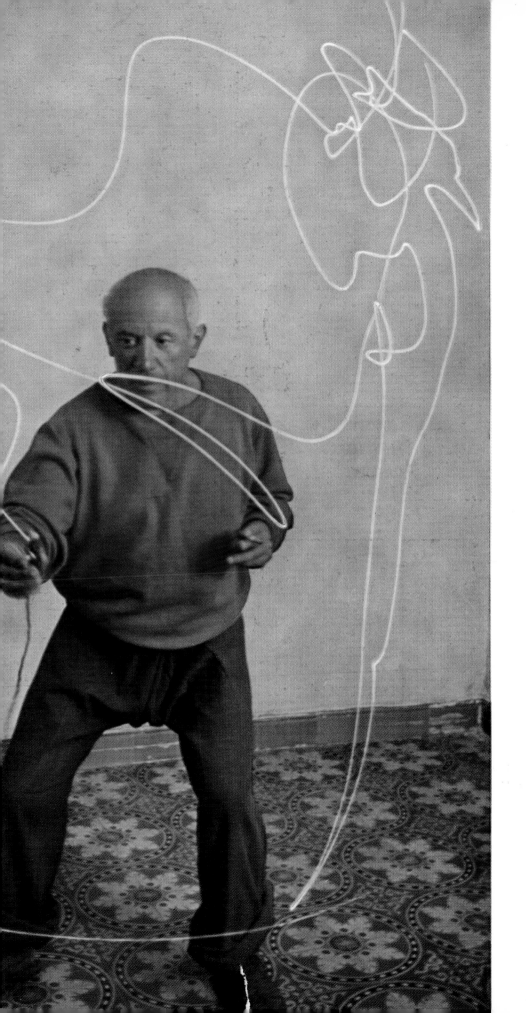

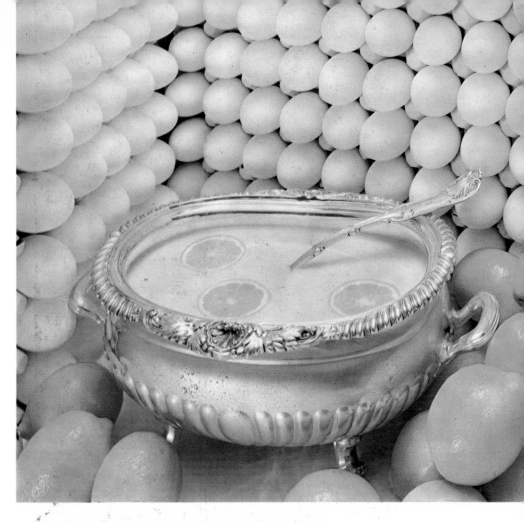

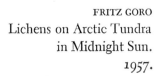

FRED LYON
Lemons and Eggs,
Soup Tureen.
1965.

FRITZ GORO
Lichens on Arctic Tundra
in Midnight Sun.
1957.

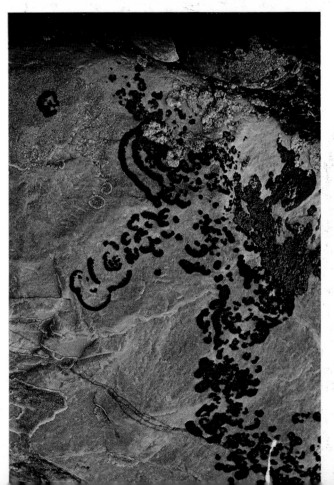

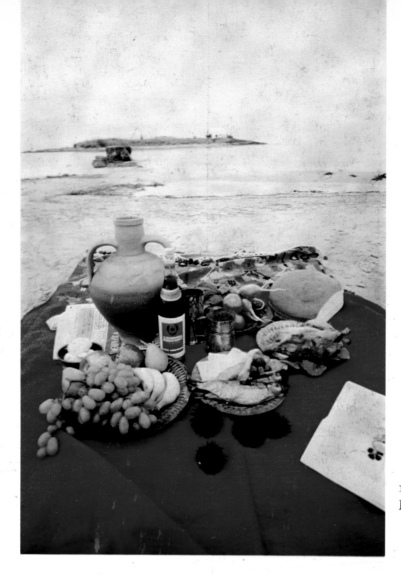

MICHAEL A. VACCARO
Picnic on Crete. *1965*.

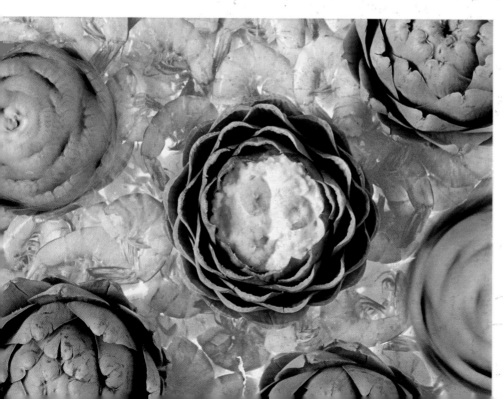

FRED LYON
Artichokes and Shrimps.
1966.

425

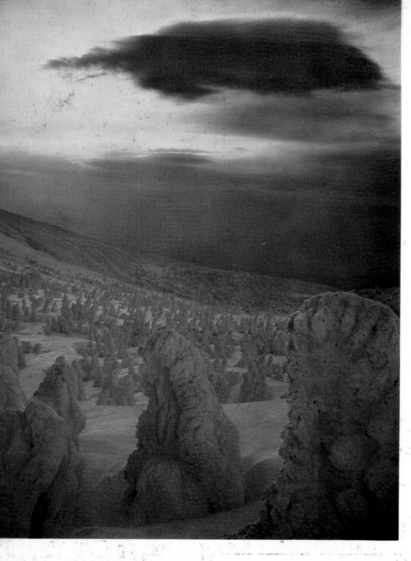

HIROSHI HAMAYA
left: Rime on Pine Forest. Mt. Zao, Japan. *1962.*
DAN BUDNICK
below: Forest of Versailles. *1960.*

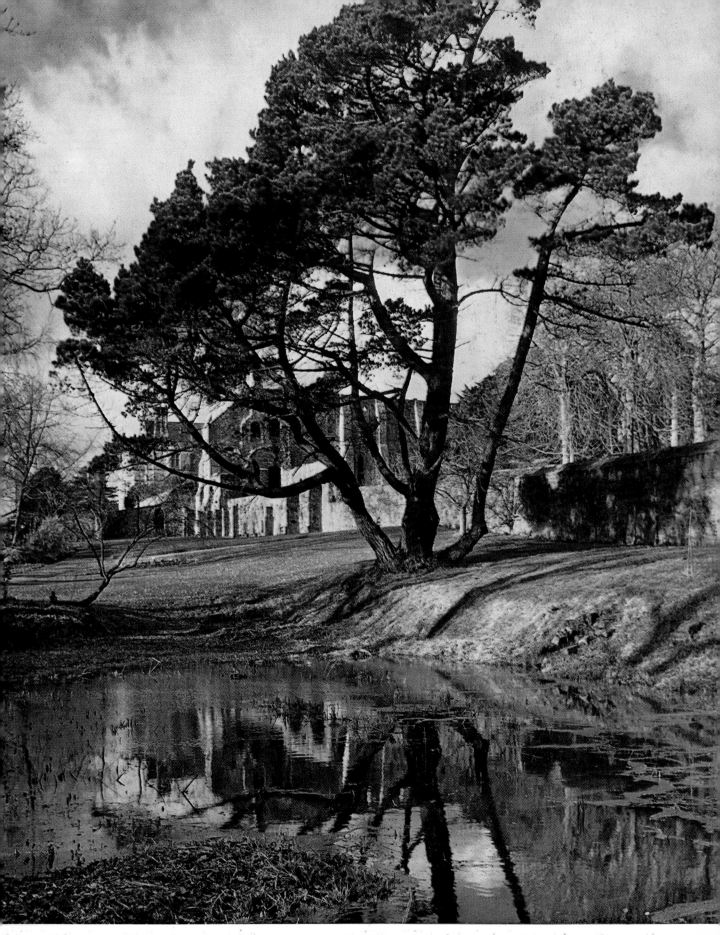

above: DMITRI KESSEL, Battle of Hastings Landscape. *1956.*
Courtesy Life Magazine, copyright Time, Inc.

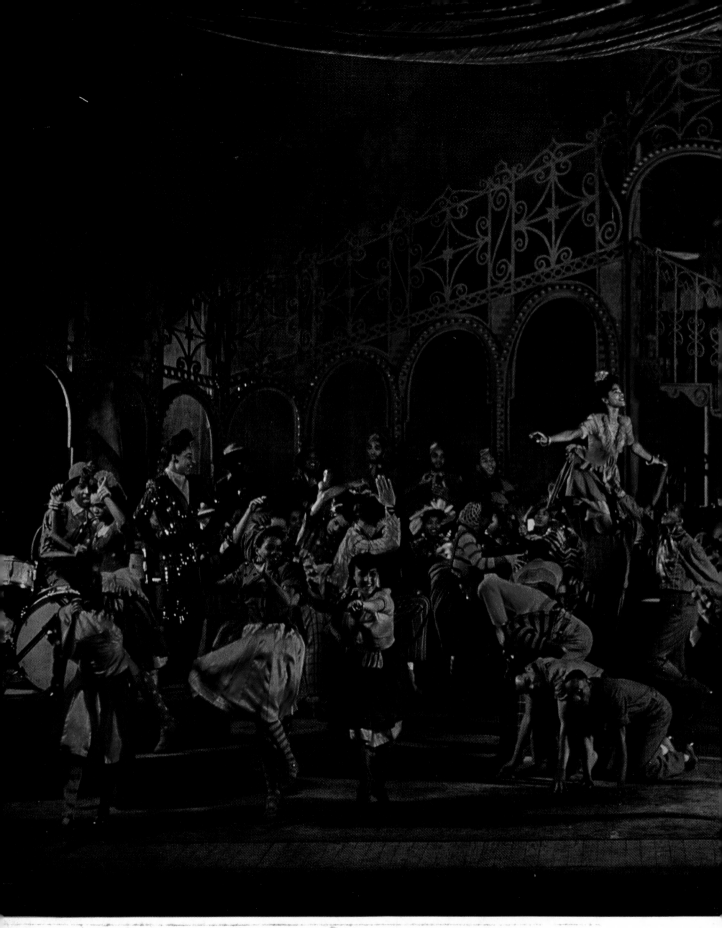

MILI, Carmen Jones, 1951. *From* The Art and Technique of Color Photography, *edited by Alexander Liberman. Courtesy Condé Nast Publications, Inc.*

below: ERWIN BLUMENFELD, Third Avenue El. 1951. *From*
The Art and Technique of Color Photography, *edited by Alexander*
Liberman. Courtesy Condé Nast Publications, Inc.

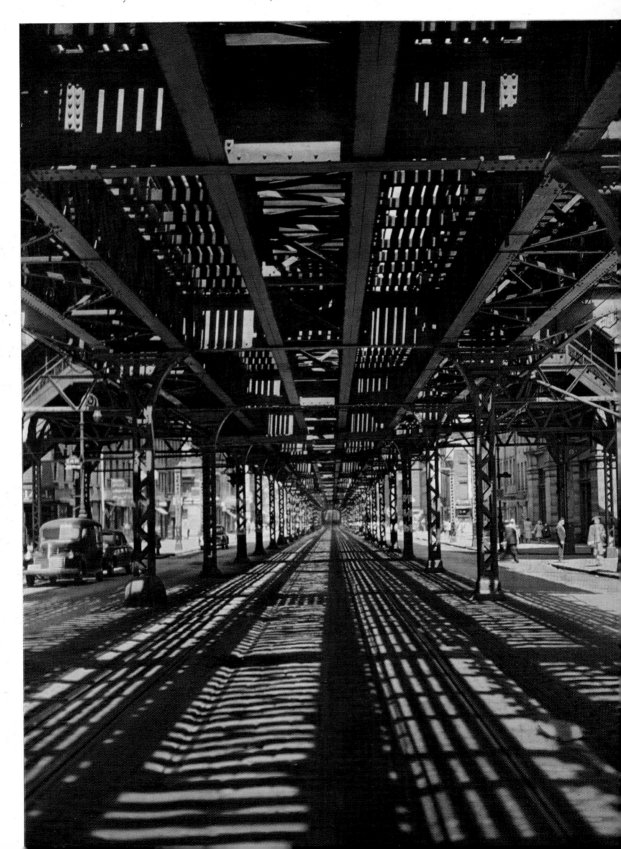

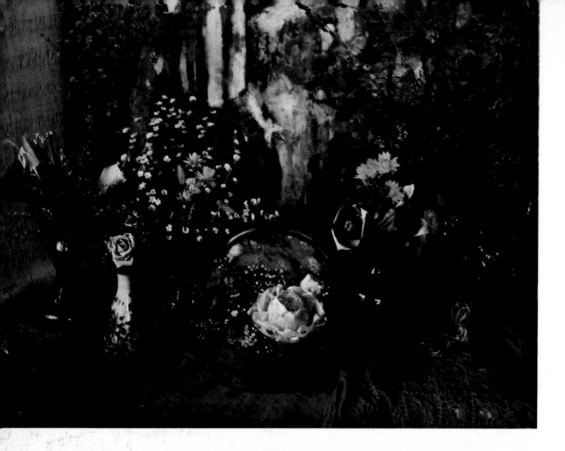

MARIE COSINDAS *is a gifted professional photographer who secures a highly personal expression using the amateur's favorite camera, Polaroid, and the 10-second color film. Avoiding the highly contrasting colors of Koda-chrome, she achieves a unique image through this medium of Polacolor: subtle tones in a low key reminiscent of a daguerreotype tinted by some master miniaturist.*

above:
Still Life. 1967.
below:
Still Life with Asparagus. 1967.
facing page:
Girl with Flowers. Vivian. 1966.

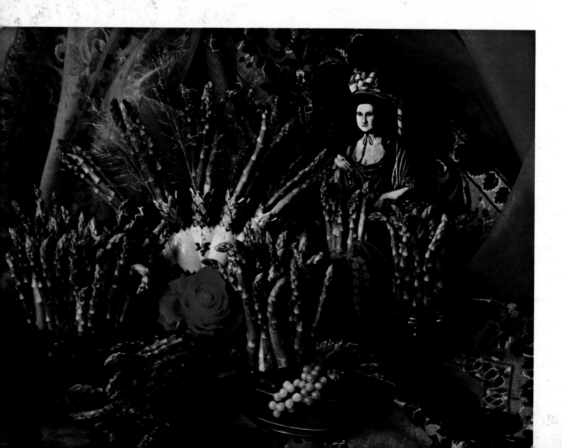

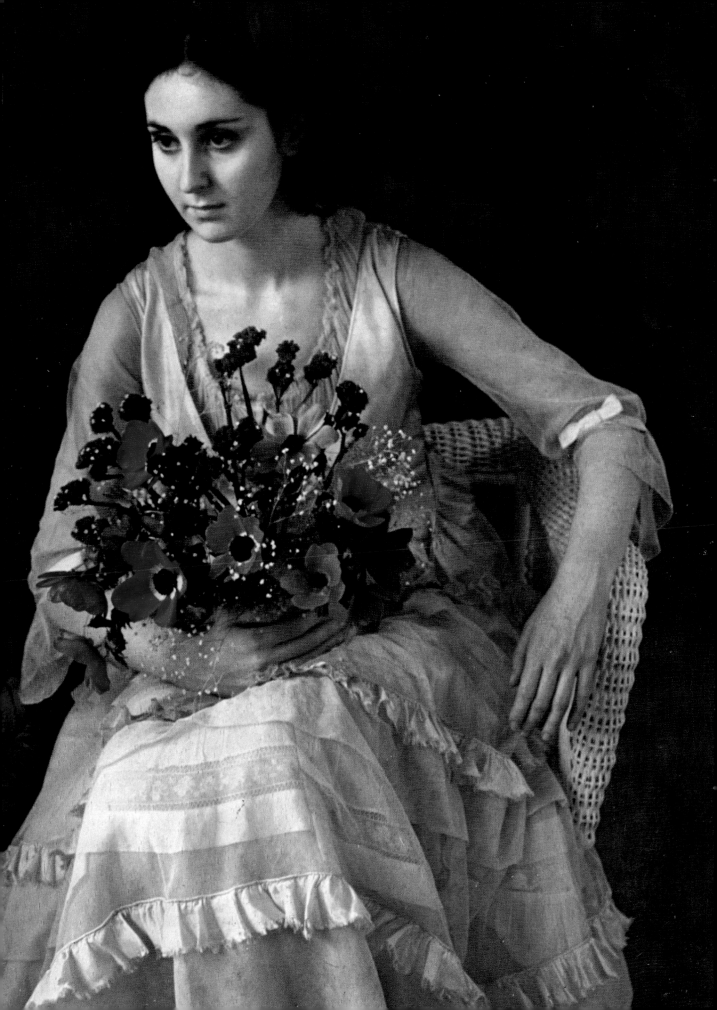

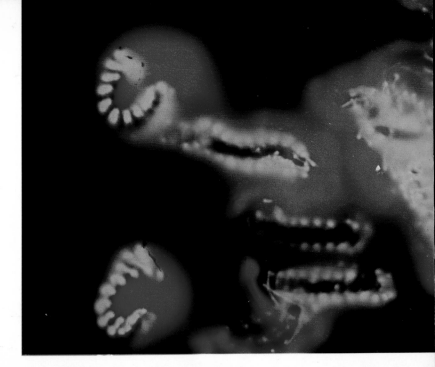

GORO

right: South American Railroad Worm,
flashing its red and yellow-green lights,
takes its own picture
in the darkroom. A "living" photogram. 1947.
below: Splitting of Uranium Atom.
Experiment of Professor Fermi.
Model as conceived and photographed
required 42 exposures
and four different lenses. 1950.

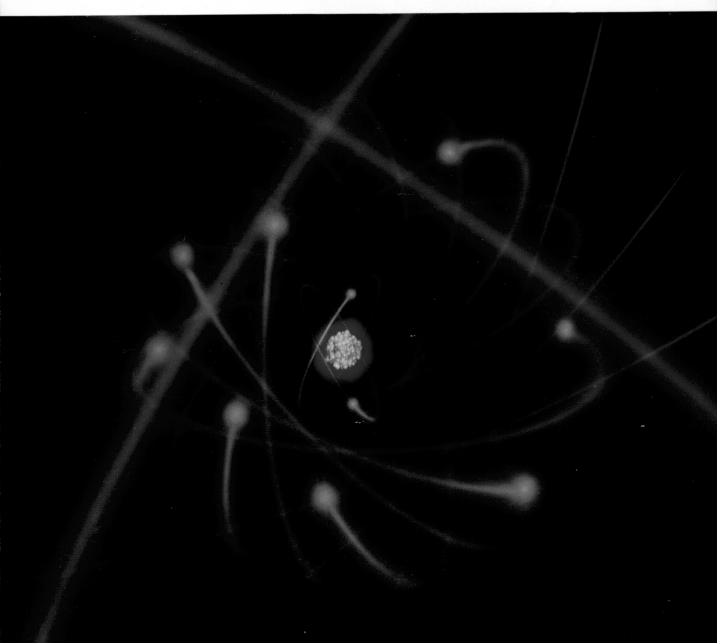

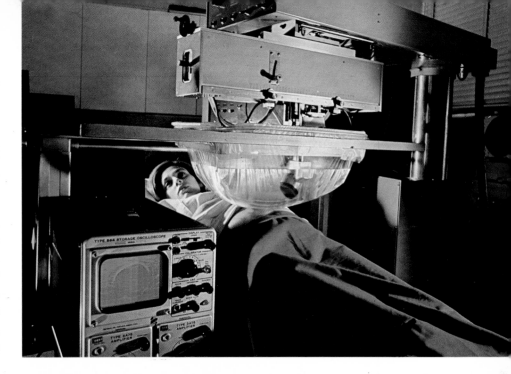

GORO

right: Control of Life.
*Supersonic device discloses position
and proportion of foetus
and size of its skull
in relation to womb.* 1958.

below: Hologram.
*The newest chapter in photography.
Three-D images in space
_ude possible by the invention of* LASER
*(Light Amplification Stimulated by
the Emission of Radiation)
photographed by the
ingenious Goro in* 1965.
(see page 440)

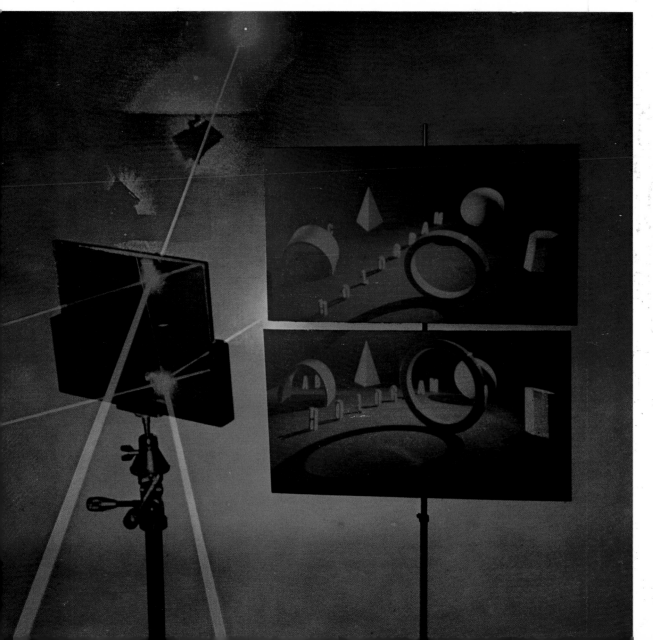

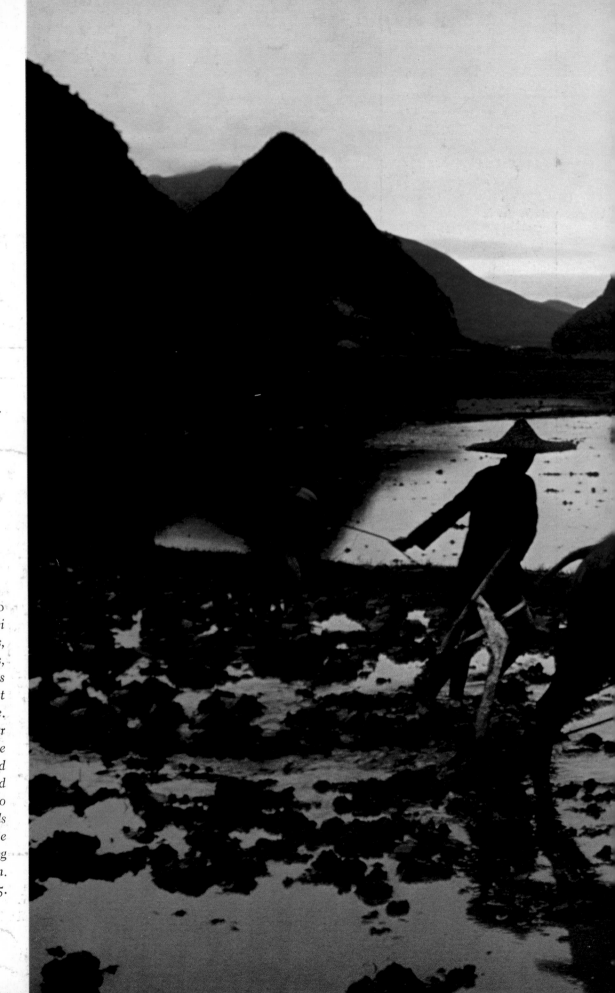

MARC RIBOUD
In Kwangsi
the buffalos,
the rice fields,
and the farmers
now are part
of the commune.
Twice a year
they make the
rain-soaked
land yield
a harvest to
fill the bowls
of the
ever-burgeoning
population.
1965.

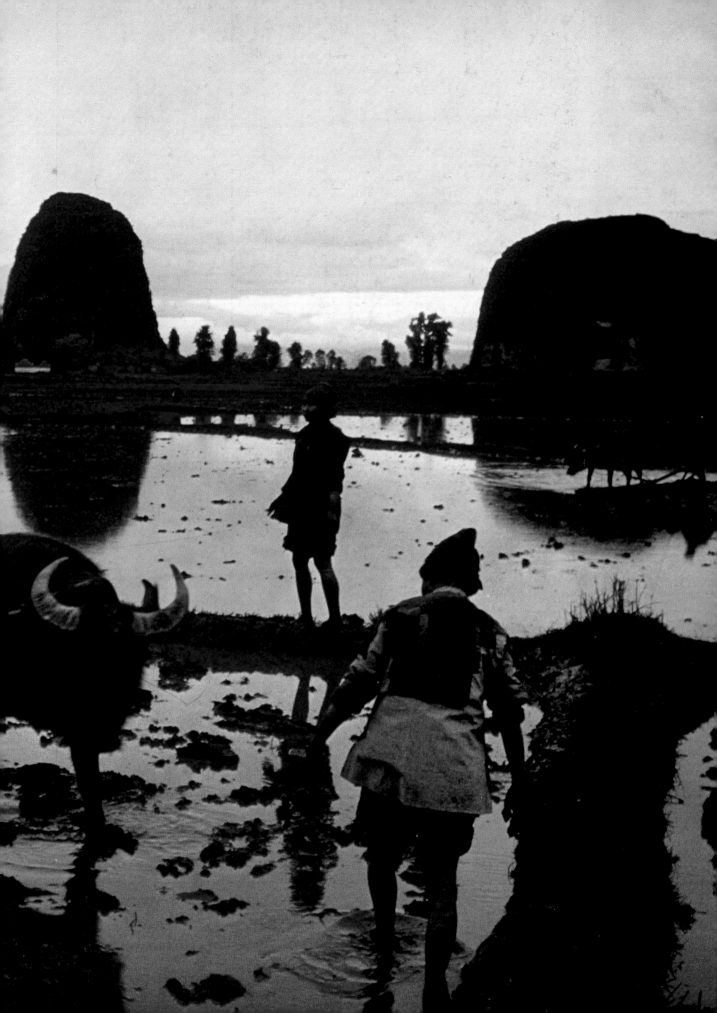

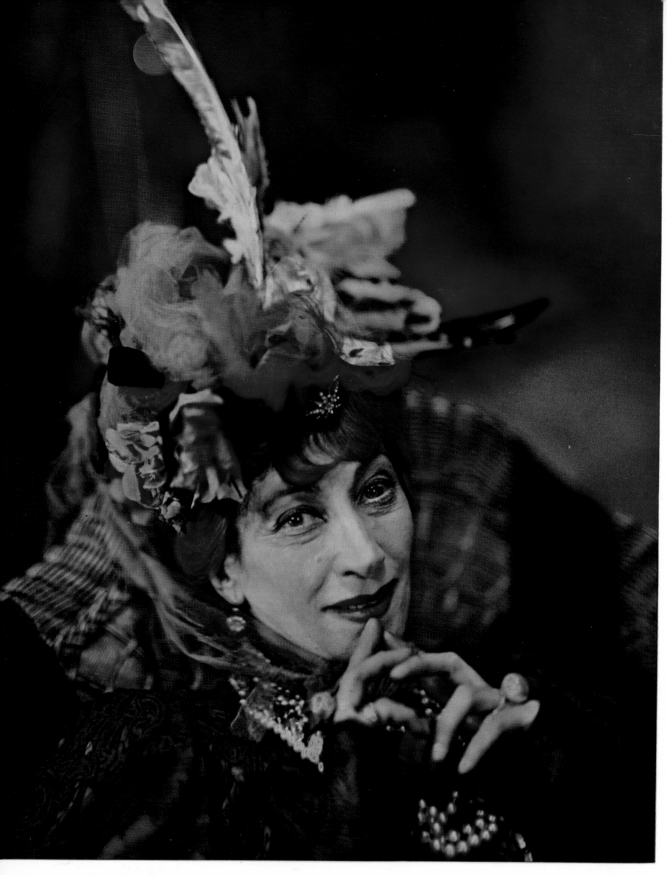

CECIL BEATON, Martita Hunt as the Madwoman of Chaillot. *1951.*
From The Art and Technique of Color Photography, *edited by*
Alexander Liberman. Courtesy Condé Nast Publications, Inc.

PART FIVE
Extending the Range of Human Vision

CHAPTER 35

Photography for Science

PHOTOGRAPHY HAS NOT ONLY GIVEN US powerful new forms of art but has found many applications in science, industry, and commerce. There it has revolutionized communications, deepened and broadened scientific research, and created new institutions of society. This process began early, for photography for practical use is as old as photography itself. Blueprints reproducing the drawings of engineers and architects were used by builders and manufacturers more than a century ago. At the same time, astronomers attached cameras to celestial telescopes in order to photograph the heavens.

Today, the extent of the photographic enterprise exceeds the wildest predictions of photographic pioneers. Processes of photomechanical reproduction of pictures sometimes rival the original photographs themselves in clarity, detail, and range of tone. Often, whole publications—text, pictures, everything—are printed by photographic means; and the printing types employed are set photographically on film rather than mechanically in metal. We photograph sounds, the paths of nuclear particles, the pattern in space traced out by dancers' feet. With wide-angle "bug-eye" lenses—their taking angle is fully 180°—we can sweep our surroundings from horizon to horizon. Using aerial cameras we make maps photographically of cities and countryside, maps so accurate in detail and contour that oil companies buy them by the hundreds for use in laying gas and oil pipelines for distances of thousands of miles. We attach cameras not only to telescopes but to rockets soaring into interplanetary space and to bathyscapes plunging into the deepest

enches of the ocean floor. We have photographed the
ar side of the moon. The combination of camera, com-
uter, and telecontrol is writing a new chapter on the
mapping of the universe, on level after level.

So advanced is the photographer's arsenal in our time
hat a magazine photographer slings around his neck a
quantity of equipment—in terms of performance—that
he great Brady, in the Civil War, could never have car-
ed in a whole train of wagons. Today's photographer
may have on his person three or four cameras equipped
with color or regular film. To one may be attached a
attery-operated stroboscope light that provides brilliant
llumination for intervals as small as a millionth of a
econd. The cameras themselves have lenses of great
ower—normal, wide-angle, and telescopic. A range-
nder coupled to the lens brings the subject into sharp
ocus within a second or two. A light meter built into the
amera frame can, automatically, provide the proper
perture for the selected shutter speed. The flick of a
nger can move an exposed frame onward and bring the
ext unexposed frame into taking position—or, if this
rocedure is too slow to match the speed of the action
eing photographed, a spring motor can do the job auto-
natically at the rate of thirty-six frames in a few seconds.
uch equipment, it may be noted, is neither rare nor
ostly. Factory-made and popularly priced, it is sold every
ay in twelve thousand shops in the United States alone.

Equipment of this kind is used by many thousands of
hotographers—amateur and professional—engaged in
bserving the world and in enabling others to observe it,
oo. This has been going on for quite some time—as
eaders of this book know, since 1839. Perhaps the great-
st contribution of photography has been its transforma-
ion of human beings. Photography has given all of us
ew power to see.

When the first photographs were made, men were ac-
ustomed only to the forms of our common perception
een straight ahead from a spot four to six feet above the
round. From time to time, of course, they saw the world
rom other angles and other distances above or below
round level. However, the images received by the eye
re fluid and temporary; the eye tends to pivot and com-
ensate for unusual angles of vision; and unfamiliar im-
ressions are wiped away when men return to normal
ositions of standing, sitting, walking, and riding.

As one might expect, the camera was at first used to
roduce familiar images, and was aimed straight ahead at
he height of a man's eye. But it was easy—too easy,
mateur photographers still discover every day—to use
he camera at other angles and from other heights; and

the images recorded were not wiped away. They were put
down in enduring form; the observer could return to
them again and again. When he looked at the pictures
made in this manner, he found that something strange
had happened: the scale and aspect of the world had
changed. The camera could see not only as men see, but
in other ways as well. And even though "swings" of lens
board and camera back were introduced into some cameras so that they could compensate as the eye does for
strange angles, the intellectual and creative possibility of
seeing the world differently, via the camera, remained.

The world, for example, could be seen as a child sees
it. Each of us, at one time, viewed things from a point
close to the ground; the world was seen tall, with grown-
ups looming like giants. We have all forgotten this experience, for the images in our heads can be reclaimed
only by our memories—notoriously unreliable and fading
rapidly from the time impressions are first made. But put
a camera down low and, from the picture that results, we
can recapture the child's-eye view, not for an instant only
but for as long as we look at the picture and as often.

In such simple ways as this it was discovered early that
cameras and photosensitive emulsions could be used to
extend human vision, both in photography the art and in
photography the scientific aid. The tool, in its potentialities, was leaving its mark upon the art. With refinement
of photographic equipment there developed unprecedented power to explore our visual surroundings.

Camera and photosensitive emulsion can now see
what the eye cannot: invisible radiation—X rays, cosmic
rays, ultraviolet rays, infra-red rays—revealing objects
cloaked in total darkness, bones beneath the skin, the
structure of the universe; things too fast for the unaided
eye—a horse winning by a nose, a bullet speeding
through the shock wave of a sound barrier, a golf ball
compressed by the head of a striking club; things too slow
—flowers and cities growing; things too big—the earth's
curvature; things too small—atoms, bacteria, metallic
crystals; things too far away—spiral nebulae and the outer
stars; things that would blind us if we looked at them—
the sun's corona and the fireball of the nuclear bomb.
Cameras can go where men would surely die—out into
space, to the bottom of sea deeps as far below the surface
as the Himalayas are above. Thus, over the past century,
photography has extended human vision and, in combination with scientific instruments, revealed thousands
upon thousands of unexpected aspects of nature on
level after level; beauty and strangeness never before
imagined.

The newest chapter in photographic description is the

wave-front reconstruction process, or *holography*. This process, discovered in England in 1947 by Dennis Gabor, underwent major advances at the hands of Emmet Leith and Juris Uptanieks at the University of Michigan following the invention of the laser (*Light Amplification Stimulated by the Emission of Radiation*) in 1960. The laser is a source of "coherent" light, i.e., light whose waves are all in phase. When an object is illuminated in coherent light and a mirror beams a portion of that light to a photographic plate, a seemingly unintelligible "interference" pattern encodes infinitely more information than any other photographic means can provide. The original waves of light can be "reconstructed" from the interference pattern, passed through a lens, and brought to a focus, thereby forming an image of the original object—a convincingly real-looking three-dimensional virtual image composed of nothing but light. One set of wave-interference patterns can be used to produce virtual images quite different in perspective. In principle, holography can be combined with cinematography or television to produce the 3D movies of the future. And, perhaps before this decade has passed, an entire exhibition of monumental sculpture can be sent through the mails in the form of an ordinary envelope. Through a variation of standard holography, a book the size of this one has been successfully stored, page by page, inside a 2-inch by 2-inch by ¼-inch potassium-bromide crystal. Theoretically, it is possible to store the contents of a major library in a hundred such crystals and retrieve any of its information with the zip of a laser beam.

In the summer of 1967 John Szarkowski of the Museum of Modern Art, with David B. Eisendrath as consultant and with the Santa Barbara Museum of Art and the University Art Museum of the University of California, Berkeley, as participating institutions, staged the important *Once Invisible* exhibition of images made accessible to our visual understanding only through photographic intercession. In focusing upon this new and marvelous source of imagery, this magnificent exhibition followed the lead of Gyorgy Kepes, who not only called attention to this material in exhibitions of his own, but, in 1956, published a wide spectrum of it in a coherent and thoughtful pioneering book: *The New Landscape In Art And Science*.

The wonders of nature now made visible are as fascinating to the observer as those that can be seen by the unaided eye. If we are interested in the world, these pictures interest us. Even a book about the art of photography would not be complete without some of

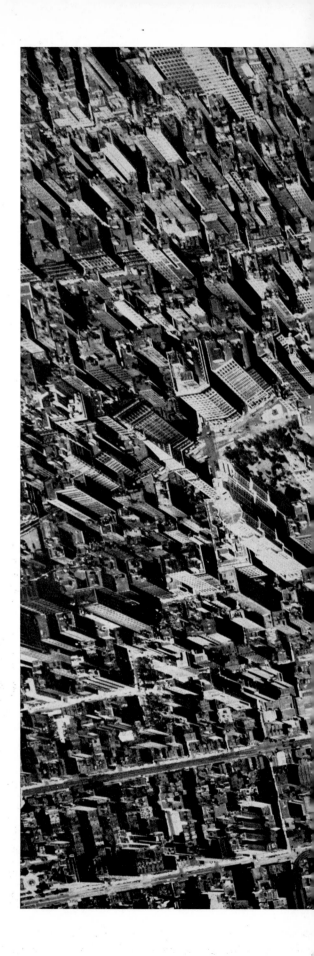

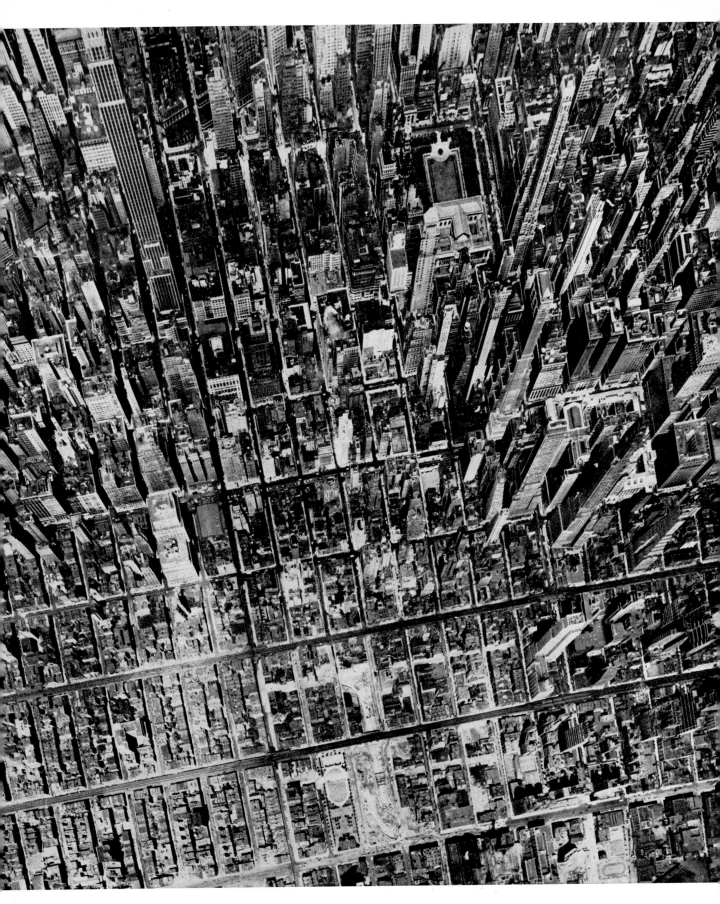

Special nine-lens aerial photograph of Manhattan, by U.S. Coast and Geodetic Survey. Courtesy Gyorgy Kepes, Cambridge, Mass.

these pictures, for the photographic artist has studied them and has extended his vision and technique through his study.

The art of still photography has been enriched by interaction with cinematic art and with applications of photography. The movie, which grew out of still photography, has in turn shown the still photographers how to master the craft of narrative, to make action sequences dramatic in their variety of motion and shifts of scene and scale. The familiar miniature camera employed for this purpose and others has been adapted from the movie camera. It has the movie camera's key structural and mechanical features: a big, fast, short-focal-length lens for great depth of focus and the ability to take pictures in dim light; 35-millimeter fine-grain roll film advanced one frame at a time by a sprocket drive—this allows dozens of pictures to be taken in rapid succession without a change of film; and a high-speed shutter that can stop almost any action. Such a camera is so small, so portable, and so versatile that it frees the photographer to go almost anywhere and take almost anything.

The telescopic lens—sometimes twenty times as long as the picture that it takes is high—provides the photographer with the opportunity to show stirring visions seen from afar. In the distance, in the back of long views seen by the human eye, there has always been a geometric realm an "infinite" distance away. There are forms and shapes, but neither perspective nor depth in space. As seen by the eye, however, the forms of this realm are vague and few, little more than hazy silhouettes. Photographers have brought this realm close and shown us fully detailed overlapping patches of windows, doors, and buildings, all apparently at the same distance from us. This is a view of the world contributed by photography confirming that of the Cubist painters. However, it also belongs to the photographer himself—by natural right if by nothing else. In documenting Cubist realities, and in providing us with images of high fantasy and bold patterning—which painters consult for Surrealism and abstraction—the photographer has enlarged our experience and made both his own art and the art of the painter more moving. He has demonstrated once again that our imaginative vision is rooted in physical and optical reality.

This vision of reality may sustain the oriented photographer-artist but not the highly trained photographer-scientist whose researches disclose images which though often beautiful, are of little or no aesthetic interest to him. These photographs are most often produced with extremely complicated mechanical gear or with completely automatic cameras taking pictures without help from scientist or photographer. Nonetheless, these functional, complex images of the invisible, non-human in origin though they may be, are the images that artists, photographers, and other sensitive persons of our day respond to, and it can be safely predicted that these new forms and visions of science will be utilized and interpreted by the artists and photographers of the future.

right: Spiral nebula, taken with 200-inch Hale telescope. Courtesy Mount Wilson and Palomar Observatories. opposite page: Clouds of gas and dust, 4,000 light years away. Photographed with 200 inch lens in red light. Courtesy Mount Wilson and Palomar Observatories.

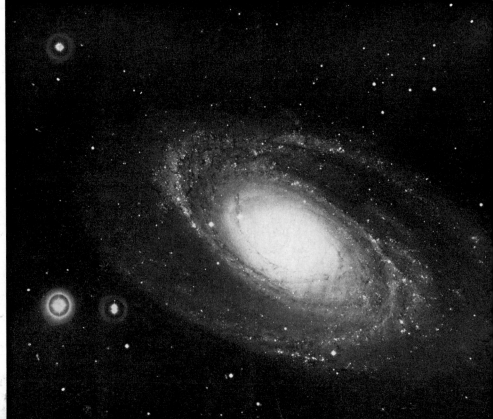

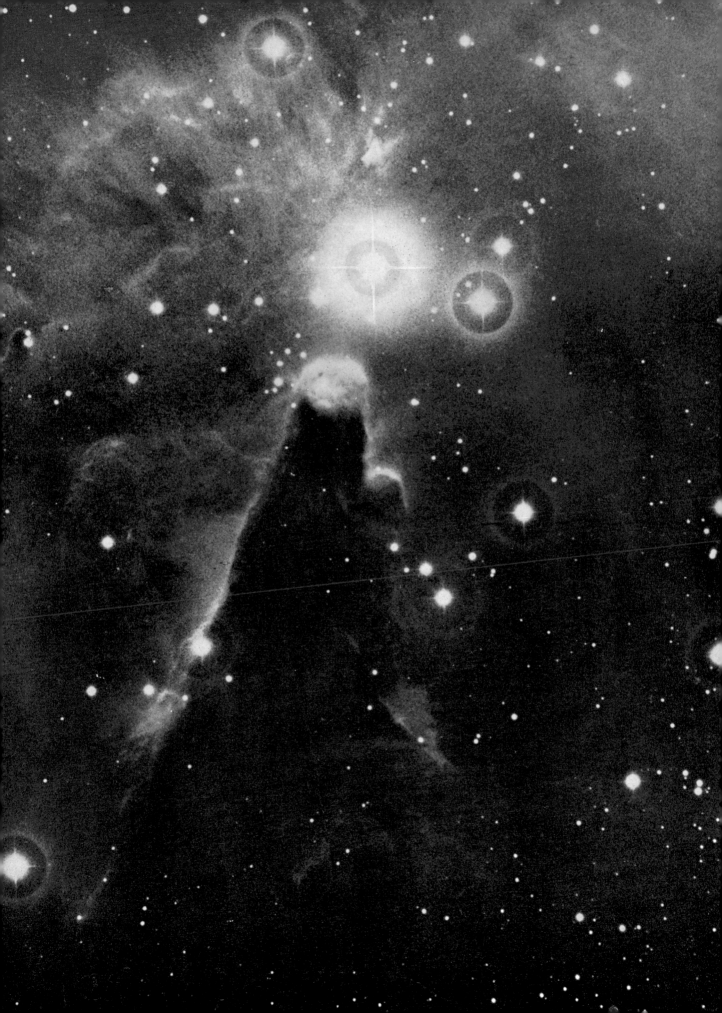

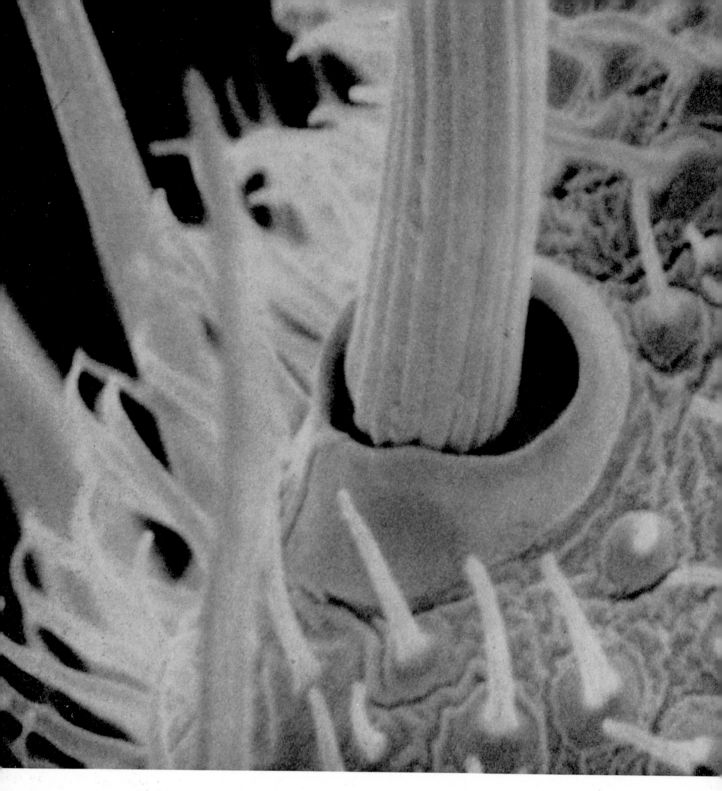

Electron micrograph scan of hair on a fly's tongue.
Original magnification 2500 X.
Courtesy Westinghouse Electric Corporation.

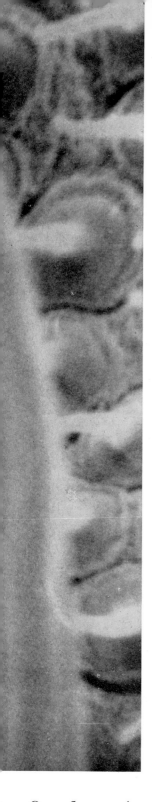

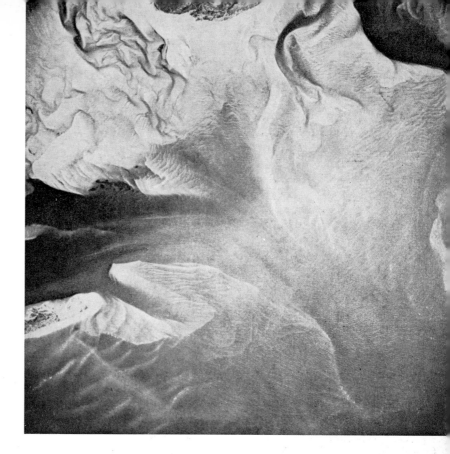

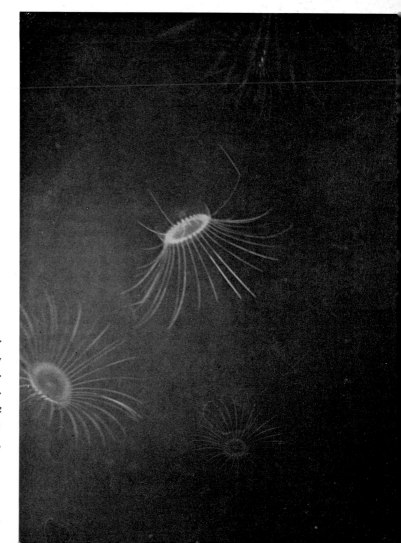

above: Ocean floor seen from three miles above water. 1948.
by Aero Service Corporation. From The New Landscape,
by Gyorgy Kepes, Paul Theobald and Co., Chicago.
Courtesy Gyorgy Kepes, Cambridge, Mass.
below: Under-sea photograph taken with the
bentograph at 970 fathoms. 1951. Courtesy Allen Hancock
Foundation for Scientific Research.

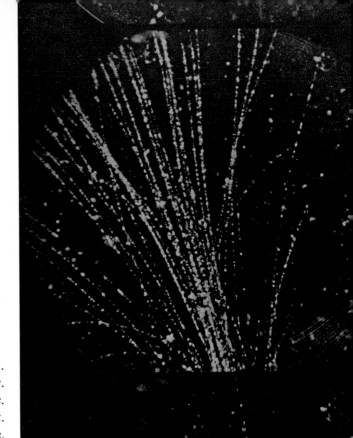

right: G. E. VALLEY, *Cloud-chamber photograph.
Taken at the Massachusetts Institute of Technology.
From* The New Landscape. *Courtesy Gyorgy Kepes.
below:* H. P. ROTH, *Uranium in polarized light.
Courtesy H. P. Roth, Nuclear Metals, Inc., Cambridge, Mass.*

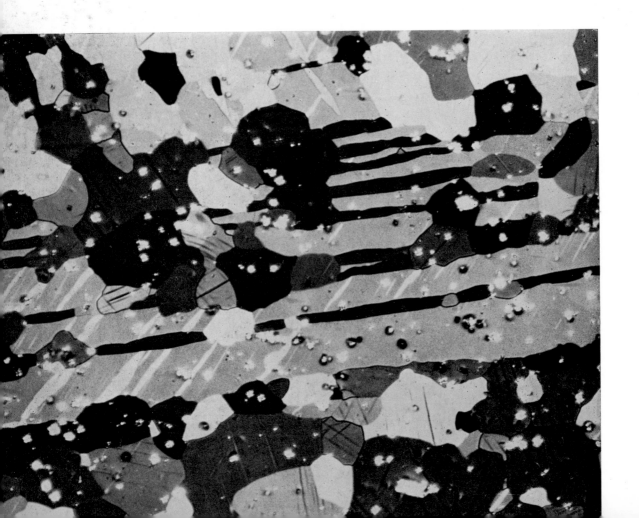

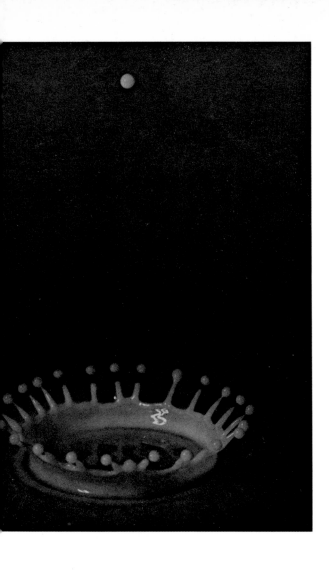

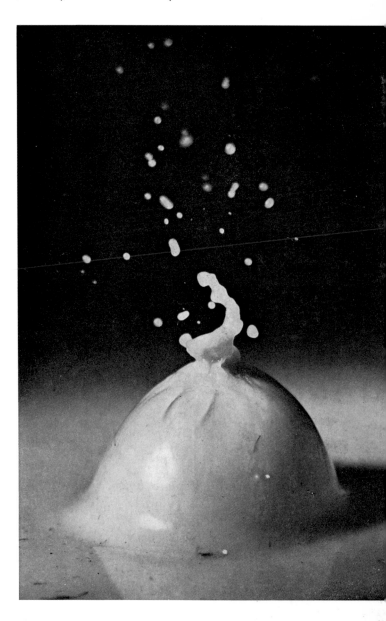

left: HAROLD EDGERTON. *High-speed
photograph of falling milk drop.
Courtesy Harold Edgerton,
Massachusetts Institute of Technology.
below: Waterdrop. High-speed photograph.
Courtesy United States Navy.*

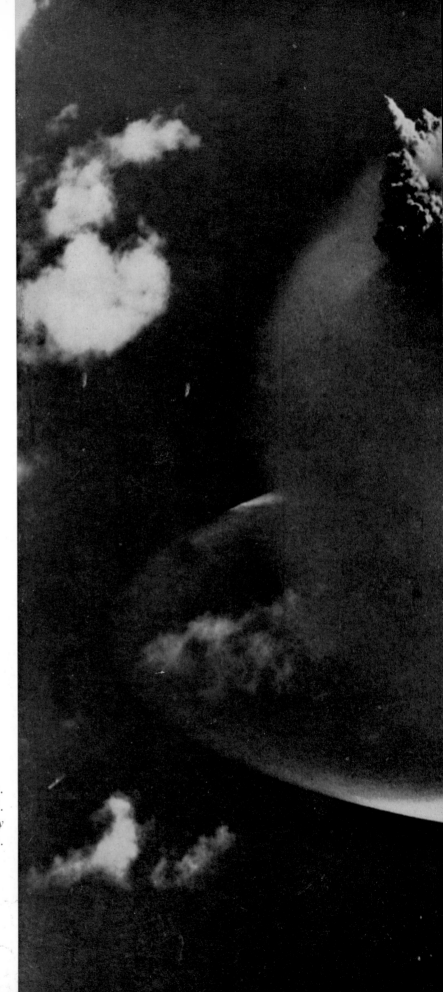

Underwater Atomic Explosion.
Bikini, "Baker Day," 1946.
Photographer unknown. Courtesy
Atomic Energy Commission.

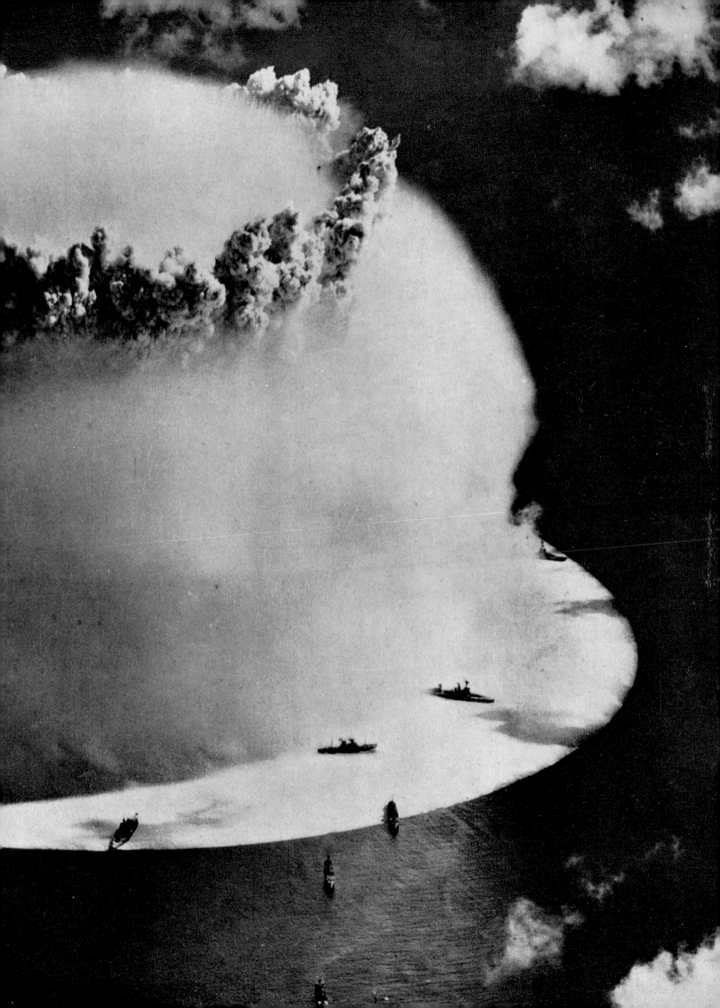

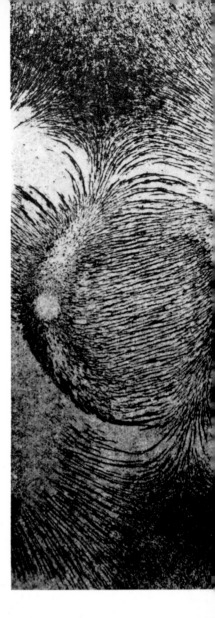

below: F. VILBIG. *Modulation disk.* From The New Landscape. *Courtesy Dr. F. Vilbig, Cambridge Research Center.*
right: FRANCIS BITTER. *Magnetic field. Courtesy Professor Francis Bitter, Massachusetts Institute of Technology.*
opposite page: *Radiograph of a snake.* From The New Landscape. *Courtesy Eastman Kodak Company, Rochester.*

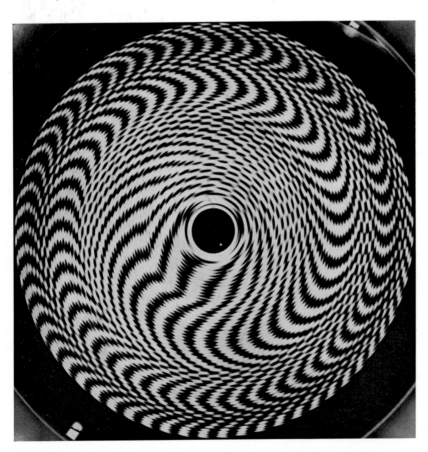

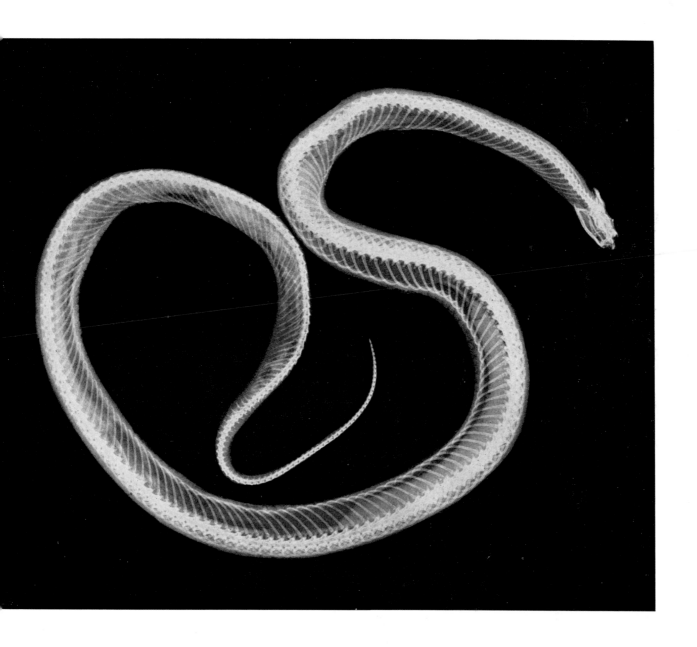

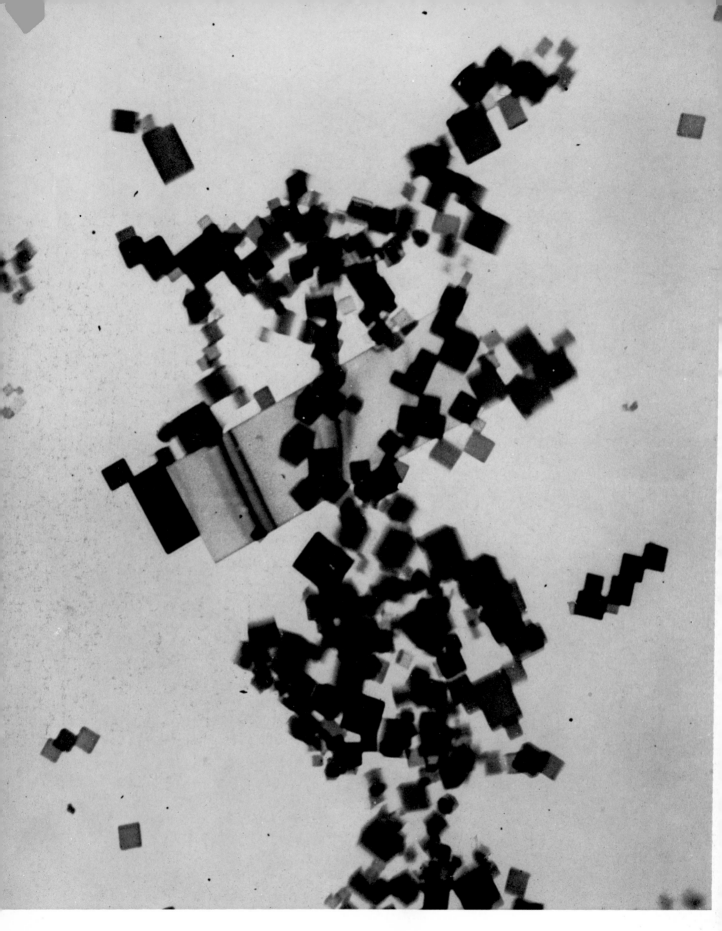

A. WATANABE, *Magnesium oxide magnified 65,000 times. Photo taken in electron microscope laboratory of Keio University, Tokyo. From* The New Landscape. *Courtesy Gyorgy Kepes.*

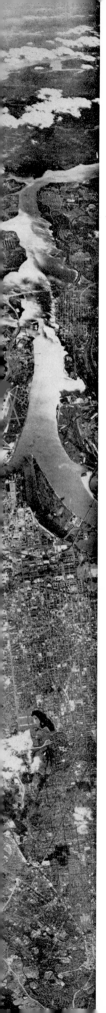

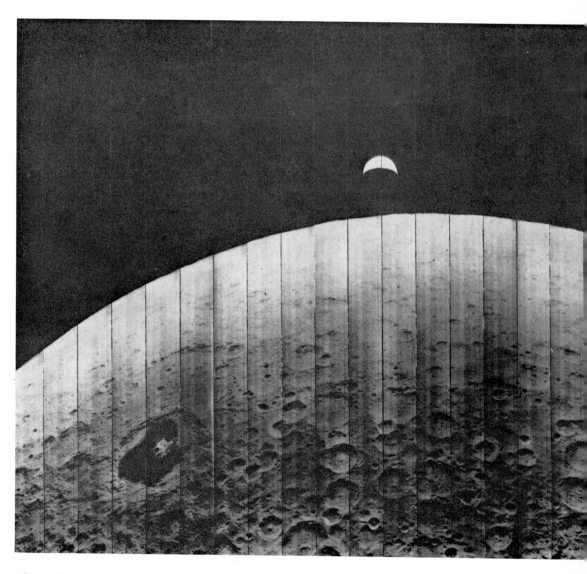

above: Earthrise from the Moon.
*Photograph transmitted to Earth August 23, 1966
from Lunar Orbiter I. Courtesy NASA.*
left: 120-degree aerial panoramic view
of Washington, D.C. from a plane
flying at high altitude. 1964.
Courtesy Perkin-Elmer Corporation.

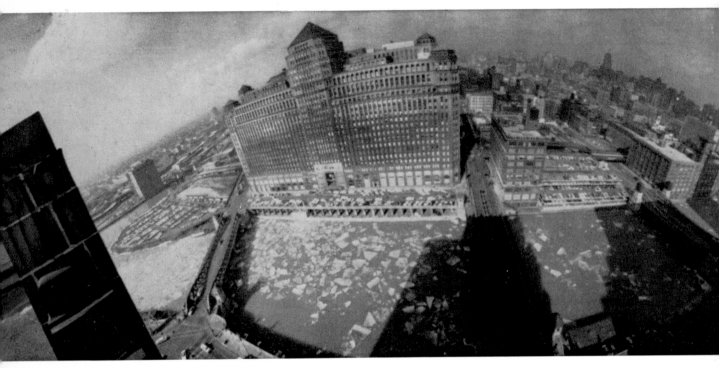

360-degree panoramic photograph of the Chicago skyline.
Courtesy Zoomar Inc.

180-degree aerial panoramic view of Verrazano Narrows Bridg
from plane flying at low altitude, 196
Side-oblique shot made on 70mm film by scanning sweep, which included strut
right and part of tail assembly at lef
Courtesy Perkin-Elmer Corporatior

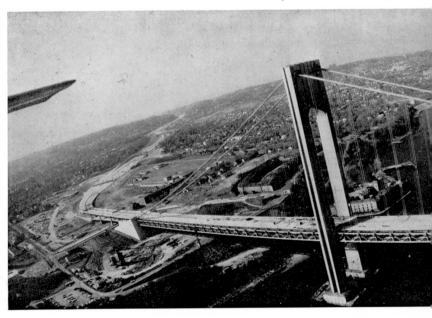

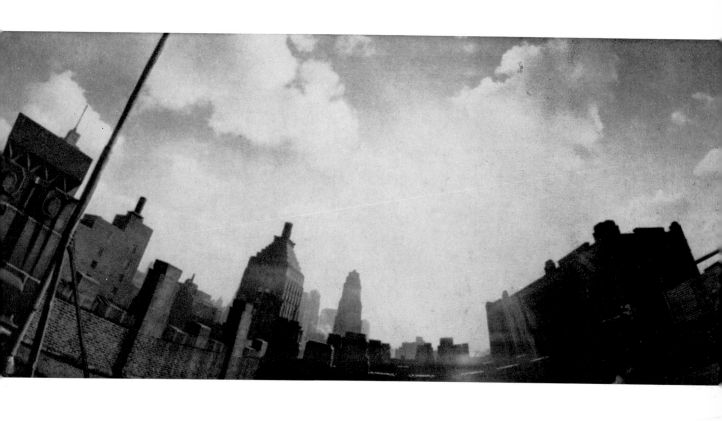

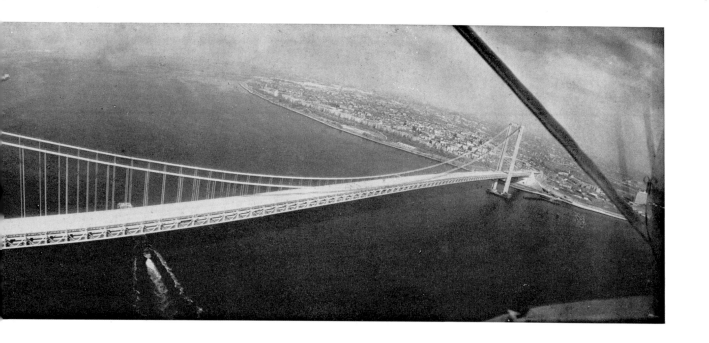

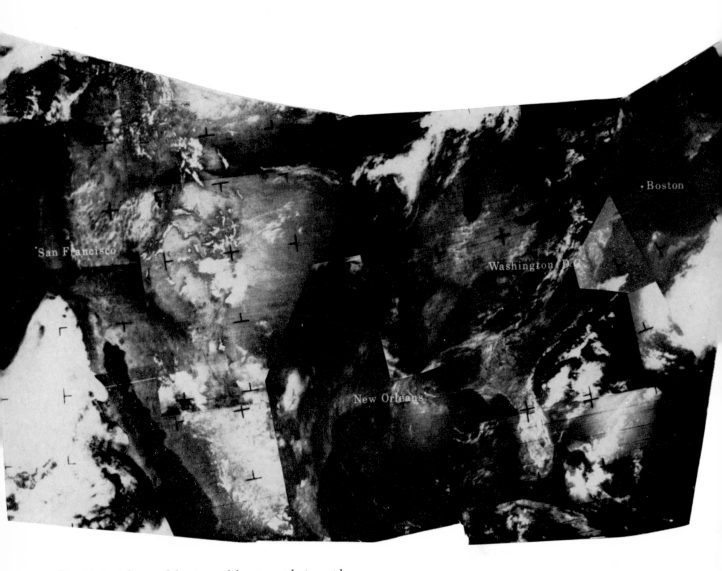

The United States. *Montage of fourteen photographs
from 700 miles above the earth.
Tape-recorded images transmitted from Nimbus II, summer 1966.
Courtesy NASA Goddard Space Flight Center.*

PART SIX

Photography Today

CHAPTER 36
Postwar Trends

SEVENTY-FIVE YEARS after Nicéphore Niepce first secured a permanent image on a sensitized metal plate, photography entered its grand classic era. A proved and tested tool of communication by 1900, by 1950 it had become an art of great range, sophistication, and power.

In 1900 the forms of photography, as created by its chief practitioners, were still tied to those of painting just as the form of the horseless carriage still echoed the form of its horse-drawn predecessor. Twenty-five years later, however, photography was autonomous and free. It had its own stylistic forms and its own expressive means. It had schools and traditions. An important museum had had a large photo exhibition. A decade later still, photography was an art of scholars and of many museums. The young and adventurous Museum of Modern Art in New York had a department of photography, with Beaumont Newhall as its first director. In 1936 photography acquired in *Life* magazine a vehicle that reached into every home and brought well-nigh universal understanding of the photographic medium. *Life* was rapidly joined by sister publications the world over and picture magazines became the key sources of public information about the world's tastes and flavors, land and peoples, habits, customs, tribulations, and triumphs.

During World War II a new generation of photographers came to the fore. The impressive body of shared photographic knowledge developed with pain and effort y their great predecessors was their birthright, which they absorbed and mastered almost as a matter of course. The technology that they found at hand a quarter-century ago has been expanding ever since at a truly astonishing rate, and technical obstacles to the realization of their creative vision have been disappearing with corresponding speed. The horizons of creative photography today seem almost limitless.

What is true of the vanguard of talented photographers is true of the photographic enterprise as a whole. Photography is the closest thing to a universal art that the world has seen. Not only are cameras sold in every gift shop and variety store, but every drugstore and newsstand sells film—half of it color film—and acts as an agency for photoprocessing. These outlets serve unassuming folk artists who number in the tens of millions and whose path to picture taking has been eased by automatic photocell-controlled diaphragms and shutters. If they use the Land Polaroid cameras and film invented in 1947, they have the satisfaction of seeing a finished print within a few seconds after making the exposure. More advanced amateurs, of course, are fewer in number, but support an industry of fantastic dimensions. In the United States of America there are twelve times as many camera shops as bookstores; and each shop is a treasury of costly but fast-selling technical marvels. Photo clubs exist everywhere, ignoring national boundaries to carry on a lively exchange of ideas and work; their members avidly study magazines and books of their opposite numbers, quite indifferent to linguistic barriers.

Professional photographers have also greatly increased in number in the last quarter-century, chiefly as a result of the broadening market in editorial and advertising photography. Photographers now receive assignments that formerly went to illustrators. The fastest-growing sector of book publishing today is the picture book that makes extensive use of good-quality photographic reproductions. And specialized magazines in scores of fields are increasingly dependent on the services of professional photographers, for never before have so many people been so eye-minded.

It cannot be said that the expansion of the market for photographs has brought unfailing prosperity to the photographers who serve it. Staff photographers of newspapers and press associations work at the same modest pay as reporters. In the 1950s freelance photographers, who shoot perhaps 150 days a year and whose studio expenses are high, were being paid as little as $30 a day on assignments from some of the largest and most moneyed users of photography. Accordingly, they banded together in the American Society of Magazine Photographers, setting a minimum rate of $100. This minimum came to be accepted in the course of time, but it tended to become a maximum as well. (The minimum day rate was raised to $150 in 1967.) The special talents of outstanding photographers, however, can command very high pay, indeed. The leading staff photographers of one or two pictures magazines do about as well as the vice-presidents of many large corporations. The international stars, however, prefer not to be staff members of any magazine. Through their own co-operative picture agencies—notably Magnum—and such privately owned firms as Rapho-Guillumette and Black Star, they supply photos to picture magazines all over the world. Through retaining rights to secondary or repeated use of their work, they manage to receive a return from their efforts that bears a realistic relation to the demand for it.

The co-operative picture agencies have not been called into being entirely because of economic motives. With the marvelous expansion of photographic culture, the editorial-photography enterprise has become part of big business at its biggest. It is institutionalized and impersonal as well as huge. Budgets, cut-and-dried editorial procedures, and accounting practices have multiplied the forces that make it difficult for the creative individual to fulfill his aims and carry his work to a satisfactory completion. The picture agencies are, above all, a means by which talented and sensitive men serve their own creative needs and keep the sources of their creative imagination intact despite the wear and tear of constant contention with a vast, impersonal communications machine.

The emergent body of photography to be seen in magazines, portfolios, exhibits, and photobooks is closely linked with the work of the first half of the century in aims, purposes, style, and subject matter, although clearly informed with a new spirit. A sixth major area of exploration—color, which is considered separately in Part IV of this volume—has been added to the five marked out by the earlier photographers of this century: "straight," abstract, symbolic, photojournalistic, and fashion and product photography. In all of these areas, a changed and changing conception of artistic truth has encouraged a vision perceptibly different from that of the 1920s and 1930s.

The photographers of the earlier twentieth century were bewitched by technique, that is, by the study of how to handle their cameras and process their films and papers in order to learn the marvels that could be accomplished by these means. The human hand is an extraordinary tool—supple, flexible, highly responsive to messages from the brain. Put a pencil or a brush in it, and it is the same hand with an extra, specialized finger. Put an instrument like a camera in it, and the ability of the brain to envisage, record, control, modify, and transform seen reality has been extended to realms beyond our ability to imagine. Our present senior statesmen of photography set themselves the task—which they discharged with great distinction—of showing what photography could do. An important means of achieving this goal—it could hardly have been achieved without it—was stark honesty in using materials and equipment. Photographic truth, inventive and imaginative as these men were, was the correspondence of the photographic image to the facts of nature. Photographic truth was fineness of grain, normality of perspective, and fullness of tonal range from black through many grays to pure white. There were men so insistent upon absolute control in composing a picture that they felt that their integrity was blemished if they made a print from anything but an uncropped full negative.

Restrictions and prescriptive rules were no longer seen as particularly useful by the photographers who came to prominence during or after World War II. On the contrary, they tried to see how far they could go in every possible direction. Or, rather, each photographer tried to see how far he could go in his own chosen direction, for photographers had become more specialized than those of the previous generation—an inevitable result of the bigger realm now occupied by photography. No discussion of photography today would be complete if note were not taken of galloping specialization. Andreas Feininger (q.v.), whose cameras and typewriter cover the whole height, depth, and breadth of modern photography, from the method of grasping a camera body to the highest levels of human experience, would have been rare in any age; today he is unique.

The "mistakes" of yesterday—graininess, contrast, distortions — are today explored as interesting values in themselves, with great potential for evocative and expressive power. Yesterday's "correct" ways of seeing and doing are being further explored—this is no more than natural—so that photographic vision is acquiring new depth as well as new breadth.

To a certain extent, the broadening of acceptable technical standards reflects a growing interest, characteristic of our day in history, in interior life—the world inside our heads as opposed to the world around us. The psychological dimension is of great importance in photography today.

PHOTOJOURNALISM

THE PHOTO ESSAY, which began with Nadar and took its present shape from Margaret Bourke-White, is now a mainstay of the news and picture magazines. Typically the photo essay is a carefully patterned sequence of pictures and captions. Sometimes the captions are merely explanatory; sometimes they carry on the thread of communication where the pictures leave off. The photographer may be a writer as well as a taker of pictures; even then he is not the sole creator of the photo essay. A picture editor selects the pictures and sizes them. This procedure is now absolutely standard; and the photographer who insists upon controlling his work from start to finish is looked upon as something of an eccentric. A great photographer, W. Eugene Smith (q.v.), has been unable to accommodate himself to the system. Although he has almost no peer as a photojournalist, and although photo editors are eager for his work, agreement between him and the magazines is not often possible. As a result his outstanding reputation is based on a comparatively small body of work.

The photo essay is a journalistic art form of great inherent power. It brings the world to us through our own senses, as it were. We see it with our own eyes and form images in our heads of sounds and smells, tastes and textures. Words alone, no matter how compelling, by comparison seem no more than secondary reports. André Malraux has called our vast and easily accessible body of magazines and book-reproduced works of art "a museum without walls." By the same token, the photo essay is a guided tour through a part of the world. In the last decade or two, the photo essay has been joined by the photo book, which expands the photo essay to add depth and breadth to impact.

The roster of distinguished photojournalists is now extensive, indeed. It is not surprising, in our unquiet times, that photographers of war and battle should rank extremely high upon that list. Combat photographers—Chim, Capa, David Duncan (all q.v.)—are a special breed and a special fellowship. They may be—they usually are—the gentlest of men, haters of violence, lovers of peace. Even more, however, they are dedicated men fascinated by the thing they hate and forced from within to follow it. Even more than other photographers, they are wanderers over the face of the earth, good comrades but not family men. Their home is the army camp and the battlefield. They submit to death and wounds with a bravery greater than that of any soldier because their discipline comes from inside. Eighty-two photographers

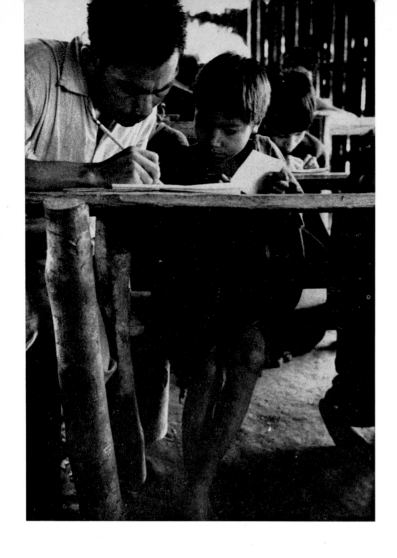

CORNELL CAPA, Teacher of Campa Indians
in Peruvian Jungle Village. 1957.
President John F. Kennedy. 1962.
*All Cornell Capa photographs
courtesy Magnum Photos.*

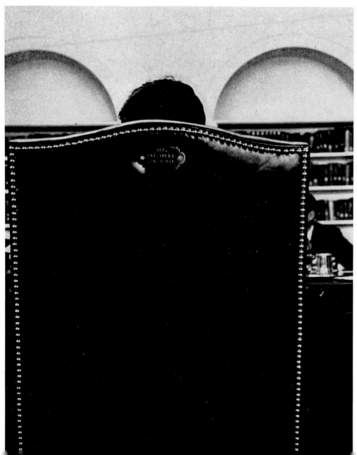

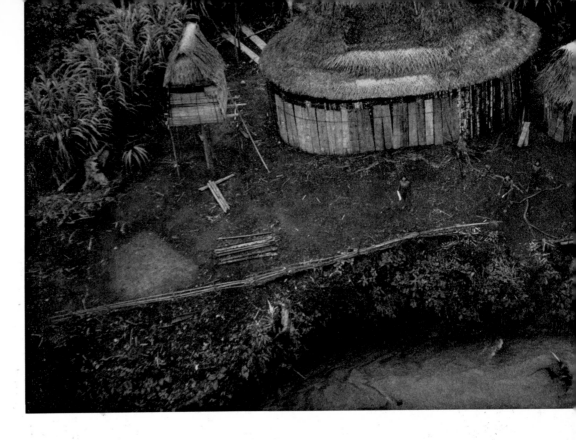

and reporters have suffered death or severe wounds in the Vietnamese War as of April 1967. In the Israeli-Arab War in June 1967, the first casualty was Paul Schutzer, staff photographer of *Life* magazine.

Other frontiers of the modern world have their equally dedicated recorders. Cornell Capa, Robert's younger brother, is one of the good ones. In his own words, he is "not a maker of images which are to be enjoyed by the viewer for their purely aesthetic value. I hope that as often as possible my pictures may have feeling, composition and sometimes beauty—but my preoccupation is with the story and not with attaining a fine-art level in the individual pictures. If I work well, my pictures mean something when connected in story form." Beyond question, however, his work attains a fine-art level in such images as his unique view of the late President Kennedy. Here we are shown the high office as well as the man, the seat of power surmounted by an identifiable bit of that well-remembered shock of hair. The hardly more detailed teacher of Torah acquires equal expressive force in Cornell's evocation of the strangely disquieting psychological climate of an all but obliterated East European world transplanted to the Williamsburg section of Brooklyn and still flickering on.

Different small worlds are evoked by Ken Heyman, whose picture stories of human relationships can be profoundly intimate, tender, and emotional, and by the Englishman Roger Mayne, who has photographed an astonishing record of yesterday's Teddy boys and their girls, giving us not a sociological exposé of delinquency but an honest, sympathetic presentation of these children of London's streets. Mayne is a comparatively detached observer who does not attempt to penetrate too deeply into humanity's interior world. But Ed Van der Elsken, Bruce Davidson, and Gordon Parks (all q.v.) evoke the anguish of spirit of groping teenagers, ghetto dwellers, and society's losers, touching the public conscience in images of uncompromising truth. In the social comment of Robert Frank we are confronted with the vision of an activist and partisan in the cause of this group, or, at least, its American branch. He flings their predicament in our faces with bitterness, anger, and carefully shaped irony.

On the contrary, in Paris the Lithuanian-born Izis tells us about people through photos that are lyrical images, zestful and humane. The Swiss-born Sabine Weiss turns her sharp eye on the innocent grace of children and cats, and on celebrities and characters. Marc and Evelyn Bernheim have chosen the new states of Africa as their field for a photojournalism that is both incisive and tender. These pictures show sensitivity toward the people and the problems of their traditional societies.

Psychological description has been carried on in

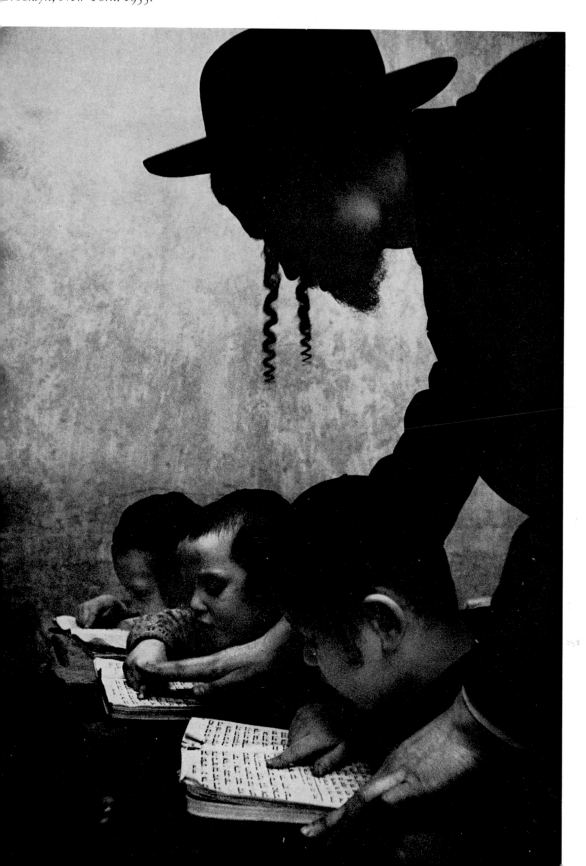

463

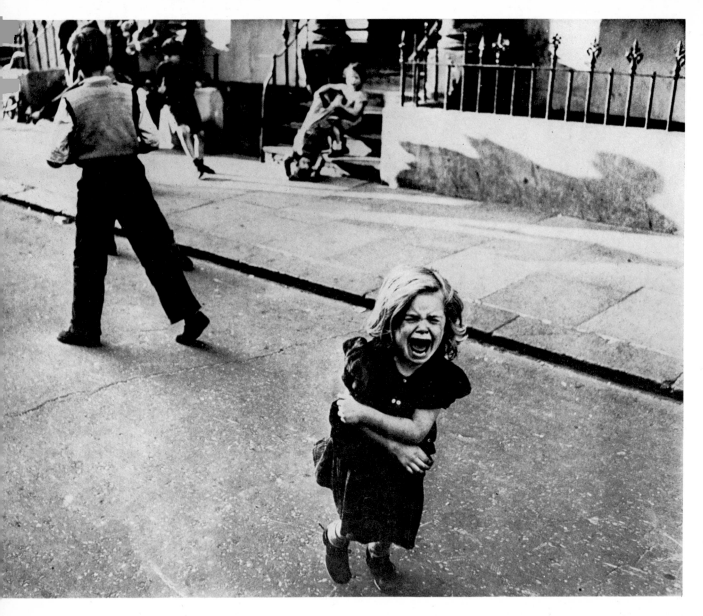

ROGER MAYNE, *above*: Tears. 1956.
right: Tension. 1956.

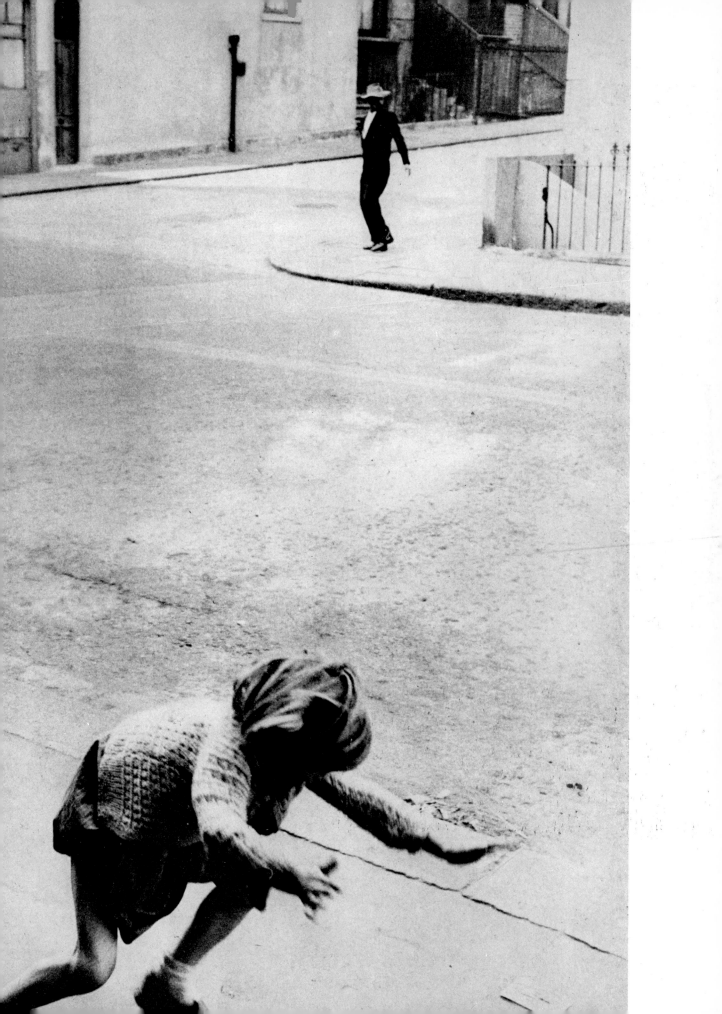

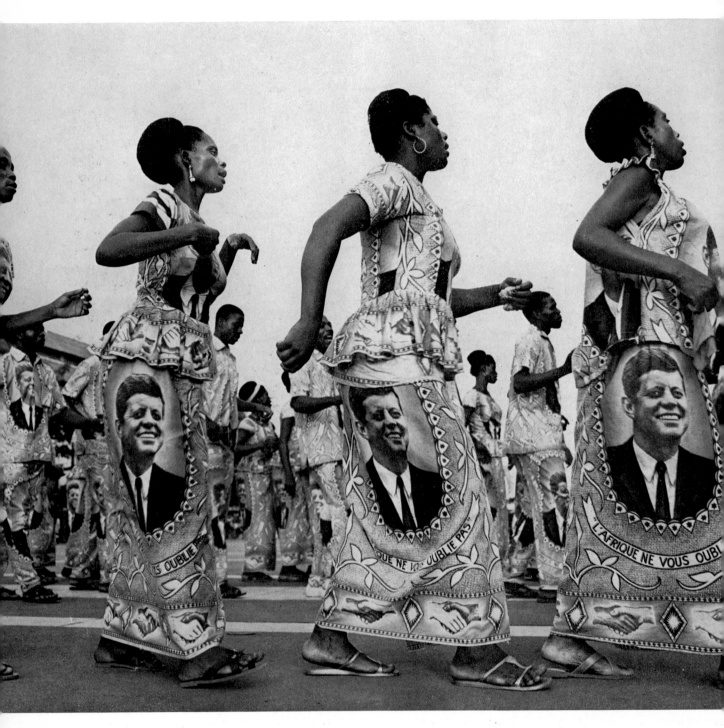

MARC AND EVELYN BERNHEIM, *Kennedy Cloth*
Ivory Coast, 1964. Courtesy Rapho-Guillumette Pictures
Paris and New York

fferent way by Yale Joel, a *Life* staffman whose 1966 cture story on psychedelic art revealed the strange perptual world of artists turned on by LSD. But, in any se, exploration of the interior world is mainly for the w. Presenting the vast, shifting panorama of world ents has absorbed the major portion of photojour-listic energies. Cartier-Bresson (q.v.) in his world avels, brings back picture stories more limited in sweep it with a well-nigh incredible freshness and immediacy. he Swiss photographer Werner Bischoff, who was lled as his jeep fell off the mountain while he was photo-aphing Machu Picchu, was matched by few men in chnical mastery. After an early career devoted to me-culously built pictures of shells and other still lifes, e took memorable news pictures of events in Central urope and Asia. His *Shinto Priests in Snow* attests to is acute responsiveness to the visual image.

Cartier-Bresson's protege Marc Riboud has so ex-nded the bounds of yesterday's photojournalism as to ititle him to be called a photohistorian. Like his men-or, he has photographed the new China, most recently 1965. His *Three Banners of China* was one of the eat publishing events of the year. Its fifty pages of color hotographs, 150 more of black-and-white, and 5,000 ords of text are the clearest, truest, and most telling icture that anyone has given us of the new China in l of its poverty, regimentation, strength, pride, and age-d beauty.

The largest pool of talented recorders of big world ories, unsurprisingly, may be found among the staffmen f *Life* magazine, a brilliant photographic-communica-on enterprise that has done more to advance the fron-ers of photography than almost any number of brilliant dividual photographers. *Life*, as its editors once put it, as founded for the purpose of harnessing "the optical onsciousness of our time." Created for readers, not for hotographers, it has set out to take its readers' eyes every-here imaginable by its imaginative editors and photog-phers. *Life* stories are not hit-or-miss: they are planned d executed like military operations. Much sophisti-ited photographic equipment and many photographic chniques have been developed specifically for the pur-ose of getting *Life* stories. Fishermen, for example, will ing remember Ralph Morse's astonishing night photos surf casting for bass off Martha's Vineyard—photos which the only precedent was set by *Life*'s oldest and ow retired photographer, Wallace Kirkland, who con-ived equipment to take in color a picture of the precise stant when a trout rises to take a fly. Morse used a full n of gear and spent days rigging lights and generators

on the beach and in boats offshore. Morse's body of expert work includes what is by far our most extensive photohistory of space exploration, and next to him in space photography come J. R. Eyerman and Fritz Goro. Goro is the incredibly inventive, science-oriented sculptor-turned-photographer who photographed the splitting of the uranium atom in 1938, and, in 1956, conceived a method of photographing a gas-laser hologram (see page 433). He and Roman Vishniac have given new dimensions to photography for science and technology, especially in color photographs of nature's marvels. Gjon Mili, an exceptionally versatile photographer, has pioneered in exploring the aesthetic possibilities of strobe photography. Dmitri Kessel has developed new lighting and filtering techniques that have made accurate color reproduction possible for old master paintings that previously did not photograph well because of their condition or location. Peter Stackpole, aqualung-equipped and carrying special cameras, swims under water for his spectacular shots; and Howard Sochurek has distinguished himself in photographing military action while parachuting as well as on the ground. *Life* photographers are producing the best pictures of the Vietnamese war through the cameras of Horst Krass and the English-born Larry Burrows, whose coverage includes a memorable color sequence of the fighting from the air. (Coverage of the war in Vietnam is not complete, for much is being left unpictured: prisoners, prison camps, patrols, Vietnamese soldiers, etc.) Other staffers no less talented have been no less active on other photographic frontiers: Ralph Crane, Carl Mydans, George Silk, Eliot Elisofon. Elisofon, a dedicated student of anthropology and an authority on primitive art, is a color photographer of rare sensibility. Memories of Melville's writings and Gauguin's paintings are touched off by his ideally beautiful, dreamlike tropical scenes (see page 411). An entire history of advanced contemporary photography could be put together from the pages of *Life*.

Photography for newspapers and wire services is almost outside the scope of this book, for the aims of news photographers are not basically different from those of other photojournalists. The differences can be seen in unusually concentrated form in the work of "Weegee" who has photographed more accidents, four-alarm fires, and murder scenes than any other photographer in history. "Weegee" is not in the least concerned with the niceties. His pictures are all action in the center and fade out to insignificance at the edges. They are unrivaled, however, for immediacy, vigor, and uncomplicated raw drama.

STRAIGHT PHOTOGRAPHY

"Photojournalism" and "straight photography" are both misnomers. These terms, nevertheless, are in such general use today that it would be more confusing than otherwise to employ substitutes for them. Straight photography, like photojournalism, is an art of the magazines, and not infrequently is extremely complex. The essential difference is that the meaning of photojournalistic work is revealed by picture sequences, whereas the meaning of straight photography is revealed by individual images. This is a boundary that photographers can traverse back and forth without great difficulty; and a number of men are equally distinguished in both branches of the art. Such a man is Elliott Erwitt, a photojournalist of great distinction and currently president of Magnum Photos. Two of his pictures illustrated here reveal extraordinary sensitivity to the individual image and show what delicacy of pattern and subtle drama of tonal contrast can be accomplished by a camera put into the hands of a master. Another such man is Art Kane. A third is Emil Schultheiss, who has given us marvelous panoramas in books on Africa, Antarctica, the Amazon, and most recently China. One of his most imaginative works is a multiple exposure of the midnight sun near the South Pole: every five minutes starting at 11:20 P.M. and finishing at 12:40 A.M. Schultheiss clicked his shutter, so that, in 17 separate positions, from right to left, the sun described more than two-thirds of its circle around the polar sky.

Within a class so inclusive as straight photography—the documentary, the nude, portraiture, abstraction, symbolism, and product and fashion are really separate categories in themselves—there are obviously many specialties, to say nothing of specialties within specialties. Thus, William Garnett's (q.v.) seen world is the upper air. Diane Arbus' pictures of religious nudists, transvestites, and Lesbians constitute a subclass within the subclass of the documentary. They show, moreover, that there is more breadth in the documentary than there was in the 1930s: truth value and shock value have been retained but, unlike Robert Frank today and unlike Dorothea Lange a generation ago, Arbus does not show her subjects as figures of misery. They are merely targets of opportunity upon whom she turned her camera. On the other hand, Janine Niepce (a collateral descendant of Nicéphore Niepce, the father of photography) treats the disenchanted and dispossessed with less curiosity and more sympathy. She sees such persons not as tragic victims but as fellow human beings.

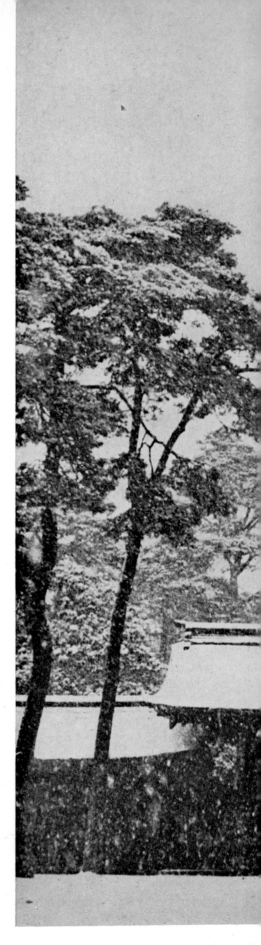

WERNER BISCHOFF, Shinto Priests in Snow. *Ja*

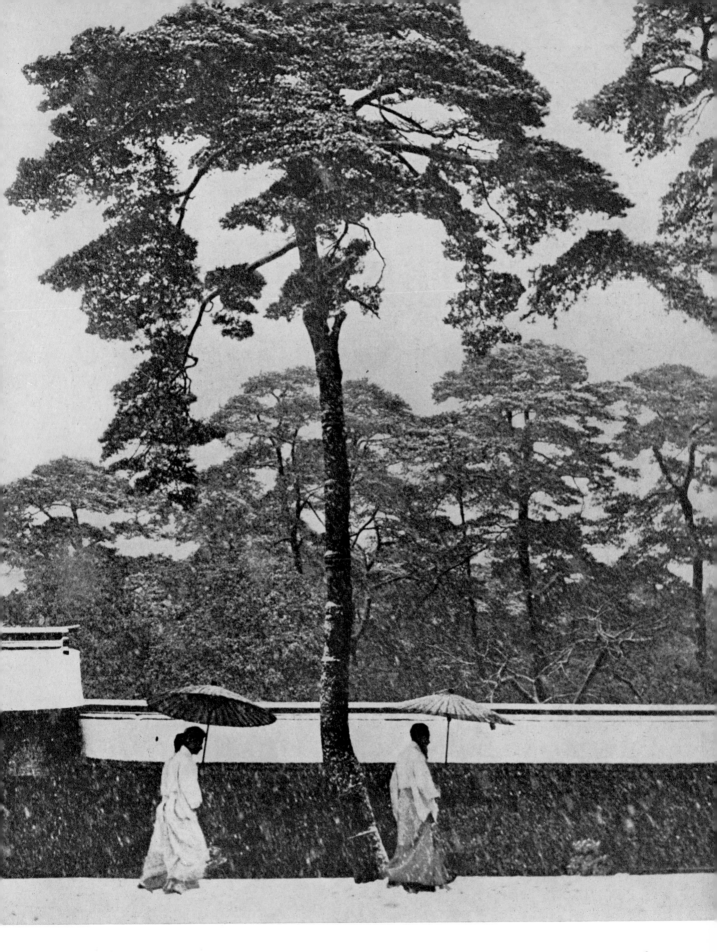

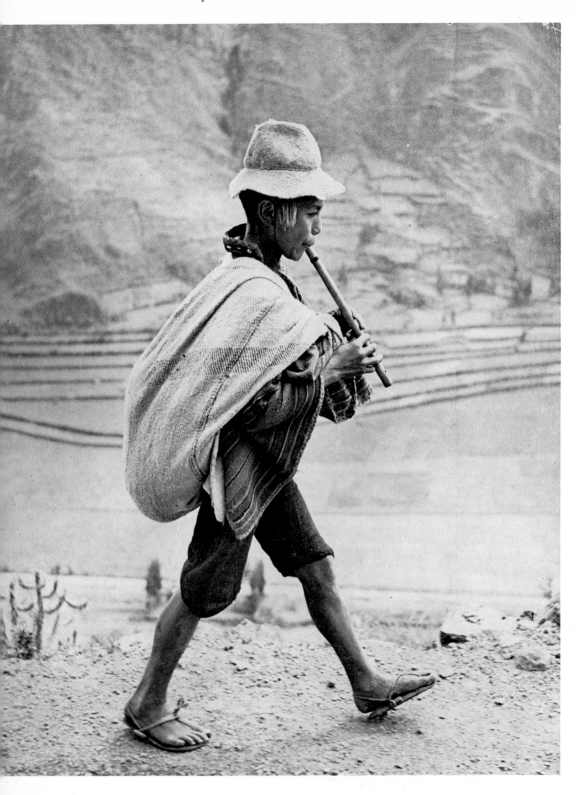

WERNER BISCHOFF, Peruvian Piper. 1954.

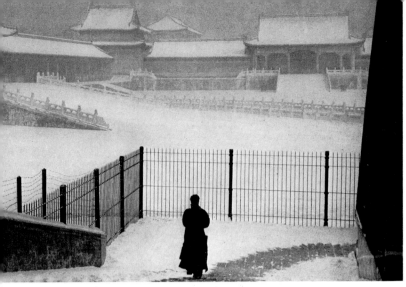

All photographs by Marc Riboud
courtesy Magnum Photos.

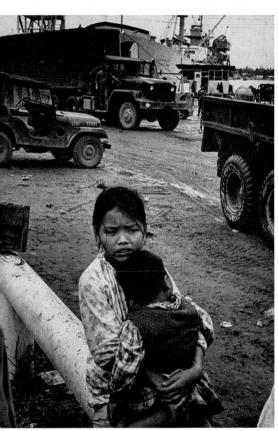

MARC RIBOUD
Palace in the Snow, Peking. 1957.
U. S. Army, Vietnam. 1967.
Haying, China. 1957.

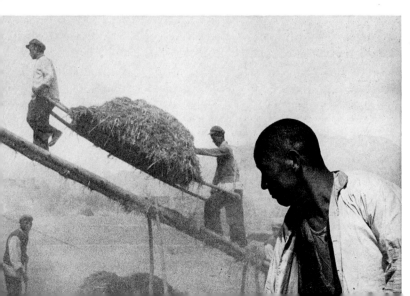

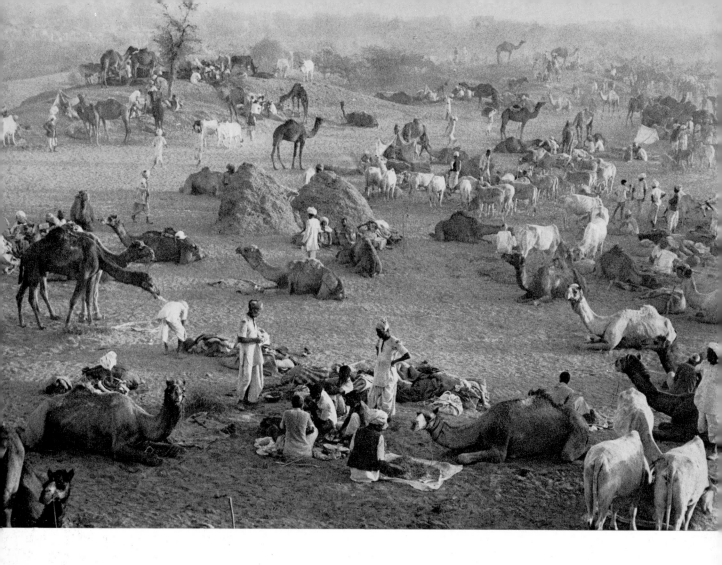

The specialty of nude photography, which presents the most difficult of problems to men whose aspirations transcend the mere description of toothsome flesh, has received a number of high practitioners in recent years. The Frenchman Lucien Clergue (q.v.) is beyond question our foremost photographer of the nude, but it is also beyond question that more great photographers of the nude are to be found in Japan than anywhere else.

Japan is today one of the leading countries in the manufacture of photographic supplies and equipment, especially lenses. Photography seems to supply a special Japanese aesthetic need; and Japanese probers and poets with the camera are among the world's best. The art of Japan is traditionally based on close observation of the moods and details of nature; and the nude female forms given us by Japanese photographers are grandly conceived, impeccably lit, and subtly evocative in form, mood, and texture. The best of them can remind us of Maillol's sculpture in their balance and stability. Some of the most sensitive are by Hoishi Hojida. Their serenity

is matched by that of Japanese landscape photographs: lighted torches carried by fishermen are delicately balanced by village lights that flicker against the night sky; logs, on a misty morning, float down the river like boats dimly drawn on an ancient scroll; the hallowed gate of a temple is silhouetted by starlight.

The Near East has joined Western Europe, America, and Japan as a center of photographic art. Dimitrios Harissiadis is a leader of a small but vigorous movement in Greek photography. His personal style is illustrated in his very characteristic *Greek Frieze*, a patterning of cleanly separated, darkly silhouetted elements set against a light background. Each element seems a unit in itself, but all are linked together in a beautifully balanced and thoroughly unified all-over composition, as in the classic Greek art to which the picture bears no superficial resemblance.

Native artistic traditions also pervade the work of Fulvio Roiter, who was born in Venice and in whom love of the seen world in all its dewy freshness seems to have filtered down from the Renaissance masters Mantegna, Giorgione, and the early Titian. The illustrated landscape scene taken in the snow-laden mountains of Central Italy is a tapestry of gray, feathery trees that almost fade into the snow; the two pack animals and the man who leads them supply darker and stronger accents, completing the composition. The artfully composed *Umbria* shows equal sensitivity to the land and the people.

Interesting developments are taking place in the United States, where more and more workshops and studios of important photographers are being moved into colleges and universities, now the principal training centers for professional photographers. This trend began in the 1930s with the establishment of departments in Moholy-Nagy's New Bauhaus, in Chicago (now merged into the Illinois Institute of Technology) and Black Mountain College in North Carolina. Both institutions were spun off from the Bauhaus in Dessau, Germany, which came to its end with the advent of Nazism in that country. College-based photographers have found an unofficial journal and forum in the magazine *Aperture*, which was founded by Minor White in 1952 and has been edited by him ever since. White, a brilliant photographer himself, teaches photography in the Department of Design of M.I.T"s School of Architecture. Oriented toward abstraction and symbolism, rigidly perfectionist, and not in the least concerned with mass aspects of photography, *Aperture* provides working photographers, teachers, students, and intellectuals the world over with reviews of photorelated books and exhibitions, articles on current developments in photography, and portfolios of current work, with special emphasis on emerging talents. Among the important young and middle-aged photographers whose work appears in *Aperture* from time to time are Brett Weston, Aaron Siskind (q.v.), Paul Caponigro,

RIBOUD
left: Camel Market, India. 1956.
below: Boatmen, Ghana. 1960.

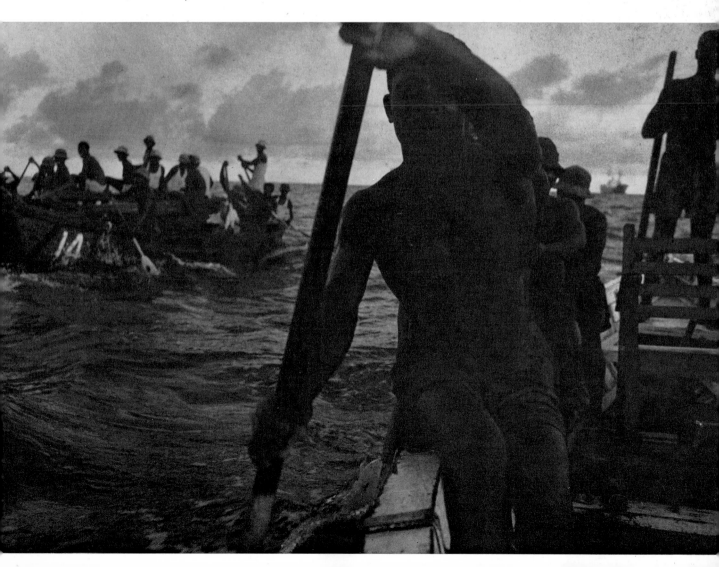

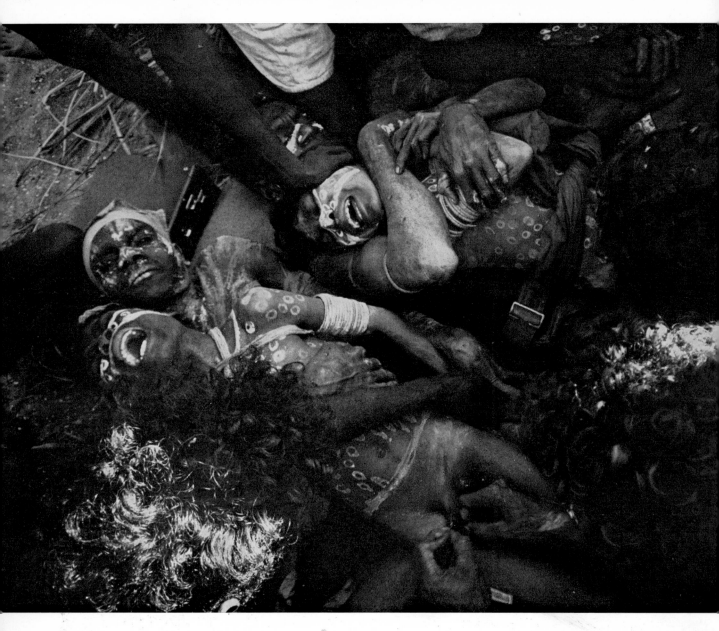

FRITZ GORO, South Sea Island Circumcision.
Courtesy Life Magazine.

Frederick Sommer, Wynn Bullock, Eugene Meatyard, Van Deren Coke, Robert Frank, Syl Labrot, John Szarkowski, Harry Callahan (q.v.), and Walter Chappell. *Aperture* has been a force not only in the raising of the general level of performance, but, in concert with the exhibition programs of George Eastman House, the Museum of Modern Art, the Worcester Museum of Art, and other institutions, in the building of an intelligent, expanding audience for photographic art.

The work of Paul Caponigro, a truly gifted Bostonian, reflects the profound love of nature inculcated in him through study with Minor White and with Benjamin Chin of San Francisco, who was a student of Ansel Adams. With this Caponigro combines a highly developed sense of composition stemming from a deep understanding of abstract photography and a lifetime attachment to music. Like Ansel Adams before him, Caponigro first planned to make his name as a concert pianist. In photography, again like Adams, Caponigro has limited himself to black-and-white, for he, too, is constantly alert to the subtle tonalities available to him in the gray scale.

Presently in Ireland on a Guggenheim grant, Caponigro has concentrated on ancient arts and monuments there and he has also turned his camera on the old megaliths of England, especially Stonehenge, and the menhirs of France. These photographs of Europe's ancient stones will appear in book form when he returns from his stay abroad.

About his profession the 35-year-old Caponigro recently wrote, "Photography's potential as a great image maker and communicator is really no different from the same potential in the best poetry, where familiar, everyday words, placed within a special context, can soar above the intellect and touch subtle reality in a unique way. . . . Some of my pictures have always been a mystery to me in terms of how I arrived at them. Even with the technical ability to produce fine prints, I am hard put to know how it happens. . . . I produce something that is a surprise to me. There are no rules. I only work and say what I have discovered."

ELLIOTT ERWITT, American Soldiers on the March. Korea. 1951.
next page: The Everlasting Sea. 1966.

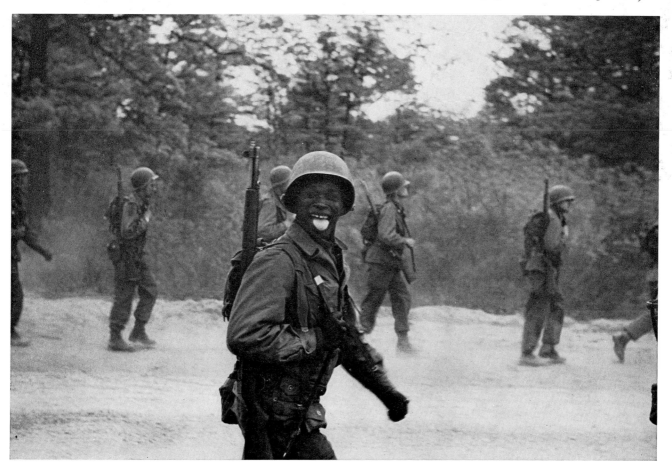

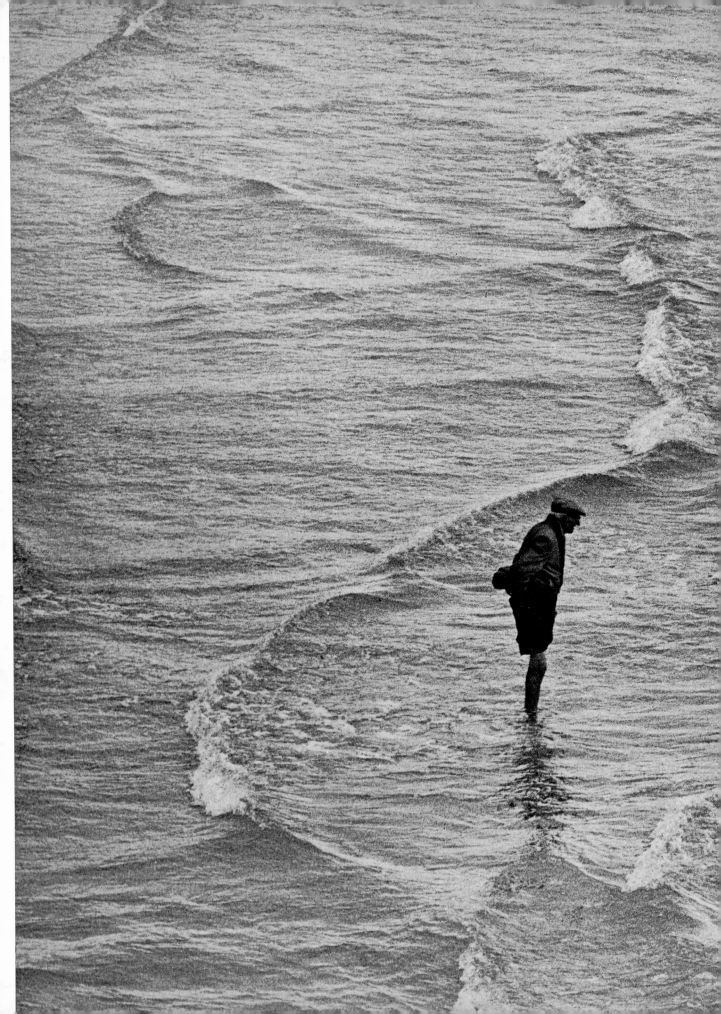

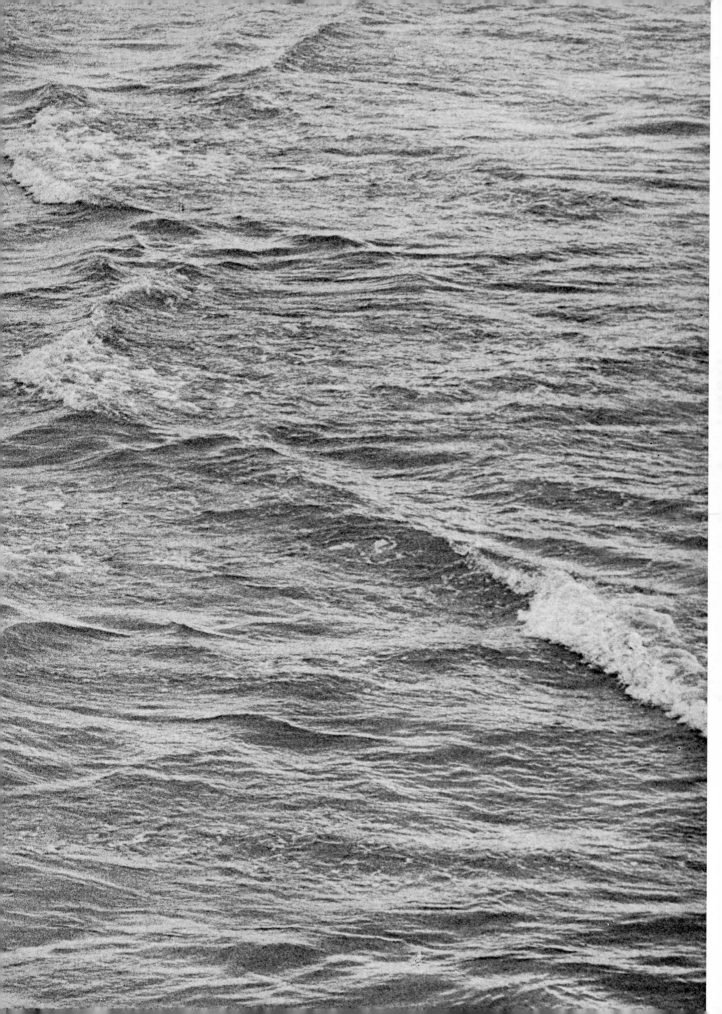

The issues on which White and *Aperture* center are rooted in the technique, style, and expression of Stieglitz, Edward Weston, and Ansel Adams. White's *Zone System Manual*, for instance, has made Adams's method of predetermining tonal structures available to any studious photographer. White has also written extensively on the theme of "equivalence," an enlargement upon ideas behind some of Stieglitz's nature studies of the early 1920s (cf. discussion of the "equivalent" on page 264). Here, the photograph is shaped so that it becomes the analogue of something within the observer. A symbol, a metaphor, it releases some "equivalent" mental image charged with memories. The theory of equivalence is rooted in one of photography's properties, a property fundamental to its existence as an independent art. Isolating nature's forms from their usual matrix of common human experience, photography persuades us to endow its images of those forms with new and different meanings.

PORTRAITURE

PHOTOGRAPHY, as we know, came about in great measure through the efforts of portrait painters to find some reliable means of getting an accurate likeness. And, as we have seen, the camera lost little time in dethroning the brush as the recorder of our faces. Portrait photography has been a big industry for practically 130 years. This is not to say that photographers have distinguished themselves in the field of portraiture. Some have, most have not—completely aside from such standard villainous images pasted inside items such as passports and the heavily retouched inanities produced by run-of-the-mill commercial studios. For portraiture is, somehow, both the easiest and the most difficult assignment for the professional photographer. It is easy because the subject can make so important a contribution. The subject made the face, after all; and a technically competent photographer can get a pretty good portrait merely by allowing a face with character to record itself. To interpret a complex personality creatively, discovering something fresh and important to say, is something else again. The roster of

ERWITT
Diana at the Metropolitan Museum. 1963.
*All photographs by Elliott Erwitt
courtesy Magnum Photos.*

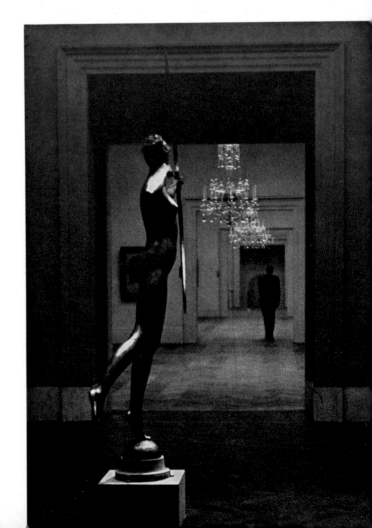

giants in portrait photography does not contain too many names. The names of Yousuf Karsh, Arnold Newman (both q.v.), and Philippe Halsman, the first a Canadian and the last two Americans, are certainly among them. Karsh has an unrivaled sense of drama; his photographs relate to the theater. Newman is a master of symbolism that underlines and reinforces his central message; his work relates to art and artists. Halsman, however, is in certain ways the most interesting member of this extremely talented group. He is not so much a "photographer" as a brilliantly inventive and witty graphic artist whose chosen medium is light, and whose work relates to literature.

Unlike Karsh and Newman, Halsman ranges far beyond the borders of portrait photography. One measure of his versatility is his 97 *Life* magazine covers—more than any other photographer, although he has never been a staffman at *Life*. Two United States postage stamps of 1966 bore his images of Adlai Stevenson and Albert Einstein. Karsh's photographs have also appeared on stamps of various other nations, particularly his wartime portrait of Churchill. But, the measure of Halsman's genius as a portraitist is measured not only by what he knows how to do but also by what he knows how not to do. That is to say, this man who projects his own personal imaginative vision so fully in so many of his images and series of images, avoids any show of self in his portraits. He is a virtuoso of graphics, but those portraits are never once displays of his dazzling graphic skill. The skill is there, of course, but it never intrudes. His mind discovers and his camera presents a small world of significant feeling and emotion. The result can be tremendous. Other great photographers, for instance, have produced splendid portraits of Judge Learned Hand—who had a photogenic face full of character—but none like Halsman's portrait (see page 421). It is one of the finest portraits in history—not only in photography but in all art.

Halsman recently said about his portraits: "I do not direct the sitter—the only thing I try is to help him over his fears and inhibitions. I therefore use the 4x5 Fairchild-Halsman camera. I invented it and had it made of wood many years ago in Paris; later the Fairchild Camera Company made a prototype in metal, but it was never marketed. This reflex camera permits a great flexibility; I can shoot fast and use small openings for a considerable depth of field, and the subject after a while doesn't even realize I am shooting his picture; and, as I can clearly see on my ground glass the fleeting expressions on the subject's face, I try to capture what I feel reflects something of his inner life. The main goal for me is not to impose my own idea of the subject, but rather to get at the psychological truth of the subject and present it in a valid form, a graphic form, if you will, but I would always sacrifice design for content."

When Halsman does inject his own personality into his pictures, as he does in his non-portraits, the result can be wildly hilarious as well as technically astonishing. The little bit of Op art on page 494 was accomplished by projecting a transparency of an all-over pattern on the bare skin of a model and then photographing the transformation of that pattern by her shapely form. The witty photo of a skull formed by seven nudes is one of a number of startling Surrealist and semisurrealist images Halsman has created with his good friend Salvador Dali. They have earned him the appellation of "brainstorm-trooper."

The Op figure and the Dali-plus-skull, of course, are high-level intellectual entertainments. But Halsman is equally successful and no less imaginative on the most popular journalistic level. His *Life* mission of 1956 to go out and photograph the world's most beautiful girls was accomplished with such éclat that six years later he was called upon for a repeat performance—this time with the world's most beautiful first ladies: queens and wives of presidents.

PRODUCT AND FASHION

IN THE 1920s, forward-looking advertising agencies were beginning to use sophisticated photographs, notably by Lejaren A. Hiller and Lewis Hine. Seemingly, however, photographers were not yet a major threat to illustrators, who dominated the visual aspects of advertising and editorial art at that time. To use a photograph on a popular magazine cover was utterly unthinkable; the early covers of *Time* magazine, for example, were a succession of charcoal portraits. All fashion pictures were drawings. Illustrations of products in consumer advertising were also drawings, but in 1927, a new cloud drifted across the advertising horizon in the form of a prize-winning still life of bananas appetizingly photographed by Shellock and Allison.

The situation changed rapidly in the 1930s. In 1931 the Abbot Kimball Advertising Agency exhibition of European advertising photography alerted American art directors to the wide range of possibilities inherent in the promising new advertising medium. In 1932—before the days of color film—Edward Steichen produced a splendid color photo of a Packard roadster. Photographed fashion models became a familiar part of the advertising scene

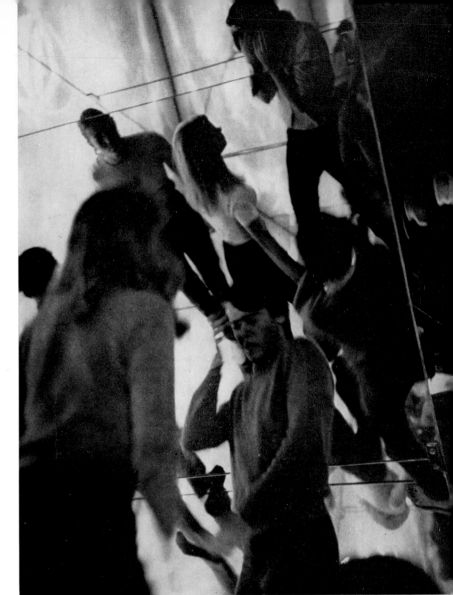

JANINE NIEPCE, Le Woum-woum.
St.-Tropez, 1966.
Courtesy Rapho-Guillumette Pictures,
Paris and New York.

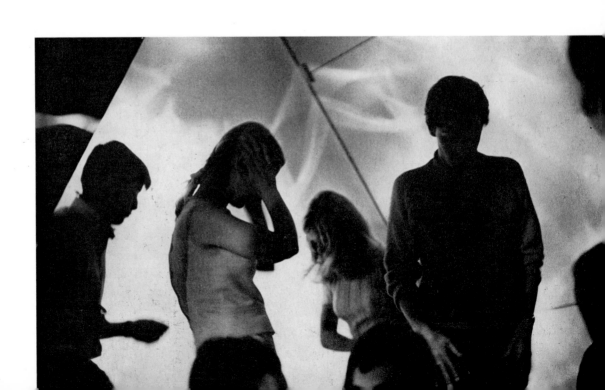

not too long after, and, in the second half of the decade, received sophisticated treatment at the hands of Munkacsi, Hoyningen-Huene, and Blumenfeld.

Photography has dominated fashion and product photography since the 1940s, when the talents of Victor Kepler, John Rawlings, Herbert Matter, Cecil Beaton, and Gjon Mili appeared. Today, the roster of fine photographers in these fields contains many names. Gordon Parks (q.v.), claimed as a master of photoportraiture and photojournalism, is no less a master of photofashion. The remarkably versatile Irving Penn is a brilliant stylist both in color and black and white, and in both fashion and product photography. His chief asset as a commercial photographer is his virtuoso flair for bold composition and unearthly grace, which he fuses into single images that are not easy to forget. Penn is one of the adventurous explorers, along with Fred Lyon of San Francisco, Michael A. Vaccaro of Rome, and Eliot Elisofon of New York, in the realm of expressive use of color for industrial purposes. Each has tried his hand in photographing the art of cooking. Penn is no less skillful in the exploitation of stark black and white, which he has employed with great effectiveness in fashion work; here, he may very well have contributed to similarly effective use of absolute black and white by photographers who are otherwise diametrically opposite in their creative vision—Lennart Olson for example. Another present-day fashion photographer of unusual capabilities is Richard Avedon, master of sophisticated softness and a unique stylist. When asked about the importance of the model in fashion photography, Avedon said, "I work with actresses—not clothes dummies or coat hangers." Through unconventional lighting, exaggerated poses, startling costumes, and exotic backgrounds, fashion photographers have created eye-catching images that have more than once changed female attire all over the world. Newly emerged talents in fashion work include Melvin Sokolsky, William Klein (who has also published photobooks documenting Tokyo—Moscow—New York) and the English photographer of way-out contemporary fashion, David Bailey, who poses men as women and women as men.

Perhaps the most difficult specialty in product photography, if it may be so called, is architecture, where the artist is called upon to evoke a full three-dimensional sense of light, space, and form in a two-dimensional transcription from the most three-dimensional of subjects. Required for membership in this select circle are a thorough knowledge of architecture, a highly developed sense of design, and the ability to plan and schedule a series of photographs taken from strategic vantage points at pinpointed moments during the course of the day or night. Mention may be made here of Ezra Stoller, G. E. Kidder Smith, and Norman F. Carver Jr., whose *Silent Cities, Mexico and the Maya*, and *Form and Space in Japanese Architecture* exemplify his exceptional talent as an architectural photographer.

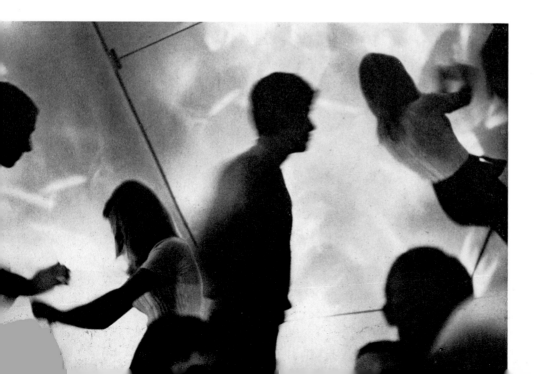

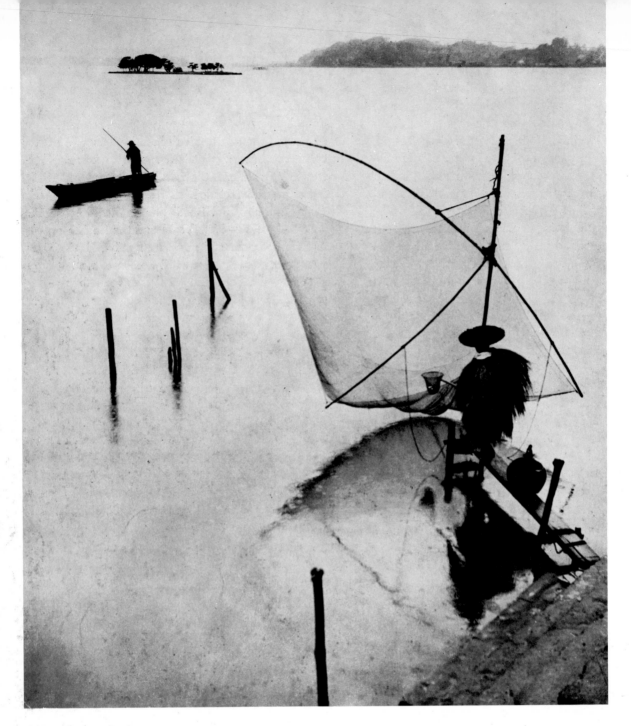

TOSHIJI MUKAI, *above*: Lake Shudoko in Rain. 1957.
right: The Valley Nagataro in May. 1957.

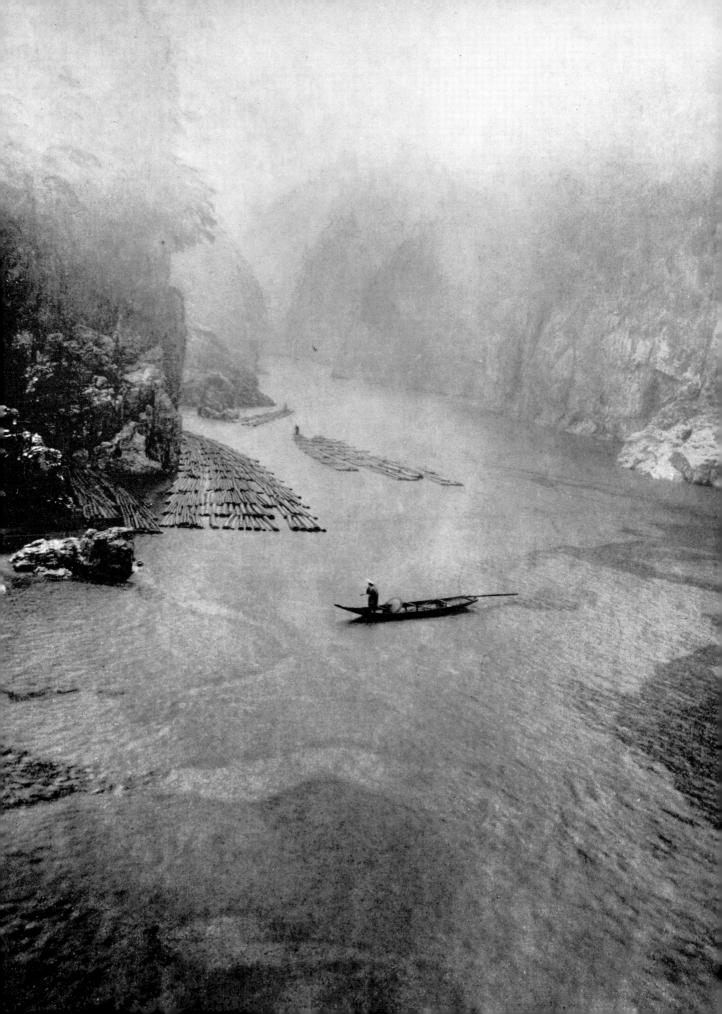

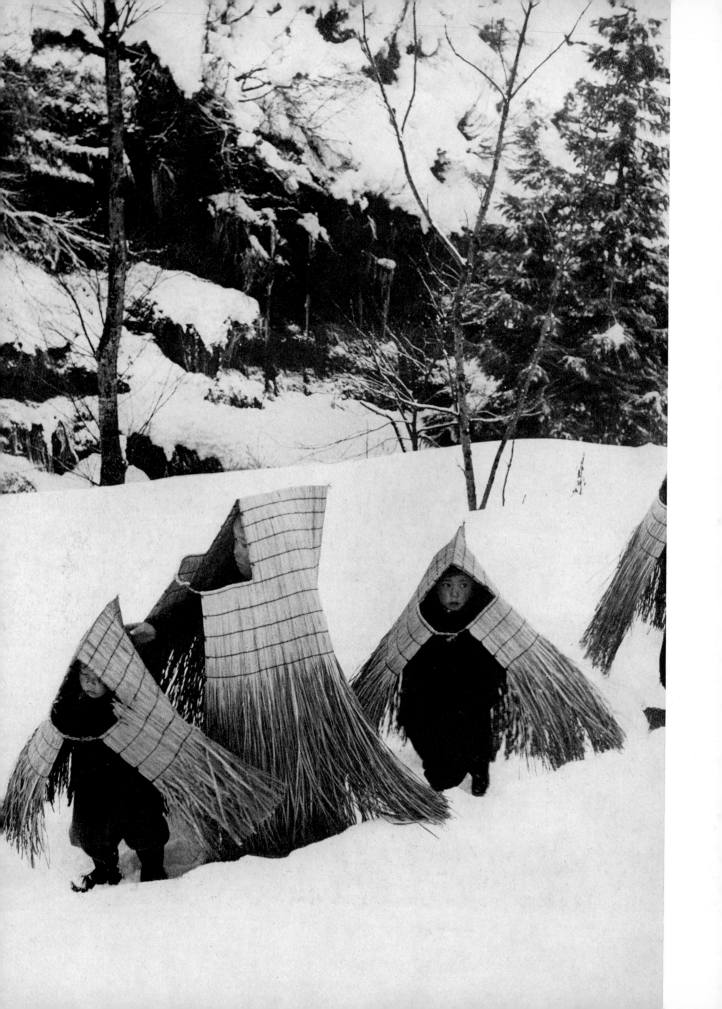

Clarence Kennedy of Smith College, Clarence John Laughlin of New Orleans, and Farrell Greham of New York, have shown individual mastery in the just as difficult specialty of photographing sculpture.

Current photographic developments raise fundamental questions about the very nature of photography itself. Why, given so high a level of technical competence and ability to observe, does our current generation of photographers present us with so astonishing a variety of photographic images? Because nature itself, as we observe it, is so various. A single small patch of nature has an infinite number of aspects, depending on our constitution and experience, upon whether we look at it steadily or fleetingly, attentively or absent-mindedly, according to its general shape or its specific detail, on the animal level of our gross, unaided senses, or on the extended levels of our extraordinary scientific instruments.

As our eyes and nature touch each other, we organize our vision. With a suitable camera and skill to match, we can record our private vision and make it public.

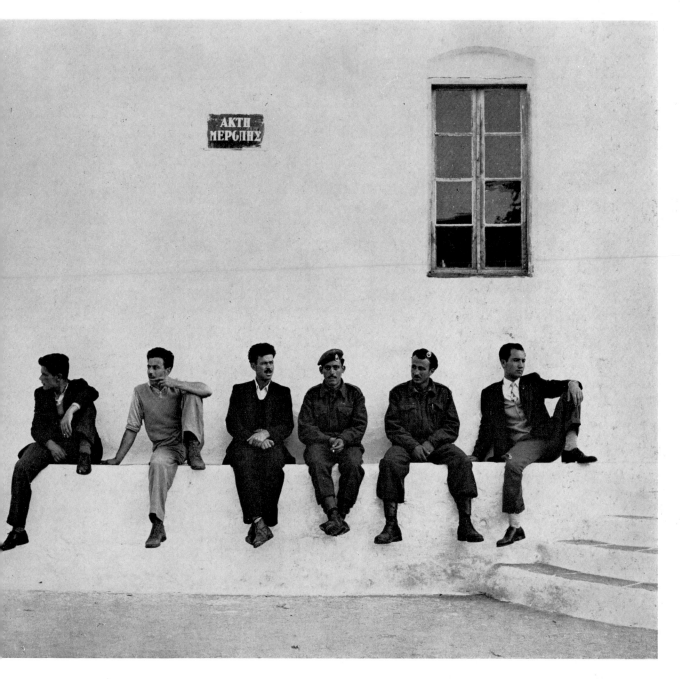

eft: HOISHI HOJIDA, Children in the Snow. *1965. Courtesy Magnum Photos.*
bove: DIMITRIOS HARISSIADIS, Greek Frieze. *1955.*

485

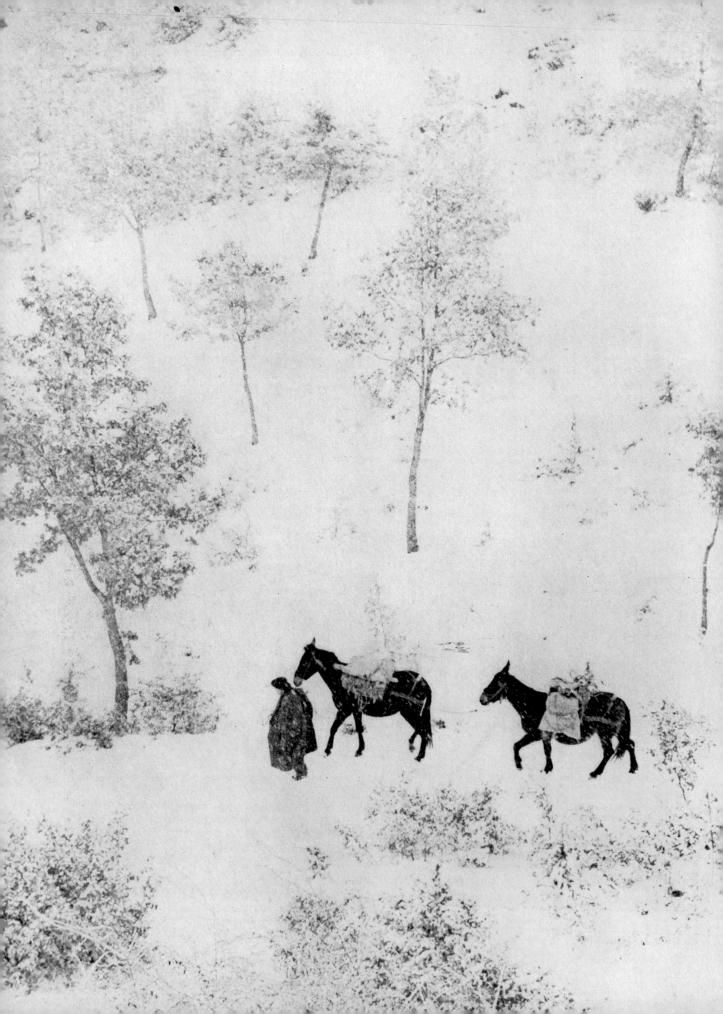

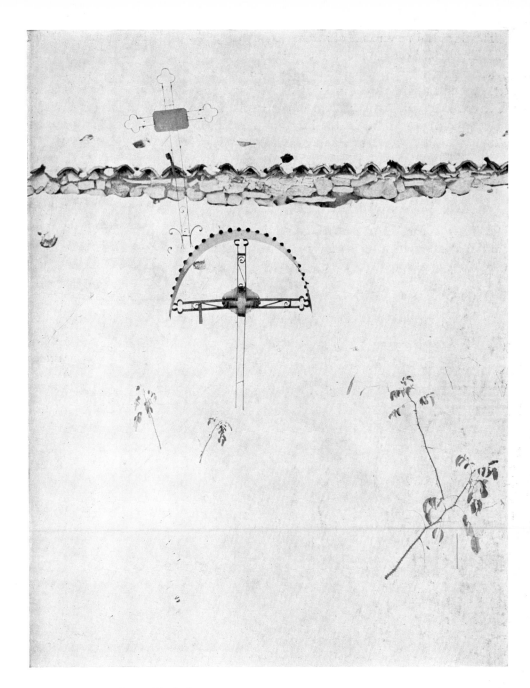

FULVIO ROITER, *above*: Umbria. *1955*
left: Umbrian Landscape. *1955*

The shifts and movements of nature are likewise infinite. The trained eye can follow the patterns of certain movements as they develop; and again, with a suitable camera and suitable photographic skill, the photographer can make public the pattern of movement that only he could see before. In the hands of a sensitive photographer, the camera shows us what is there—yes—but it shows far more than just that, for it requires an exquisitely honed understanding to reveal the chosen meaning out of the many possible.

This kind of organization of nature's forms and meanings is the essence of photographic creativeness. The creative photographer does not invent forms as the creative painter or sculptor does. He discovers them in natural or man-made things. The photograph is a true statement of the world rather than *about* it. In this respect, photography is like science. The creative scientist, too, discovers what is there. But photography is like its fellow visual arts of painting and sculpture in its control, discipline, and organization of forms drawn from nature. Indeed, photography gives us basic information about the realities of all visual art. Feininger's New York recorded by a telescopic lens from far-off Jersey City or his compressed spatial vision taken within the city, Yale Joel's and Gjon Mili's recorded flow of movement, and Ernst Haas's architectural geometries and coruscating images of the city show us that the created abstract, cubist visions of modern artists are rooted in the seen reality of

MINOR WHITE, *From* Rural Chapels. 195

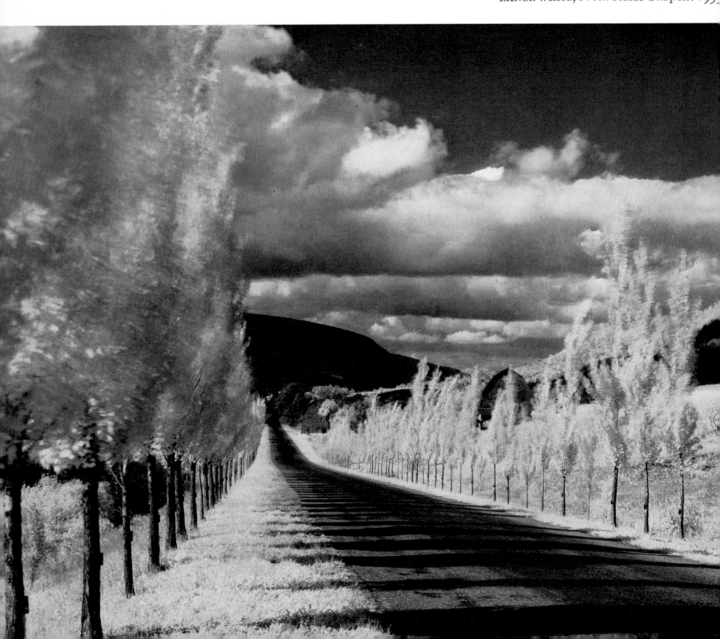

the modern cityscape. Lucien Clergue's stalks of grass and reflections in a marsh; William Garnett's laminated world of air, land, water, and land below the water; Harry Callahan's trees and woods; Aaron Siskind's and Edward Weston's eroded rocks; Minor White's peeling paint, and Walter Chappel's ice-coated twigs, all disclose nature's counterparts of the patterns, signs, and woven strokes of such painters as Rothko, Klee, and Kline.

Photography, which unites art and science, was a child of the industrial revolution. It was the first art in history to depend upon a scientific instrument for its fruits. Photography's broadening and deepening as an art followed upon developments in science and technique, for creative photographers have used every new invention to make more meaningful images. Is this a virtue? It is the greatest of virtues. Photography is, perhaps, the most confident and optimistic art that we have. Most painters and poets see our scientific and industrial civilization as an expanding nightmare that menaces the very possibility of a truly human existence. Unwilling to explore and discover its poetry, they forbear to provide our visually chaotic society with the visual discipline and imagination so badly needed. The photographers have not stayed their hands, and photography may yet be the saving of its sister arts. It is an artistic medium of tremendous flexibility and power, charged with reality on many levels. It has become the characteristic art of the machine age.

MINOR WHITE
From sequence
The Book of Infinity.
1959.

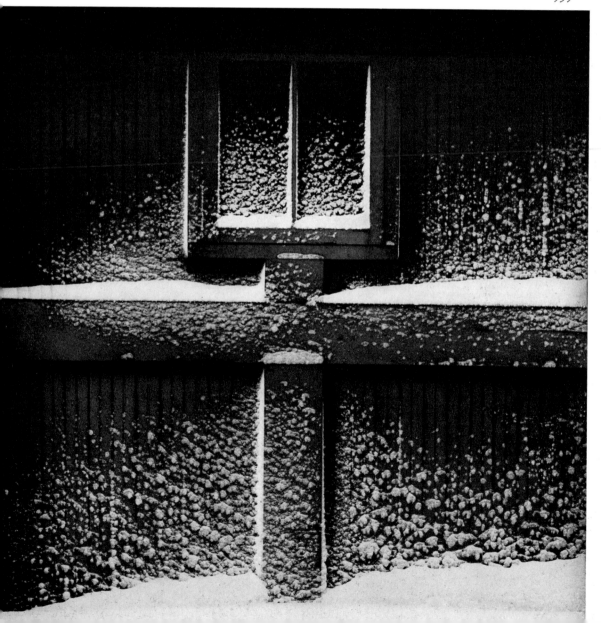

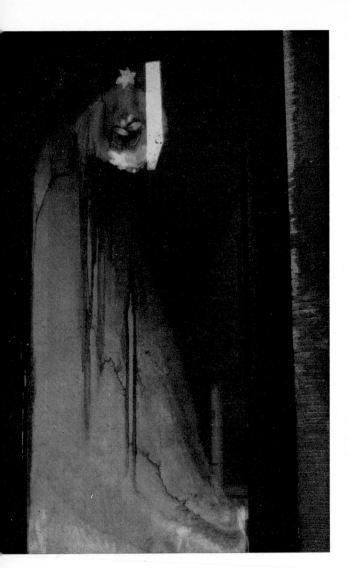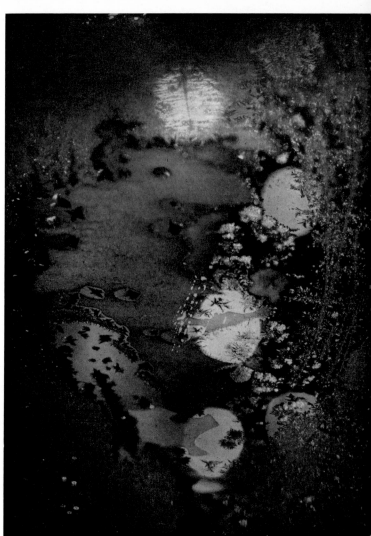

MINOR WHITE, *left*: The Sound of One Hand Clapping. *1958.*
right: Beginnings. *Rochester, 1961.*

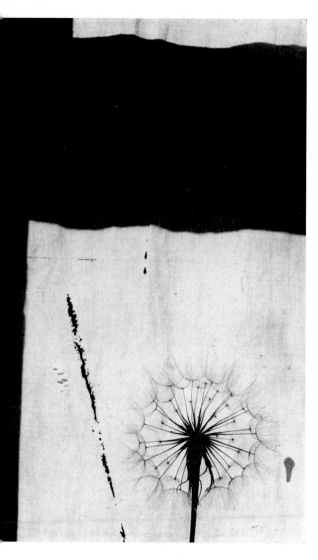

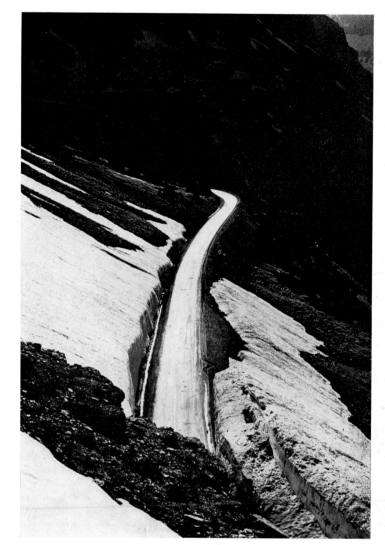

PAUL CAPONIGRO, *left:* Dandelion 2. 1958.
right: Road in Glacier National Park. *Montana.* 1959.
Both photographs courtesy
Museum of Modern Art, New York.

491

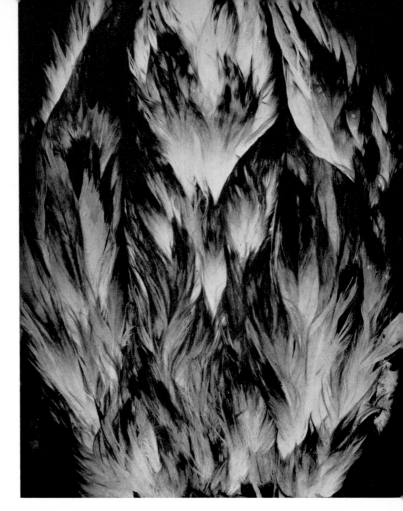

CAPONIGRO, Feather-Flame. *1963*.
Courtesy Grace M. Mayer.
below: Soaped Window. *1959.*
Courtesy Museum of Modern Art, New York.

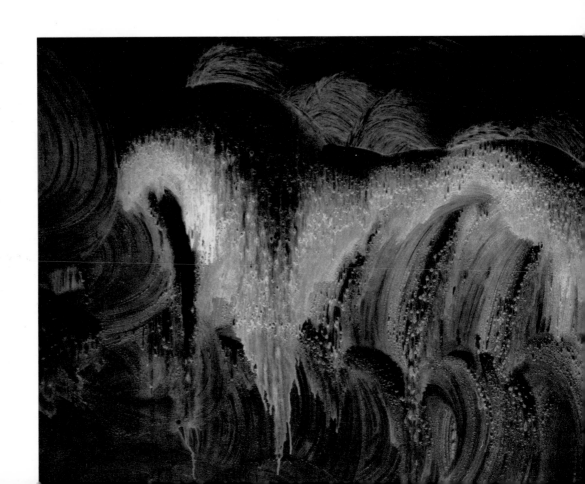

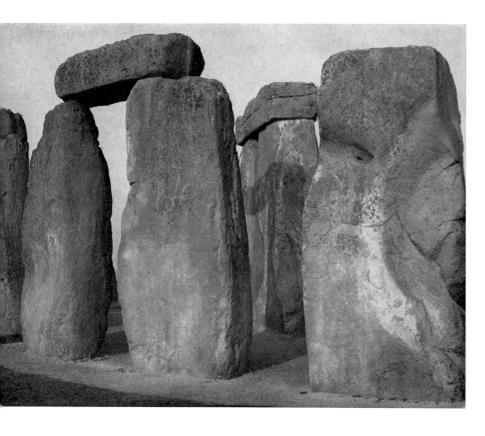

CAPONIGRO
Stonehenge.
1967.

It would be wrong to think of science-minded Andreas Feininger, Fritz Goro, Roman Vishniac, and Lennart Nilsson as cold and factual reporters of the modern world —mere hands and eyes. They are poets who have drawn upon technology at its most advanced to reveal the poetry of an emerging world of thought and feeling— even heroes of a kind. Feininger's explorations over the years of the functional forms in nature, from sea shells to spider webs, from glacier-cut valleys to a fly's eye; Goro's picture essays in such diverse fields as botany, biology, physics, anthropology, and the Arctic; Vishniac's explorations in the realm of microbiology; are comparable to the years of creative thought spent by Nilsson on his color photographs depicting a baby inside its mother's womb, inventing new equipment for the job including lights of various kinds and sizes. His womb pictures can be compared to the wall paintings of the caves of Alta-

mira, on which Stone Age bisons were given birth before the fires of the first artists—womb pictures made before the horizon line was conceived and the natural world became an enclosure for man.

Who is the creative artist? He is an explorer and a discoverer above all. The creative impulse leaps from vehicle to vehicle, according to the needs and aspirations of the times. Once the hand tool was the centrally important art form, then the decorated human skin, the cave mural, the royal tomb, the temple of the gods, the statue, the illuminated manuscript, the great cathedral, the easel painting. The photograph is but the latest to become a housing for the creative spirit, and its possibilities for art have only begun to be exploited. It would appear that a future of unimaginable richness lies ahead for creative photography—individually created, mass-viewed, the central art of the twenty-first century.

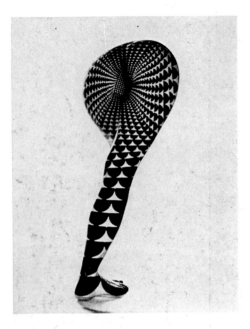

PHILIPPE HALSMAN
Homage to Op Art. 1965.
Dali and the Seven Nudes. 1951.

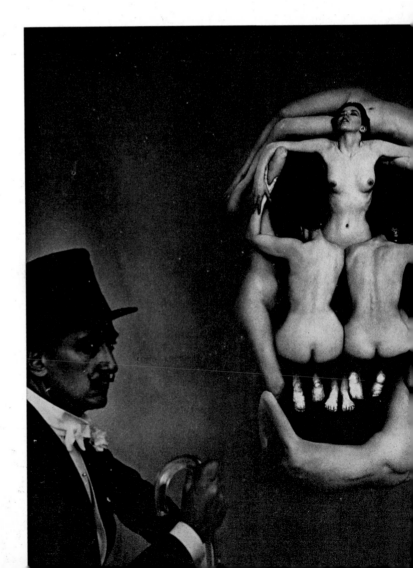

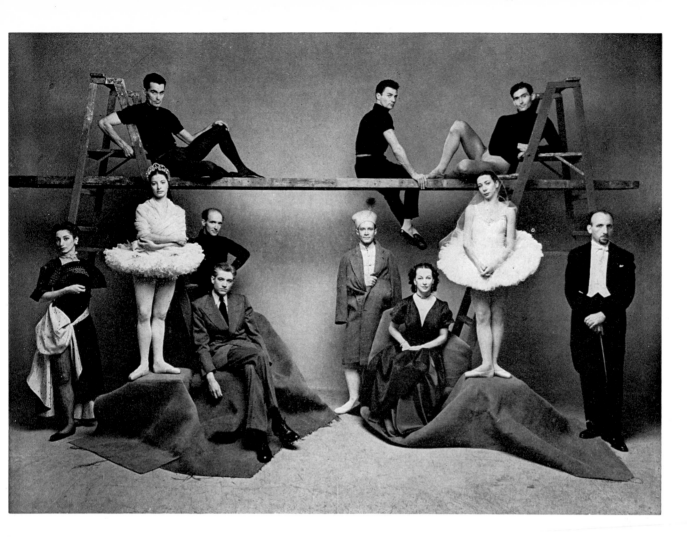

IRVING PENN, Ballet Theatre Group. 1948.
Girl in Black and White. 1950.
Paris Fashion. 1950.
All courtesy Condé Nast Publications.

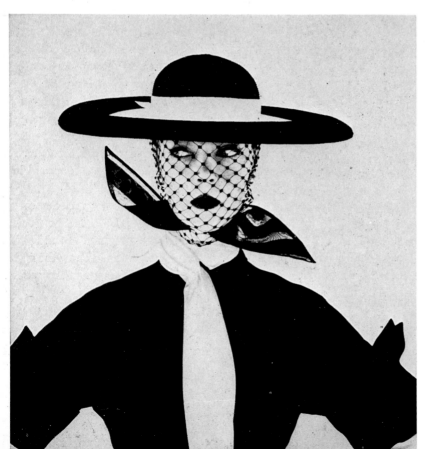

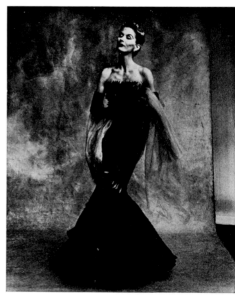

CHAPTER 37

Doisneau: Humorist with a Camera

ROBERT DOISNEAU has the true Parisian's habit of strolling—but never aimlessly. He is always alert, his camera always set for the light and the site, ready for use. He walks seeking the incongruous, the ludicrous, the humorous, the ironic, and the satirical to be found in life. He is a rarity among cameramen, a photographer with a puckish sense of humor; what he secures in his seeing is often really funny, really witty, with nothing forced or faked. Amusing situations come into focus; his reaction is automatic—he laughs and shoots the picture at the same time. There is a range to his human comedy: a goose farmer who resembles his force-fed geese; a statue of a nude seemingly shivering in the snow; American soldiers on leave, one snapping a photograph of a second who beams as he sits in the lap of a Maillol sculpture of a nude; Saul Steinberg, the American artist, posed in a curio shop that recalls his celebrated drawings.

In London's Hotel Claridge the droll French photographer tried to capture the way men looked at women, but was utterly defeated by the discretion of the British. He was more successful at the Crillon in Paris; the appreciative reactions of the boulevardiers made the series a successful story for the illustrated weeklies.

Doisneau's wit is never sardonic, never caustic. Collectors fascinate him but not those who attend art auctions to buy prestige names or hedges against inflation.

Those whom he photographs are original eccentrics; one collects useless objects such as electric sockets and old bottle caps, which he methodically arranges and displays with pride as he wears a wig made of corks; another, a doorman in a Montparnasse night club, prides himself on his artistic taste, dressing up with monocle and astrakhan fur headpiece as he poses in front of his littered collection of questionable canvases.

Doisneau's Paris is not the tourists' paradise, though he follows the sight-seeing buses and joins the international groups to seek entertaining situations that usually go unobserved and unrecorded. In a night club near the Bastille, Doisneau trained his Leica on a blonde apache dancer who, when flung across the floor, rested her weary elbow on the knee of a delighted elderly tourist while his wife glowered at "such goings on."

These whimsical tableaux he often anticipates. In Romi's gallery on the Left Bank he photographed expressions of people who suddenly discovered a female figure, nude but for stockings, painted from the rear as she peers through a window drapery. Doisneau caught a series of comical expressions which were published in the world's press. He received letters from all over addressed simply, "Romi, Paris," all asking to buy the painting.

His pictures are in a really universal language, the situations appeal to people everywhere. Postmen and porters wait for a pedicure shop to open; a sentinel in front of the President's palace holds bayonet poised as he intently ponders a bunch of balloons; in a three-sided wrestling match even the referee joins the grimacing mock battle.

Doisneau writes of his work, "The marvels of daily life are exciting; no movie director can arrange the unexpected that you find in the street." The concrete streets

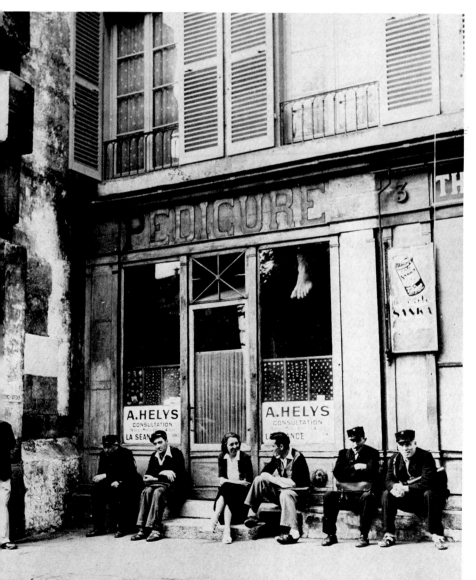

ROBERT DOISNEAU, Porters and Postmen Waiting for Pedicure Shop to Open. 1953.

497

DOISNEAU, Tourists and Apache Dance. 1952

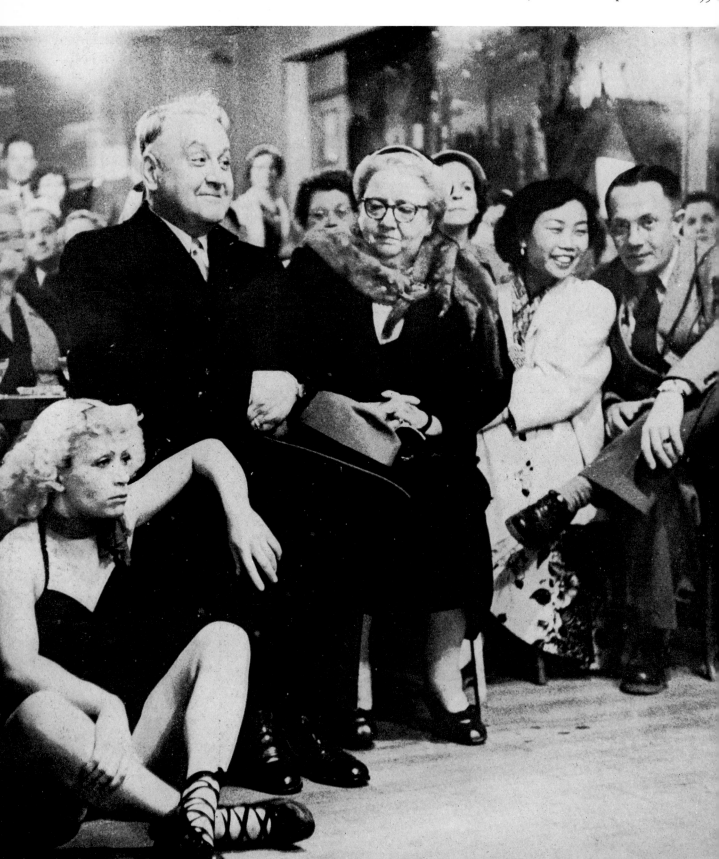

of the workingmen's suburbs know him as well as the paving stones of Paris. Blaise Cendrars, one-armed poet and writer of piquant prose, writes in the preface to Doisneau's book *Banlieue de Paris (The Suburbs of Paris)*, "He is an astonishing little guy. I imagine him as an artisan worker joining the other artisans, sculptors and stained-glass-window makers, as they build Chartres Cathedral." The association is quite valid, for Doisneau was born in the spiritually inspiring cathedral city of the Beauce in 1912 and was raised in the shadow of its jeweled windows. Cendrars considers Doisneau a man of the Middle Ages and writes, "Every artist who pays attention to the small people of the street goes back to the tradition, and for a Frenchman the tradition is always the Middle Ages of the small craftsman. They are the same people, the people in today's suburbs and the people who built Chartres." He concludes that Doisneau is too humble to make any comparison of his work with those of the artisans, but, writes Cendrars, "as a sculptor with a camera he builds up character and atmosphere . . . he fills himself with irony and laughter so your heart is captured. Spring is blossoming in all the gardens and the flower pots of the concierge are gay . . . it is a day when there's kissing in the streets."

Doisneau took a thousand pictures of people kissing—while walking in the streets, riding in tricycle or automobile, in amusement parks, subway trains, boats along the Seine: a spectacle of love in which uninhibited Frenchmen indulge everywhere. Another series of photographs was of the bread carriers; Doisneau caught bread in Frenchmen's hands carried as a cane, as a pointer, under the arm, on the head, on the back of a bicycle, broken in two, nibbled on while strolling—hardly ever covered by wrapping paper or a bag.

His gifted off-beat seeing is also evident in his journalistic assignments. For international picture magazines he has taken such diverse stories as the most costly, social costumed party seen in Venice in a generation and the economic life of small manufacturers in France. Industrial photography was his first experience with the camera when he worked for the Renault automobile company in 1935. Three years later he left the inflexible routine of photographing machine parts as he had earlier left the minute art of engraving, in which he was also an expert. Assignments of all kinds for the next several years taught him complete mastery of a wide variety of cameras, but by the time the war started his favorites were the Leica and the Rolleiflex. He carried a camera while a foot soldier, but in the Resistance his photographs of the occupation and the liberation served as a springboard for his reputation in the front ranks of photography in France.

Doisneau is a seasoned professional who always gives their money's worth to editor and patron on any of his assignments. His two real loves, however, which keep him from traveling much, are Paris and its people. With fast film and lenses he takes them as they are. Many of these pictures go into books; five books have been published to date, although not as yet translated into English. These are not the romantic, picturesque, and enchanting picture books of Paris brought back by tourists as souvenirs. Doisneau's explorations with his camera show his city exciting, honest, gay, alive, and direct with a sensitivity and breadth of humor distinctly his.

DOISNEAU, Sentry in Front of President's Palace. 1951.

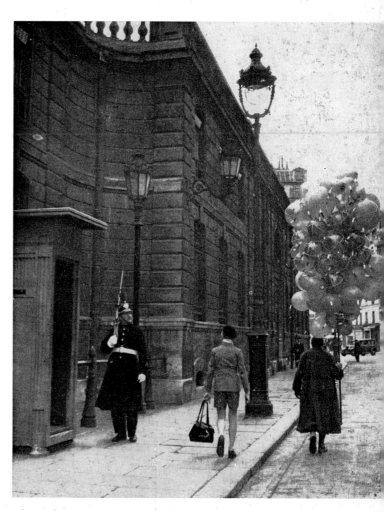

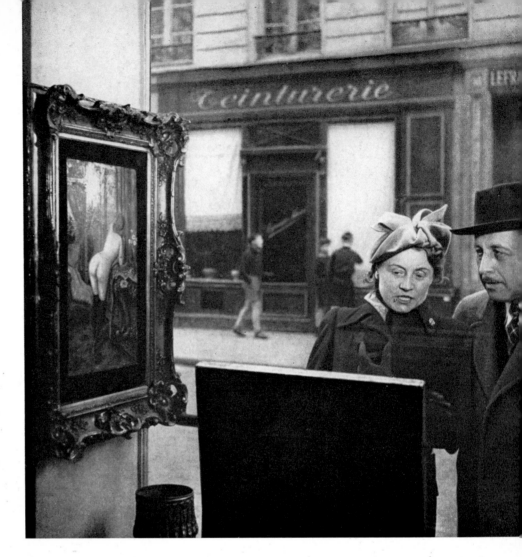

DOISNEAU, *top*: Side Glance. 1953.
below: The Blind Accordionist. 1953.
opposite page: Saul Steinberg. 1953.

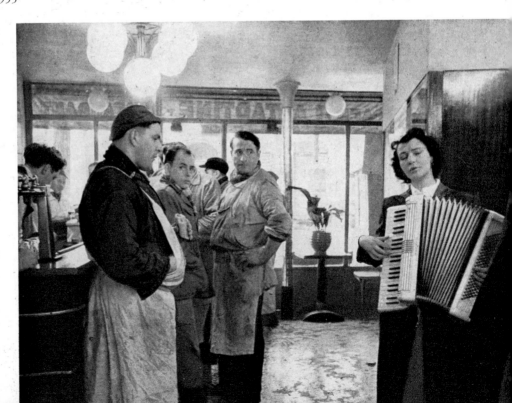

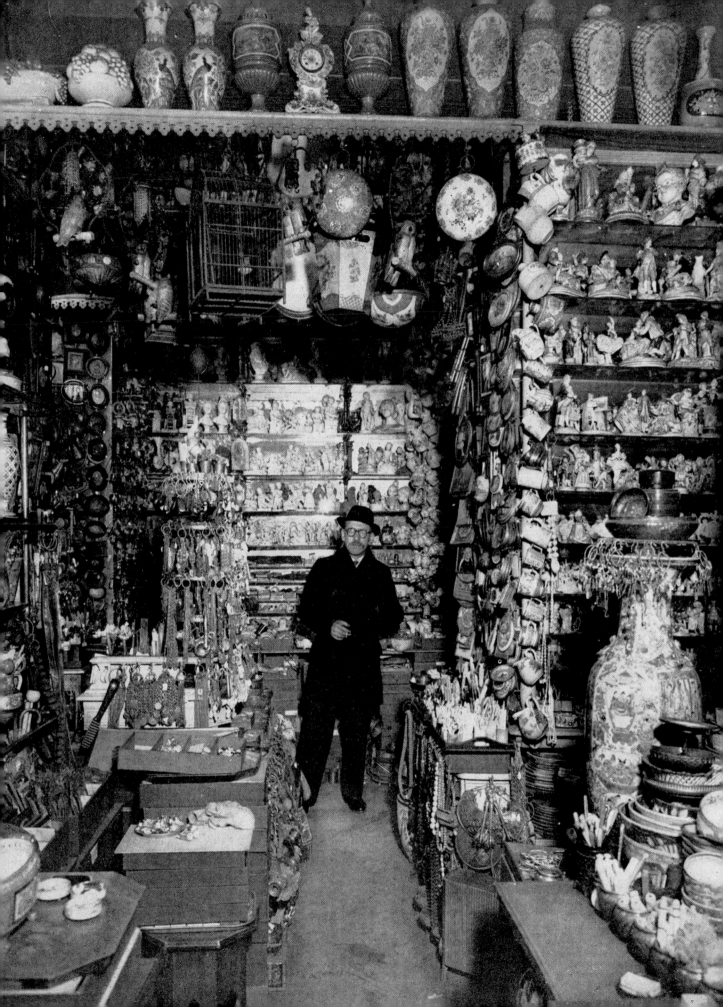

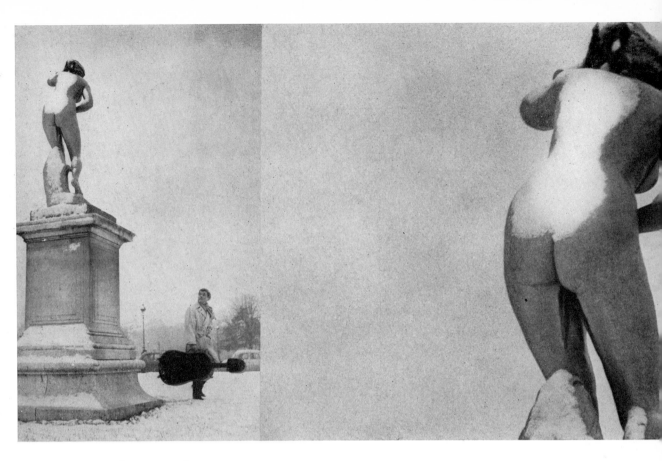

ROBERT DOISNEAU, *four scenes from sequence*
The Skier and His Cello. 1958.

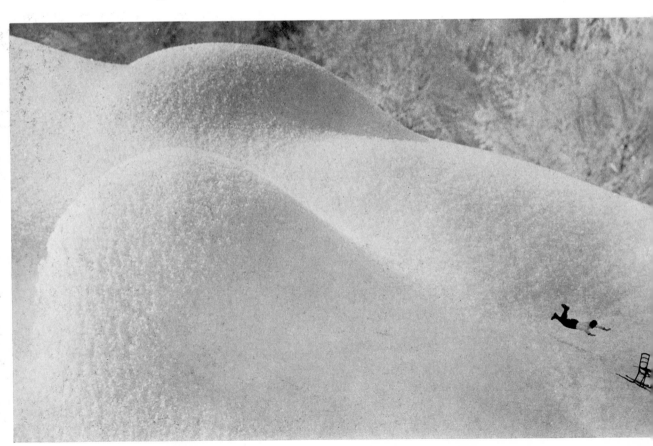

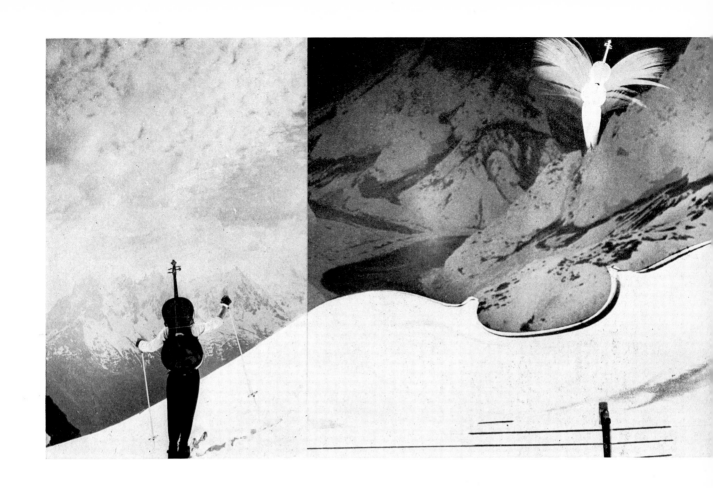

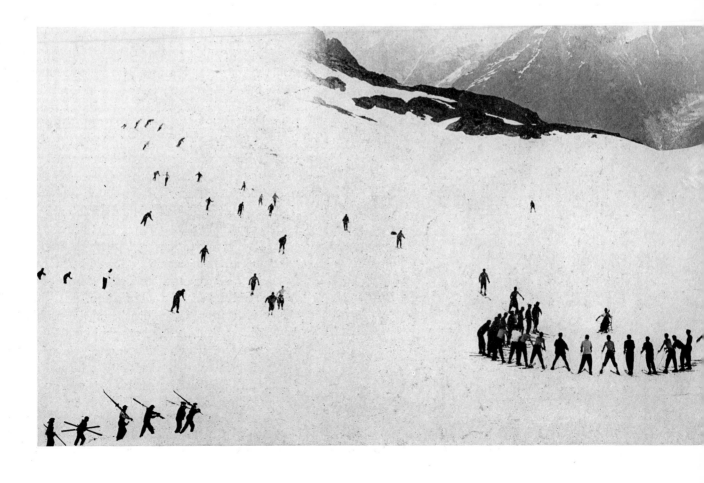

CHAPTER 38

David Douglas Duncan: Lensman of the Marines

DAVID DOUGLAS DUNCAN, an ex-marine whose reckless exploits with carbine and camera had earned him the title "The Legendary Lensman" in World War II, carried only a camera (for *Life* magazine) in the Korean War. He marched with the marines of the encircled First Division, his old outfit, in their bitter withdrawal from the border of Communist China to the Korean Sea. Icy winds of below-zero temperatures froze his gloved fingers and his camera shutters, and he thawed both out against his body. When he could feel that the shutter was working again he would quickly take a picture or two. He had to protect each roll of exposed film until he could put it aboard a plane for New York to be processed in *Life*'s darkroom.

Communist snipers picked off the soldiers' bent bodies as they marched across icy mountain trails and the snow-packed valleys of the ravaged peninsula into the cold wind mile after mile from the Changjin Reservoir at the Yalu River. Along a road he took a picture of dead feet frozen solid and sticking out of a jeep.

The intimacy of the soldiers' struggle was his. Often he was in front of them, photographing their unforgettable faces as they came into range. During vivid scenes of fighting in small pitched battles he waited beside them, catching their expressions as a trigger was squeezed or a hand grenade thrown. They kept marching back toward the sea and freedom. Commanding officer General Oliver Smith said, "Retreat! Hell, we're just fighting in another direction," and the fighting men cheered, held, and went on doggedly.

Duncan took close-up shots of the eyes of men completely oblivious to him. He came up close to take a picture of a man crying, of men with empty, staring eyes, as mentally beat as they were physically exhausted. He took memorable pictures of men in hand-to-hand combat, the killing at point-blank despite the misery inflicted by the elements. Duncan photographed the inexhaustible courage of the marines with a sympathy and honesty that make his photographs some of the best taken in any war.

Outnumbered 5 to 1, in the ten terrible days of withdrawal, the First Marine Division lost more than two thousand men. Duncan and his camera became to those marines what Ernie Pyle and his typewriter had been to the G.I.'s of World War II. A historian with a camera, Duncan secured an epic picture of American military heroism. His imposing photographs of the retreat were published in a book, *This is War*, along with his earlier photographs of the troops' first attack on the hill of the Pusan Perimeter and of the landing of the transports at Inchon. These are pictures of the troops in full strength, fighting their way to liberate the heavily fortified city of Seoul before the debacle at the Chinese border. Duncan was the last man off the beach at Hungnam when the retreat ended.

Duncan instinctively takes truthful, telling pictures. The factual, the emotional, and the spiritual are fused into stark symbols of war, as graphically intense as Gardner's *Dead Rebel* of the Civil War.

His photographs are uncaptioned, but the pungent prose of his essays matches the graphic power of his seeing. He writes in the preface, "This book is an effort to completely divorce the word 'war' as flung dramatically down off the highest benches of every land, from the look in a man's eyes who is taking his last puff on perhaps his last cigarette, perhaps forever, before he grabs his rifle, his guts and his dreams, and attacks an enemy position above him." He includes four hard-hitting, terse reports describing General Douglas MacArthur's first visit to the Korean front and questioning his gamble in military strategy that accounted for the devastating retreat. Duncan describes his flight in an Air Force jet-attack mission (the first ever made by a war correspondent), a snafu attack by R.O.K. troops, and the marines' first action in Korea.

Duncan's exploit in Korea was a continuation of his incredible adventures in World War II with Fijian guerrillas who marched across the island of Bougainville to set up a base and harass the Japanese troops behind the lines. In this sixty-day campaign he fought alongside the fierce, bushy-haired Fiji Islanders.

After more than a year in the South Seas he was sent to Washington, where he wangled orders for travel anywhere in the Pacific theater with his cameras. This was now his kind of war. He flew twenty-eight missions over Okinawa, three of them in a stifling, plexiglass belly tank which he attached under the wing of a P38. He secured a spectacular shot of a Corsair firing all of its eight 5-inch rockets over Japanese positions on Okinawa. This earned him a D.F.C. One of his best known photographs taken at this time was of a defecting Japanese lieutenant in an American plane, talking into a microphone as he guides an American attack on his own former base.

Those roving papers allowed 2d Lt. David Duncan to range all over the Pacific. He was the only marine photographer aboard the U.S.S. Missouri during the signing of the historic surrender in Tokyo Bay. He returned to the States in 1946 covered with ribbons: another D.F.C., three air medals, six battle stars, and a Purple Heart for a flak wound received in a flight in which the pilot over whose shoulder he was snapping his shutter was killed by a bursting shell.

Early in 1946, still in uniform and on terminal leave, Duncan joined *Life* magazine's staff, and three days later he was bound for Iran to cover the Azerbaijan incident. From Persia he went to Palestine to photograph the growing Zionist-Arab tension, then to Bulgaria for a view behind the Iron Curtain. By the end of 1947 he had photographed the partition of India and Pakistan and the Hindu-Moslem riots, and was back in the States with a wife whom he had married in Cairo. During the following eight years with *Life*, he was on assignments in practically every country of the Middle and Far East, taking pictures of small and big wars, incidents, happenings, and revolutions. His stories regularly appeared in *Life*, and dealt with the Greek Civil War, the Gaza Strip, the Egyptian Revolt, the Vietminh affair, Hindu pilgrims, Japanese sculpture, Egyptian archaeology, and the Islamic religion.

How did this intrepid peripatetic photographer-writer become what he is? Born in Kansas City, Missouri, in 1916, he was an ardent collector of snakes by the time he had finished high school and he had rambled in a jalopy all over the United States and parts of Canada. In 1933 he entered the University of Arizona to study archaeology, with visions of following field expeditions all over the world. A Kodak folding camera given him as a present he used for the first time on a fire which destroyed the hotel in Tucson. He photographed an unknown man in the crowd; it turned out to be the notorious criminal, John Dillinger. This was the beginning of his being in the right place at the right time with his camera ready. A year of dry-bones search and he was on his way to study marine zoology and deep-sea diving at the University of Miami. He was the first man to broadcast over a radio from the bottom of the sea while wearing an open diving helmet. His undersea pictures sold, bringing him the first money he realized as a photographer. Until then he had gladly given his photographs away just to see them published.

In 1936 the lean and wiry six-foot Duncan boxed more than forty bouts as middle and welterweight, winning most of them on decision. The same year his photograph of a fishing scene was awarded second prize in a national snapshot contest. After graduating from college with an A.B., he was off immediately on a friend's two-masted schooner headed for deep-sea fishing in the Caribbean. While he was climbing a limestone cliff on Swan Island south of Cuba, hunting iguanas, the rock gave way, cutting his right upper arm and wrist. With a barbless fishhook and rough sail thread he sewed up the nasty gash. Doctors later praised the stitching. A signed article and set of pictures about turtles in the Caribbean were sold to *National Geographic*. He had found his profession.

During the next few years he roamed all over the western hemisphere, from Nova Scotia to Argentina, always with his cameras ready. By now these were Leicas equipped with the fastest lenses available. He photographed the Mayan ruins of Yucatan for Pan American Airways. He was official cameraman for the Michael Lerner, Chile-Peru Expeditions of the American Museum of Natural History, catching giant squid and swordfish, whale-sharks and marlin, and for a hunting trip to British Columbia also sponsored by Lerner.

In late 1942 he was sent by Nelson Rockefeller's Office of Inter-American Affairs to make photographs in the interest of hemisphere solidarity. Mexico permitted him to take photographs for the first time of defense installations. He continued on through Central America, survived a plane crash in the jungle, but was hospitalized for an emergency operation when he arrived in Panama. While the doctors were sewing up his left side under local anaesthesia he asked that they take out his appendix as well. Though it didn't hurt him, it might some day, and he wanted no more of hospitals.

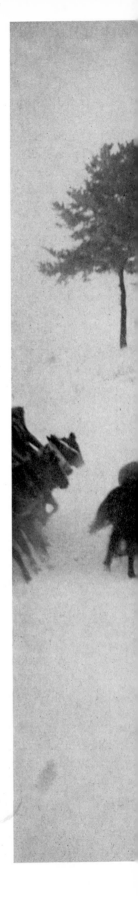

DAVID DOUGLAS DUNCAN, "Black Avni" Turkish Cavalry on Maneuvers. 1948.

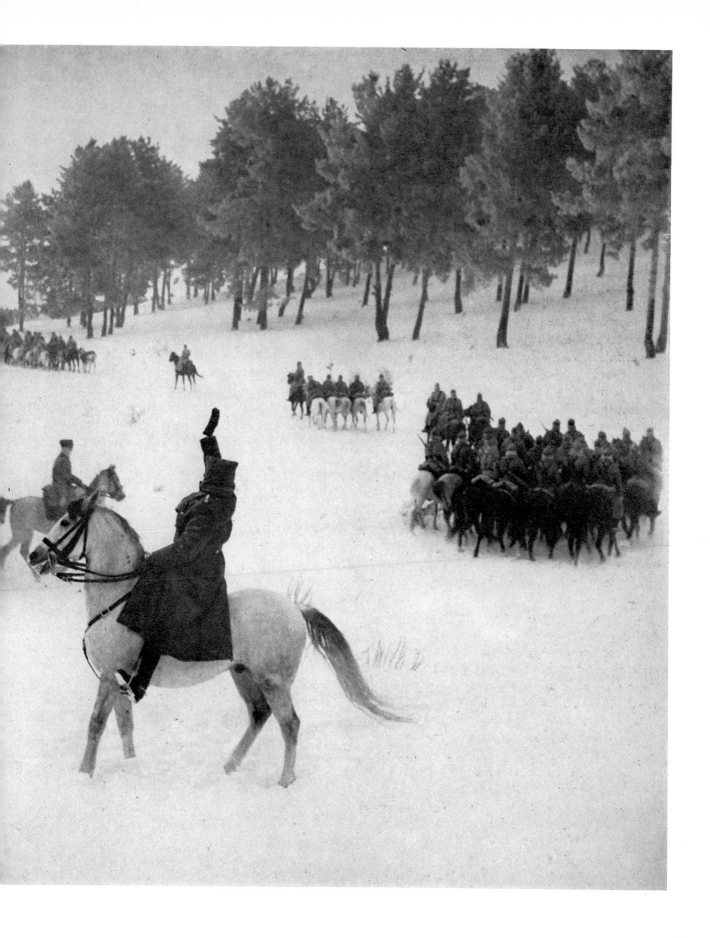

In 1956 he quit *Life* to join *Collier's* and go with John Gunther to Russia. When *Collier's* closed, he sold to *Life* the color pictures he had taken of Russian art treasures, to the *Saturday Evening Post* the brazen portraits he had taken close-up with flash of the Kremlin hierarchy, and to *Look* magazine another photograph for a cover. A book also resulted from this trip—*The Kremlin*, which was published in 1960, and republished with additions as *Treasures of The Kremlin* in 1969.

In 1957 Duncan lived in Picasso's chateau in Cannes for months, producing a unique picture story about the great Spanish artist that proved a best seller in half a dozen languages. *Picasso's Picassos*, a magnificent book of colorplates of paintings withheld by Picasso from the world's art markets, was published in 1963. The works reproduced were the paintings to which Picasso is personally the most attached; some day they will be the core collection of a Picasso museum.

A trip to Paris in 1965 resulted in a color sequence of multiple, repeated images for which *McCall's* paid $50,000, the highest price ever paid for a single picture story.

In 1966, to close the record of a photographer who had reached the half-century mark, Duncan published *Yankee Nomad*, the autobiography of a gentle, dedicated artist who had clothed his life with violence. The record was not to be closed, however, for fate decreed that in August 1967 he would sign with *Life* and ABC to cover the war in Vietnam. Fifty-one years of age or not, he felt that whenever American marines took to the field, anywhere in the world, it was his duty to be among them, patiently securing a distinguished pictorial record that told the world what those determined men endure by their own choice.

Duncan was revolted and disillusioned by what he experienced with the marines at Khesanh, and wrote a thoroughly angry book, *I Protest*, published in 1968. *I Protest* denounced the political and military direction of the war and the sufferings inflicted upon the Vietnamese people. This great book of the war might well have become a handbook for peace-loving Americans, but it appeared on the very day that President Johnson announced his intention of de-escalating the conflict and seeking a negotiated settlement. In the future, perhaps, "Lucky" Duncan, the chronicler of man-to-man mortal combat, will photograph only art and artists.

The uncaptioned pictures which follow were taken by David Douglas Duncan in the Korean War during 1950. All, courtesy Life Magazine, copyright Time, Inc.

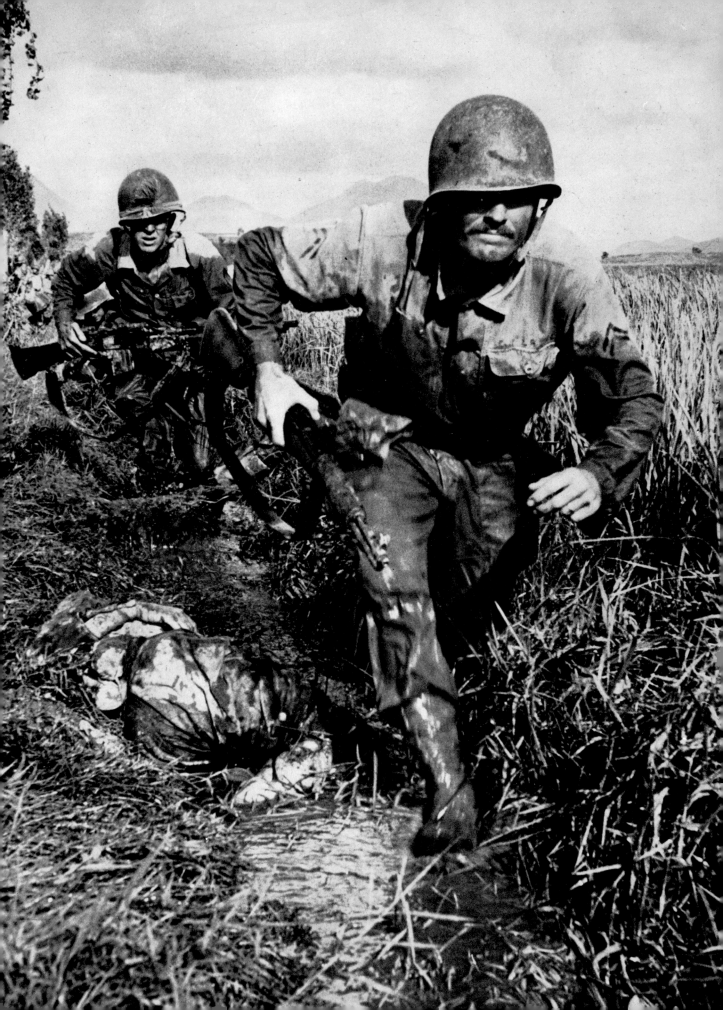

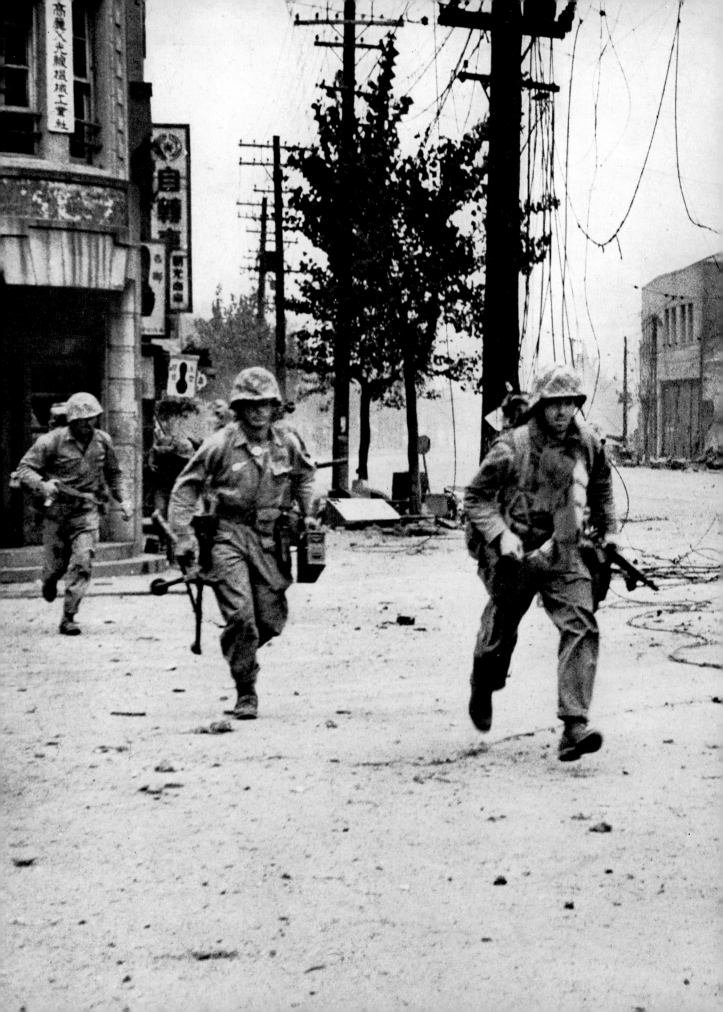

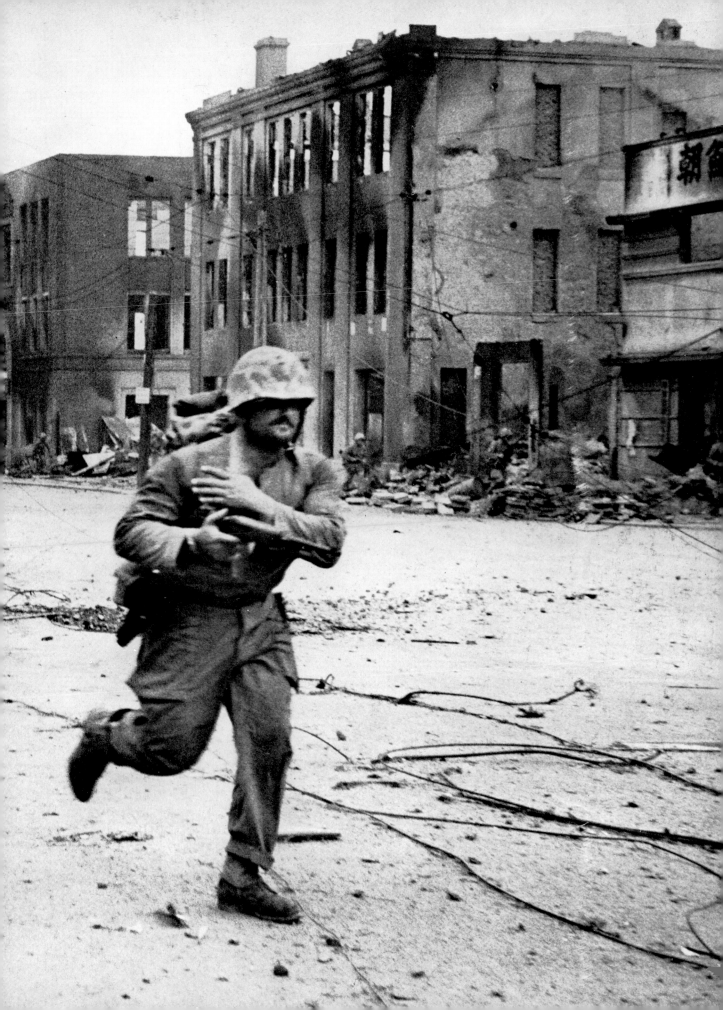

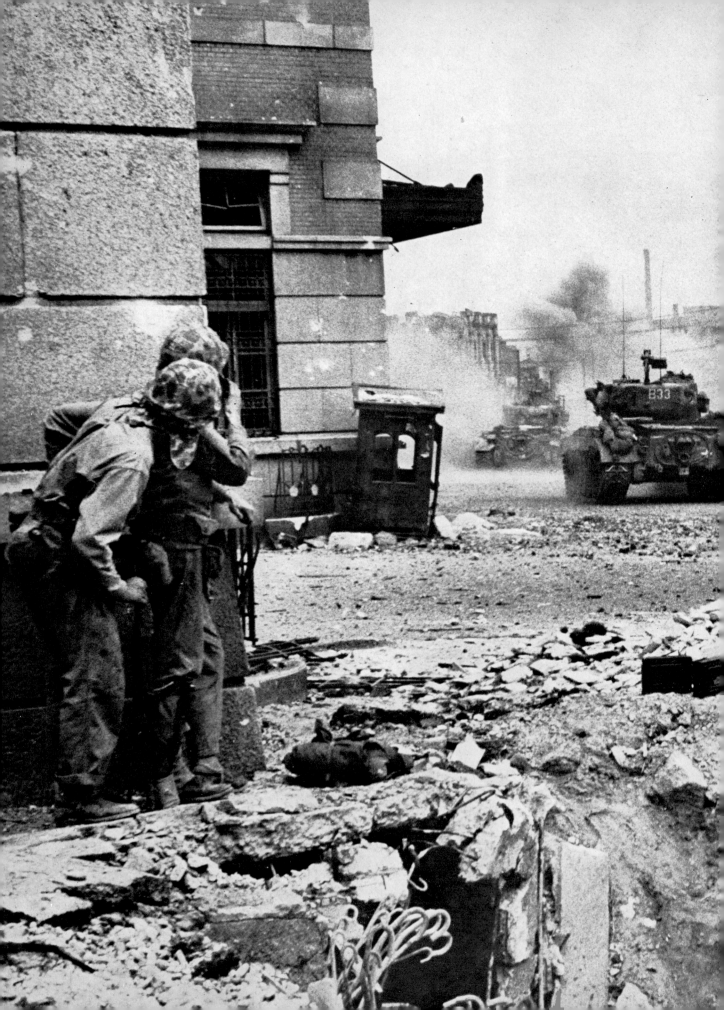

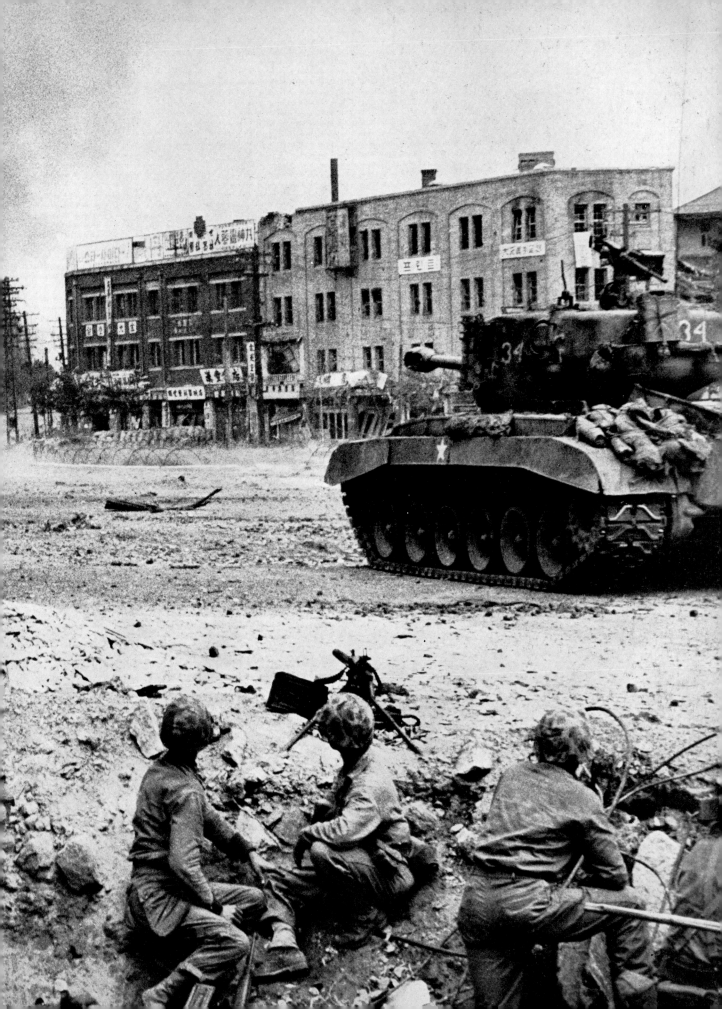

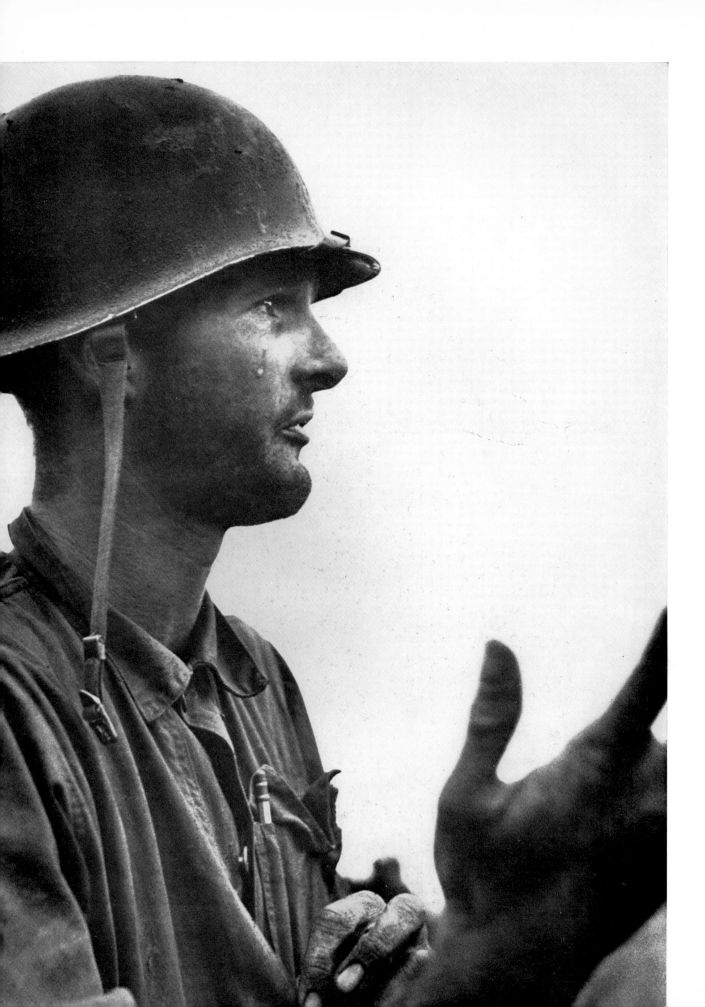

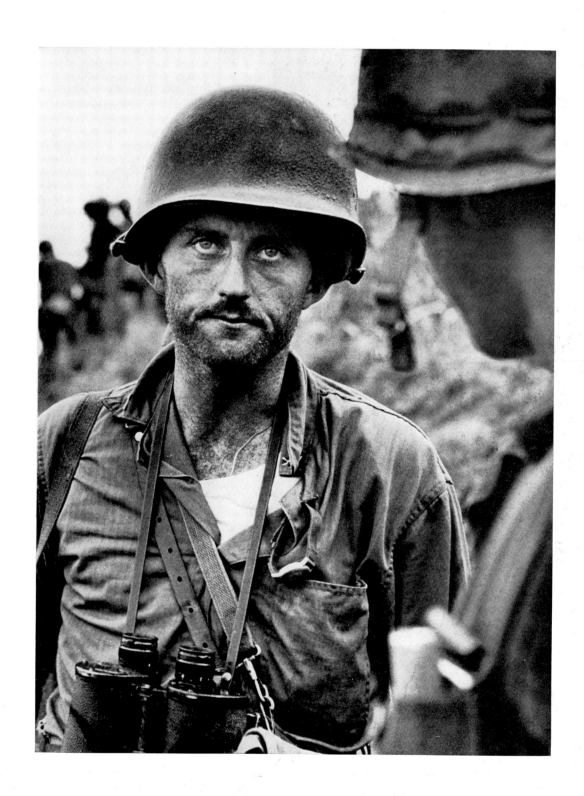

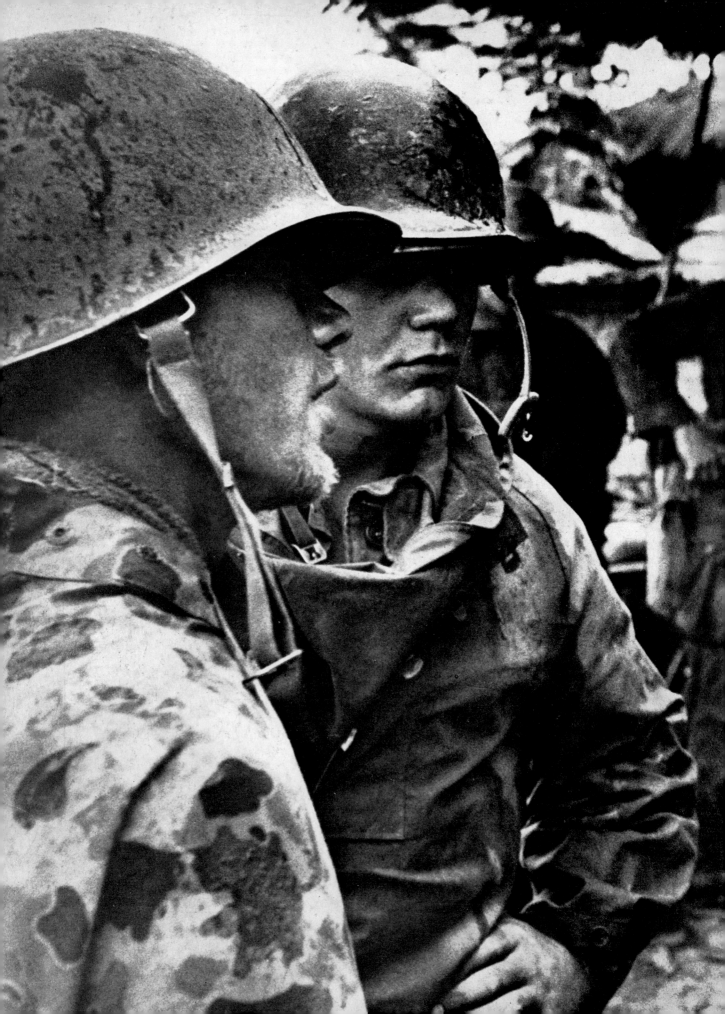

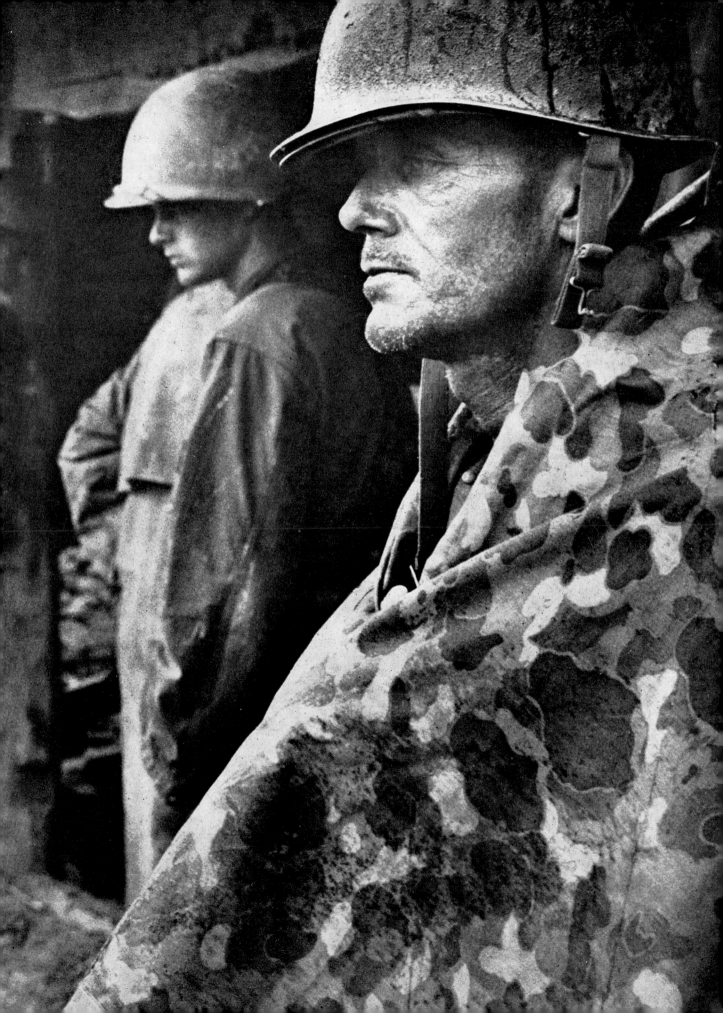

CHAPTER 39

Brassai's Probing Vision

GYULA HALASZ he was christened. The year 1899; the place Brasso, Transylvania. To the world of photography he is Brassai, a Frenchman. That is as he would have it though he has taken the town in which he was born for his name. French literature, painting, theater, and the city of Paris he loves as did his father, who had studied at the Sorbonne and had become professor of French literature at the University of Brasso. He brought the future photographer to Paris at the age of four. They lived there a year and the boy, too, fell under the spell of the city. He was taken to the popular theatre, to the Champs-Elysées, the Grand Boulevard, and the Bois; he saw the horses and carriages, the people parading in the Luxembourg Gardens and eating in the markets and restaurants where he sat with his father. (The father in 1968—aged 92—has begun at long last writing his autobiography.) This was the year that formed his future.

Twenty years later he came back, after two years' study at the École des Beaux-Arts in Budapest and an additional two years' study at the Art Academy in Berlin. Strangely, for the next eight years, he left art for journalism. To pin down certain aspects of Paris after dark he borrowed a camera from a fellow Hungarian, André Kertesz a well-known photographer in Paris.

"Why didn't you sketch what you wanted as illustrations?" I recently asked Brassai. "Why did you turn to photography?"

He answered, "How I became interested in photography reminds me of a story Isadora Duncan once told me. She was in love with an extremely wealthy man she called Lohengrin. He hired for her an accomplished pianist who played perfectly as an accompanist to her dances but whom she detested. His face drove her to such distraction that she had a screen placed between them when she practiced. Her disaffection grew steadily worse. One day they found themselves in a carriage sitting opposite each other, face to face; there was no avoiding him. It was a rough, curving road. The carriage came to an abrupt stop and she was catapulted into his arms. She said to me, 'I stayed there; I understood it was to be the greatest love of my life. In fact for years he had rooms in another part of Lohengrin's castle.'"

Brassai ended the story, "So too with me and the camera. I once detested her."

He haunted the streets entranced with what he saw through his camera. What he saw was too much for his pencil or brush; only the camera, he knew, could capture the whole fantastic world of Montparnasse. It was there he went night after night for months, for years. The paving stones, the bridges, the tourists, and the people who lived in the district he met in his wanderings, all took on a special meaning for him and his lens. He was searching for truthful photography. In 1921, from among the thousands of pictures he had taken, a publisher put together a book, *Paris de Nuit*, which rapidly sold out. A reviewer wrote, "Among the thousands of photographs that could be taken from the same point of view, there is one, signed Brassai, that gives the impression of freshness, of something new born through its style."

Publishers, impressed with the success of this book wanted Brassai to do London, Berlin, Rome at night. Brassai said he didn't want to become a specialist in any one kind of photography, that he had exhausted the theme of city streets at night. He started to photograph people indoors, what they did, how they lived, people dancing, people kissing, unaware of him and his camera.

"I make no comments with my camera," he says. "My camera sees all the different kinds of people and with impartiality transfixes them on the negative. Here they are, the apaches, the male and female homosexuals, the eccentrics. Whatever I see and I feel about people the camera sees—this is the result."

It became his second book. It was supposed to have been a big book with text by M. MacOrlan, but a mercenary publisher issued hastily an inadequate, plastic-bound, popular-priced booklet, *Voluptes de Paris*. Said Brassai, "I am so ashamed of this volume I never mention it in my list of books." Nevertheless, it contains an invaluable collection of his essential pictures probing the night life of Paris, curiously unsalacious despite the subjects. Here is a photographer with daring vision, profound in his understanding of people and their environment, of the prosaic, the incongruous, the ridiculous. His unfailing eye discovers his kind of a picture. He shows us glimpses down the side streets and alleys he knows intimately; he has been called "the eye of Paris." It is a revelation of every stratum. "The creative moment," Brassai has said, "lies in the selection of the subject."

The day that the Nazis entered Paris, June 13, 1940, Brassai left the city by subway. He took cover in the fields from the low-flying planes that were machine-gunning the roads as he walked and hitchhiked his way to Cannes 400 miles away. He would perhaps have sat out the occupation on the Riviera had he not happened to fall into conversation with a fellow tenant of the apartment building they shared in Paris. He learned that the basement where he had hidden his negatives was not waterproof. The security of a decade's work became more important than his own safety. He returned to Paris and rescued his negatives.

During the occupation his kind of photography was curtailed, and he resumed sketching. He drew Amazon-proportioned figures, emphasizing continued rounds and curvaceous forms of the nude. He showed these drawings to Picasso, who said, "Why did you give up drawing for the camera, Brassai? You have a gold mine and instead you exploit a silver mine." An exhibition of his drawings was held in 1945 at Renou et Colle Gallery; the artist Segonzac bought one. The fish-eye view of the camera can be detected as an influence in his sketches of the nude figure, a heightened triangular composition with limbs and thighs exaggerated as in some ancient fertility sculpture. An edition of his drawings with a poem by Jacques Prévert was published. Later he executed immense straight photographic backdrops for Prévert's ballet, "Le Rendezvous," which were considerably praised in Paris and London where the ballet was seen for several years.

During the occupation he turned also to sculpture, experimenting in three-dimensional stone carvings of the nude figure. The bulky flowing forms and solidity of sculpture taught him to see figures in space and to achieve a similar rounded effect in his two-dimensional photographs.

Brassai, like the well-rounded man of the Renaissance, has been able to create in all the arts. A poem entitled *Histoire de Marie* is a Surrealist-Existentialist work in which he attempts to produce the mood of night life in Paris "by ear, not by eye." I prefer the eye of Brassai. Henry Miller writes, in his preface to *Marie*, "There's not a subject of which he has not some knowledge . . . A wall covered with scribbled drawings can absorb his attention as much as the Venus de Milo."

New York's Museum of Modern Art, during 1956 exhibited a series of Brassai's *graffiti*, photographs of the scrawls and carvings he found on the walls of Paris. Symbols of what the young in the streets think, the *graffiti* show animals, birds, faces, gallows, hearts and arrows, and two black hollows that inevitably become empty sockets of staring death heads. Ever the consummate craftsman, Brassai waited for the cross lighting of the late afternoon sun to secure detail and deep, dramatic shadows on the wall.

Still another graphic art Brassai attempted was the motion picture; he made a twelve-minute film in the Paris zoo, which is now being circulated in American movie theatres. It concerns itself with the movement of animals; there is a ballet sequence of the intricate, graceful movements of giraffes' necks and of chimpanzees swinging from limb to limb, going in and out of focus, and creating weird patterns of flight. In discussing still photography and the cinema, Brassai said, "The true cinema is movement. The photograph is the contrary of movement; it is always the stopping of movement. The screen is always an image in transition, and we demand that it transform itself unceasingly. The fixed image and the arrested image of a single movie frame, is the rectangle of the plastic art where always has been inscribed the artist's drawing, painting and engraving and now photography. Each lives in the shape of the rectangle and adapts itself to it."

Brassai conceives flawless compositions within the rectangle of his Leica and Voigtländer cameras as well as on the square film used by his Rolleiflex. In all his photographs there is a sensitivity to patterns, color values, tensions created between objects in space and an accent of rhythms controlling the entire image. He selects and carefully arranges the visual stimulation which he considers as the isolated image, ever related to the outward dimensions of the picture.

Brassai works differently from the usual documentary photographer. His work is more static; into the instantaneous he injects his unique element of meditation, of revery. He seems not so much interested in the flux and action of a given picture as in holding the image— as in *Crosswalk on the Rue de Rivoli* or *The White Umbrella*.

In Spain several years ago he and his camera secured an absorbing chronicle, a vast photographic panorama of Spanish life published in France as *Seville en fête*.

In the summer of 1957 he was in the United States for the first time. He said, "I have always opposed color in photography, but at the same time I discovered America I discovered color. I've done something different, something distinctive with it, I hope. A new book may result. It is a good way to record life in the places I visit, a living series of pictures of what moves me."

In a lecture Brassai gave before the Societé française de photographie, he said, "To keep from going stale you must forget your professional outlook and rediscover the virginal eye of the amateur. Do not lose that eye; do not lose your own self. The great Japanese artists changed their names and their status ten or even twenty times in their ceaseless efforts to renew themselves . . . it is not right that the originality of that first vision should become a trick of the trade, a formula a thousand times repeated."

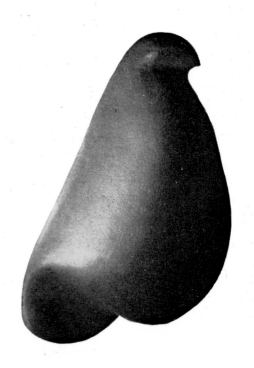

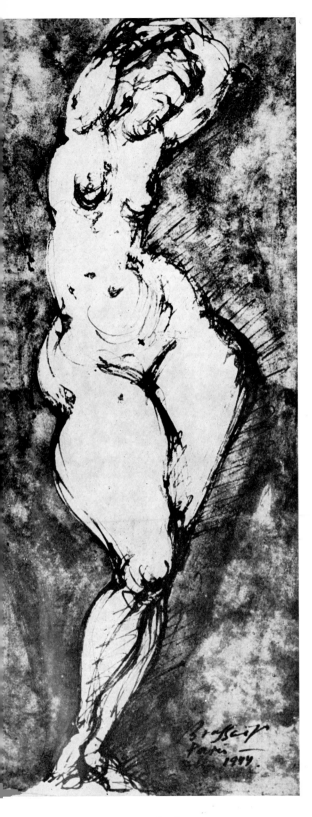

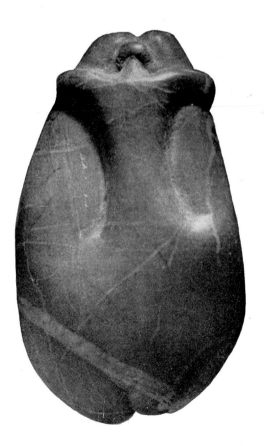

RASSAI, A Drawing and Two Sculptures. *1943-1947.*

Brassai and Picasso became close friends during the Nazi occupation of Paris, when Brassai (illegally) made a photographic record of Picasso's works, which were in danger of confiscation by the enemy. In 1966 Brassai published a biographical memoir centering on the experience: *Picasso & Co.* "If you want to know about me," Picasso has said, "read Brassai's book." It is appropriate that a photographer was the author of *Picasso & Co.*, in which the subject takes his own picture, as it were, through his own recorded words.

In 1967 a comprehensive exhibition of Brassai's works was held in Lacoste, in southern France. Featured in the exhibition were a number of unusual images produced in the 1930s—"transmutations"—Brassai's word for prints he made from photographic glass negatives on which he cut lines and patterns with a sharp tool. The "transmutation," thus, is a combination of a camera image and the *cliché verre* of Corot and Millet. In Brassai's supremely creative hands, both types of image are not only greatly enriched but brought into new and unexpected unity; each such fused image seems almost like a carved form which Brassai has seen as latent in some stone found upon the beach and which he has released from the material that imprisons it. The onlooker cannot fail to be impressed by the inventiveness of this extraordinary man who here epitomizes the protean, gifted amateur whom he himself holds in such great respect.

BRASSAI
below: Backdrop for Ballet "Le Rendezvous," *1947.*
Made from photographs by Brassai.
right: Two Apaches, Paris. *1934.*

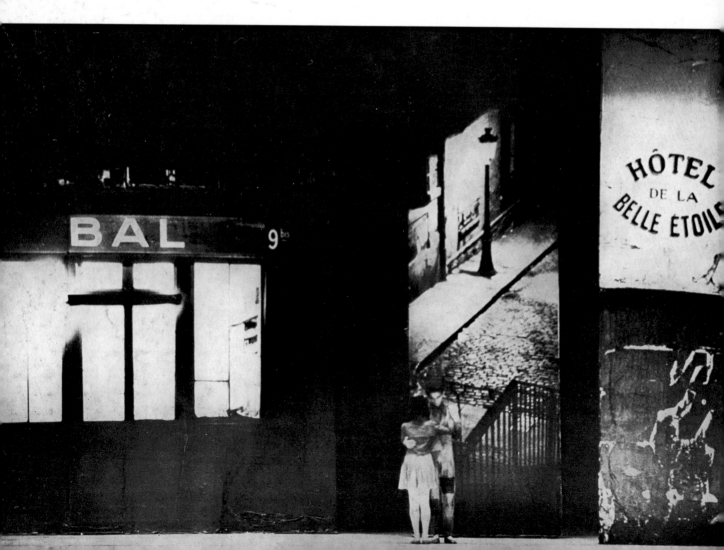

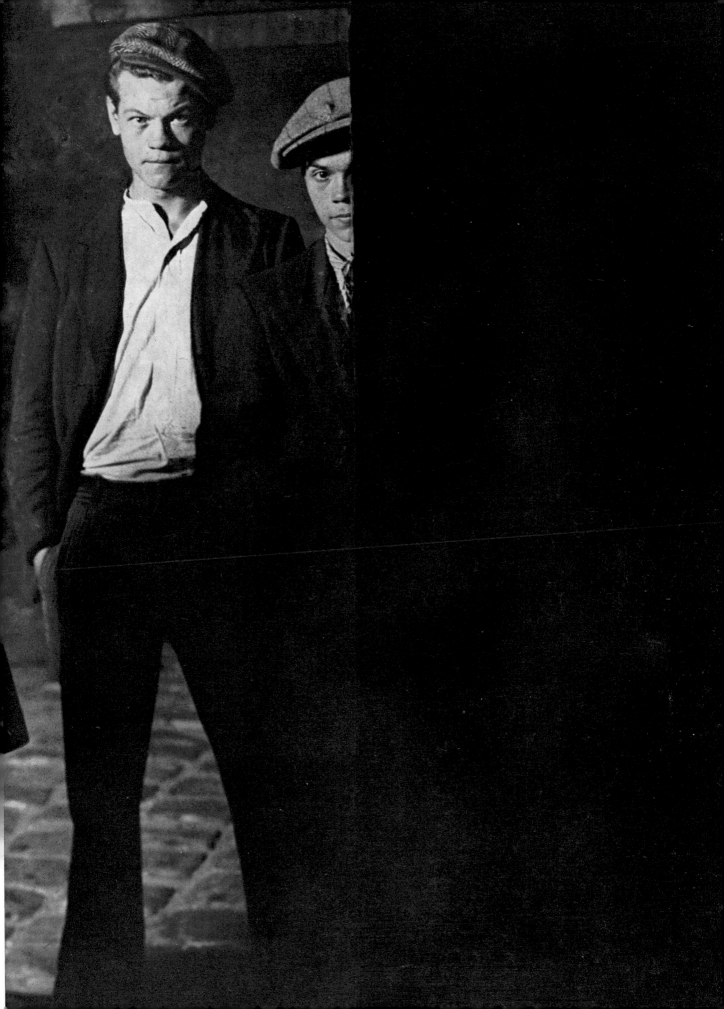

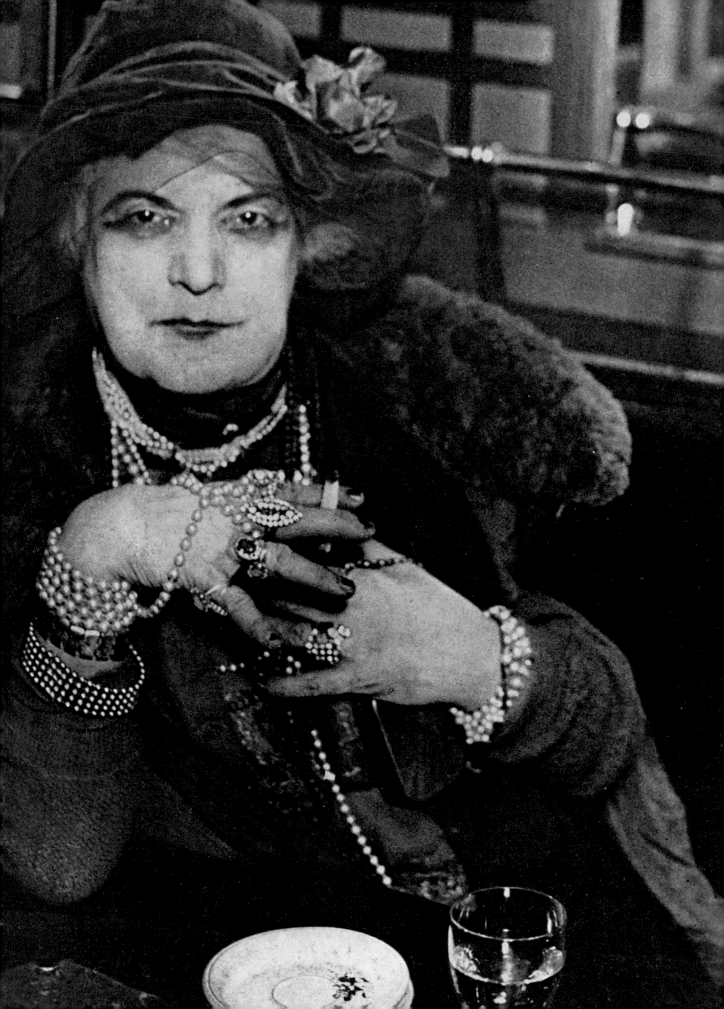

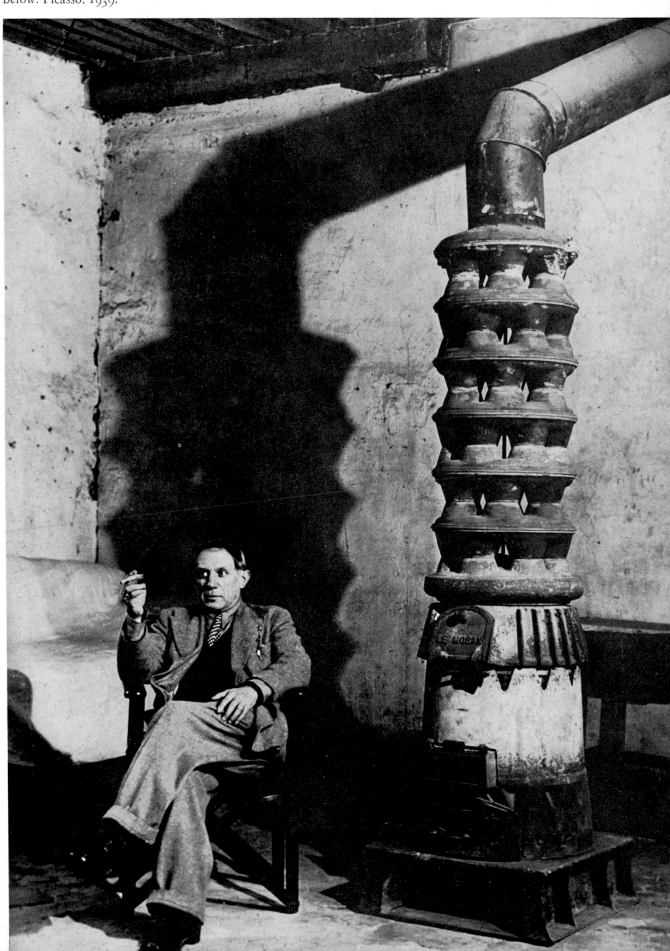

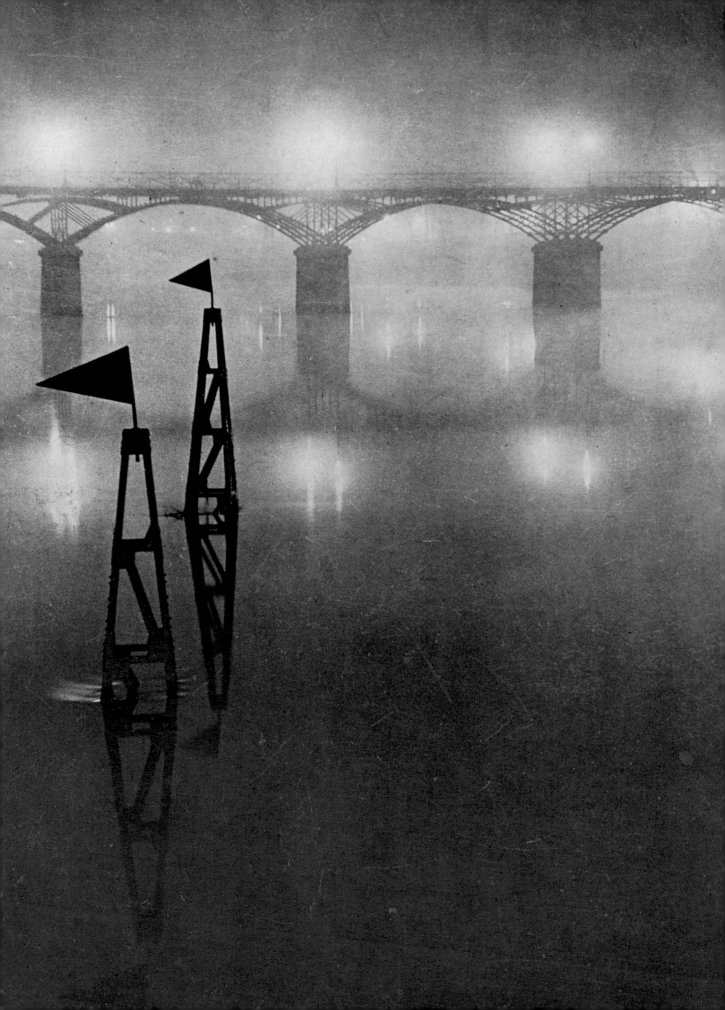

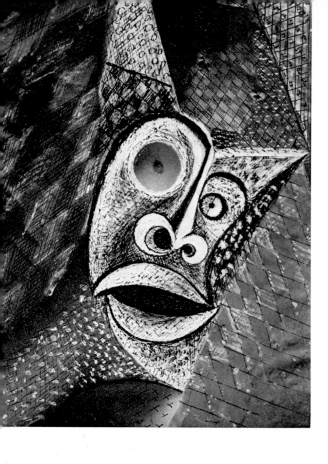

BRASSAI, *left: Transmutation*, Temptation of St. Anthony. 1934.
below: Transmutation, Dreaming Girl. 1934-35.

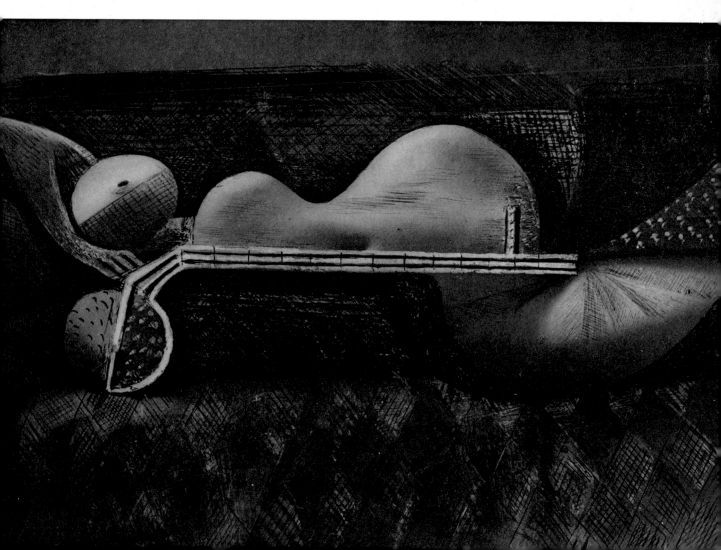

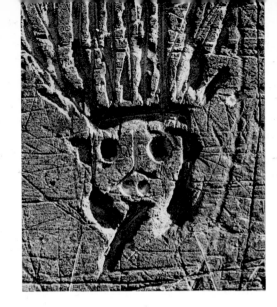
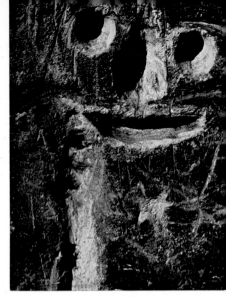
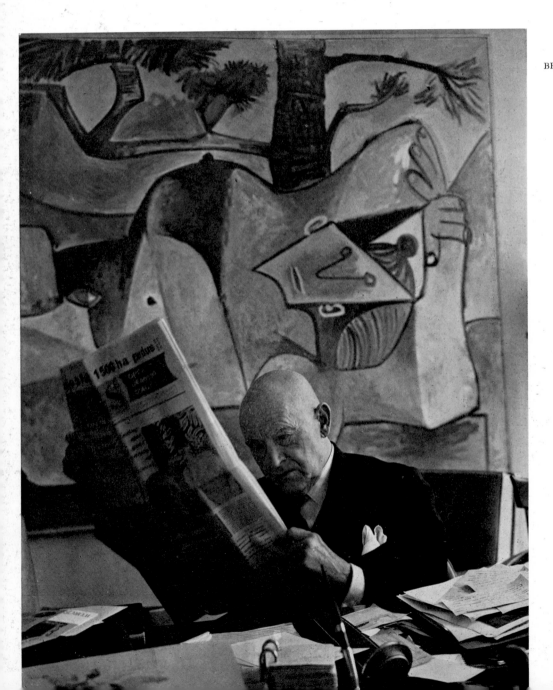

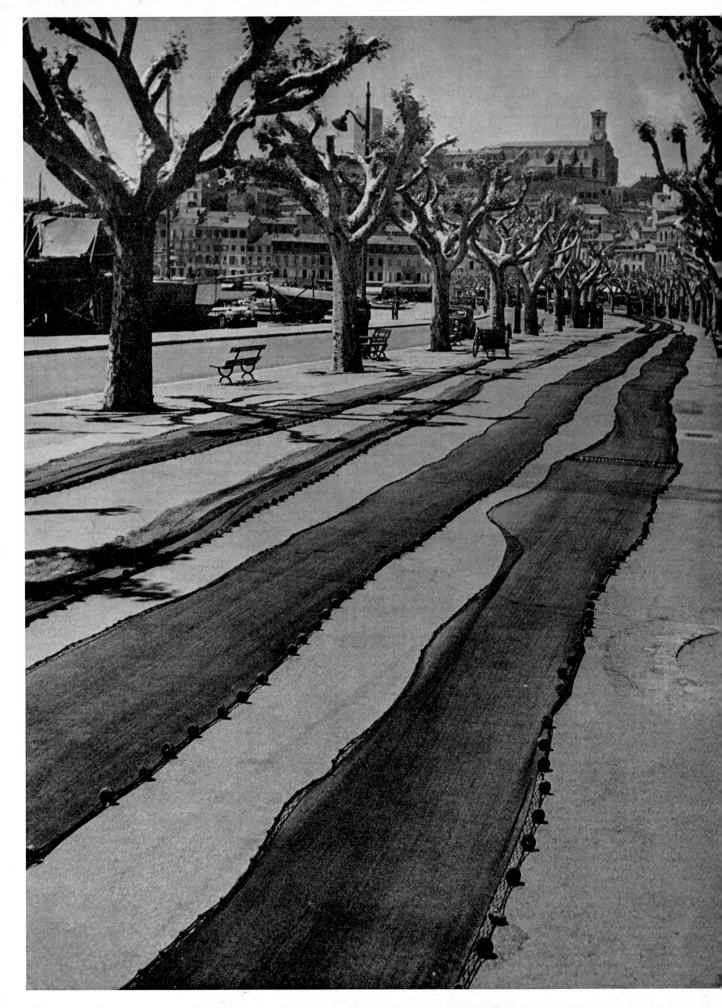

CHAPTER 40

Callahan and Siskind:
The Magic of the Commonplace

HARRY CALLAHAN

HARRY CALLAHAN, whom one critic termed "photog
rapher of the obscure and the insignificant," grows out
of two traditions of photography, the interpretive and
the constructive. The first influence is the tradition o
Edward Weston, Paul Strand, and Walker Evans, inter
preters of the commonplace, who transform into aesthe
tic visions unaesthetic objects found in nature—vege
tables, eroded rocks, etc.—and in the man-made scene—
fences, signs, dilapidated houses, and dirty city streets
The second influence is the tradition of Moholy-Nagy
and Man Ray, creators of photograms, nonobjective
images created in the darkroom by combining and
arranging shapes on a piece of sensitized paper and using
a flashlight to expose.

In Callahan's pictures there is the fusion of these two
traditions, the documentary and the abstract. He di
gested and integrated these influences into a persona
vision, seeing things adventurously and saying them suc
cinctly with his camera.

Callahan opens our eyes to the familiar and the com
monplace: sights of no beauty in themselves he make
beautiful. An upturned waste basket silhouetted in the
dust; a desolate park bench in winter; a water fountain
and a concrete step in the snow; a lowly weed consisting

f three delicate, tapering lines subtle as any seen in a master drawing; all taken with straight photography. With his camera he captures an intimate portrait of the inanimate, which he makes emotionally effective.

His pictures do not show us more and more of nature, like those of many cameramen. Callahan deliberately shows us less; he makes photographic discoveries by reduction, by simplification, and by isolation. The insignificant image becomes important. He has conquered the technical problems of his medium. He experiments with multiple exposures or moves his camera to superimpose images, thereby achieving repeated patterns of varying tones and interplay of lines and movements in the resultant textures.

In all his experiments Callahan retains contact with reality. The exact image cannot be foreseen when a camera is moved or a plate exposed several times, but the accidental effects can be anticipated and controlled. The photographer must take advantage of the accident; often an alert photographer will make the artistic accident repeat itself.

Callahan has a profound feeling for the façades of buildings, of which he makes original graphic statements. The buildings are rarely shown with people; they are peopled with inhabitants who do not show their faces but who make themselves felt—through a window reflection, a fluttering piece of lace curtain, a still life of edibles on a window sill. The building commands us to see what the photographer saw, the proportions, the play of planes, the gradations of tones. The awesome, the fearsome, and the tawdry behind the façade are sensed only upon deeper penetration of the photograph. The emotional intensities in Callahan's photographs come through with a still kind of reticence.

Callahan is not slavishly devoted to nature, with horizon line in place and perspectives respected. The finished photograph is the criterion. This is neither a picture of a trivial natural form nor a record of a dramatic slum dwelling. Unlike Walker Evans's photographs of social criticism, Callahan's pictures carry no social message. His pictures supersede the source of his inspiration: the overstressed and the overdramatic are filtered out; the essence of the subject remains. He stresses single aspects of nature to reveal his artistic purpose: lines simple,

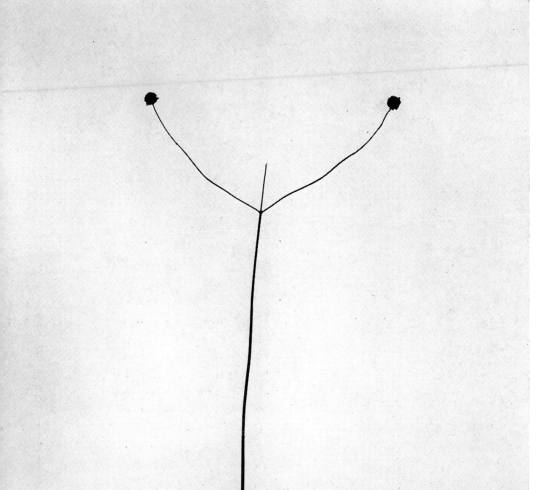

HARRY CALLAHAN
A Weed. 1951.

straight, and of varying breadth, skeins of lines or multiple superimposed lines in various tones, whites permitted to peep through various shades of black and gray. Callahan is concerned to control patterns, textures, rhythms, contrasts, and composition, but, beyond technique, he is involved with an intuitive and sensitive interpretation of his subject.

In Callahan's multiple-exposure pictures of buildings, much as in Cubist paintings, the background and the foreground no longer suggest perspective or depth. The subject is deliberately changed by superimposing several images on the negative so that a repetition of forms appears, multiplied and dislocated but making for dynamic movement in the space of the picture plane.

The image, no matter how hackneyed, commands the camera view, and there is no altering after exposure. Callahan's work repudiates the pictorial, but his photographs are never total abstractions. He stops short of eliminating subject matter entirely. Through his intrinsic artistry and unique vision he has advanced the tradition of photography.

All of his subjects to date have been taken in the United States, mostly in Chicago where he is head of the photography department of the Institute of Design of the Illinois Institute of Technology. In 1957, Callahan received a $10,000 grant from the Graham Fellowship, the largest sum ever awarded a photographer for experimental study. This fellowship enabled him to spend more than a year in Europe, where he continued his investigation of hitherto unseen marvels within commonplace forms in nature, eschewing romantic and historical subjects. Following his return to the United States, an exhibition of his photographs was held by the Museum of Modern Art. In 1964 a comprehensive showing of his work was circulated in Europe, the Far East, and the United States after its first showing in the galleries of the Hallmark Card Co. Since 1963 Harry Callahan has been in charge of the photography department at the Rhode Island School of Design.

All photographs in this section
courtesy Harry Callahan, Chicago.

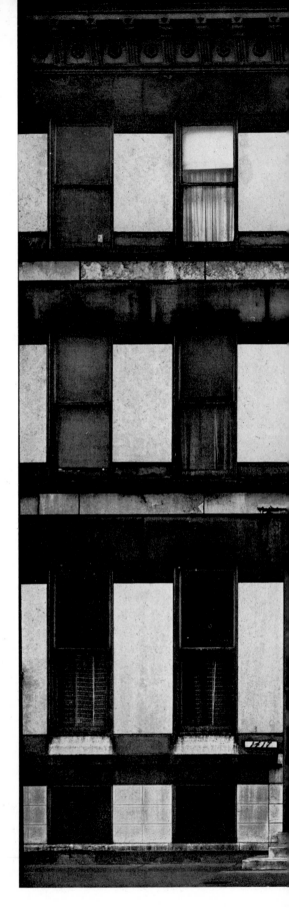

CALLAHAN, Dearborn Street, Chicago. *About 1953.*

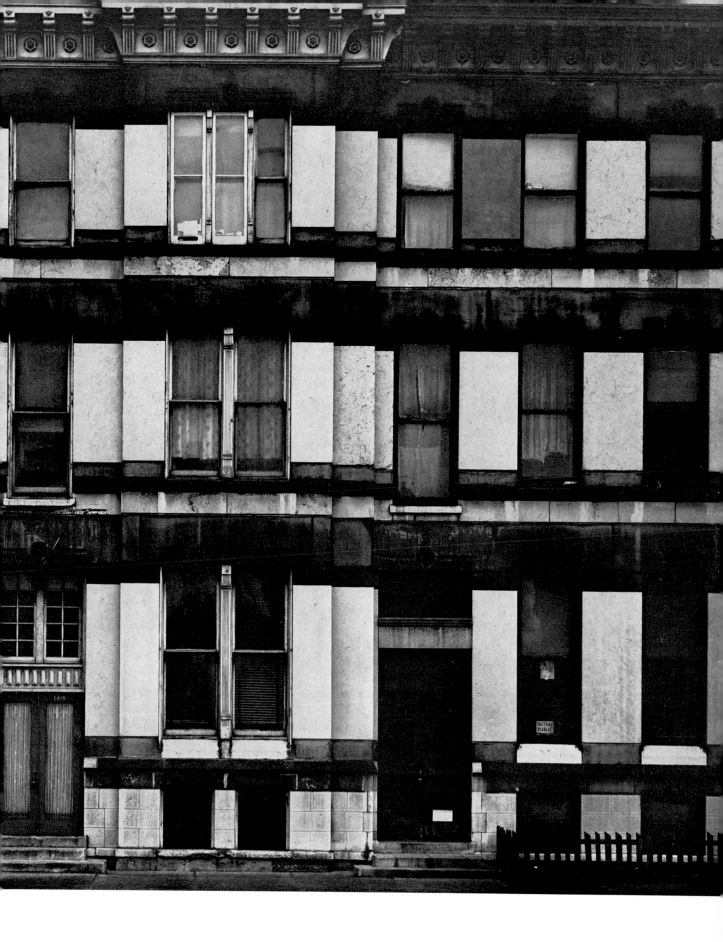

CALLAHAN, *below*: A Plant. *About 1951.*
right: Chicago Loop. *Multiple exposure, 1952.*

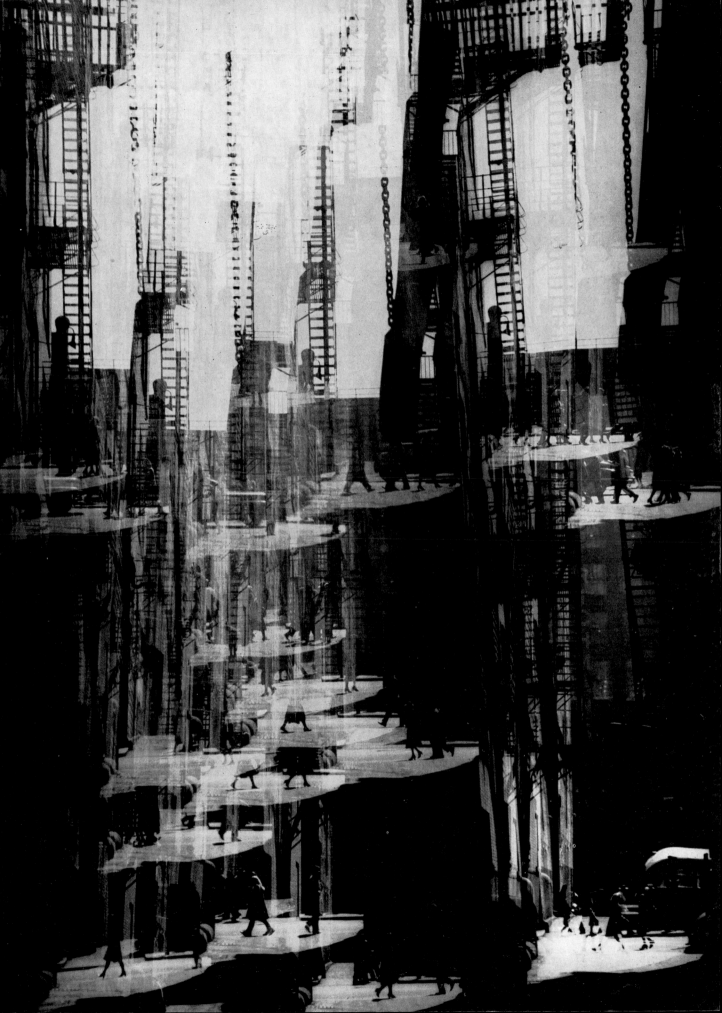

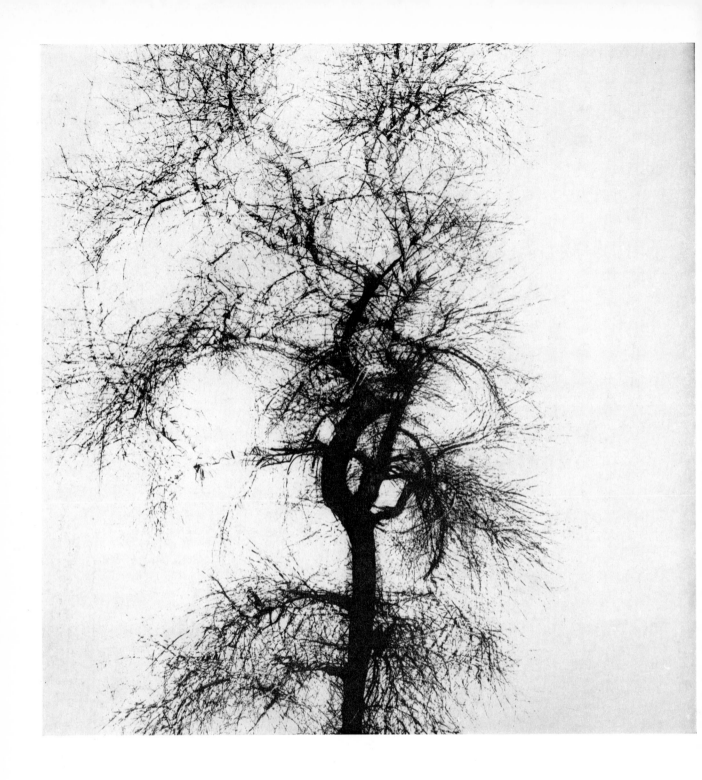

CALLAHAN, *below:* Weeds in Snow. *About 1951.*
left: Tree in Winter. *Multiple exposure, 1956.*

CALLAHAN, Airplane Hangar. *About 1955.*

AARON SISKIND, Degraded Sign. *New York City, 1951.*

AARON SISKIND

AARON SISKIND, just turned sixty years old, was born in New York City. For the past fifteen years he has been teaching at the Institute of Design (founded by Moholy-Nagy as the Chicago Bauhaus, now part of the Illinois Institute of Technology), where he has been one of the powerful influences on the students who are today's avid proponents of modern art and design.

Siskind has not always photographed in his current abstract idiom. He originally won recognition as a documentary photographer, especially for his series depicting New York's Harlem, Martha's Vineyard, and Bucks County, Pennsylvania. He now says about this long apprenticeship in craftsmanship and realism, "I found I wasn't saying anything. Special meaning was not in the pictures but in the subject. I began to feel reality was something that existed only in our minds and feelings."

He turned for this "new reality" to abstract images that he found in lowly objects ordinarily ignored. Siskind's work now bears striking similarity to Abstract Expressionist paintings of our day, particularly to those canvases that emphasize big unrelated forms, nongeometric abstractions, or strong textures and patterns in colors subdued almost to black and white. It is contemporary aesthetics with a camera. The photographer suggests plastic ideas to the painters, just as modern artists such as Willem de Kooning, Robert Motherwell, Franz Kline, James Brooks, and the late Jackson Pollock through their paintings suggest ideas to the photographer. Siskind with his camera, however, does not compete with the brush nor does he attempt to emulate or imitate painting. His work is an idiomatic photographic expression of the *avant-garde* conceptions of modern art.

One great difference between photographer and painter is that Siskind does not make his image in a darkroom; no matter how abstract there is a foothold in reality. One of his motifs, to which he often returns, is the wall. To him it is never just a wall; the various forms seen in the wall come alive. Defaced and marked, the wall asserts itself far more than a blatant neon sign. It commands, like the marked walls of the public gardens in ancient Greece, where everyone was interested in the message; or like a school yard wall covered with messages that have meaning to children. Siskind with his camera seeks to capture meanings, not so much the message as the originality young artists display in making drawings on roughly textured walls with purloined chalk, combined with meaningful words or letters resembling some primitive writing. Wall images have their own reality which Siskind wills into becoming a photograph. He sees the human element in these images and instills it in his pictures. He responds to the shape, form, and mood of a wall and to the feel and sight of weathered wood, jagged glass, peeled paint, rusted metal, sand and seaweed, and to the effect of time and the elements on concrete, paint, paper, plaster, and brick.

Here is invention through selection of nontraditional

visual stimuli. Siskind searches for photographic inspirations in the useless dregs of the city, rejecting the usual formal and accepted motifs. He discloses the excitement to be found in the relationship of irregular blobs and whorls, accidental lines, roughly hewn textures, and broken patterns. The inconsequential comes alive through his artistry. His photographs are personal experiences developed between him and the subject, but the photograph lives as an object apart from the subject. The photograph is a created graphic print. The composition he selects has to have complete unity, the required light and no more, for there is no elimination or retouching once the exposure is made. Siskind photographs what he finds as it lies, without rearranging it. Though the photograph may be nonrepresentational there are movement, repetitious and complementary forms, textures varying from delicate and soft to harsh and violent, gradations of light and shadow, and an over-all design to control the finished result as a work of art.

This is true of all of Siskind's photographs, whether the subject is an oily paper bag, lichens on rocks, weathered billboards, or rusty metals. They are works of art wrested from a surrounding world of junk and chaos. His work transcends the subject, but recognition of the subject heightens the emotional response to his artistic interpretation.

Though Siskind's cryptic ideas may be communicable to comparatively few, the image, with its sensuous surfaces and its structural unity, may readily be enjoyed by many. He recently said of his work, "I regard the photograph as a new object to be contemplated for its own meaning and its own beauty."

Siskind has the rare gift of converting and transforming a subject into a stimulating expression of his own vision, a picture born in the imagination as he discovers it in the abandoned rubbish heaps of the city or in the unimpressive manifestations of nature.

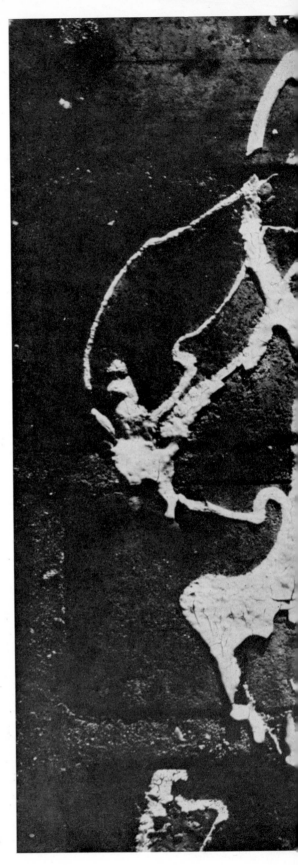

SISKIND, Paint on Brick Wall. *Chicago, 1948.*

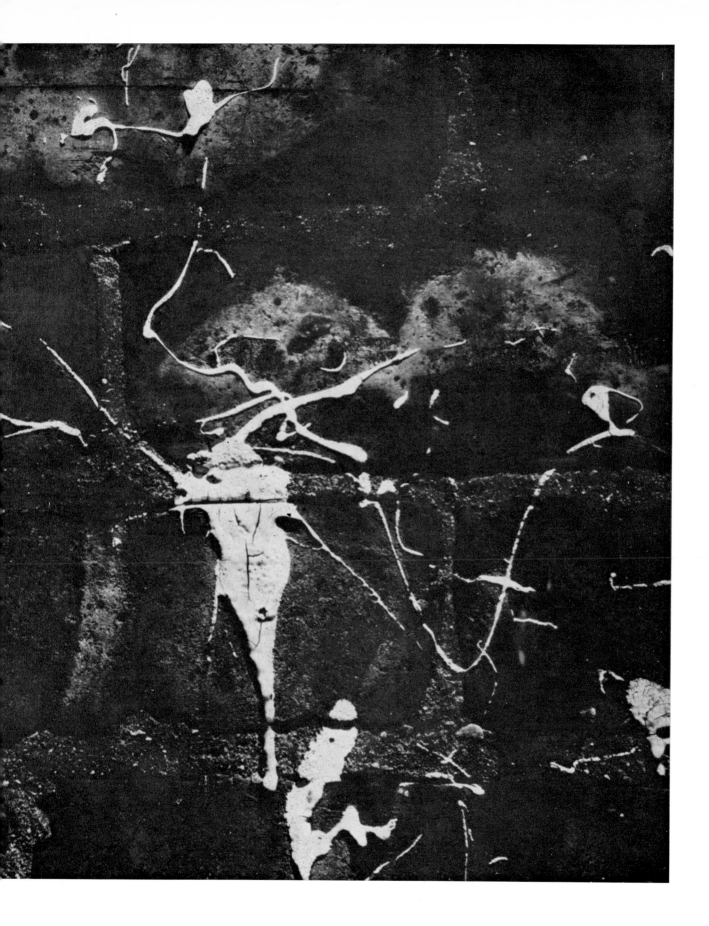

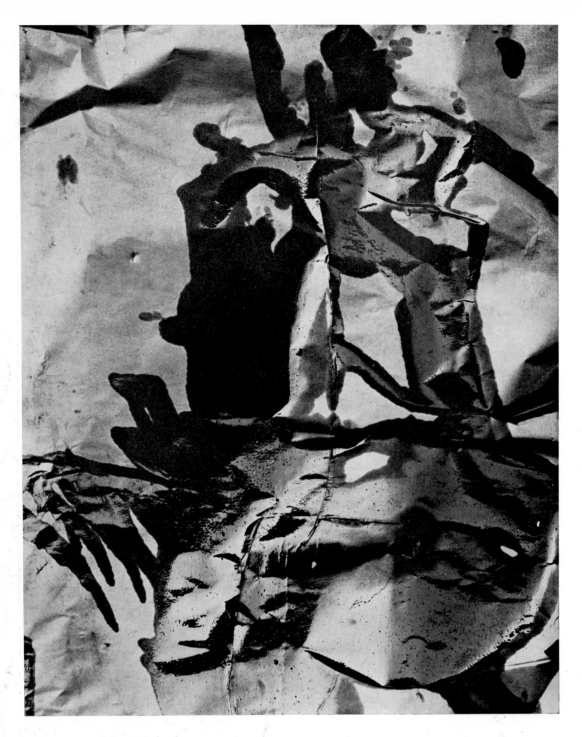

SISKIND, *above:* Oil Stains on Paper. *New York City, 1950.*
right: Stone Fence. *Martha's Vineyard, Massachusetts, 1954.*

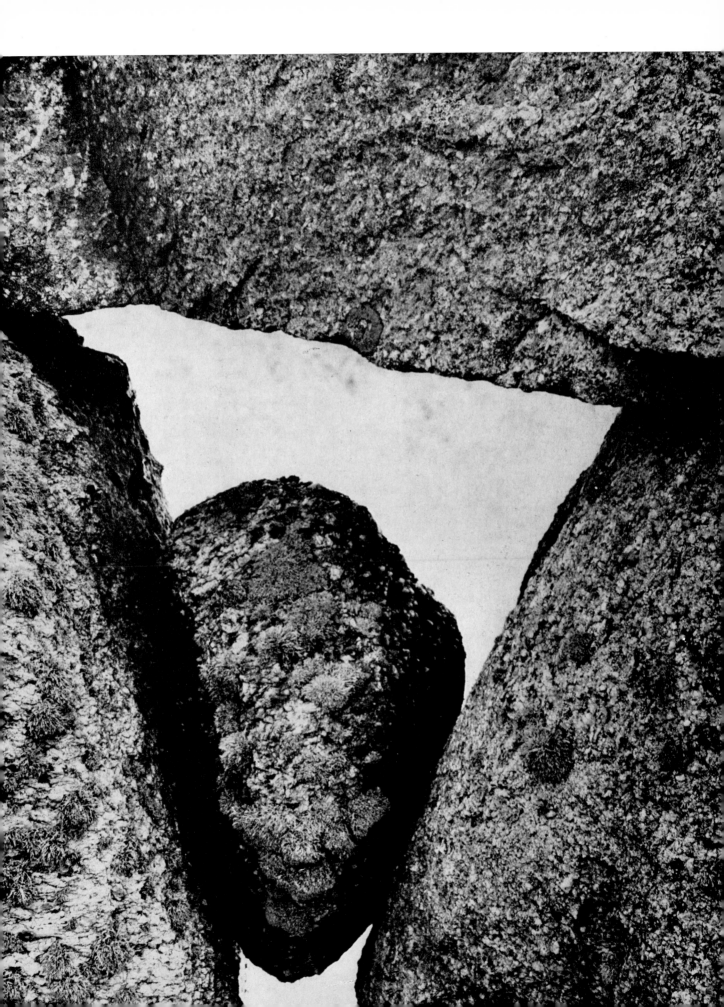

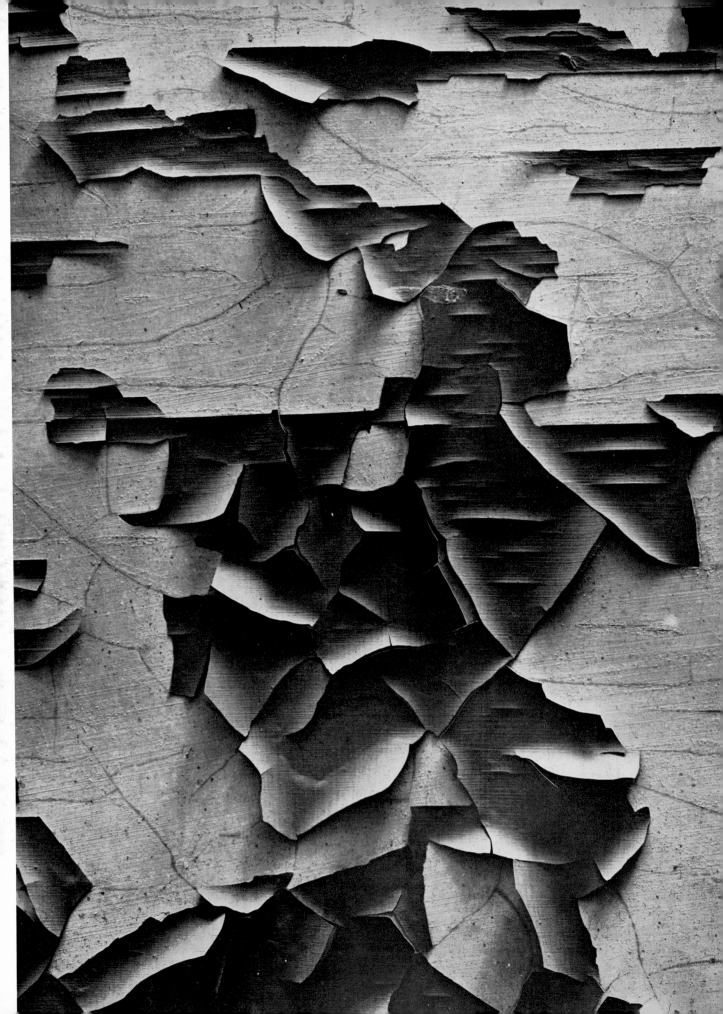

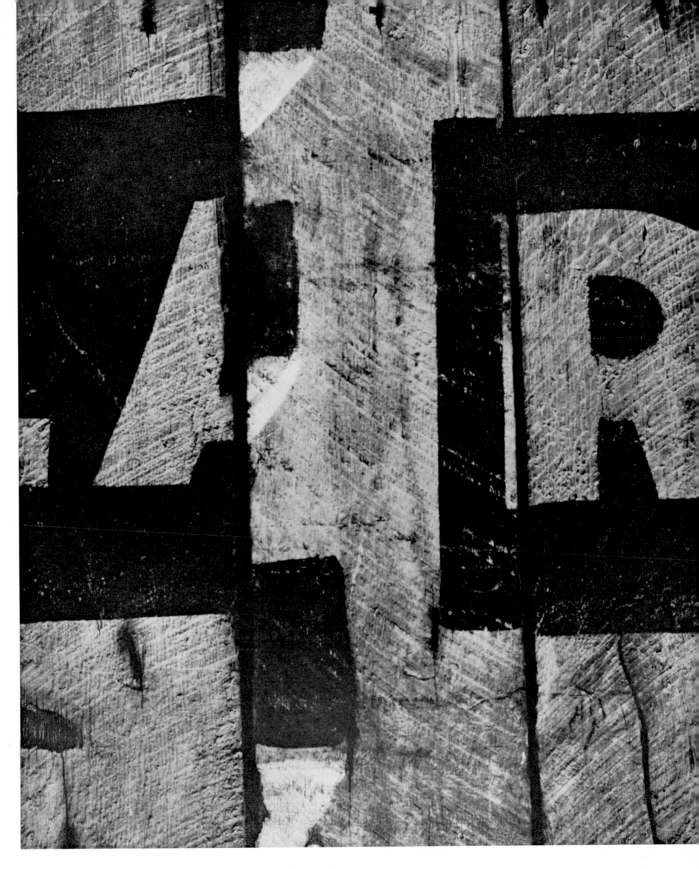

SISKIND, *above*: Scrambled Fence. *Harlan, Kentucky, 1951.*
left: Peeling Paint on Wall. *Jerome, Arizona, 1949.*

SISKIND, *below:* Side of Old Barn. *Martha's Vineyard, Massachusetts, 1947.*
right: Rock by Ocean. *Gloucester, Massachusetts, 1944.*

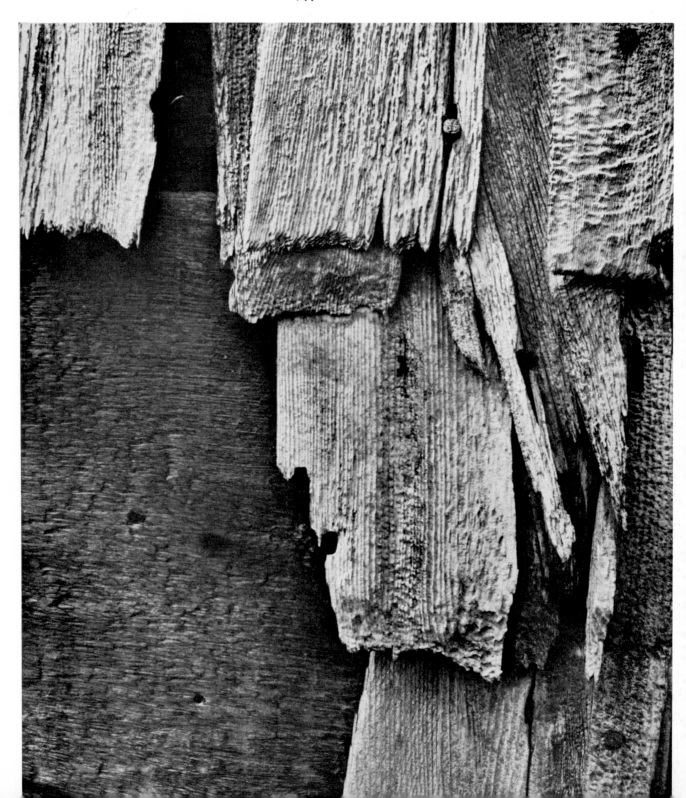

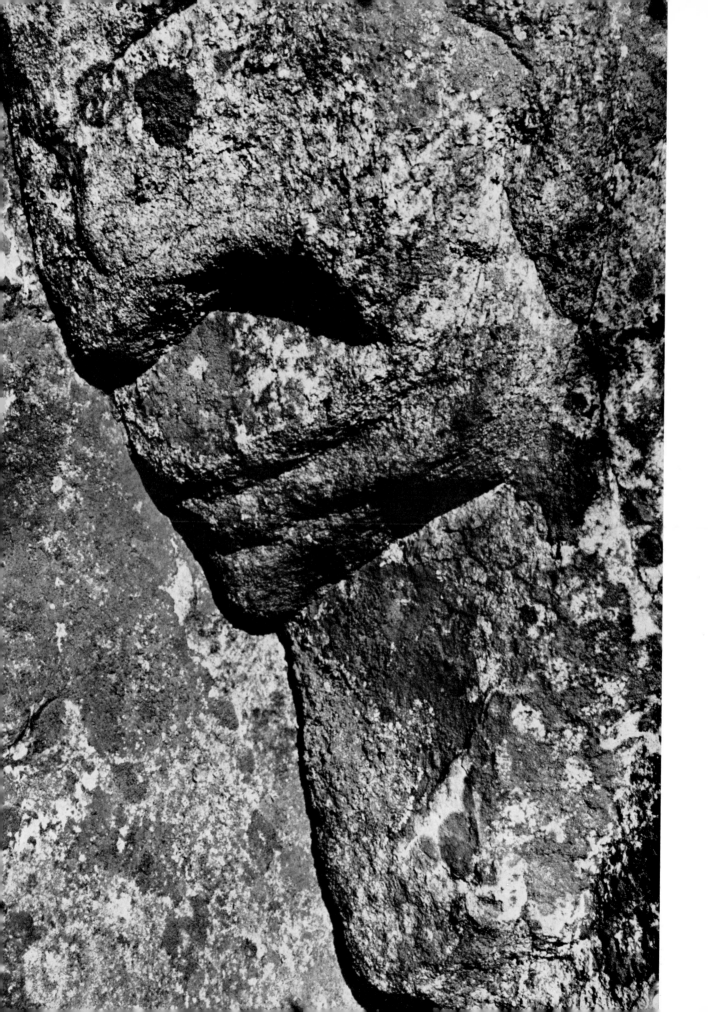

CHAPTER 41

Van der Elsken: Storyteller in Photographs

GREENWICH VILLAGE can never equal the Left Bank of Paris and, in particular, the district of Saint-Germain des-Prés. No other place on earth means what the Left Bank has meant to the artist, the student, the expatriate, the "would-be," and the "flawed."

The romantic mood of Trilby or Tricotrin in Leonard Merrick's *Chair on the Boulevard* is now faded. F. Scott Fitzgerald's lost generation has gone; rich Canadians and Argentinians have replaced the sons and daughters of America's industrialists who once gloried in the reckless life that was "Parisienne" in the roaring twenties. The district still supports the studio of Moreau and the Atelier Suisse, but the ateliers of the late Fernand Léger and Ossip Zadkine are now close by; and in the Beaux Arts more foreigners are enrolled than French students.

The district, despite all these changes and despite inflation of the franc, still has its seventh-floor single rooms at $2 a week with water and toilet three floors down; but there is a difference. Instead of a Mimi or Rudolph dwelling in the garrets there is a photographer, who hauls his water up three perilous flights of stairs to develop his negatives.

Ed van der Elsken was a photographer who in 1950 did not have $2 for one of these rooms. When he arrived in Paris he was less than twenty-five years old. In his native Amsterdam he had been an art student, had endured the Nazi occupation, and, at the end of the war, had turned to the camera. A year of darkroom work, and he was a ready-made free-lancer with no jobs.

In Paris he slept first under the bridges amidst the offal and filth of the derelicts, the "clochards" of the Seine. He learned quickly to rest during the long night sitting in a café chair. He listened to the youths of the district speaking their own peculiar brand of French, and once in a while he took a picture, unobserved. He had only two rolls of 35mm film when he arrived. He made each shot count and he held on to his Leica even when he was starving. Night after night he sat in the cafés, observing, taking his few precious pictures. Then one morning he went to work. He had tried to write, but words were not sharp enough for his tastes. A 1.5 lens was, and he needed film. He found work in a photographer's darkroom where he did every conceivable kind of job. It was all to the good; he learned many subtleties in technique that he applied to his own work.

He found a seventh-floor room; took a job as a photographer—correspondent for a Dutch paper, taking pictures he disliked—but it released him from being what he termed a "darkroom slave." He now had time to take photographs day and night. He started to assemble a direct, unposed, total picture of youth in Saint-Germain-des-Prés. The district by now had forgotten he had a camera in his hands. He took thousands of pictures, filing each negative carefully. Editors who saw these prints were not interested. The papers back home wanted pictures of visitors in front of the Eiffel Tower or the Opera. These hack sales kept him going.

A picture story began in his mind one night when he met an attractive young girl from Australia who had come to Paris with ambitions to become a singer. Here was a girl who seemed to symbolize all the rebellious young talent annually drawn to the fabled Latin Quarter. He took pictures of her with the many men she attracted, art students, American sailors, Senegalese musicians, and

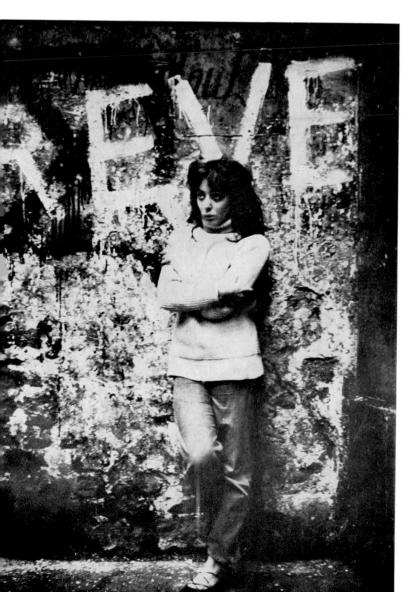

*All photographs in this chapter courtesy
Ed van der Elsken, Amsterdam.*

ED VAN DER ELSKEN, "Dreams" in Saint-Germain-des-Prés. *1953.*

the man who convinced her to shout a song in a café rather than sing it on a stage.

Van der Elsken followed her for two years with his camera. He took pictures of her smoking marijuana, of her drunk and of her sober. He caught her in all her moods, and the camera worshipped her beauty. In his hand it never lied; he made it tell what the lens saw, honestly. She had become so accustomed to his being there that she was unaware of his camera. It pictured her wearing a turtle-neck sweater that emphasized her bizarre beauty; it captured an unexpected picture of narcissism as she contemplated her soft-cheeked reflection in a frighteningly pitted mirror and as she kissed her intoxicated, Medusa-haired likeness in a rain-steamed window.

She tried a song-and-dance act teamed with another girl. Paris cafés pay little, but the experience was new, something different. The shocking became hilarious and the Existentialist caves welcomed the diversion. Painters found her a fascinating model.

She planned to stay in Paris, but one day in 1953 she left the Left Bank—fortunately not before Van der Elsken had caught his final picture of her. "Pregnancy and Saint-Germain-des-Prés wouldn't work," she told him. She went home.

In 1967 she was being shown as "Vali—the Witch of Positano" in a film at the Bleecker Street Cinema, New York. "A creature of nighttime streets," George Plimpton was quoted as saying of her, "a missing link. A personalization of something torn and loose and deep-down primitive in all of us."

He stayed on, photographing what he vowed would be a complete picture of the district. And then he, too, suddenly was gone. He was home in Holland. He had his story, but no editor wanted it. "Too immoral, too stark," they said. The story told itself in pictures. It needed only a few words. He would write them himself and perhaps it would make a book, he reasoned. Book publishers thought so too. A *Love Story in Saint-Germain-des-Prés* appeared in Dutch in 1956, a novel in pictures of people's lives graphically portrayed and told without moralizing or sensationalism.

An autobiographical novel in pictures gleaned from the tremendous number of Van der Elsken's negatives is still to be published as *We Wait Till This Door Opens*. It was preceded by another picture book titled *Bagara* gleaned from months spent with a tribe in central Africa in the heart of the sub-Sahara.

The complete picture book, a story to be read in pictures with a few words merely to indicate direction, is a comparatively new art form in photography. Van der Elsken uses this demanding medium like a novelist, describing a cast of characters, a place, a mood, time, plot,

VAN DER ELSKEN
right: Singing with the Senegalese. 1953.
opposite page: Students in the Café. 1952.

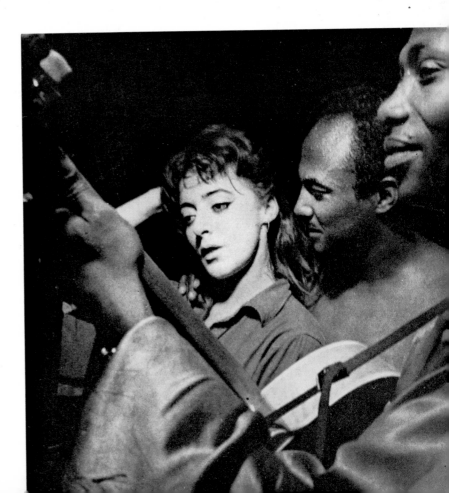

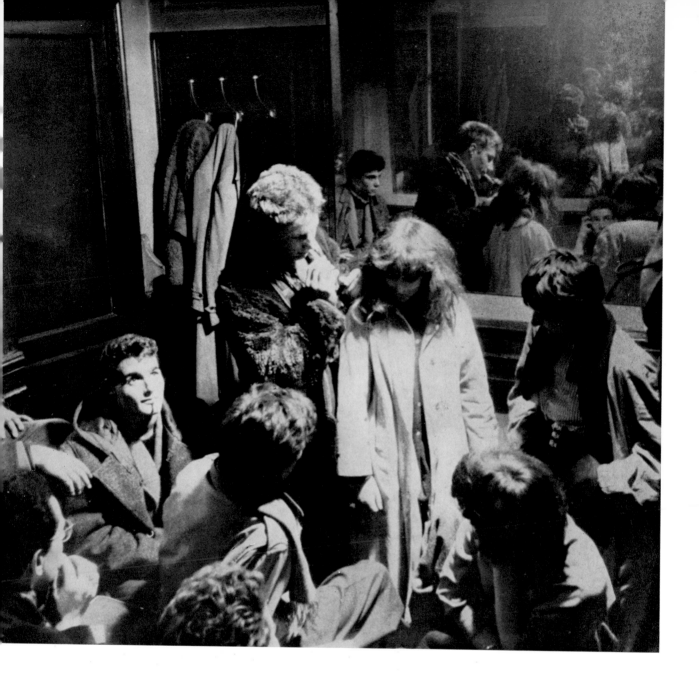

nd dramatic development. Van der Elsken's unique picture style appeals long after the story is fully understood, for he does not pose or direct the subjects; there s nothing faked in his story. The camera discloses the many-faceted character of each individual. The writing does not influence the pictures; the text exposes related acts while the pictures disclose the meaning and feeling nd are entities in themselves. The result is a book of pictures with some few words of text that function like illustrations in a novel; the pictures carry the story and ave a life of their own.

Holland accepts Van der Elsken in 1968 as one of her fine artist-photographers. Several years ago a Dutch television station and a shipping line enabled him and his wife to circumnavigate the globe with cameras and tape recorder. The trip yielded highly dramatic telecasts and an intimate travel book dedicated to the ship *Sweet Life*, on which they traveled through the Philippines. The book is unusual in the travel genre for its deliberate coarse-grain photography, with highlights and halos applied in the darkroom. It shows the beholder harsh and starkly realistic images charged with emotion.

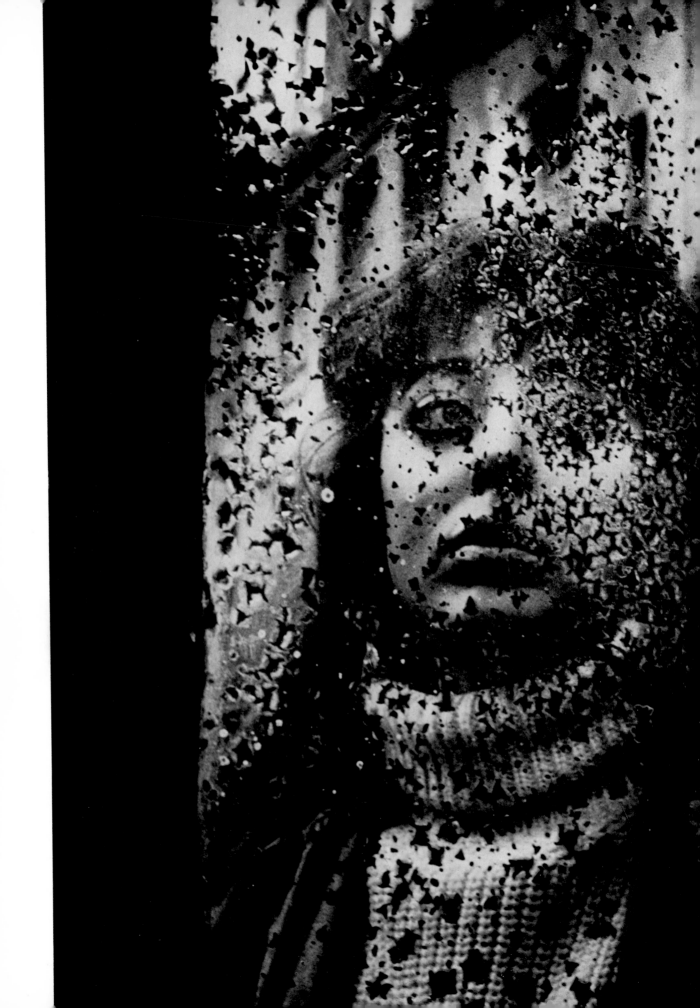

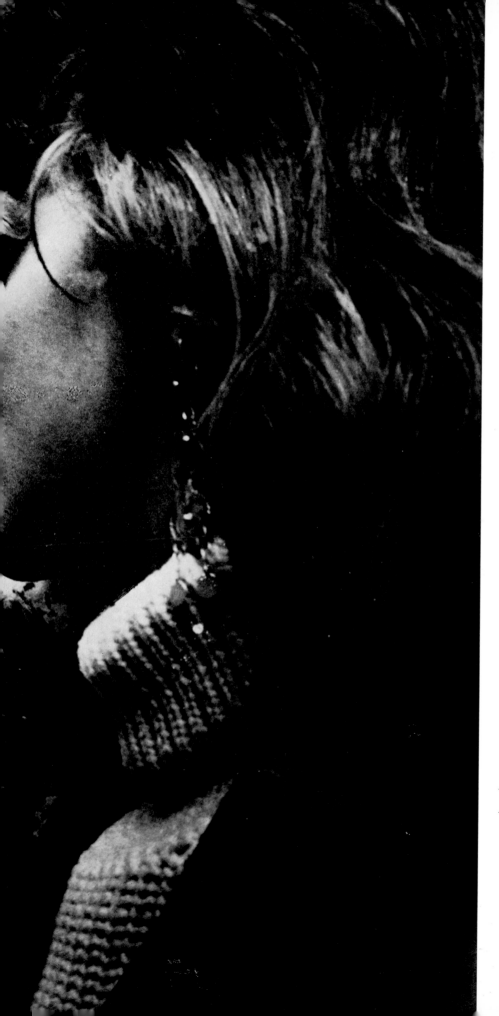

VAN DER ELSKEN
A Pitted Mirror. 1953.

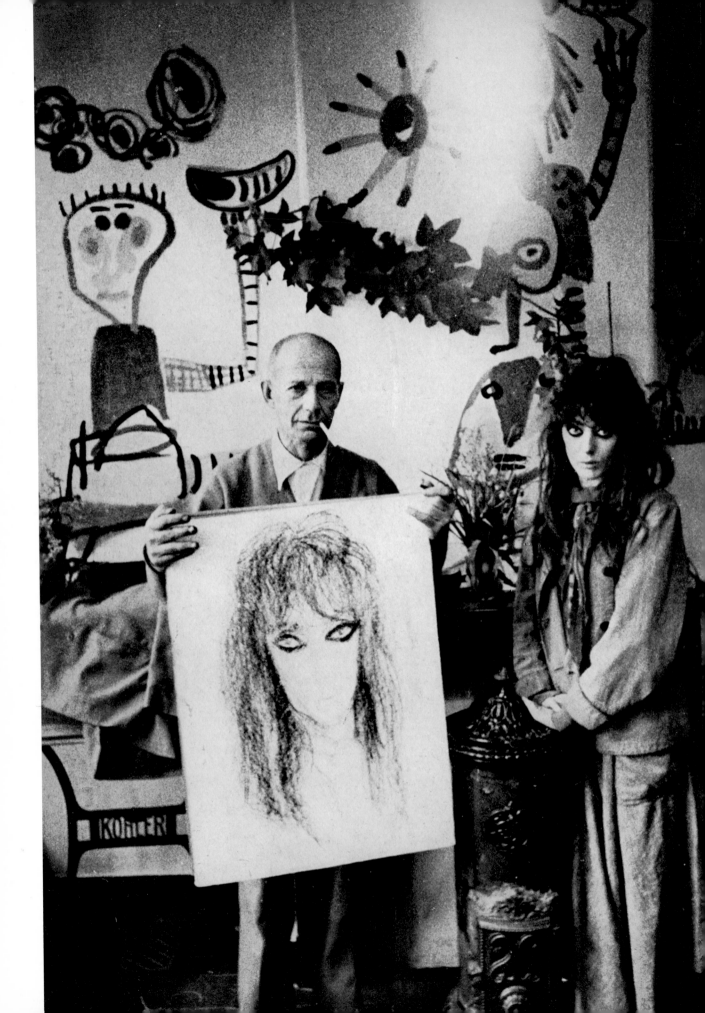

VAN DER ELSKEN
left: Her Bizarre Beauty Appealed to Artists. *1952.*
below: "Pregnancy and Saint-Germain-des-Prés
Won't Work," She Said, and Left Paris. *1953.*

next page, left: VAN DER ELSKEN, Beggar, Kuala Lumpur.
right: Chamula Indians, Mexico.
Both photographs from Sweet Life, *1966.*

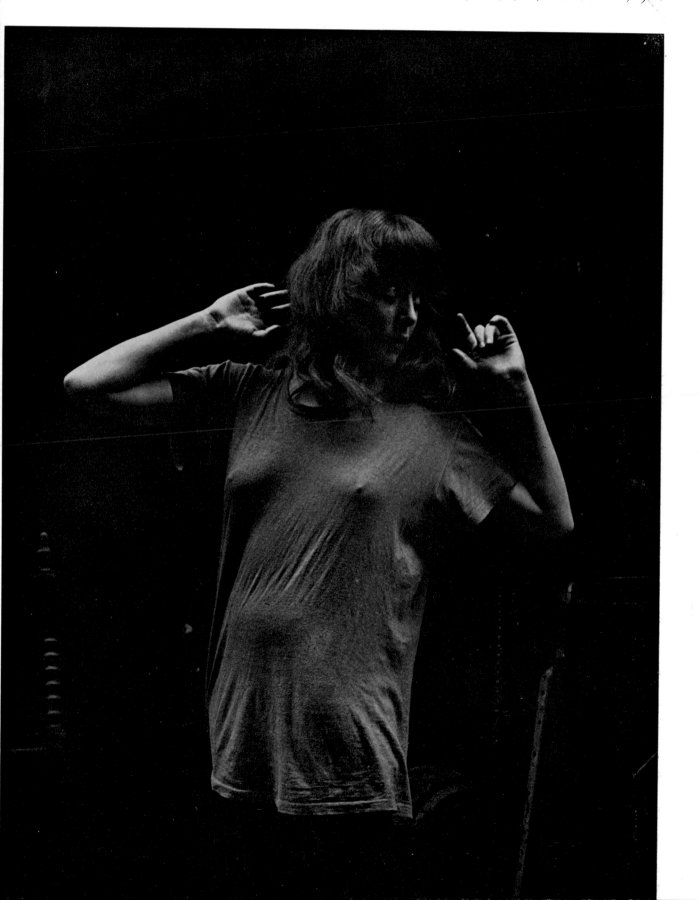

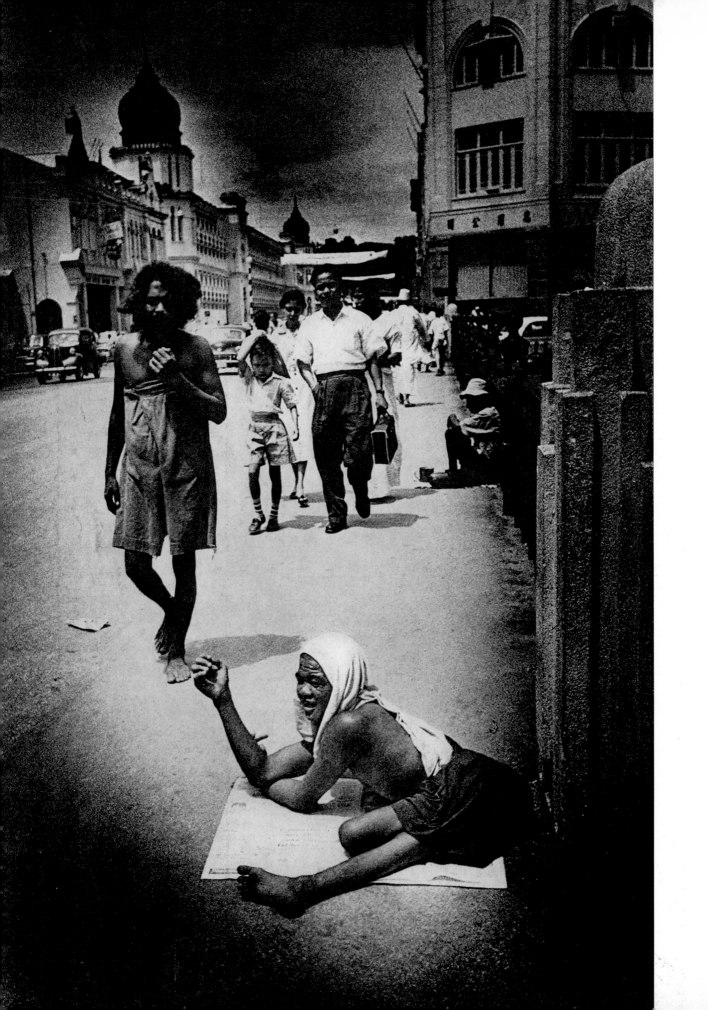

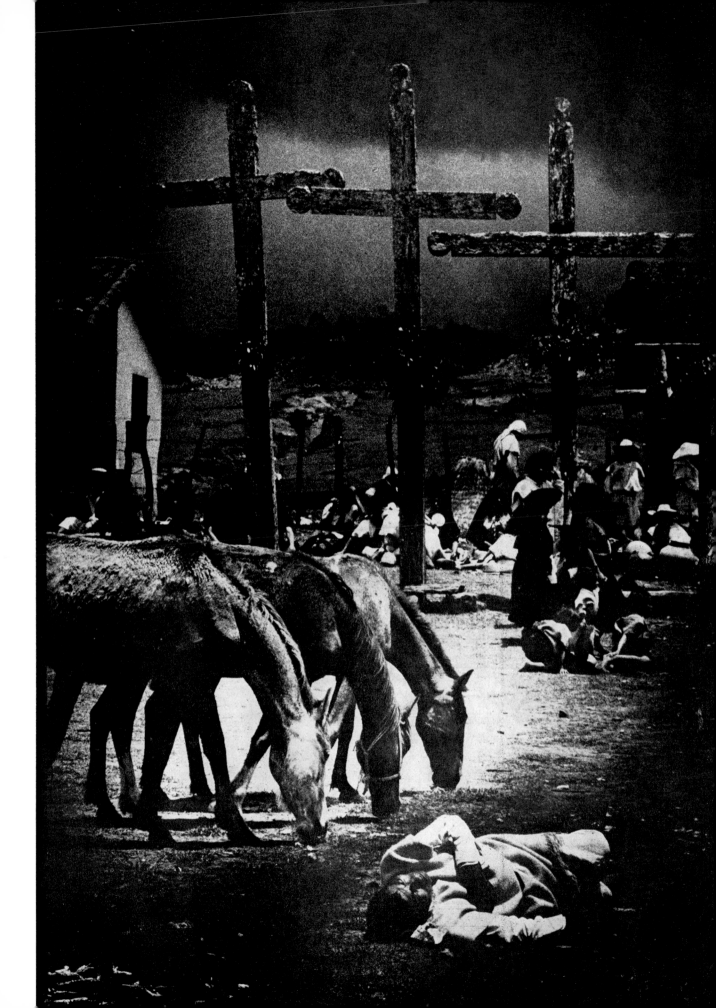

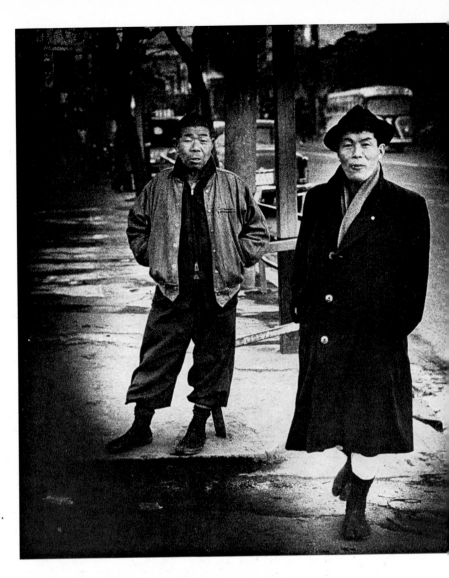

VAN DER ELSKEN, Underworld Characters, Japan.
From Sweet Life, *1966.*
below: African Harangue. *1961*.

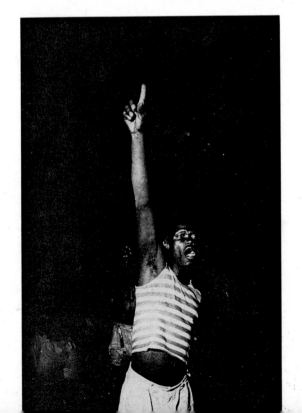

Kamangasaki, Japan.
From Sweet Life, 1966.

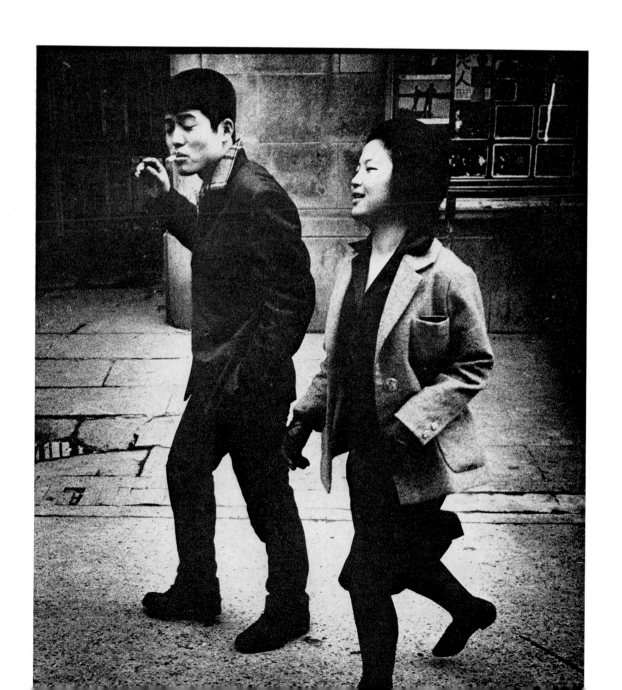

CHAPTER **42**

Cartier-Bresson
and the Human Comedy

HENRI CARTIER-BRESSON is the perfect detective with a camera: the man who never intrudes. He has the extraordinary ability to make himself part of a setting; he belittles himself whenever a subject becomes conscious of him and his camera by saying, "I'm just one of those camera bugs; I won't bother."

It would never enter his head to ask a person to move or pose or to change a setting by adding or eliminating a prop. One time in Texas he and Eliot Elisofon were assigned by *Life* magazine to cover an annual meeting of the American Federation of Arts. Elisofon had a large bronze sculpture moved outdoors, placed in lower-right foreground so that it focused on the ground glass two-thirds of the way up the film. He continued composing by asking a lady wearing a round red hat to sit with back to camera in lower left. Within that designed framework Elisofon waited for a spontaneous action of people who entered the scene, unaware of the camera, to group themselves into a balanced composition, a harmonious color arrangement, and a play of forms that would express the idea of a garden party for art. Cartier-Bresson, fascinated by Elisofon's method, lauded it, but it was contrary to anything he would have done.

Cartier-Bresson searches for the meaning, the essential characteristic of the picture he instinctively sees in front of him. To make sure he sees it as a complete composi tion and not as some superficial charming expression or gesture, he peers through a reversing prism set on top of the ever-present Leica that he uses exclusively. The image is upside down; the bold forms stand out; when these flow into an acceptable composition he presses the shutter. It is by now a reflex action. The entire frame is filled with the picture (he rarely crops). He sees through the lens as a sniper sees through the telescopic sight on his rifle. Cartier-Bresson has repeatedly said that his right eye looks out onto the exterior world while his left eye looks inside to his personal world. The two obviously fuse in the one eye of the lens. He once wrote about this, "To me photography is the simultaneous recognition in a fraction of a second of the significance of an event, as well as the precise organization of forms that give that event its proper expression."

His are poignant pictures: his camera searches out the joys and sorrows of people everywhere. The immediacy of his seeing makes it possible for him to grasp evanescent sights and fleeting emotions. Vision and conception are one; technique never gets in his way. It is by now automatic; he explains that he is no more conscious of changing shutter speeds or f-stops than he is of shifting gears while driving a car. He never uses flash bulbs, for he never can be sure he will get the picture he *sees*. Flash takes its own picture: it flattens space; it disembodies the vision; and the resultant picture is a distortion of the emotions as well as of the photographer's vision. In portraits Cartier-Bresson uses the same silent, unobtrusive method. He waits patiently until the subject stands revealed in the existing light, then he presses the shutter.

Cartier-Bresson is universally respected for his magnificent photoreporting. In 1933 he took his first unforgettable picture: hilarious children chasing a wildly laughing, crippled child on crutches playing in the ruins of a stucco building in Seville. The poignancy of this scene became a characteristic of his clear, unique style; concrete pictures which in their visual poetry command attention and continue to evoke emotional responses even after many viewings. This quality made him one of the world's best known and highest paid photojournalists. Reporter of the human comedy, he is concerned with the typical rather than the unusual, fascinated by people and their natural actions. Dull, unimpressive scenes he conceives as striking pictures. He is not concerned with recording the historical event itself, as most newspaper photographers must be—necessarily they stop the very center of an action to make it serve as an illustration for the day's news. In 1938, when Cartier-Bresson photographed the coronation of George VI, he turned his camera away from the picturesque procession of England's pageantry to search the multitude's anonymous face for human, touching incidents.

He explains that it is a journalist's duty to recognize what is important though he does not know in advance what that will be. Cartier-Bresson's camera is ready to take that picture the instant it takes shape. As the movement unfolds he perceives the precise instant when all the transitory elements form his kind of photograph. He concentrates on securing a series of dramatic photographs which, coupled with his notes, become a precise account of what took place. He clearly articulates this intention by saying, "Photography implies the recognition of a rhythm in the world of real things. What the eye does is find and focus on the particular subject within the mass of reality, what the camera does is simply to register on film the decision made by the eye."

He finds his pictures at eye level; fish-eye and bird's-eye perspectives he considers odd, tricky angles. The only valid angles, he claims, "are the angles of the geometry of composition," not realizing that valid geometric compositions can be photographed from any angle and that any creative photographer has the freedom to make his own kind of picture. But his rules, he has persistently said, apply only to himself, not to others.

Cartier-Bresson has circled the earth many times; he and his wife, a Javanese dancer named Ratna Mohini, whom he married in 1937, seem at home anywhere. He has discovered great photographs in all parts of the world. The Far East and Europe, however, yield more penetrating pictures for his camera than the United States. He seems more attuned to ancient civilizations, to the incongruities inherent in the extremes of society, and to buildings and streets that have withstood millenia of treading feet. His book *The Europeans* attests to this keen rapport with his people, as does, in a lesser way, his book, *The Russians*. In his earlier volume, *The Decisive Moment*, the panorama he captured of China, Java, India, and North Africa, is more penetrating and more convincing than his pictures of the States. Some of his finest photographs appear in these volumes and in his *From One China to Another*, in which he traces pictorially the last changing days of the old regime and the beginnings of Communist China. In the tradition of Emerson, Stieglitz, and Adams, but without their vehement demands for fine reproduction, Cartier-Bresson believes in publishing his photographs in book form to attract the widest audience possible for his work.

Through these books and through traveling exhibitions of his photographs more people have seen his work than that of almost any other photographer. A retrospective exhibition, consisting of four hundred photographs encompassing the years 1930 to 1955, opened in the Louvre in Paris (destroying a century of official prejudice held against photography) and has since been circulating in major museums on both hemispheres.

Cartier-Bresson's original intention was to become a painter. In 1928, at the age of twenty, he studied painting with André Lhôte; the next year pursued it further in Cambridge, England, where he added the study of literature. The year 1930 he spent in the West African bush, where he contracted blackwater fever and began his lifetime interest in photography. While recuperating in Paris in 1932 he acquired a Leica, which became, he wrote, "the extension of my eye." He traveled with it to Poland, Germany, and Italy, testing what he could do with the camera, making himself master of its very response. The results of this trip and his next year's travel in Spain he showed in his first exhibition, held in Madrid and later shown in New York.

In 1934 he joined an expedition for a year's travel in Mexico where he held a joint exhibition with Mexico's Alvarez-Bravo in the Palace of Fine Arts. The succeeding year he shared gallery space with Walker Evans in a two-man exhibition which presented their personal styles as documentary photographers. Then followed his first sojourn in the States, the year he discovered Harlem, Brooklyn, and Coney Island.

He returned to France to make his first moving picture with Jean Renoir. In 1937 he took the documentary film, *Return to Life*, depicting medical aid to hospitals during the Spanish Civil War. The same year he photographed in the south of France with Robert Capa and David Seymour (Chim) who were to become organizers of Magnum Photos with him a decade later.

Cartier-Bresson entered the French Army in 1939, just after completing another film with Jean Renoir. As a corporal in the army's film and photo unit he was taken prisoner by the Nazis at the collapse of France. For the next thirty-six months he was a prisoner of war, escaping successfully only after the third try. He reached Paris and, for the balance of the war, served in the Underground assisting ex-prisoners of war. He organized French press photographers to cover the occupation and the retreat of the Nazis after liberation. Immediately after World War II ended in Europe, he resumed work as a cameraman for the United States Office of War Information, filming the return of war prisoners to France.

In 1946 he came again to New York, to attend the first comprehensive exhibition of his work held at the Museum of Modern Art. He stayed here for the ensuing twelve months, traveling throughout the nation to acquaint himself with the immense pictorial canvas of the country. On his return to Paris he and his two good friends, Capa and Chim (both of whom were to die in war—Capa in Indo-China and Chim in Egypt—while pursuing stories for Magnum) founded the independent photo agency Magnum Photos. Magnum is owned as a cooperative by its outstanding photographers, who supply illustrated journals and magazines of all the world with single photographs or complete picture essays. Cartier-Bresson has had to take the position of president of Magnum Photos since the death of Chim, who held that office when he was killed.

For Magnum, Cartier-Bresson has taken all kinds of picture stories, including specific assignments for *Life*, *Picture Post*, and *Paris Match*. The quality of his work continues to develop as his vision and understanding of humanity deepen with the passing years. He sums up his belief in photography by saying, "For me, content cannot be separated from form. By form I mean a rigorous organization of the interplay of surfaces, lines, and values. It is in this organization alone that our conceptions and emotions become concrete and communicable. In photography, visual organization can stem from a developed instinct." Photography to the modest, unassuming Cartier-Bresson is a way of life, a creative mode of expression in which he can record the story of man with uncanny awareness, sympathy, and poetic imagination.

In his native France Cartier-Bresson is *maitre*—the title of respect reserved for such as the sculptor Rodin or the painter Matisse. In January 1967 the Musée des Arts Décoratifs of the Louvre broke all precedents by presenting Henri Cartier-Bresson's photographs in a second one-man show. The 260 works on view included 60 photographs from the 1955 exhibition. The rest were chosen from the large number he has taken since. First exhibited in Tokyo (the Far Eastern pictures grew out of an assignment from the Japanese newspaper *Shimbun*), the exhibition was shown in New York's Museum of Modern Art in 1968 and later that year at the Worcester Museum of Art.

All photographs in this chapter from The Decisive Moment, *by Henri Cartier-Bresson, published by Simon and Schuster, Inc., New York, courtesy the photographer and Magnum Photos, New York.*

HENRI CARTIER-BRESSON, Allée du Prado, Marseille. 1932.

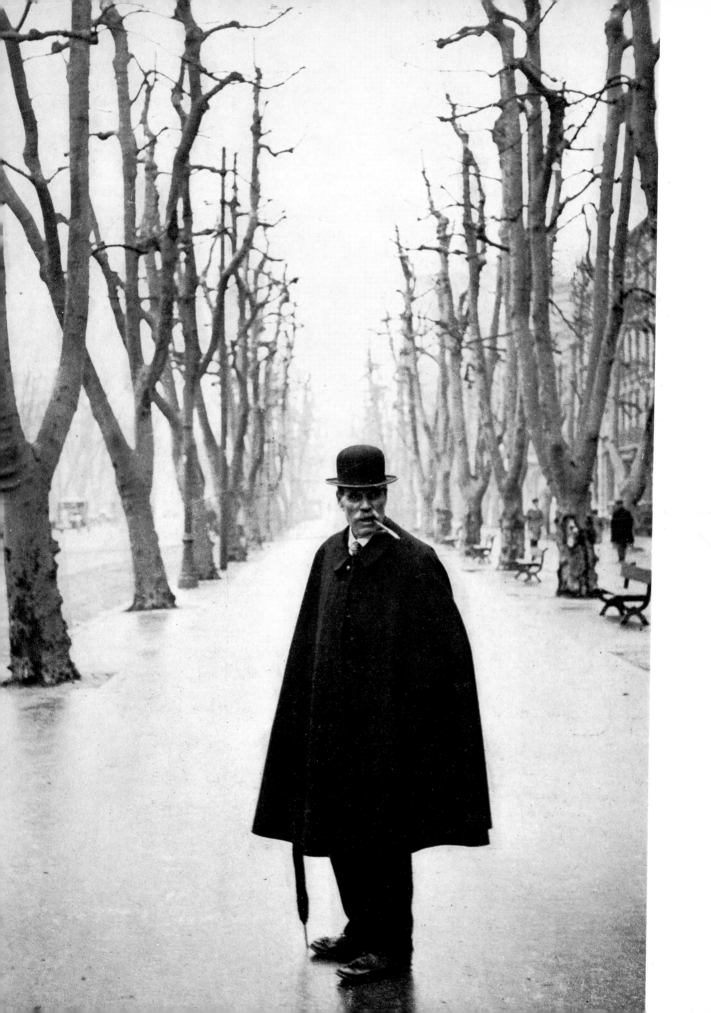

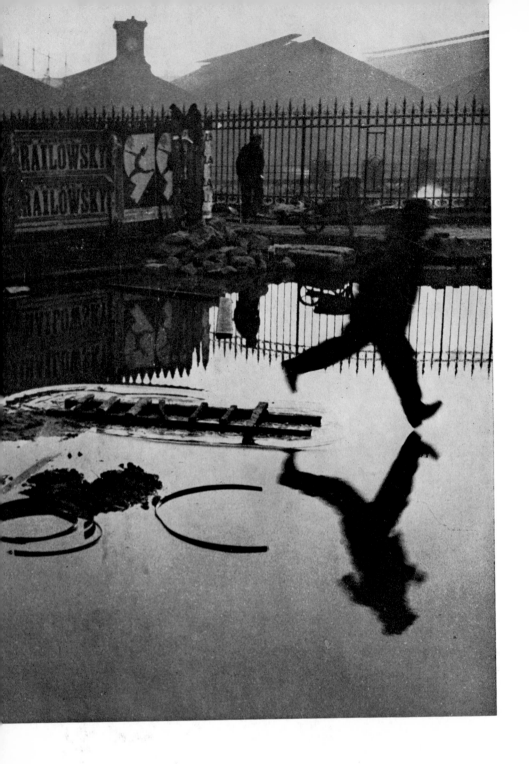

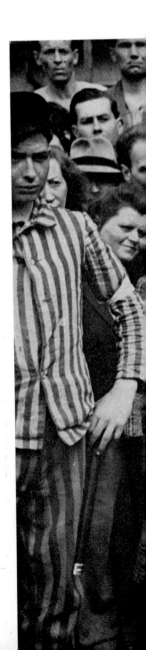

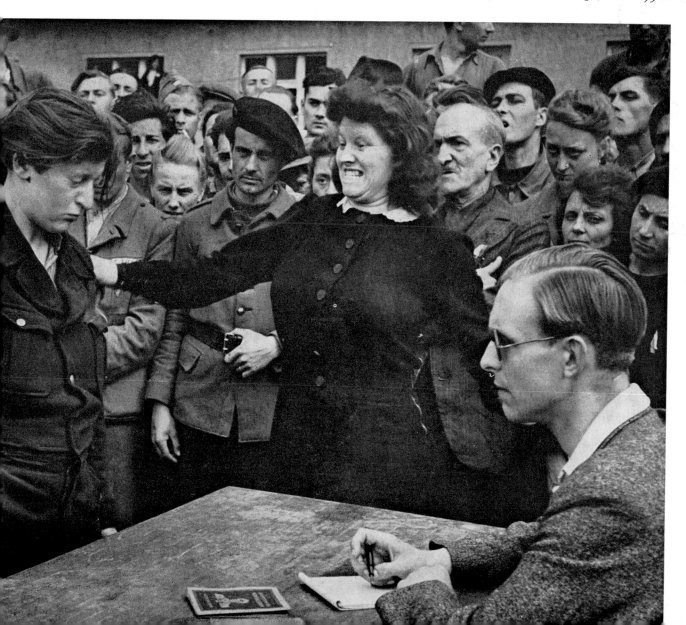

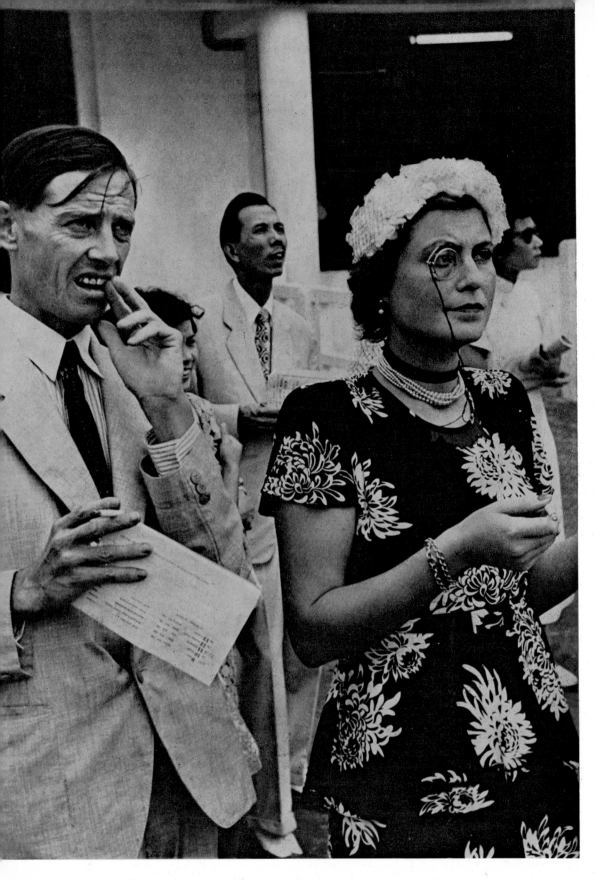

CARTIER-BRESSON, *above:* Day at the Races. *Hong Kong, 1949.*
right: Coronation of George VI. *London, 1937.*

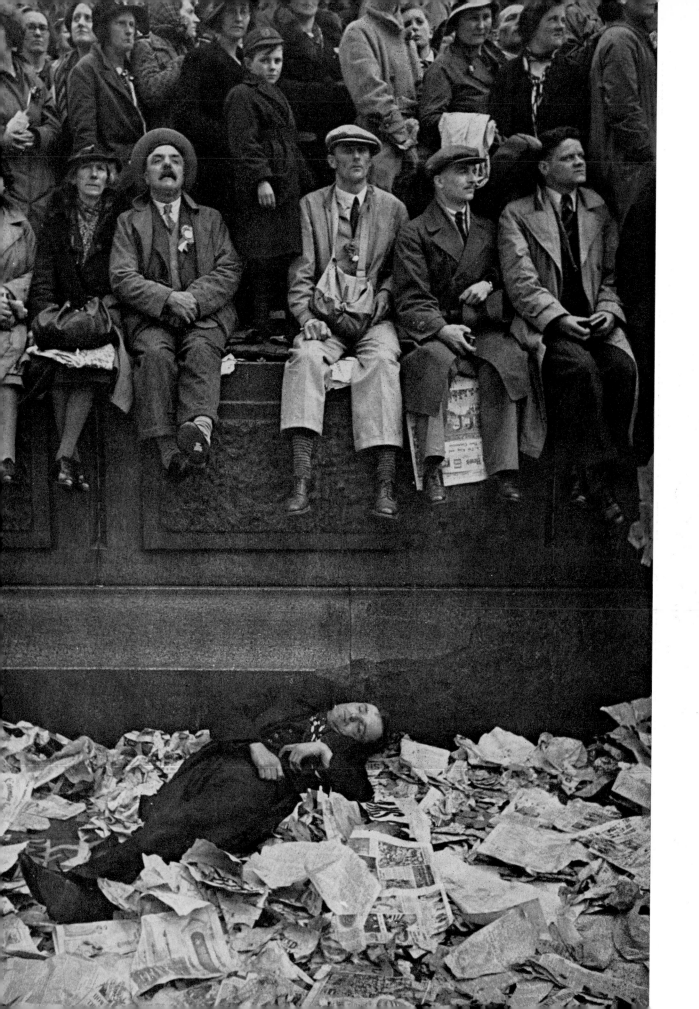

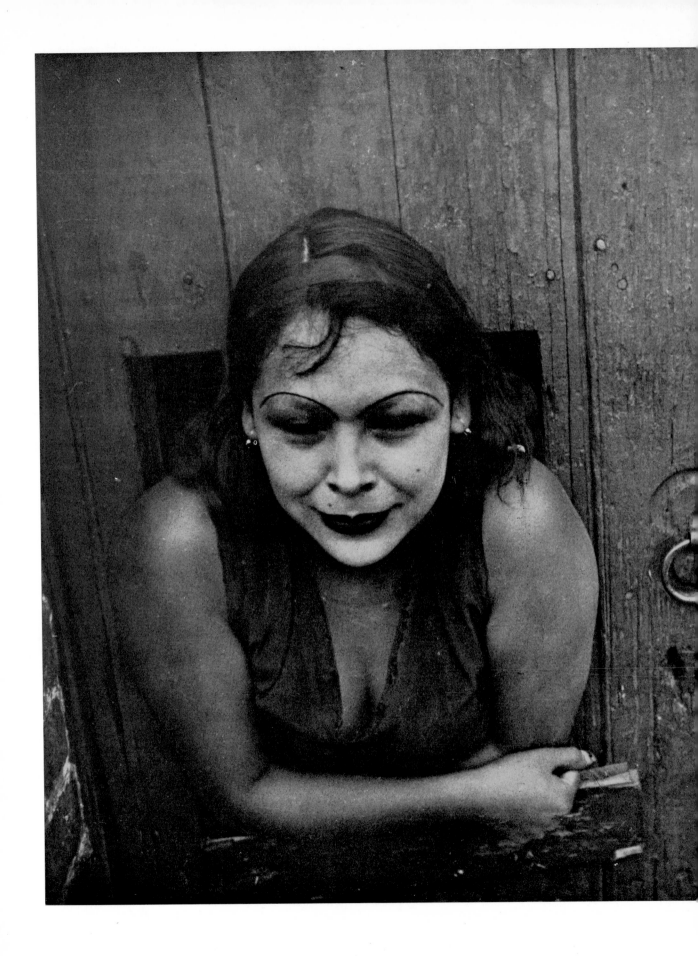

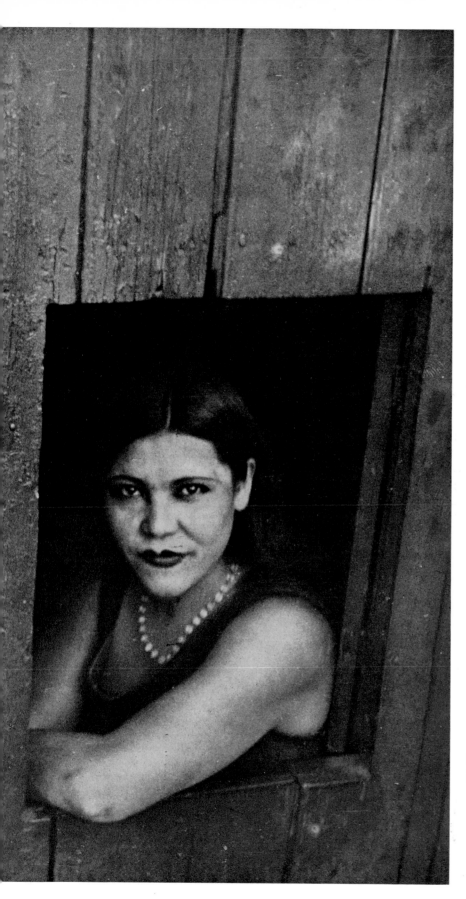

CARTIER-BRESSON, Two Prostitutes' Cribs.
Mexico City, 1934.

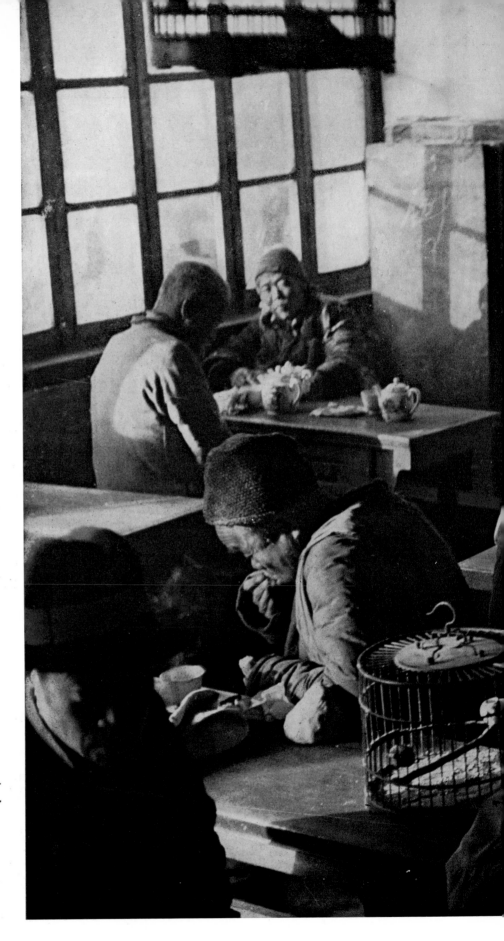

CARTIER-BRESSON, Tea House in Peking.
China, 1949.

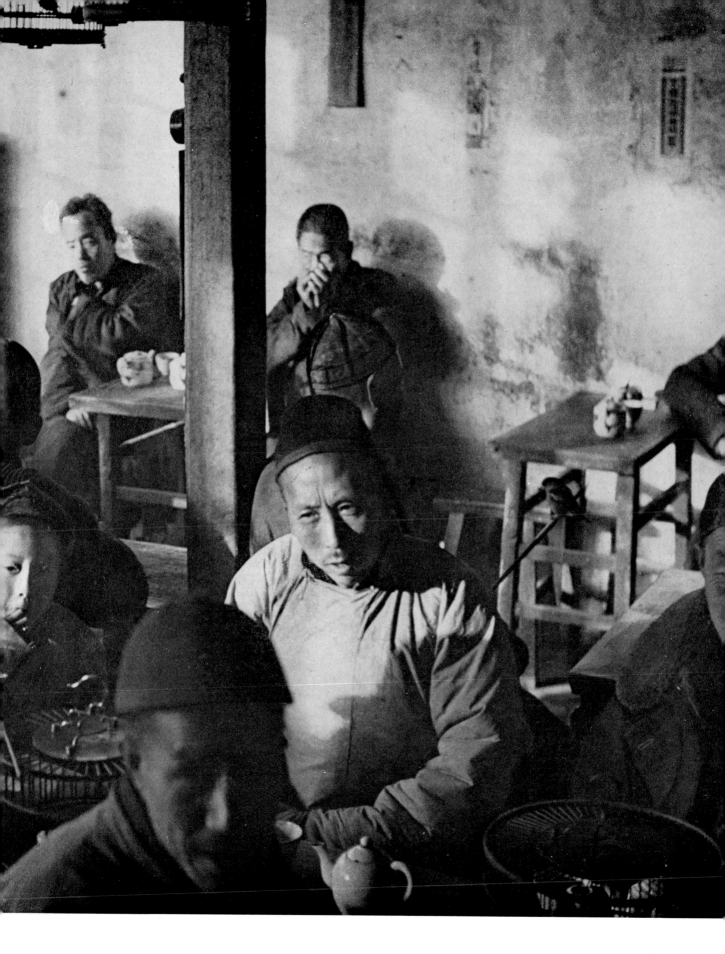

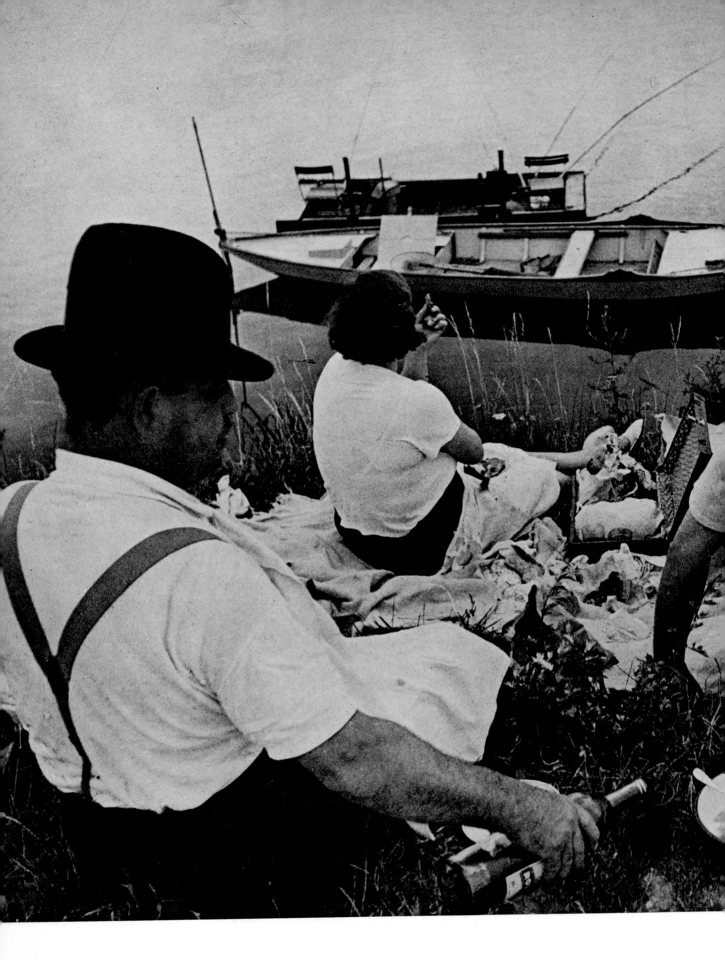

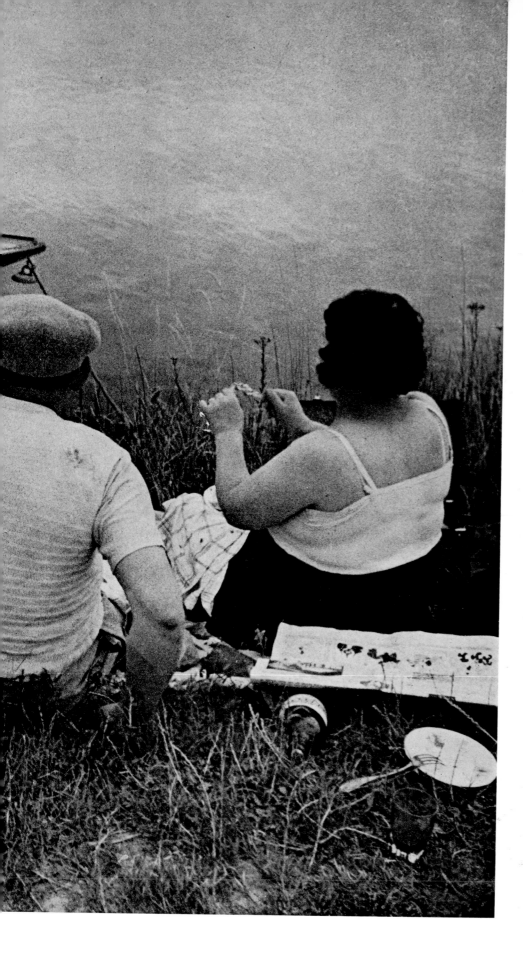

CARTIER-BRESSON
Sunday on the
Banks of the Marne.
1938.

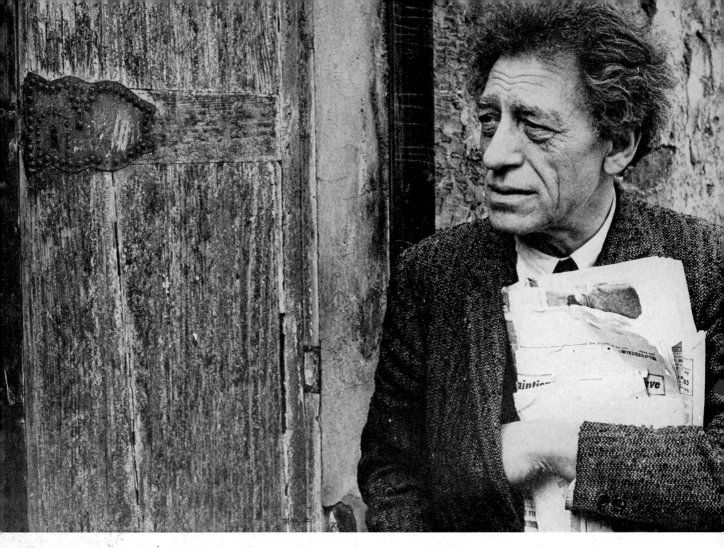

CARTIER-BRESSON, Alberto Giacometti. 1963.
opposite page: Palais Royale. 1960.

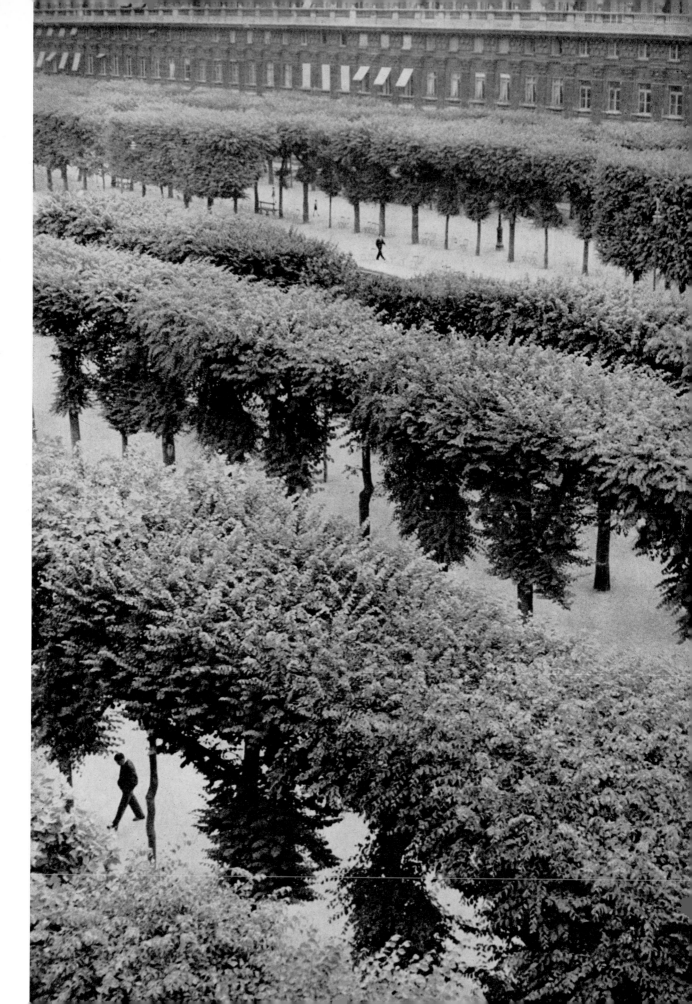

CHAPTER **43**

Yousuf Karsh: Faces of Destiny

YOUSUF KARSH, in his powerful portraits, transforms the human face into legend. Future historians covering the period between World War II and Sputnik II will turn for illumination to the perceptive, psychological portraits Karsh has made of statesmen, scientists, and artists whose faces have changed the face and tastes of the world.

A superb photographic craftsman, Karsh fills his portraits with multiple meanings that yield their full import only upon continued, concentrated observation. His terse and intimate characterizations convey insight into the subjects' will power, leadership, creative intensity, or spiritual stature. Although the image remains faithful to objective reality, through emphasizing features, hands, or body, Karsh achieves a visual idealization as well as an expressive interpretation of the subject's character.

Karsh composes each photograph carefully, paying as much attention to background as to modeling the structure of the face and figure with light. The portrait is organized within the picture space. A dominant feature becomes the focal point, drawing the spectator's eye through the composition and back to the objective center. The lighting appears natural, but number and sizes of light sources are carefully considered, so that the subject seems to sit in the diffused atmosphere of a courtyard lit by beams of unblinding sunlight. Each part of the picture is harmoniously linked by a balanced relation ship of forms and masses, of dark areas and areas of light.

Karsh does not use decorative sweeps of drapery or painted props for backgrounds. He creates the proper background with light, and correlates it with the clothes worn by his sitter. In his photographs of Nehru, Sibelius, and Marian Anderson, the subject detaches itself to become a strongly framed light mass isolated by contrast from the dark costume worn, and from the solid black background. In his photographs of Shaw and Churchill, Karsh achieves space and depth through highlighted areas made effective by the position of head and hands, clothes and accessories.

Karsh seems to follow the precept of Goya, who wrote, "I see [in nature] only forms that advance, forms that recede, masses in light and shadow." This play of forms Karsh achieves purposefully through subtle modeling of the dominant characteristics he finds in the uneven human face.

There is no academic, repetitious formula to his work. In *Faces of Destiny*, published by Ziff-Davis at the close of World War II, his versatility is evident. His photographs clearly reveal the diverse attitudes and personalities of the men who brought the Allies to victory; they convey effectively strength of purpose, intellectual breadth, and sense of power.

When asked about his method of capturing the greatness, the individuality of each sitter, Karsh declared, "I have tried for years to define for myself the ingredients of successful portraiture, but it defies definition . . . Though perception of what is right must be instantaneous, continuous practice does not make portrait photography a matter of near automatic perfection."

Karsh's masterful technique can create but superficially what does not exist in the subject's character. His portrait style applied to financial giants has resulted in overdramatized, brilliant photographs of apparent outer strength without the concomitant inner force.

To secure a portrait Karsh will travel halfway across the globe to spend sometimes only one hour in productive work with his subject.

When he flew to Finland to photograph the distinguished composer Sibelius, Karsh took with him his 8 x 10-inch camera and hundreds of pounds of equipment, only to find the electric current available was insufficient. Until permission from the authorities was secured to tap the main line, Sibelius regaled Karsh with stories told with infectious gaiety. Karsh's lens probed to find the image, a divine mask with eyes closed that reflected the spirit and genius of the venerable composer.

Karsh photographed Einstein in his little study at Princeton's Institute for Advanced Study. A verbatim record of Karsh's questions and Einstein's answers demonstrates Karsh's technique of drawing the subject into realms of profound thought until he forgets the presence of the camera. Karsh asked, "Are you optimistic about the future of mankind?" Einstein replied, "I cannot say that I am optimistic, but this I will say, that if there is not found in the near future a solution to the security program, then there will be a disaster on a scale unimaginable to us."

"To what source should we look for the hope of the future of the world?" asked Karsh. Einstein answered simply and softly, "To ourselves."

Most people sit for Karsh either in his Ottawa or in his New York studio. Twenty-five years ago, in 1933, he arrived in the Canadian capital, debating with himself whether to study surgery or to open a photographic studio. Karsh was born in the town of Mardin in the Armenian part of Turkey. He was ten years old when the massacres of 1918 ravaged his home town. He escaped a year or two later to find a home with his uncle, a photographer operating in Sherborne, Quebec, where Karsh learned the rudiments of his profession. Later he was apprenticed for three years to John H. Garo in Boston, a fellow Armenian whom Karsh remembers as "a stimulating and inspiring teacher as well as a photographer of distinction." From Boston he moved to Ottawa, where he established his home.

Ottawa grew rapidly and the studio of young Yousuf Karsh grew with it. His skill as a portrait photographer was soon recognized by Lord Duncannon, son of the governor general of Canada, Lord Bessborough. Karsh was introduced to members of the government, to visiting dignitaries, and also to the Ottawa Little Theatre Group where Karsh met his future wife, the talented actress Solange Gauthier.

Prime Minister W. L. Mackenzie King, a close friend and patron of Karsh, in December, 1941, arranged to have Winston Churchill pause to be photographed immediately after his speech before the combined houses of the Canadian Parliament. Karsh was given two minutes to take one shot. Churchill entered and stood impatiently, smoking a freshly lit cigar. Karsh, who had no intention of including the cigar in the portrait, walked up to him and said, "Sir, here is an ashtray." Getting no result, he said, "Pardon me," simultaneously taking the cigar from Churchill and snapping the shutter. Churchill walked over, shook hands, and remarked, "Well, you can certainly make a roaring lion stand still to be photographed." Eleanor Roosevelt, when she heard of the incident, commented, "It must have been Churchill's first major defeat."

This was the picture that made Karsh famous. Published again and again, it became a symbol of England's will to fight. The strength and power of Churchill's face stiffened the resolution of the English people, who were then bearing the full weight of Nazi bombings. The people loved the photograph; it was easy to imagine Churchill's stirring speeches issuing from this indomitable face.

At the request of the Canadian government, Karsh went to England to take a series of photographs that included King George VI and Lord Beaverbrook, who said, "Karsh, you have immortalized me." *Life* magazine assigned him to photograph American war leaders; one of an unsmiling, determined General Eisenhower was as effective for the pursuit of the war as the picture of Churchill.

Since the war's end, leaders of the mind and the spirit, creative people in all fields, have claimed Karsh's interest. To his gallery of statesmen, military men, and royalty he has added artists, architects, scientists, humanitarians, and musicians. Karsh, with his keen sense of judgment, seeks the intrinsic character of his subject. He caught the expression on Marian Anderson's face just as she finished humming her favorite spiritual "The Crucifixion." The audacious George Bernard Shaw said to Karsh, "Armenian? Good. I have many friends among the Armenians. To keep strong and healthy they should be exterminated every little while." Frank Lloyd Wright, another magnificent egocentric, disapproved violently of everything Karsh was doing, but invited him to Taliesen to take his picture in his Wisconsin home.

When Karsh photographed President Franklin D. Roosevelt, he clicked a gadget attached to his camera that made it appear that he had tripped the shutter. Roosevelt relaxed; then Karsh really took the picture. He used the same procedure with Lord Tweedsmuir and occasionally with other famous personalities.

Karsh writes of his profession, "If there is a driving purpose to my work, it is to record the best in people and, in so doing, remain true to myself. . . . It has been my good fortune to meet many of the world's great men and women. People who will leave their mark on our time. I have used my camera to portray them as they appeared to me and as I felt they have impressed themselves on their generation."

Karsh's great photographs of them will impress future generations, who will know through his artistry the look of the celebrated persons of this period of history.

All photographs in this chapter copyright Yousuf Karsh, Ottawa.

YOUSUF KARSH, Winston S. Churchill. 194[

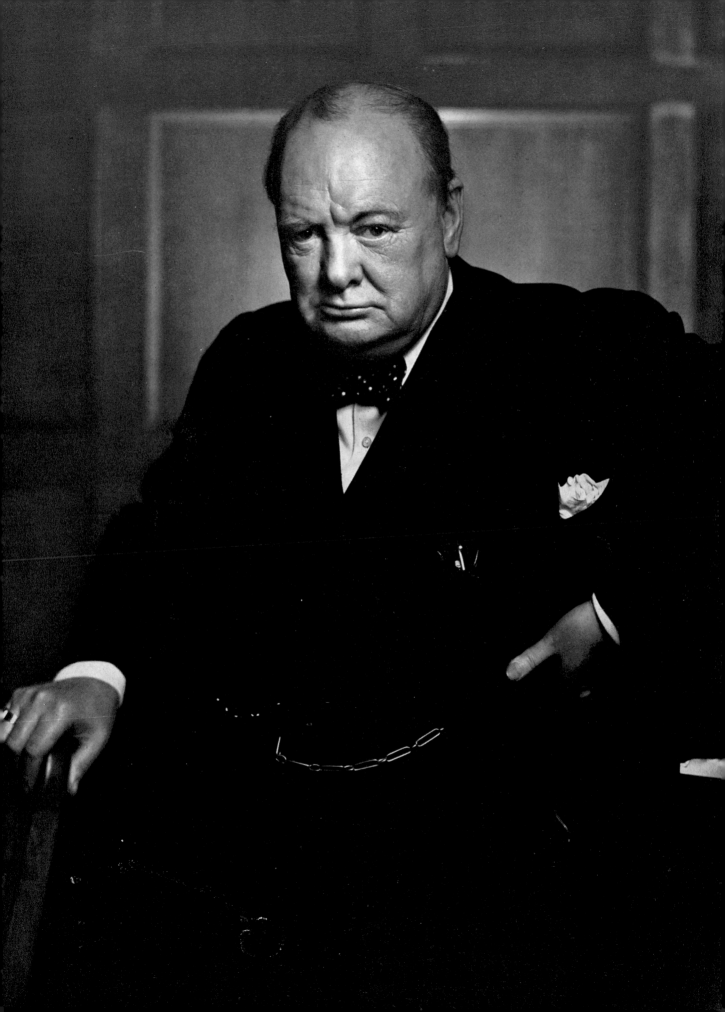

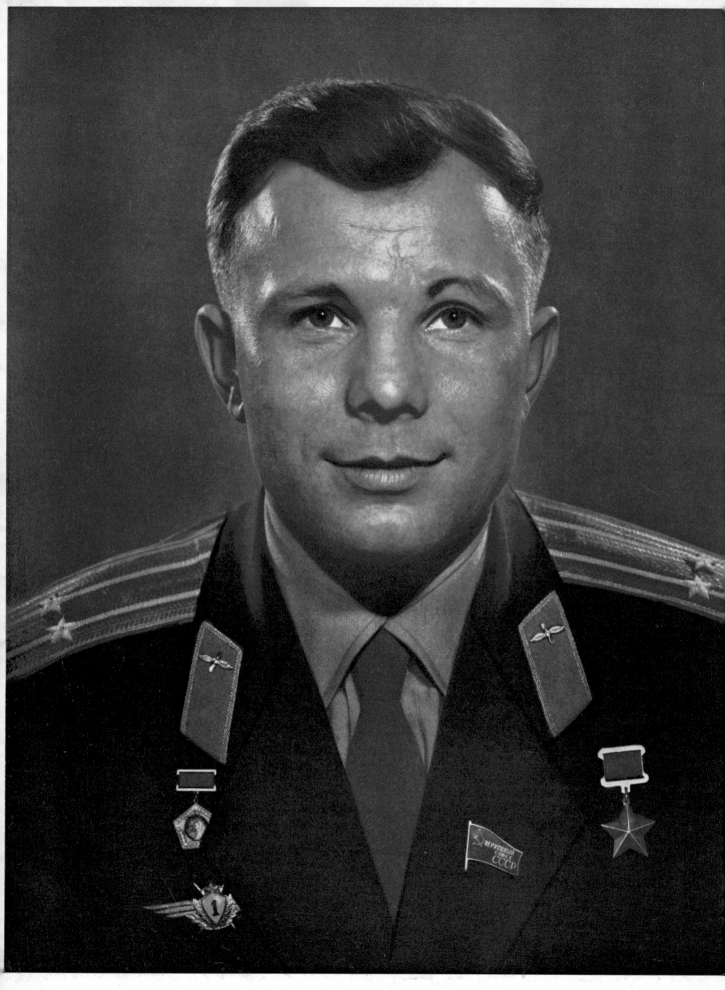

KARSH, Yuri Alexeyevich Gagarin.

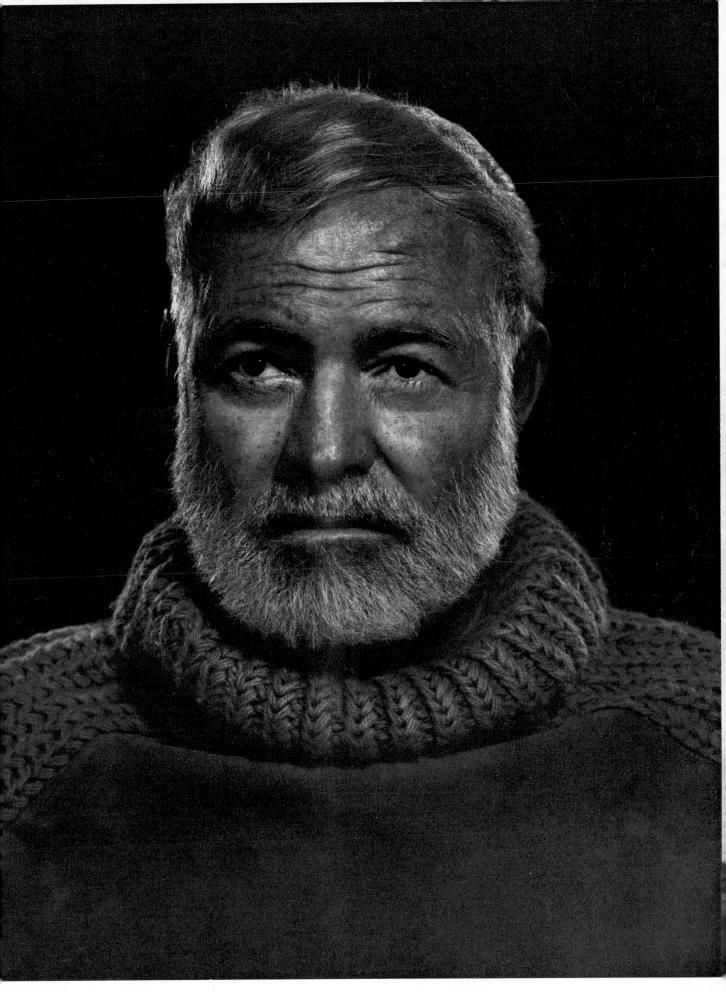

KARSH, Ernest Hemingway. 1958.

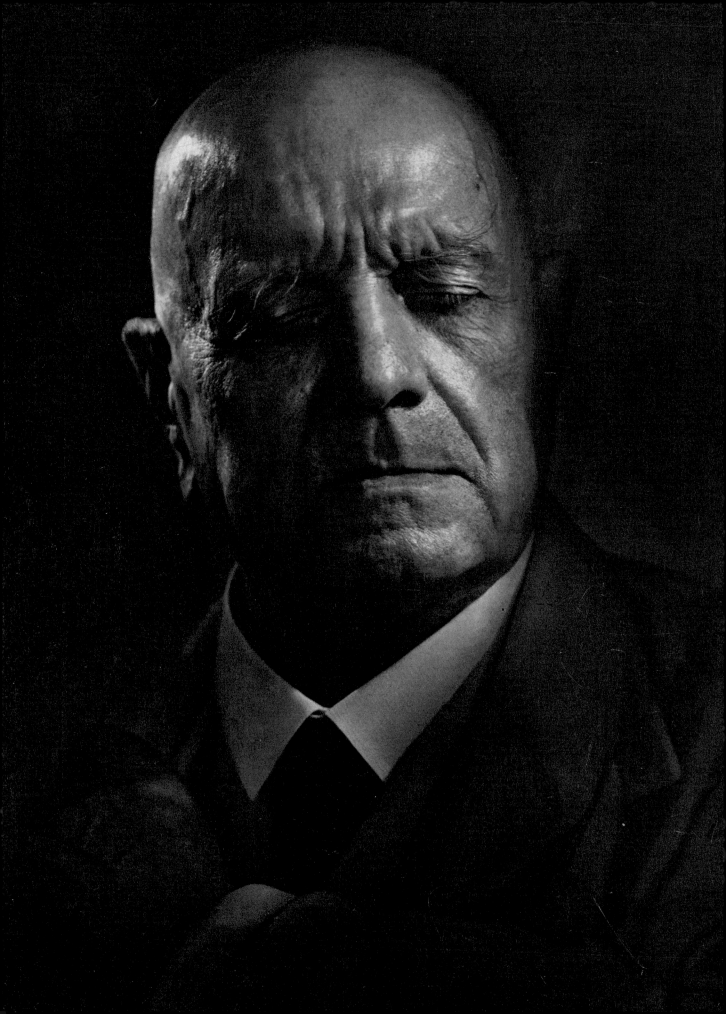

KARSH, *below*: Frank Lloyd Wright. *1945*.
left: Jan Sibelius. *1949*.

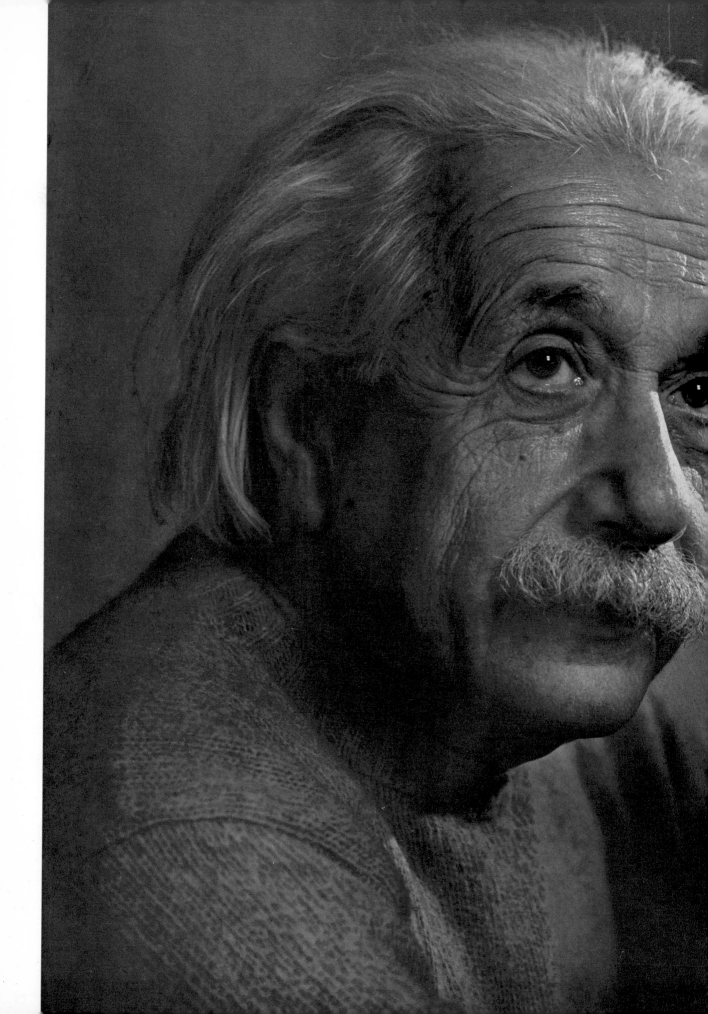

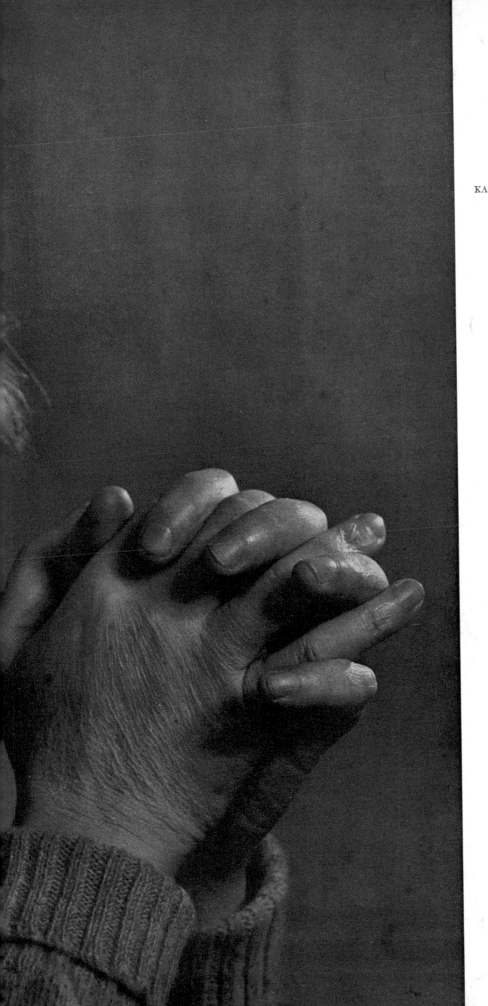

KARSH, Albert Einstein. *1948*.

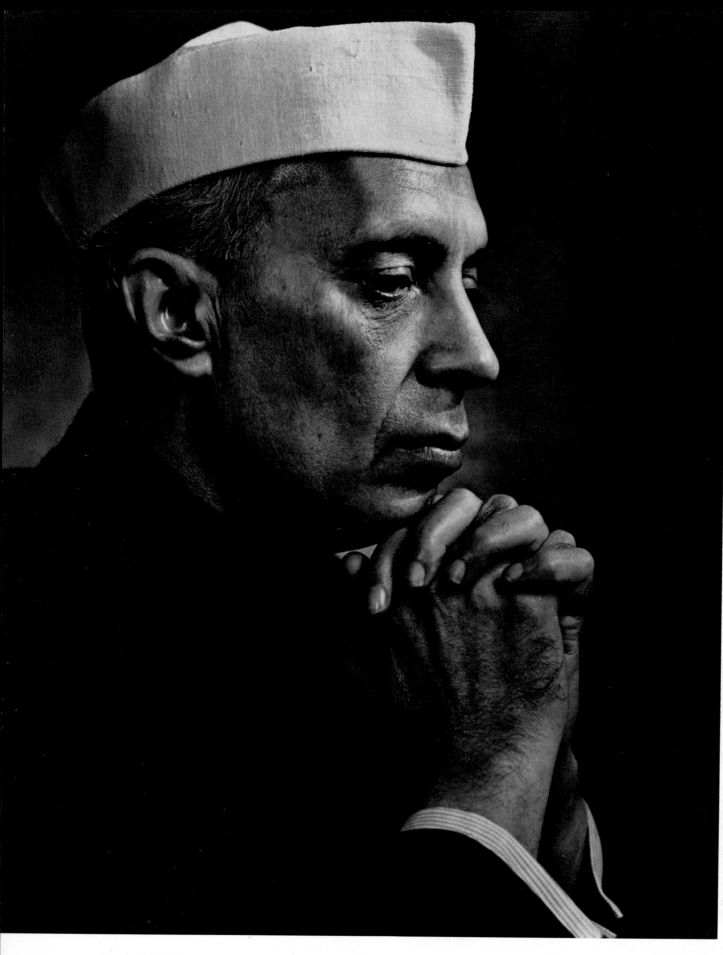

KARSH, Jawaharlal Nehru. 1949.

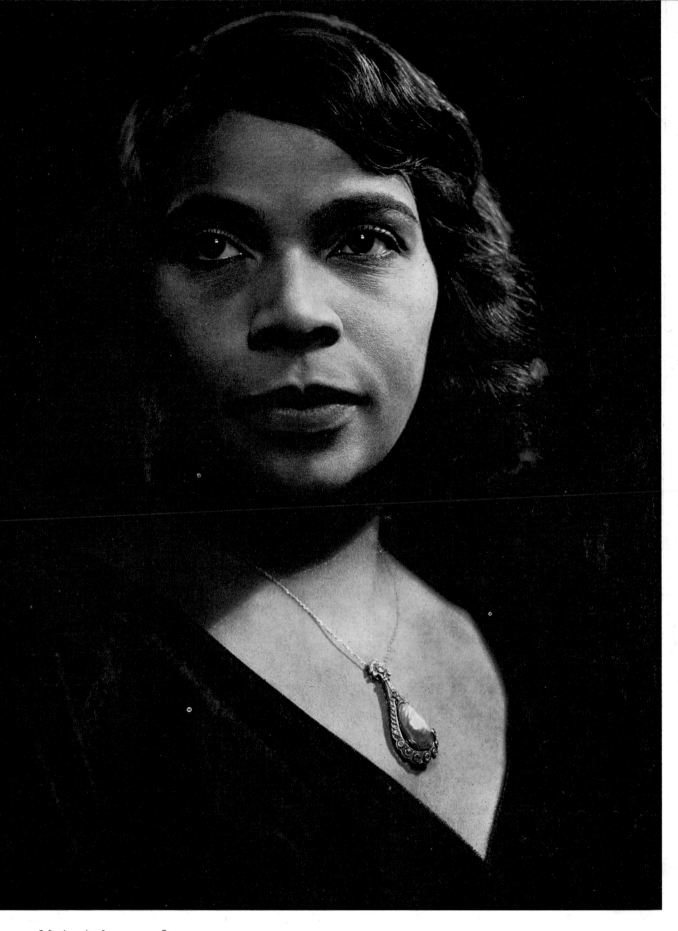

KARSH, Marian Anderson. *1948*.

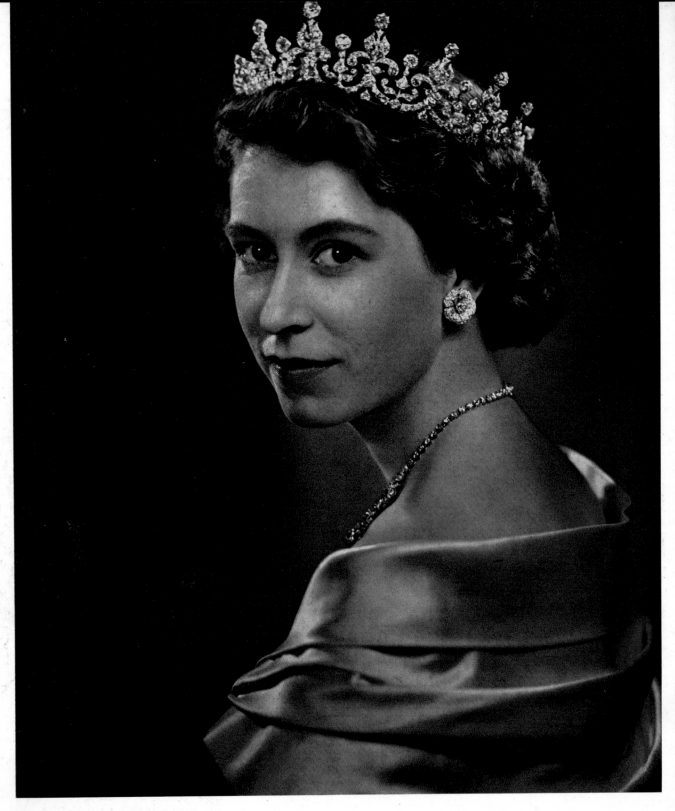

KARSH, *above:* Queen Elizabeth II. *1951.*
right: George Bernard Shaw. *1943.*

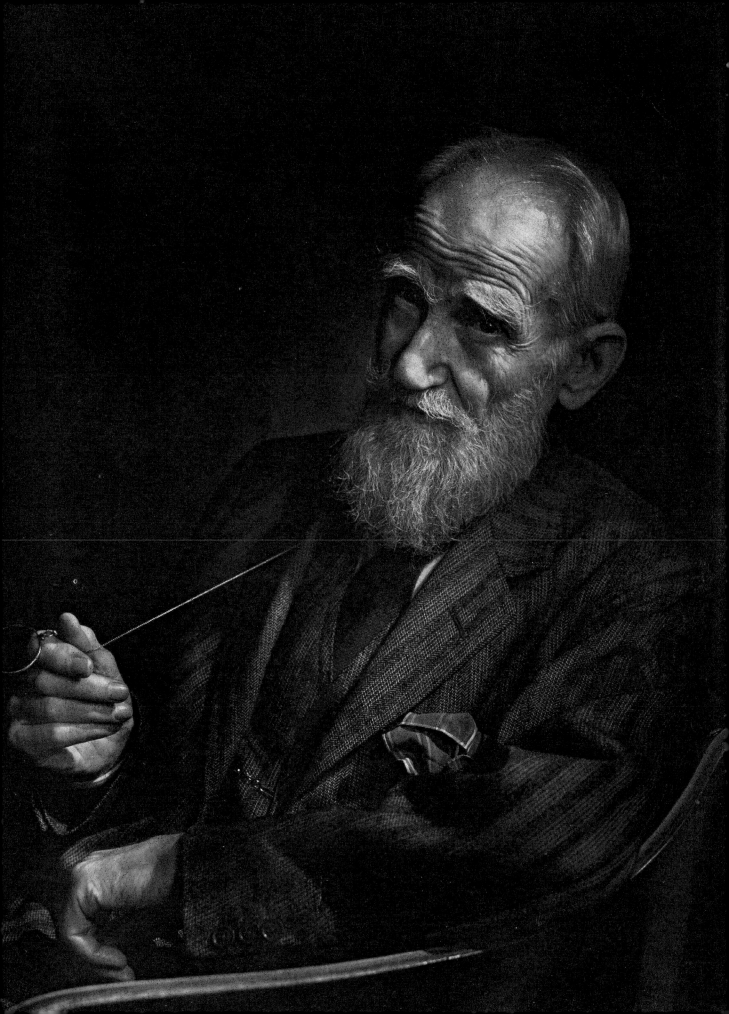

CHAPTER 44

Andreas Feininger

WHEN ANDREAS FEININGER was born in Paris in 1906 there was no question about whether he was destined for a career in the arts. His paternal grandparents were musicians; his mother was a painter; his father, Lyonel Feininger, was not only a great painter but a highly original composer. Lyonel Feininger was moved to awe and wonder by the eternal mystery of light—he endowed his youngest son, Theodore, with the middle name Lux, which is Latin for "light"—with which he transmuted the rational, geometric world of Cubism into luminous mystic visions. Unlike his father, Andreas is completely in the grip of outer nature, whose secrets he unravels. An analyst among photographers, he scans both natural and man-made vistas on every possible level of magnitude and complexity from telescopic to the microscopic. Enlarging the scope of our normal, unaided vision, he assists us to observe the anatomy of our surroundings in unexpected forms and new beauty, as in the dramatic pattern of a Gabon viper's uncoiling skeleton or the marvelous woodcarvings created by the jaws of the carpenter ant. Andreas Feininger intensifies our perception of nature's processes, enabling us, for example, to see with our own eyes a pond in the process of freezing. Half scientist, all artist, he is the most scholarly of photographers and applies his encyclopedic knowledge of photographic techniques with schooled intelligence and highly disciplined control.

Feininger has received more from his father than might appear on the surface, in particular his father's reverence for light—an orientation that may well have influenced his selection of a photographic career. He has a deep understanding of light in all its nuanced properties and its great power to affect. And he has his father's profound insight into form, structure, and space.

Although there is no aspect of photography of which Feininger is not a master, he is at his most brilliant and original when he evokes the majesty and strength of the urban-industrial cityscape, where he envisions modern civilization at its most heroic. Here he creates forms so sweeping and grand that *Life* magazine, of which he was a staff member from 1943 to 1963, has always been hard put to reproduce a Feininger horizontal photograph in a format smaller than two pages. (The editor of this book, it is plain to see, has met with a like difficulty.) Unsurprisingly, Andreas is known to his friends and colleagues as "Double-truck Feininger."

Feininger uses a telephoto lens, thereby eliminating extraneous detail. Or he bores close in to the subject, thereby also eliminating extraneous detail. These two conceptions of photographic procedure, with both of which he has become identified and both of which give him just the detail he wants, are exemplified first by his beautiful telephoto views of New York City and second by his spectacular views of nature's microarchitecture, close up and greatly enlarged, taken with special attachments he has constructed himself. "With a short lens," he says, "I can reveal the hidden things near at hand, with a long lens the hidden things far away. The telephoto lens provides a new visual sensation for people: it widens their horizons. And, conversely, the things under our nose invariably look good when blown up really big."

Asked whether he ever wanted to become a painter, Feininger answered, "No! The photographer has almost as much control over his subject as a painter does. He can control light and shade, form and space, pattern and texture, motion and mood, subject selection—everything except composition." Perhaps not the impeccably resolved composition that Lyonel Feininger constructed; nevertheless, Andreas' sensitivity to what he sees on the ground glass makes possible a degree of compositional control that the common, garden variety of painter—or photographer—would give his soul to possess. Andreas' compositions, in point of fact, belong to a three-dimensional conception of space that reminds us more of architecture and environmental design than of the flat world of painting. Thus, we are not surprised to learn that he was trained as an architect and worked as one for several years before turning to photography.

Until now, most professional photographers seem to have taken up the camera professionally only after having mastered another line of work. A good many have come to photography from painting and sculpture, others from social work, medicine, and writing, and some few from the building trades and the crafts. The trained craftsman conscious of design and of the techniques of a trade has an edge in learning photography. Feininger's apprenticeship to a cabinetmaker and subsequent graduation from a technical school in his preparation for his formal training and study in architecture (he was graduated *summa cum laude* from the Bauschule in Zerbst, Germany, in 1928) stood him in good stead when he took up the camera.

In Sweden in 1933, after a year of further architectural study in Paris, where he worked in Le Corbusier's studio, Feininger decided to give up architectural practice. He became an architectural photographer for Sweden's top architects and architectural magazines, and an industrial photographer for manufacturers of ceramics.

His writing also began in Sweden, where, between 1933 and 1936, he produced a flood of magazine articles on photography and no fewer than nine photograph manuals and picture books. Since coming to New York in 1939, he has increased this list of book titles to the impressive number of 21; and he currently devotes all his working time to putting out new books.

Feininger's *Complete Photographer*, published in 1965, is a totally reorganized and updated compendium of all his former manuals. Its title is no misnomer, for the book touches competently and in detail on every important aspect of photography, from aesthetic philosophy to detailed advice on procedure and equipment. Andreas himself considers *Forms of Nature and Life*, 1966, for which he both wrote the text and took the pictures, to be the best of his books, but there are those who prefer *New York*, a picture book with text by Kate

ANDREAS FEININGER, *next pages:* Brooklyn Bridge. 1948.
New York, 42nd Street. 1947.
Coney Island. 1948.

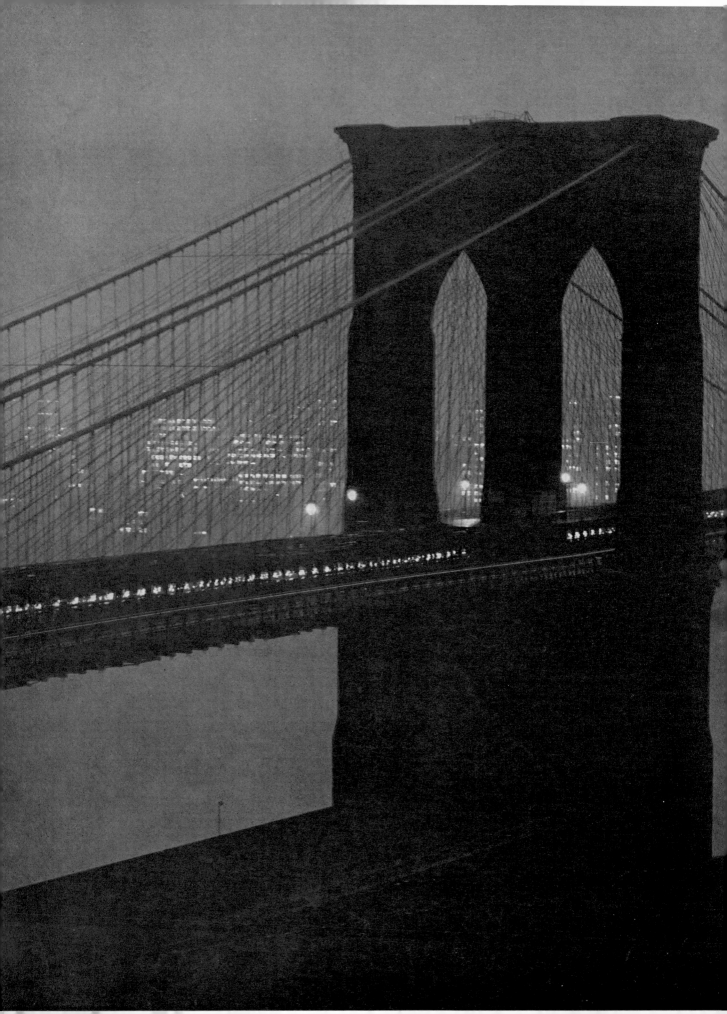

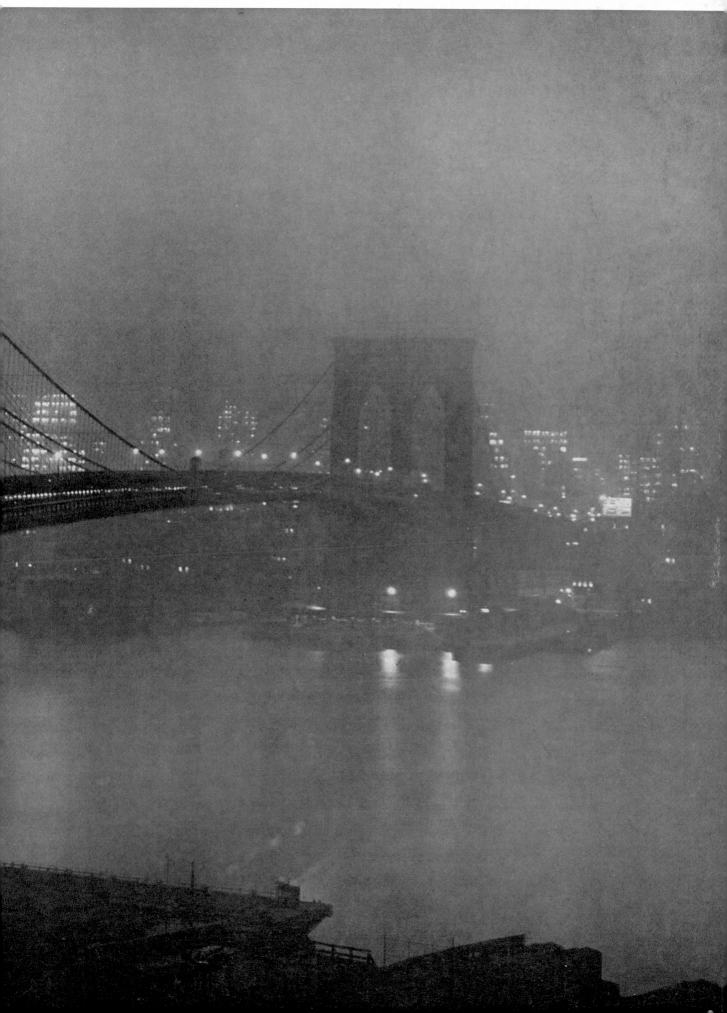

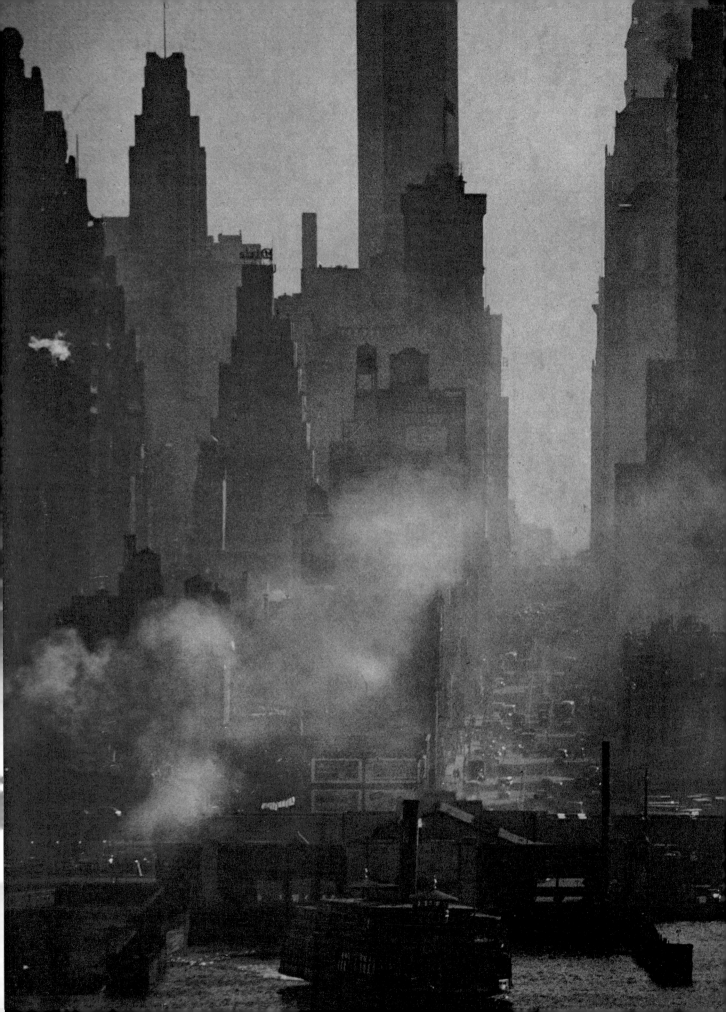

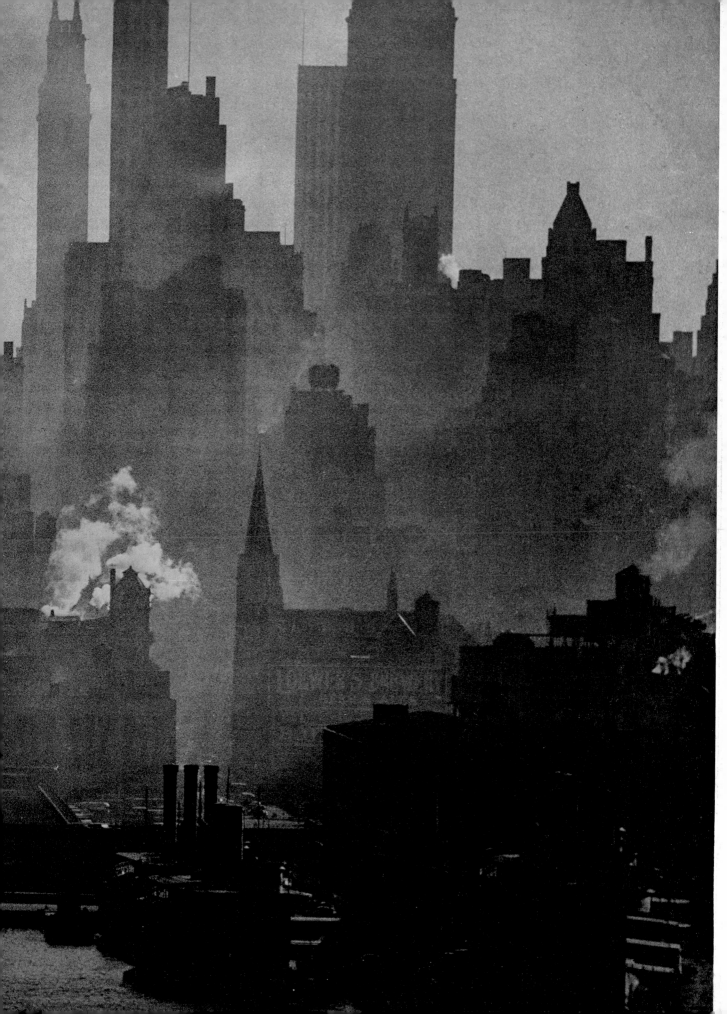

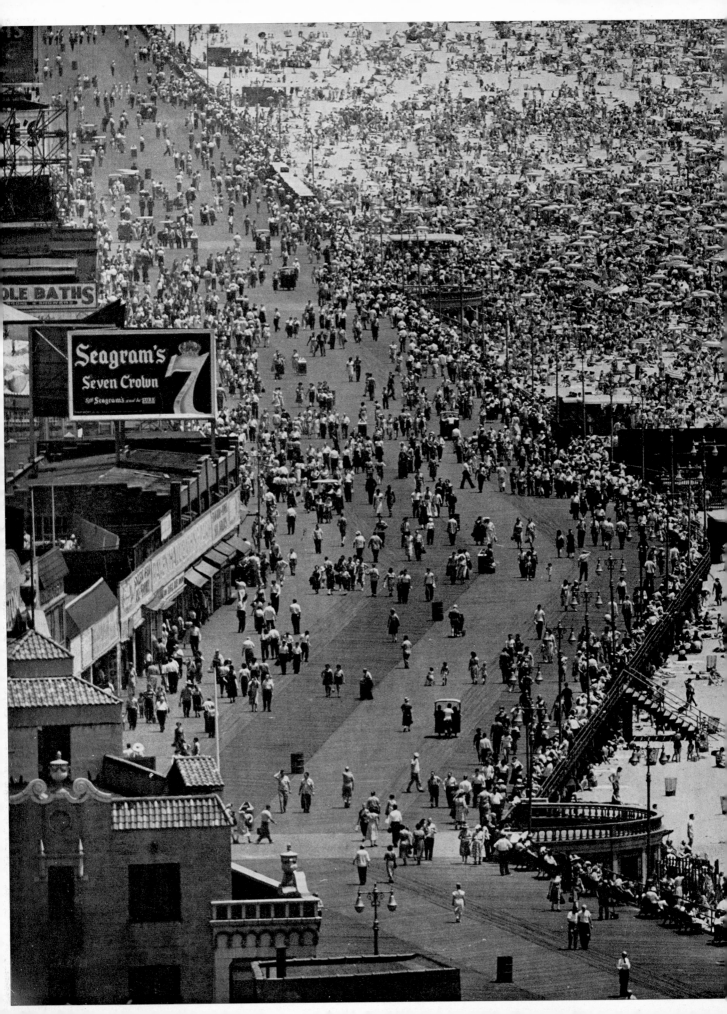

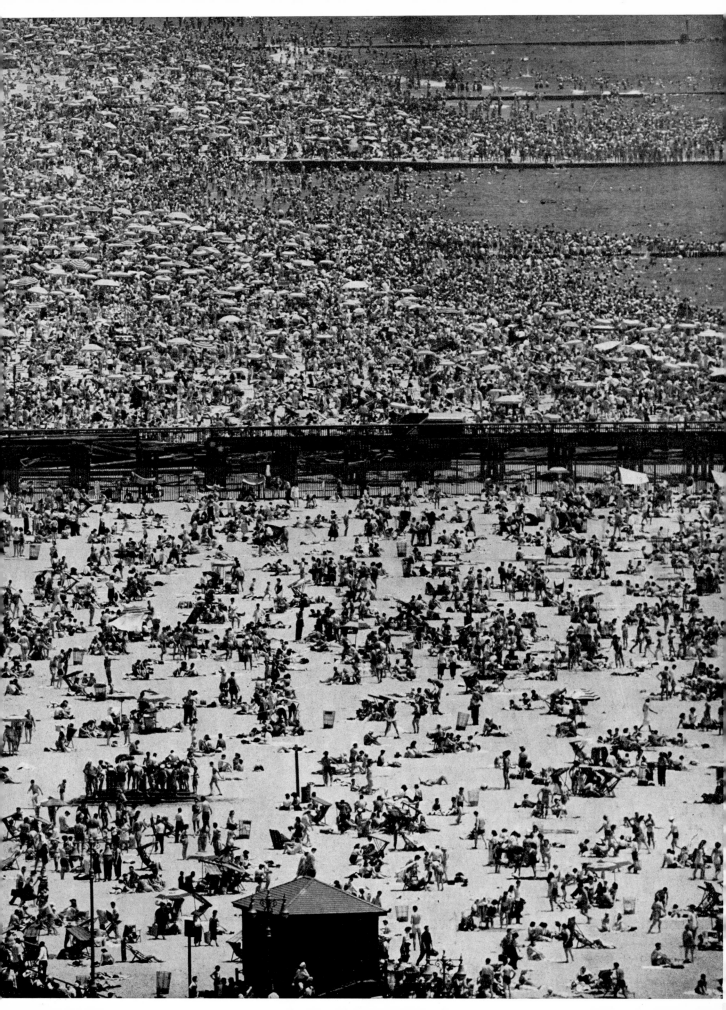

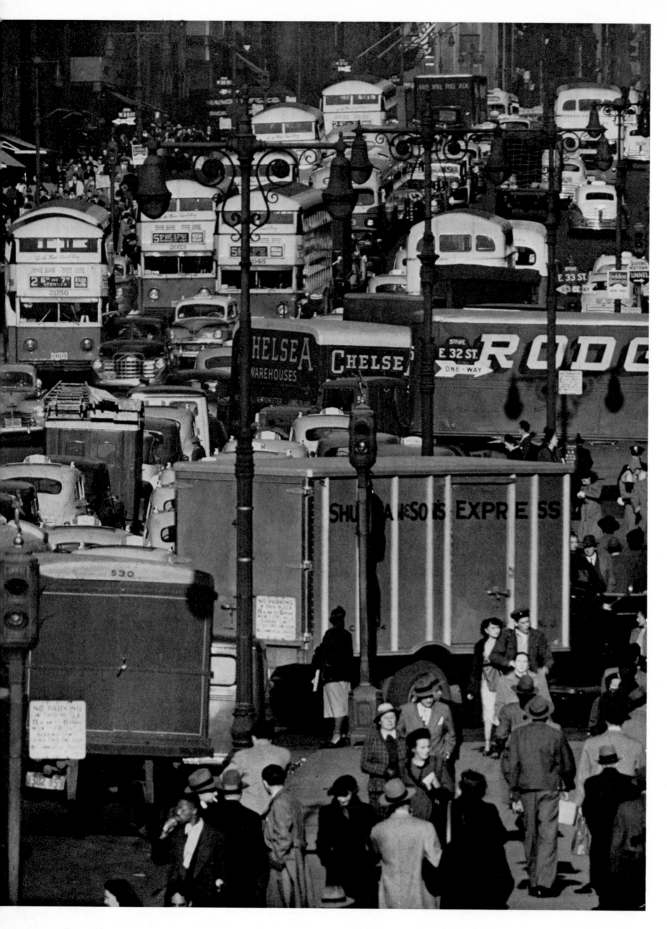

Simon, published in 1964. Among his other outstanding books are *The Anatomy of Nature; Changing America; Maids, Madonnas, and Witches;* and *Feininger on Photography.*

Feininger believes that for photographers—whom he expects to be color photographers from now on—nothing will be more valuable than interchange of ideas and stimulation between the arts of painting and photography.

"The camera," he says, "can push the new medium to its limits—and beyond. It is there—in the 'beyond'—that the imaginative photographer will compete with the imaginative painter. Painting must return to the natural world from time to time for renewal of the artistic vision. The key sector of renewal of vision today is the new vistas revealed by science. Here photography, which is not only art but science also, stands on the firmest ground."

FEININGER, *opposite page:*
Fifth Avenue, New York. *1948.*
right: Cemetery, New York. *1948.*
All photographs by Andreas Feininger courtesy Life Magazine.

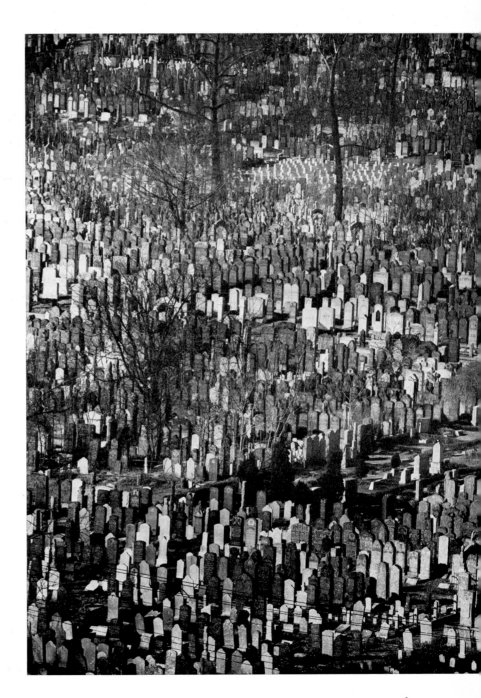

CHAPTER 45

Robert Capa:
Men in Combat

ROBERT CAPA was the foremost combat photographer of his time. A man who loved peace, hated violence and terror, and longed for a time in which there would be no wars for him to record, he dedicated his adult life to close and intimate study of men in mortal combat. His commitment to this task was passionate and complete. In 1936 he went to Spain with Chim and Gerda Taro, also a photojournalist and the woman he loved, to cover the Spanish Civil War. Carrying a camera instead of a gun, he characteristically moved along with the front-line troops, and almost immediately took his classic photograph of the death of a Loyalist soldier at the instant of the bullet's impact. Within a year, Gerda Taro was crushed to death by a tank, and, three wars and seventeen years later, Capa himself met violent death. Although a cautious and battle-wise veteran who never took an uncalculated risk, he took a mortal risk when a wished-for picture demanded it. In 1954, driving well ahead of French troops so that he could photograph the column as they moved along, he drove over a Vietminh land mine and was blown to bits.

He was born Andrei Friedmann in Budapest in 1913. When still in his teens, he left his native Hungary, then in the grip of Admiral Horthy's oppressive dictatorship, and went to Paris, by way of Berlin, where his compatriot Gyorgy Kepes lent him an old Voigtländer camera.

hus enabling Capa to discover that he and photography ad been made for each other. In Paris, Capa began a felong friendship with Chim and Cartier-Bresson. The aree youths worked together, often on the same stories, nd shared darkroom space. Together, they developed he concept of what Cartier-Bresson, the most polished raftsman of the three, was later to call "the decisive noment." Capa's pictures, as John Steinbeck was to rite, "were made in his brain—the camera only completed them." That is, Capa knew what to look for. Great events reveal their significance in small details and in bits of action. Every action has its pattern of movement—a beginning, a middle, an end—and at some point the meaning of the pattern is at a peak. At that point, photographers like Capa, Chim, and Cartier-Bresson snap the shutter. Thus, in photographing a 1936 parade of French World War I veterans, Capa waited for the wheelchair contingent; the picture he took speaks for itself. And so does the even more remarkable picture of exhausted and grimy GIs sitting around in the debris before the village church of Nicosia, Sicily, a town they had just captured. To the right, oblivious of their dis-

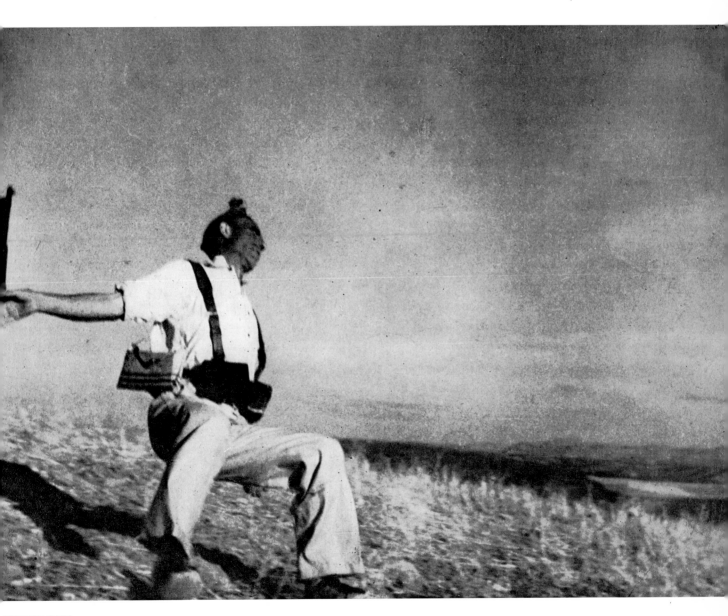

ROBERT CAPA
Death of a Loyalist Soldier. 1936.

603

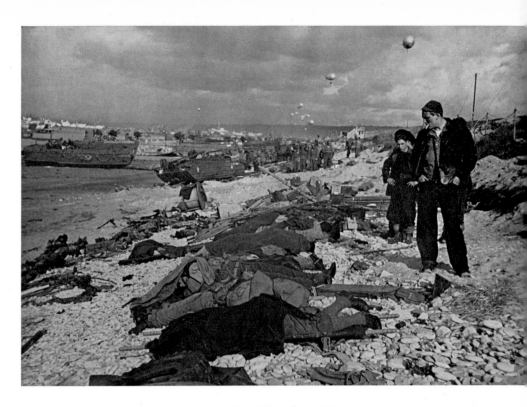

CAPA, D-Day Plus One: The Dead on Normandy Beach. 1944

enchantment, a winged statue of Victory rides heroically above the ruins to proclaim the glory of war with baroque ostentation. But there is nothing wry about Capa's famous picture of the Normandy beachhead assault. Its swift blur shows us, as no sharp and richly detailed picture ever could, the incredible violence of war.

After the war, Capa became what he happily called an "unemployed war photographer." In 1947, with Chim and Cartier-Bresson, he founded Magnum Photos, the international co-operative agency for photojournalists, and divided his energies between building Magnum and encouraging and instructing a new generation of photog-

raphers. And, twice again, he became an employed war photographer, photographing the fiery birth of Israel in 1948 and France's war in Vietnam in 1954. His Vietnamese assignment, unfortunately, was his last. With his death, the world of photography lost one of its most colorful personalities. He may not have been one of the greatest technicians—to him the picture story came first —but he undoubtedly was one of photojournalism's most dedicated sons. His dramatic pictures of the wars he covered in his time have become classics—reproduced again and again by editors of the most diverse political convictions.

CAPA
O-Day Normandy Beachhead.
944.

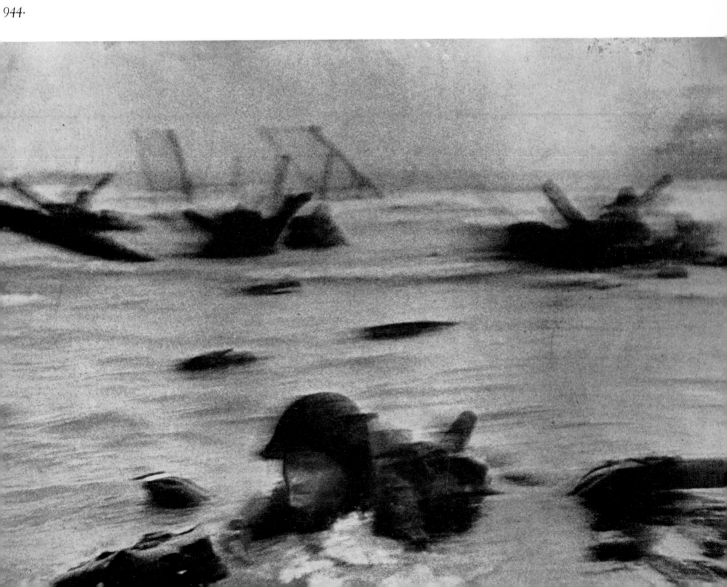

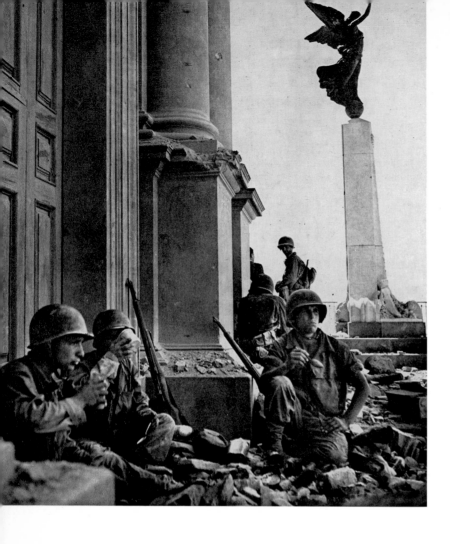

above: CAPA, Allied Victory in Nicosia, Italy. 1943.
right: A Day in the Liberation of Paris. 1944.

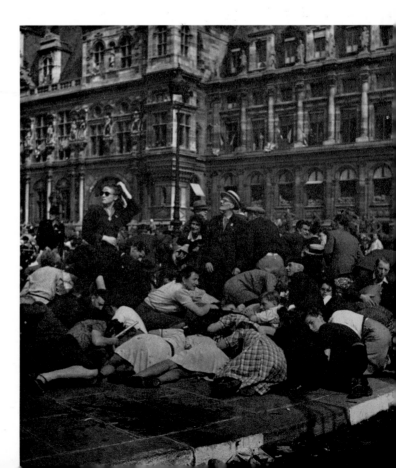

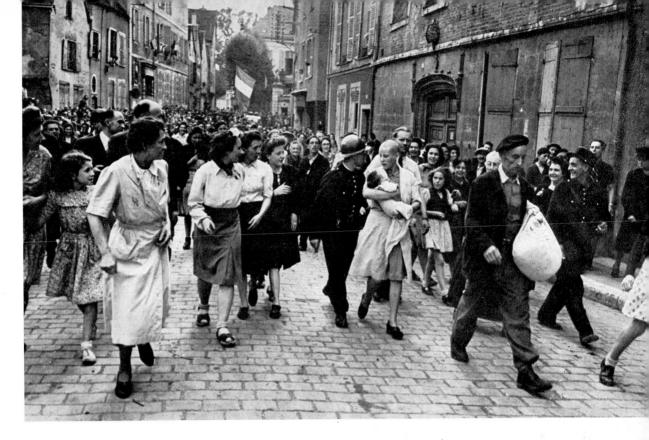

above: CAPA, A Collaborator and Her Baby
Escorted Out of Town.
Chartres, France. 1944.

left: Vietnamese Widows Grieving.
*One of Capa's last photographs
before stepping on a mine while
photographing French troop movements. 1954.
Courtesy Magnum Photos.*

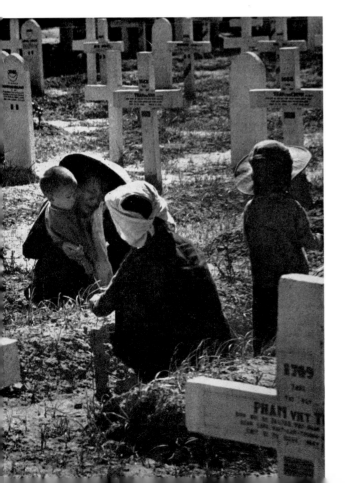

CHAPTER **46**

Eugene Smith

*Editorial layout, all photographs
and captions for this chapter
courtesy W. Eugene Smith.*

WHO IS OUR GREATEST photojournalist at this moment? Most photographers, if asked, would reply, "Gene Smith."

In many ways, W. Eugene Smith would seem an unlikely candidate for this universal, if unofficial honor. He is a near-perfect technician, but by no means the only one. And hardly any other photojournalist has proved so unadaptable to the workings of magazine-photography publishing as constituted today. Nevertheless, Smith is an awesome hero of photography in his own time, and his influence, always great, is constantly growing.

The reason for Smith's acknowledged importance is actually not hard to find. This brooding, temperamental man is a moral force. As a practical matter, other men cannot make the demands upon themselves that Eugene Smith makes. If they did, they would become impoverished; the disciplined teamwork of the communication enterprise would founder; and the printing presses could no longer run. But Smith gives photographers a standard of moral and artistic responsibility in executing assignments that serves as a guide to the entire profession in communicating truthfully.

"The photographer," Smith writes, "must bear the responsibility for his work and its effect." For "photographic journalism, because of the tremendous audience reached by publications using it, has more influence on public thinking than any other branch of photography."

Smith is awed by this power and overwhelmed by this responsibility; he sees understanding—deep, broad, on level after level—as an inescapable obligation. And he sees any compromise with that understanding as a betrayal of his trust. He will research a project as long as need be with every ounce of his formidable intelligence and with a determinedly open mind before taking a shot. He will then work with the utmost care which does not preclude and may even demand the utmost speed—to bring his hard-earned insight to his finished pictures. The living actuality of the subject itself is the only guide whose authority he will recognize in shaping his photographic interpretations. He will not allow instructions and suggestions from photo editors to coerce a subject into a preconceived pattern. Not only does Smith insist on taking, developing and printing individual pictures in his own way, but also—and particularly—on selecting and arranging picture sequences and their captions to provide what he regards as a true and faithful vision.

Obviously, Smith is no team man, and, just as obviously, photo editors are not so self-effacing as to bow out completely after handing a photographer a story assignment. Editors, too, are capable and talented communicators and, as well, dedicated men with strong convictions about the ways in which photographs are to be used. They would hardly be where they are if they did not recognize talent and make every effort to use it. Smith, thus, was associated with *Life* magazine off and on between 1939 (he was only 21 years old then and already a professional photographer for six years) and 1954. The years 1942 to 1954 were a running battle and an extraordinary love-hate relationship with Wilson Hicks, *Life*'s picture editor. Largely because of mutual exhaustion, the connection with *Life* was terminated amicably at the end of this period, Smith became a freelance photographer, and has remained one ever since.

It would be difficult to blame either Hicks or Smith for the storminess of Smith's term at *Life*; in the nature of

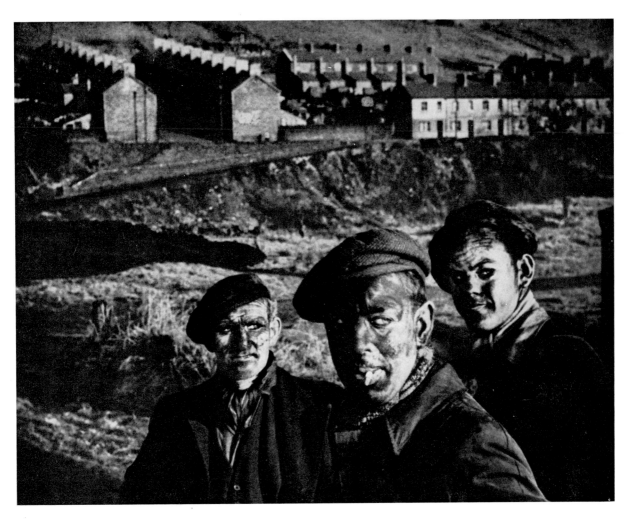

Welsh Miners. *Made as part of my reportage of the English Election of 1950.*

Smoky City. Pittsburgh, 1955. After resigning from Life *over the Schweitzer essay (some at* Life *said I would never again do another major project, and some tried to make it stick) I began the experimental Pittsburgh essay, the most extended I have ever tried. It was the city as the individual—the city to be known, reflective of its inhabitants but knowing no human intimately. To some extent, it celebrated the city's battle against smog, a remarkable battle, but the photograph we are using was a reminder that the "miracle" was less than perfect. Much remained to be accomplished.*

I approached the photograph from editorial and informational points that I believed needed to be made. (From such beginnings I then strive to make these points in a photograph that has its own separate validity.) There was the pollution, the suggestion of river dependence as well as other topographical characteristics. Beyond these are lead-ins for discussion of education, religion, and, of course, its commercial aspects. Careless viewers, especially editors, in feeling the emotional aspects of many of my photographs, conclude that the editorial points are accidental rather than the result of journalistic disciplines.

The essay itself was only partially successful, the writing as such (as published) ending in a flabby incompleteness—a compromise—for I was caught between my difficult circumstances and my respect for a deadline (plus a very deep exhaustion).

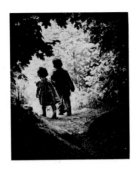

*The two children walking through the woods—*The Walk to Paradise Garden—*this, the first exposure I made after two years of hospitals and operations as a result of war wounds. (I received the wounds on Okinawa.)* 1947.

things, the two men were fated to pursue a collision course from the beginning of their association. But, from the perspective of 1967 and 35 years of Smith's work, it can be said that Smith is no less talented a photo editor than he is a photographer and that he seems, in all actuality, to be the best editor of his own work. (For this reason, and with my freely accorded assent, the normal page-layout procedure of this volume has been abandoned for the 14 pages accompanying this profile and the picture layout has been provided by Eugene Smith himself. I might add that Smith would never have dreamed of exercising the least control over the text.)

Some of Smith's greatest picture stories—*The Doctor, Midwife, Spanish Village, Albert Schweitzer*—were done for *Life* and Hicks. *Spanish Village* has been called "a new outpost in photographic journalism . . . rendered with some of the pictorial splendor of Spanish painting." After arriving in Spain in 1952 with a general assignment of doing a picture story on that country, Smith researched his subject for many weeks, reading a whole library of books on Spanish culture and politics, soaking up the moods, tastes, and flavors of the land and the people, and traveling 7,000 miles. In the ancient village of Deleitosa he found Spain at its most distilled and concentrated. The alarmed authorities of Deleitosa—Falangist to a man—were more than uncooperative. They

forbade Smith to take notes, ransacked his room, and demanded that he submit his films for their inspection. Smith and his assistant had to make a hasty departure for the French border in order to save the story from censorship or confiscation.

Perhaps the most splendid image of *Spanish Village* is *Woman Spinning*, which is so convincingly authentic that she seems to have stepped out of a genre painting by the youthful Velázquez. Of this picture Spaniards who saw the picture essay in *Life* said, "It's an insult to the weaving industry." Of the picture of a woman carrying loaves of bread on her head, they said, "It's an insult to the baking industry." It was thus a joy to Smith when he began to receive requests for prints from the Spanish embassy in Washington.

Smith's most astonishing photo essay, perhaps, is *Labyrinthian Walk*, a "personal interpretation" of Pittsburgh published in 1959 in *Popular Photography*, a magazine for which he had been a war correspondent from 1942 to 1944, before becoming a war correspondent for *Life* and suffering crippling wounds at Okinawa.

To encompass the life of a small village is one of the most difficult of tasks. To encompass the life of a great city is a thousand times as difficult, for—in Smith's own words—"to portray a city is beyond ending; to begin such an effort is itself a grave conceit." True. The metropoli-

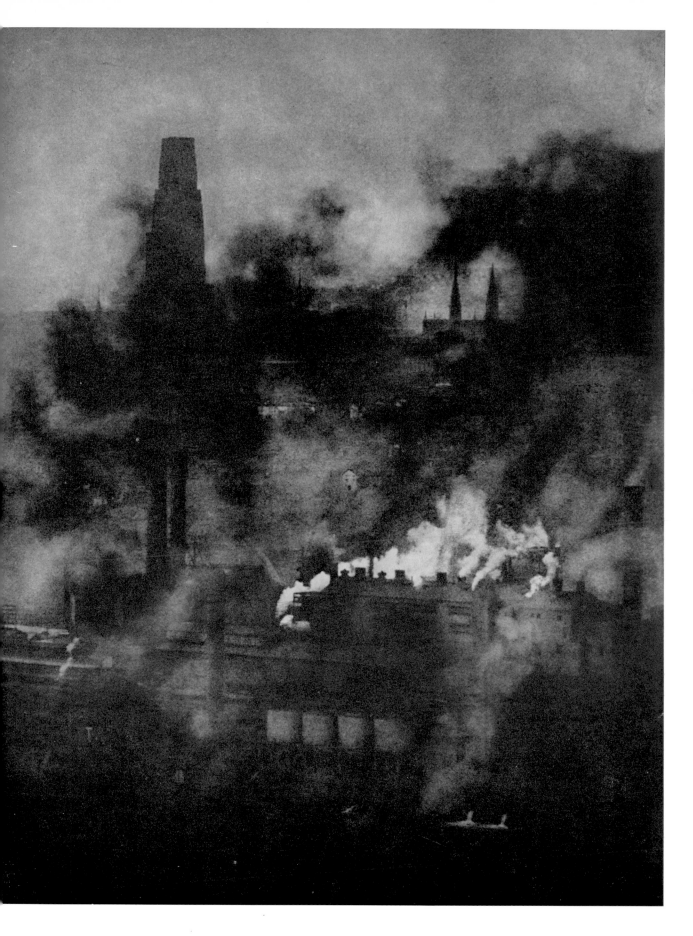

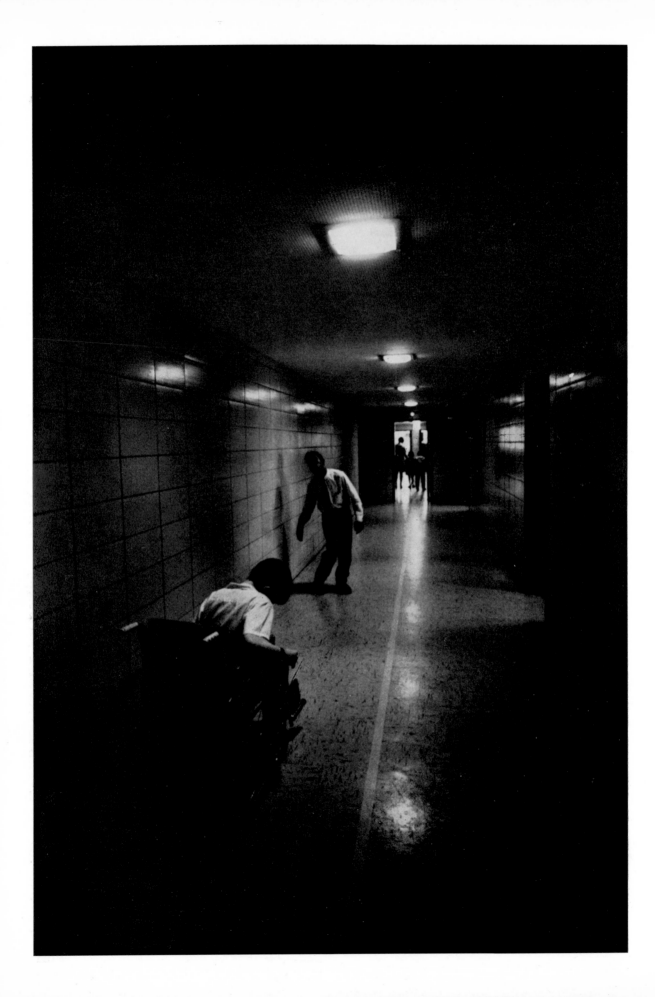

tan city form is so big and complex that it is beyond the limits of human perception. But we can move in it, remember parts of it, watch its people, note its landmarks, and catch its moods. No one before Smith had ever tried to do this—just a few aspects of a city had been all that any photographer had dared to take on. A film-making genius, perhaps, with unlimited funds and an army of motion-picture photographers could do an almost adequate job of portraying a city. *Labyrinthian Walk*, in fact, is extremely cinematic, with many shifts of topic, emphasis, and scale. If *Spanish Village* was a new outpost in photographic journalism, *Labyrinthian Walk* was a major breakthrough in human vision, a landmark of perception and communication.

"I am constantly torn," Smith has written, "between the attitude of the conscientious journalist who is a recorder and interpreter of the facts and of the creative artist who often is necessarily at poetic odds with the literal facts." Only a man with two such sides to his nature and profoundly aware of it could so have blended and reconciled them in photojournalism's boldest thrust toward the future.

The School Hallway. 1966. *Photographed in a section of a public school (New York City) devoted to the handicapped—part of an effort (a brochure) to raise money for the Hospital for Special Surgery.*

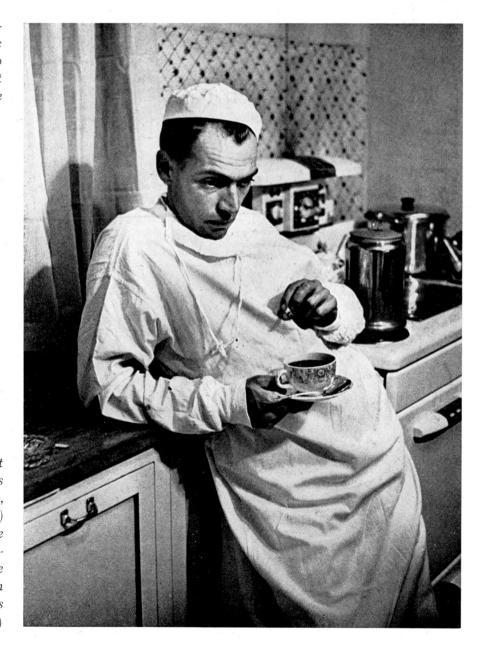

Country Doctor. 1948. *An essay that grew out of 23 days and 23 nights with a country doctor at Kremling, Colorado. Many suggest (or concede) that this story did much to change the course of photographic journalism. It at least helped to break the terrible habit of pre-scripting such "feature" stories. (The layout was terrible, however.)*

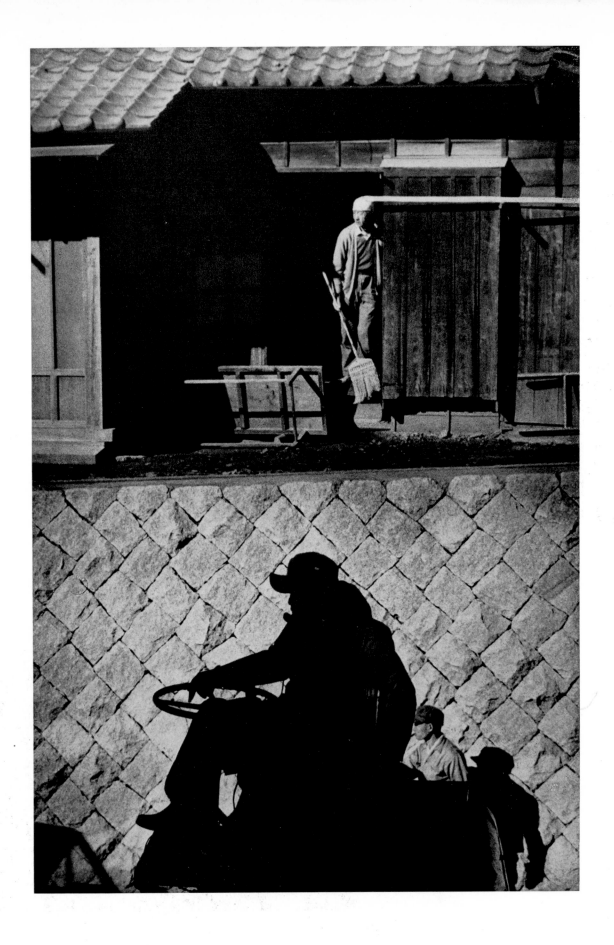

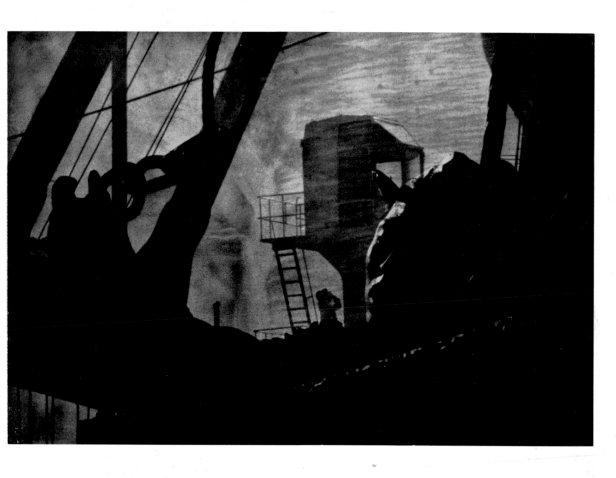

Japan (*3 photographs*): *From the book*
Japan—a Chapter of Image
sponsored and printed in a limited edition
by Hitachi, a Japanese electronics company.

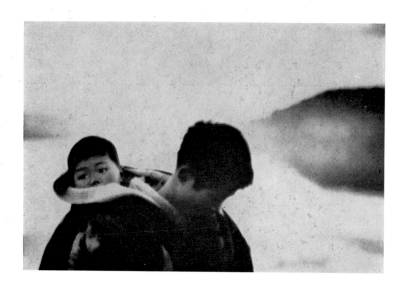

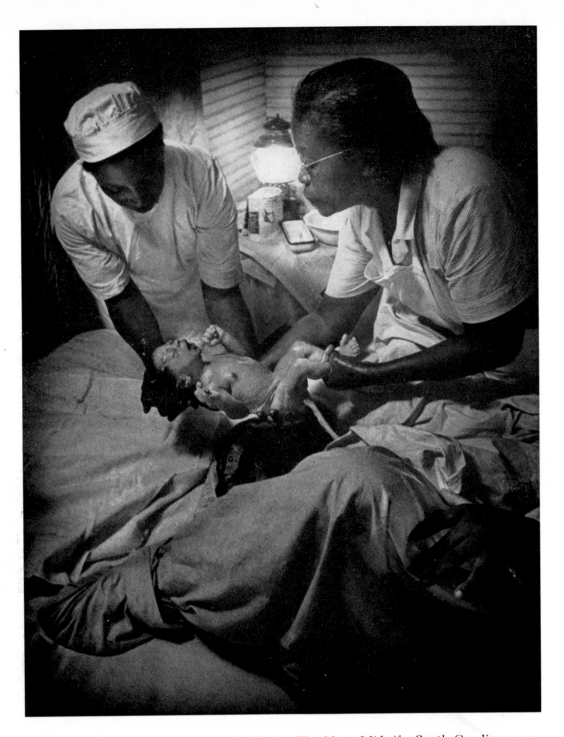

The Nurse-Midwife. *South Carolina, 1951.*
My own favorite essay. Many believed that I was a Negro—
that only a Negro could have approached
the subject so closely,
without discomfort.

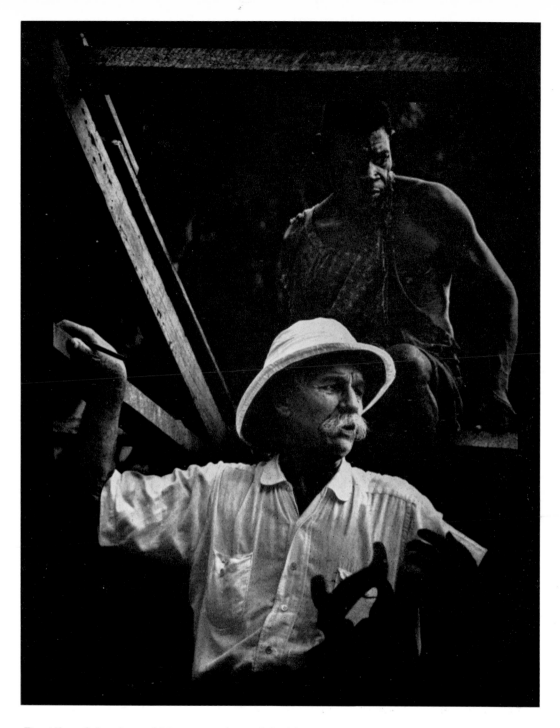

Dr. Albert Schweitzer. Africa, 1954. At work building a leper village near his hospital. The worker near him is a leper. "No one knows me who does not know me in Africa" —and this is what I tried to do. I believed my responsibility to be a cutting through of the myths and the malarkey—stating the story of a remarkable man at work in his African place, so that both those who gave him adulation as well as those who called him fraud would have a reasonable basis for beginning a re-evaluation of the man as a mortal. It would have cut away romance, but it was not a debunking. A farce of circumstance threatened the one importance of the story—I resigned in an effort to save it. The printed result was a rough and confusing semi-indication of what the essay should have been. The printed result was a failure.

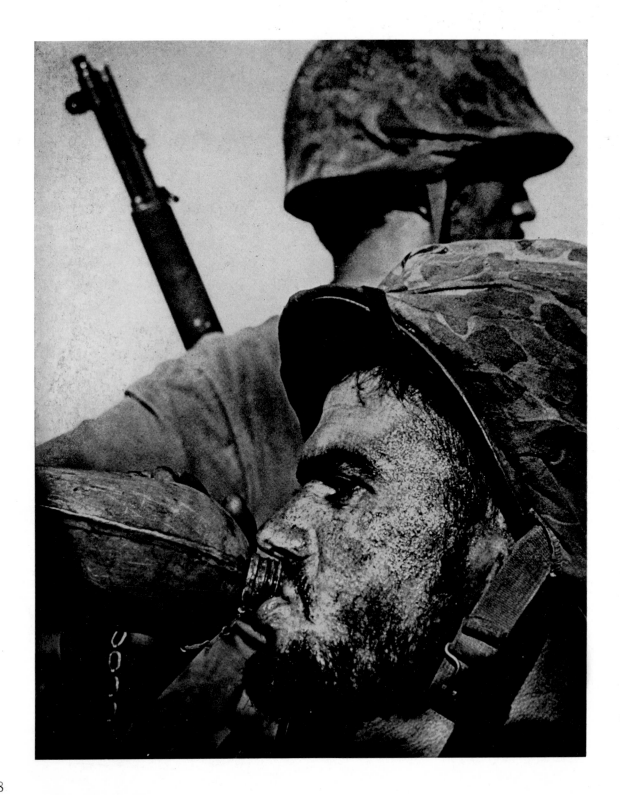

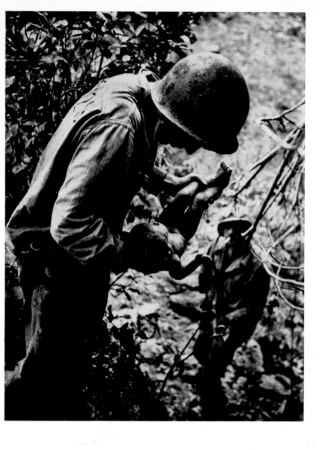

World War II. *The soldier drinking and the marine holding the baby were photographed on Saipan, 1943(?). The marine on the stretcher was on Okinawa, 1945, a few days before I was injured (on my thirteenth invasion, which included 26 combat flights and several invasion landings, all in the Pacific).*

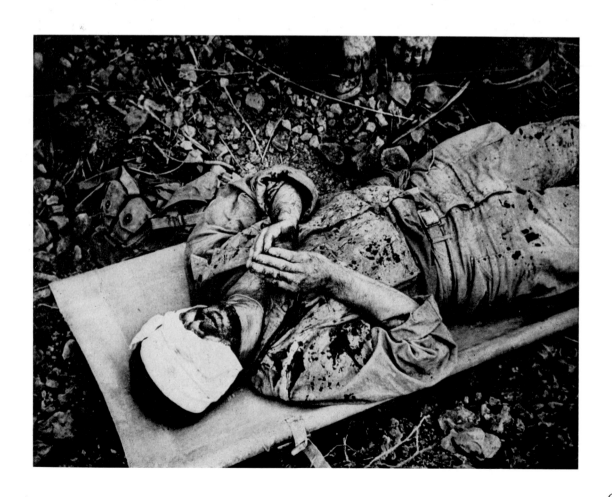

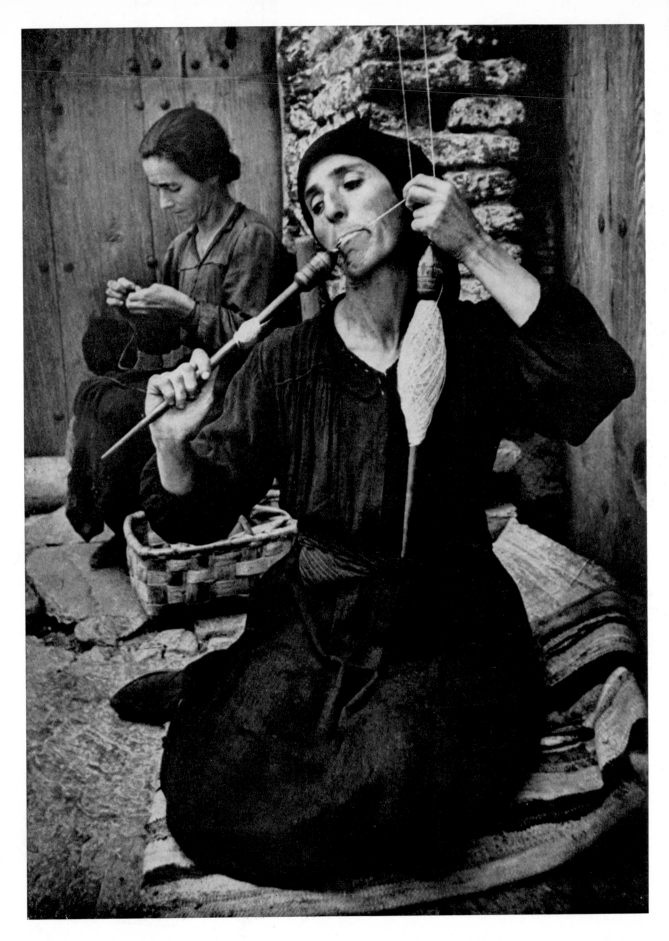

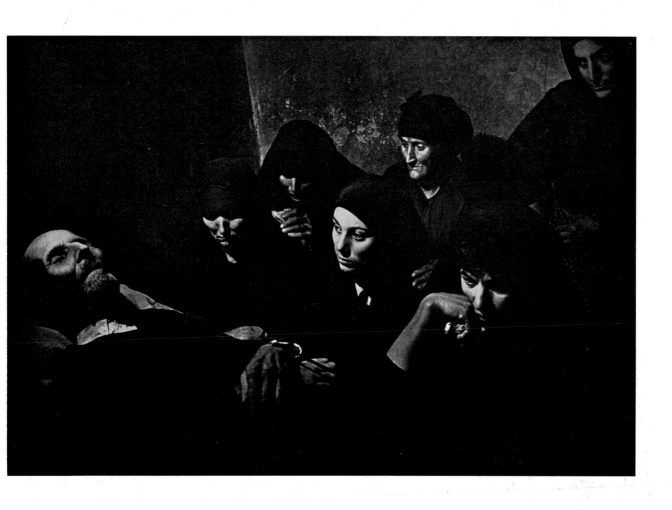

Spanish Village. 1950. *All were in one small village, not a typical village but an individual village that reflected many characteristics common to other villages.*

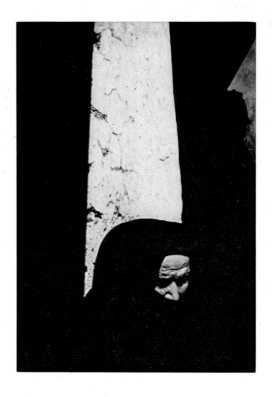

CHAPTER 47

'Chim' –David Seymour

BORN IN POLAND, David Seymour—"Chim"—completed his education in Germany and France, and died an American citizen. In Mexico when World War II broke out, he crossed the border to the United States speaking seven languages but no English. Volunteering in the U.S. Army, he served three years in the European theater of war as a photo interpreter for the Air Corps. Toward the end of the war he received a field promotion to lieutenant.

No man was more deeply loved among international photographers. A gentle soul, a gourmet of exquisite cultivation, Chim was devoted to children. He was single and 45 years old when he was killed in 1956, a casualty of the Israeli-Egyptian War of that year, which saw England and France as the allies of Israel. Except for one sister, Chim's own family had been entirely destroyed by the Nazis in the gas chambers. The wars that he covered (and he covered many wars) he saw as enormous crimes against the world's children. He revealed the horrors of war in the faces of children, photographing the lost, the hurt, the maimed, and the parentless, their starved bodies and their indelibly seared souls. He adopted children wherever he was. He sent money for their support. He remembered their birthdays and he saw them as often as he could. Whenever possible, he placed them in the homes of his friends.

Chim's professional career as a photographer began in 1933 in Paris, where he shared a darkroom with Robert Capa and Henri Cartier-Bresson. From 1936 to 1938 he covered the Spanish Civil War and events in North Africa and Czechoslovakia. When he could, he turned his camera away from the armies and the impersonal destruction of bricks, mortar, and bodies, photographing the faces of the people and showing us the personal, human consequences of the war. In 1939 he covered the voyage of Spanish Loyalist refugees to Mexico. Caught in Mexico at the outbreak of World War II, he went to New York and worked as a darkroom technician before his army enlistment. In 1944, wearing the uniform of an American army officer, he returned to cover the liberation of Paris, where he met his friends from all over Europe who had found refuge there.

At the end of the war, Chim co-founded Magnum Photos with Capa and Cartier-Bresson, becoming its president after Capa's death in 1954. Chim's first post-war years were spent documenting the children of Europe's devastated areas for UNESCO. His pictures were exhibited first at the Art Institute of Chicago, then circulated internationally, and later published as a photo-book. They touched the conscience of the world. Our illustration of a blind, armless boy reading Braille with his lips has come from these pages. After covering the foundation of Israel in 1948, Chim spent eight years on a great love affair with Italy, photographing the cities, villages, countryside, and people and producing marvelously intimate and revealing portraits of Lollobrigida, Toscanini, and Bernard Berenson. From time to time, he returned to Israel. His many pictures of that little state include our illustration of a Yemenite Jewish worker, whose bearded face has come straight out of the Old Testament of the patriarchs but who is engaged in the thoroughly twentieth-century occupation of pipeline welder.

When the war in Suez was launched in 1956, Chim went to cover it. Four days after the armistice, he and Jean Roy, a French photographer, took a jeep to the Suez Canal to cover an exchange of prisoners. A nervous Egyptian machine-gunner mowed them down.

Ten years after Chim's death, a cache of his Spanish Civil War and French Popular Front negatives was found. Several are now reproduced for the first time in this volume. They are a brilliant record of the harrowing days that preceded World War II.

DAVID SEYMOUR (CHIM)
Loyalist Troops, Spanish Civil War. 1936.

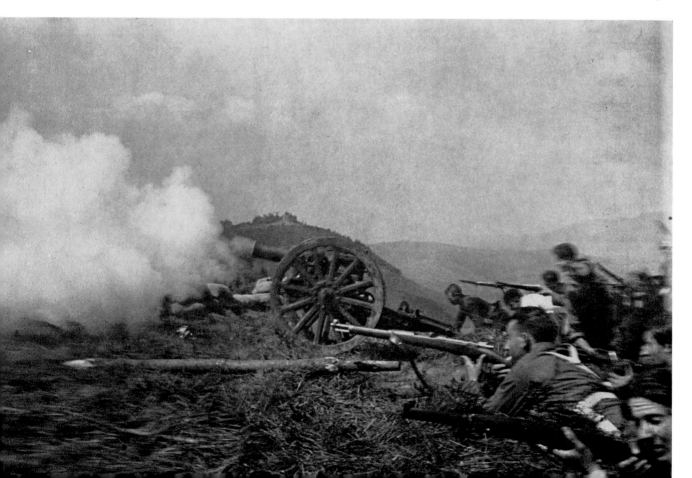

CHIM
below: Popular Front Sit-down Strikers. *Paris,* 1936.
right: Barcelona Air Raid. 1936.

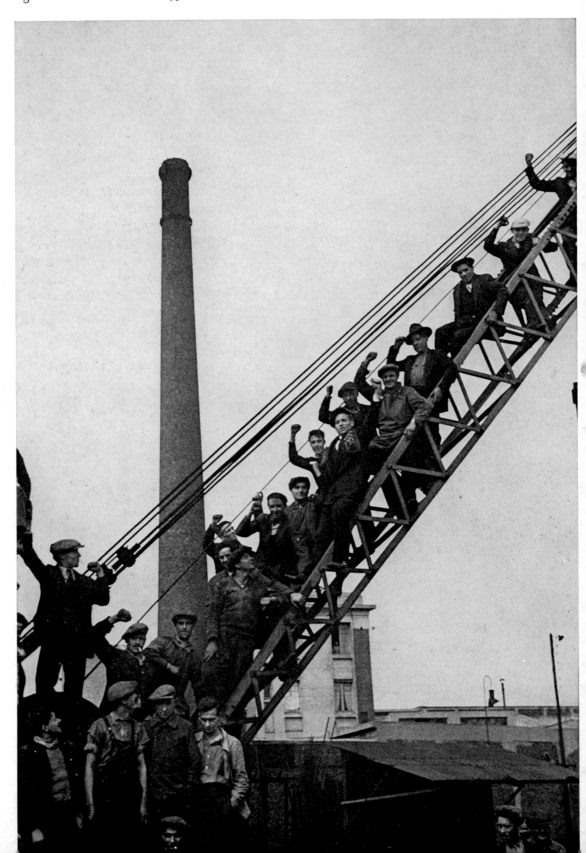

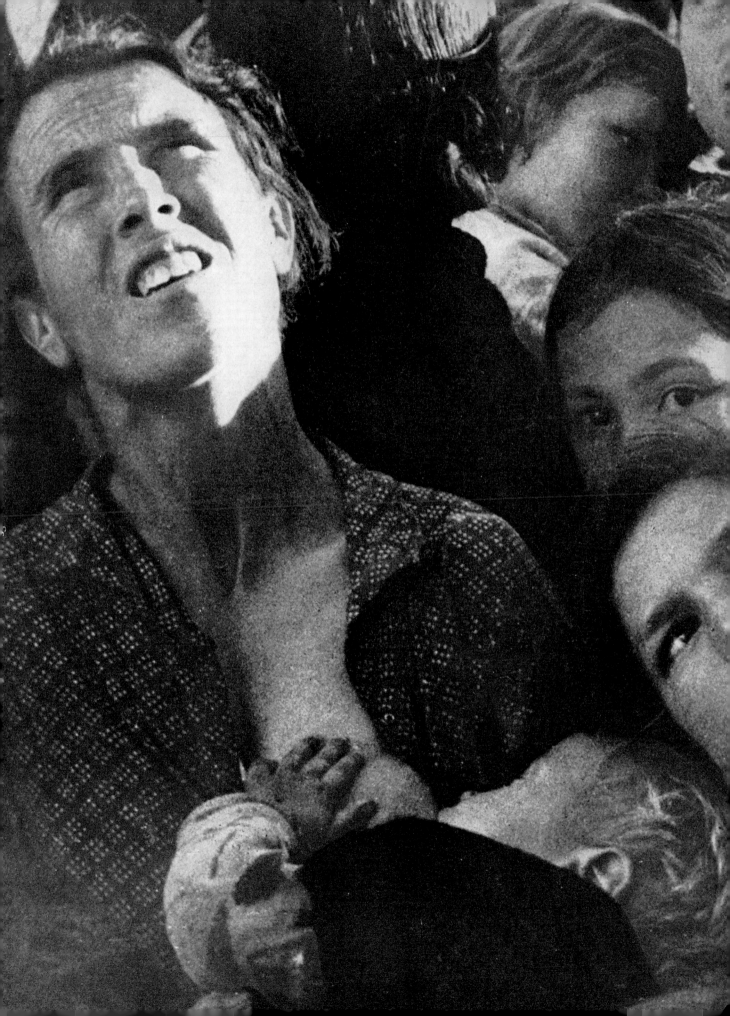

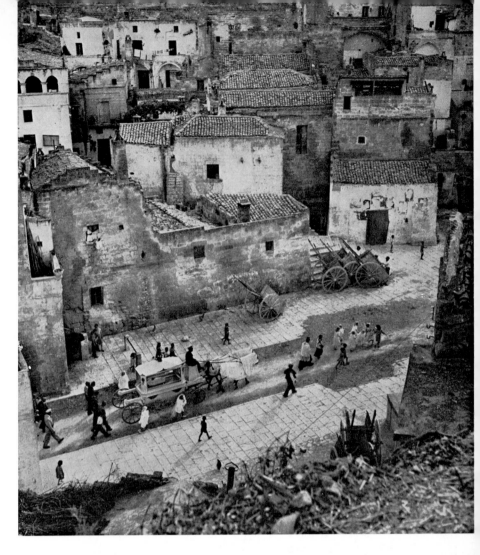

CHIM
Funeral of a Child.
Italy, 1948.

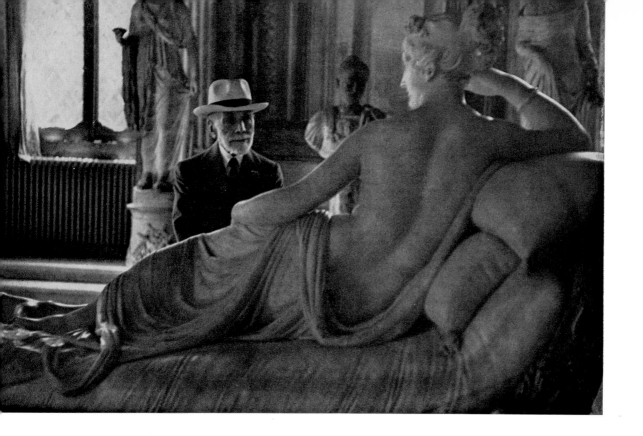

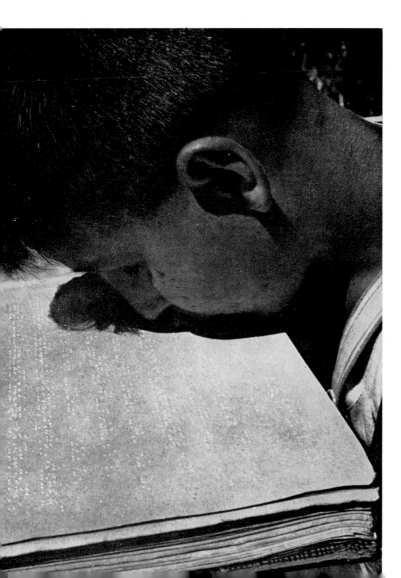

CHIM, *above:* Bernard Berenson
in Borghese Gallery, Rome. *1955.*
left: Handless Blind Boy
Reading Braille with His Lips.
Italy, 1948.

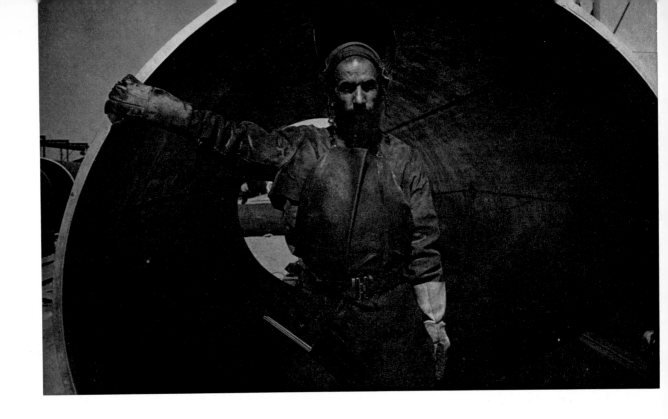

CHIM, *above:* Orthodox Jewish Welder. *Israel, 1954.*
right: Port Said. *1956.*

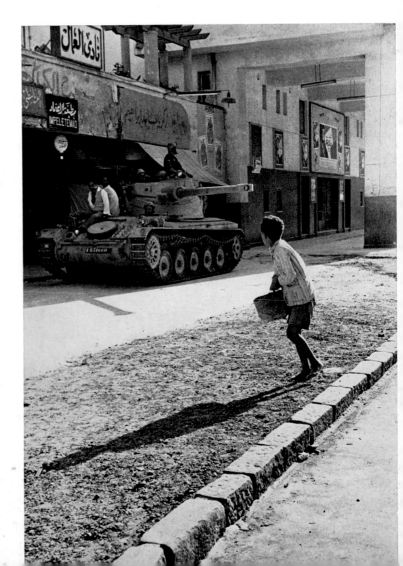

CHIM, Port Said during Suez Campaign.
1956.

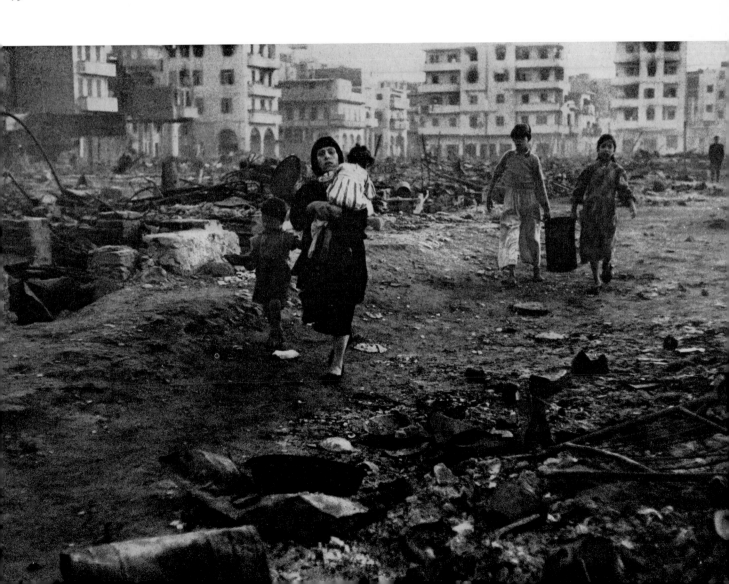

CHAPTER **48**

William Garnett:
The World from Upper Air

WILLIAM GARNETT SHARES Ansel Adams' sensitivity to the beauty of the outdoors and Feininger's interest in natural structure, but on a different level. He looks at the world from the twentieth-century perspective of the upper air, revealing the earth's forms and textures from above in pictures of extraordinary technical skill. He learned to fly in order to exercise full control over both camera and plane at the critical moment of shooting—accident was not to be allowed to select a subject and frame it within his viewfinder.

Garnett has come to know and understand the laminated world of air, land, water, and land below the water as Renaissance artists came to know the human body and its articulated structure of bones, muscles, skin, and hair. He discloses the transparency of lake and sea, describing the configurations of the shore and of the beds underneath the water surface; the ripple of the sand dunes; and the texture of plowed land, woodland, grassland, and hill. From high up he shows us the lively patterning of terrain—the maplike structure of the earth. Only such familiarity with the upper reaches of our natural environment could have produced his remarkable picture of a flock of geese where the pattern of the white birds is echoed in a double set of shadows—first in gray on the water's surface, and then in black in the ocean bed below.

The mountains, sand dunes, and deserts of his native

California and the adjoining states he has interpreted innumerable times from the air, always seeking that instant in time when the light of the sun and his own inner light of recognition were in inexplicable accord. Garnett finds inexhaustible inspiration from the bird's-eye-view effects which are uniquely his. He can envision them not only in the highly dramatic contours of Death Valley or the rugged Sierra Madre Mountains, but also in the lush farmland and worn foothills of New England. *Life* magazine, in March 1967, published his splendid picture essay on New England as the first in its series *To See This Land—To See America*.

Garnett's noble and sensuous forms, flat patterns, hovering mists, and subdued colors remind us of the landscape worship so deeply ingrained in Far Eastern artists. We find a magnificent blending of the purposes of precamera Oriental art and the most advanced Western technology in picture making. Garnett flattens his perspective, reduces space, accentuates patterns, emphasizes particular details. The photographs he took in Japan from the air have an innate resemblance to the painting of a wave or mountain by Hokusai. For, in Garnett as in Hokusai, nature is all. The landscape is never a mere background for man.

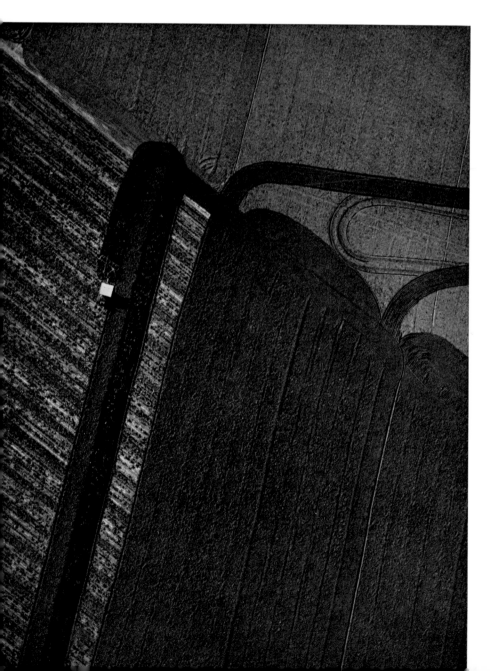

WILLIAM GARNETT
Tractor Plowing, Arvin, California.
1952.

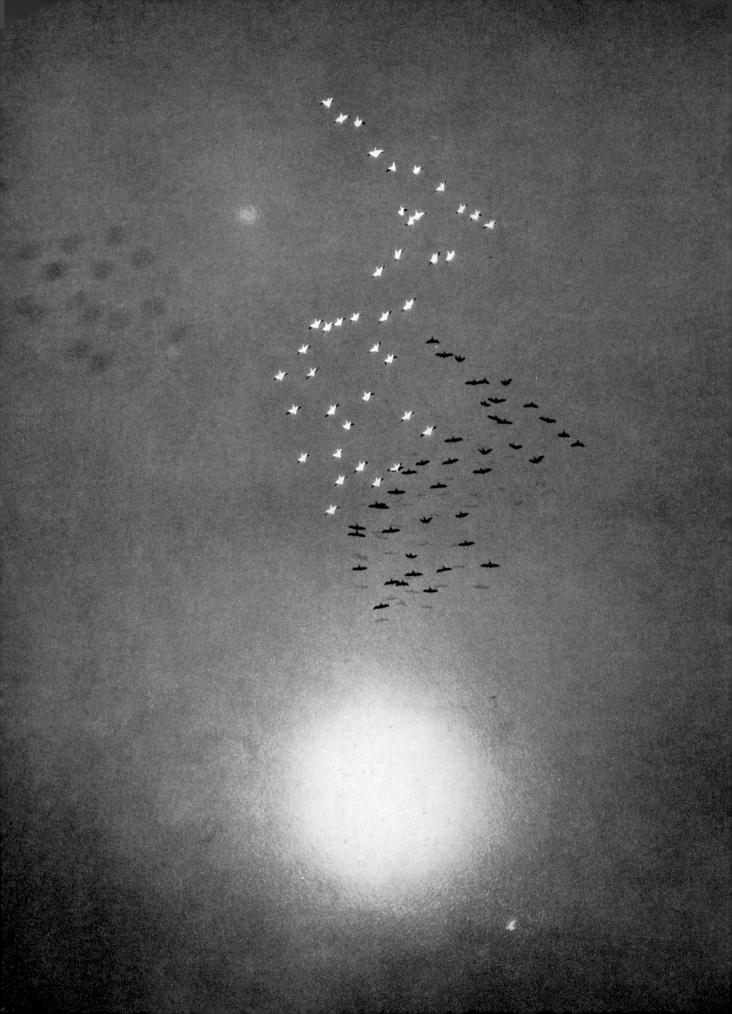

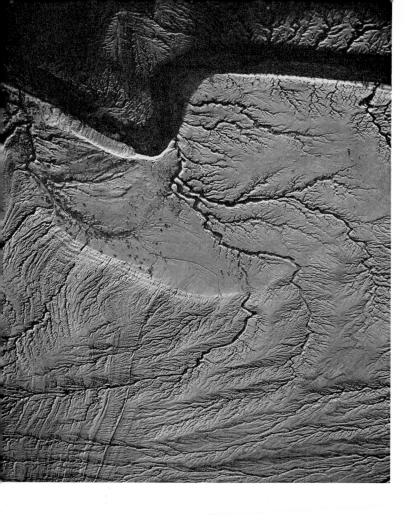

WILLIAM GARNETT
facing page:
Snow Geese over Buena Vista Lake, California. 1953.
left:
Erosion, Salton Sea, California. 1956.
below:
Tembler Mountains, Maricopa, California. 1957.

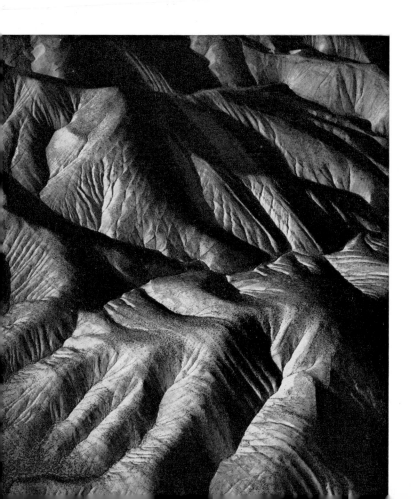

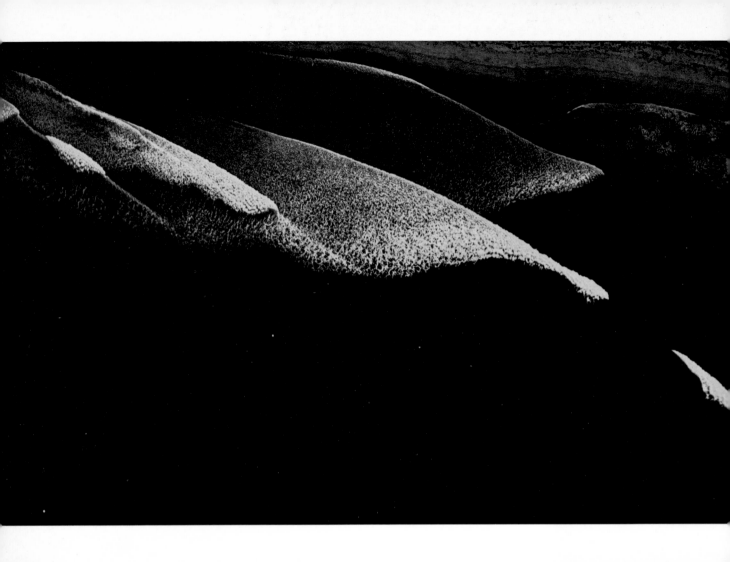

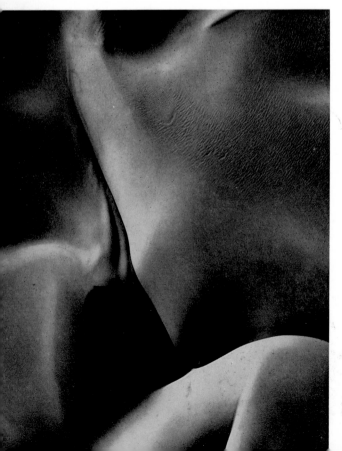

WILLIAM GARNETT
above: Surf at Oceanside,
California. *1957*.
left: Nude Dune,
Death Valley, California.
1954.

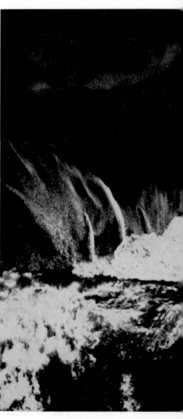

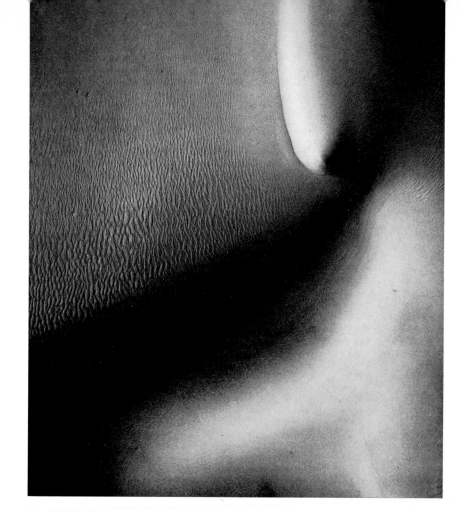

WILLIAM GARNETT
left: Sand Dunes, Death Valley,
California. 1956.
below: Surf, Point Reyes,
California. 1956.

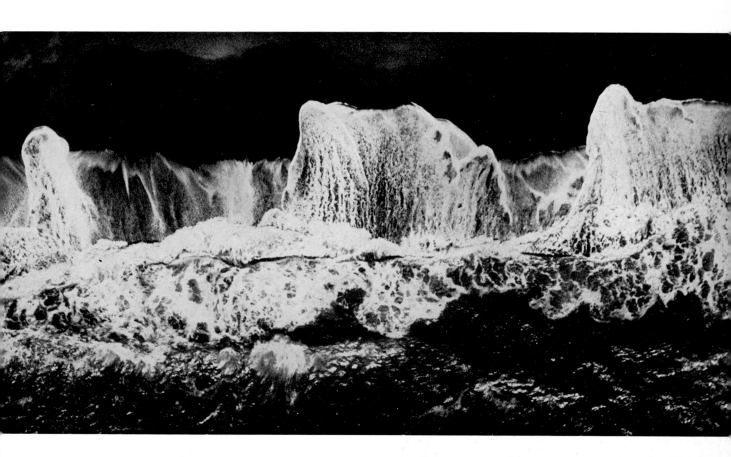

CHAPTER 49

Bill Brandt

BILL BRANDT IS ONE OF THE best-rounded and one of the most effective cameramen working in Britain. An architectural and landscape photographer par excellence, he is also a social commentator with the camera, a satirist of the incongruous social structure that was England before World War II. After photographing a memorable document in still pictures of the human misery he saw in the jobless, depression-bound mining towns of Wales, he turned to photojournalism when the war broke out.

When the blitz came to London, Brandt stayed. He haunted the shelters where the people escaped into sleep from the pounding above. Turning his camera on the silent forms, Brandt recorded their patterned distributions along the subway platforms, and he photographed them as they lay on the cold stone floors of church crypts and cellars, huddled together for warmth. His images of those harassed, courageous people have the monumental strength we also find in Henry Moore's drawings of the same scenes.

Brandt often came out of the shelters while the bombs were still falling to photograph the streets of London in the blackout. Lit by moonlight, the houses stand eerie and lonely; St. Paul's Cathedral looms steadily above the rubble, giving hope and courage to all. These pictures are indeed memorable, for Bill Brandt's mastery resurrects a true and feeling-charged image of that frightful time.

After the war Brandt made a series of photographs of the nude female figure using a wide-angle anamorphic lens. They are fascinating designs. By means of his distorting lens Brandt was able to alter familiar perspective and thereby create anatomical images of distorted shape or exaggerated mass. His conceptions of the human form approached those of Maillol's sculptures and El Greco's mystical attenuated figures. These photographs testify to Brandt's power as an inventor of forms.

In more recent times, Bill Brandt has photographed his personal pantheon, a gallery of celebrated portraits comprising Edith and Osbert Sitwell, Dylan and Caitlin Thomas, Graham Greene, Robert Graves, Cyril Connolly, Alec Guinness, Peter Sellers, Henry Moore, Picasso, Braque, and a few others. This unique set of portraits

exemplifies Brandt's driving concern to reveal the precise personalities he has come to know.

Brandt has published six photobooks. The first five were: *The English at Home, A Night in London, Camera in London, Literary Britain,* and *Perspective of Nudes.* The latest, published in 1966, is entitled *Shadow of Light.* This is a collection of photographs taken over a period of 35 years, showing the full range of his stylistic development from the time he acquired a camera in 1929 and went to work in the Paris darkroom of Man Ray, whom we have already met as one of the inventors of abstract photography.

This comprehensive book of Brandt's pictures shows us that a great photographer cannot be pigeonholed as documentary, abstractionist, social realist, or photojournalist. A great photographer is a thorough artist, one who imprints his intelligence, will, and understanding on what he takes. Such a man is Bill Brandt.

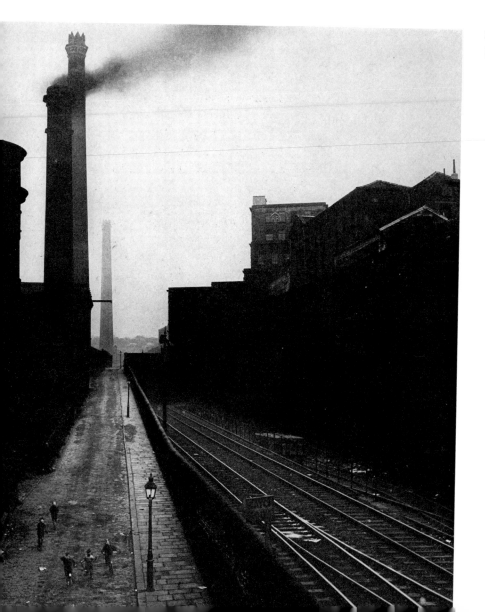

BILL BRANDT
Halifax. 1936.

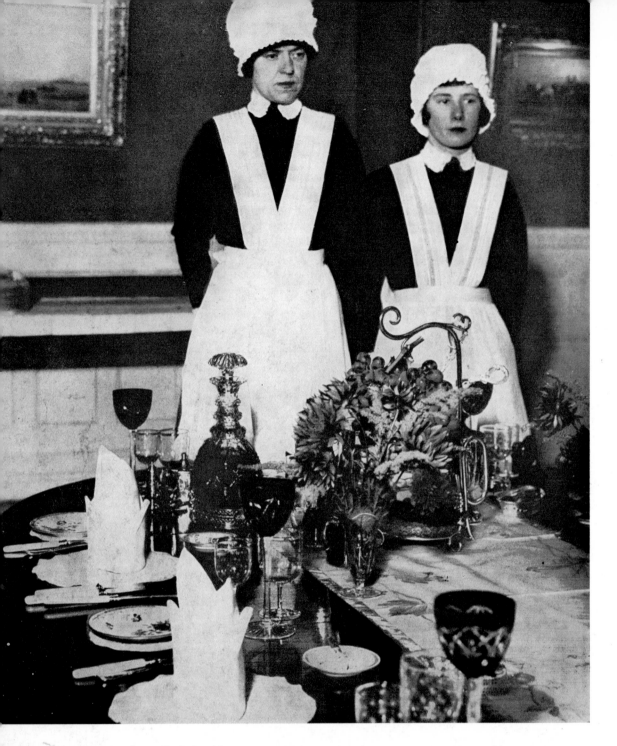

BILL BRANDT, *above*: Parlormaids. *1932*.
opposite page: "Wuthering Heights." *1945*.

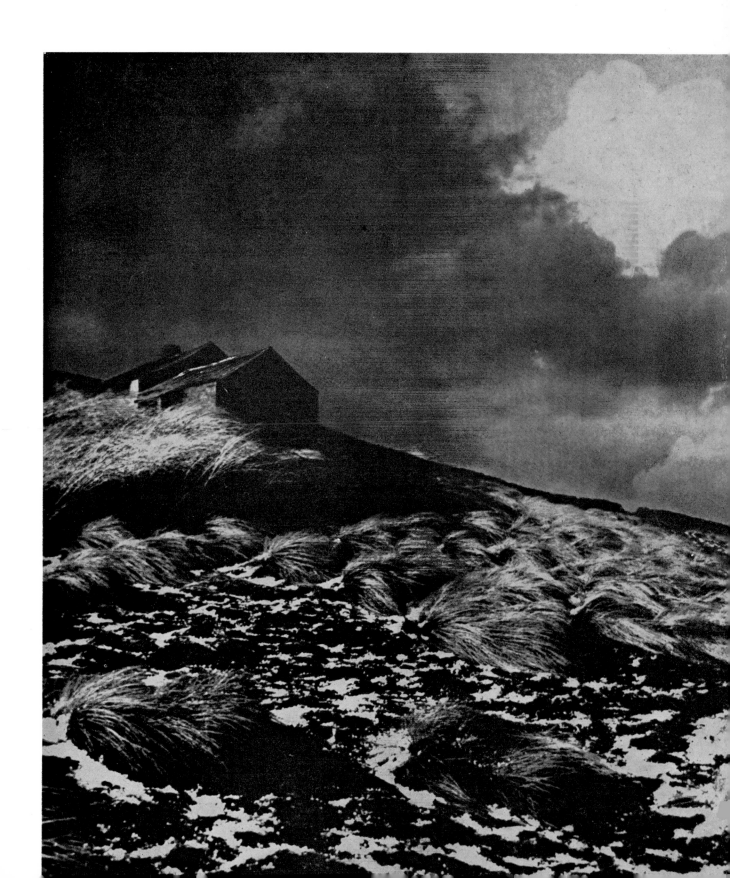

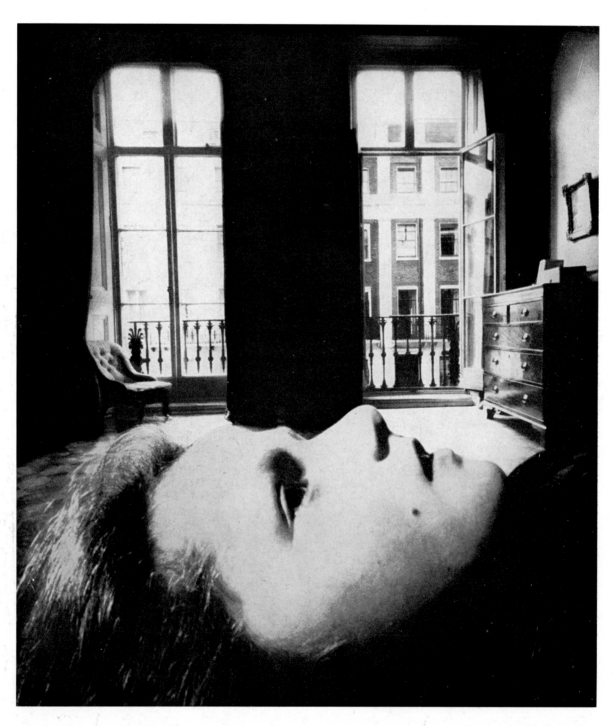

BRANDT, London Child. 1955.

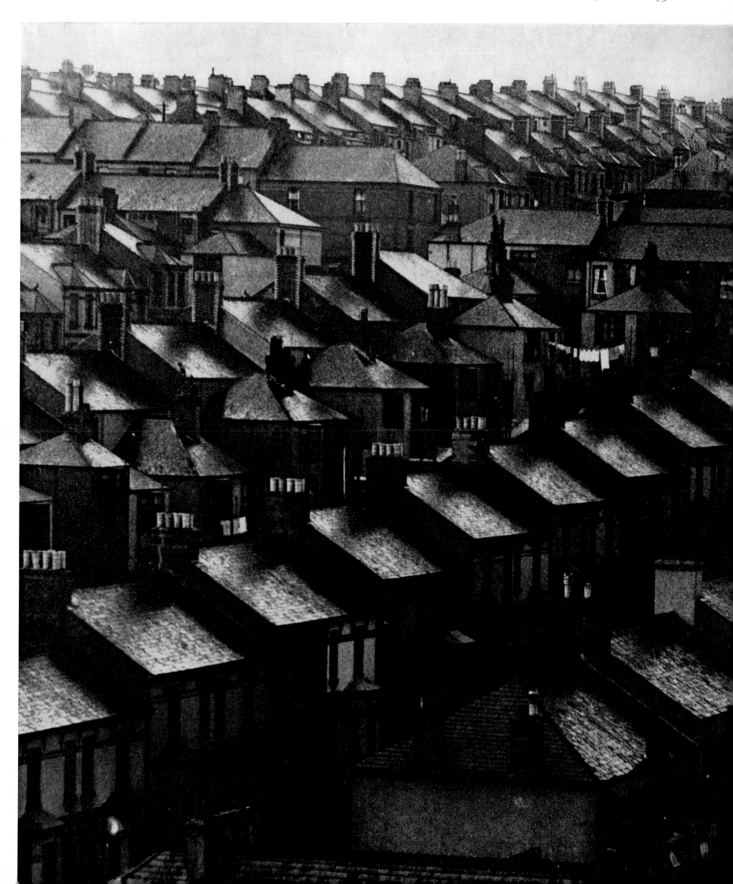

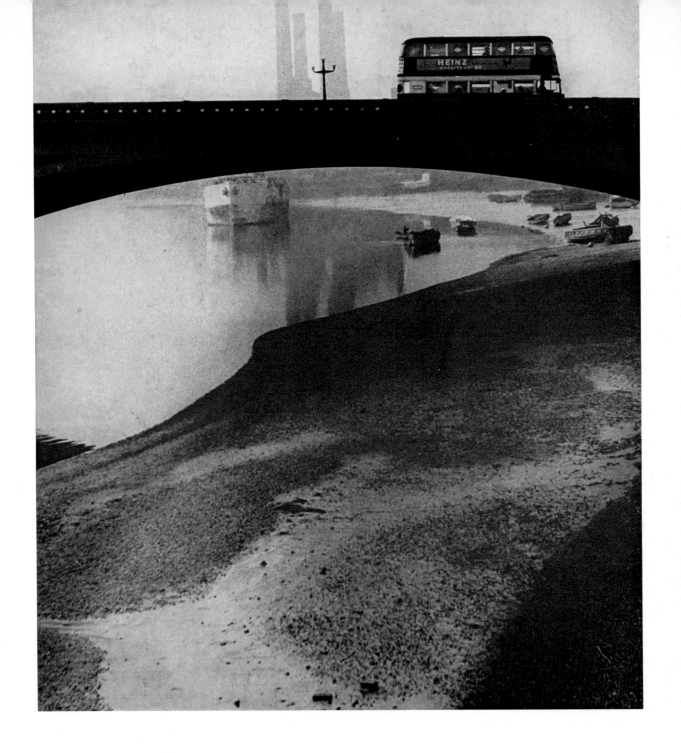

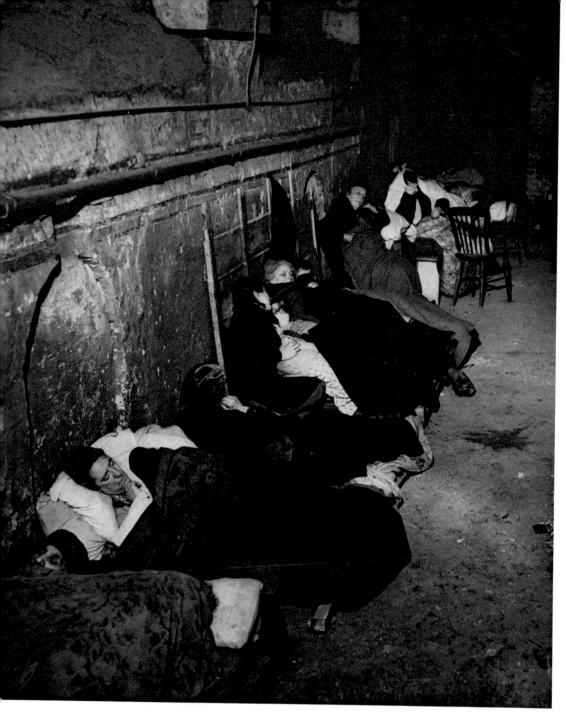

BILL BRANDT
facing page:
Battersea Bridge. 1937.
above:
Christ Church Crypt, Stepney.
1940.

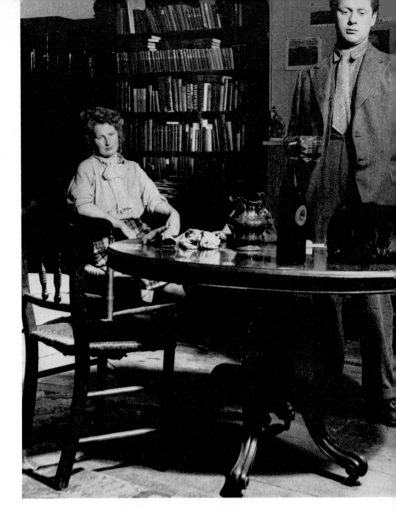

BILL BRANDT
Dylan and Caitlin Thomas.
1944.

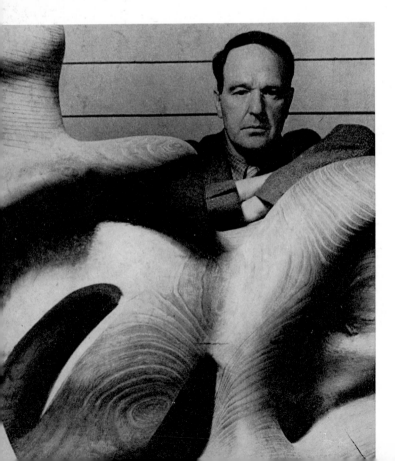

left: Henry Moore. *1946.*
facing page: Shadow of Light. *1959.*

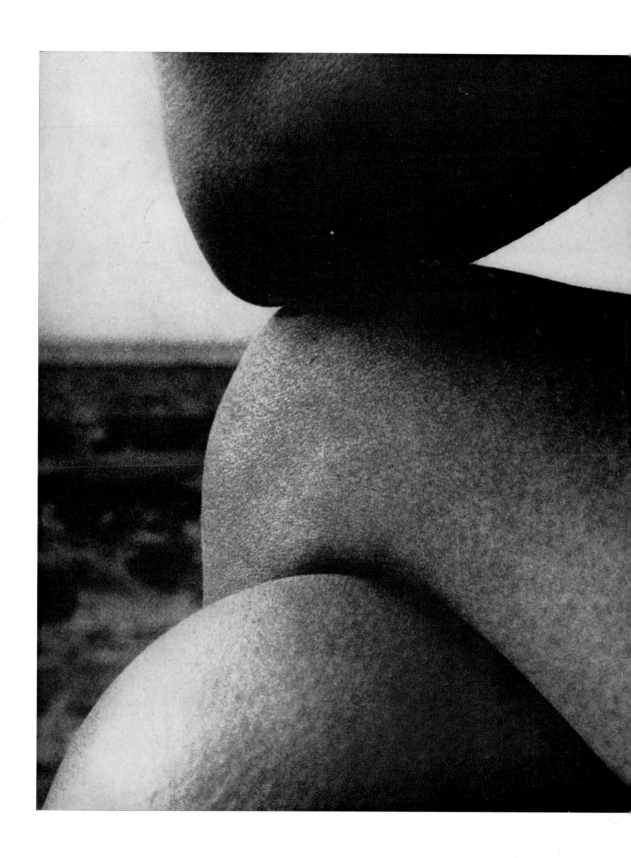

CHAPTER 50

Arnold Newman

ARNOLD NEWMAN SPECIALIZES in portraiture: grandly patterned, superbly composed pictures of which parts are symbolic objects that signify the sitter's occupation or other importance in the world. Newman reveals with a great degree of objectivity rarely seen sides of the sitter's personality. He seems to have the ability, amounting almost to extrasensory perception, of finding that infinitesimally brief moment in time when an important aspect of a personality stands clearly revealed. Arnold denies possession of this gift—but he has it nevertheless, like certain other portrait photographers before him. Sarony also had it, though he looked only for momentary drama rather than for the disclosure of a personality or for the sudden revelation of a hidden face that exposes the subject's inner character.

Newman has trained himself to observe deeply, to penetrate below the surface. He is particularly interested in the relation between a man's personality and his life's work. He wants to know what there is about them that makes them important in our time, and searches for symbols that suggest their involvement. His attitude towards the sitter seems to be: "You are the sum of the work you've done. Therefore, in my pictures, I shall say something about the field you have made your life's work and, most important of all, how you feel toward it."

A photographer could do this easily enough, perhaps,

through exaggeration, through caricaturing a salient feature of the sitter's face or body, or by prettifying, glossing over, or dramatically enobling him. Arnold's exaggerations are used only for the sake of design, not for characterization. He waits patiently for the sitter to reveal an aspect he has pre-envisioned as the most characteristic. He has anticipated that aspect, and never misses it when it appears. In that instant he records the pictorial image that he knew would come.

Though Arnold Newman had some training as an artist (he attended the University of Miami) and as a portrait photographer is the servant of images and ideas, he does not attempt to force his sitter's likenesses into great noble pictures resembling masterpieces in portraiture of the past. He wants to make his own kind of picture. And a Newman portrait is now invariably recognized for what it is.

Arnold is a master of lighting. He works extremely fast when on an assignment outside his studio. When he photographed President Lyndon B. Johnson he was allowed 1½ hours to set up his lights but only fifteen minutes with the President to take the pictures; he took 30 minutes, nevertheless. Arnold used two cameras—an 8 x 10 and a 4 x 5—for black-and-white and color film respectively. He posed his subject so that the architectural features of the President's office in the White House completed the consciously controlled elements of his composition, producing a photograph that LBJ selected as the official portrait of the Chief Executive.

Arnold said, "Weeks before I leave on an assignment the editors and I thrash out the creative concepts. I take both color and black-and-white film with me—there are too many differences in European films even in those of the same manufacturer. I carry filters, cameras, lenses, repair kits, duplicate parts, etc., all the equipment I can imagine I will need on an assignment—and I try to anticipate such problems as differences in electric voltage, lighting needs that I cannot satisfy in many countries, etc. I find I always bring some things I don't need and forget some things I need very badly—but you make do and get, or try to get, the kind of a picture you imagined before you left, but I always try to remain alert to see a picture I never even imagined."

The camera now dominates the domain of portraiture. Painters finally relinquished this once most important aspect of their profession around the turn of the century, when Cézanne admonished his sitters to sit as still as an apple. To him portraiture was a branch of still life. The late C. J. Bulliet, art critic for the *Chicago Daily News*, was wont to say, speaking for modern artists: "An apple by Cézanne is a Madonna by Raphael." Portraits became a matter of an artist's invention rather than the faithful description of a person, after Picasso's experiments in simultaneous views of the sitter became popular among artists of the twenties. In our own day, painters eschew the likeness practically in its entirety; closed to painters, the field of portraiture has been left open for photographers. Modern artists, moreover, seem to feel that portraiture is a lesser field, beneath their dignity. What they do not realize is that to the fine photographer the likeness is no more a criterion of a successful portrait than it is to them. The photographer can make it smooth and well-groomed, as do society's slick portrait painters. Many of these actually copy the photograph to get that more-than-lifelike picture. How differently Ingres, Delacroix, and Degas used photographs as documents for their creative portraits!

The cameraman can range from the maker of a "true image," an untouched real-life 35 mm picture, to the manipulator of form who imposes his style on the piece of film inside the box, even a Brownie, which Edward Weston once demonstrated he could do and took a fine photograph (see his Rosa Covarrubias on the roof of her house in Mexico). Karsh and Newman use more complicated gear to create images that endure, as in the former's portrait of Churchill or the latter's portrait of Stravinsky. In the work of such men obvious physical appearance, likeness, is subordinated to the all-over intent, the total image. This can be done whether the photographer is shooting candid at a thousandth of a second with a miniature camera or is working in a formal studio with a "Big Bertha" 8 x 10 camera. The effectiveness of the portrait depends upon the photographer's conception and his capability of realizing it. Unfortunately, too many portrait photographers through stereotyped lighting and pancake makeup produce images that are masks, not people. We are all familiar with their work, their wooden impoverished countenances—the profundity of the human personality and the mystery of the human face drowned in a sea of worn-out conventions.

The life a man has lived is marked in his face, which reflects his inner depths. It may not be there on the surface, for people hide their miseries, their areas of darkness. But not to gifted and sensitive students of the *visage de l'homme*—a colleague of Thomas Eakins once said that he'd never pose for him, for parts of him would be exposed that he had been hiding for years and did not want the world to see.

Newman's early work reflects his intense interest in abstract art and artists, particularly his series *Artists Look*

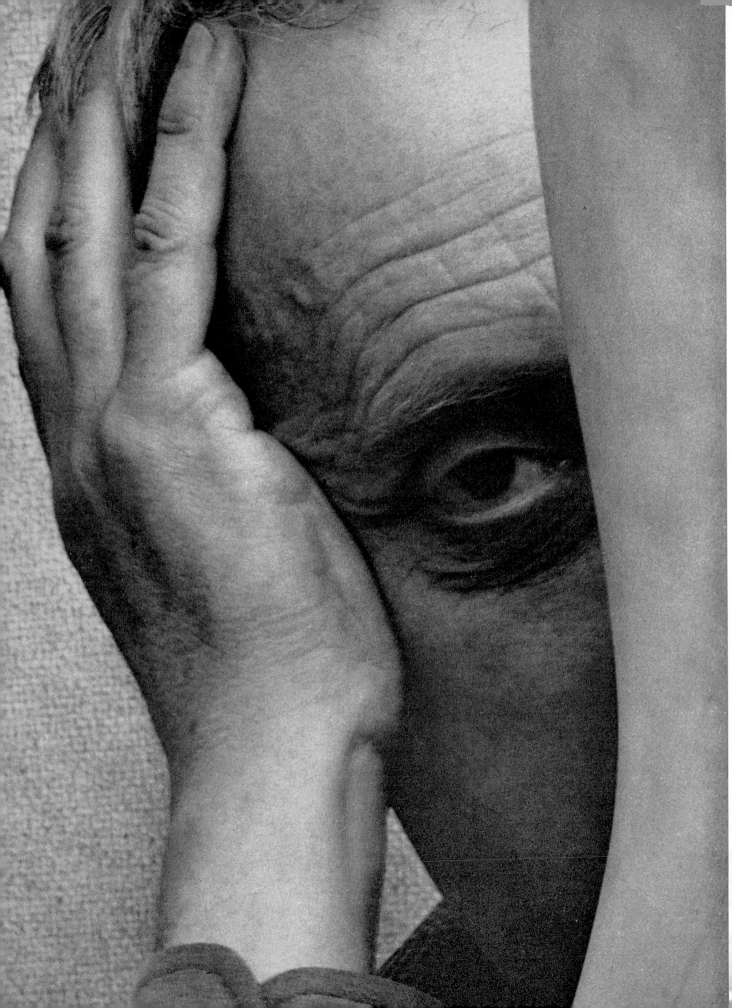

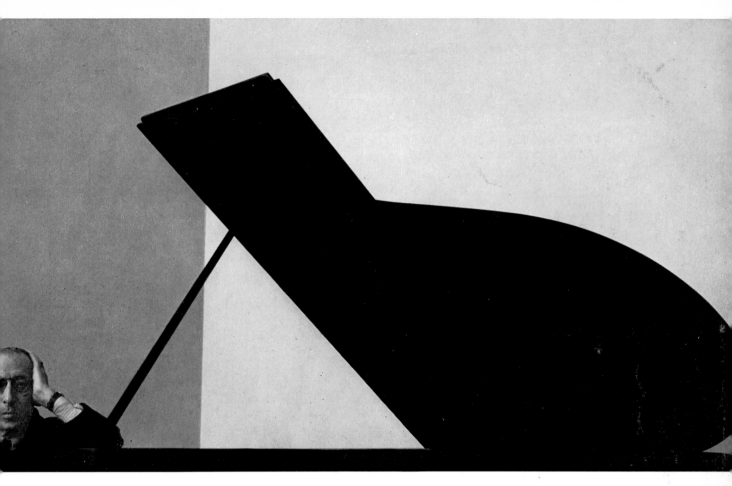

ARNOLD NEWMAN
Igor Stravinsky. 1946.
facing page:
Jean Arp. 1949

Like This, which was exhibited in 1946 at the Philadelphia Museum of Art. Newman is still preoccupied with art and artists, especially abstractionists, whose experiments in bold geometric forms, positive and negative space, arbitrary forms, and oddly shaped canvases he has found somewhat comparable to his own experiments in photography. Running throughout the entire body of his work is a connecting thread of abstraction from nature, a vision of images as bold, large patterns. The boldest pattern elements are the symbols with which he sees people surrounded.

"Memories of real tragedy are found in my portraits," he says. "In 1960 my wife Augusta and I met Otto Frank, father of Anne Frank, while he was in Amsterdam to dedicate the house—now world-famous as a memorial. . . . He quietly showed us the few tender mementos pinned and drawn on the wall . . . memories of a family

murdered by the Nazis. His present wife and mine remained below as we climbed to upper areas of the hideout to take the photographs. As we worked, the church bells nearby began to ring. He turned to me, a lonely figure, and choked: 'Those are the bells Anne wrote about . . . she . . .' We both broke down and wept. No more photographs could be taken that day."

Newman prefers big cameras for his portraits. He works deliberately and carefully; he designs on the ground glass, controls perspective, planes, his space of 4 x 5 proportions, and distorts and exaggerates subject or symbol as he decides. He recently said, "I use the camera as a creative tool as well as a recording device.

"When I photograph someone like Chagall, the turbulent character of both the man's personality and his work is indicated, I hope, by the turbulent, exciting, continuous movement within the composition. With Mon-

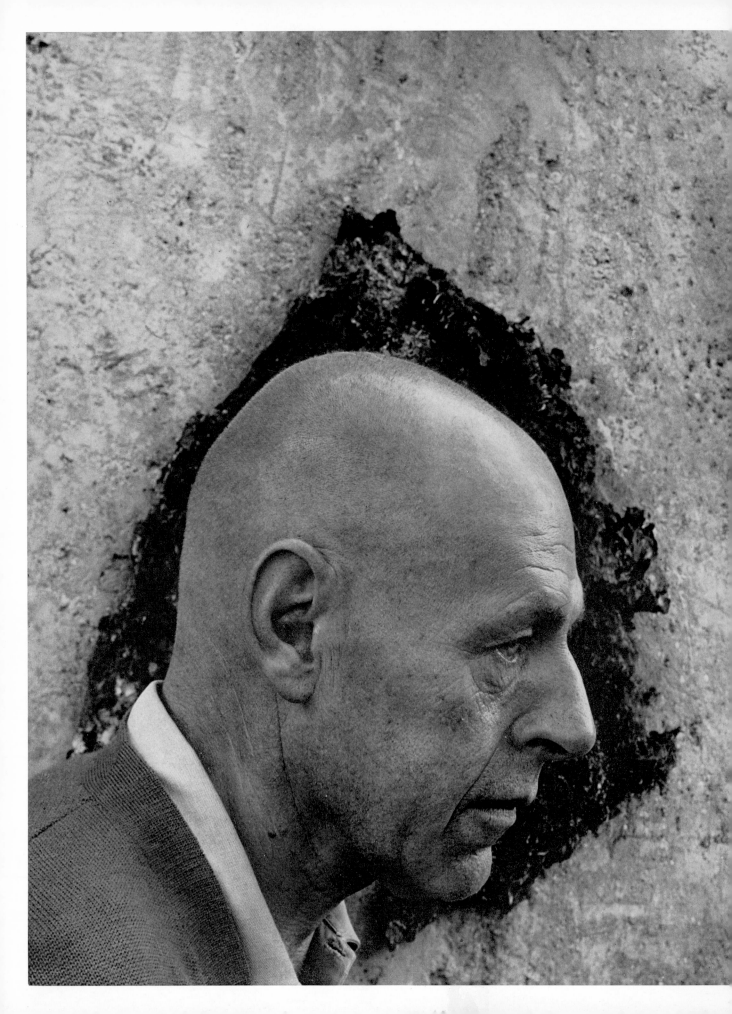

drian I used a very severe, very linear approach—again to indicate the man and his work. There are people whose personalities are placid—I try to be placid with this type of composition . . . the composition is just another one of the means of conveying my feelings about a subject.

"I think photography is a matter of controlling what's in front of you and making it do your will. This, of course, implies absolute mastery over camera, medium, techniques, and the ability to work with the subject and get him willingly and happily without any self-conscious feeling to fall into those things which are natural to him. This is a very complicated thing to do in portraiture. Mine are deliberately self-conscious portraits and therefore contain no forced feeling of candidness . . . the subject is unaware of the fact that I am waiting—things begin to happen—the man begins to reveal himself.

"If the background becomes overwhelming and you lose the personality, then I have not made a good portrait and it is not a good picture. I think the world is full of intelligent people who are not really trying to be flattered; what they really want is to be understood.

"The more I get to know my subject the more he gets to know me, and so often the pictures taken at the end of a sitting are much better both creatively and interpretively. . . . A photographer is always in a state of preparing himself for a given moment . . . we have only an instant in which to think and act."

The 50-year-old-photographer was born in New York and raised and educated in Florida, where he once ran a photographer's studio. He has seen his work reproduced in the world's major picture magazines and has exhibited in the world's major art museums. His photographs are in most of the important national public and private collections.

Arnold Newman was recently appointed acting curator of the photographic collection of the National Museum of Art of Israel in Jerusalem.

Two major books of his are scheduled to appear soon. The first, on Stravinsky, will contain photographs of the great composer in his eighty-fourth year. The second will be a selection of Newman's most famous portraits.

NEWMAN, *facing page:*
Jean Dubuffet.
1956.

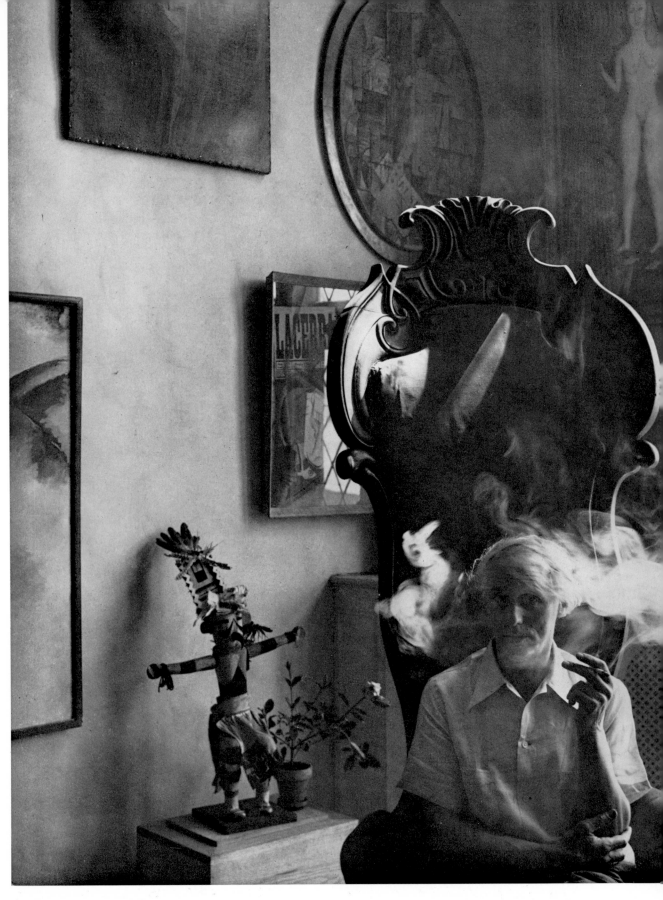

NEWMAN
Max Ernst. 1942.

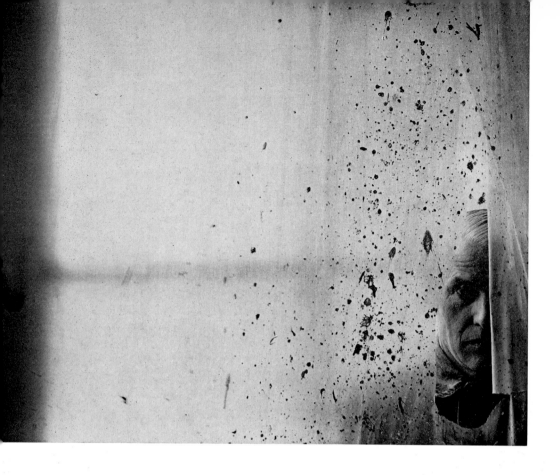

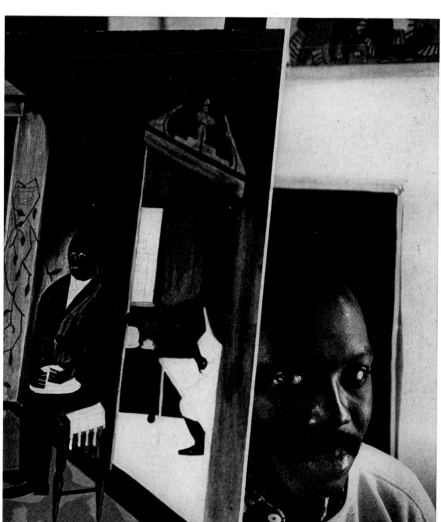

NEWMAN
above: Willem de Kooning. 1959.
left: Jacob Lawrence. 1959.

653

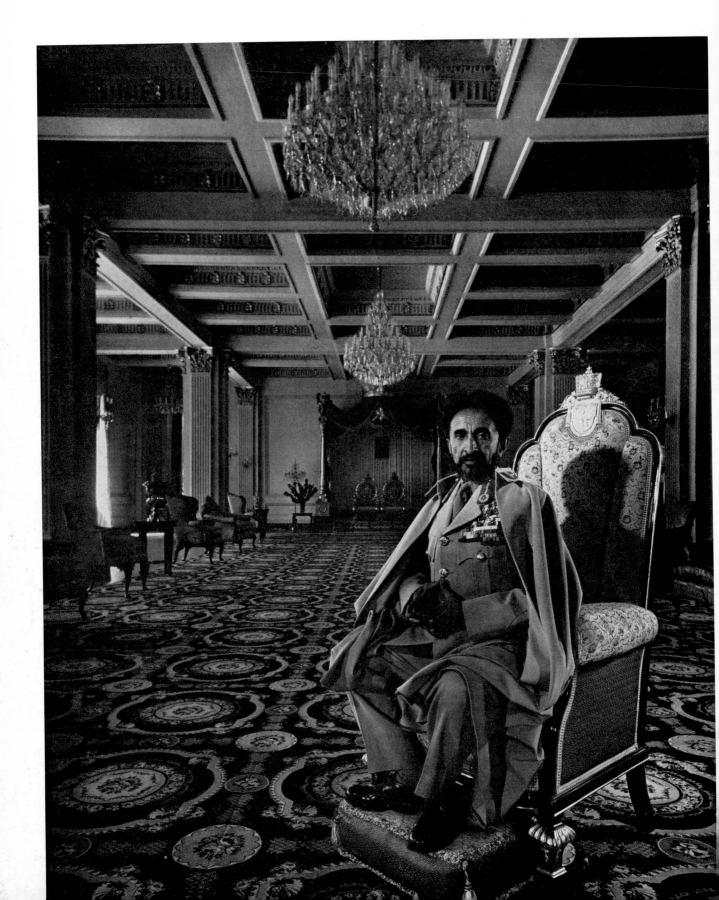

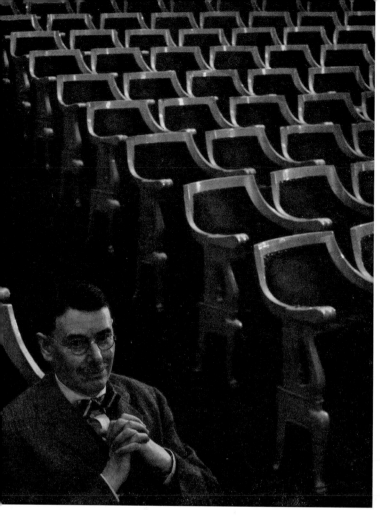

NEWMAN
facing page: Emperor Haile Selassie. *1958.*
above: Brooks Atkinson. *1951.*
right: Piet Mondrian. *1942.*

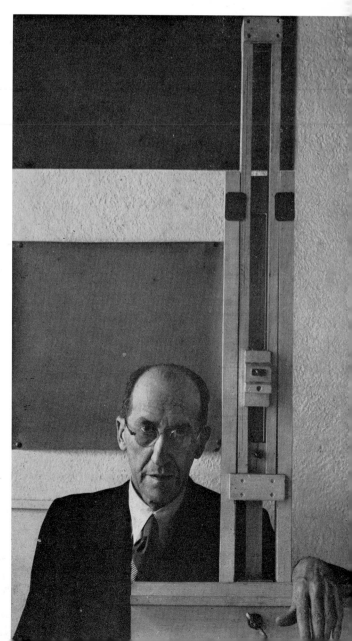

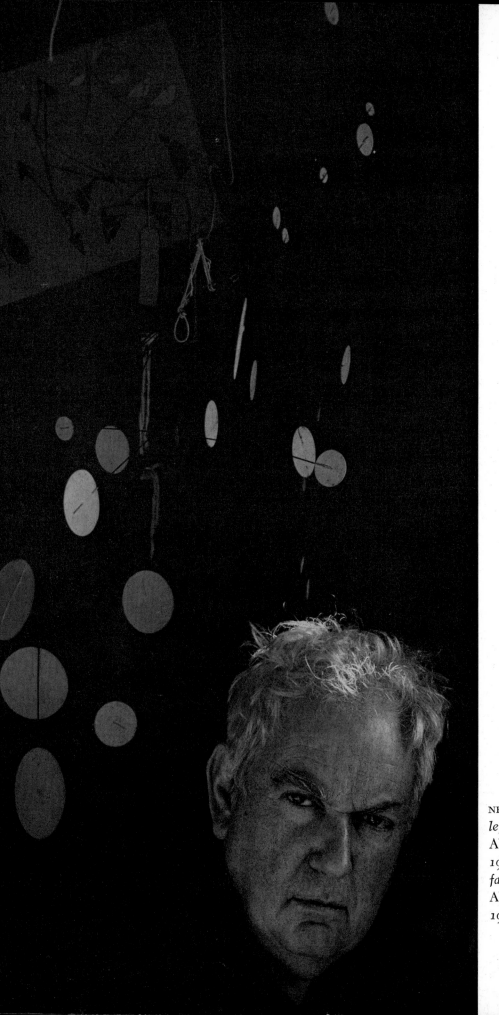

NEWMAN
left:
Alexander Calder.
1957.
facing page:
Alfried Krupp.
1963.

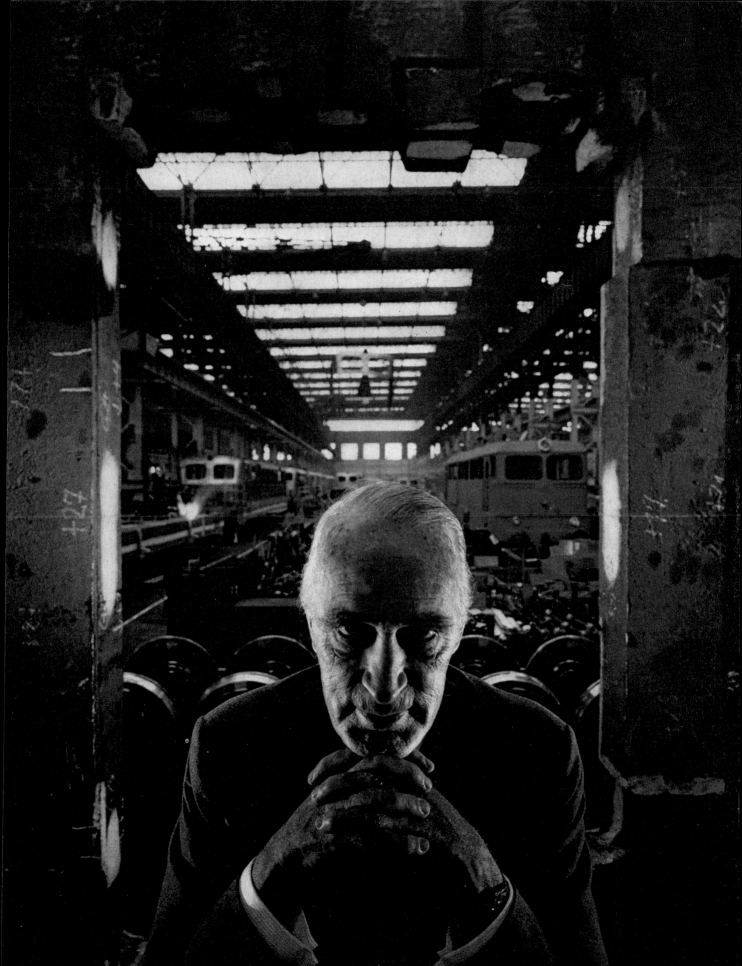

CHAPTER 51

Todd Webb

TODD WEBB IS A PHOTOGRAPHER of places—places shaped by the lives of men. He was first brought to public notice through his fascination with the city of New York, where he arrived in 1945 after having served three years as a photographer in the South Pacific with the Seventh Fleet. He was deeply moved by the incredibly complex configurations of New York by day and by night, its streets, buildings, squares, windows, and alleys, its broad panoramas and small details, its doorways, lamps, bridges, street cars, and even its tombstones. Surrounded by people on every side when aboard ship, he rarely turned his camera on people in New York. He photographed inanimate objects that reflected the presence of those gobs and marines he had known so well, putting together a whole series of photographs of doorways from each of which flew a service flag and a printed banner bought at the five and ten proclaiming "Welcome Home, Vito"— or John, or Isidore, or any one of a hundred first names— an hysterically happy banner that flouted the death each householder had feared for his son. In 1946 a group of these prints was included in Todd Webb's first one-man show, which was held at the Museum of the City of New York. During his next four years in Manhattan he pursued his masterful compositions of inanimate objects. He tramped from Harlem to the Battery, at first carrying a heavy 5 x 7 camera and tripod. Soon he acquired a less cumbersome Speed Graphic, and then, in the summer of 1946, he at long last got an 8 x 10 Deardorff. He could then really take the pictures he sought.

He discovered the store-front churches of Harlem, the city's bridges, especially the Brooklyn Bridge; and, though more often than not we see no people, their traces are there. People or no people, we are given a powerful indication of the way New Yorkers lived. These pictures Todd Webb took for himself. He would show them time and again in exhibitions all over the United States and Europe, and once in a while in the nation's magazines. He took an assignment from *Fortune* magazine in the fall of 1946, and thereafter sporadic assignments from various publications in order to raise funds with which to continue his own personal explorations.

When Roy Stryker set up the photography file for Standard Oil of New Jersey in 1947, Todd Webb was one of the seven photographers recruited for his staff. Under Stryker Todd mastered the Rollei and the 35mm cameras, and could now accept all kinds of assignments. One of them he remembers with enthusiasm: making the still photographs during Robert Flaherty's filming of *Louisiana Story*.

In 1949, after two years with Esso, Todd Webb left for Paris, which he made his headquarters for the following four years. He went all over Europe on assignments for the Marshall Plan, Esso, and the picture magazines. Most important, he had the time to pursue his own photography. Like Atget before him, he walked the streets with a big camera on a tripod, taking such unpromising objects as doorways, lamps, stoves, etc., catching the subtle light of Paris as it played over the surface of its streets and the details of its buildings.

During Webb's stay abroad, the American Embassy in Paris, the Painting Gallery in Munich, and the National Museum in Tokyo presented his Paris and New York photographs. Eastman House in Rochester, the Art Institute of Chicago, and the Museum of Modern Art in

TODD WEBB
Storefront Church, Harlem. *1946.*

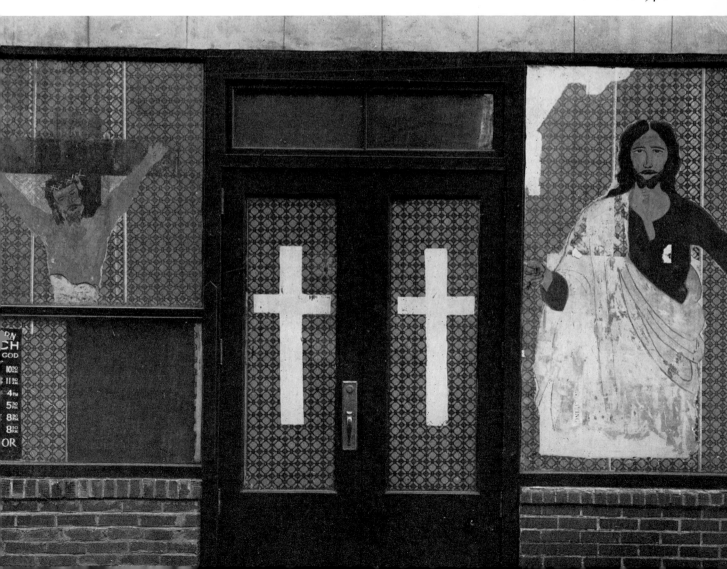

New York showed them in the United States soon after his return.

In looking around his own land, Todd Webb developed a strong interest in the westward expansion of the nineteenth century. He applied for a Guggenheim Fellowship for 1955 and 1956 with which to study the emigrant trails to Oregon and California. Receiving the award, he became an avid interpreter of the West, which he saw with the same intense, personal vision with which he had scanned New York and Paris. He pored over the visual relics of the pioneers still to be found along the trails. He photographed the few little settlements still remaining and the lost, forgotten ghost towns. This remarkable series of photographs resulted in two books: *Gold Strikes and Ghost Towns*, 1961, and *The Gold Rush Trail and the Road to Oregon*, 1963. The long trek across the country with his cameras brought him out of

the city and reminded him of his early love of the land, for he had studied mining engineering in college and had spent years during the depression prospecting for gold in the Southwest. He gave up city life and has resided in Santa Fe for the past decade.

Todd Webb is a master of design. He treats the space within a photograph as though modeled by a sculptor's hand. His work has an indestructible unity, for everything superfluous is excluded. He loves the subtleties inherent in the gray scale, unlike Lennart Olson and a number of younger photographers who eschew grays for the bolder solid black-and-white photograph. Webb refines contrasts, heightening the drama of a picture by suppressing disturbing features to show us a unique image filled with an artistry that he imposes upon it. Todd Webb makes visible to us astonishing images of things easily overlooked by lesser eyes.

TODD WEBB
First Spiritual Psychic
Science Church, Harlem.
1946.

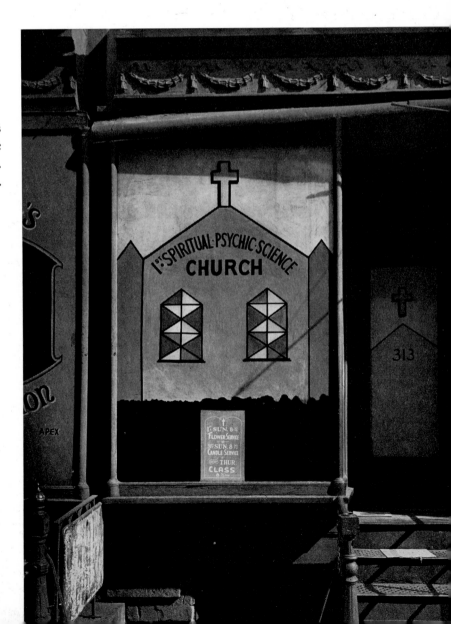

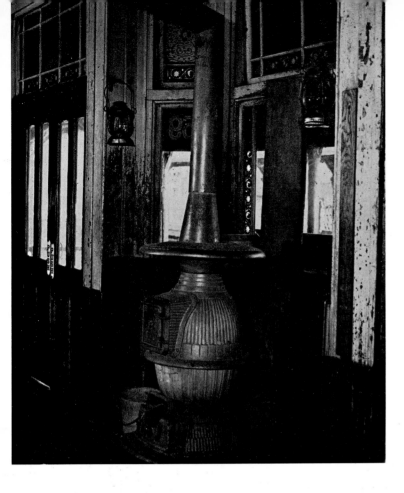

TODD WEBB
"L" Station Stove, Paris. 1950.
below: Studio Stove, Paris. 1950.

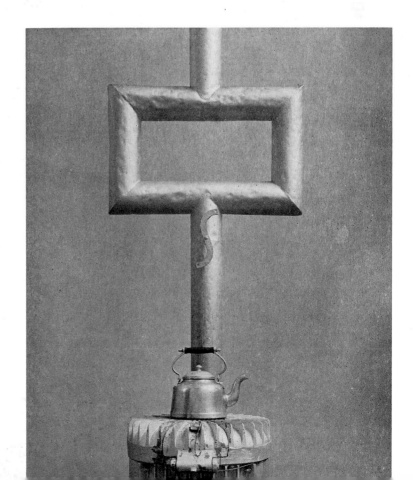

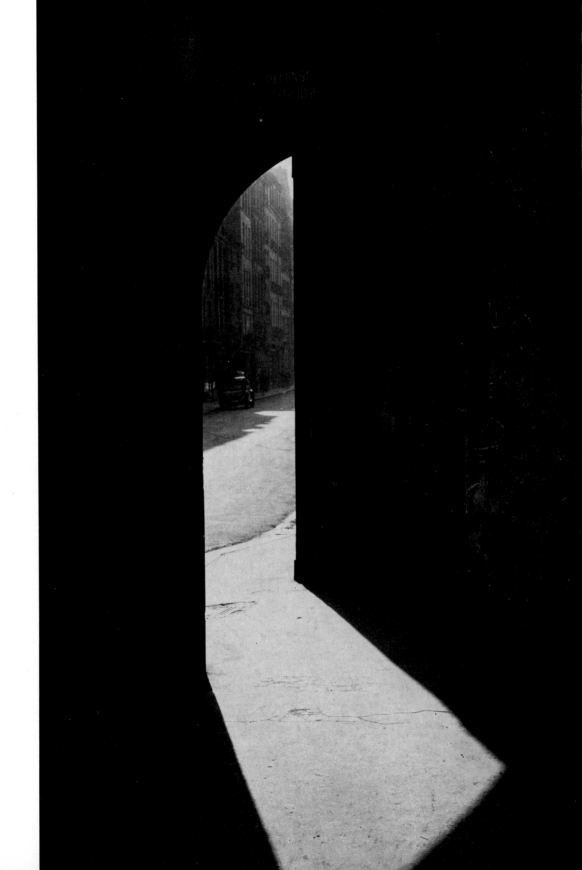

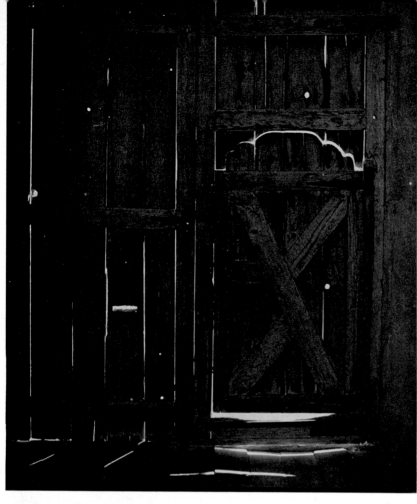

TODD WEBB
facing page:
Doorway to Rue de la Seine, Paris. *1949.*
left:
Patio Door in Georgia O'Keeffe's
Ranch House, Abiqui, New Mexico. *1964.*
below:
Doorway and Court, Rue du Bac,
Paris. *1949.*

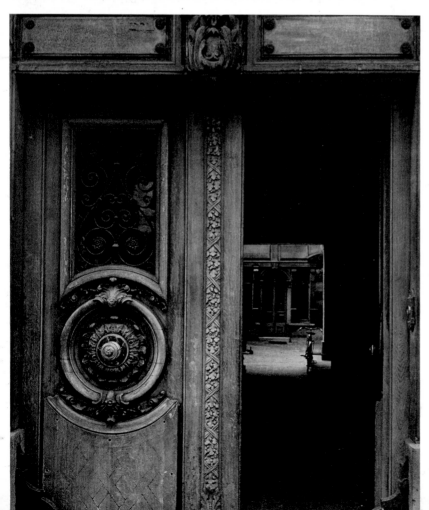

CHAPTER 52

Lucien Clergue

CEZANNE ONCE SAID as he sat looking over his easel at Mt. Ste.-Victoire in Aix, that he had but to turn his head to find a fit subject for his brush. Stieglitz spoke of finding his best subjects within a block or two of his house. And Edward Weston once told me that he did not wait for weather to clear nor did he concern himself about a place for shooting—he took his best photographs right where he was, near his home in the mountains behind Carmel or near his shack above the Pacific.

Lucien Clergue lives according to this tradition, and to find the precise subject he seeks he needs to take no more than a few steps inside the territory he considers home base. This territory is the city of Arles, in southern France, and the sea nearby. The themes he has made his own are limited to the nude female figure, invariably taken near water—salt or fresh, moving or still—at any time of the day or night; the marshes with fearful images of sterile, starved stalks caked in salt and mud, reflecting lights from sun or moon; dead cats and birds half buried in sand or stagnant pools; and the bullfight. This Spanish ceremony of life and death is played out in an ancient Roman amphitheater in which Caesar's legions once watched gladiators fight to the death. Arles today is one of the few French cities to which Spain sends her finest toreros to perform for aficionados as dedicated as any in Madrid or Mexico City.

Vincent van Gogh loved Arles and its visual delights, painting its bridges, burial grounds, bordellos, billiard parlors and his own small yellow bedroom. The Mistral, the south wind from the Sahara, crosses the Mediterranean and during the summer months blows incessantly in Arles, baking the marshes into a bleak lunar landscape. Fascinating textures appear in the caked and crackled mud. Bone-dry stalks seemingly stuck in cement rise up to a cloudless sky. Birds lie dead, half-covered by the sand and dust. This strange landscape is home to Lucien Clergue, and he roams it with his camera.

Clergue was born in Arles in 1934. He learned photography from the town baker. By the age of sixteen he was out of school, working as a clerk in some business firm. Two years later his mother died. His first series of photographs was of dead animals, followed by his first pictures of the ballet of the bullring, capturing his best photographs of the slaughter of the dull-witted beautiful beasts.

Morbid subjects, however, did not hold Clergue's total attention. He loved the female figure and the sea with an exalted intensity exceeding his fascination with the dead and the dying. His "Nus de la Mer," begun in 1956, have in a decade become a glorified exhibition of the female nude shown in many exhibitions all over the world and was published in book form in the spring of 1967. Jean Cocteau, on being shown the collection, said, "Clergue has witnessed the birth of Aphrodite."

Picasso, when he looked at the nude female figure of a Clergue photograph, with its shimmer of highlights from the foaming sea, said, "He is the Monet of the camera." And, indeed, Clergue shares the Impressionists' feeling for light but he is even more interested in the figure as a sculptural mass. He uses light to make his memorable forms and shapes come alive; Clergue's Venus rising from the sea is three-dimensional. Her thighs, buttocks, and breasts are islands of tenderness. Her navel is a depthless pool. A billion bubbles of light are trapped in her hair. Altogether she is an exalted image, the divine woman whom a hundred generations have seen in their dreams since Greek sailors first put out to sea.

Through photographic magic Clergue transforms soft, sensuous forms into polished marble, into such shapes as sculptors carve in order to exploit the effects of light. He gives up these impressive effects, nevertheless, when he concentrates on the textures of the female figure. He purposely lets his models become chilled so that they are all gooseflesh, then he places them against coarse sands of varying shades, achieving dramatic distinctions in tactile values.

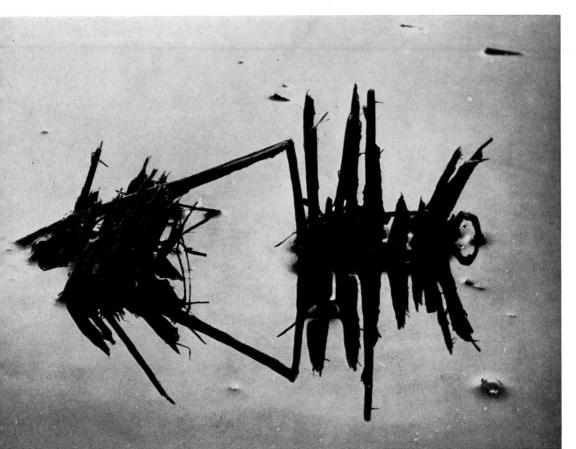

LUCIEN CLERGUE
Weeds in La Camargue, a Marshy Island near Arles, France. 1960.

665

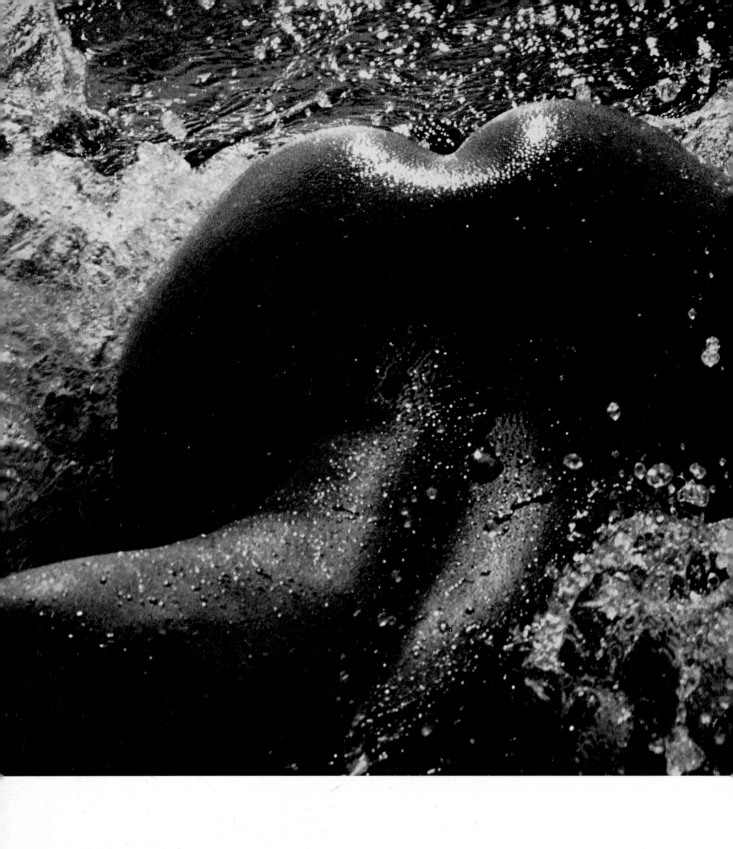

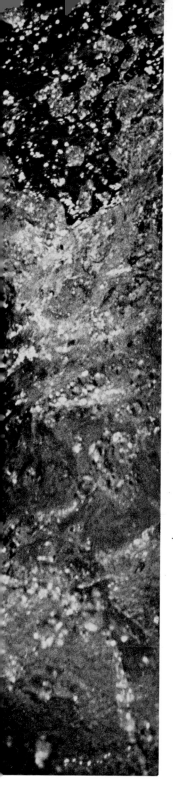

CLERGUE
left: Nude in the Sea. 1964.
below: Nude in the Sea. 1958.

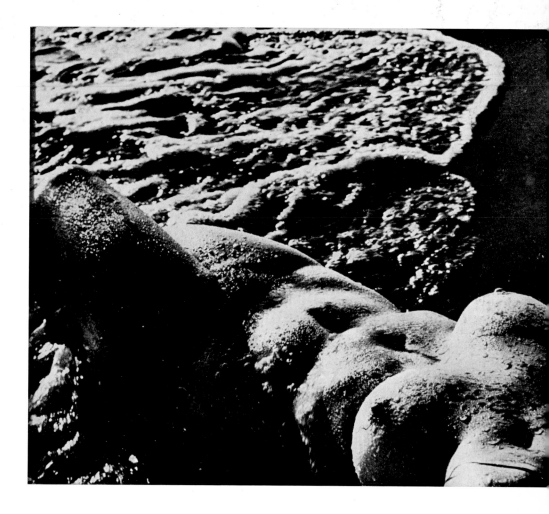

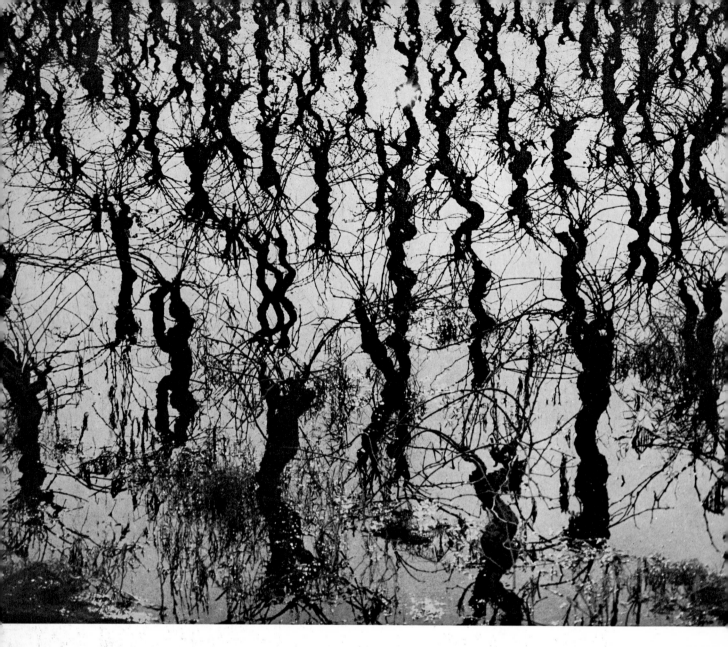

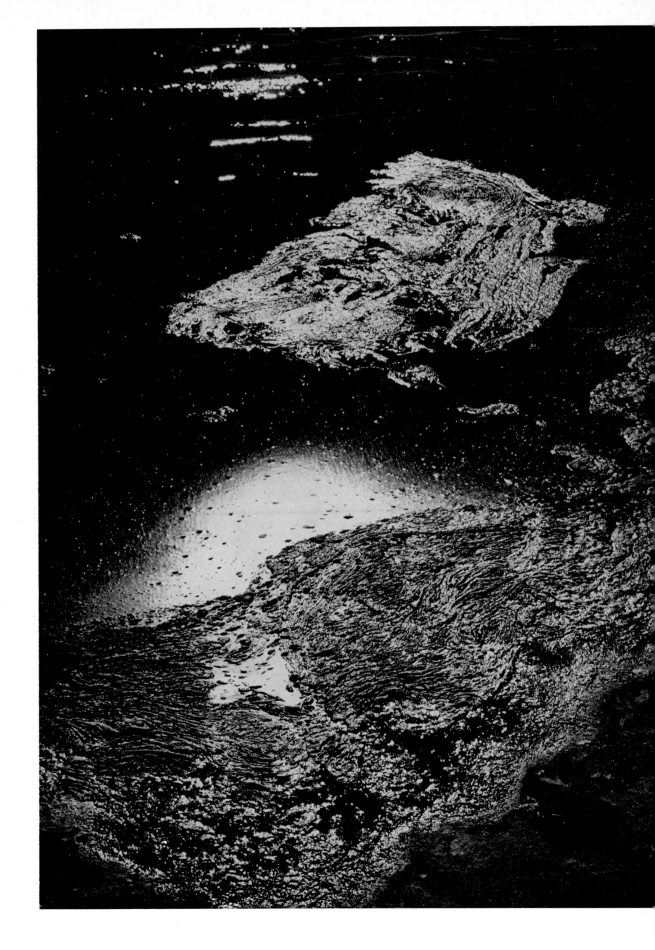

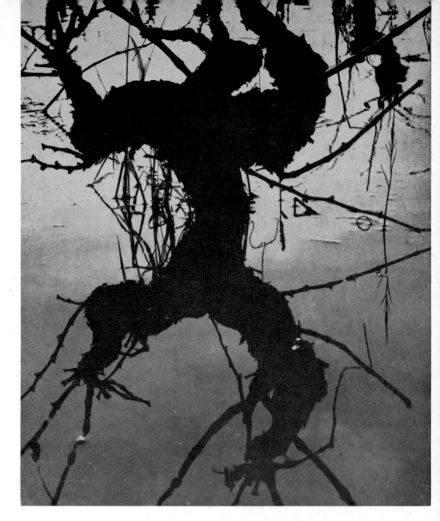

CLERGUE
right: Vines. 1960.
facing page: Reflections in Marsh of
La Camargue, Arles.
1964.

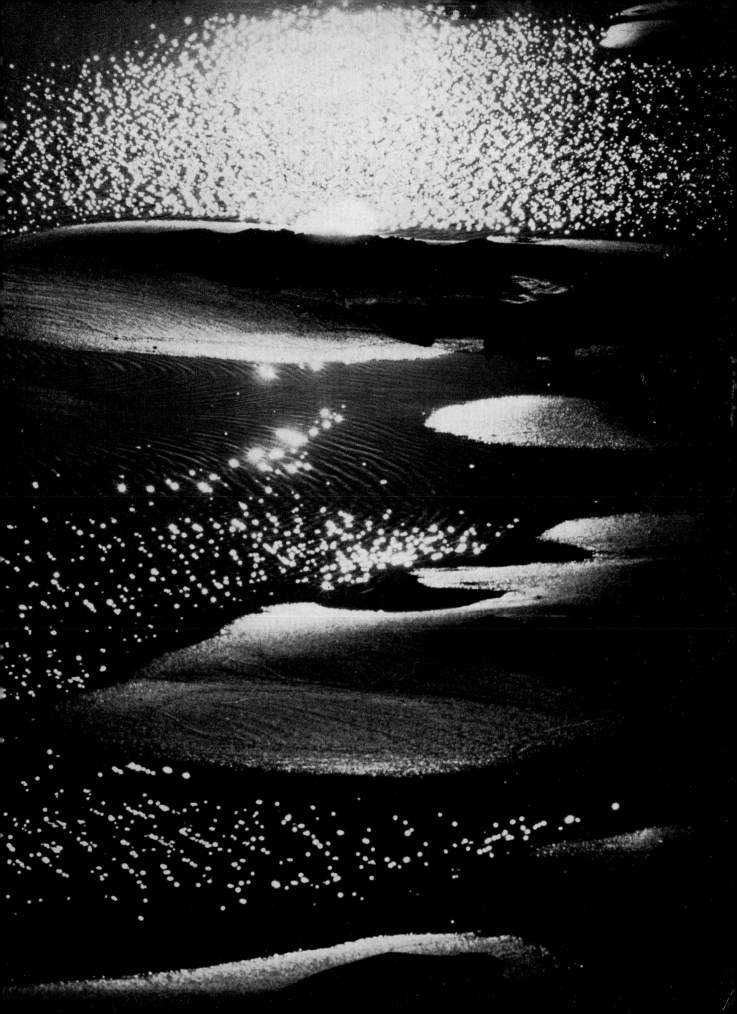

CHAPTER 53
Gordon Parks

I HAVE A MENTAL PICTURE of Gordon Parks that invariably comes to my mind whenever I run across one of his picture stories in *Life* magazine. He is on skis, slaloming down some steep hill in Minnesota: a young man with brown skin, black mustache, white suit, and a red scarf, racing downhill, very much alone, alert to every obstacle on the run. He is cool and detached, maneuvering around obstacles almost without effort and keeping an eye out for careless humans who might wander into his path. Parks maneuvers his cameras with equal skill through the dangerous twists and turns on the steep slopes of human relations—of race relations especially.

The deeper Parks's involvement with photography the greater became his ability to remain in character. He interprets what he sees and experiences with detachment and honesty, in pictures, and in pictures and words. He has become the perfect analyst of his people, seeing them with love but not hating white men any more than he hated the rocks, stumps, and other obstacles he encountered on the ski lanes.

Parks learned to move smoothly in every situation at a very early age. Gripped by poverty when he was sixteen and had just arrived in St. Paul from his native Kansas, he worked at a dozen jobs, from playing the piano in honkytonks to professional basketball, lumberjacking in the North Woods, and waiting on table in a railroad dining car traveling to and from the West Coast. Fortunately he found a camera in his hands in 1937, when he was 25, and his real career began. Three years later he was in Chicago taking fashion and arty photographs. He eked out a bare existence until 1942 when he was awarded a Julius Rosenwald Fellowship. The fellowship enabled him to work for one year with the legendary Farm Security Administration photography unit in Washington so brilliantly directed by Roy Stryker. This former Columbia University professor was Parks's great teacher in photography. He taught Parks to see deeply, putting him into situations that subjected him to the discrimination then prevalent in our nation's capitol. Parks, never losing his innate dignity but profoundly moved by what he saw for the first time, deliberately photographed the seamiest side of Washington in sections of the city where the dome of the Capitol was visible above scenes of appalling misery.

Parks went all over the country for FSA, shooting the agony of the Depression. After the outbreak of World War II he was transferred to the Office of War Information, overseas division, as a war correspondent-cameraman. At the end of the war, he rejoined Stryker to become a member of a seven-man photographic team that made documentaries for Standard Oil Company of New Jersey. Photography for one industry has never been realized so well as by the photographers Stryker called together for this purpose; and though the subject of oil could not be portrayed so emotionally as depression and war, Gordon traveled from the Arctic to Saudi Arabia photographing the drama of oil and oil installations.

All these experiences in technical and personal development were vital preparation for Gordon's career as photographer for *Life* magazine, which he joined in 1949. His byline as photographer-reporter has since appeared over many major stories ranging from Harlem

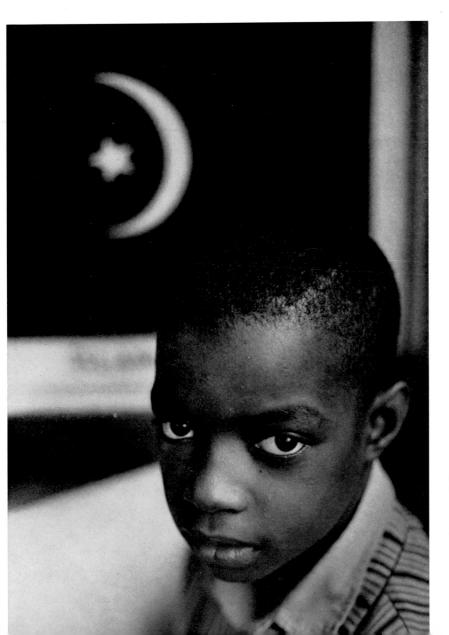

GORDON PARKS
Youngest of the Black Muslims.
*The first to be given an African name,
Mahmoud, in 1963.*

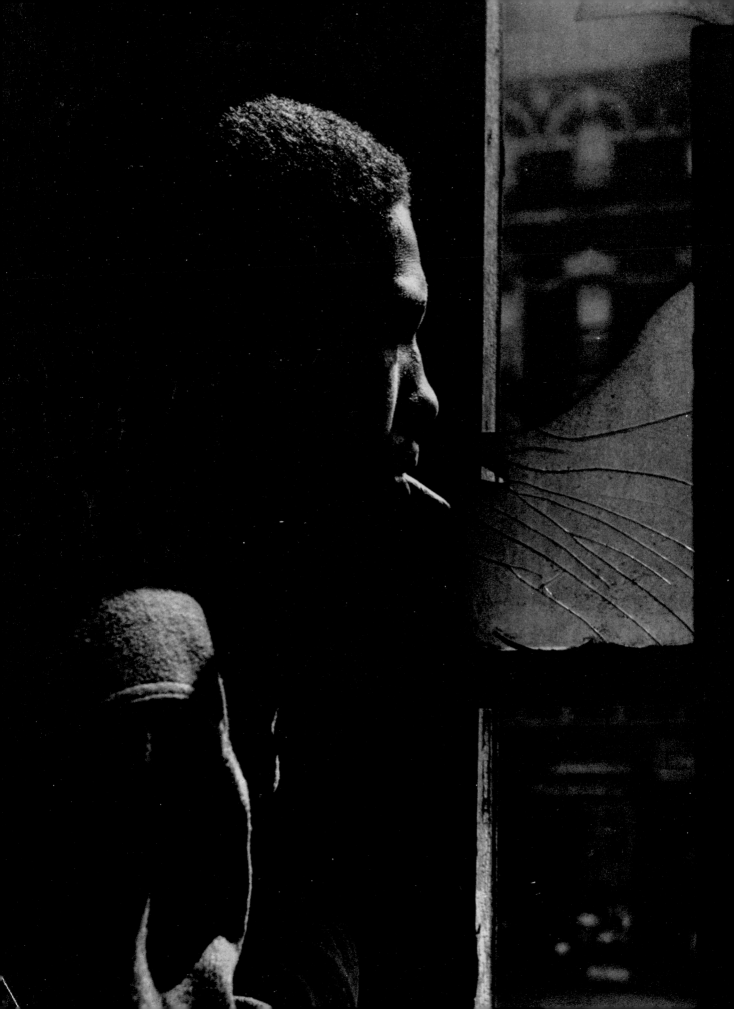

gangs and their violent turf rumbles to Flavio, a tubercular boy in Brazil living amid death and poverty on a hillside of muddy shacks. So much attention was attracted to the boy's plight and to Brazil's sociological problems that the money sent to Parks by many Americans brought Flavio to a Denver sanitorium where he was cured. The Brazilian government was prompted to take steps to alleviate the misery in the ghetto.

Within the last several years Parks's stories in *Life* have included penetrating essays and forceful photographs about the various American Negro movements and their leaders. Parks was given unprecedented permission to photograph the belligerently chauvinistic Black Muslims in their mosques, schools, tactical training centers, and Elijah Muhammad himself, the self-proclaimed messenger of a "Black Allah." Parks interviewed black supremacy's powerful orator, Malcolm X (who was to be killed two years later, in 1965), then second in command. In a soul-searching report Parks reported on "What Their Cry Means To Me." He concluded with, "I don't intend to join the Muslims. I sympathize with much of what they say, but I also disagree with much of what they say. I wouldn't follow Elijah Muhammad or Malcolm X into a Black State— even if they achieved such a complete separation.... nor will I condemn all whites for the violent acts of their brothers against the Negro. Not just yet, anyway.... Nevertheless, to the Muslims I acknowledge that the circumstance of common struggle has willed us brothers. I know that if unholy violence should erupt—and I pray it won't—this same circumstance will place me, reluctantly, beside them."

Life published Parks's essay on the death of Malcolm X, whom he had interviewed just two days before the assassination. "Is it really true that the Black Muslims are out to get you?" he asked, and the other man replied, "It's as true as we are standing here. They've tried it twice in the last two weeks."

Cover stories by Parks as well as long essays in pictures and words continue to appear with great regularity not only in *Life* but in many other of the world's magazines. They touch upon a variety of subjects and ideas, some conceived by him alone, others on assignments from editors (at this writing he has just completed a picture essay on Black Power and Stokely Carmichael). Excerpts from his two latest books—both autobiographical—*The Learning Tree* and *A Choice of Weapons*, have appeared with special pictures he took to make for a unique kind of picture story.

Parks has received numerous awards for his photo-

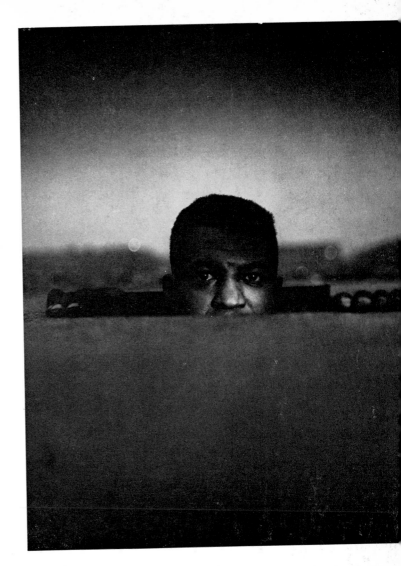

PARKS

facing page: Red Jackson. 1948.
above: Invisible Man. 1956.

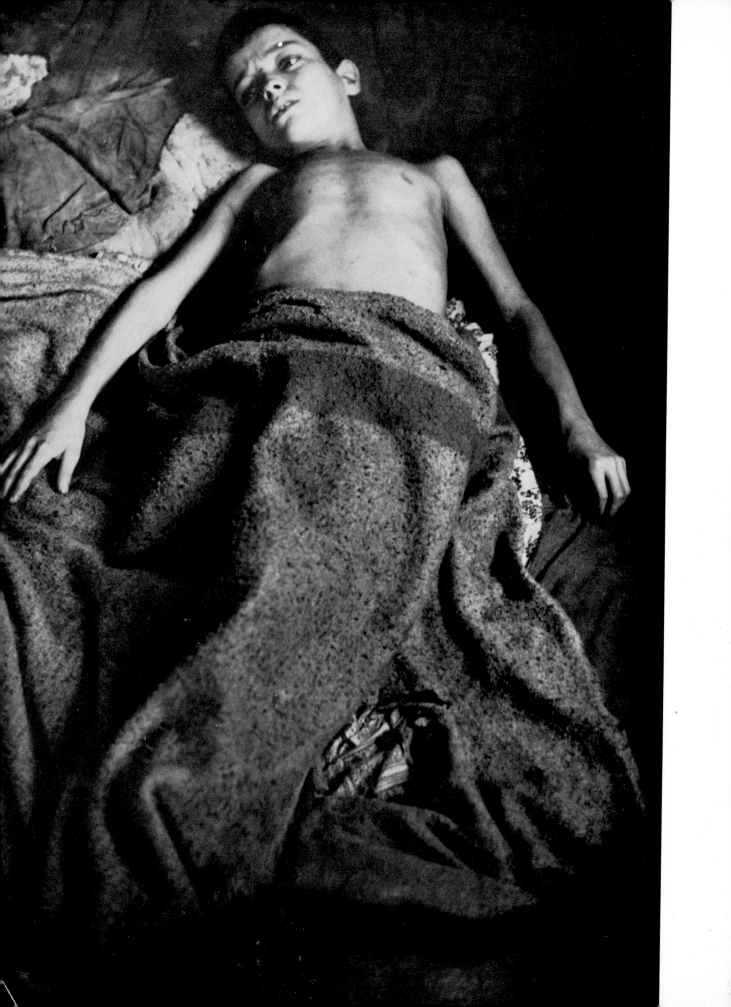

graphs from such organizations as the National Conference of Christians and Jews, the Syracuse University School of Journalism, and the American Society of Magazine Photographers. He has had innumerable one-man exhibitions in the nation's major museums; and, on occasion of the one I assembled of his work for the Art Institute of Chicago, he wrote me: "The camera is a forthright, honest and powerful medium of self-expression, and its potentialities are far reaching and unpredictable. A good picture may not always be in focus or best in compositions, but in it you are always aware of a specific moment, which has been recorded truthfully. As a photographer I relentlessly search for that specific moment."

In the spring of 1968 Parks signed a contract with Paramount to produce and direct his autobiography, *The Learning Tree*, the first of four films he will do within the next three years for Hollywood producers. His honesty as a still photographer will be evident in his role as a movie director.

PARKS
facing page: Flavio. *Rio de Janeiro, 1961.*
A *Life Magazine Cover.*
below: "Favela"—Slum in Rio de Janeiro.
Child with Dead Man. 1961.

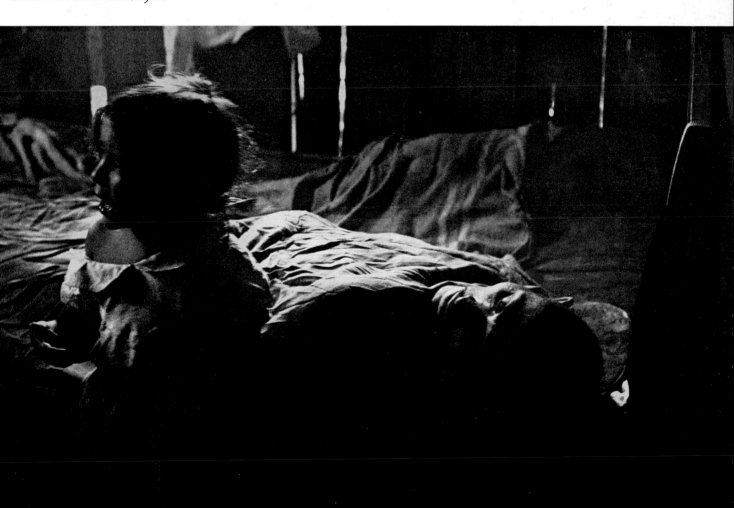

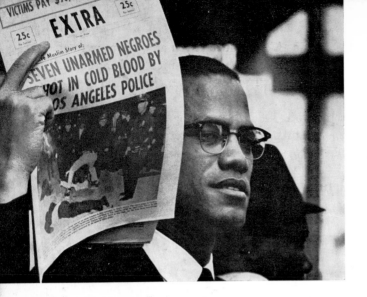

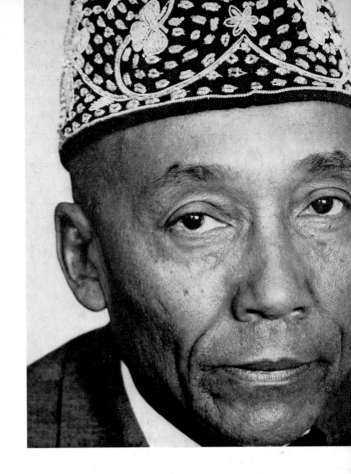

PARKS *above left:* Malcolm X. *1963.*
When second in command to Elijah Muhammad,
two years before he was murdered.
above right: Elijah Muhammad,
Leader of the Black Muslims. *1963.*
below: Black Muslim Demonstration. *1963.*
facing page: Lonely Man in Harlem.
1958.

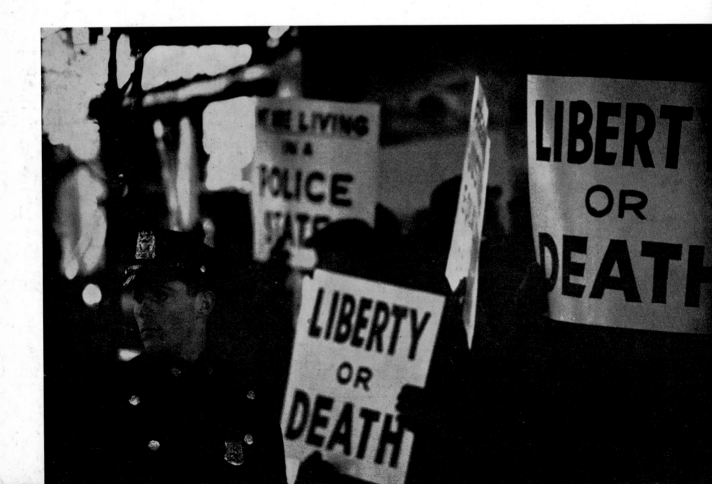

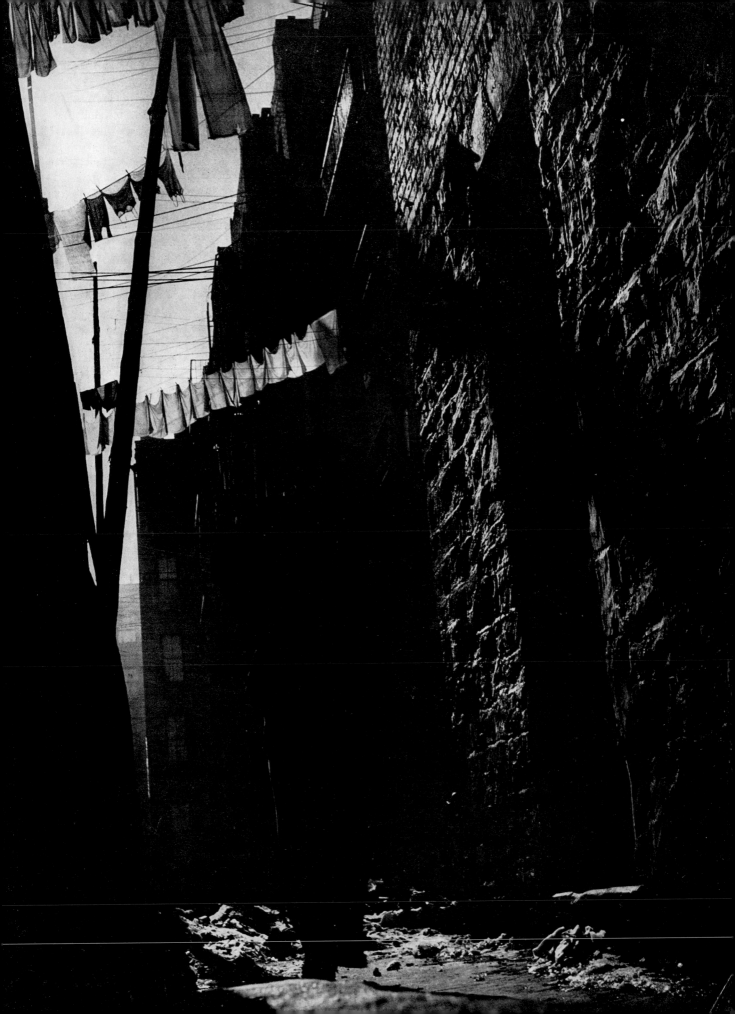

CHAPTER 54

Lennart Olson

LENNART OLSON WAS ONLY seventeen years old when, in 1942, he decided to make photography his life's work. In the following decade he pushed his camera into the fields of architectural, industrial, and magazine photography. He soon developed his own unique personal style, in which he reduced what he saw to very simple terms, abstracting the 1200 tones in the gray scale to a handful. He now consistently strives for relationships of stygian blacks and dazzling whites, finding photographic values in suppressing the nuances of gray tones. He conceives images that are architecturally bold: strongly geometric patterns of black structures—bridges, buildings, roads— thrusting into white space. His meticulously balanced photographs are often five or six times as wide as they are high. Even his murals are conceived in these spectacular proportions: they are long, narrow strips made complete as compositions by the desks and the seated people continuing the space suggested by the photograph. He completed his first mural in 1957 and since then has made four others for a bank, hospital, cafeteria, and industrial plant—all in his native Sweden.

In Olson's regular photographs, as in his murals, horizontal sweep is interrupted by solid black vertical shapes that create accents, tensions, or rests for the eye as our gaze follows the rhythm and beat of his dynamic patterns. Such a shape might be a steel beam or an array of round electric bulbs glowing in a soft semi-circle of light on the black asphalt pavement of a cloverleaf intersection in his native Stockholm.

Olson is a member of TIO ("ten" in Swedish), a group of ten talented photographers among whom are Pal Nils Nilsson, Hans Hammarskiold, Rune Hassner, and George Oddner. Olson modestly says about TIO, "I am but one." His vision, however, is personal and unique; it may carry him far as a still photographer if he does not become completely involved with movies and television.

In November 1966 he was in the United States following the late Senator Robert F. Kennedy around the country as he politicked. Olson was on the chartered plane for weeks doing a film on assignment for Swedish TV. "I'm rather impressed with Kennedy," Olson said to me. "I didn't know much about him, only that he was the younger brother. We had heard in Sweden that he was an important factor in U.S. politics, but nobody knew

why. Now I can understand why. He chats with people in an unconventional way, but he is very much aware when photographers are taking pictures of him. He lets his wishes be known in no uncertain terms, especially when he's first welcomed by some group of city officials. On the stage he appears to be very informal: he departs from his written paper; he answers in a very personal, easy way; he surprised us all, reporters and cameramen who traveled with him. And what he does particularly well is develop a quick rapport with the questioning students in his audience."

"How does this compare with photographing Swedish politicians on the go?" I asked him. He replied, "It's not so complicated. The same standards of politicians operate all over the world, no? But in Sweden there's not this vast country; there are not so many different kinds of people, or such big problems to contend with. In Sweden the politicians take it easier. TV gives each politician the same amount of time, so the whole country hears them

LENNART OLSON
Dragon Jets. Sweden.
1963.

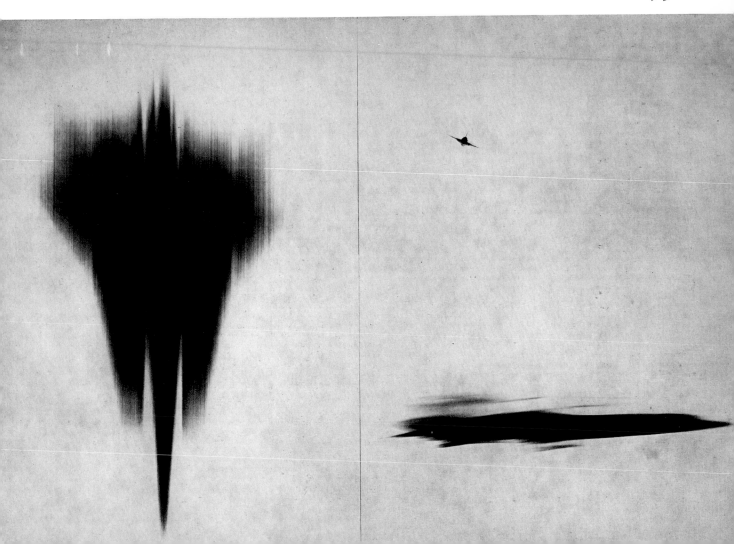

all. And the photographer doesn't have to follow him around the way it's done in the United States; this makes for a different kind of photographic coverage."

"What's this exciting and lucrative medium going to do to you as a still and mural photographer?"

"I don't think I'll stop," he answered. "I see people through a movie camera. In still photography I see design. It's the mural I'm particularly interested in as a medium, and I hope to return to it whenever I can. Photomurals have become important in Sweden; and it is all due to an art critic named Alf Hard Af Segerstad of the *Svenska Dagbladet,* who has embraced photography as an art in his columns. Architects have followed his lead. Museums have opened their doors to photography and industry has started to give us commissions. If it can happen in Sweden it surely can happen in other parts of the world.

"This may be the answer for many photographers who have financial problems," he concluded, "especially for those among us who are losing interest in advertising or architectural still photography because the possibility of creating our own work in these fields becomes too limited as the client's demands become too much for us."

OLSON
The Tjorn Bridge.
1962.

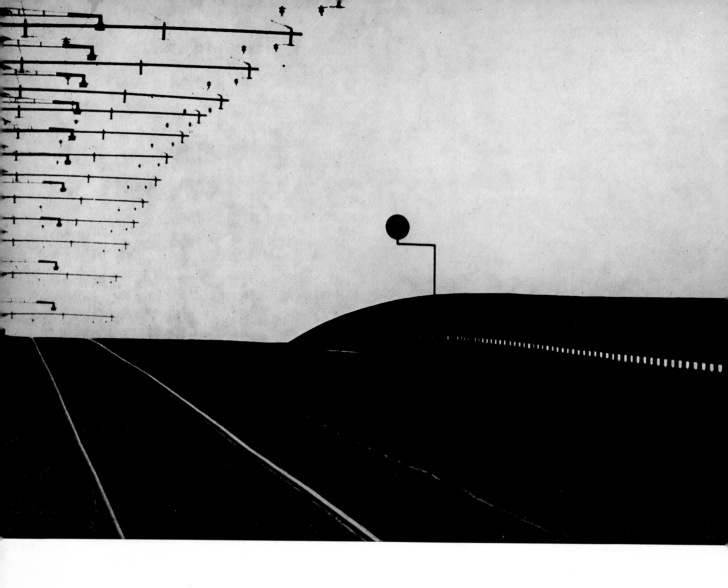

OLSON, *above:* The West Bridge, Stockholm. VI. 1954.
right: Mural, Stockholm: Bridges of Sweden. 1963.

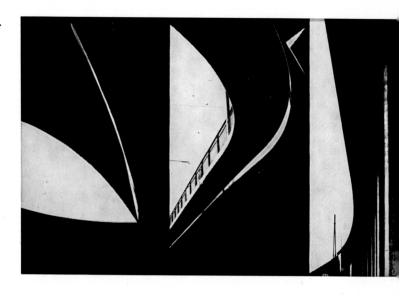

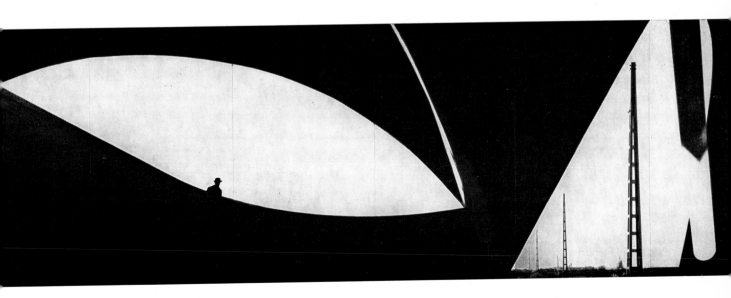

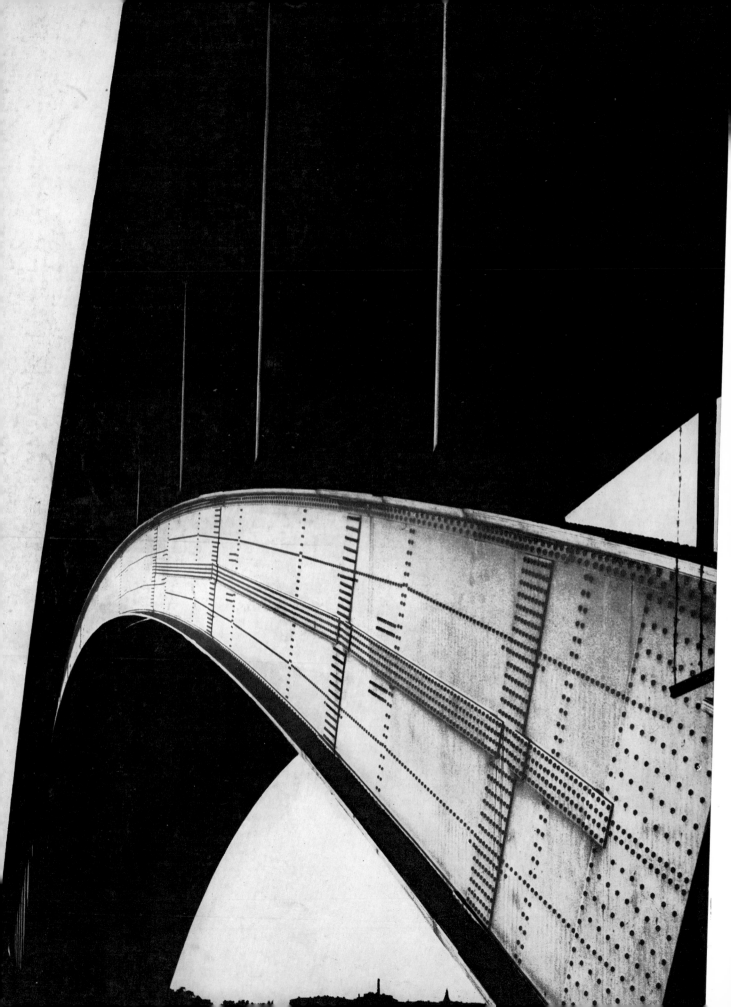

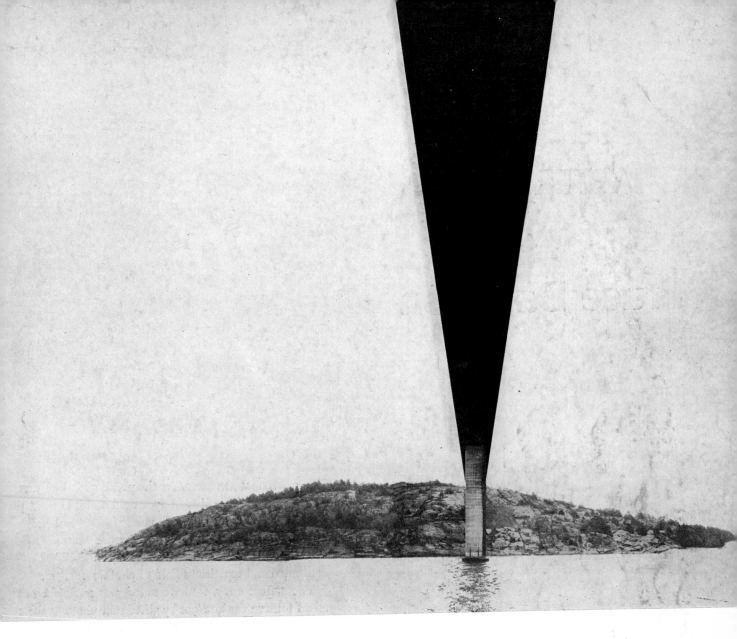

OLSON

left: The West Bridge, Stockholm. I. 1954.
above: The Tjorn Bridge. 1966.

CHAPTER 55

Bruce Davidson

THE PHOTOGRAPHS TAKEN over the past decade by Bruce Davidson, who was thirty-five years old on his last birthday, are extraordinary for their poetic feeling and depth of mood, and have won for their author a most enviable reputation as an original talent in the terribly overcontrolled and repetitious field of photojournalism.

The picture essay, we have noted, was established as an art form in the late '30s by gifted staff photographers on *Life* and similar picture magazines. The younger people subsequently hired by the picture magazines, although just as competent as their predecessors, were less original, because forced to run on the same tracks. Opportunities for personal interpretation were now limited, for they depended on the wisdom of the picture editor— the inspiration and direction he gave the photographers and the freedom he allowed them.

Bruce Davidson, an individualist in the tradition of the pioneer picture-essay photographers, did not go to work as a magazine staffman. In 1958, after studying art and philosophy at Yale, he joined Magnum Photos. Accordingly, he has had the freedom to pursue picture stories of his own conception—for example, *Brooklyn Gang*, *Selma March*, *Central Park*, *In the Footsteps of Christ*—and Magnum has placed these unique photoessays in the world's picture magazines. In 1962, he was awarded a Guggenheim Fellowship to do a photographic study of the American Negro.

His previous work included photo-essays on England's beaches, resorts, wax museums, amusement parks, and children at play. In Wales he photographed the lives of people in the depressing soot-covered hill towns, miners and their families playing, getting married, and dying. In Los Angeles he photographed the people in that surprisingly overcrowded horizontal city's ghettos. In New York he has never ceased to pursue the city's many subcultures, especially those of its teenagers, jazz-hungry youths, and the hordes that take the subway out to Coney Island.

Davidson's young people do not burn with frustration and rage. They are not aghast at the evils and miseries to to be seen all around them; astonishingly they accept these things without a great show of emotion. The pain-

ful feelings impressed on us are the photographer's. Davidson's every wounded sensibility is recorded as he photographs with compassion the painful situations to which people are subjected in various parts of the country and endure because of jobs they cannot leave.

Bruce Davidson emphasizes the young people's underplayed expression of emotions by using harsh available light. He combines strong contrasts with large dim areas. He softens the pattern of lighting by using slow film, exploiting its possibilities by printing in grainy textures. On occasion he suggests movement through blurring of the image, foregoing the crisp, sharply defined planes and lovingly described detail of more classic-minded picture-essay photographers. But Davidson is no less sensitive than they to the visual wonders of pictorial images, although, by comparison with his fellow photojournalists, he is something of a romantic.

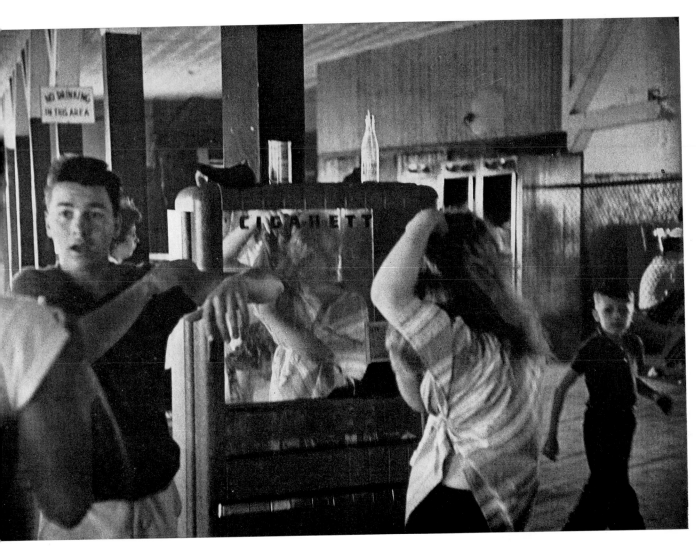

BRUCE DAVIDSON
Bathhouse, Coney Island. 1960.
next page: Coney Island Embrace. 1960.

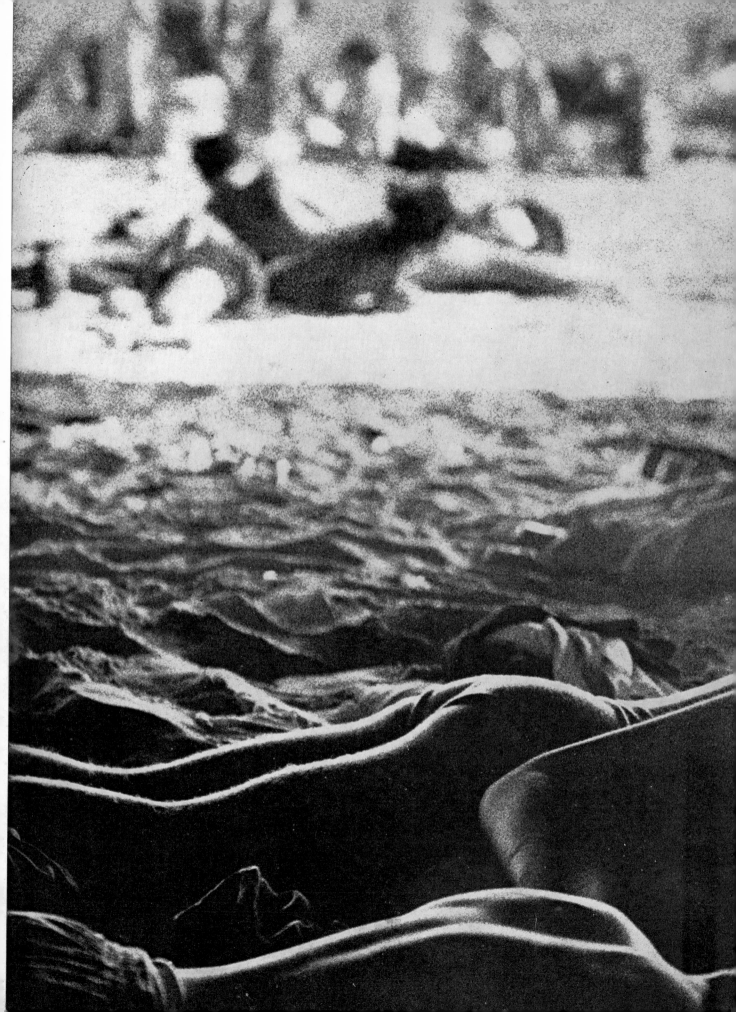

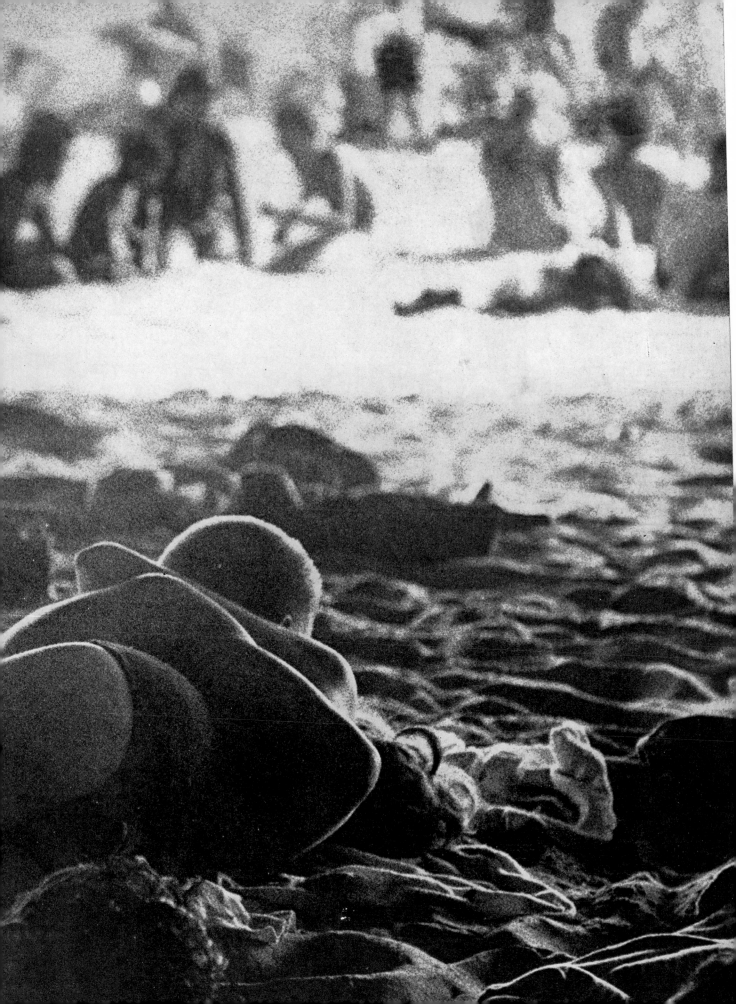

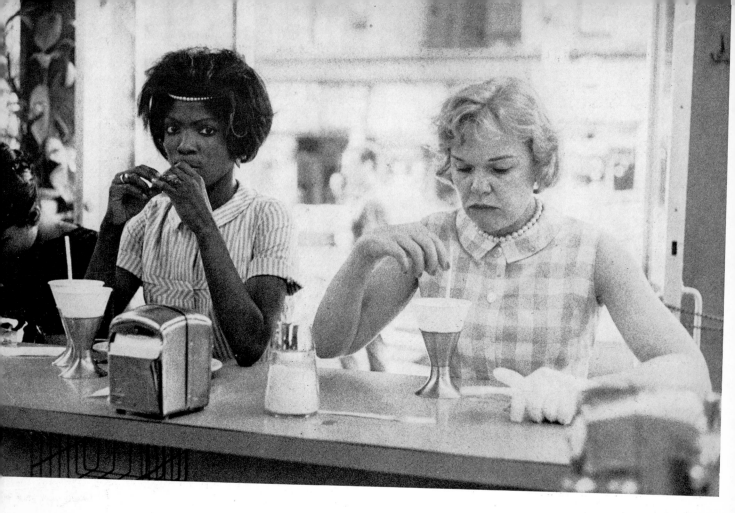

DAVIDSON
5 & 10-Cent Store Lunch Counter.
1963.

John Szarkowski, Curator of Photography of New York's Museum of Modern Art, wrote in the catalogue of his one-man show of Bruce Davidson's work, "Few contemporary photographers give us their observation so unembellished—so free of apparent craft or artifice. In his work formal and technical concerns remain below the surface, all but invisible. The presence that fills these pictures seems the presence of life that is described, scarcely changed by its transmutation into art."

Bruce Davidson's photographs have been exhibited in some of the nation's major museums, which have acquired many of his prints for their permanent collections. His *Brooklyn Gang* is the only photo story on display since 1964 at the Steichen Center in the Museum of Modern Art. He has had one-man shows at the Art Institute of Chicago, Eastman House, and the De Young Museum, and another is now circulating among a number of churches. His photographs have appeared in sev-

eral books: *The Bridge; The Negro American* (foreword by President Lyndon B. Johnson); and a volume is now in preparation to be entitled *England*.

Bruce Davidson is indeed one of the gifted young photojournalists now working, and is reputed to be the photographer who has the most profound influence and impact on those young people leaving college who are considering photography as a vocation. Davidson teaches a photography seminar in his studio to a group of these talented young people.

Without the financial help of any foundation, Davidson spent 18 months documenting the life on 110th Street, New York City, using camera and tape recorder to achieve a remarkable study of Puerto Rican families residing in the slums of Harlem. *Life* magazine is to publish a picture story and Harvard University Press in 1969 a complete book of this latest effort by Bruce Davidson.

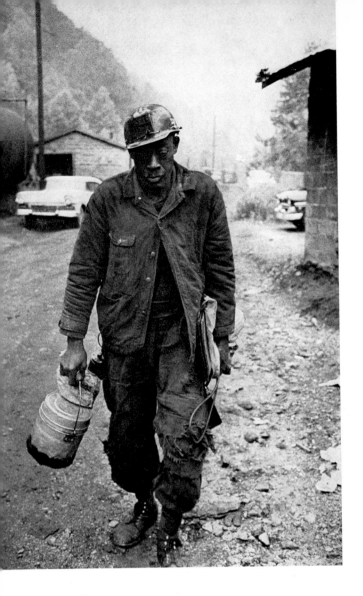 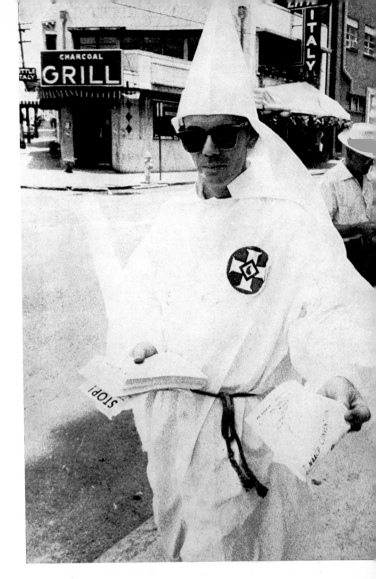

DAVIDSON, *above left*: Miner. 1965.
above right: Ku Kluxer Selling Klan Literature. 1963.

*All photographs in this chapter courtesy
Magnum Photos.*

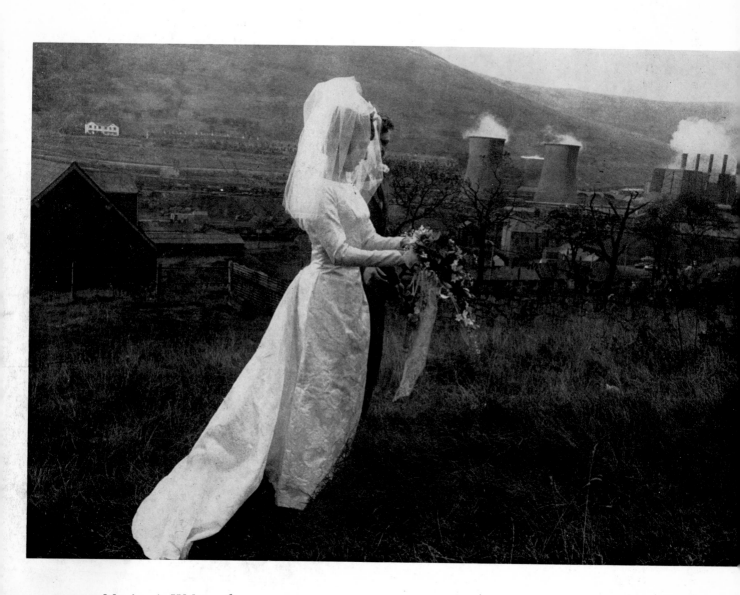

DAVIDSON, Marriage in Wales. *1961.*

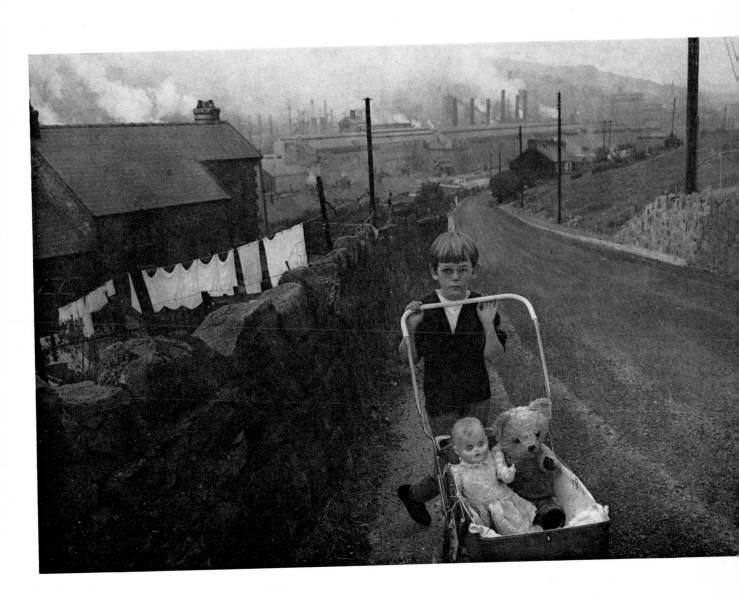

DAVIDSON, Child Playing, Welsh Mining Town. 1961.

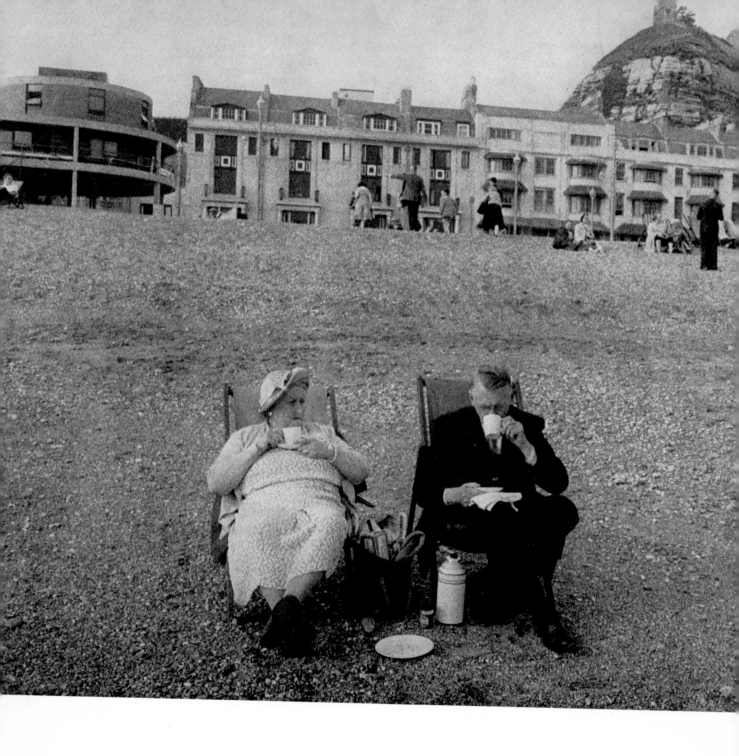

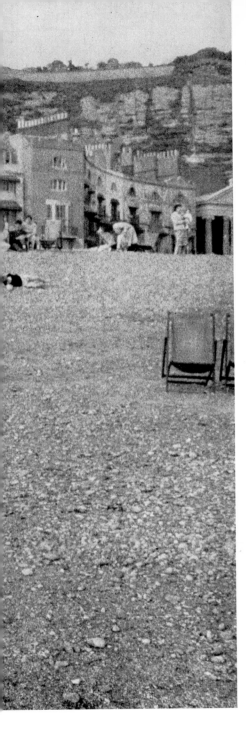

DAVIDSON
Tea, Wales.
1961.

BIBLIOGRAPHY

BOOKS

Abbott, Berenice. *The World of Atget.* New York, 1964.

Ackerman, Carl W. *George Eastman.* New York, 1930.

Adams, Ansel. Basic Photo Series, 6 vols.: *Camera and Lens, The Negative, The Print, Natural Light Photography, Artificial Light Photography, Twelve Photographic Problems.* Polaroid-Land Photography Manual, 1963.

America and Alfred Stieglitz. New York, 1934.

Angers, George W. *Balloon Posts in the Siege of Paris, 1870–1871.* Springfield, Mass., 1952.

————. *Carrier Pigeons during the Siege of Paris.* Springfield, Mass., 1952.

Archer, Frederick Scott. *A Manual of the Collodion Process.* London, 1852.

Armitage, Merle, editor. *The Art of Edward Weston.* New York, 1940.

Avedon, Richard, *Nothing Personal.* New York, 1965.

Beny, Roloff. *The Thrones of Earth and Heaven.* New York, 1959.

Bihalji-Merin, Oto. *The World from Above.* New York, 1967.

Blanquart-Evrard, L. D. *Traité de photographie sur papier.* Paris, 1851.

Boni, Albert. *Photographic Literature.* Hastings-on-Hudson, 1963.

Bourke-White, Margaret. *Portrait of Myself.* New York, 1963.

Brandt, Bill. *Perspective of Nudes.* New York, 1961.

————. *Shadow of Light.* New York, 1966.

Brassai. *Paris de nuit.* Paris, 1933.

————Volupté de Paris. Paris, 1935.

————. *Trente dessins.* Paris, 1946. With a poem by Jacques Prévert.

————. *Camera in Paris.* London, 1949.

————. *Histoire de Marie.* Introduction by Henry Miller. Paris, 1949.

————. *Seville en fête.* Paris, 1954.

————. *Graffiti.* Stuttgart, 1960.

————. *Picasso & Co.* Garden City, 1968.

Bravie, Michael F. *A Social History.* New York, 1966.

Brown, Mark Herbert, and W. R. Felton. *The Frontier Years: L. A. Huffman, Photographer of the Plains.* New York, 1955.

————. *Before Barbed Wire: L. A. Huffman, Photographer on Horseback.* New York, 1955.

Bry, Doris. *Alfred Stieglitz, Photographer.* Museum of Fine Arts, Boston, 1965.

Bullock, Wynn. *Three Photographers.* With Aaron Siskind and David Vestal. Institute of Arts, Kalamazoo, 1961.

Callahan, Harry. *Photographs: Harry Callahan.* Santa Barbara, 1964.

Capa, Robert. *Images of War.* New York, 1964.

Capote, Truman. *Observations.* With photos by Richard Avedon. New York, 1959.

Cartier-Bresson, Henri. *The World of Henri Cartier-Bresson.* New York, 1968.

Chapman, Ronald. *The Laurel and the Thorn: a Study of G. F. Watts.* London, 1947.

Chesterton, Gilbert Keith. *G. F. Watts.* London, 1904.

Clerc, L. P. *Photography: Theory and Practice.* 3d ed., New York, 1954.

Clergue, Lucien. *The Birth of Aphrodite.* New York, 1966.

Coke, Van Deren. *The Painter and the Photograph.* Albuquerque, 1964.

Deschin, Jacob. *Say It with Your Camera.* New York, 1960.

_____. *Photography in Your Future.* New York, 1965.

Duncan, David Douglas. *The Private World of Pablo Picasso.* New York, 1958.

_____. *This Is War.* New York, 1961.

_____. *Yankee Nomad.* New York, 1966.

_____. *I Protest.* New York, 1968.

_____. *Great Treasures of the Kremlin.* New York, 1969.

Eder, Joseph Maria. *History of Photography.* Translated by Edward Epstean. New York, 1945.

Elisofon, Eliot. *Color Photography.* New York, 1961.

_____. *The Nile.* New York, 1964.

Elliott, George. *Dorothea Lange. A Harvest of Truth.* The Museum of Modern Art, New York, 1966.

Emerson, Peter Henry. *Naturalistic Photography.* 3d ed., London, 1889.

Feininger, Andreas. *The Face of New York.* New York, 1954.

_____. *Successful Photography.* New York, 1954.

_____. *Changing America.* New York, 1955.

_____. *The Creative Photographer.* New York, 1955.

_____. *The Anatomy of Nature.* New York, 1956.

_____. *Total Picture Control.* New York, 1961.

_____. *The World Through My Eyes.* New York, 1963.

_____. *The Complete Photographer.* Englewood Cliffs, 1965.

_____. *Forms of Nature and Life.* New York, 1966.

Focal Press. *Focal Encyclopedia of Photography.* London, New York, 1956. Also publishes books on photography, particularly on techniques and science.

Genthe, Arnold. *As I Remember.* New York, 1936.

Gernsheim, Helmut. *New Photo Vision.* London, 1942.

_____. *The Man Behind the Camera.* London, 1948.

_____. *Julia Margaret Cameron.* London, 1948.

_____. *Lewis Carroll, Photographer.* London, 1949.

_____. *Masterpieces of Victorian Photography.* London, 1951.

_____. *Historic Events 1839–1939.* London, 1960.

_____. *Creative Photography.* London, 1962.

Gernsheim, Helmut, and Alison Gernsheim. *Roger Fenton, Photographer of the Crimean War.* London, 1954.

_____. *The History of Photography from the Earliest Use of the Camera Obscura in the Eleventh Century up to 1914.* London, 1955.

_____. *L. J. M. Daguerre: The History of the Diorama and the Daguerreotype.* London, 1955.

Goodrich, Lloyd. *Thomas Eakins, His Life and Work.* New York, 1933.

Halsman, Philippe. *Halsman on the Creation of Photographic Ideas.* New York, 1961.

Hammer, Mina Fisher. *History of the Kodak and Its Continuations.* New York, 1940.

Hentoff, Nat. *Jazz Street.* With photos by Dennis Stock. Garden City, 1961.

Horan, James D. *Mathew Brady, Historian with a Camera.* New York, 1955.

Hunt, Robert. *A Manual of Photography.* 3d ed., London, 1853.

Huxley, Matthew. *A Farewell to Eden.* With photos by Cornell Capa. New York, 1964.

Karsh, Yousuf. *Faces of Destiny.* New York, 1946.

_____. *In Search of Greatness.* New York, 1962.

_____. *Portfolio.* Toronto, 1967.

Kepes, Gyorgy. *The Education of Vision.* New York, 1965.

Kerouac, Jack. *The Americans.* With photos by Robert Frank. New York, 1959.

Kertesz, André. *André Kertesz Photographs.* New York, 1966.

Klein, William. *Rome: The City and Its People.* London, 1957.

_____. *Tokyo.* London, 1964.

Lartigue, Jacques Henri. *The Boyhood Photos of J. H. Lartigue. The Family Album of a Gilded Age.* Lausanne, 1966.

Lécuyer, Raymond. *Histoire de la photographie.* Paris, 1945.

Liberman, Alexander, editor. *The Art and Technique of Color Photography: a Treasury of Color Photographs by the Staff Photographers of Vogue, House & Garden, and Glamour.* New York, 1951.

Litchfield, R. *Tom Wedgwood, the First Photographer.* London, 1903.

Lossing, Benson J. *The History of the Civil War.* New York, 1912.

Lyons, Nathan. *Photographers on Photography.* Englewood Cliffs, 1966.

———. *Contemporary Photographers Toward a Social Landscape,* Horizon Press and George Eastman House, 1966.

———. *Seeing Photographically.* Englewood Cliffs, 1966.

Mack, J. E., and M. J. Martin. *The Photographic Process.* New York, 1939.

Man Ray. *Self Portrait.* Boston, 1963.

Mayer, Grace M. *Once Upon a City.* New York, 1958.

Mead, Margaret. *Family.* With photos by Ken Heyman. New York, 1965.

Meredith, Roy. *Mr. Lincoln's Camera Man, Mathew B. Brady.* New York, 1946.

Messer, Thomas. *The Emergent Decade.* With photos by Cornell Capa. Ithaca and New York, 1965–66.

Museum of the City of New York. *Battle with the Slum: Fifty Photographic Prints: Exhibition.* New York, 1947.

Muybridge, Eadweard. *Animal Locomotion.* 11 vols. University of Pennsylvania, Philadelphia, 1887.

Newhall, Beaumont. *The History of Photography from 1839 to the Present Day.* New York, 1949.

———. *On Photography.* New York, 1956.

———. *The Daguerreotype in America.* New York, 1961.

———. *Frederick H. Evans.* Rochester, 1964.

——— and Nancy Newhall. *Masters of Photography.* New York, 1958.

Newhall, Nancy. *Photographs, 1915–1945: Paul Strand.* New York, 1945.

———. *The Photographs of Edward Weston.* New York, 1946.

———. *Alvin Langdon Coburn. A Portfolio of Sixteen Photographs.* Rochester, 1962.

Parks, Gordon. *Flash Photography.* New York, 1947.

———. *The Learning Tree.* New York, 1963.

———. *A Choice of Weapons.* New York, 1966.

Pawek, Karl. *World Exhibition of Photography.* Circulating exhibition, first shown in Hamburg. 1966.

Penn, Irving. *Moments Preserved.* New York, 1960.

Pocock, Philip J. *The Camera as Witness.* International Exhibition of Photography, EXPO 67, Montreal, 1967.

Porter, Eliot. *In Wilderness Is the Preservation of the World.* San Francisco, 1962.

Potoniée, Georges. *The History of the Discovery of Photography.* Translated by Edward Epstean. New York, 1936.

Riboud, Marc. *The Three Banners of China.* New York, 1966.

Robinson, Henry Peach. *Pictorial Effect in Photography.* London, 1869.

Roh, Franz, editor. *60 Fotos von L. Moholy-Nagy.* Berlin, 1930.

Sandburg, Carl. *Steichen, the Photographer.* New York, 1929.

Schultheiss, Emil. *Antarctica.* New York, 1961.

Schwarz, Heinrich. *David Octavius Hill, Master of Photography.* New York, 1932.

Sipley, Louis Walton. *Collector's Guide to American Photography.* Philadelphia, 1957.

Siskind, Aaron. *Aaron Siskind.* New York, 1959.

Soby, James Thrall. "Four Photographers," *Modern Art and the New Past,* Chapter 11. Norman, Okla., 1957. Articles on Stieglitz, Cartier-Bresson, Evans, and Strand, reprinted from *The Saturday Review.*

Steichen, Edward. *A Life in Photography.* Garden City, 1962.

Stenger, Erich. *The History of Photography: Its Relation to Civilization and Practice.* Translated by Edward Epstean. Easton, Pa., 1939.

Szarkowski, John. *The Face of Minnesota.* Minneapolis, 1958.

———. *The Photographer and the American Landscape.* New York, 1963.

———. *A. Kertesz, Photographer.* New York, 1964.

Taft, Robert. *Photography and the American Scene: A Social History, 1839–1899.* New York, 1938.

Tissandier, Gaston. *A History and Handbook of Photography.* 2d ed., London, 1878.

Tugwell, Rexford Guy, Munro Thomas, and R. E. Stryker. *American Economic Life.* New York, 1925.

Uris, Leon. *Exodus Revisited.* With photos by Dimitrios Harissiadis. Garden City, 1960.

Van der Elsken, Ed. *Love on the Left Bank.* London, 1956.

———. *Jazz.* Amsterdam, 1959.

———. *Bagara.* London, 1961.

———. *Sweet Life.* New York, 1965.

Weimar, Wilhelm. *Die Daguerreotype in Hamburg, 1839–1860: Ein Beitrag zur Geschichte der Photographie.* Hamburg, 1915. (Hamburgische wissenschaftliche Anstalten. Beiheft zum Jahrbuch. Jahrg. 321.)

Weston, Charis Wilson, and Edward Weston. *California and the West.* New York, 1940.

Weston, Edward. *Day Books.* Vol. 1. Edited by Nancy Newhall. Rochester, 1962.

Whiting, John R. *Photography Is a Language.* Chicago, 1946.

Wolff, Paul. *My First Ten Years with the Leica.* New York, 1935.

Woolf, Virginia, and Roger Fry. *Victorian Photographs of Famous Men & Fair Women.* London, 1926.

ARTICLES

Abbott, Berenice. "Eugène Atget," *Creative Art,* September, 1929.

Adams, Ansel. "Edward Weston," *Creative Art,* May, 1933.

L'ARC, Spring, 1963.

Caponigro, Paul. *Aperture,* special issue, 1967.

Clark, Sir Kenneth. "Relation of Photography to Painting," *Aperture,* 1954.

Coke, Van Deren. "The Art of Photography in College Teaching," *College Art Journal,* June, 1960.

Dobell, Byron. "A Conversation with Cartier-Bresson," *Popular Photography,* September, 1957.

Goldsmith, Arthur. "The Ambiguity of the Photographic Image," *Infinity,* March, 1964.

———. "Elliott Erwitt. Improbable Photographs," *Infinity,* August, 1965.

———. "How to Look at a Photograph," *Photography Annual,* 1965.

Grehan, Farrell. "Photographs of Rodin's Sculptures," *Infinity,* February, 1966.

Ivins, W. M. "Photography of Stieglitz," *Metropolitan Museum of Art Bulletin,* February, 1929.

Mayor, A. Hyatt. "Daguerreotypes and Photographs," *Metropolitan Museum of Art Bulletin,* November, 1939.

———. "Photographs by Eakins and Degas," *Metropolitan Museum of Art Bulletin,* July, 1944.

———. "The Photographic Eye," *Metropolitan Museum of Art Bulletin,* July, 1946.

———. "The World of Atget: Photographs from the Collection of Berenice Abbott," *Metropolitan Museum of Art Bulletin,* February, 1952.

"Modern Photography," *Studio Magazine,* special issue, Autumn, 1936.

Newhall, Beaumont. "The Photographs of Moholy-Nagy," *Kenyon Review,* summer, 1941.

———. "The Photographic Inventions of George Eastman," *Journal of Photographic Science,* vol. 3, 1955.

———. "Photography, the Reality of the Abstract," *New Directions,* no. 15, 1955.

———. "Photography as Art in America," *Perspectives USA,* no. 15, 1956.

———. "The Search for Color," *Color Photography Annual,* 1956.

———. "Paul Strand, Traveling Photographer," *American Artist,* 1964.

Rivera, Diego. "Edward Weston and Tina Modotti," *Mexican Folkways,* April, 1926.

Schwarz, Heinrich. "Art and Photography," *Magazine of Art,* December, 1949.

Siegel, Arthur. "Fifty Years of Documentary Portraits," *American Photography,* January, 1951.

Stackpole, Peter. "The Return of Eugene Smith," *U. S. Camera,* January, 1964.

Techniques Graphiques. Each issue has one or more articles on photography.

"12 Photographers of the American Social Landscape," Brandeis University, Boston, 1967.

Weiss, Margaret. "Creative Vision: Six Decades of the Photographer's Art," *Saturday Review,* September 22, 1962.

———. "The Photographer and the American Landscape," *Saturday Review,* September 28, 1963.

Weston, Edward. "From My Day Book," *Creative Art,* August, 1928.

———. "My Photographs of California," *Magazine of Art,* January, 1939.

INDEX

22 PL